FOSTER ON
EU Law

Fifth Edition

PROFESSOR NIGEL FOSTER, FRSA

*Visiting Professor of European Law, Europa Institut,
Universität des Saarlandes, Saarbrücken, Germany and
Programme Leader for the LLM in International Business Law,
Robert Kennedy College, Switzerland.*

OXFORD

UNIVERSITY PRESS

OXFORD
UNIVERSITY PRESS

Great Clarendon Street, Oxford, OX2 6DP,
United Kingdom

Oxford University Press is a department of the University of Oxford.
It furthers the University's objective of excellence in research, scholarship,
and education by publishing worldwide. Oxford is a registered trade mark of
Oxford University Press in the UK and in certain other countries

Second Edition 2009
Third Edition 2011
Fourth Edition 2013

Impression: 1

Published in the United States of America by Oxford University Press
198 Madison Avenue, New York, NY 10016, United States of America

British Library Cataloguing in Publication Data
Data available

Library of Congress Control Number: 2015939039

ISBN 978–0–19–872759–0

Printed in Great Britain by Ashford Colour Press Ltd, Gosport, Hampshire

To Lynsey and Alexander
I will remember the moments you were born all of my life
and will love you equally as long.
Dad

Revised Preface for the Fifth Edition

The Preface is where the author writes why he or she has written the book, and provides embarrassing details of the deprivations suffered by him or her, and especially his or her family, whilst undergoing the self-imposed purgatory of seemingly endless days and nights putting the words on the screen, driven—nay, possessed—by the conception that it is for the better good of mankind that the book is written. Sometimes there is an interruption when the spouse produces some children to kiss/chasten, or to whom to say 'hello'/'goodbye'. One only finds time to comment: 'My—don't the children look small today?' The reply comes: 'No, those are your grandchildren. Our children left home during an earlier book. Would you like to play with the grandchildren?' The answer: 'Umm, yes—but perhaps later. I just have to finish this chapter!'

There follows thanks for the almost, if not entirely, unending patience of the publisher's staff and, in particular, the editor in charge—or should I say the two, or three, or four, or five editors who have been overseeing the project or counting the missed deadlines (the writing having taken so long that the earlier editors have had time to produce their own dynasty of potential book purchasers).

So, after that first paragraph, will I do something completely different? Nope: it's tradition, and here is my version of it.

I've taught EC and EU law for 30 years now (and, hey, I studied it before that both at undergraduate and postgraduate levels!) and, from the beginning, I thought that there was a need for a manageable single-text course book. In 1983, there were very few on the market and there was no credible one-stop shop; now, there are a number. However, I think the original premise holds true. Throughout the years, my colleagues and I have failed to recommend wholeheartedly a single text and instead we have jointly recommended a number of texts. So, to a large extent, this is why I thought the market was still there—and indeed growing—for a new mid-range textbook. It is my clear belief, backed up by an awful lot of experience, that students want a single accessible book that covers the course they are taking (or at least 90 per cent of it) and which can be absorbed easily. Obviously, a few will wish to read much more widely—those who have a real interest; for them, a number of books exist and are excellent. Most students, though, simply want to pass the exam as well as they can, but with the minimum of effort—and I don't blame them: it's perfectly rational behaviour. Who can blame them when most university managements have pursued exactly the same policy for the REF,[1] and anything else by which they may be assessed? Effort is concentrated on securing the best result in the exercise because the result is more important than the journey—that is, the end justifies the means, even if that means diverting resources from teaching to increase research output. But watch out: the era of higher student fees is starting to focus attention back on to students and rightly so—and that is the focus of this, a student textbook, pure and simple!

So, on to the book itself. I should mention the numbering policy used in the book for the treaties, even more challenging now following the entry into force of the Lisbon Treaty. For the most part, the present numbers of the Treaty on European Union (TEU) and

---

[1] The Research Assessment Exercise, and now the Research Excellence Framework, which determine the share-out of government research monies to the universities.

Treaty on the Functioning of the European Union (TFEU) only will be used, with reference in parentheses to the immediate past numbers of the pre-Lisbon EC and EU Treaties only where vital to aid understanding, and exceptionally to the old pre-Amsterdam Treaty numbers. This will be mainly in respect of case law. This fifth edition is in production at a time when, again, great uncertainty has been cast on the future progress of the EU, this time by the political promise by David Cameron, the UK prime minister, of his hope to re-negotiate the terms of UK membership. If the other 27 member states are willing to make any concessions, which itself is a massive 'if', a referendum will be held on continued membership or withdrawal in 2017! I would welcome a referendum. It would provide a chance for the UK electorate to debate full information about the EU and the pros and cons of membership alongside, no doubt, piles of garbage printed by the papers. Furthermore, when in 1975 we had a referendum on the terms and continued membership, after all the information that had been disseminated had been weighed and evaluated by the UK electorate, a two-thirds against in the opinion polls was converted into a two-thirds for vote on the day. That's why I welcome a referendum. The UK electorate will vote on the long-term interests of the UK and not the short-term interests of a prime minister to placate a minority of MPs on his backbenches who are Eurosceptic or to placate voters lured by UKIP. With the results of the 2015 election announced on 8th May, there is now a majority Conservative Government in the UK and it looks very much as if we are now cast into a very uncertain future until 2017, which is far from being in the best interests of the Country. We can only wait and see if sense will prevail.

The thanks bit . . .

Thanks to many staff of Oxford University Press who have participated in the conception and production of this book, now into its fifth edition. Thanks are due to Jane Kavanagh, Claire Brewer, Angela Griffin, Kate Whetter, Penelope Woolf, and Sarah Viner.

Then, Alex Clabburn took over as editor of this title, and following him, Anna Winstanley, then Abbey Nelms, and now Emily Spicer. Thanks also to Elisa Cozzi in production and Clare Weaver in marketing for their work on the book. Thanks to Jeremy Langworthy and Geraldine Ferguson at copy-editing and proof stages.

But most of all my thanks and love go to my family who have witnessed my self-imposed isolation with good humour and understanding, particularly so whilst continuing to update four titles on EU law.

Quite rightly, this book in first edition was dedicated to my two children, Lynsey and Alexander, whom I continue to love with equal passion; that sentiment and dedication remains.

I acknowledge with thanks the permission of the European Union to reproduce material taken historically from the Official Journal printed volumes. More recent provisions and additions have been taken from the online EUR-Lex website and, likewise, permission to reproduce these is gratefully acknowledged, but with the clear proviso that 'Only European Union legislation in the online edition of the *Official Journal of the European Union* is deemed authentic'. UK legislation is reproduced with the permission of HMSO.

I have tried to state the law accurately up to January 2015; however, it is always possible that I did not get things entirely correct. For errors and omissions, I am solely responsible. I would gratefully receive advice of any errors discovered and also any general comments in respect of coverage, treatment, or any other aspect of the book.

Nigel Foster
Saarbrücken, Germany, and Cardiff
May 2015

New to this Edition

The fifth edition has been revised to incorporate the numerous, nay hundreds if not thousands of individual changes throughout the book since the last edition, which in addition to new cases include:

- the reorganization of Chapter 4, in particular the hierachy of EU law sources;
- further reorganization of Chapter 9 and, in particular, considerable change to the section on citizenship and the rearranging of subsections on welfare, family, and TCN rights;
- following its reintroduction in the fourth edition, enhanced coverage of competition law and the addition of a section on state aids;
- amended and increased coverage on human rights aspects;
- extended coverage of case law throughout the book.

Outline Contents

Guide to the Online Resource Centre   xix

Alphabetical Table of Cases   xx

Numerical Table of Cases   xxxviii

Table of National Legislation   liv

Table of International Legislation   lvi

Table of EU Treaties   lvii

Table of EU Secondary Legislation   lxiii

Table of Decisions   lxvii

Table of Opinions   lxvii

Abbreviations   lxviii

Part I Introduction to the Institutional and Procedural Law of the European Union

1 The History and Constitutional Basis of the European Union   3

2 The Union Institutions   42

3 The Empowerment of the Union: Transfer, Division, and Control of Powers   71

4 EU Law: Sources, Forms, and Law-making   93

5 The Supremacy of EU Law   138

6 Ensuring EU Laws Are Effective: Remedies and Art 267 TFEU   170

7 The Direct Jurisdiction of the Court of Justice   211

Part II Introduction to the Substantive Law of the European Union

8 The Free Movement of Goods   255

9 The Free Movement of Persons   299

10 An Introduction to EU Competition Policy and Law   356

11 Sex Discrimination Law   398

Index   435

Detailed Contents

Guide to the Online Resource Centre   xix

Alphabetical Table of Cases   xx

Numerical Table of Cases   xxxviii

Table of National Legislation   liv

Table of International Legislation   lvi

Table of EU Treaties   lvii

Table of EU Secondary Legislation   lxiii

Table of Decisions   lxvii

Table of Opinions   lxvii

Abbreviations   lxviii

Part I Introduction to the Institutional and Procedural Law of the European Union

1 The History and Constitutional Basis of the European Union   3

1.1 Introduction   3

1.2 The Motives for European Integration   4

1.3 The Founding of the European Communities   5
    1.3.1 The Schuman Plan (1950)   6
    1.3.2 The Proposed European Defence Community and European
        Political Community   7
    1.3.3 Progress Nevertheless   8

1.4 The Relationship of the UK with the European Communities and Union   9
    1.4.1 The Early Relationship   9
    1.4.2 From Membership Acceptance to Date   10

1.5 The Basic Objectives and Nature of the European Union   12
    1.5.1 Intergovernmentalism, Supranationalism, and Federalism 14
    1.5.2 Progress to a Federal Europe?   14

1.6 The Widening and Deepening of the Communities and Union   16
    1.6.1 The Widening of the Union   16
    1.6.2 The European Economic Area and the 1995 Expansion 17
    1.6.3 The 2004 and 2007 Expansions   18
    1.6.4 Future Widening   19
    1.6.5 The EU and the World: External Relations   23
    1.6.6 The Deepening of the Union   25
    1.6.7 The First Radical Change: The Single European Act 28
    1.6.8 The Maastricht Treaty on European Union   31
    1.6.9 The Amsterdam Intergovernmental Conference and Treaty 33
    1.6.10 The Nice Intergovernmental Conference and Treaty 35

1.6.11 The Constitutional Treaty for Europe 37
1.6.12 The 2007 Lisbon Treaty 38

1.7 Future Developments and Conclusions 39

2 The Union Institutions 42

2.1 Introduction: The Institutional Framework 42

2.2 The Commission 43
2.2.1 Composition of the Commission 43
2.2.2 Appointment and Removal 44
2.2.3 Tasks and Duties 46

2.3 The Council (of Ministers) of the European Union 47
2.3.1 Functions and Powers 47
2.3.2 The Presidency of the Council 48
2.3.3 Role and Voting in the Legislative Procedures 48
2.3.4 Council General Law-making Powers 52
2.3.5 The Committee of Permanent Representatives (COREPER)
and the Council Secretariat 52

2.4 The European Council 53
2.4.1 The European Council President 53
2.4.2 The High Representative of the Union for Foreign Affairs
and Security Policy 54

2.5 The European Parliament 54
2.5.1 Membership 55
2.5.2 Functions and Powers 56

2.6 The Court of Justice of the European Union 60
2.6.1 Composition and Organization 60
2.6.2 Procedure 61
2.6.3 Jurisdiction 62
2.6.4 Methodology: Interpretation and Precedent 64
2.6.5 The General Court 65
2.6.6 Specialized Courts 66
2.6.7 The European Central Bank 67
2.6.8 The Court of Auditors 67

2.7 The Union's Advisory Bodies 67
2.7.1 The European Economic and Social Committee 67
2.7.2 The Committee of the Regions 68

2.8 Other Union Bodies 68

2.9 Union Financing 68
2.9.1 The Budgetary Procedure 69

2.10 Chapter Summary 69

3 The Empowerment of the Union: Transfer, Division, and Control of Powers 71

3.1 Introduction 71

3.2 The Transfer of Sovereign Powers 71

3.3 Democracy in the Union 72
3.3.1 The Democratic Credentials of the Union 72
3.3.2 Transparency and Open Governance 73

3.4   The Constitutional Basis of the Union   74
    3.4.1   The Community and Union Treaties   74
    3.4.2   The Abandoned Constitutional Treaty   76

3.5   Competences, their Division, and Subsidiarity   78
    3.5.1   The Conferral and Division of Competences   78
    3.5.2   Exclusive, Concurrent, and Complimentary Competences   79
    3.5.3   Extension of Competences   81
    3.5.4   Residual Powers   82
    3.5.5   Implied Powers   84
    3.5.6   The Principle of Subsidiarity   86
    3.5.7   Restrictive Drafting   89
    3.5.8   Proportionality   89
    3.5.9   The Lisbon Treaty and the Division and Control of Competences   90

4   EU Law: Sources, Forms, and Law-making   93

4.1   Introduction   93

4.2   The EU Legal System   93
    4.2.1   The Style of the EU Legal System   94
    4.2.2   The Classification of the Elements of EU Law   95

4.3   The Sources and Forms of EU Law   97

4.4   Primary EU Law   99
    4.4.1   The Treaties   99
    4.4.2   The Protocols Attached to the Treaties   100
    4.4.3   Declarations   101
    4.4.4   The EU Charter of Fundamental Rights   101
    4.4.5   General Principles and Other Fundamental Rights   104

4.5   Secondary Sources of EU Law   105
    4.5.1   International Agreements, Treaties, and Conventions   105
    4.5.2   EU Secondary Legislation   107

4.6   The Court of Justice's Contribution   110
    4.6.1   Human or Fundamental Rights   111
    4.6.2   The EU and the ECHR   113
    4.6.3   Equality and Non-discrimination   116
    4.6.4   General Principles of Procedural Law and Natural Justice   117
    4.6.5   Summary   121

4.7   'Soft Law'   122

4.8   The Participation of the Institutions in the Legislative Processes   123
    4.8.1   The Legal Base for Legislative Proposals   123

4.9   Law-making Principles and Procedures   126
    4.9.1   The Law-making Procedures   127
    4.9.2   Why so Many Changes to the Legislative Procedures?   131

4.10   The Delegation of Powers   132

4.11   The Community Method, the Open Method of Communication, and Governance Issues   134

4.12   Law-making: Getting the Balance Right   135

5 The Supremacy of EU Law 138

5.1 The Supremacy of EU Law 138

5.2 The View of the Court of Justice 138
    5.2.1 Supremacy and Member State Constitutional Law 140
    5.2.2 Supremacy and International Law 143

5.3 EU Law in the Member States 145
    5.3.1 Theories of Incorporation of International Law: Monism and Dualism 145

5.4 EU Law in the UK 146
    5.4.1 The 'Unwritten' Constitution 146
    5.4.2 The Dualist Approach to International Law 146
    5.4.3 The Doctrine of Parliamentary Supremacy 147
    5.4.4 UK Entry and the European Communities Act 1972 147
    5.4.5 Judicial Reception of Community and EU Law in the UK 149
    5.4.6 The European Union Act 2011 153

5.5 Reception of EU Law in Other Member States 155
    5.5.1 Belgium 155
    5.5.2 Germany 155
    5.5.3 Italy 159
    5.5.4 France 160
    5.5.5 The Czech Republic 162
    5.5.6 Denmark 163
    5.5.7 Hungary 164
    5.5.8 Ireland 164
    5.5.9 Poland 165
    5.5.10 Spain 166

5.6 Summary on Reception: Sufficient Evidence of an Emerging Trend? 166

6 Ensuring EU Laws Are Effective: Remedies and Art 267 TFEU 170

6.1 Introduction 170

6.2 An Introduction to Art 267 TFEU 170

6.3 Direct Applicability and Direct Effects 170
    6.3.1 Definitions and the Distinction between Directly Applicable and Direct Effects 170
    6.3.2 Direct Applicability 171
    6.3.3 Direct Effects 171
    6.3.4 Overcoming the Lack of Horizontal Direct Effect for Directives 177

6.4 State Liability: The Principle in *Francovich* 184
    6.4.1 The Principle of State Liability Developed 185
    6.4.2 The Extension of the *Francovich* State-liability Principle 187

6.5 Article 267 TFEU: The Preliminary Ruling Procedure 188
    6.5.1 Which Law-adjudicating Bodies Can Refer? 189
    6.5.2 The Question Referred: Relevance and Admissibility 191
    6.5.3 A Discretion or Obligation to Refer? 195
    6.5.4 The Discretion of Lower Courts 195
    6.5.5 The Timing of the Reference 196
    6.5.6 Courts of Last Instance 197
    6.5.7 Avoiding the Obligation to Refer: The Development of Precedent and *Acte Clair* 197

6.5.8   The Effect of an Art 267 TFEU Ruling   200
6.5.9   The Evolution of Art 267 TFEU References   201
6.5.10 Reforms and Future   202
6.5.11 Interim Measures within an Art 267 TFEU Reference   203

6.6   **National Procedural Law and the System of Remedies**   203
6.6.1   The Principle of National Procedural Autonomy   204
6.6.2   Further Intervention by the Court of Justice   205
6.6.3   A More Balanced Approach   206
6.6.4   Conclusions   208

7   **The Direct Jurisdiction of the Court of Justice**   211

7.1   Introduction   211

7.2   Actions against Member States   211
7.2.1   Enforcement Actions by the Commission   211
7.2.2   Article 258 TFEU Procedure   214
7.2.3   Actions Brought by One Member State against Another   220

7.3   Alternative Actions to Secure Member States' Compliance   222

7.4   Actions to Annul EU Acts   222
7.4.1   Admissibility   223
7.4.2   *Locus Standi* for Non-privileged Applicants   226
7.4.3   Direct and Individual Concern   228
7.4.4   Interest Groups and Party Actions   230
7.4.5   The Challenge to Regulatory Acts   231
7.4.6   Merits or Grounds for Annulment   232
7.4.7   The Effect of a Successful Action and Annulment   233
7.4.8   A Restrictive Approach?   234
7.4.9   Alternatives to Art 263 TFEU   235

7.5   Action for Failure to Act: Art 265 TFEU   237
7.5.1   Admissibility and *Locus Standi*   237
7.5.2   Acts Subject to an Art 265 TFEU Action   238
7.5.3   Procedural Requirements   238

7.6   Non-contractual Liability of the EU   239
7.6.1   Admissibility   240
7.6.2   An Autonomous or Independent Action   241
7.6.3   The Requirements of Liability   241
7.6.4   The Standard of Liability and Fault   241
7.6.5   A New Single Test for Liability?   246
7.6.6   Individual (Non-legislative) Acts   247
7.6.7   Liability for Lawful Acts   247
7.6.8   The Damage   248
7.6.9   The Causal Connection   248
7.6.10 Concurrent Liability/Choice of Court   249

7.7   The Plea of Illegality   249
7.7.1   *Locus Standi*   249
7.7.2   Acts that Can Be Reviewed   250
7.7.3   Grounds of Review   250
7.7.4   Effect of a Successful Challenge   250

7.8   Actions against Natural or Legal Persons   251

Part II Introduction to the Substantive Law of the European Union

8 **The Free Movement of Goods**   255

   8.1 Introduction   255

   8.2 Legislative Provisions   256
     8.2.1 Treaty Articles   256
     8.2.2 Secondary Legislation   257

   8.3 Progress Towards the Treaty Goals   257
     8.3.1 A Free Trade Area   257
     8.3.2 A Customs Union   257
     8.3.3 A Common Market   257
     8.3.4 An Economic Union   258
     8.3.5 Which Stage Has the EU Reached?   258

   8.4 Integration Methods   259
     8.4.1 Negative Integration   259
     8.4.2 Positive Integration   261
     8.4.3 Methods of Harmonization   262
     8.4.4 Alternatives to Legislative Harmonization   263

   8.5 The Establishment of the Internal Market   264
     8.5.1 The Common Commercial Policy and the Common Customs Tariff   264
     8.5.2 The Prohibition of Customs Duties   264
     8.5.3 A Charge Having Equivalent Effect (CHEE)   265
     8.5.4 The Distinction between Internal Taxation and CHEEs   268

   8.6 The Prohibition of Discriminatory Taxation   270
     8.6.1 Direct and Indirect Taxation   270
     8.6.2 'Similar' or 'Other Products'   271

   8.7 Summary on Tariff Barriers   273

   8.8 Quantitative Restrictions and Measures Having Equivalent Effect   273
     8.8.1 The General Scope of the Treaty Prohibition   274
     8.8.2 What Are 'Measures' for the Purposes of Art 34 TFEU?   275
     8.8.3 The Meaning of 'Quantitative Restrictions'   275
     8.8.4 Measures Having Equivalent Effect (MHEE)   276
     8.8.5 The Scope of the Prohibition   277

   8.9 The Derogations of Art 36 TFEU   278
     8.9.1 General Purpose and Scope   279
     8.9.2 Public Morality   279
     8.9.3 Public Policy   280
     8.9.4 Public Security   280
     8.9.5 The Protection of the Health or Life of Humans or Animals   280
     8.9.6 Artistic, Historic, or Archaeological Heritage   282
     8.9.7 The Protection of Industrial or Commercial Property   282
     8.9.8 Article 36 TFEU Second Sentence   283
     8.9.9 Decision 3052/95 and Regulation 764/2008   284

   8.10 Equally Applicable Measures (Indistinctly Applicable Measures)   284
     8.10.1 The *Cassis de Dijon* Case   285
     8.10.2 The Application of the Rule of Reason: The Requirements in Detail   286
     8.10.3 Technical Standards and Legislative Interventions   288

	8.10.4 Summary of *Cassis de Dijon*	289
	8.10.5 Equal Burden/Dual Burden	289
8.11	*Keck and Mithouard*: Certain Selling Arrangements	291
	8.11.1 Post-*Keck* Case Law	292
	8.11.2 Market Access or Discrimination, or Both?	293
	8.11.3 Restriction on Use Rules	294
8.12	Overall Summary	295
9	**The Free Movement of Persons**	299
9.1	Introduction	299
9.2	The Legal Framework: Primary and Secondary Legislation	302
	9.2.1 Treaty Provisions	302
	9.2.2 Secondary Legislation	303
	9.2.3 The Basic Right of No Discrimination	303
9.3	The Scope of the Basic Rights	304
	9.3.1 Personal Scope	304
9.4	The Material Scope of the Rights	314
	9.4.1 Secondary Legislation: Introduction	314
	9.4.2 Rights of Entry, Residence, and Exit	314
	9.4.3 The Rights Provided by Regulation 492/2011 and Directive 2004/38	317
	9.4.4 Education and Carer Rights	320
	9.4.5 Right to Remain	321
9.5	Free Movement Rights of the Self-employed	322
	9.5.1 The Intervention of the Court of Justice	322
	9.5.2 Legislative Developments	326
	9.5.3 The Free Movement of Lawyers	327
9.6	Derogations from the Free Movement Regimes	329
	9.6.1 Procedural Safeguards	329
	9.6.2 Restrictions on the Grounds of Public Policy, Security, and Health	330
	9.6.3 The Public Service Proviso	332
9.7	The Extension of Free Movement Rights	334
	9.7.1 Receiving Services	334
	9.7.2 The General Free Movement Directives	336
	9.7.3 European Citizenship	337
	9.7.4 Case Law on the Citizenship Articles	338
	9.7.5 Citizenship and Welfare Rights	340
9.8	Citizenship and Family Rights (including TCN Family Members)	343
9.9	The Wholly Internal Rule	346
9.10	Third-country Nationals—Legislative Moves	350
9.11	Concluding Remarks	352
10	**An Introduction to EU Competition Policy and Law**	356
10.1	Introduction	356
10.2	Competition Law Relevance to the EU	357
	10.2.1 Basic Outline of EU Competition Policy	357
	10.2.2 Legislative Outline	359
	10.2.3 Application and Interpretation	360

10.3 Article 101 TFEU (Anti-competitive Behaviour)   361
    10.3.1   Article 101(1) Definitions   361
    10.3.2   The Object or Effect of Restricting or Distorting Competition   365
    10.3.3   Types of Prohibited Agreements   366
    10.3.4   Which May Affect Trade between Member States   366
    10.3.5   Exemptions from Art 101(1) TFEU   368

10.4 Article 101(2) TFEU and the Consequence of a Breach   370

10.5 Article 101(3) TFEU Exemptions   371
    10.5.1   Individual Notification   371
    10.5.2   Negative Clearance and Comfort Letters   372
    10.5.3   Block Exemptions   373

10.6 Article 102 TFEU and the Abuse of a Dominant Position   374
    10.6.1   Article 102 TFEU Requirements   374
    10.6.2   Definition of Undertakings   375

10.7 The Relationship between Arts 101 and 102 TFEU   381

10.8 State Aid   383
    10.8.1   Defining State Aid   383
    10.8.2   Exceptions   384
    10.8.3   Procedures under Articles 108 and 109 TFEU   385

10.9 The Enforcement of EU Competition Law   387
    10.9.1   Council Regulation 1/2003   387
    10.9.2   Leniency Notice and Settlements   390
    10.9.3   Judicial Review of Enforcement   390
    10.9.4   Private Enforcement   391

10.10 Conflict of EU and National Law   391

10.11 EU Merger Control   392
    10.11.1   The Mergers Regulations (4064/89 and 139/04)   393
    10.11.2   Enforcement of Regulation 139/04   395

10.12 Summary   396

11 Sex Discrimination Law   398

11.1 Introduction   398

11.2 A General Principle of Equality in EU Law?   398
    11.2.1   Article 18 TFEU   399

11.3 The Reasons for the Original Inclusion of Sex Discrimination
Provisions in the Treaty   399

11.4 The Legislative Framework   401
    11.4.1   Treaty Articles   401
    11.4.2   Secondary Legislation   402

11.5 Article 157 TFEU and the Scope of the Principle of Equal Pay   403
    11.5.1   The Meaning of 'Pay'   404
    11.5.2   The Original Equal Pay Directive 75/117   408
    11.5.3   The Basis of Comparison   408
    11.5.4   Comparison Revisited   409
    11.5.5   Part-time Work and Indirect Discrimination   410
    11.5.6   Work of Equal Value   412
    11.5.7   Enforcement and Remedies   414

11.6   Equal Treatment   414
       11.6.1   The Concept of Equal Treatment/No Discrimination on
                the Grounds of Sex   415
       11.6.2   The Scope of Equal Treatment   417
       11.6.3   Equality with Regard to Employment Access, Working Conditions,
                Dismissal, and Retirement Ages   417
       11.6.4   Member States' Ability to Exempt Certain Occupations   419
       11.6.5   The Protection of Women Regarding Childbirth and Maternity   420
       11.6.6   The Promotion of Equal Opportunity by Removing Existing Inequalities
                Affecting Opportunities   424
       11.6.7   Judicial Enforcement and Remedies   426

11.7   Social Security Directive 79/7   427

11.8   Directive 92/85   428

11.9   Related Secondary Legislation   428
       11.9.1   Occupational Pensions   428
       11.9.2   Self-employed Equal Treatment   429
       11.9.3   The Part-time Workers Directive 97/81   429
       11.9.4   Summary of Secondary Legislation   429

11.10 Article 19 TFEU: The Expansion of EU Equality Law   430
       11.10.1 Secondary Legislation Enacted under Art 19 TFEU   430
       11.10.2 Directive 2004/113   430

11.11 The Lisbon Treaty and Equality Rights   432

11.12 Concluding Comments   433

Index   435

Guide to the Online Resource Centre

This book is accompanied by an Online Resource Centre offering a range of resources and materials to support teaching and learning.

www.oxfordtextbooks.co.uk/orc/foster5e/

An interactive map of the European Union
An interactive map provides a useful summary of each member state's involvement in the EU, plus essential facts and figures that are ideal for students new to the subject and for revision.

Interactive timeline
An interactive timeline allows you to trace the development of the EU through key dates and events, providing a useful source of accurate information for learning and revision.

Regular updates
Regular updates are an indispensable resource, allowing you to access changes and developments in the law that have occurred since publication of the book.

Exam advice
Exam advice from the author helping you to plan and prepare your revision.

Video clips
Video clips from the European Commission showing the key moments in EU legal history.

Alphabetical Table of Cases

Where case names are duplicated e.g. Commission v Belgium, cases are filed in numerical order

Abdoulaye v Regie Nationale des Usines Renault SA (C-218/98) [1999] ECR I-5723; [2001] 2 CMLR 18 . . . 425

Abrahamsson (Katarina) & Leif Anderson v Elisabet Fogelqvist (C-407/98) [2000] ECR I-5539 . . . 425

Accrington Beef (C-241/95) [2004] ECR I-873; [2004] 1 CMLR 35 . . . 236

Adams v Commission (145/83) [1985] ECR 3539; [1986] 1 CMLR 506 . . . 240, 242

Adeneler v ELOG (C-212/04) [2006] ECR I-6057 . . . 181, 188

Admenta v Federfarma [2006] 2 CMLR 47 . . . 160

Adoui and Cornuaille v Belgian State (115–16/81) [1982] ECR 1665; [1982] 3 CMLR 631 . . . 329, 331

Advocaten voor de Wereld VZW v Leden van de Ministerraad (C-303/05) [2008] All ER (EC) 317; [2007] 3 CMLR 1 . . . 117

Ahlstrom v Commission (89, 104, 114, 116, 117 and 125–9/85) [1994] ECR I-99 . . . 362, 364

Airtours plc v Commission (T-342/99) [2004] ECR II-1785 . . . 379, 396

Aklagaren v Mickelsson and Roos (C-142/05) [2009] ECR I-4273 . . . 295

Akrich *see* Secretary of State for the Home Department v Akrich

Aktien-Zuckerfabrik Schöppenstedt v Council (5/71) [1971] ECR 975 . . . 186, 240, 243, 244, 246

AKZO Chemie BV v Commission (53/85) [1986] ECR 1965; [1987] 1 CMLR 231 . . . 118

AKZO Nobel Chemicals v Commission (C-550/07 P) [2010] ECR I-8301 . . . 118, 389

AKZO Nobel v Commission (C-97/08) [2009] ECR I-8237 . . . 362

AKZO v Commission (62/86) [1991] ECR I-3359 . . . 380

Albany International (C-67/96) [1999] ECR I-5751 . . . 368

Alfa Vita Vassilopoulos AE v Greece (C-158/04 & 159/04) [2006] ECR I-8135; [2007] 2 CMLR 2 . . . 294

Alliance for Natural Health v Secretary of State for Health (C-154 and 155/04) [2005] ECR I-6451; [2005] 2 CMLR 61 . . . 88, 90

Allonby v Accrington and Rossendale College (C-256/01) [2004] ECR I-873; [2004] 1 CMLR 35 . . . 311, 409

Alluè and Coonan v Università degli Studi di Venezia (33/88) [1989] ECR 1591; [1991] 1 CMLR 283 . . . 303, 333

Almelo (C-393/92) [1994] ECR I-1477 . . . 265

Alpine Investments BV v Minister of Finance (C-384/93) [1995] ECR I-1141; [1995] 2 CMLR 209 . . . 311, 325, 353

AM & S Europe Ltd v Commission (155/79) [1982] ECR 1575; [1982] 2 CMLR 264 . . . 117, 389

Amylum NV v Council of the European Communities (Amylum and Tunnel Refineries) (116, 124 & 143/77) [1978] ECR 893; [1979] ECR 3497; [1982] 2 CMLR 590 . . . 245

Angonese v Cassa di Risparmio di Bolzano SpA (C-281/98) [2000] All ER (EC) 577; [2000] ECR I-4139; [2000] 2 CMLR 1120 . . . 302, 336, 348, 352

Anker v Germany (C-47/02) [2003] ECR I-10447; [2004] 2 CMLR 35 . . . 333

Antonissen (R v Immigration Appeal Tribunal *ex p*) (C-292/89) [1991] ECR I-745; [1991] 2 CMLR 373 . . . 309, 316, 331, 340

AOIP v Beyrard Decision [1976] 1 CMLR D14 . . . 361

AOK Bundesverband (C-264/01) [2004] ECR I-2493 . . . 361

Apple and Pear Development Council v Lewis (222/82) [1983] ECR 4083; [1984] 3 CMLR 733 . . . 274, 277

Arbeiterwohlfahrt der Stadt Berlin v Monika Botel (C-360/90) [1992] ECR I-3589 . . . 405

Arcaro *see* Criminal Proceedings against Arcaro

Arcelor (T-16/04) [2010] ECR II-211 . . . 244, 247

AROW v BNIC Decision OJ 1982 L379/1; [1983] 2 CMLR 240 . . . 363

Arsenal FC v Matthew Reed (C-206/01) [2003] Ch 454; [2003] 3 WLR 450 . . . 201

Asnef-Equifax (C-238/05) [2006] ECR I-11125 . . . 368

Association de Mediation Sociale (AMS) (C-176/12) ECLI:EU:C:2014:2 . . . 173

Associazione Italiana Tecnico Economica del Cemento (AITEC) v Commission (T-447-9/93) [1995] ECR II-1971 . . . 230

Asturcom v Rodriguez Noguiera (C-40/08) [2009] ECR I-9579 . . . 206

Atlanta Fruchthandelsgesellschaft (C-465–6/93) [1995] ECR I-3761; [1996] 1 CMLR 575; [1995] ECR I-3799 . . . 157, 203

Audiolux SA v GBL (C-101/03) [2009] ECR
  I-9823 . . . 98, 105

B&Q Ltd v Shrewsbury BC [1990] 3 CMLR
  535 . . . 291
Bacardi-Martini SAS v Newcastle United
  Football Co Ltd (C-318/00) [2003] ECR I-905;
  [2003] 1 CMLR 26 . . . 193
Bananenmarktverordnung of 7 June 2000
  BVerfG–2 BvL 1/97 . . . 157
Barber v Guardian Royal Exchange (C-262/88)
  [1990] ECR 1944; [1990] 2 CMLR 513 . . . 81,
  118, 404, 406, 407, 408, 428
BASF AG v Commission (T-79/89) [1992] ECR
  II-315; [1992] 4 CMLR 357 . . . 225
BAT and Reynolds v Commission (142 and
  156/84) [1987] ECR 4487 . . . 382, 393, 394
Bauhuis v The Netherlands (46/76)
  ECLI:EU:C:1977:6 . . . 267
Baumbast v Secretary of State for the Home
  Department (C-413/99) [2002] ECR I-7091;
  [2002] 3 CMLR 23 . . . 113, 320, 321, 336, 339,
  343, 344
Bayerische HNL Vermehrungsbetriebe GmbH
  & Co KG v Commission (83/76) [1978] ECR
  1209; [1978] 3 CMLR 566 . . . 244, 245
BBV v Commission (T-138/89) [1992] ECR
  II-2181 . . . 227
Becker v Finanzamt Münster-Innenstadt
  (C-8/81) [1982] ECR 53; [1982] 1 CMLR
  499 . . . 176, 178, 182, 183
Belgapom Groupement National des
  Négociants en Pommes de Terre de Belgique
  v SA ITM Belgium (C-63/94) [1995] ECR
  I-2467 . . . 292
Belgium v Humbel (263/86) [1988] ECR 5365;
  [1989] 1 CMLR 393 . . . 95, 334
Belgium v Spain (C-388/95) [2000] ECR I-3123;
  [2002] 1 CMLR 26 . . . 221, 278, 283
Bergaderm see Laboratoires Pharmaceutiques
  Bergaderm SA v Commission
Bergman v Grows-Farm (Skimmed milk pow-
  der) (114/76) [1977] ECR 1211; [1979] 2 CMLR
  83 . . . 116
Bernini (MJE) v Netherlands Ministry of
  Education and Science (C-3/90) [1992]
  ECR I-1071 . . . 318
Bethell (Lord) v Commission (C-246/81)
  [1982] ECR 2277; [1982] 3 CMLR
  300 . . . 215, 236
Bettray v Staatssecretaris van Justitie (344/87)
  [1989] ECR 1621; [1991] 1 CMLR 459 . . . 307
Bickel see Criminal Proceedings against Bickel
Bidar (C-209/03) [2005] ECR I-2119; [2005] 2
  CMLR 3 . . . 311, 335, 342
Bilka-Kaufhaus GmbH v Weber von Harz
  (170/84) [1986] ECR 1607; [1986] 2 CMLR
  701 . . . 406, 408, 411, 413
Blaizot v University of Liège (24/86) [1988] ECR
  379; [1989] 1 CMLR 57 . . . 95, 334

Bleis v Ministry of Education, Proceedings of
  the ECJ (C-4/91) [1991] ECR I-5627; [1994] 1
  CMLR 793 . . . 333
Bluhme (C-67/97) [1998] ECR I-8033; [1999] 1
  CMLR 612 . . . 289
Bobie Getrankevertrieb GmbH v Hauptzollamt
  Aachen-Nord (127/75) [1976] ECR
  1079 . . . 270
Boisdet, Re [1990] 1 CMLR 3 . . . 161
Bond van Adverteerders v Netherlands
  (C-352/85) [1988] ECR 2085; [1989] 3 CMLR
  113 . . . 330
Bonsignore v Oberstadtdirektor der Stadt
  Köln (67/74) [1975] ECR 297; [1975] 1 CMLR
  472 . . . 331
Borker, Re (138/80) [1980] ECR 1975; [1980] 3
  CMLR 638 . . . 190
Bosman see Union Royale Belge des Sociétés de
  Football Association (ASBL) v Bosman
Brasserie de Haecht v Wilkin (23/67) ECR
  407 . . . 365, 367
Brasserie du Pêcheur SA v Germany (C-46/93)
  [1996] QB 404 . . . 158, 185, 246
BRB v Pickin [1974] AC 765 . . . 1
Bresciani v Amministrazione delle Finanze
  (87/75) [1976] ECR 129; [1976] 2 CMLR
  62 . . . 176, 267
Bressol (C-73/08) [2010] ECR I-2735 . . . 335
Briheche (C-319/03) [2004] ECR I-8807 . . . 424
Brinkmann Tabakfabriken GmbH v
  Skatteministeriet (C-319/96) [1998] ECR
  I-5255; [1998] 3 CMLR 673 . . . 186
Broekmeulen v Huisarts Registratie Commissie
  (C-246/80) [1981] ECR 2311; [1982] 1 CMLR
  91 . . . 190
Brown v Rentokil (C-394/96) [1998] ECR I-4186;
  [1998] 2 CMLR 1049 . . . 335, 424
Brown v Secretary of State for Scotland (197/86)
  [1988] ECR 3205; [1988] 3 CMLR 403 . . . 310
BRT v SABAM (127/73) [1974] ECR 313 . . . 361
Brunner et al v The Federal Republic of
  Germany . . . 157, 162, 165, 166
Busch v Klinikum Neustadt GmbH & Co
  Betriebs KG (C-320/01) [2003] ECR I-2041;
  [2003] 2 CMLR 15 . . . 422

Cadman (C-17/05) [2007] All ER (EC) 1; [2006]
  ECR I-9583; [2007] 1 CMLR 16 . . . 414
Café Vabre, Re [1975] 2 CMLR 336 . . . 160
Calfa see Criminal Proceedings against Calfa
Campus Oil Ltd v Minister for Industry and
  Energy (238/82) [1984] ECR 2727; [1984] 3
  CMLR 544 . . . 280
Campus Oil Ltd v Minister for Industry and
  Energy (72/83) [1984] ECR 2727; [1984] 3
  CMLR 544 . . . 279
Cantina v Commission (T-166/98) [2004] ECR
  II-3991 . . . 244
Carbonati Apuani (C-72/03) [2004] ECR
  I-8027 . . . 266

Carlsen v Prime Minister Rasmussen (Case I 361/1997) 6/4/1998, [1999] ECR I-49; [1999] 3 CMLR 854 . . . 163, 164

Carpenter v Secretary of State for the Home Department (C-60/00) [2002] ECR I-6279; [2002] 2 CMLR 64 . . . 336, 343, 348, 352

Cartesio Oktató és Szolgáltató (C-210/06) [2008] ECR I-9641 . . . 192, 313

Carvel (T-194/94) [1995] ECR II-2765; [1995] 3 CMLR 359 . . . 73

Casagrande v Landeshauptstadt München (9/74) [1974] ECR 773; [1974] 2 CMLR 423 . . . 320

Cassis de Dijon see Rewe-Zentral AG v Bundesmonopolverwaltung für Branntwein

Castelli v ONPTS (261/83) [1984] ECR 3199; [1987] 1 CMLR 465 . . . 319

Cement Association case see Vereeniging van Cementhandelaren v Commission

Centrafarm cases (15–16/74) [1974] ECR 1147; [1974] 2 CMLR 480 . . . 282

Centre Public d'Aide Sociale de Courcelles v Lebon (316/85) [1987] ECR 2811; [1989] 1 CMLR 337 . . . 308, 318, 319

Centros Ltd v Erhvervs-og Selskabsstyrelsen (C-212/97) [1999] ECR I-1459; [1999] 2 CMLR 551 . . . 313

Chatzi (C-149/10) [2010] ECR I-8489 . . . 116, 399

Chen v Secretary of State for the Home Department (C-200/02) [2004] ECR I-9925; [2004] 3 CMLR 48 . . . 321, 345, 350

Chevalley v Commission (15/70) [1975] ECR 975 . . . 237

Chiron Corporation v Murex Diagnostics Ltd (No 8) [1995] All ER (EC) 88; [1995] FSR 309 . . . 197

CIA Security International SA v Signalson SA (C-194/94) [1996] ECR I-2201 . . . 182

CILFIT Srl v Ministero della Sanita (283/81) [1982] ECR 3415; [1983] 1 CMLR 472 . . . 197, 198

Cinéthèque SA v Fédération Nationale des Cinémas Français (60–1/84) [1985] ECR 2605; [1986] 1 CMLR 365 . . . 286, 290

Claro v Milenium SL (C-168/05) [2006] ECR I-10421 . . . 206

Clean Car Autoservice (C-350/96) [1998] ECR I-2521 . . . 305

CNAVTS v E Thibault (C-136/95) [1998] ECR I-2011 . . . 418

Codorniu v Commission (Spanish wine producers) (C-309/89) [1994] ECR I-1853 . . . 230

Collins v Imtrat Handelsgesellschaft mbH (C-92/92) [1993] ECR I-5145; [1993] 3 CMLR 773 . . . 174

Collins v Secretary of State for Work and Pensions (C-138/02) [2004] ECR I-2703; [2004] 2 CMLR 8 . . . 309, 310, 335, 336, 341, 342, 352

Comet BV v Produktschap Voor Siergewassen (45/76) [1976] ECR 2043 . . . 204, 207

Commission v Assidomän (C-310/97 P) [1999] ECR I-5363 . . . 65, 234

Commission v Austria (C-147/93) [1995] ECR I-4125 . . . 335

Commission v Austria (C-150/00) [2004] ECR I-3887 . . . 278

Commission v Austria (C-147/03) [2005] ECR I-5969 . . . 216

Commission v Austria (C-205/06) [2009] ECR I-1301 . . . 143, 144

Commission v Austria (C-54/08) [2011] ECR I-4355 . . . 333

Commission v Austria (C-28/09) [2011] ECR I-13525 . . . 288, 294

Commission v Bayer (C-2 and 3/01P) [2004] ECR I-0023 . . . 362

Commission v Belgium (77/69) (Stamp Tax on Timber) [1970] ECR 237; [1974] 1 CMLR 203 . . . 213, 217

Commission v Belgium (156/77) [1978] ECR 1881 . . . 250

Commission v Belgium (Re: Public employees) (149/79) [1980] ECR 3881; [1981] 2 CMLR 413 . . . 333

Commission v Belgium (Customs Warehouses) (132/82) [1983] ECR 1649 . . . 266

Commission v Belgium (C-227–30/85) [1988] ECR 1 . . . 214

Commission v Belgium (293/85) (University Fees) [1988] ECR 305; [1989] 2 CMLR 527 . . . 215, 216, 218

Commission v Belgium (C-2/90) (Imports of Waste) [1992] ECR I-4431; [1993] 1 CMLR 365 . . . 265

Commission v Belgium (C-344/95) [1997] ECR I-1035; [1997] 2 CMLR 187 . . . 315

Commission v Belgium (C-47/08) [2011] ECR I-4105 . . . 333

Commission v Belgium and Luxembourg (90–1/63) [1996] ECR I-4115; [1997] 2 CMLR 289 . . . 162, 217, 266

Commission v Council (ERTA) (22/70) [1971] ECR 263; [1971] CMLR 335 . . . 24, 78, 84, 109, 224

Commission v Council (81/72) (Staff Salaries) [1973] ECR 575; [1973] CMLR 639 . . . 119

Commission v Council (16/88) (Re: Management Committee Procedure) [1988] ECR 3457 . . . 133

Commission v Council (C-300/89) (Re: Titanium Dioxide Directive) [1990] ECR I-2867 . . . 125

Commission v Council (C-155/91) (Waste Directive) [1993] ECR I-939 . . . 124

Commission v Council (C-24/94) [1996] ECR I-3989 . . . 223

Commission v Council (C-94/03) [2006] ECR I-1 . . . 125

Commission v Council (C-176/03) [2005] ECR I-7879 . . . 125

Commission v Council (C-440/05) [2007] ECR
    I-9097 . . . 126
Commission v Council (C-370/07) [2009] ECR
    I-8917 . . . 125
Commission v Denmark (106/84) [1986] ECR
    833 . . . 272
Commission v Denmark (Disposable Beer Cans)
    (302/86) [1988] ECR 4607; [1989] 1 CMLR
    619 . . . 122, 286
Commission v Denmark (Prohibition of
    Marketing of Enriched Foods) (C-192/01)
    [2003] ECR I-9693; [2003] 3 CMLR 29 . . . 281
Commission v Edith Cresson (C-432/04) [2006]
    ECR I-06387; [2006] All ER (D) 141 . . . 45
Commission v Finland (Air Transport)
    (467–9/98) [2002] ECR I-9519–9627 . . . 85
Commission v Finland (C-118/07) [2009] ECR
    I-10889 . . . 143, 144
Commission v France (163/73) [1974] ECR
    359 . . . 219
Commission v France (167/73) (French
    Merchant Seamen) [1974] ECR 359; [1974] 2
    CMLR 216 . . . 212, 217, 302
Commission v France (Advertising of Alcoholic
    Beverages) (152/78) [1980] ECR 2299; [1981] 2
    CMLR 743 . . . 222
Commission v France (Import of Lamb)
    (232/78) [1979] ECR 2729; [1980] 1 CMLR
    418 . . . 216, 217, 221
Commission v France (Re: Reprographic
    Machines) (90/79) [1981] ECR 283; [1981] 3
    CMLR 1 . . . 268, 270
Commission v France (Re: Italian Table Wines)
    (42/82) [1983] ECR 1013; [1984] 1 CMLR
    160 . . . 281, 283
Commission v France (Franking Machines)
    (21/84) [1985] ECR 1355 . . . 275
Commission v France (Re: French Nurses)
    (307/84) [1986] ECR 1734; [1987] 3 CMLR
    555 . . . 333
Commission v France (Re: Protection of
    Women) (C-312/86) [1988] ECR 6315; [1989] 1
    CMLR 408 . . . 418, 425
Commission v France (C-334/94) [1996] ECR
    I-1307 . . . 219
Commission v France (C-196/95) . . . 270
Commission v France (C-265/95) (Spanish
    Strawberries) [1997] ECR I-6959 . . . 212, 214,
    217, 275
Commission v France (Foie Gras) (C-184/96)
    [1998] ECR I-6197; [2000] 3 CMLR
    1308 . . . 264, 277
Commission v France (C-230/99) [2001] ECR
    I-1169 . . . 215
Commission v France (C-1/00) [2001] ECR
    I-3493 . . . 221
Commission v France (C-147/00) [2001] ECR
    I-2387 . . . 216
Commission v France (Cigarettes) (C-302/00)
    [2002] ECR I-2055 . . . 271

Commission v France (C-304/02) [2005] ECR
    I-6263; [2005] 3 CMLR 13 . . . 220
Commission v France (C-77/07) [2007] ECR
    I-158 . . . 220
Commission v France (C-50/08) [2011] ECR
    4195 . . . 333
Commission v Germany (70/72) [1973] ECR
    813 . . . 249
Commission v Germany (29/84) [1985] ECR
    1661 . . . 217
Commission v Germany (Re: Beer Purity Law)
    (178/84) [1987] ECR 1262; [1988] 1 CMLR
    780 . . . 120, 281, 288
Commission v Germany (Re: Insurance
    Services) (205/84) [1986] ECR 3755; [1987] 2
    CMLR 69 . . . 312, 323
Commission v Germany (Migration Policy)
    (281, 283–5, 287/85) [1987] ECR 3203 . . . 84
Commission v Germany (Re: Lawyers' Services)
    (427/85) [1988] ECR 1123; [1989] 2 CMLR
    677 . . . 327, 347
Commission v Germany (Animal Inspection
    Fees) (18/87) [1988] ECR 5427; [1990] 1 CMLR
    561 . . . 267
Commission v Germany (Sausage Purity Law)
    (274/87) [1989] ECR 250; [1989] 2 CMLR
    733 . . . 281
Commission v Germany (C-5/89) [1990] ECR
    I-3437 . . . 387
Commission v Germany (C-195/90) [1990] ECR
    I-2715 . . . 218
Commission v Germany (C-191/95) [1998] ECR
    I-5449 . . . 215
Commission v Germany (C-387/99) [2004] ECR
    I-3751 . . . 278
Commission v Germany (C-463/01) [2004] ECR
    I-11705 . . . 122
Commission v Germany (C-61/08) [2011] ECR
    I-4399 . . . 333
Commission v Greece (C-240/86) [1988] ECR
    1835; [1989] 3 CMLR 578 . . . 216
Commission v Greece (Re: Taxation
    of Motor Cars) (C-132/88) [1991]
    3 CMLR 1 . . . 269, 271
Commission v Greece (C-293/89) [1992] ECR
    I-4577 . . . 281
Commission v Greece (C-391/92) [1995] ECR
    I-1621; [1996] 1 CMLR 359 . . . 292
Commission v Greece (C-187/96) [1998] ECR
    I-1095 . . . 317
Commission v Greece (C-387/97) [2000] ECR
    I-5047 . . . 220
Commission v Ireland (61/77 R) (Sea Fishery
    Restrictions) [1977] ECR 1411 . . . 218
Commission v Ireland (Excise payments)
    (55/79) [1980] ECR 481; [1980] 1 CMLR
    734 . . . 271
Commission v Ireland (Metal Objects)
    (113/80) [1981] ECR 1625; [1982] 1 CMLR
    706 . . . 277, 279, 287

Commission v Ireland (Re: Buy Irish campaign) (249/81) [1982] ECR 4005; [1983] 2 CMLR 104 . . . 214, 274, 275, 277

Commission v Ireland (Dundalk Water Supply) (45/87) [1988] ECR 4929; [1989] 1 CMLR 225 . . . 265

Commission v Italy (7/61) (Pigmeat Imports) [1961] ECR 317; [1962] CMLR 39 . . . 217, 224, 279

Commission v Italy (Art Treasures) (7/68) [1968] ECR 423; [1969] CMLR 1 . . . 219, 265, 282

Commission v Italy (Statistical Levy) (24/68) [1969] ECR 193; [1971] CMLR 611 . . . 265

Commission v Italy (48/71) (Tax on Art Treasures No 2) [1972] ECR 529; [1972] CMLR 699 . . . 219

Commission v Italy (39/72) (Slaughtered Cows) [1973] ECR 101; [1973] CMLR 439 . . . 108, 171, 216

Commission v Italy (78/82) [1983] ECR 1955 . . . 278

Commission v Italy (274/83) [1987] 1 CMLR 345 . . . 215

Commission v Italy (101/84) [1985] ECR 2629 . . . 217

Commission v Italy (Italian Fruit) (184/85) [1987] ECR 2013 . . . 268, 272

Commission v Italy (22/87) [1989] ECR 143 . . . 184, 217

Commission v Italy (Re: Italian Customs Posts) (340/87) [1989] ECR 1483; [1991] 1 CMLR 437 . . . 266

Commission v Italy (Cheese fat content) (210/89) [1990] ECR 3704; [1992] 2 CMLR 1 . . . 281

Commission v Italy (C-424/98) [2000] ECR I-4001 . . . 336

Commission v Italy (C-212/99) [2001] ECR I-4923 . . . 220

Commission v Italy (C-129/00) [2003] ECR I-14637 . . . 214

Commission v Italy (C-110/05) (Italian Trailers) [2009] ECR I-519 . . . 288, 294, 295

Commission v Jego-Quere (C-263/02 P) [2004] ECR I-3425; [2004] 2 CMLR 12 . . . 65, 201, 235

Commission v Luxembourg (C-193/05) [2006] ECR I-8673 . . . 329

Commission v Luxembourg (C-53/08) [2011] ECR I-4309 . . . 333

Commission v Luxembourg & Belgium (Gingerbread) (2–3/62) [1962] ECR 425; [1963] CMLR 199 . . . 265

Commission v Netherlands (Re: Entry Requirements) (C-68/89) [1991] ECR I-2637, Proceedings of the ECJ 11/91, p. 4 . . . 315

Commission v Portugal (C-84/98) [2000] ECR I-5215; [2000] ECR I-5171 . . . 143, 144

Commission v Portugal (C-265/06) [2008] I-2245 . . . 295

Commission v Portugal (C-52/08) [2011] ECR 4275 . . . 333

Commission v Portugal (C-438/08) [2009] ECR I-10219 . . . 333

Commission v Spain (C-278/01) [2003] ECR I-14141 . . . 204

Commission v Spain (C-442/04) [2008] ECR I-3517 . . . 233

Commission v Spain (C-154/08) [2009] ECR I-187 . . . 188, 200, 214

Commission v Sweden (C-167/05) [2008] ECR I-2127 . . . 273

Commission v Sweden (C-249/06) [2009] ECR I-1335 . . . 143, 144

Commission v UK (53/77) (Pig Producers) [1977] ECR 921; [1977] 2 CMLR 359 . . . 218

Commission v UK (128/78) (Re Tachographs) [1979] ECR 419; [1979] 2 CMLR 45 . . . 108, 171, 217

Commission v UK (Re: Excise Duties on Wine (No 2)) (170/78) [1983] ECR 2263; [1983] 3 CMLR 512 . . . 272

Commission v UK (Import of Potatoes) (231/78) [1979] ECR 1447; [1979] 2 CMLR 427 . . . 275

Commission v UK (Re: Equal Pay for Equal Work) (61/81) [1982] ECR 2601; [1982] CMLR 377 . . . 413

Commission v UK (Re: UHT Milk) (124/81) [1983] ECR 203; [1983] 2 CMLR 1 . . . 276, 280, 283, 285, 287

Commission v UK (Re: Turkeys) (40/82) [1982] ECR 2793; [1982] 3 CMLR 497 . . . 97

Commission v UK (Re: Equal Treatment) (165/82) [1983] ECR 3431; [1984] 1 CMLR 44 . . . 419

Commission v UK (60/86) (Dim-Dip Car Lights) [1988] ECR 3921; [1988] 3 CMLR 437 . . . 262

Commission v UK (C-146/89) (Fishing Limits) [1991] ECR I-3533; [1991] 3 CMLR 649 . . . 162

Commission v UK (Nationality of Fishermen) (C-246/89 R) [1989] ECR 3125; [1989] 3 CMLR 601 . . . 218, 303

Commission v UK (C-466/98) [2002] ECR I-9427 . . . 144

Commission v Volkswagen (C-74/04 P) [2006] ECR I-6585 . . . 363

Compagnie Continentale France v Council of the European Communities (169/73) [1975] ECR 117; [1975] 1 CMLR 578 . . . 240, 248

Compagnie Maritime Belge Transports (C-395 and 396/96 P) [2000] ECR I-1365 . . . 379, 382

Comptoir National Technique Agricole (CNTA) SA v Commission (74/74) (No 1) [1975] ECR 533; [1977] 1 CMLR 171 . . . 244, 249

Conegate v Customs and Excise Commissioners (121/85) [1986] ECR 1007; [1986] 1 CMLR 739 . . . 279

Conforama (C-312/89) [1991] ECR I-997; [1993] 3 CMLR 746 . . . 291

Consten & Grundig v Commission (56 and
    58/64) [1966] ECR 299 . . . 362, 366, 370
Continental Can *see* Europemballage
    Corporation v Commission (6/72)
Coote v Granada (C-185/97) [1998] ECR I-5199;
    [1998] 3 CMLR 958 . . . 427
Corbiau (Pierre) v Administration des
    Contributions (C-24/92) [1993] ECR
    I-1277 . . . 190
Costa v ENEL (6/64) [1964] ECR 1141; [1964]
    CMLR 425 . . . 13, 28, 64, 65, 75, 141, 143, 148,
    160, 166, 187, 192, 197, 204
Council v Commission (242/87) (Erasmus)
    [1989] ECR 1425; [1991] 1 CMLR 478 . . . 84
Council v European Parliament (34/86) (1986
    Budget) [1986] ECR 2155; [1986] 3 CMLR
    94 . . . 59, 223
Courage Ltd v Crehan (C-453/99) [2001] ECR
    I-6297; [2001] 5 CMLR 28 . . . 187, 391
Cowan v The French Treasury (186/87) [1989]
    ECR 195; [1990] 2 CMLR 613 . . . 334
Criminal Proceedings against Arcaro
    (C-168/95) [1996] ECR I-4705; [1997]
    1 CMLR 179 . . . 179
Criminal Proceedings against Bickel
    (C-274/96) [1998] ECR I-7637; [1999]
    1 CMLR 348 . . . 338
Criminal Proceedings against Calfa (C-348/96)
    [1999] ECR I-11; [1999] 2 CMLR 1138 . . . 332
Criminal Proceedings against Lemmens
    (C-226/97) [1998] ECR I-3711; [1998] 3 CMLR
    261 . . . 182
Criminal Proceedings against Lyckeskog
    (C-99/00) [2002] ECR I-4839; [2004] 3 CMLR
    29 . . . 197
Criminal Proceedings against Marchandise
    (C-332/89) [1991] ECR I-997; [1993] 3 CMLR
    746 . . . 286, 291
Criminal Proceedings against Prantl
    (16/83) [1984] ECR 1299; [1985] 2 CMLR
    238 . . . 286, 288
Crotty v An Taoiseach [1987] 2 CMLR
    666 . . . 165
Cullet (Henri) v Centre Leclerc, Toulouse
    (231/83) [1985] ECR 305; [1985] 2 CMLR
    524 . . . 260

D and Sweden v Council (C-125/99 P) [2008] 3
    CMLR 17 . . . 416
Da Costa en Schaake NV v Nederlandse
    Belastingadministratie (28-30/62) [1963] ECR
    61; [1963] CMLR 224 . . . 65, 198, 201, 202
Daily Mail (81/87) [1988] ECR 5483 . . . 313
de Coster (C-17/00) [2001] ECR I-9445 . . . 325,
    336, 349
De Cuyper (C-406/04) [2006] ECR I-6947;
    [2006] 3 CMLR 44 . . . 342
de Geus v Bosch *see* Robert Bosch GmbH
    v Kleding Verkoopbedrijf de Geus en
    Uitdenbogerd

De Groot v Staatssecretaris van Financiën
    (C-385/00) [2004] STC 1346; [2002] ECR
    I-11819; [2004] 3 CMLR 21 . . . 307, 318
Decker v Caisse de maladie des employés privés
    (C-120/95) [1998] ECR I-1831 . . . 286
Defrenne v Belgium (No 1) (80/70) [1971] ECR
    445; [1971] 1 CMLR 494 . . . 403, 404, 405, 407
Defrenne v Sabena (No 2) (43/75) [1976] ECR
    455; [1976] 2 CMLR 98 . . . 118, 173, 201, 400,
    403, 404, 406, 407
Defrenne v Sabena (No 3) (149/77) [1978] ECR
    1365; [1978] 3 CMLR 312 . . . 400, 403
Dekker v Stichting VJM Centram (C-177/88)
    [1990] ECR I 3941; [1989] 3 CMLR 454 . . . 418
Delhaize v Promalvin, Proc of the Court
    of Justice 17/92 (C-47/90) [1992] ECR
    I-3669 . . . 278
Delimitis v Henniger Bräu (C-234/89) [1991]
    ECR I-935 . . . 370
Denkavit Loire Sarl v France (132/78) [1979]
    ECR 1928; [1979] 3 CMLR 605 . . . 269, 270
Dereci (C-256/11) [2011] ECR I-11315 . . . 346
Deutsche Grammophon Gesellschaft v Metro
    Grossmarkt (78/70) [1971] ECR 487; [1971]
    CMLR 631 . . . 282
Deutsche Lufthansa and Frankfurt-Hahn
    Airport (C-284/12) [2013] ECR I-755 . . . 387
Deutsche Telekom AG v Schroder (C-50/96)
    [2000] ECR I-743; [2002] 2 CMLR 25 . . . 400
Deutsche Telekom v Vick (C-324 & 325/96)
    [1998] ECR I-1333 . . . 96, 400
Deutscher Apothekerverband eV v 0800
    DocMorris NV (C-322/01) [2003] ECR
    I-14887; [2005] 1 CMLR 46 . . . 280
Deutscher Handballbund eV v Kolpak
    (C-438/00) [2003] ECR I-4135; [2004] 2
    CMLR 38 . . . 304
Deutscher Komponistenverband eV v
    Commission (8/71) [1971] ECR 705; [1973]
    CMLR 902 . . . 239
DGV v Commission and Council (241, 242,
    245–50/78) [1979] ECR 3017 . . . 245
D'Hoop v Office National de l'Emploi
    (C-224/98) [2002] ECR I-6191; [2002] 3 CMLR
    12 . . . 338, 339, 341
Diatta v Land Berlin (267/83) [1985] ECR 567;
    [1986] 2 CMLR 674 . . . 319, 320, 344
Digital Rights Ireland et al (Joined Cases
    C-293/12 and C-594/12) Judgment of 16 May
    2014, not yet reported . . . 159
Dillenkofer v Germany (C-178/94) [1996] ECR
    I-4845; [1996] 3 CMLR 469 . . . 187
DIP SpA v Comune di Bassano del Grappa
    (C-140/94) [1995] I-3257 . . . 292
Dorsch Consult Ingenieurgesellschaft mbH
    v Bundesbaugesellschaft Berlin mbH
    (C-54/96) [1997] ECR I-4961; [1998] 2 CMLR
    237 . . . 190
Dorsch Consult v Council (C-237/98) [2000]
    ECR I-4549 . . . 247

Dory v Germany (C-186/01) [2003] ECR I-2479;
[2003] 2 CMLR 26 ... 420, 426

Doughty v Rolls Royce plc [1992] 1 CMLR 1045;
[1992] ICR 538, CA ... 178

Dow Benelux Landewyck Sarl v Commission
(209–15 & 218/78) [1980] ECR 3125; [1981] 3
CMLR 134 ... 118, 389

Dow Benelux v Commission (85/87) [1989]
ECR 3137 ... 389

Draehmpaehl (Nils) v Urania
Immobilienservice (C-180/95) [1997]
ECR I-2195 ... 427

Dublin Regulation case see NS v Secretary of
State for the Home Department

Dubois v Commission (T-113/96) [1998] ECR
II-125 ... 240

Dubois v Council & Commission (C-95/98)
[1999] ECR I-4835 ... 240

Duke v GEC Reliance Ltd [1988] AC 618; [1988]
1 All ER 626; [1988] 2 WLR 359 (HL) ... 150,
160, 176, 179

Dumortier Frères SA v Council (64/76) [1982]
ECR 1733 ... 244, 245, 248

Dumortier Frères SA v Council (Gritz and
Quellmehl) (64 and 113/76) [1982] ECR
1748 ... 230, 245, 248

Dyestuffs see ICI v Commission (Dyestuffs)

Dynamic Medien Vertriebs GmbH v
Avides Media AG (C-244/06) [2008] ECR
I-505 ... 286

Dzodzi v Belgium (C-297/88) [1990] ECR
I-3763 ... 191, 194

Dzodzi v Belgium (C-197/89) [1990] ECR
I-3763 ... 191, 194

Eau de Cologne v Provide (C-150/88) [1989] ECR
3831 ... 194, 195

Echternecht and Moritz v Netherlands Minister
for Education and Science (389 & 390/87)
[1989] ECR 723; [1990] 2 CMLR 305 ... 343

Eco Swiss China Time Ltd v Benetton
International NV (C-126/97) [1999] ECR
I-3055 ... 357

EEC Seed Crushers and Oil Processors
Federation (FEDIOL) v Commission
(70/87) [1989] ECR 1781; [1991]
2 CMLR 489 ... 177

Elf Aquitaine v Commission (T-299/08) [2011]
ECR II-2149 ... 362

Einfuhr und Vorratsstelle für Getreide und
Futtermittel v Köster, Berodt & Co (25/70)
[1970] ECR 1161; [1972] CMLR 255 ... 133

Eman and Sevinger (C-300/04) [2006] ECR
I-8055 ... 55

Emmott v Minister for Social Welfare
(C-208/90) [1991] ECR I-4269; [1991]
3 CMLR 894 ... 205, 206, 207

Enderby v Frenchay Health Authority
(C-127/92) [1993] ECR I-5535; [1994]
1 CMLR 8 ... 412, 413

European Night Services (T-374-5/94) [1998]
ECR II-3141 ... 370

European Parliament v Council (Students
Residence Directive) (295/90) [1992] ECR
I-4193 ... 59, 226, 234

European Parliament v Council (13/83)
(Transport Policy) [1985] ECR 1513; [1986] 1
CMLR 138 ... 59, 238, 239

European Parliament v Council (C-302/87)
(Comitology) [1988] ECR 5615 ... 59, 133, 238

European Parliament v Council (C-70/88)
(Chernobyl) [1990] ECR I-2041; [1992] 1
CMLR 91 ... 59, 65, 226

European Parliament v Council (C-295/90)
(Students' Residence) [1992] ECR I-4193;
[1992] 3 CMLR 281 ... 226, 234

European Parliament v Council (C-65/93) [1995]
ECR I-643; [1996] 1 CMLR 4 ... 130

European Parliament v Council (C-540/03)
(Family Reunion Directive) [2007] All ER
(EC) 193; [2006] ECR I-5769 ... 103

Europemballage Corporation v Commission
(Continental Can) (6/72) [1973] ECR 215;
[1973] CMLR 199 ... 95, 377, 379, 380, 382,
392, 393

Eurotunnel (C-408/95) [1997] ECR I-6315;
[1998] 2 CMLR 293 ... 236

Evans Medical (C-324/93) ... 144

Even (207/78) ... 318

Extramet Industrie SA v Council of the
European Communities (C-358/89) [1991]
ECR I-2501; [1993] 2 CMLR 619 ... 230

Fabbrica Pisana Decision 80/334 ... 388

Faccini Dori v Recreb Srl (C-91/92)
[1994] ECR I-3325; [1995] 1 CMLR
665 ... 180, 182, 185

Factortame cases ... 2, 64, 149, 151, 152, 153,
185, 187, 218, 246, 254 see also R v Secretary of
State for Transport, ex p Factortame Ltd

Fantask A/S v Industriministeriet
(Erhvervsministeriet) (C-188/95) [1997] ECR
I-6783; [1998] 1 CMLR 473 ... 206

Fédération Charbonniere de Belgique v High
Authority of the European Coal and Steel
Community (Admissibility) (8/55) [1955] ECR
201; [1954–56] ECR 245 ... 84, 233

Federolio v Commission (T-122/96) [1997] ECR
II-1559 ... 230

FENIN v Commission (C-205/03 P) [2006] ECR
I-6295 ... 361

FIAMM v Council of the European Union
(T-69/00) [2005] ECR II-5393; [2006] 2 CMLR
9 ... 244, 247, 248

FIAMM v Council of the European Union
(C-120/06 P) [2008] ECRI-6513 ... 247, 248

Fiorini aka Christini v SNCF (32/75) [1975] ECR
1085; [1975] 1 CMLR 573 ... 317

Firma E Kampfmeyer v Commission (5, 7,
13 & 24/66) [1967] ECR 245 ... 244, 248, 249

Firma Foto Frost v Hauptzollamt Lubeck-Ost (314/85) [1987] ECR 4199; [1988] 3 CMLR 57 . . . 199, 234

Foglia v Novello (104/79) [1981] ECR 745; [1980] ECR 745 . . . 193, 194

Foglia v Novello (No 2) (244/80) [1981] ECR 3045 . . . 193

Ford v Commission (25-26/84) [1985] ECR 2725 . . . 362, 364

Ford Espana v The Spanish State (C-170/88) [1989] ECR 2307 . . . 267

Förster v IB-Groep (C-158/07) [2008] ECR I-8507 . . . 311, 342

Foster v British Gas plc (C-188/89) [1990] ECR I-3313; [1990] 2 CMLR 833 . . . 176, 177, 178

Fra.bo SpA v DVGW (C-171/11) . . . 274, 278

Fragd v Amministrazione delle Finanze [1985] ECR 1605 . . . 160

France v Commission (C-325/91) [1993] ECR I-3283 . . . 110, 233

France v Commission (C-327/91) [1994] ECR I-3641; [1994] 5 CMLR 517 . . . 232

France v Commission (C-68/94) [1998] ECR I-1375 . . . 383, 394

France v Commission (C-57/95) [1997] ECR I-1627; [1997] 2 CMLR 935 . . . 224, 232

France v Commission (T-425, 444, 450, and 456/04) . . . 384

France v European Parliament (Re Brussels Meetings) (358/85) [1986] ECR 2149 . . . 55

France v European Parliament (Re Meetings Facilities) (51/86) [1988] ECR 4821 . . . 55

France v European Parliament (C-345/95) [1997] ECR I-5215 . . . 55

France v European Parliament (C-237–8/11) Judgment of the Court (Third Chamber) of 13 December 2012 . . . 55

France v United Kingdom (141/78) (Fishing Net Mesh Sizes) [1979] ECR 2923; [1980] 1 CMLR 6 . . . 221

Franchet et al v Commission (T-391/03 & T-700/04) [2006] ECR II-2023 . . . 74

Francovich v Italy (C-6/90 & C-9/90) [1991] ECR I-5357; [1993] 2 CMLR 66 . . . 65, 95, 161, 180, 184, 185, 187, 205, 207, 217, 243, 391

Fransson (C-617/10) Judgment of 26 February 2013 (OJ (2013) C280) . . . 104

Fratelli Cucchi v Avez SpA (77/76) [1987] ECR 987 . . . 269

Frontini v Ministero delle Finanze [1974] 2 CMLR 372 . . . 160

G Badeck et al v Land Hessen (C-158/97) [2000] ECR I-1875 . . . 425

Gaal see Landesamt für Ausbildungsförderung Nordrhein-Westfalen v Gaal

Galileo International Technology and Others v Commission (T-279/03) [2006] ECR II-1291 . . . 248

Gallagher (C-175/94) [1995] ECR I-4253 . . . 330

Garcia Avello (C-148/02) [2003] ECR I-11613 . . . 349

Garland v British Rail Engineering Ltd (12/81) [1982] 2 All ER 402; [1982] ECR 359 . . . 201, 403, 404

Garland v British Rail Engineering Ltd [1982] ICR 420 (HL) . . . 149, 150

GB-INNO-BM (13/77) [1977] ECR 2115 . . . 392

Gebhard v Consiglio dell'Ordine degli Avvocati (C-55/94) [1995] ECR I-4165; [1996] 1 CMLR 603 . . . 261, 312, 324

Geddo see Riseria Luigi Geddo v Ente Nazionale Risi

GEMA v Commission (125/78) [1979] ECR 3173; [1980] 2 CMLR 177 . . . 239

Gencor v Commission (T-102/96) [1999] ECR II-753 . . . 395

Germany v Commission (24/62) (Tariff Quota on Wine) [1963] ECR 63; [1963] CMLR 347 . . . 233

Germany v Council (C-280/93) [1994] ECR I-4973 . . . 158, 177

Germany v European Parliament (C-376/98 & C-74/99); R v Secretary of State for Health ex p Imperial Tobacco Ltd (Tobacco Advertising) [2000] ECR I-8419 . . . 82, 88, 126, 232, 261

Germany v European Parliament and Council (C-380/03) [2007] All ER (EC) 1016; [2007] 2 CMLR 1 . . . 82, 126, 261

Gestoras (C-354/04 P) [2007] I-1579 . . . 101

Geven v Land Nordrhein-Westfalen (C-213/05) [2008] All ER (EC) 1196; [2007] 3 CMLR 45 . . . 308

Giangregorio v Secretary of State for the Home Department [1983] 3 CMLR 472 . . . 317

Gibraltar v Council (C-298/89) [1993] ECR I-3605 . . . 227

Giuffrida v Council (105/75) [1976] ECR 1395 . . . 233

Glaverbel v Commission (62/87) [1988] ECR 1573 . . . 384

Gourmet International Products see Konsumentombudsmannen (KO) v Gourmet International Products AB

Grad v Finanzamt Traunstein (9/70) [1971] CMLR 1 . . . 171, 172, 174, 176

Granital v Amministrazione delle Finanze Judgment of 8 June 1984 [1984] 1 Giui It 1521 . . . 160

Grant v South West Trains (C-249/96) [1998] 1 CMLR 993 . . . 416

Gravier v City of Liège (293/83) [1985] ECR 593; [1985] 3 CMLR 1 . . . 95, 334

Greenpeace International v Commission (T-585/93) [1995] ECR II-2205 . . . 231

Greenpeace International v Commission (C-321/95 P) [1998] ECR I-1651 . . . 231

Grimaldi v Fonds des Maladies Professionelles (C-322/88) [1989] ECR 4407; [1991] 2 CMLR 265 . . . 110, 122

Groener v Minister of Education and the City
of Dublin Vocational Education Committee
(379/87) [1989] ECR 3967; [1990] 1 CMLR
401 . . . 315

Grogan see Society for the Protection of Unborn
Children (Ireland) Ltd (SPUC) v Grogan

Grzelczyk (C-184/99) [2001] ECR I-6193;
[2002] 1 CMLR 19 . . . 310, 334, 335, 336, 338,
339, 340

Guerlain SA, Rochas SA, Lanvin SA and Nina
Ricci SA (235/78 and 1–3/79) [1980] ECR
2327 . . . 372

Gul v Regierungsprasident Dusseldorf (131/85)
[1986] ECR 1573; [1987] 1 CMLR 501 . . . 320

Habermann-Beltermann (Gabriele) v
Arbeiterwohlfahrt Bezirksverband (C-421/92)
[1994] ECR I-1657; [1994] 2 CMLR 242 . . . 421

Haegemann v Belgium (181/73) [1974] ECR 449;
[1975] 1 CMLR 515 . . . 106

Haim v Kassenzahnärztliche Vereinigung
Nordrhein (C-424/97) [2000] ECR
I-5123 . . . 185

Handels-og Kontorfunktionaerernes Forbund
i Danmark v Dansk Arbejdsgiverforening
(Danfoss) (109/88) [1989] ECR 3199; [1991] 1
CMLR 8 . . . 414

Hartmann v Freistaat Bayern (C-212/05)
[2008] All ER (EC) 1166; [2008]
3 CMLR 38 . . . 308

Harz v Tradex (79/83) [1984] ECR 1921; [1986] 2
CMLR 430 . . . 179

Hauer v Land Rheinland-Pfalz (44/79) [1979]
ECR 3727; [1980] 3 CMLR 42 . . . 103, 112

Hauptzollamt Mainz v CA Kupferberg & Cie KG
aA (104/81) [1982] ECR 3641; [1983] 1 CMLR
1 . . . 176

Hautala, Heidi v Council (C-353/99 P) [2001]
ECR I-9565; [2002] 1 CMLR 15 . . . 73, 121

Hedley Lomas see R v Ministry of Agriculture,
Fisheries and Food ex p Hedley Lomas
(Ireland) Ltd

Hellmut Marschall v Land Nordrhein-Westfalen
(C-409/95) [1997] ECR I-6363; [1998] 1 CMLR
547 . . . 425

Helmig (C-399/92) [1994] ECR I-5727 . . . 412

Hennessy/Henkel Decision [1981] 1 CMLR
601 . . . 366

Herrero v Instituto Madrileño de la Salud
(Imsalud) (C-294/04) [2006] ECR
I-1513 . . . 421

Hertz v Aldi (C-179/88) [1990] ECR
I-3979 . . . 423, 424

Hilti A G v Commission (T-30/89) [1990] ECR
II-163; [1990] 4 CMLR 16 . . . 118, 389

Hoechst (46/87 and 227/88) [1989] ECR
2859 . . . 388

Hoekstra v Bestuur der Bedrijfsvereniging voor
Detailhandel en Ambachten (75/63) [1964]
ECR 177; [1964] CMLR 319 . . . 305, 308

Hoffmann-La Roche (85/76) [1979] ECR
461 . . . 377, 379, 380, 382

Hoffmann-La Roche Decision 2003/2 . . . 390

Hofmann v Barmer Ersatzkasse (184/83) [1984]
ECR 3047; [1986] 1 CMLR 242 . . . 421

Höfner and Elser v Macrotron GmbH (C-41/90)
[1991] ECR I-1979 . . . 361

Holcim (Deutschland) AG v Commission
(C-282/05 P) [2007] ECR I-2941 . . . 244, 247

Honeywell case, FCC Judgment 6 July 2010
(2 BvR 2261/06) BVerfGE 126, 286 . . . 159

Hüls AG v Commission (C-199/92 P) [1999] ECR
I-4287 . . . 362

Humblet v Belgium (6/60) [1960] ECR 559;
[1960] ECR 1125 . . . 65

Humblot v Directeur des Services Fiscaux
(112/84) [1987] ECR 1367; [1985] ECR 1367;
[1986] 2 CMLR 338 . . . 271

Hunermund (C-292/92) [1983] ECR
6787 . . . 292

Hungary v Slovak Republic (C-364/10)
ECLI:EU:C:2012:630 . . . 221

Hurd v Jones (Inspector of Taxes) (44/84) [1986]
ECR 29; [1986] 2 CMLR 1 . . . 173

HZA Bremerhafen v Massey Ferguson (8/73)
[1973] ECR 89 . . . 83

Ianelli & Volpi SpA v Meroni (74/76) [1977] ECR
557; [1977] 2 CMLR 688 . . . 274

IATA see R v Dept of Transport ex p
International Air Transport Association and
European Low Fares Airline Association

IAZ International Belgium NV v Commission
(C-96/82) [1983] ECR 3369 . . . 363

ICI v Commission (Dyestuffs) (48, 49 & 51–7/69)
[1972] ECR 619; [1972] CMLR 557 . . . 362, 363

ICI Commercial Solvents v Commission (6 and
7/73) [1974] ECR 223 . . . 360, 362, 375, 377,
380, 381

IFAW v Commission (T-168/02) [2004] ECR
II-4135 . . . 74

Ilonka Sayn-Wittgenstein v Landeshauptmann
von Wien (C-208/09) . . . 349

Impact v Minister for Agriculture and Food and
Others (C-268/06) [2008] ECR I-2483 . . . 180

IN.CO.GE.'90 (C-10-22/97) [1998] ECR
I-6307 . . . 142

Ingrid Rinner-Kuhn v FWW
Spezial-Gebaudereiningung (C-171/88) [1989]
ECR 2743; [1989] IRLR 493 . . . 404, 412

Inspire Art (C-167/01) [2003] ECR I-10155;
[2005] 3 CMLR 34 . . . 313

Institute of the Motor Industry v Customs and
Excise Commission (C-149/97) [1998] ECR
I-7053; [1999] 1 CMLR 326 . . . 99

Intel v Commission (T-286/09) not yet
reported . . . 379, 381

Intel v Commission (C-413/14 P) [2014] ECR
I-547 and appeal pending . . . 251, 379,
381, 390

Intermills v Commission (323/82) [1984] ECR
3809 . . . 384
International Chemical Corp SpA v
Amministrazione delle Finanze dello Stato
(66/80) [1981] ECR 1191; [1983] 2 CMLR
593 . . . 199, 201, 251
International Fruit Co v Produktschap voor
Groenten en Fruit (No 3) (21–2/72) [1972]
ECR 27; [1975] 2 CMLR 1 . . . 176
International Fruit Co NV v Commission
(41–4/70) [1971] ECR 411; [1975] 2 CMLR
515 . . . 106, 228, 229, 277
International Transport Workers' Federation v
Viking Line ABP (C-438/05) [2008] All ER
(EC) 127; [2008] 1 CMLR 51 . . . 325
Internationale Handelsgesellschaft (11/70)
[1970] ECR 1125; [1972] CMLR 255 . . . 112,
119, 140, 142
Internationale Handelsgesellschaft case (Solange
I) (BVerfGE 37, 271) . . . 156
Interquell v Commission and Council (C-261
and 262/78) [1979] ECR 3045 . . . 245
Intertanko (C-308/06) [2008] ECR
I-4057 . . . 177
Inuit (T-18/10) (not yet reported) . . . 230, 231
Inuit v EP & Council (C-583/11 P) . . . 230, 231
Ioannidis (C-256/04) [2005] ECR I-8275; [2005]
3 CMLR 47 . . . 341, 342
Ireks-Arkady GmbH v Council of Ministers
and Commission (238/78) [1979] ECR
2955 . . . 245
Irish Creamery Milk Suppliers (36/80 and 76/80)
[1981] ECR 81 . . . 196
Isoglucose cases see Amylum NV v Council of
the European Communities (Amylum and
Tunnel Refineries)
Italian Flat Glass, Re (T-68 and 77–8/89) [1992]
ECR II-1403 . . . 368, 375
Italy v Watson and Belmann (118/75) [1976] ECR
1185; [1976] 2 CMLR 619 . . . 316
ITC Innovative Technology Center GmbH v
Bundesagentur für Arbeit (C-208/05) [2007]
ECR I-181 . . . 305

Jackson v AG [2006] AC 262 . . . 153
Jany v Staatssecretaris van Justitie (C-268/99)
[2001] ECR I-8615; [2003] 2 CMLR
1 . . . 311, 312
JCB v Commission (T-67/01) [2004] ECR
II-0049 . . . 374
Jego-Quere & Cie SA v Commission
(T-177/01) [2004] ECR I-3425; [2004]
2 CMLR 12 . . . 235
Jenkins v Kingsgate (Clothing Productions)
Ltd (96/80) [1981] ECR 911; [1981] 2 CMLR
241 . . . 411
Jia v Migrationsverket (C-1/05) [2007] QB 545;
[2007] 2 WLR 1005; [2007] All ER (EC) 575;
[2007] 1 CMLR 41 . . . 320, 345
Jipa (C-33/07) [2008] ECR I-5157 . . . 332

John Walker & Sons Ltd v Ministeriet for Skatter
og Afgifter (243/84) [1986] ECR 875 . . . 272
Johnston v Chief Constable RUC (222/84)
[1986] ECR 1651; [1986] 3 CMLR 240 . . . 117,
176, 419

Kadi and Al Barakaat v Council (C-402/05 P
& C-415/05) [2008] I-6351 . . . 76, 83, 113,
144, 177
Kalanke v Freie Hansestadt Bremen (C-450/93)
[1995] ECR I-3051; [1996] 1 CMLR 175 . . . 425
Katsarou v Greek State Judgment 3457/1998 of
25 September 1998 . . . 199
Kaur see R v Secretary of State for the Home
Department ex p Kaur (Manjit)
KB v NHS Pensions Agency (C-117/01) [2004]
ECR I-541; [2004] 1 CMLR 28 . . . 407, 416
Keck and Mithouard (C-267–8/91) [1993] ECR
I-3283; [1995] 1 CMLR 101 . . . 65, 291, 292,
295, 297, 325
Kempf v Staats Secretaria van Justitie (139/85)
[1986] ECR 1741; [1987] 1 CMLR 764 . . . 306
Kirsamer Hack (C-189/91) [1993] ECR
I-6185 . . . 384
Kleinwort Benson (C-346/93) [1995]
I-615 . . . 191
Kloppenburg Case Bundesfinanzhof 25 April
1985, NJW 1988, 1459; [1988] 3 CMLR
1 . . . 156
Köbler v Austria (C-224/01) [2003] ECR I-10239;
[2003] 3 CMLR 28 . . . 118, 188, 200, 202, 214
Kodak, Re [1970] CMLR D9 . . . 361
Kolpnghuis see Public Prosecutor v Kolpnghuis
Nijmegan
Koninklijke Vereeniging ter Bevordering van
de Belangen des Boekhandels v Free Record
Shop BV (C-39/96) [1997] ECR I-2303 . . . 372
Konsumentombudsmannen (KO) v De Agostini
(C-34–6/95) [1997] ECR I-3843; [1998] 1
CMLR 32 . . . 293
Konsumentombudsmannen (KO) v Gourmet
International Products AB (C-405/98) [2001]
All ER (EC) 308; [2001] ECR I-1795; [2001] 2
CMLR 31 . . . 293
Köster see Einfuhr und Vorratsstelle für
Getreide und Futtermittel v Köster,
Berodt & Co
Kowalska v Hamburg (C-33/89) [1990] ECR
2607; [1990] IRLR 447 . . . 405
Kreil v Germany (C-285/98) [2000] ECR I-69;
[2002] 1 CMLR 36 . . . 420
Kremzow v Austria (C-299/95) [1997] ECR
I-2629; [1997] 3 CMLR 1289 . . . 310
Krohn v Commission (175/84) [1986] ECR 753;
[1987] 1 CMLR 745 . . . 240, 249
KSH v Council and Commission (101/76) [1977]
ECR 797 . . . 233, 235
Kühne & Heitz NV v Productschap voor
Pluimvee en Eieren (C-453/00) [2004] ECR
I-837; [2006] 2 CMLR 17 . . . 201

Kuhner (33 & 59/79) [1980] ECR 1677 . . . 117

Kükükdeveci (C-555/07) [2010]
ECR I-365 . . . 116, 174, 175, 180, 181, 182, 433

Kupferberg see Hauptzollamt Mainz v CA
Kupferberg & Cie KGaA

Kziber see Office National de l'Emploi v Kziber

Laboratoires Pharmaceutiques Bergaderm
SA v Commission (C-352/98 P) [2000] ECR
I-5291 . . . 187, 242, 243, 244, 246, 247

Lair v Universität Hannover (39/86) [1988] ECR
3161; [1989] 3 CMLR 545 . . . 95, 309, 318

Lancome SA v ETOS BV (99/79) (Perfumes)
[1980] ECR 2511; [1981] 2 CMLR 164 . . . 123

Land Baden-Württemberg v Tsakouridis
(C-145/09) [2010] ECR I-11979 . . . 332

Land Nordrhein-Westfalen v Uecker & Jacquet
(C-64/96) [1997] ECR I-3171; [1997]
3 CMLR 963 . . . 347

Land Rheinland-Pfalz v Alcan (C-24/95) [1997]
ECR I-1591 . . . 386

Landtová (C-399/09) [2011] ECR I-415 . . . 163

Lancry (C-363/93) [1994] ECR I-3957 . . . 266

Larsson v Dansk Handel & Service, acting for
Fotex Supermarked A/S (C-400/95) [1997]
ECR I-2757; [1997] 2 CMLR 915 . . . 422,
423, 424

Laval un Partneri Ltd v Svenska
Byggnadsarbetareforbundet (C-341/05)
[2008] All ER (EC) 166; [2008] 2 CMLR
9 . . . 325

Lawrence v Regent Office Care Ltd (C-320/00)
[2002] ECR I-7325; [2002] 3 CMLR 27 . . . 409

Lawrie-Blum v Land Baden-Würtemberg
(66/85) [1986] ECR 2121; [1987] 3 CMLR
389 . . . 306, 333

Leclerc-Siplec v TF1 Publicite SA (C-412/93)
[1995] ECR I-179; [1995] 3 CMLR
422 . . . 194, 293

Leclere v Caisse Nationale des Prestations
Familiales (C-43/99) [2001] ECR I-4265;
[2001] 2 CMLR 49 . . . 308, 318

Legros (C-163/90) [1992] ECR I-4625 . . . 121

Lemmens see Criminal Proceedings against
Lemmens

Leonesio v Italian Ministry of Agriculture and
Forestry (93/71) [1972] ECR 287; [1973]
CMLR 343 . . . 174

Les Verts see Parti Ecologiste v European
Parliament and Council

Leur-Bloem (C-28/95) [1997] ECR I-4161 . . . 194

Levez v TH Jennings (Harlow Pools) Ltd
(C-326/96) [1998] ECR I-7835; [1999] 2 CMLR
363 . . . 207

Levin v The Minister of State for Justice
(53/81) [1982] ECR 1035; [1982] 2 CMLR
454 . . . 305, 306

Lindorfer v Council (C-227/04) [2008]
Pens. LR 15 . . . 181

Lisbon Judgment case 2 BvE 2/08 . . . 158

Litster v Forth Dry Dock & Engineering
Co Ltd [1990] 1 AC 546; [1989]
2 WLR 634 . . . 151

Lommers v Minister van Landbouw,
Natuurbeheer en Visserij (C-476/99) [2002]
ECR I-2891; [2004] 2 CMLR 49 . . . 426

Luisi v Ministero del Tesoro (286/82) [1984] ECR
377; [1985] 3 CMLR 52 . . . 334

Lütticke (Alfons) GmbH v Commission
(C-48/65) [1966] ECR 27; [1966] CMLR
378 . . . 172, 215, 224, 238

Lütticke v Commission (4/69) [1971] ECR
325 . . . 200, 236

Lütticke v Hauptzollamt Saarlouis (57/65) [1966]
ECR 205; [1971] CMLR 674 . . . 270

Luxembourg v European Parliament (230/81)
[1983] ECR 255; [1983] 2 CMLR 726 . . . 223

Luxembourg v European Parliament (108/83)
[1984] ECR 1945 . . . 55

Lyckeskog see Criminal Proceedings against
Lyckeskog

Macarthys Ltd v Smith (129/79) [1980] ECR
1275; [1980] 2 CMLR 205 . . . 408, 409

Macarthys v Smith [1979] 3 All ER
325 . . . 149, 152

McCarthy (Shirley) v Secretary of State for
the Home Department (C-434/09) (not yet
reported) . . . 346

McKenna (C-191/03) [2006] All ER (EC) 455;
[2005] ECR I-7631; [2006] 1 CMLR 6 . . . 424

Magnavision v General Optical Council (No
2) [1987] 2 CMLR 262 . . . 197

Mahlberg (C-207/98) [2000] ECR I-3201; [2001]
3 CMLR 40 . . . 421

Maizena GmbH v Council (Roquette Frères)
(138-9/79) [1980] ECR 3393 . . . 130, 226,
229, 233

Manfredi v Lloyd Adriatico Assicurazioni SpA
(C-295-298/04) [2007] Bus LR 188; [2007] All
ER (EC) 27 . . . 187

Mangold v Helm (C-144/04) [2006] All ER
(EC) 383; [2005] ECR I-9981; [2006] 1 CMLR
43 . . . 116, 174, 175, 180, 181, 182, 433

Mannesmannröhren-Werke AG v Commission
(T-112/98) [2001] ECR II-729 . . . 121

Marchandise see Criminal Proceedings against
Marchandise

Marks & Spencer plc v Customs and Excise
Commissioners (C-62/00) [2002] ECR I-6325;
[2002] 3 CMLR 9 . . . 175, 199

Marks & Spencer plc v Customs and Excise
Commissioners (C-309/06) [2008] STC 1408;
[2008] 2 CMLR 42 . . . 120, 121

Marks & Spencer plc v David Halsey (Her
Majesty's Inspector of Taxes) (C-446/03)
[2005] ECR I-10837 . . . 313

Marleasing SA v La Comercial Internacionale
de Alementacion SA (C-106/89) [1990] ECR
I-4135; [1992] 1 CMLR 305 . . . 99, 179

Marrosu and Sardino (C-53/04) [2006]
ECR I-7213 . . . 179

Mars see Verein Gegen Unwesen in Handel und
Gewerbe Koln eV v Mars GmbH

Marshall v Southampton and South West
Hampshire AHA (No 1) (152/84) [1986] ECR
723; [1986] 1 CMLR 688 . . . 150, 151, 175, 176,
177, 179, 182, 403, 405, 418

Marshall v Southampton and South West
Hampshire AHA (No 2) (C-271/91) [1993]
ECR I-4367; [1993] 3 CMLR 293 . . . 205,
403, 426

Martinez Sala v Freistaat Bayern (C-85/96)
[1998] ECR I-2691 . . . 338

Mary Murphy v An Bord Telecom Eireann
(157/86) [1988] ECR 673; [1988] 1 CMLR
879 . . . 409, 413

Masdar (UK) v Commission (C-47/07 P) [2008]
ECR I-9761 . . . 244

Mattheus v Doego Fruchtimport und
Tiefkuhlkost eG (93/78) [1978] ECR 2203;
[1979] 1 CMLR 551 . . . 192, 196

Mayr v Backerei und Konditorei Gerhard
Flockner OHG (C-506/06) [2008] All ER (EC)
613; [2008] 2 CMLR 27 . . . 423

ME v Refugee Applications Commissioner
(C-411/10, 493/10) [2012] 2 CMLR 9 . . . 103

Meilicke v ADV/ORGA AG (C-83/91) [1992]
ECR I-4871 . . . 192

Melgar v Ayuntamiento de Los Barrios
(C-438/99) [2001] ECR I-6915; [2003] 3 CMLR
4 . . . 422, 428

Melki and Abdeli (C-188 and 189/10) [2010] ECR
I-5667 . . . 162, 208

Melloni (C-399/11) Judgment of 26 February
2013, not yet reported . . . 104, 142

Meroni & Co Industrie Metallurgiche SpA v
High Authority of the European Coal and
Steel Community (9/56) [1958] ECR 11;
[1957–58] ECR 133 . . . 133, 232, 250

Meroni & Co v High Authority of the European
Coal and Steel Community (14/60) [1961]
ECR 161; [1961] ECR 321 . . . 242

Metock et al (C-127/08) [2008] ECR
I-6241 . . . 320, 345

Metro SB-Grossmarkte GmbH & Co KG v
Commission (26/76) [1977] ECR 1875; [1978]
2 CMLR 1 . . . 229, 360, 366, 369

Metropole Television v Commission (T-112/99)
[2001] ECR II-2459 . . . 368

Meyers v Adjudication Officer (C-116/94) [1995]
ECR I-2131; [1996] 1 CMLR 461 . . . 383

Micheletti (C-369/90) [1992] ECR I-4239 . . . 337

Michelin v Commission (322/81) [1983] ECR
3461 . . . 377

Microban (T-262/10) [2011] ECR
II-7697 . . . 231, 232

Microsoft Case COMP/C–3/37.792 . . . 390

Microsoft Corp v Commission (T-201/04) [2007]
ECR II-3601 . . . 379, 380

Minister for Economic Affairs v SA Fromagerie
'Le Ski' [1972] CMLR 330 . . . 155

Minister of the Interior v Cohn-Bendit [1980]
1 CMLR 543 . . . 161

Ministère Public v Mutsch (137/84) [1985]
ECR 2681; [1986] 1 CMLR 648 . . . 318

Ministre de l'Interieur v Oteiza Olazabal
(C-100/01) [2002] ECR I-10981; [2005] 1
CMLR 49 . . . 332

Ministry of Justice v Cornelius Kramer
(3, 4 and 6/76) [1976] ECR 1279; [1977]
2 CMLR 440 . . . 286

Miret (Wagner) v Fondo de Garantia Salarial
(C-334/93) [1993] ECR I-6911; [1995] 2 CMLR
49 . . . 179, 180

Mobistar (C-544/03) [2005] ECR
I-7723 . . . 336, 350

Molkerei-Zentrale Westfalen/Lippe v
Hauptzollamt Paderborn (28/76) [1968] ECR
143; [1968] CMLR 187 . . . 270

Morellato see Tommaso Morellato v Unita
Sanitaria Locale (Usl) N 11 di Pordenone

Morgan and Bucher (C-11–12/06) [2008] All ER
(EC) 851; [2009] 1 CMLR 1 . . . 342

Morgenbesser v Consiglio dell'Ordine degli
Avvocati di Genova (C-313/01) [2003] ECR
I-13467; [2004] 1 CMLR 24 . . . 324, 329

Morson and Jhanjan v Netherlands
(35 and 36/82) [1982] ECR 3723; [1983]
2 CMLR 221 . . . 347

Moulins de Pont a Mousson (Maize, Gritz,
and Quellmehl cases) (124/76 & 20/77)
[1977] ECR 1795 . . . 245

Mouvement contre le Racisme, l'Antisemitisme
et la Xenophobie ASBL (MRAX) v Belgium
(C-459/99) [2002] ECR I-6591; [2002]
3 CMLR 25 . . . 113, 316, 344

Mr and Mrs F v The Belgian State (7/75) [1975]
ECR 679; [1975] 2 CMLR 442 . . . 95

Mr and Mrs Richard Meade (238/83) [1984]
ECR 2631 . . . 350

Mulder v Council of the European
Communities (C-104/89 & C-37/90) [2000]
ECR I-203 . . . 233, 246

Munoz v Frumar Ltd (C-253/00) [2002] ECR
I-7289 . . . 174

Mutsch see Ministère Public v Mutsch

My Travel Group plc v Commission (T-212/03)
[2008] ECR II-1967 . . . 246

National Panasonic v Commission (136/79)
[1980] ECR 2033; [1980] 3 CMLR
169 . . . 118, 388

Neath v Hugh Steeper (C-152/91) [1993] ECR
I-6935; [1995] 2 CMLR 357 . . . 407

Netherlands v Council (C-58/94) [1996] ECR
I-2169 . . . 121

Netherlands v European Parliament and
Council (C-377/98) (Biotechnology Directive)
[2001] ECR I-7079 . . . 82, 88

Netherlands v P Bakker Hillegom BV
(C-111/89) [1990] ECR I-1735; [1990]
3 CMLR 119 . . . 268

Netherlands v Reed (59/85) [1986] ECR 1283;
[1987] 2 CMLR 448 . . . 303, 319, 344

Nicolo [1990] 1 CMLR 173 . . . 161

Nimz v Hamburg (C-184/89) [1991] ECR
I-297 . . . 404

Ninni-Orasche v Bundesminister für
Wissenschaft, Verkehr und Kunst (C413/01)
[2004] All ER (EC) 765; [2003] ECR I-13187;
[2004] 1 CMLR 19 . . . 306

Noordwijks Cement Accord (8–11/66) [1967]
ECR 93; [1967] CMLR 77 . . . 109, 224

Nordgetreide v Commission (42/71) [1972] ECR
105 . . . 238

Nordsee Deutsche Hochseefischerei GmbH v
Reederei Mond Hochseefischerei Nordstern
AG & Co KG (102/81) [1982] ECR 1095 . . . 190

NS v Secretary of State for the Home
Department (C-411/10) [2012] 2 CMLR
9 . . . 103

NTN v Council (113/77 R) [1977] ECR
1721 . . . 218

Nygard (C-234/99) [2002] ECR I-3657 . . . 270

Office National de l'Emploi (ONE) v Deak
(94/84) [1985] ECR 1873 . . . 318

Office National de l'Emploi (ONE) v Kziber
(C-18/90) [1991] ECR I-199 . . . 176

O'Flynn v Adjudication Officer (C-237/94)
[1996] ECR I-2617; [1996] 3 CMLR 103 . . . 318

Olazabal see Ministre de l'Interieur v Oteiza
Olazabal

Omega Spielhallen v Bonn (C-36/02) [2004] ECR
I-9609; [2005] 1 CMLR 5 . . . 158

Openbaar Ministerie v Van Tiggele (82/77)
[1978] ECR 25 . . . 278

Orkem v Commission (374/87) [1989] ECR
3283 . . . 389

Oscar Bronner GmbH & Co KG v Mediaprint
Zeitungs- und Zeitschrift enverlag GmbH &
Co (C-7/97) [1998] ECR I-7791 . . . 380

O, S & L (C-356–7/11)
ECLI:EU:C:2012:776 . . . 346

Otto BV v Postbank NV (C-60/92) [1993] ECR
I-5683 . . . 121

Outokumpu OY (C-213/96) [1998] ECR
I-1777 . . . 271

P v S and Cornwall County Council (C-13/94)
[1996] ECR I-2143; [1996] 2 CMLR 247 . . . 415

Paquay v Société d'Architectes Hoet + Minne
SPRL (C-460/06) [2008] 1 CMLR 12; [2008]
ICR 420 . . . 423

Parker Pen case see Viho Europe BV v
Commission (Parker Pen case)

Parti Ecologiste v European Parliament and
Council (294/83) (Les Verts) [1986] ECR 1339;
[1987] 2 CMLR 343 . . . 59, 76, 222, 223, 224

Patented Feedstuffs, Re NJW 1988, 1456; [1989]
2 CMLR 902 . . . 156

Pecastaing v Belgium (98/79) [1980] ECR 691;
[1980] 3 CMLR 685 . . . 330

Perreux (2009) 30 October 2009, Conseil d'État,
No 298348 . . . 161

Peterbroeck Van Campenhout & Cie SCS v
Belgium (C-312/93) [1995] ECR I-4599; [1996]
1 CMLR 793 . . . 195, 207

Petrie (T-191/99) [2001] ECR II-3677 . . . 216

Pfeiffer v Deutsches Rotes Kreuz Kreisverband
Waldshut eV (C-397/01-401/01) [2004] ECR
I-8835; [2005] 1 CMLR 44 . . . 179

Philip Morris v Commission (730/79) [1980]
ECR 2671 . . . 384

Pickstone v Freemans plc [1989] AC 66; [1988] 3
WLR 265 . . . 151

Pigs Marketing Board (Northern Ireland) v
Redmond (83/78) [1978] ECR 2347; [1979] 1
CMLR 177 . . . 149, 274

Piraiki-Patraiki Cotton Industry AE v
Commission (11/82) [1985] ECR 207; [1985] 2
CMLR 4 . . . 228

Plaumann v Commission (C-25/62) [1963] ECR
95; [1964] CMLR 29 . . . 65, 200, 201, 227, 228,
230, 235

Polyelectrolyte Producers Group v Council
and Commission (T-376/04) [2005] ECR
II-3007 . . . 240

Polypropylene Cartel Community v ICI
Decision [1988] 4 CMLR 347 . . . 361, 362

Portugal v Council (C-149/96) [1999] ECR
I-8395 . . . 176

Prais v Council (130/75) [1976] ECR
1589 . . . 116

Prantl see Criminal Proceedings against Prantl

Pretore di Salo v Persons Unknown
(14/86) [1987] ECR 2545; [1989] 1 CMLR
71 . . . 194, 196

Pringle v Ireland (C-370/12) [2012] ECR-I
756 . . . 60

Procureur de la Republique v Waterkeyn
(C-314–16/81) [1982] ECR 4337; [1983] 2
CMLR 145 . . . 222

Procureur du Roi v Dassonville (8/74) [1974]
ECR 837; [1974] 2 CMLR 436 . . . 274, 276, 277,
284, 285, 291, 292, 295, 367

Promusiciae (C-275/06) 2008 I-00271 . . . 103

Pronuptia v Schillgalis (161/84) [1986] ECR
353 . . . 366, 368

Pubblico Ministero v Ratti (148/78) [1979] ECR
1629; [1980] 1 CMLR 96 . . . 175, 181

Public Prosecutor v Kolpnghuis Nijmegan
(80/86) [1987] ECR 3969; [1989] 2 CMLR
18 . . . 119, 179

Quelle AG v Bundesverband der
Verbraucherzentralen und
Verbraucherverbände (C-404/06) [2008]
ECRI-2685 . . . 180

R v Bouchereau (30/77) [1977] ECR 1999; [1977] 2 CMLR 800 . . . 331

R v Dept of Transport *ex p* International Air Transport Association and European Low Fares Airline Association (C-344/04) [2004] EWHC 1721 (Admin); [2004] 3 CMLR 20 . . . 90, 191

R v Henn & Darby (34/79) [1979] ECR 3795; [1980] 1 CMLR 246 . . . 275, 279

R v HM Treasury *ex p* British Telecommunications plc (C-392/93) [1996] ECR I-1631; [1996] 2 CMLR 217 . . . 186

R v Immigration Appeal Tribunal *ex p* Antonissen (C-292/89) [1991] ECR I-745; [1991] 2 CMLR 373 . . . 309, 316, 331

R v Immigration Appeal Tribunal and Surinder Singh *ex p* Secretary of State for the Home Department (C-370/90) [1992] ECR I-4265; [1992] 3 CMLR 358 . . . 348

R v Intervention Board for Agricultural Produce *ex p* Man (181/84) [1985] ECR 2889; [1985] 3 CMLR 759 . . . 120

R v Kirk (63/83) [1984] ECR 2689; [1984] 3 CMLR 522 . . . 113, 118, 233

R v London Boroughs' Transport Committee [1991] 1 WLR 828 . . . 199

R v Ministry of Agriculture, Fisheries and Food *ex p* Hedley Lomas (Ireland) Ltd (C-5/94) [1997] QB 139; [1996] 3 WLR 787; [1996] All ER (EC) 493; [1996] ECR I-2553; [1996] 2 CMLR 39 . . . 187

R v Pharmaceutical Society of Great Britain (266 & 267/87) [1989] ECR 1295; [1989] 2 CMLR 751 . . . 274, 278

R v Pieck (159/79) [1980] ECR 2171; [1980] 3 CMLR 220 . . . 120, 316, 340

R v Saunders (Vera Ann) (175/78) [1979] ECR 1129; [1979] 2 CMLR 216 . . . 347

R v Secretary of State for Employment *ex p* EOC (C-9/91) [1992] 3 CMLR 233 . . . 152

R v Secretary of State for Employment *ex p* Seymour-Smith (C-167/97) [1999] ECR I-623; [1999] 2 CMLR 273 . . . 405, 412

R v Secretary of State for Health *ex p* Gallagher (C-11/92) [1993] ECR I-3545 . . . 263

R v Secretary of State for Health *ex p* Swedish Match (C-210/03) [2004] ECR I-11893; [2005] 1 CMLR 26 . . . 82, 126

R v Secretary of State for the Home Department *ex p* Kaur (Manjit) (C-192/99) [2001] ECR I-1237 . . . 101, 305

R v Secretary of State for the Home Department *ex p* Santillo (131/79) [1980] 2 CMLR 308 . . . 171

R v Secretary of State for Transport, *ex p* Factortame and ors (No 1) [1990] 2 AC 85 . . . 148, 151, 196

R v Secretary of State for Transport, *ex p* Factortame Ltd (No 1) (C-213/89) [1990] ECR I-2433; [1990] 3 CMLR 1 . . . 140, 142, 151, 203, 205, 208

R v Secretary of State for Transport, *ex p* Factortame Ltd (No 2) (C-221/89) [1991] ECR I-3905 . . . 138, 140, 151, 152, 204, 311

R v Secretary of State for Transport, *ex p* Factortame Ltd (No 3) (C-48/93) [1996] ECR I-1029 . . . 140, 152, 185, 186

R v Thompson et al (7/78) [1978] ECR 2247; [1979] 1 CMLR 47 . . . 280

Racke v Hauptzollamt Mainz (98/78) [1979] ECR 69 . . . 119

Racke v Hauptzollamt Mainz (C-162/96) [1998] ECR I-3655 . . . 143

Ratti *see* Pubblico Ministero v Ratti

Rau *see* Walter Rau v BALM

Raulin v Minister van Onderwijs en Wetenschappen (C-357/89) [1992] ECR I-1027; [1994] 1 CMLR 227 . . . 306, 310

Razzouk and Beydoun v Commission (75 & 117/82) [1984] ECR 1509; [1984] 3 CMLR 470 . . . 116

Rechberger v Austria (C-140/97) [1999] ECR I-3499 . . . 187

Renato Albini v Council & Commission (33/80) [1981] ECR 2141 . . . 249

Rewe-Handelsgesellschaft Nord mbH v Hauptzollamt Kiel (C-158/80) [1981] ECR 1805; [1982] 1 CMLR 449 . . . 204

Rewe-Zentral AG v Bundesmonopolverwaltung für Branntwein (120/78) (Cassis de Dijon) [1978] ECR 649; [1979] 3 CMLR 494 . . . 65, 81, 86, 135, 259, 260, 263, 264, 277, 285, 286, 287, 289, 290, 291, 292, 293, 294, 295, 296, 297, 303

Rewe-Zentralfinanz eG v Landwirtschaftskammer für das Saarland (33/76) [1976] ECR 1989; [1977] 1 CMLR 533 . . . 204, 207

Rey Soda v Cassa Conguaglio Zucchero (23/75) [1975] ECR 1279; [1976] 1 CMLR 185 . . . 133

Reyners v Belgian State (2/74) [1974] ECR 631; [1974] 2 CMLR 305 . . . 258, 303, 323, 326, 333

Reynolds Tobacco Holdings Inc v Commission (C-131/03 P) [2006] ECR I-7795; [2007] 1 CMLR 1 . . . 225

Rheinmühlen-Dusseldorf v Einfuhr- und Vorratsstelle für Getreide und Futtermittel (146 & 166/73) [1974] ECR 33; [1974] 1 CMLR 523 . . . 195

Riccardo Tasca (65/75) [1976] ECR 291 . . . 278

Richards (C-423/04) [2006] ECR I-3585; [2006] 2 CMLR 49 . . . 416

Richez Parise v Commission (19, 20, 25 & 30/69) [1970] ECR 325 . . . 242

Rieser Internationale Transporte GmbH v Autobahnen- und Schnellstrassen Finanzierungs AG (ASFINAG) (C-157/02) [2004] ECR I-1477 . . . 178

Rinner-Kuhn (Ingrid) v FWW
Spezial-Gebäudereiningung (C-171/88) [1989]
ECR 2743; [1989] IRLR 493 . . . 404, 412

Riseria Luigi Geddo v Ente Nazionale Risi (2/73)
[1973] ECR 865; [1974] 1 CMLR 13 . . . 275

Robert Bosch GmbH v Kleding Verkoopbedrijf
de Geus en Uitdenbogerd (13/61) [1962] ECR
89; [1962] CMLR 1 . . . 195, 196

Roberts v Cleveland Area Health Authority
[1979] 2 All ER 1163; [1979] ICR 558 . . . 150

Roberts v Tate and Lyle (151/84) [1986] ECR 703;
[1986] 1 CMLR 714 . . . 418

Robins v Secretary of State for Work and
Pensions (C-278/05) [2007] All ER (EC) 648;
[2007] 2 CMLR 13 . . . 187

Roca Alvaraz (C-109/09) [2010] ECR
I-08661 . . . 421

Roquette Frères see Maizena GmbH v Council
(Roquette Freres)

Rosengren and Others v Riksäklagaren
(C-170/04) [2007] 3 CMLR 10 . . . 280, 283

Rothley v European Parliament (C167/02 P)
[2004] ECR I-3149; [2004] 2 CMLR 11 . . . 235

Rothmans & Philip Morris Tobacco and
Arizona Tobacco [1993] 1 CMLR 93 . . . 161

Rottmann (C-135/08) [2010] ECR
I-1499 . . . 305, 337

Royal Scholten-Honig (Holdings) Ltd v
Intervention Board for Agricultural Produce
(103 & 145/77) [1978] ECR 2037; [1979] 1
CMLR 675 . . . 236, 244, 245

Rucksdeschel (117/76 and 16/77) [1977] ECR
I-753 . . . 245

Rummler v Dato-Druck GmbH (237/85) [1986]
ECR 2101; [1987] 3 CMLR 127 . . . 413

Rush Portuguesa Lda v Office National
d'Immigration (C-113/89) [1990] ECR I-1417;
[1991] 2 CMLR 818 . . . 173

Rutili v Minister of Interior (36/75) [1975] ECR
1219; [1975] 1 CMLR 140 . . . 120, 316, 347

Säger v Dennemeyer and Co Ltd (C-76/90) [1991]
ECR I-4221; [1993] 3 CMLR 639 . . . 324

Saint-Gobain Glass France SA and Others v
European Commission (T-56/09 and T-73/09)
(2014) ECLI:EU:T:2014:160 . . . 251, 390

Salah Oulane (C-215/03) [2005] ECR
I-1215 . . . 315

Samenwerkende Elektriciteits-
produktiebedrijven (Sep) NV v
Commission (C-36/92 P) [1994] ECR
I-1911 . . . 118, 389

Santillo see R v Secretary of State for the Home
Department ex p Santillo

SAT v Eurocontol (C-364/92) [1994] ECR
I-43 . . . 361

Sayag v Leduc (9/69) [1969] ECR 329 . . . 243

Schempp v Finanzamt Munchen V (C-403/03)
(C-403/03) [2005] SC 1792; [2005] ECR
I-6421; [2005] 3 CMLR 37 . . . 348

Schmidberger Internationale Transporte
Planzuge v Austria (C-112/00) [2003] ECR
I-5659; [2003] 2 CMLR 34 . . . 275, 286

Schnitzer (C-215/01) [2003] ECR I-14847 . . . 312

Schnorbus v Land Hessen (C-79/99) [2000] ECR
I-10997; [2001] 1 CMLR 40 . . . 420, 426

Scholz v Opera Universitaria di Cagliari
(C-419/92) [1994] ECR I-505; [1994] 1 CMLR
873 . . . 307, 348

Schöppenstedt see Aktien-Zuckerfabrik
Schöppenstedt v Council

Schöttle and Söhne OHG v Finanzamt
Freudenstadt (20/76) [1977] ECR 247; [1977] 2
CMLR 98 . . . 269, 270

Schul (15/81) [1982] ECR 1409 . . . 258

Schul (C-461/03) [2005] ECR I-10513 . . . 199

Schumacher v Hauptzollamt Frankfurt (215/87)
[1989] ECR 617; [1990] 2 CMLR 465 . . . 282

Schutzverband gegen Unlauteren Wettbewerb v
TK-Heimdienst Sass GmbH (C-254/98) [2000]
ECR I-151; [2002] 1 CMLR 25 . . . 294, 297

Schwarze v Einfuhr-und Vorratsstelle für
Getreide und Futtermittel (16/65) [1965] ECR
1081; [1966] CMLR 172 . . . 191

SDDDA v Commission (T-47/96) [1996] ECR
II-1559 . . . 213

Secretary of State for the Home Department v
Akrich (C-109/01) [2003] ECR I-9607; [2003]
3 CMLR 26 . . . 113, 114, 320, 345, 349

Segi v Council (C-355/04P) [2008] All ER (EC)
65; [2007] 2 CMLR 23 . . . 117

Sgarlata v Commission (40/64) [1965] ECR 279;
[1966] CMLR 314 . . . 112

Simmenthal (106/77) [1978] ECR 629; [1978]
3 CMLR 263 . . . 139, 140, 141, 160, 185,
192, 204

Simmenthal SpA v Commission (C-92/78) [1979]
ECR 777; [1978] ECR 1129 . . . 236, 250

Simutenkov v Ministerio de Educacion y
Cultura (C-265/03) [2006] All ER (EC) 42;
[2005] ECR I-2579 . . . 106

Sirdar v Army Board (C-273/97) [1999] ECR
I-7403; [1999] 3 CMLR 559 . . . 420

Skoma-Lux (C-161/09) [2007] ECR
I-10841 . . . 107

Slob (J) v Productschap Zuivel (C-236/02) [2004]
ECR I-1861 . . . 191

Sociaal Fonds voor de Diamantarbeiders,
Antwerp v SA Ch Brachfeld & Sons, Antwerp
(2/69 & 3/69) [1969] ECR 211; [1969] CMLR
335 . . . 266

Sociedade Agricola (C-258/13)
ECLI:EU:C:2013:810 . . . 104

Société Comateb v Directeur Général des
Douanes et Droits Indirects (C-192/95) [1997]
STC 1006; [1997] ECR I-165; [1997] 2 CMLR
649 . . . 120, 121

Société Commerciale des Potasses et de l'Azote
(SCPA) v Commission (C-30/95) [1998] ECR
I-1375 . . . 383, 394

Société Technique Minière v Maschinenbau
Ulm (STM case) (56/65) ECR 235 . . . 362, 365,
367, 369, 370

Society for the Protection of Unborn Children
(Ireland) Ltd (SPUC) v Grogan (C-159/90)
[1991] ECR I-4685; [1991] 3 CMLR
849 . . . 164, 301

Sofiane Fahas v Council of the European Union
(T-49/07) [2010] ECR II-5555 . . . 230

Sofrimport Sarl v Commission (C-152/88) [1990]
ECR I-2477; [1990] 3 CMLR 80 . . . 229, 248

Solange I see Internationale Handelsgesellschaft
case (Solange I)

Solange II see Wünsche Handelsgesellschaft
decision (Solange II)

Sotgui v Deutsche Bundespost (152/73) [1974]
ECR 153 . . . 333

Souliotis v Commission (T-380/11)
ECLI:EU:T:2013:420 . . . 232

South Ayrshire Council v Morton [2002] IRLR
256 . . . 410

Spain v Council (Spanish Cotton Subsidies)
(C-310/04) [2006] ECR I-7285 . . . 90

Spain v UK (C-145/04) [2006] ECR I-7917 . . . 55, 221

Spedition Welter (C-306/12) [2013] ECR
I-650 . . . 180

Spijker Kwasten BV v Commission (231/82)
[1983] ECR 2559; [1984] 2 CMLR 284 . . . 228

Star Fruit Co SA v Commission (C-247/87)
[1989] ECR 291; [1990] 1 CMLR
733 . . . 213, 215

Stauder v City of Ulm (26/69) [1969] ECR 419;
[1970] CMLR 112 . . . 112

Stauffer (C-386/04) [2006] ECR I-8203 . . . 312

Steenhorst-Neerings v Bestuur van de
Bedrijfsvereniging voor Detailhandel,
Ambachten en Huisvrouwen (C-338/91)
[1993] ECR I-5475; [1995] 3 CMLR 323 . . . 206

Steenkolenmijnen v HA (30/59) [1961] ECR
1 . . . 384

Steff-houlberg Export (366/95) [1998] ECR
I-2661; [1999] 2 CMLR 250 . . . 121

Steinike und Weinlig v Germany (C-78/96)
[1977] ECR 595; [1977] 2 CMLR 688 . . . 269

Steymann v Staatssecretaris van Justitie (196/87)
[1988] ECR 6159; [1989] 1 CMLR 449 . . . 307

STM case see Société Technique Minière v
Maschinenbau Ulm (STM case)

Stoke-on-Trent City Council v B&Q plc
(C-169/91) [1992] ECR I-6635; [1993] 1 CMLR
426 . . . 291

Stork v High Authority (1/58) [1959] ECR
17 . . . 112

Sugar Export v Commission (88/76) [1977] ECR
709 . . . 119, 380

Sugar Export v Commission (132/77) [1978]
ECR 1061 . . . 248

Suiker Unie (Sugar Union) v Commission (40–8,
50, 43, 56, 111 and 113–14/73) [1973] ECR
1465 . . . 363, 389

Surinder Singh see R v Immigration Appeal
Tribunal and Surinder Singh ex p Secretary of
State for the Home Department

Sweden v Commission (C-64/05 P) [2008] QB
902; [2008] 3 WLR 756 . . . 73

Sweden & Turco v Council (C-39/05 & C-52/05)
[2008] ECR I-4723 . . . 74

Swedish Journalists (T-174/95) [1998] ECR
II-2289 . . . 73

Syfait v GlaxoSmithKline (C-53/03) [2005] ECR
I-4609; [2005] 5 CMLR 1 . . . 190

T Mobile (C-8/08) [2009] ECR I-4529 . . . 365

T Port GmbH & Co KG v Bundesanstalt für
Landwirtschaft und Ernahrung (C-68/95)
[1996] ECR I-6065; [1997] 1 CMLR
1 . . . 158, 238

T Port GmbH & Co v Hauptzollamt
Hamburg-Jonas (C-364/95) [1998] ECR
I-1023 . . . 158

Tankstation 't Heukste vof and JBE Boermans
(C-401 and 402/92) [1994] ECR I-2199; [1995]
3 CMLR 501 . . . 292

Technische Glaswerke Ilmenau v Commission
(T-237/02) [2006] ECR II-5131 . . . 74

Tele Danmark A/S v Handels- og
Kontorfunktionaerernes Forbund I Danmark
(HK) (C-109/00) [2001] ECR I-6993; [2002] 1
CMLR 5 . . . 422

Telefónica v Commission (C-274/12 P), judgment
of 19 December 2013, not yet reported . . . 232

Telemarsicabruzzo SpA v Circostel (C-320/90)
[1993] ECR I-393 . . . 192

Ten Oever v Stichting Bedriftspensioenfonds
voor het Glazenwassers (C-109/91) [1993] ECR
I-4879; [1995] 2 CMLR 357 . . . 407

Tepea v Commission (28/77) [1978] ECR
1391 . . . 362

Test-Achats (C-236/09) [2011] ECR
I-773 . . . 103, 431

Tetra Pak International SA v Commission
(T-83/91) [1994] ECR II-755 . . . 192, 380

Tetra Pak International SA v Commission
(C-333/94 P) [1996] ECR I-5951; [1997] 4
CMLR 662 . . . 251, 380, 390

Tetra Pak Rausing SA v Commission
(T-51/89) [1990] ECR II-309; [1991] 4 CMLR
334 . . . 251, 390, 393

Thieffry v Paris Bar Council (71/76) [1977] ECR
765; [1977] 2 CMLR 373 . . . 323

Thorburn v Sunderland City Council [2002] 1
CMLR 50 . . . 147, 153

Timex Corp v Council of the European
Communities (C-264/82) [1985] ECR 849;
[1985] 3 CMLR 550 . . . 229

Tommaso Morellato v Comune di Padova
(C-416/00) [2003] ECR I-9343 . . . 294

Tommaso Morellato v Unita Sanitaria Locale
(Usl) N 11 di Pordenone (C-358/95) [1997]
ECR I-1431 . . . 281

Töpfer v Commission (106–7/63) [1965] ECR
405; [1966] CMLR 1 . . . 119
Töpfer v Commission (112/77) [1978] ECR
1019 . . . 119, 233
Torfaen Borough Council v B&Q plc
(C-145/88) [1989] ECR 3851; [1990] 1 CMLR
337 . . . 290, 291
Traghetti del Mediterraneo SpA v Italy
(C-173/03) [2006] All ER (EC) 983; [2006]
ECR I-5177; [2006] 3 CMLR 19 . . . 188,
200, 202
Transocean Marine Paints Association v
Commission (17/74) [1974] ECR 1063;
[1974] 2 CMLR 459 . . . 117, 233
Transportes Urbanos y Servicios Generales
(C-118/08) [2010] ECR I-635 . . . 166, 205, 206
Trojani v Centre Public d'Aide Sociale de
Bruxelles (CPAS) (C-456/02) [2004] All ER
(EC) 1065; [2004] ECR I-7573; [2004] 3 CMLR
38 . . . 307
TWD Textilwerke Deggendorf GmbH v
Germany (C-188/92) [1994] ECR I-833;
[1995] 2 CMLR 145 . . . 193, 236

Uberseering BV v Nordic Construction Co
Baumanagement GmbH (NCC) (C-208/00)
[2002] ECR I-9919; [2005] 1 CMLR 1 . . . 313
UK v Commission (C-106/96) [1998] ECR
I-2729; [1998] 2 CMLR 981 . . . 109, 225, 234
UK v Council (68/86) (Hormones) [1988] ECR
855; [1988] 2 CMLR 453 . . . 124
UK v Council (C-84/94) (Working Time
Directive) [1996] ECR I-5755; [1996]
3 CMLR 671 . . . 88, 89, 125, 263
UK v Council and Parliament (Network and
Information Security Agency) (C-217/04)
[2006] ECR I-3771; [2006] 3 CMLR 2 . . . 262
UK v Council and Parliament (Smoked
Flavourings) (C-66/04) [2006] All ER
(EC) 487; [2005] ECR I-10553; [2006]
3 CMLR 1 . . . 261
UNECTEF v Heylens et al (222/86) [1987] ECR
4097; [1989] 1 CMLR 901 . . . 113, 117
Unibet (London) Ltd v Justitiekanslern
(C-432/05) [2008] All ER (EC) 453; [2007] 2
CMLR 30 . . . 103, 207
Unilever Italia SpA v Central Food SpA
(C-443/98) [2000] ECR I-7535; [2001] 1 CMLR
21 . . . 183
Union de Pequeños Agricultores v Council
of the European Union (UPA) (C-50/00 P)
[2002] ECR I-6677; [2002] 3 CMLR
1 . . . 201, 235
Union Depart. des Syndicats CGT de l'Aisne v
Sidef Conforama, judgment of 28 February
1991 . . . 286
Union Royale Belge des Sociétés de Football
Association (ASBL) v Bosman (C-415/93)
[1995] ECR I-4921; [1996] 1 CMLR
645 . . . 106, 293, 304

United Brands v Commission (27/76) [1978]
ECR 207 . . . 375, 376, 377, 379, 380, 381
Unitel Decision 78/516 . . . 361
Universitat Hamburg v Hauptzollamt
Hamburg-Kehrwieder (216/82) [1983] ECR
2771 . . . 250
US v Syufy Case No 89-15475 US Court of
Appeals for the Ninth Circuit . . . 356

Vacuum Interrupters, Re [1977] 1 CMLR
D67 . . . 368
Vaassen (61/65) [1966] ECR 261 . . . 190
Van Binsbergen v Bestuur van de
Bedrijfsvereniging voor de Metaalnijverheid
(33/74) [1974] ECR 1299; [1975] 1 CMLR
298 . . . 323
Van der Elst v Office des Migrations
Internationales (OMI) (C-43/93) [1994] ECR
I-3803; [1995] 1 CMLR 513 . . . 351
Van Duyn v Home Office (41/74) [1974] ECR
1337; [1975] 1 CMLR 1 . . . 161, 174, 331
Van Gend en Loos (26/62) NV Algemene
Transport en Expeditie Onderneming Van
Gend en Loos v Nederlandse Administratie
der Belastingen [1963] ECR 1; [1963] CMLR
105 . . . 13, 28, 64, 65, 75, 78, 79, 99, 138, 139,
166, 172, 174, 182, 184, 185, 187, 192, 198, 234,
254, 258, 260, 265, 391
Van Schijndel v Stichting Pensioenfonds voor
Fysiotherapeuten (C-430/93 and C-431/93)
[1996] All ER (EC) 259; [1995] ECR I-4705;
[1996] 1 CMLR 801 . . . 207
Vassallo v Azienda Ospedaliera Ospedale San
Martino di Genova e Cliniche Universitarie
Convenzionate (C180/04) [2006] ECR
I-7251 . . . 179
VAT Exemption, Re NJW 1988, 2173; [1989] 1
CMLR 113 . . . 156
Vatsouras and Koupatantze v ARGE Nürnberg
(C-22 and 23/08) [2009] ECR I-4585 . . . 342
Verbond van Nederlandse Ondernemingen v
Inspecteur der Invoerrechten en Accijnzen
(51/76) [1977] ECR 113; [1977] 1 CMLR
413 . . . 175
Vereeniging van Cementhandelaren v
Commission (Cement Association case)
(8/72) [1972] ECR 977 . . . 363, 366, 367, 368
Verein Gegen Unwesen in Handel und Gewerbe
Koln eV v Mars GmbH (C-470/93) [1995] ECR
I-1923; [1995] 3 CMLR 1 . . . 292, 294
Vereinigte Familiapress Zeitungsverlags- und
vertriebs GmbH v Heinrich Bauer Verlag
(C-368/95) [1997] ECR I-3689; [1997] 3 CMLR
1329 . . . 286, 293, 297
Viho Europe BV v Commission (Parker Pen
case) (C-73/95P) [1996] ECR I-5457 . . . 361
Vinal SpA v Orbat SpA (C-46/80) [1981] ECR 77;
[1981] 3 CMLR 524 . . . 194
Virgin/British Airways (T-219/99) [2003] ECR
II-5917 . . . 379

Vlassopoulou v Justice Ministry, Baden-
  Württemburg (340/89) [1992] 1 CMLR
  625 . . . 324
Vodafone and others (C-58/08) [2010] ECR
  I-4999 . . . 88, 89, 90
Volk v Vervaecke (5/69) [1969] ECR 295 . . . 370
Volswagen, Commission Decision 98/273 . . . 390
Volkswagen AG v Commission (T-62/98) [2000]
  ECR II-2707 . . . 251
Von Colson v Land Nordrhein-Westfahlen
  (14/83) [1984] ECR 1891; [1986] 2 CMLR
  430 . . . 95, 1178, 179, 180, 181, 205, 254, 426
Voss (Ursula) v Land Berlin (C-300/06) [2007]
  ECR I-10573 . . . 412
Vroege v NCIV Instituut (C-57/93) [1994] ECR
  I-4541; [1995] 1 CMLR 881 . . . 408

Wachauf v Federal Republic of Germany (5/88)
  [1989] ECR 2609; [1991] 1 CMLR 328 . . . 113
Walrave v Association Union Cycliste
  Internationale (36/74) [1974] ECR 1405; [1975]
  1 CMLR 320 . . . 173, 302
Walt Wilhelm v Bundeskartellamt (14/68) [1969]
  ECR 1 . . . 392
Walter Rau Lebensmittelwerke v De Smedt
  PVBA (261/81) [1982] ECR 3961; [1983] 2
  CMLR 496 . . . 278, 287, 289
Walter Rau v BALM (133/85) [1987] ECR
  2289 . . . 236
Webb v EMO Air Cargo (UK) Ltd (C-32/93)
  [1994] ECR I-3567; [1994] 2 CMLR 729 . . . 421
Weber's Wine World Handels GmbH v
  Abgabenberufungskommission Wien
  (C-147/01) [2005] All ER (EC) 224; [2003] ECR
  I-11365; [2004] 1 CMLR 7 . . . 120
Wells v Secretary of State for Transport
  (C-201/02) [2004] ECR I-723 . . . 184

Werhahn Hansamuhle v Council of the
  European Communities (63–9/72) [1973]
  ECR 1229 . . . 240
Werner A Bock KG v Commission (62/70)
  (Chinese Mushrooms) [1971] ECR 897; [1972]
  CMLR 160 . . . 228, 229
Willame v Commission (110/63) [1965] ECR 803;
  [1966] CMLR 231 . . . 248
Wippel v Peek & Cloppenburg (C-313/02) [2004]
  ECR I-9483 . . . 306, 409
Wirth v Stadt Hannover (C-109/92) [1993] ECR
  I-6447 . . . 334
Wöhrmann v Commission (31/62 & 33/62)
  [1962] ECR 965; [1963] CMLR 152 . . . 249
Woodpulp cases see Ahlstrom v Commission
Worringham v Lloyds Bank Ltd (69/80) [1981]
  ECR 767; [1981] 2 CMLR 1 . . . 406
Wouters (C-309/99) [2002] ECR I-1577 . . . 363
Wünsche Handelsgesellschaft decision (Solange
  II) (BVerfGE 73, 339) . . . 156, 158
Wünsche v Germany (69/85) [1986] ECR
  947 . . . 201
WWF UK (World Wide Fund for Nature)
  v Commission (T-105/95) [1997] ECR
  II-313 . . . 216

Zambrano v ONEM (C-34/09) [2011] ECR
  I-1177 . . . 345, 346
Zbiral (2012) 49 CML Rev (2012) 1475 . . . 163
Ziolkowski and Szeja (C-424–5/10) [2011] ECR
  I-14035 . . . 322
Zuckerfabrik Schöppenstedt see
  Aktien-Zuckerfabrik Schöppenstedt v
  Council
Zuckerfabrik Süderdithmarschen AG v
  Hauptzollamt Itzehoe (C-143/88) [1991] ECR
  I-415; [1993] 3 CMLR 1 . . . 203

Numerical Table of Cases

Court of Justice

8/55 Fédération Charbonniere de Belgique v
High Authority of the European Coal and
Steel Community (Admissibility) [1955] ECR
201; [1954–56] ECR 245 . . . 84, 233

9/56 Meroni & Co Industrie Metallurgiche SpA
v High Authority of the European Coal and
Steel Community [1958] ECR 11; [1957–58]
ECR 133 . . . 133, 232, 250

1/58 Stork v High Authority [1959] ECR 17;
[1959] ECR 43 . . . 112

30/59 Steenkolenmijnen v HA [1961] ECR 1 . . . 384

6/60 Humblet v Belgium [1960] ECR 559; [1960]
ECR 1125 . . . 65

14/60 Meroni & Co v High Authority of the
European Coal and Steel Community [1961]
ECR 161; [1961] ECR 321 . . . 242

7/61 Commission v Italy (Pigmeat Imports)
[1961] ECR 317; [1962] CMLR 39 . . . 217,
224, 279

13/61 Robert Bosch GmbH v Kleding
Verkoopbedrijf de Geus en Uitdenbogerd
[1962] ECR 89; [1962] CMLR 1 . . . 195, 196

2–3/62 Commission v Luxembourg & Belgium
(Gingerbread) [1962] ECR 425; [1963] CMLR
199 . . . 265

24/62 Germany v Commission (Tariff Quota
on Wine) [1963] ECR 63; [1963] CMLR
347 . . . 233

25/62 Plaumann v Commission [1963] ECR 95;
[1964] CMLR 29 . . . 65, 200, 201, 227, 228,
230, 235

26/62 NV Algemene Transport en Expeditie
Onderneming Van Gend en Loos v
Nederlandse Administratie der Belastingen
[1963] ECR 1; [1963] CMLR 105 . . . 13, 28,
64, 65, 75, 78, 79, 99, 138, 139, 166, 172, 174,
182, 184, 185, 187, 192, 198, 234, 254, 258, 260,
265, 391

28-30/62 Da Costa en Schaake NV v
Nederlandse Belastingadministratie [1963]
ECR 61; [1963] CMLR 224 . . . 65, 198,
201, 202

31/62 & 33/62 Wöhrmann v Commission [1962]
ECR 965; [1963] CMLR 152 . . . 249

75/63 Hoekstra v Bestuur der Bedrijfsvereniging
voor Detailhandel en Ambachten [1964] ECR
177; [1964] CMLR 319 . . . 305, 308

90–1/63 Commission v Belgium and
Luxembourg [1964] ECR 625 . . . 162, 217, 266

106–7/63 Töpfer v Commission [1965] ECR 405;
[1966] CMLR 1 . . . 119

110/63 Willame v Commission [1965] ECR 803;
[1966] CMLR 231 . . . 248

6/64 Costa v ENEL [1964] ECR 1141; [1964]
CMLR 425 . . . 13, 28, 64, 65, 75, 139, 141, 143,
148, 160, 166, 187, 192, 197, 204

40/64 Sgarlata v Commission [1965] ECR 279;
[1966] CMLR 314 . . . 112

56 and 58/64 Consten & Grundig v Commission
[1966] ECR 299 . . . 362, 366, 370

16/65 Schwarze v Einfuhr- und Vorratsstelle für
Getreide und Futtermittel [1965] ECR 1081;
[1966] CMLR 172 . . . 191

48/65 Lütticke (Alfons) GmbH v Commission
[1966] ECR 27; [1966] CMLR 378 . . . 172, 215,
224, 238

56/65 Société Technique Minière v
Maschinenbau Ulm (STM case) ECR
235 . . . 362, 365, 367, 369, 370

57/65 Lütticke v Hauptzollamt Saarlouis [1966]
ECR 205; [1971] CMLR 674 . . . 270

61/65 Vaassen [1966] ECR 261 . . . 190

5, 7, 13 & 24/66 Firma E Kampfmeyer v
Commission [1967] ECR 245 . . . 244,
248, 249

8–11/66 Noordwijks Cement Accord [1967] ECR
93; [1967] CMLR 77 . . . 109, 224

23/67 Brasserie de Haecht v Wilkin ECR
407 . . . 365, 367

7/68 Commission v Italy (Art Treasures) [1968]
ECR 423; [1969] CMLR 1 . . . 219, 265, 282

14/68 Walt Wilhelm v Bundeskartellamt [1969]
ECR 1 . . . 392

24/68 Commission v Italy (Statistical Levy)
[1969] ECR 193; [1971] CMLR 611 . . . 265

2/69 & 3/69 Sociaal Fonds voor de
Diamantarbeiders, Antwerp v SA Ch
Brachfeld & Sons, Antwerp [1969] ECR 211;
[1969] CMLR 335 . . . 266

4/69 Lütticke v Commission [1971] ECR
325 . . . 200, 236

5/69 Volk v Vervaecke [1969] ECR 295 . . . 370

9/69 Sayag v Leduc [1969] ECR 329 . . . 243

19, 20, 25 & 30/69 Richez Parise v Commission
[1970] ECR 325 . . . 242

26/69 Stauder v City of Ulm [1969] ECR 419;
[1970] CMLR 112 . . . 112

48, 49 & 51-7/69 ICI v Commission (Dyestuffs)
[1972] ECR 619; [1972] CMLR 557 . . . 362, 363

77/69 Commission v Belgium (Stamp Tax on
Timber) [1970] ECR 237; [1974] 1 CMLR
203 . . . 213, 217

9/70 Grad v Finanzamt Traunstein [1971]
CMLR 1 . . . 171, 172, 174, 176

11/70 Internationale Handelsgesellschaft [1970] ECR 1125; [1972] CMLR 255 . . . 112, 119, 140, 141, 142

15/70 Chevalley v Commission [1975] ECR 975 . . . 237

22/70 Commission v Council (ERTA) [1971] ECR 263; [1971] CMLR 335 . . . 24, 78, 84, 109, 224

25/70 Einfuhr und Vorratsstelle für Getreide und Futtermittel v Köster, Berodt & Co [1970] ECR 1161; [1972] CMLR 255 . . . 133

41–4/70 International Fruit Co NV v Commission [1971] ECR 411; [1975] 2 CMLR 515 . . . 106, 228, 229, 277

62/70 Werner A Bock KG v Commission (Chinese Mushrooms) [1971] ECR 897; [1972] CMLR 160 . . . 228, 229

78/70 Deutsche Grammophon Gesellschaft v Metro Grossmarkt [1971] ECR 487; [1971] CMLR 631 . . . 282

80/70 Defrenne v Belgium (No 1) [1971] ECR 445; [1971] 1 CMLR 494 . . . 403, 404, 405, 407

5/71 Aktien-Zuckerfabrik Schöppenstedt v Council [1971] ECR 975 . . . 186, 240, 243, 244, 246

8/71 Deutscher Komponistenverband eV v Commission [1971] ECR 705; [1973] CMLR 902 . . . 239

42/71 Nordgetreide v Commission [1972] ECR 105 . . . 238

48/71 Commission v Italy (Tax on Art Treasures No 2) [1972] ECR 529; [1972] CMLR 699 . . . 219

93/71 Leonesio v Italian Ministry of Agriculture and Forestry [1972] ECR 287; [1973] CMLR 343 . . . 174

6/72 Europemballage Corporation v Commission (Continental Can) [1973] ECR 215; [1973] CMLR 199 . . . 95, 377, 379, 380, 382, 392, 393

8/72 Vereeniging van Cementhandelaren v Commission (Cement Association case) [1972] ECR 977 . . . 363, 366, 368

21–2/72 International Fruit Company v Produktschap voor Groenten en Fruit (No 3) . . . 176

39/72 Commission v Italy (Slaughtered Cows) [1973] ECR 101; [1973] CMLR 439 . . . 108, 171, 216

63–9/72 Werhahn Hansamuhle v Council of the European Communities [1973] ECR 1229 . . . 240

70/72 Commission v Federal Republic of Germany [1973] ECR 813 . . . 249

81/72 Commission v Council (Staff Salaries) [1973] ECR 575; [1973] CMLR 639 . . . 119

2/73 Riseria Luigi Geddo v Ente Nazionale Risi [1973] ECR 865; [1974] 1 CMLR 13 . . . 275

6 and 7/73 ICI Commercial Solvents v Commission [1974] ECR 223 . . . 360, 362, 375, 377, 380, 381

8/73 HZA Bremerhafen v Massey Ferguson [1973] ECR 89 . . . 83

40–8, 50, 43, 56, 111 and 113–14/73 Suiker Unie (Sugar Union) v Commission [1973] ECR 1465 . . . 363, 389

127/73 BRT v SABAM [1974] ECR 313 . . . 361

146/73 Rheinmuhlen-Düsseldorf v Einfuhr- und Vorratsstelle für Getreide und Futtermittel [1974] ECR 33; [1974] 1 CMLR 523 . . . 183

152/73 Sotgui v Deutsche Bundespost [1974] ECR 153 . . . 333

163/73 Commission v France [1974] ECR 359 . . . 219

166/73 Rheinmuhlen-Düsseldorf v Einfuhr- und Vorratsstelle für Getreide und Futtermittel [1974] ECR 33; [1974] 1 CMLR 523 . . . 195

167/73 Commission v France (French Merchant Seamen) [1974] ECR 359; [1974] 2 CMLR 216 . . . 212, 217, 302

169/73 Compagnie Continentale France v Council of the European Communities [1975] ECR 117; [1975] 1 CMLR 578 . . . 240, 248

181/73 Haegemann v Belgium [1974] ECR 449; [1975] 1 CMLR 515 . . . 106

2/74 Reyners v Belgian State [1974] ECR 631; [1974] 2 CMLR 305 . . . 258, 303, 323, 326, 333

8/74 Procureur du Roi v Dassonville [1974] ECR 837; [1974] 2 CMLR 436 . . . 274, 276, 277, 284, 285, 291, 292, 295, 367

9/74 Casagrande v Landeshauptstadt München [1974] ECR 773; [1974] 2 CMLR 423 . . . 320

15–16/74 Centrafarm cases [1974] ECR 1147; [1974] 2 CMLR 480 . . . 282

17/74 Transocean Marine Paints Association v Commission [1974] ECR 1063; [1974] 2 CMLR 459 . . . 117, 233

33/74 Van Binsbergen v Bestuur van de Bedrijfsvereniging voor de Metaalnijverheid [1974] ECR 1299; [1975] 1 CMLR 298 . . . 323

36/74 Walrave v Association Union Cycliste Internationale [1974] ECR 1405; [1975] 1 CMLR 320 . . . 173, 302

41/74 Van Duyn v Home Office [1974] ECR 1337; [1975] 1 CMLR 1 . . . 161, 162, 174, 331

67/74 Bonsignore v Oberstadtdirektor der Stadt Köln [1975] ECR 297; [1975] 1 CMLR 472 . . . 331

74/74 Comptoir National Technique Agricole (CNTA) SA v Commission (No 1) [1975] ECR 533; [1977] 1 CMLR 171 . . . 244, 249

7/75 Mr and Mrs F v The Belgian State [1975] ECR 679; [1975] 2 CMLR 442 . . . 95

23/75 Rey Soda v Cassa Conguaglio Zucchero [1975] ECR 1279; [1976] 1 CMLR 185 . . . 133

32/75 Fiorini aka Christini v SNCF [1975] ECR 1085; [1975] 1 CMLR 573 . . . 317

36/75 Rutili v Minister of Interior [1975] ECR
1219; [1975] 1 CMLR 140 . . . 120, 316, 347

43/75 Defrenne v Sabena (No 2) [1976] ECR 455;
[1976] 2 CMLR 98 . . . 118, 173, 201, 400, 403,
404, 406, 407

65/75 Riccardo Tasca [1976] ECR 291 . . . 278

87/75 Bresciani v Amministrazione delle
Finanze [1976] ECR 129; [1976] 2 CMLR
62 . . . 176, 267

105/75 Giuffrida v Council [1976] ECR
1395 . . . 233

118/75 Italy v Watson and Belmann [1976] ECR
1185; [1976] 2 CMLR 619 . . . 316

127/75 Bobie Getrankevertrieb GmbH v
Hauptzollamt Aachen-Nord [1976] ECR
1079 . . . 270

130/75 Prais v Council [1976] ECR 1589 . . . 116

3, 4, 6/76 Ministry of Justice v Cornelius Kramer
[1976] ECR 1279; [1977] 2 CMLR 440 . . . 286

20/76 Schöttle and Söhne OHG v Finanzamt
Freudenstadt [1977] ECR 247; [1977] 2 CMLR
98 . . . 269, 270

26/76 Metro SB-Grossmarkte GmbH & Co KG v
Commission [1977] ECR 1875; [1978] 2 CMLR
1 . . . 229, 360, 366, 369

27/76 United Brands v Commission [1978] ECR
207 . . . 375, 376, 377, 379, 380, 381

28/76 Molkerei-Zentrale Westfalen/Lippe v
Hauptzollamt Paderborn [1968] ECR 143;
[1968] CMLR 187 . . . 270

33/76 Rewe-Zentralfinanz eG v
Landwirtschaft-skammer für das
Saarland [1976] ECR 1989; [1977] 1 CMLR
533 . . . 204, 207

45/76 Comet BV v Produktschap Voor
Siergewassen [1976] ECR 2043 . . . 204, 207

46/76 Bauhuis v The Netherlands
ECLI:EU:C:1977:6 . . . 267

51/76 Verbond van Nederlandse
Ondernemingen v Inspecteur der
Invoerrechten en Accijnzen [1977] ECR 113;
[1977] 1 CMLR 413 . . . 175

64 and 113/76 Dumortier Frères v Council
(Gritz and Quellmehl) [1982] ECR
1748 . . . 245, 248

64/76 Dumortier Frères SA v Council [1982]
ECR 1733 . . . 244, 245, 248

71/76 Thieffry v Paris Bar Council [1977] ECR
765; [1977] 2 CMLR 373 . . . 323

74/76 Ianelli & Volpi SpA v Meroni [1977] ECR
557; [1977] 2 CMLR 688 . . . 274

77/76 Fratelli Cucchi v Avez SpA [1987] ECR
987 . . . 269

82/77 Openbaar Ministerie v Van Tiggele [1978]
ECR 25 . . . 278

83/76 Bayerische HNL Vermehrungsbetriebe
GmbH & Co KG v Commission [1978] ECR
1209; [1978] 3 CMLR 566 . . . 244, 245

85/76 Hoffmann-La Roche [1979] ECR
461 . . . 377, 379, 380, 382

88/76 Sugar Export v Commission [1977] ECR
709 . . . 119, 380

101/76 KSH v Council and Commission [1977]
ECR 797 . . . 233, 235

114/76 Bergman v Grows-Farm (Skimmed milk
powder) [1977] ECR 1211; [1979] 2 CMLR
83 . . . 116

117/76 and 16/77 Rucksdeschel [1977] ECR
I-753 . . . 245

124/76 & 20/77 Moulins de Pont a Mousson
(Maize, Gritz, and Quellmehl cases) [1977]
ECR 1795 . . . 245

13/77 GB-INNO-BM [1977] ECR 2115 . . . 392

28/77 Tepea v Commission [1978] ECR
1391 . . . 362

30/77 R v Bouchereau [1977] ECR 1999; [1977] 2
CMLR 800 . . . 331

53/77 Commission v UK (Pig Producers) [1977]
ECR 921; [1977] 2 CMLR 359 . . . 218

61/77 R Commission v Ireland (Sea Fishery
Restrictions) [1977] ECR 1411 . . . 218

103 & 145/77 Royal Scholten-Honig (Holdings)
Ltd v Intervention Board for Agricultural
Produce [1978] ECR 2037; [1979] 1 CMLR
675 . . . 236, 244, 245

106/77 Simmenthal [1978] ECR 629; [1978]
3 CMLR 263 . . . 139, 140, 141, 160, 185,
192, 204

112/77 Töpfer v Commission [1978] ECR
1019 . . . 119, 233

113/77R NTN v Council [1977]
ECR 1721 . . . 218

116, 124 & 143/77 Amylum NV v Council of
the European Communities (Amylum and
Tunnel Refineries) [1978] ECR 893; [1979]
ECR 3497; [1982] 2 CMLR 590 . . . 245

132/77 Sugar Export v Commission [1978] ECR
1061 . . . 248

149/77 Defrenne v Sabena (No 3) [1978] ECR
1365; [1978] 3 CMLR 312 . . . 400, 403

156/77 Commission v Belgium [1978] ECR
1881 . . . 250

7/78 R v Thompson et al [1978] ECR 2247; [1979]
1 CMLR 47 . . . 280

83/78 Pigs Marketing Board (Northern Ireland)
v Redmond [1978] ECR 2347; [1979] 1 CMLR
177 . . . 149, 274

92/78 Simmenthal SpA v Commission (8) [1979]
ECR 777; [1978] ECR 1129 . . . 236, 250

93/78 Mattheus v Doego Fruchtimport und
Tiefkuhlkost eG [1978] ECR 2203; [1979] 1
CMLR 551 . . . 192, 196

98/78 Racke v Hauptzollamt Mainz [1979] ECR
69 . . . 119, 136

120/78 Rewe-Zentral AG v
Bundesmonopolverwaltung für Branntwein
(Cassis de Dijon) [1978] ECR 649; [1979] 3
CMLR 494 . . . 65, 81, 86, 135, 259, 260, 263,
264, 277, 285, 286, 287, 289, 290, 291, 292, 293,
294, 295, 296, 297, 303

125/78 GEMA v Commission [1979] ECR 3173; [1980] 2 CMLR 177 . . . 239

128/78 Commission v UK (Re: Tachographs) [1979] ECR 419; [1979] 2 CMLR 45 . . . 108, 171, 217

132/78 Denkavit Loire Sarl v France [1979] ECR 1928; [1979] 3 CMLR 605 . . . 269, 270

141/78 France v United Kingdom (Fishing Net Mesh Sizes) [1979] ECR 2923; [1980] 1 CMLR 6 . . . 221

148/78 Pubblico Ministero v Ratti [1979] ECR 1629; [1980] 1 CMLR 96 . . . 175, 181

152/78 Commission v France (Advertising of Alcoholic Beverages) [1980] ECR 2299; [1981] 2 CMLR 743 . . . 222

170/78 Commission v UK (Re: Excise Duties on Wine (No 2)) [1983] ECR 2263; [1983] 3 CMLR 512 . . . 272

175/78 R v Saunders (Vera Ann) [1979] ECR 1129; [1979] 2 CMLR 216 . . . 347

207/78 Even . . . 318

209–15 & 218/78 Dow Benelux Landewyck Sarl v Commission [1980] ECR 3125; [1981] 3 CMLR 134 . . . 118, 389

231/78 Commission v UK (Import of Potatoes) [1979] ECR 1447; [1979] 2 CMLR 427 . . . 275

232/78 Commission v France (Import of Lamb) [1979] ECR 2729; [1980] 1 CMLR 418 . . . 216, 217, 221

238/78 Ireks-Arkady GmbH v Council of Ministers and Commission [1979] ECR 2955 . . . 245

241, 242, 245–50/78 DGV v Commission and Council [1979] ECR 3017 . . . 245

253/78 and 1–3/79 Guerlain SA, Rochas SA, Lanvin SA and Nina Ricci SA [1980] ECR 2327 . . . 372

261 and 262/78 Interquell v Commission and Council [1979] ECR 3045 . . . 245

33 & 59/79 Kuhner [1980] ECR 1677 . . . 117

34/79 R v Henn & Darby [1979] ECR 3795; [1980] 1 CMLR 246 . . . 275, 279

44/79 Hauer v Land Rheinland-Pfalz [1979] ECR 3727; [1980] 3 CMLR 42 . . . 103, 112

55/79 Commission v Ireland (Excise Payments) [1980] ECR 481; [1980] 1 CMLR 734 . . . 271

90/79 Commission v France (Re: Reprographic Machines) [1981] ECR 283; [1981] 3 CMLR 1 . . . 268, 270

98/79 Pecastaing v Belgium [1980] ECR 691; [1980] 3 CMLR 685 . . . 330

99/79 Lancome SA v ETOS BV (Perfumes) [1980] ECR 2511; [1981] 2 CMLR 164 . . . 123

104/79 Foglia v Novello [1981] ECR 745; [1980] ECR 745 . . . 193, 194

129/79 Macarthys Ltd v Smith [1980] ECR 1275; [1980] 2 CMLR 205 . . . 408, 409

131/79 R v Secretary of State for the Home Department, ex p Santillo [1980] 2 CMLR 308 . . . 171

136/79 National Panasonic v Commission [1980] ECR 2033; [1980] 3 CMLR 169 . . . 118, 388

138–9/79 Maizena GmbH v Council (Roquette Frères) [1980] ECR 3393 . . . 130, 226, 229, 233

149/79 Commission v Belgium (Re: Public Employees) [1980] ECR 3881; [1981] 2 CMLR 413 . . . 333

155/79 AM & S Europe Ltd v Commission [1982] ECR 1575; [1982] 2 CMLR 264 . . . 117, 389

159/79 R v Pieck [1980] ECR 2171; [1980] 3 CMLR 220 . . . 120, 316, 340

730/79 Philip Morris v Commission [1980] ECR 2671 . . . 384

33/80 Renato Albini v Council & Commission [1981] ECR 2141 . . . 249

36/80 and 76/80 Irish Creamery Milk Suppliers [1981] ECR 81 . . . 196

46/80 Vinal SpA v Orbat SpA [1981] ECR 77; [1981] 3 CMLR 524 . . . 194

66/80 International Chemical Corp SpA v Amministrazione delle Finanze dello Stato [1981] ECR 1191; [1983] 2 CMLR 593 . . . 199, 201, 251

69/80 Worringham v Lloyds Bank Ltd [1981] ECR 767; [1981] 2 CMLR 1 . . . 406

96/80 Jenkins v Kingsgate (Clothing Productions) Ltd [1981] ECR 911; [1981] 2 CMLR 241 . . . 411

113/80 Commission v Ireland (Metal Objects) [1981] ECR 1625; [1982] 1 CMLR 706 . . . 277, 279, 287

138/80 Borker, Re [1980] ECR 1975; [1980] 3 CMLR 638 . . . 190

158/80 Rewe-Handelsgesellschaft Nord mbH v Hauptzollamt Kiel [1981] ECR 1805; [1982] 1 CMLR 449 . . . 204

244/80 Foglia v Novello (No 2) [1981] ECR 3045 . . . 193

246/80 Broekmeulen v Huisarts Registratie Commissie [1981] ECR 2311; [1982] 1 CMLR 91 . . . 190

8/81 Becker v Finanzamt Munster-Innenstadt [1982] ECR 53; [1982] 1 CMLR 499 . . . 176, 178, 182, 183

12/81 Garland v British Rail Engineering Ltd [1982] 2 All ER 402; [1982] ECR 359 . . . 149, 201, 403, 404

15/81 Schul [1982] ECR 1409 . . . 258

53/81 Levin v The Minister of State for Justice [1982] ECR 1035; [1982] 2 CMLR 454 . . . 305, 306

61/81 Commission v UK (Re: Equal Pay for Equal Work) [1982] ECR 2601; [1982] CMLR 377 . . . 413

102/81 Nordsee Deutsche Hochseefischerei GmbH v Reederei Mond Hochseefischerei Nordstern AG & Co KG [1982] ECR 1095 . . . 190

104/81 Hauptzollamt Mainz v CA Kupferberg & Cie KG aA [1982] ECR 3641; [1983] 1 CMLR 1 . . . 176

115–16/81 Adoui and Cornuaille v Belgian State [1982] ECR 1665; [1982] 3 CMLR 631 . . . 329, 331

124/81 Commission v UK (Re: UHT Milk) [1983] ECR 203; [1983] 2 CMLR 1 . . . 276, 280, 283, 285, 287

230/81 Luxembourg v European Parliament [1983] ECR 255; [1983] 2 CMLR 726 . . . 223

246/81 Bethell (Lord) v Commission [1982] ECR 2277; [1982] 3 CMLR 300 . . . 215, 236

249/81 Commission v Ireland (Re: Buy Irish Campaign) [1982] ECR 4005; [1983] 2 CMLR 104 . . . 214, 274, 275, 277

261/81 Walter Rau Lebensmittelwerke v De Smedt PVBA [1982] ECR 3961; [1983] 2 CMLR 496 . . . 278, 287, 289

283/81 CILFIT Srl v Ministero della Sanita [1982] ECR 3415; [1983] 1 CMLR 472 . . . 197, 198

314-16/81 Procureur de la Republique v Waterkeyn [1982] ECR 4337; [1983] 2 CMLR 145 . . . 222

322/81 Michelin v Commission [1983] ECR 3461 . . . 377

11/82 Piraiki-Patraiki Cotton Industry AE v Commission [1985] ECR 207; [1985] 2 CMLR 4 . . . 228

35 and 36/82 Morson and Jhanjan v Netherlands [1982] ECR 3723; [1983] 2 CMLR 221 . . . 347

40/82 Commission v UK (Re: Turkeys) [1982] ECR 2793; [1982] 3 CMLR 497 . . . 97

42/82 Commission v France (Re: Italian Table Wines) [1983] ECR 1013; [1984] 1 CMLR 160 . . . 281, 283

75 & 117/82 Razzouk and Beydoun v Commission [1984] ECR 1509; [1984] 3 CMLR 470 . . . 116

78/82 Commission v Italy [1983] ECR 1955 . . . 278

96/82 IAZ International Belgium NV v Commission [1983] ECR 3369 . . . 363

132/82 Commission v Belgium (Customs Warehouses) [1983] ECR 1649 . . . 266

165/82 Commission v UK (Re: Equal Treatment) [1983] ECR 3431; [1984] 1 CMLR 44 . . . 419

216/82 Universitat Hamburg v Hauptzollamt Hamburg-Kehrwieder [1983] ECR 2771 . . . 250

222/82 Apple and Pear Development Council v Lewis [1983] ECR 4083; [1984] 3 CMLR 733 . . . 274, 277

231/82 Spijker Kwasten BV v Commission [1983] ECR 2559; [1984] 2 CMLR 284 . . . 228

231/83 Cullet (Henri) v Centre Leclerc, Toulouse [1985] ECR 305; [1985] 2 CMLR 524 . . . 260

238/82 Campus Oil Ltd v Minister for Industry and Energy [1984] ECR 2727; [1984] 3 CMLR 544 . . . 280

264/82 Timex Corp v Council of the European Communities [1985] ECR 849; [1985] 3 CMLR 550 . . . 229

286/82 Luisi v Ministero del Tesoro [1984] ECR 377; [1985] 3 CMLR 52 . . . 334

323/82 Intermills v Commission [1984] ECR 3809 . . . 384

13/83 European Parliament v Council (Transport Policy) [1985] ECR 1513; [1986] 1 CMLR 138 . . . 59, 238, 239

14/83 Von Colson v Land Nordrhein-Westfahlen [1984] ECR 1891; [1986] 2 CMLR 430 . . . 95, 178, 179, 180, 181, 205, 254, 426

16/83 Criminal Proceedings against Prantl [1984] ECR 1299; [1985] 2 CMLR 238 . . . 286, 288

63/83 R v Kirk [1984] ECR 2689; [1984] 3 CMLR 522 . . . 113, 118, 233

72/83 Campus Oil Ltd v Minister for Industry and Energy [1984] ECR 2727; [1984] 3 CMLR 544 . . . 279

79/83 Harz v Tradex [1984] ECR 1921; [1986] 2 CMLR 430 . . . 179

108/83 Luxembourg v European Parliament [1984] ECR 1945 . . . 55

145/83 Adams v Commission [1985] ECR 3539; [1986] 1 CMLR 506 . . . 240, 242

184/83 Hofmann v Barmer Ersatzkasse [1984] ECR 3047; [1986] 1 CMLR 242 . . . 421

231/83 Cullet v Centre Leclerc Toulouse . . . 280

238/83 Mr and Mrs Richard Meade [1984] ECR 2631 . . . 350

261/83 Castelli v ONPTS [1984] ECR 3199; [1987] 1 CMLR 465 . . . 319

267/83 Diatta v Land Berlin [1985] ECR 567; [1986] 2 CMLR 674 . . . 319, 320, 344

274/83 Commission v Italy [1987] 1 CMLR 345 . . . 215

293/83 Gravier v City of Liège [1985] ECR 593; [1985] 3 CMLR 1 . . . 95, 334

294/83 Parti Ecologiste v European Parliament and Council (Les Verts) [1986] ECR 1339; [1987] 2 CMLR 343 . . . 59, 76, 222, 223, 224

21/84 Commission v France (Franking Machines) [1985] ECR 1355 . . . 275

25-26/84 Ford v Commission [1985] ECR 2725 . . . 362, 364

29/84 Commission v Germany [1985] ECR 1661 . . . 217

44/84 Hurd v Jones (Inspector of Taxes) [1986] ECR 29; [1986] 2 CMLR 1 . . . 173

60–1/84 Cinéthèque SA v Fédération Nationale des Cinémas Français [1985] ECR 2605; [1986] 1 CMLR 365 . . . 286, 290

94/84 Office National de l'Emploi (ONE) v Deak [1985] ECR 1873 . . . 318

101/84 Commission v Italy [1985] ECR 2629 . . . 217

106/84 Commission v Denmark [1986] ECR 833 . . . 272

112/84 Humblot v Directeur des Services Fiscaux [1987] ECR 1367; [1985] ECR 1367; [1986] 2 CMLR 338 . . . 271

137/84 Ministere Public v Mutsch [1985] ECR 2681; [1986] 1 CMLR 648 . . . 318

142 and 156/84 BAT and Reynolds v Commission [1987] ECR 4487 . . . 382, 393, 394

151/84 Roberts v Tate and Lyle [1986] ECR 703; [1986] 1 CMLR 714 . . . 418

152/84 Marshall v Southampton and South West Hampshire AHA (No 1) [1986] ECR 723; [1986] 1 CMLR 688 . . . 150, 151, 175, 176, 177, 179, 182, 403, 405, 418

161/84 Pronuptia v Schillgalis [1986] ECR 353 . . . 366, 368

170/84 Bilka-Kaufhaus GmbH v Weber von Harz [1986] ECR 1607; [1986] 2 CMLR 701 . . . 406, 408, 411, 413

178/84 Commission v Germany (Re: Beer Purity Law) [1987] ECR 1262; [1988] 1 CMLR 780 . . . 120, 281, 288

175/84 Krohn v Commission [1986] ECR 753; [1987] 1 CMLR 745 . . . 240, 249

178/84 Commission v Germany (Beer Purity) . . . 281, 288

181/84 R v Intervention Board for Agricultural Produce, ex p Man [1985] ECR 2889; [1985] 3 CMLR 759 . . . 120

205/84 Commission v Germany (Re: Insurance Services) [1986] ECR 3755; [1987] 2 CMLR 69 . . . 312, 323

222/84 Johnston v Chief Constable of the RUC [1986] ECR 1651; [1986] 3 CMLR 240 . . . 116, 176, 419

243/84 John Walker & Sons Ltd v Ministeriet for Skatter og Afgifter [1986] ECR 875 . . . 272

307/84 Commission v French Republic (Re: French Nurses) [1986] ECR 1734; [1987] 3 CMLR 555 . . . 333

53/85 AKZO Chemie BV v Commission [1986] ECR 1965; [1987] 1 CMLR 231 . . . 118, 356

59/85 Netherlands v Reed [1986] ECR 1283; [1987] 2 CMLR 448 . . . 303, 319, 344

66/85 Lawrie-Blum v Land Baden-Würtemberg [1986] ECR 2121; [1987] 3 CMLR 389 . . . 306, 333

69/85 Wünsche v Germany [1986] ECR 947 . . . 201

89, 104, 114, 116, 117 and 125–9/85 Ahlstrom v Commission [1994] ECR I-99 . . . 201, 362, 364

121/85 Conegate v Customs and Excise Commissioners [1986] ECR 1007; [1986] 1 CMLR 739 . . . 279

131/85 Gül v Regierungspräsident Düsseldorf [1986] ECR 1573; [1987] 1 CMLR 501 . . . 320

133/85 Walter Rau v BALM [1987] ECR 2289 . . . 236

139/85 Kempf v Staats Secretaria van Justitie [1986] ECR 1741; [1987] 1 CMLR 764 . . . 306

184/85 Commission v Italy (Italian Fruit) [1987] ECR 2013 . . . 268, 272

227–30/85 Commission v Belgium [1988] ECR 1 . . . 214

237/85 Rummler v Dato-Druck GmbH [1986] ECR 2101; [1987] 3 CMLR 127 . . . 413

281, 283–5, 287/85 Commission v Germany (Migration Policy) [1987] ECR 2303; [1988] 2 CMLR 11 . . . 84

293/85 Commission v Belgium (University Fees) [1988] ECR 305; [1989] 2 CMLR 527 . . . 215, 216, 218

314/85 Firma Foto Frost v Hauptzollamt Lubeck-Ost [1987] ECR 4199; [1988] 3 CMLR 57 . . . 199, 235

316/85 Centre Public d'Aide Sociale de Courcelles v Lebon [1987] ECR 2811; [1989] 1 CMLR 337 . . . 308, 318, 319

352/85 Bond van Adverteerders v Netherlands [1988] ECR 2085; [1989] 3 CMLR 113 . . . 330

358/85 France v European Parliament (Re Brussels Meetings) [1986] ECR 2149 . . . 55

427/85 Commission v Germany (Re: Lawyers' Services) [1988] ECR 1123; [1989] 2 CMLR 677 . . . 327, 347

14/86 Pretore di Salo v Persons Unknown [1987] ECR 2545; [1989] 1 CMLR 71 . . . 194, 196

24/86 Blaizot v University of Liège [1988] ECR 379; [1989] 1 CMLR 57 . . . 95, 334

34/86 Council v European Parliament (1986 Budget) [1986] ECR 2155; [1986] 3 CMLR 94 . . . 59, 223

39/86 Lair v Universität Hannover [1988] ECR 3161; [1989] 3 CMLR 545 . . . 95, 309, 318

51/86 France v European Parliament (Re Meetings Facilities) [1988] ECR 4821 . . . 55

60/86 Commission v United Kingdom (Dim-Dip Car Lights) [1988] ECR 3921; [1988] 3 CMLR 437 . . . 262

62/86 AKZO v Commission [1991] ECR I-3359 . . . 380

68/86 UK v Council (Hormones) [1988] ECR 855; [1988] 2 CMLR 453 . . . 124

80/86 Public Prosecutor v Kolpnghuis Nijmegan [1987] ECR 3969; [1989] 2 CMLR 18 . . . 124, 119, 179

157/86 Mary Murphy v An Bord Telecom Eireann [1988] ECR 673; [1988] 1 CMLR 879 . . . 409, 413

197/86 Brown v Secretary of State for Scotland [1988] ECR 3205; [1988] 3 CMLR 403 . . . 310

222/86 UNECTEF v Heylens et al [1987] ECR 4097; [1989] 1 CMLR 901 . . . 113, 117

240/86 Commission v Greece [1988] ECR 1835;
[1989] 3 CMLR 578 . . . 216

263/86 Belgium v Humbel [1988] ECR 5365;
[1989] 1 CMLR 393 . . . 95, 334

302/86 Commission v Denmark (Disposable
Beer Cans) [1988] ECR 4607; [1989] 1 CMLR
619 . . . 122, 286

312/86 Commission v France (Re: Protection
of Women) [1988] ECR 6315; [1989] 1 CMLR
408 . . . 418, 425

18/87 Commission v Germany (Animal
Inspection Fees) [1988] ECR 5427; [1990] 1
CMLR 561 . . . 267

22/87 Commission v Italy [1989] ECR
143 . . . 184, 217

45/87 Commission v Ireland (Dundalk Water
Supply) [1988] ECR 4929; [1989] 1 CMLR
225 . . . 265

46/87 and 227/88 Hoechst [1989] ECR
2859 . . . 388

62/87 Glaverbel v Commission [1988] ECR
1573 . . . 384

70/87 EEC Seed Crushers and Oil Processors
Federation (FEDIOL) v Commission [1989]
ECR 1781; [1991] 2 CMLR 489 . . . 177

81/87 Daily Mail [1988] ECR 5483 . . . 313

85/87 Dow Benelux v Commission [1989] ECR
3137 . . . 389

186/87 Cowan v The French Treasury [1989]
ECR 195; [1990] 2 CMLR 613 . . . 334

196/87 Steymann v Staatssecretaris van
Justitie [1988] ECR 6159; [1989] 1 CMLR
449 . . . 307

215/87 Schumacher v Hauptzollamt
Frankfurt [1989] ECR 617; [1990] 2 CMLR
465 . . . 282

242/87 Council v Commission (Erasmus) [1989]
ECR 1425; [1991] 1 CMLR 478 . . . 84

247/87 Star Fruit Co SA v Commission [1989]
ECR 291; [1990] 1 CMLR 733 . . . 213, 215

266 & 267/87 R v Pharmaceutical Society of
Great Britain [1989] ECR 1295; [1989] 2
CMLR 751 . . . 274, 278

274/87 Commission v Germany (Sausage
Purity Law) [1989] ECR 250; [1989] 2 CMLR
733 . . . 281

302/87 European Parliament v Council
(Comitology) [1988] ECR 5615 . . . 59,
133, 238

340/87 Commission v Italian Republic
(Re: Italian Customs Posts) [1989] ECR 1483;
[1991] 1 CMLR 437 . . . 248

344/87 Bettray v Staatssecretaris van Justitie
[1989] ECR 1621; [1991] 1 CMLR 459 . . . 307

374/87 Orkem v Commission [1989] ECR
3283 . . . 389

379/87 Groener v Minister of Education and
the City of Dublin Vocational Education
Committee [1989] ECR 3967; [1990] 1 CMLR
401 . . . 315

389 & 390/87 Echternecht and Moritz v
Netherlands Minister for Education and
Science [1989] ECR 723; [1990] 2 CMLR
305 . . . 343

5/88 Wachauf v Federal Republic
of Germany [1989] ECR 2609; [1991]
1 CMLR 328 . . . 113

16/88 Commission v Council (Re: Management
Committee Procedure) [1988] ECR
3457 . . . 133

33/88 Alluè and Coonan v Università degli Studi
di Venezia [1989] ECR 1591; [1991] 1 CMLR
283 . . . 303, 333

70/88 European Parliament v Council
(Chernobyl) [1990] ECR I-2041; [1992] 1
CMLR 91 . . . 59, 65, 226

109/88 Handels-og Kontorfunktionaerernes
Forbund i Danmark v Dansk
Arbejdsgiverforening (Danfoss) [1989] ECR
3199; [1991] 1 CMLR 8 . . . 414

132/88 Commission v Greece (Re: Taxation of
Motor Cars) [1991] 3 CMLR 1 . . . 269, 271

143/88 Zuckerfabrik Süderdithmarschen AG
v Hauptzollamt Itzehoe [1991] ECR I-415;
[1993] 3 CMLR 1 . . . 203

145/88 Torfaen Borough Council v B&Q
plc [1989] ECR 3851; [1990] 1 CMLR
337 . . . 290, 291

C-150/88 Eau de Cologne v Provide [1989] ECR
3831 . . . 194, 195

152/88 Sofrimport Sarl v Commission
[1990] ECR I-2477; [1990] 3 CMLR
80 . . . 229, 248

170/88 Ford Espana v The Spanish State [1989]
ECR 2307 . . . 267

171/88 Ingrid Rinner-Kuhn v FWW
Spezial-Gebaudereiningung [1989] ECR 2743;
[1989] IRLR 493 . . . 369, 376

177/88 Dekker v Stichting VJM Centram [1990]
ECR I 3941; [1989] 3 CMLR 454 . . . 418

179/88 Hertz v Aldi [1990] ECR
I-3979 . . . 423, 424

227/88 Hoechst [1989] ECR 2859 . . . 355

262/88 Barber v Guardian Royal Exchange
[1990] ECR 1944; [1990] 2 CMLR 513 . . . 81,
118, 404, 406, 407, 408, 428

C-70/88 European Parliament v Council
(Chernobyl) [1990] ECR I-2041 . . . 226

C-297/88 Dzodzi v Belgium [1990] ECR
I-3763 . . . 191, 194

C-322/88 Grimaldi v Fonds des Maladies
Professionelles [1989] ECR 4407; [1991] 2
CMLR 265 . . . 110, 122

C-5/89 Commission v Germany [19990] ECR
I-3437 . . . 387

C-33/89 Kowalska v Hamburg [1990] ECR 2607;
[1990] IRLR 447 . . . 405

C-68/89 Commission v Netherlands (Re: Entry
Requirements), Proceedings of the ECJ
11/91, 315

C-95 and C-293/89 Commission v Italy and Greece . . . 281

C-104/89 & C-37/90 Mulder v Council of the European Communities [2000] ECR I-203 . . . 233, 246

C-106/89 Marleasing SA v La Comercial Internacionale de Alementacion SA [1990] ECR I-4135; [1992] 1 CMLR 305 . . . 99, 179

C-111/89 Netherlands v P Bakker Hillegom BV [1990] ECR I-1735; [1990] 3 CMLR 119 . . . 268

C-113/89 Rush Portuguesa Lda v Office National d'Immigration [1990] ECR I-1417; [1991] 2 CMLR 818 . . . 173

C-146/89 Commission v UK (Fishing Limits) [1991] ECR I-3533; [1991] 3 CMLR 649 . . . 162

C-184/89 Nimz v Hamburg [1991] ECR I-297 . . . 404

C-188/89 Foster v British Gas plc [1990] ECR I-3313; [1990] 2 CMLR 833 . . . 176, 177, 178

C-197/89 Dzodzi v Belgium [1990] ECR I-3763 . . . 191, 194

C-210/89 Commission v Italy, (Cheese Fat Content) [1990] ECR 3704; [1992] 2 CMLR 1 . . . 281

C-213/89 R v Secretary of State for Transport, ex p Factortame Ltd (No 1) [1990] ECR I-2433; [1990] 3 CMLR 1 . . . 140, 142, 151, 203, 205, 208

C-221/89 R v Secretary of State for Transport ex p Factortame Ltd (No 2) [1991] ECR I-3905 . . . 138, 140, 151, 152, 204, 311

C-234/89 Delimitis v Henniger Bräu [1991] ECR I-935 . . . 370

C-246/89 R Commission v United Kingdom (Nationality of Fishermen) [1989] ECR 3125; [1989] 3 CMLR 601 . . . 218, 303

C-292/89 Antonissen (R v Immigration Appeal Tribunal ex p) [1991] ECR [1991] 2 CMLR 373 . . . 309, 316, 331, 340

C-293/89 Commission v Greece [1992] ECR I-4577 . . . 281

C-298/89 Gibraltar v Council [1993] ECR I-3605 . . . 227

C-300/89 Commission v Council (Re: Titanium Dioxide Directive) [1990] ECR I-2867 . . . 125

C-309/89 Codorniu v Commission (Spanish wine producers) [1994] ECR I-1853 . . . 230

C-312/89 Conforama [1991] ECR I-997; [1993] 3 CMLR 746 . . . 291

C-332/89 Criminal Proceedings against Marchandise [1991] ECR I-997; [1993] 3 CMLR 746 . . . 286, 291

C-340/89 Vlassopoulou v Justice Ministry, Baden-Württemburg [1992] 1 CMLR 625 . . . 324

C-357/89 Raulin v Minister van Onderwijs en Wetenschappen [1992] ECR I-1027; [1994] 1 CMLR 227 . . . 306, 310

C-358/89 Extramet Industrie SA v Council of the European Communities [1991] ECR I-2501; [1993] 2 CMLR 619 . . . 230

C-2/90 Commission v Belgium (Imports of Waste) [1992] ECR I-4431; [1993] 1 CMLR 365 . . . 265

C-3/90 Bernini (MJE) v Netherlands Ministry of Education and Science [1992] ECR I-1071 . . . 318

C-6/90 & C-9/90 Francovich v Italy [1991] ECR I-5357; [1993] 2 CMLR 66 . . . 64, 95, 161, 180, 184, 185, 187, 205, 207, 217, 243, 391

C-18/90 Office National de l'Emploi (ONE) v Kziber [1991] ECR I-199 . . . 176

C-41/90 Höfner and Elser v Macrotron GmbH [1991] ECR I-1979 . . . 361

C-47/90 Delhaize v Promalvi, Proc of the Court of Justice 17/92 . . . 278

C-76/90 Säger v Dennemeyer and Co Ltd [1991] ECR I-4221; [1993] 3 CMLR 639 . . . 324

C-129/00 Commission v Italy [2003] ECR I-14637 . . . 214

C-159/90 Society for the Protection of Unborn Children (Ireland) Ltd (SPUC) v Grogan [1991] ECR I-4685; [1991] 3 CMLR 849 . . . 164, 301

C-1693/90 Legros [1992] ECR I-4625 . . . 121

C-195/90 Commission v Germany [1990] ECR I-2715 . . . 218

C-208/90 Emmott v Minister for Social Welfare [1991] ECR I-4269; [1991] 3 CMLR 894 . . . 205, 206, 207

C-295/90 European Parliament v Council (Students' Residence) [1992] ECR I-4193; [1992] 3 CMLR 281 . . . 59, 226, 234

C-320/90 Telemarsicabruzzo SpA v Circostel [1993] ECR I-393 . . . 192

C-360/90 Arbeiterwohlfahrt der Stadt Berlin v Monika Botel [1992] ECR I-3589 . . . 405

C-369/90 Micheletti [1992] ECR I-4239 . . . 337

C-370/90 R v Immigration Appeal Tribunal and Surinder Singh ex p Secretary of State for the Home Department [1992] ECR I-4265; [1992] 3 CMLR 358 . . . 348

C-4/91 Bleis v Ministry of Education [1991] ECR I-5627; [1994] 1 CMLR 793 . . . 333

C-9/91 R v Secretary of State for Employment, ex p EOC [1992] 3 CMLR 233; [1992] ECR I–4297 . . . 152

C-83/91 Meilicke v ADV/ORGA AG [1992] ECR I-4871 . . . 192

C-109/91 Ten Oever v Stichting Bedriftspensioenfonds voor het Glazenwassers [1993] ECR I-4879; [1995] 2 CMLR 357 . . . 407

C-152/91 Neath v Hugh Steeper [1993] ECR I-6935; [1995] 2 CMLR 357 . . . 407

C-155/91 Commission v Council (Waste Directive) . . . 124

C-169/91 Stoke-on-Trent City Council v B&Q
plc [1992] ECR I-6635; [1993] 1 CMLR
426 . . . 291

C-189/91 Kirsamer Hack [1993] ECR
I-6185 . . . 384

C-267–8/91 Keck and Mithouard [1993] ECR
I-3283; [1995] 1 CMLR 101 . . . 65, 291, 292,
295, 297, 325

C-271/91 Marshall v Southampton and South
West Hampshire AHA (No 2) [1993] ECR
I-4367; [1993] 3 CMLR 293 . . . 205, 403, 426

C-325/91 France v Commission [1993] ECR
I-3283 . . . 110, 233

C-327/91 France v Commission [1994] ECR
I-3641; [1994] 5 CMLR 517 . . . 232

C-338/91 Steenhorst-Neerings v Bestuur van
de Bedrijfsvereniging voor Detailhandel,
Ambachten en Huisvrouwen [1993] ECR
I-5475; [1995] 3 CMLR 323 . . . 206

C-11/92 R v Secretary of State for Health ex p
Gallagher [1993] ECR I-3545 . . . 263

C-24/92 Corbiau (Pierre) v Administration des
Contributions [1993] ECR I-1277 . . . 190

C-36/92 P Samenwerkende Elektriciteits-
produktiebedrijven (Sep) NV v Commission
[1994] ECR I-1911 . . . 118, 389

C-60/92 Otto BV v Postbank NV [1993] ECR
I-5683 . . . 121

C-91/92 Faccini Dori v Recreb Srl [1994] ECR
I-33325; [1995] 1 CMLR 665 . . . 180, 182, 185

C-92/92 Collins v Imtrat Handelsgesellschaft
mbH [1993] ECR I-5145; [1993] 3 CMLR
773 . . . 174, 318, 319

C-109/92 Wirth v Stadt Hannover [1993] ECR
I-6447 . . . 334

C-127/92 Enderby v Frenchay Health Authority
[1993] ECR I-5535; [1994] 1 CMLR
8 . . . 412, 413

C-140/94 DIP SpA v Comune di Bassano del
Grappa . . . 271

C-188/92 TWD Textilwerke Deggendorf GmbH
v Germany [1994] ECR I-833; [1995] 2 CMLR
145 . . . 193, 236

C-199/92 P Hüls AG v Commission [1999] ECR
I-4287 . . . 362

C-292/92 Hunermund [1983] ECR 6787 . . . 292

C-334/92 Miret v Fondo de Garantia Salarial
[1993] ECR I-6911; [1995] 2 CMLR 49 . . . 179

C-364/92 SAT v Eurocontol [1994] ECR
I-43 . . . 361

C-391/92 Commission v Greece [1995] ECR
I-1621; [1996] 1 CMLR 359 . . . 292

C-393/92 Almelo [1994] ECR I-1477 . . . 265

C-399/92 Helmig [1994] ECR I-5727 . . . 412

C-401 and 402/92 Tankstation 't Heukste vof
and JBE Boermans [1994] ECR I-2199; [1995]
3 CMLR 501 . . . 292

C-419/92 Scholz v Opera Universitaria di
Cagliari [1994] ECR I-505; [1994] 1 CMLR
873 . . . 307, 348

C-421/92 Habermann-Beltermann (Gabriele)
v Arbeiterwohlfahrt Bezirksverband [1994]
ECR I-1657; [1994] 2 CMLR 242 . . . 421

C-32/93 Webb v EMO Air Cargo (UK) Ltd
[1994] ECR I-3567; [1994] 2 CMLR 729 . . . 385

C-43/93 Van der Elst v Office des Migrations
Internationales (OMI) [1994] ECR I-3803;
[1995] 1 CMLR 513 . . . 351

C-46/93 Brasserie du Pêcheur SA v Germany
[1996] QB 404 . . . 158, 185, 246

C-48/93 Factortame III v UK [1996] ECR
I-1029 . . . 140, 152, 185, 186

C-57/93 Vroege v NCIV Instituut [1994] ECR
I-4541; [1995] 1 CMLR 881 . . . 408

C-65/93 European Parliament v Council [1995]
ECR I-643; [1996] 1 CMLR 4 . . . 130

C-147/93 Commission v Austria [1995] ECR
I-4125 . . . 335

C-280/93 Germany v Council [1994] ECR
I-4973 . . . 158, 177

C-312/93 Peterbroeck Van Campenhout & Cie
SCS v Belgium [1995] ECR I-4599; [1996] 1
CMLR 793 . . . 195, 207

C-324/93 Evans Medical . . . 144

C-334/93 Miret v Fondo de Garantia Salarial
[1993] ECR I-6911; [1995] 2 CMLR 49 . . . 180

C-346/93 Kleinwort Benson [1995] I-615 . . . 191

C-363/93 Lancry [1994] ECR I-3957 . . . 266

C-384/93 Alpine Investments BV v Minister of
Finance [1995] ECR I-1141; [1995] 2 CMLR
209 . . . 311, 325, 353

C-392/93 R v HM Treasury ex p British
Telecommunications plc [1996] ECR I-1631;
[1996] 2 CMLR 217 . . . 186

C-412/93 Leclerc-Siplec v TF1 Publicite
SA [1995] ECR I-179; [1995] 3 CMLR
422 . . . 194, 293

C-415/93 Union Royale Belge des Sociétés de
Football Association (ASBL) v Bosman [1995]
ECR I-4921; [1996] 1 CMLR 645 . . . 106,
293, 304

C-430/93 and C-431/93 Van Schijndel
v Stichting Pensioenfonds voor
Fysiotherapeuten [1996] All ER (EC)
259; [1995] ECR I-4705; [1996] 1 CMLR
801 . . . 207

C-450/93 Kalanke v Freie Hansestadt
Bremen [1995] ECR I-3051; [1996] 1 CMLR
175 . . . 425

C-465–6/93 Atlanta Fruchthandelsgesellschaft
[1995] ECR I-3761; [1996] 1 CMLR 575; [1995]
ECR I-3799 . . . 157, 203

C-470/93 Verein Gegen Unwesen in Handel und
Gewerbe Koln eV v Mars GmbH [1995] ECR
I-1923; [1995] 3 CMLR 1 . . . 292, 294

C-5/94 R v Ministry of Agriculture, Fisheries
and Food ex p Hedley Lomas (Ireland) Ltd
[1997] QB 139; [1996] 3 WLR 787; [1996] All
ER (EC) 493; [1996] ECR I-2553; [1996] 2
CMLR 39 . . . 187

C-13/94 P v S and Cornwall County Council C13/94 [1996] ECR I-2143; [1996] 2 CMLR 247 . . . 415

C-24/94 Commission v Council [1996] ECR 1–3989 . . . 223

C-55/94 Gebhard v Consiglio dell'Ordine degli Avvocati [1995] ECR I-4165; [1996] 1 CMLR 603 . . . 261, 312, 324

C-58/94 Netherlands v Council [1996] ECR I-2169 . . . 121

C-63/94 Belgapom Groupement National des Négociants en Pommes de Terre de Belgique v SA ITM Belgium [1995] ECR I-2467 . . . 292

C-68/94 France v Commission [1998] ECR I-1375 . . . 383, 394

C-84/94 UK v Council (Working Time Directive) [1996] ECR I-5755; [1996] 3 CMLR 671 . . . 88, 89, 125, 263

C-116/94 Meyers v Adjudication Officer [1995] ECR I-2131; [1996] 1 CMLR 461 . . . 383

C-140/94 DIP SpA v Comune di Bassano del Grappa [1995] I-3257 . . . 292

C-175/94 Gallagher [1995] ECR I-4253 . . . 330

C-178/94 Dillenkofer v Germany [1996] ECR I-4845; [1996] 3 CMLR 469 . . . 187

C-194/94 CIA Security International SA v Signalson SA [1996] ECR I-2201 . . . 182

C-237/94 O'Flynn v Adjudication Officer [1996] ECR I-2617; [1996] 3 CMLR 103 . . . 318

C-333/94P Tetra Pak International SA v Commission [1996] ECR I-5951; [1997] 4 CMLR 662 . . . 251, 379, 380, 390

C-334/94 Commission v France [1996] ECR I-1307 . . . 219

C-24/95 Land Rheinland-Pfalz v Alcan [1997] ECR I-1591 . . . 386

C-28/95 Leur-Bloem [1997] ECR I-4161 . . . 194

C-30/95 Société Commerciale des Potasses et de l'Azote (SCPA) v Commission [1998] ECR I-1375 . . . 383, 394

C-34–6/95 Konsumentombudsmannen (KO) v De Agostini [1997] ECR I-3843; [1998] 1 CMLR 32 . . . 293

C-57/95 French Republic v Commission [1997] ECR I-1627; [1997] 2 CMLR 935 . . . 224, 232

C-68/95 T Port GmbH & Co KG v Bundesanstalt für Landwirtschaft und Ernährung [1996] ECR I-6065; [1997] 1 CMLR 1 . . . 158, 238

C-73/95 P Viho Europe BV v Commission (Parker Pen case) [1996] ECR I-5457 . . . 361

C-120/95 Decker v Caisse de maladie des employés privés [1998] ECR I-1831 . . . 286

C-136/95 CNAVTS v E Thibault [1998] ECR I-2011 . . . 418

C-168/95 Criminal Proceedings against Arcaro [1996] ECR I-4705; [1997] 1 CMLR 179 . . . 179

C-180/95 Nils Draehmpaehl v Urania Immobilienservice [1997] ECR I-2195 . . . 427

C-188/95 Fantask A/S v Industriministeriet (Erhvervsministeriet) [1997] ECR I-6783; [1998] 1 CMLR 473 . . . 206

C-191/95 Commission v Germany [1998] ECR I-5449 . . . 215

C-192/95 Societe Comateb v Directeur General des Douanes et Droits Indirects [1997] STC 1006; [1997] ECR I-165; [1997] 2 CMLR 649 . . . 120, 121

C-196/95 Commission v France . . . 270

C-241/95 Accrington Beef [2004] ECR I-873; [2004] 1 CMLR 35 . . . 236

C-265/95 Commission v France (Spanish Strawberries) [1997] ECR I-6959 . . . 212, 214, 217, 275, 280

C-299/95 Kremzow v Austria [1997] ECR I-2629; [1997] 3 CMLR 1289 . . . 347

C-321/95 P Greenpeace International and Others v Commission [1998] ECR I-1651 . . . 231

C-344/95 Commission v Belgium [1997] ECR I-1035; [1997] 2 CMLR 187 . . . 315

C-345/95 France v European Parliament [1997] ECR I-5215 . . . 55

C-358/95 Tommaso Morellato v Unita Sanitaria Locale (Usl) N 11 di Pordenone [1997] ECR I-1431 . . . 281

C-364/95 T Port GmbH v Hauptzollamt Hamburg-Jonas [1998] ECR I-1023 . . . 158

C-366/95 Steff-houlberg Export [1998] ECR I-2661; [1999] 2 CMLR 250 . . . 121

C-368/95 Vereinigte Familiapress Zeitungsverlags- und vertriebs GmbH v Heinrich Bauer Verlag [1997] ECR I-3689; [1997] 3 CMLR 1329 . . . 286, 293, 297

C-388/95 Belgium v Spain [2000] ECR I-3123; [2002] 1 CMLR 26 . . . 221, 278, 283

C-400/95 Larsson v Dansk Handel & Service, acting for Fotex Supermarked A/S [1997] ECR I-2757; [1997] 2 CMLR 915 . . . 422, 423, 424

C-408/95 Eurotunnel [1997] ECR I-6315; [1998] 2 CMLR 293 . . . 236

C-409/95 Hellmut Marschall v Land Nordrhein-Westfalen [1997] ECR I-6363; [1998] 1 CMLR 547 . . . 425

C-39/96 Koninklijke Vereeniging ter Bevordering van de Belangen des Boekhandels v Free Record Shop BV [1997] ECR I-2303 . . . 372

C-50/96 Deutsche Telekom AG v Schroder [2000] ECR I-743; [2002] 2 CMLR 25 . . . 400

C-54/96 Dorsch Consult Ingenieurgesellschaft mbH v Bundesbaugesellschaft Berlin mbH [1997] ECR I-4961; [1998] 2 CMLR 237 . . . 190

C-64/96 Land Nordrhein-Westfalen v Uecker & Jacquet [1997] ECR I-3171; [1997] 3 CMLR 963 . . . 347

C-67/96 Albany International [1999] ECR I-5751 . . . 368

C-78/96 Steinike und Weinlig v Germany [1977] ECR 595; [1977] 2 CMLR 688 . . . 269

C-85/96 Martinez Sala v Freistaat Bayern [1998] ECR I-2691 . . . 338

C-106/96 UK v Commission [1998] ECR I-2729; [1998] 2 CMLR 981 . . . 109, 225, 234

C-149/96 Portugal v Council [1999] ECR I-8395 . . . 177

C-162/96 Racke v Hauptzollamt Mainz [1998] ECR I-3655 . . . 143

C-184/96 Commission v France (Foie Gras) [1998] ECR I-6197; [2000] 3 CMLR 1308 . . . 264, 277

C-187/96 Commission v Greece [1998] ECR I-1095 . . . 317

C-213/96 Outokumpu OY [1998] ECR I-1777 . . . 271

C-249/96 Grant v South West Trains [1998] 1 CMLR 993 . . . 416

C-274/96 Criminal Proceedings against Bickel [1998] ECR I-7637; [1999] 1 CMLR 348 . . . 338

C-319/96 Brinkmann Tabakfabriken GmbH v Skatteministeiet [1998] ECR I-5255; [1998] 3 CMLR 673 . . . 186

C-324 & 325/96 Deutsche Telekom v Vick [1998] ECR I-1333 . . . 96, 400

C-326/96 Levez v TH Jennings (Harlow Pools) Ltd [1998] ECR I-7835; [1999] 2 CMLR 363 . . . 207

C-348/96 Criminal Proceedings against Calfa [1999] ECR I-11; [1999] 2 CMLR 1138 . . . 332

C-350/96 Clean Car Autoservice [1998] ECR I-2521 . . . 305

C-394/96 Brown v Rentokil [1998] ECR I-4186; [1998] 2 CMLR 1049 . . . 335, 424

C-395 and 396/96 P Compagnie Maritime Belge Transports [2000] ECR I-1365 . . . 379, 382

C-7/97 Oscar Bronner GmbH & Co KG v Mediaprint Zeitungs- und Zeitschrift enverlag GmbH & Co [1998] ECR I-7791 . . . 380

C-10–22/97 IN.CO.GE.'90 [1998] ECR I-6307 . . . 142

C-67/97 Bluhme [1998] ECR I-8033; [1999] 1 CMLR 612 . . . 289

C-126/97 Eco Swiss China Time Ltd v Benetton International NV [1999] ECR I-3055 . . . 357

C-140/97 Rechberger v Austria [1999] ECR I-3499 . . . 187

C-149/97 Institute of the Motor Industry v Customs and Excise Commission [1998] ECR I-7053; [1999] 1 CMLR 326 . . . 99

C-158/97 G Badeck et al v Land Hessen [2000] ECR I-1875 . . . 425

C-167/97 R v Secretary of State for Employment, ex p Seymour-Smith [1999] ECR I-623; [1999] 2 CMLR 273 . . . 405, 412

C-185/97 Coote v Granada [1998] ECR I-5199; [1998] 3 CMLR 958 . . . 427

C-212/97 Centros Ltd v Erhvervs-og Selskabsstyrelsen [1999] ECR I-1459; [1999] 2 CMLR 551 . . . 313

C-226/97 Criminal Proceedings against Lemmens [1998] ECR I-3711; [1998] 3 CMLR 261 . . . 182

C-273/97 Sirdar v Army Board [1999] ECR I-7403; [1999] 3 CMLR 559 . . . 420

C-310/97 P Commission v Assidomän [1999] ECR I-5363 . . . 65, 234

C-387/97 Commission v Greece [2000] ECR I-5047 . . . 220

C-424/97 Haim v Kassenzahnärztliche Vereinigung Nordrhein [2000] ECR I-5123 . . . 185

C-84/98 Commission v Portugal [2000] ECR I-5215; [2000] ECR I-5171 . . . 143, 144

C-95/98 Dubois v Council & Commission [1999] ECR I-4835 . . . 240

C-207/98 Mahlberg [2000] ECR I-3201; [2001] 3 CMLR 40 . . . 421

C-218/98 Abdoulaye v Regie Nationale des Usines Renault SA [1999] ECR I-5723; [2001] 2 CMLR 18 . . . 425

C-224/98 D'Hoop v Office National de l'Emploi [2002] ECR I-6191; [2002] 3 CMLR 12 . . . 338, 339, 341

C-237/98 P Dorsch Consult v Council [2000] ECR I-4549 . . . 247

C-254/98 Schutzverband gegen Unlauteren Wettbewerb v TK-Heimdienst Sass GmbH [2000] ECR I-151; [2002] 1 CMLR 25 . . . 294, 297

C-281/98 Angonese v Cassa di Risparmio di Bolzano SpA [2000] All ER (EC) 577; [2000] ECR I-4139; [2000] 2 CMLR 1120 . . . 302, 336, 348, 352

C-285/98 Kreil v Germany [2000] ECR I-69; [2002] 1 CMLR 36 . . . 420

C-352/98 P Laboratoires Pharmaceutiques Bergaderm SA v Commission [2000] ECR I-5291 . . . 187, 242, 243, 244, 246, 247

C-376/98 & C-74/99 Germany v European Parliament; R v Secretary of State for Health ex p Imperial Tobacco Ltd (Tobacco Advertising) [2000] ECR I-8419 . . . 82, 88, 126, 232, 261

C-377/98 Netherlands v European Parliament and Council (Biotechnology Directive) [2001] ECR I-7079 . . . 82, 88

C-405/98 Konsumentombudsmannen (KO) v Gourmet International Products AB [2001] All ER (EC) 308; [2001] ECR I-1795; [2001] 2 CMLR 31 . . . 293

C-407/98 Katarina Abrahamsson & Leif Anderson v Elisabet Fogelqvist [2000] ECR I-5539 . . . 425

C-424/98 Commission v Italy [2000] ECR I-4001 . . . 336

C-443/98 Unilever Italia SpA v Central
Food SpA [2000] ECR I-7535; [2001]
1 CMLR 21 . . . 183

C-466/98 Commission v UK [2002] ECR
I-9427 . . . 144

C-467–9/98 Commission v Finland (Air
Transport) [2002] ECR I-9518–9627 . . . 85

C-43/99 Leclere v Caisse Nationale des
Prestations Familiales [2001] ECR I-4265;
[2001] 2 CMLR 49 . . . 308, 318

C-79/99 Schnorbus v Land Hessen [2000] ECR
I-10997; [2001] 1 CMLR 40 . . . 420, 426

C-125/99 P D and Sweden v Council [2008] 3
CMLR 17; [1996] ECR I–2143 . . . 416

C-184/99 Grzelczyk [2001] ECR I-6193; [2002] 1
CMLR 19 . . . 310, 334, 335, 336, 338, 339, 340

C-192/99 R v Secretary of State for the Home
Department ex p Kaur (Manjit) . . . 101, 305

C-212/99 Commission v Italy [2001] ECR
I-4923 . . . 220

C-230/99 Commission v France [2001] ECR
I-1169 . . . 215

C-234/99 Nygard C-234/99 . . . 270

C-268/99 Jany v Staatssecretaris van Justitie
[2001] ECR I-8615; [2003] 2 CMLR
1 . . . 311, 312

C-309/99 Wouters [2002] ECR I-1577 . . . 363

C-353/99 P Hautala, Heidi v Council [2001] ECR
I-9565; [2002] 1 CMLR 15 . . . 73, 121

C-387/99 Commission v Germany [2004] ECR
I-3751 . . . 278

C-413/99 Baumbast v Secretary of State for
the Home Department [2002] ECR I-7091;
[2002] 3 CMLR 23 . . . 113, 320, 321, 336, 339,
343, 344

C-438/99 Melgar v Ayuntamiento de Los
Barrios [2001] ECR I-6915; [2003] 3 CMLR
4 . . . 422, 428

C-453/99 Courage Ltd v Crehan [2001] ECR
I-6297; [2001] 5 CMLR 28 . . . 187, 391

C-459/99 Mouvement contre le Racisme,
l'Antisemitisme et la Xenophobie ASBL
(MRAX) v Belgium [2002] ECR I-6591; [2002]
3 CMLR 25 . . . 113, 316, 344

C-476/99 Lommers v Minister van Landbouw,
Natuurbeheer en Visserij [2002] ECR I-2891;
[2004] 2 CMLR 49 . . . 426

C-1/00 Commission v France [2001] ECR
1–3493 . . . 221

C-17/00 de Coster [2001] ECR I-9445 . . . 325,
336, 349

C-50/00 P Union de Pequeños Agricultores v
Council of the European Union (UPA) [2002]
ECR I-6677; [2002] 3 CMLR 1 . . . 201, 235

C-60/00 Carpenter v Secretary of State for the
Home Department [2002] ECR I-6279; [2002]
2 CMLR 64 . . . 336, 343, 348, 352

C-62/00 Marks & Spencer plc v Customs and
Excise Commissioners [2002] ECR I-6325;
[2002] 3 CMLR 9 . . . 175, 199

C-99/00 Criminal Proceedings against
Lyckeskog [2002] ECR I-4839; [2004] 3 CMLR
29 . . . 197

C-109/00 Tele Danmark A/S v Handels- og
Kontorfunktionaerernes Forbund I Danmark
(HK) [2001] ECR I-6993; [2002] 1 CMLR
5 . . . 422

C-112/00 Schmidberger Internationale
Transporte Planzuge v Austria [2003] ECR
I-5659; [2003] 2 CMLR 34 . . . 275, 286

C-129/00 Commission v Italy [2003] ECR
I-14637 . . . 199

C-147/00 Commission v France [2001] ECR
I-2387 . . . 216

C-150/00 Commission v Austria [2004] ECR
I-3887 . . . 278

C-159/00 Sapod Audic v Eco-Emballages SA
[2002] ECR I-5031 . . . 183

C-208/00 Uberseering BV v Nordic
Construction Co Baumanagement GmbH
(NCC) [2002] ECR I-9919; [2005] 1 CMLR
1 . . . 313

C-253/00 Munoz v Frumar Ltd [2002] ECR
I-7289 . . . 174

C-302/00 Commission v France (Cigarettes)
[2002] ECR I-2055 . . . 271

C-318/00 Bacardi-Martini SAS v Newcastle
United Football Co Ltd [2003] ECR I-905;
[2003] 1 CMLR 26 . . . 193

C-320/00 Lawrence v Regent Office
Care Ltd [2002] ECR I-7325; [2002]
3 CMLR 27 . . . 409

C-385/00 De Groot v Staatssecretaris van
Financien [2004] STC 1346; [2002] ECR
I-11819; [2004] 3 CMLR 21 . . . 307, 318

C-416/00 Tommaso Morellato v Comune di
Padova [2003] ECR I-9343 . . . 294

C-438/00 Deutscher Handballbund eV v Kolpak
[2003] ECR I-4135; [2004] 2 CMLR 38 . . . 304

C-453/00 Kühne & Heitz NV v Productschap
voor Pluimvee en Eieren [2004] ECR I-837;
[2006] 2 CMLR 17 . . . 201

C-2 and 3/01 P Commission v Bayer [2004] ECR
I-0023 . . . 362

C-100/01 Ministre de l'Interieur v Oteiza
Olazabal [2002] ECR I-10981; [2005] 1 CMLR
49 . . . 332

C-109/01 Secretary of State for the Home
Department v Akrich [2003] ECR I-9607;
[2003] 3 CMLR 26 . . . 113, 114, 320, 345, 349

C-117/01 KB v NHS Pensions Agency [2004]
ECR I-541; [2004] 1 CMLR 28 . . . 407, 416

C-147/01 Weber's Wine World Handels GmbH v
Abgabenberufungskommission Wien [2005]
All ER (EC) 224; [2003] ECR I-11365; [2004] 1
CMLR 7 . . . 120

C-167/01 Inspire Art [2003] ECR I-10155; [2005]
3 CMLR 34 . . . 313

C-186/01 Dory v Germany [2003] ECR I-2479;
[2003] 2 CMLR 26 . . . 420, 426

C-192/01 Commission v Denmark (Prohibition of Marketing of Enriched Foods) [2003] ECR I-9693; [2003] 3 CMLR 29 . . . 281

C-206/01 Arsenal FC v Matthew Reed [2003] Ch 454; [2003] 3 WLR 450 . . . 201

C-215/01 Schnitzer [2003] ECR I-14847 . . . 312

C-224/01 Köbler v Austria [2003] ECR I-10239; [2003] 3 CMLR 28 . . . 118, 188, 200, 202, 214

C-256/01 Allonby v Accrington and Rossendale College [2004] ECR I-873; [2004] 1 CMLR 35 . . . 311, 409

C-264/01 AOK Bundesverband [2004] ECR I-2493 . . . 361

C-278/01 Commission v Spain [2003] ECR I-14141 . . . 204

C-313/01 Morgenbesser v Consiglio dell'Ordine degli Avvocati di Genova [2003] ECR I-13467; [2004] 1 CMLR 24 . . . 324, 329

C-320/01 Busch v Klinikum Neustadt GmbH & Co Betriebs KG [2003] ECR I-2041; [2003] 2 CMLR 15 . . . 422

C-322/01 Deutscher Apothekerverband eV v 0800 DocMorris NV [2003] ECR I-14887; [2005] 1 CMLR 46 . . . 280

C-397/01–401/01 Pfeiffer v Deutsches Rotes Kreuz Kreisverband Waldshut eV [2004] ECR I-8835; [2005] 1 CMLR 44 . . . 179

C-413/01 Ninni-Orasche v Bundesminister für Wissenschaft, Verkehr und Kunst [2004] All ER (EC) 765; [2003] ECR I-13187; [2004] 1 CMLR 19 . . . 306

C-463/01 Commission v Germany [2004] ECR I-11705 . . . 122

C-36/02 Omega Spielhallen v Bonn [2004] ECR I-9609; [2005] 1 CMLR 5 . . . 158

C-47/02 Anker v Germany [2003] ECR I-10447; [2004] 2 CMLR 35 . . . 333

C-138/02 Collins v Secretary of State for Work and Pensions [2004] ECR I-2703; [2004] 2 CMLR 8 . . . 309, 310, 335, 336, 341, 342, 352

C-148/02 Garcia Avello [2003] ECR I-11613 . . . 349

C-157/02 Rieser Internationale Transporte GmbH v Autobahnen- und Schnellstrassen Finanzierungs AG (ASFINAG) . . . 178

C-167/02 P Rothley v European Parliament [2004] ECR I-3149; [2004] 2 CMLR 11 . . . 235

C-200/02 Chen v Secretary of State for the Home Department [2004] ECR I-9925; [2004] 3 CMLR 48 . . . 321, 345, 350

C-201/02 Wells v Secretary of State for Transport [2004] ECR I-723 . . . 184

C-236/02 J Slob v Productschap Zuivel [2004] ECR I-1861 . . . 191

C-263/02 P Commission v Jego-Quere [2004] ECR I-3425; [2004] 2 CMLR 12 . . . 65, 201, 235

C-304/02 Commission v France [2005] ECR I-6263; [2005] 3 CMLR 13 . . . 220

C-313/02 Wippel v Peek & Cloppenburg [2004] ECR I-9483 . . . 306, 409

C-456/02 Trojani v Centre Public d'Aide Sociale de Bruxelles (CPAS) [2004] All ER (EC) 1065; [2004] ECR I-7573; [2004] 3 CMLR 38 . . . 307

C-53/03 Syfait v GlaxoSmithKline [2005] ECR I-4609; [2005] 5 CMLR 1 . . . 190

C-72/03 Carbonati Apuani [2004] ECR I-8027 . . . 266

C-94/03 Commission v Council [2006] ECR I-1 . . . 125

C-101/03 Audiolux SA v GBL [2009] ECR I-9823 . . . 98

C-131/03 P Reynolds Tobacco Holdings Inc v Commission [2006] ECR I-7795; [2007] 1 CMLR 1 . . . 225

C-147/03 Commission v Austria [2005] ECR I-5969 . . . 216

C-173/03 Traghetti del Mediterraneo SpA v Italy [2006] All ER (EC) 983; [2006] ECR I-5177; [2006] 3 CMLR 19 . . . 188, 200, 202

C-176/03 Commission v Council [2005] ECR I-7879 . . . 125

C-191/03 McKenna [2006] All ER (EC) 455; [2005] ECR I-7631; [2006] 1 CMLR 6 . . . 424

C-205/03 P FENIN v Commission [2006] ECR I-6295 . . . 361

C-209/03 Bidar [2005] ECR I-2119; [2005] 2 CMLR 3 . . . 311, 335, 342

C-210/03 R v Secretary of State for Health, ex p Swedish Match [2004] ECR I-11893; [2005] 1 CMLR 26 . . . 82, 126

C-215/03 Salah Oulane [2005] ECR I-1215 . . . 315

C-265/03 Simutenkov v Ministerio de Educacion y Cultura [2006] All ER (EC) 42; [2005] ECR I-2579 . . . 106

C-319/03 Briheche [2004] ECR I-8807 . . . 424

C-380/03 Germany v EP and Council [2007] All ER (EC) 1016; [2007] 2 CMLR 1 . . . 82, 126, 261

C-403/03 Schempp v Finanzamt Munchen V (C-403/03) [2005] SC 1792; [2005] ECR I-6421; [2005] 3 CMLR 37 . . . 348

C-446/03 Marks & Spencer plc v David Halsey (Her Majesty's Inspector of Taxes) [2005] ECR I-10837 . . . 313

C-461/03 Schul [2005] ECR I-10513 . . . 199

C-540/03 Parliament v Council (Family Reunion Directive) [2007] All ER (EC) 193; [2006] ECR I-5769 . . . 103

C-544/03 Mobistar [2005] ECR I-7723 . . . 336, 350

C-53/04 Marrosu and Sardino [2006] ECR I-7213 . . . 179

C-66/04 UK v Council and EP (Smoked Flavourings) [2006] All ER (EC) 487; [2005] ECR I-10553; [2006] 3 CMLR 1 . . . 261

C-74/04 P Commission v Volkswagen [2006] ECR I-6585 . . . 363

C-144/04 Mangold v Helm [2006] All ER (EC) 383; [2005] ECR I-9981; [2006] 1 CMLR 43 . . . 116, 174, 175, 180, 181, 182, 433

C-145/04 Spain v UK [2006] ECR
I-7917 . . . 55, 221

C-154 & 155/04 Alliance for Natural Health
v Secretary of State for Health [2005] ECR
I-6451; [2005] 2 CMLR 61 . . . 88, 90

C-158 & 159/04 Alfa Vita Vissilopoulos AE v
Greece [2006] ECR I-8135; [2007] 2 CMLR
2 . . . 294

C-170/04 Rosengren and Others v
Riksäklagaren [2007] 3 CMLR 10 . . . 280, 283

C-180/04 Vassallo v Azienda Ospedaliera
Ospedale San Martino di Genova e Cliniche
Universitarie Convenzionate [2006] ECR
I-7251 . . . 179

C-212/04 Adeneler v ELOG [2006] ECR
I-6057 . . . 181, 188

C-217/04 UK v Council and Parliament
(Network and Information Security Agency)
[2006] ECR I-3771; [2006] 3 CMLR 2 . . . 262

C-227/04 Lindorfer v Council [2008] Pens. LR
15 . . . 181

C-256/04 Ioannidis [2005] ECR I-8275; [2005] 3
CMLR 47 . . . 341, 342

C-294/04 Herrero v Instituto Madrileño de la
Salud (Imsalud) [2006] ECR I-1513 . . . 421

C-295–8/04 Manfredi v Lloyd Adriatico
Assicurazioni SpA [2007] Bus LR 188; [2007]
All ER (EC) 27 . . . 187

C-300/04 Eman and Sevinger [2006]
I-8055 . . . 55

C-310/04 Spain v Council (Spanish Cotton
Subsidies) [2006] ECR I-7285 . . . 90

C-344/04 R v Dept of Transport, ex p
International Air Transport Association and
European Low Fares Airline Association
[2004] EWHC 1721 (Admin); [2004] 3 CMLR
20 . . . 90, 191

C-354/04P Gestoras [2007] I-1579 . . . 101

C-355/04 P Segi v Council [2008] All ER (EC)
65; [2007] 2 CMLR 23 . . . 117

C-386/04 Stauffer [2006] ECR I-8203 . . . 312

C-406/04 De Cuyper [2006] ECR I-6947; [2006]
3 CMLR 44 . . . 342

C-423/04 Richards [2006] ECR I-3585; [2006] 2
CMLR 49 . . . 416

C-432/04 Commission v Edith Cresson [2006]
ECR I-06387; [2006] All ER (D) 141 . . . 45

C-442/04 Commisssion v Spain [2008] ECR
I-3517 . . . 233

C-1/05 Jia v Migrationsverket (C-1/05) [2007]
QB 545; [2007] 2 WLR 1005; [2007] All ER
(EC) 575; [2007] 1 CMLR 41 . . . 320, 345

C-17/05 Cadman [2007] All ER (EC) 1; [2006]
ECR I-9583; [2007] 1 CMLR 16 . . . 414

C-39/05 & C-52/05 Sweden & Turco v Council
[2008] ECR I-4723 . . . 74

C-64/05 P Sweden v Commission [2008] QB
902; [2008] 3 WLR 756 . . . 73

C-110/05 Commission v Italy (Italian Trailers)
[2009] ECR I-519 . . . 288, 294, 295

C-142/05 Aklagaren v Mickelsson and Roos
[2009] ECR I-4273 . . . 295

C-167/05 Commission v Sweden [2008] ECR
I-2127 . . . 273

C-168/05 Claro v Milenium SL [2006] ECR
I-10421 . . . 206

C-193/05 Commission v Luxembourg [2006]
ECR I-8673 . . . 329

C-208/05 ITC Innovative Technology Center
GmbH v Bundesagentur für Arbeit [2007]
ECR I-181 . . . 305

C-212/05 Hartmann v Freistaat Bayern [2008]
All ER (EC) 1166; [2008] 3 CMLR 38 . . . 308

C-213/05 Geven v Land Nordrhein-Westfalen
[2008] All ER (EC) 1196; [2007] 3 CMLR
45 . . . 308

C-238/05 Asnef-Equifax [2006] ECR
I-11125 . . . 368

C-278/05 Robins v Secretary of State for Work
and Pensions [2007] All ER (EC) 648; [2007] 2
CMLR 13 . . . 187

C-282/05 P Holcim (Deutschland) AG v
Commission [2007] ECR I-2941 . . . 244, 247

C-303/05 Advocaten voor de Wereld VZW v
Leden van de Ministerraad [2008] All ER
(EC) 317; [2007] 3 CMLR 1 . . . 117

C-341/05 Laval un Partneri Ltd v Svenska
Byggnadsarbetareforbundet [2008] All ER
(EC) 166; [2008] 2 CMLR 9 . . . 325

C-402/05 P & C-415/05 Kadi and Al Barakaat v
Council . . . 76, 83, 113, 144, 177

C-432/05 Unibet (London) Ltd v Justitiekanslern
[2008] All ER (EC) 453; [2007] 2 CMLR
30 . . . 103, 207

C-438/05 International Transport Workers'
Federation v Viking Line ABP [2008] All ER
(EC) 127; [2008] 1 CMLR 51 . . . 325

C-440/05 Commission v Council [2007] ECR
I-9097 . . . 126

C-11–12/06 Morgan and Bucher [2009] 1 CMLR
1 . . . 342

C-120/06 P FIAMM v Council of the European
Union [2008] ECR I-6513 . . . 247, 248

C-205/06 Commission v Austria [2009] ECR
I-1301 . . . 143, 144

C-210/06 Cartesio Oktató és Szolgáltató [2008]
ECR I-9641 . . . 192, 313

C-244/06 Dynamic Medien Vertriebs GmbH v
Avides Media AG [2008] ECR I-505 . . . 286

C-249/06 Commission v Sweden [2009] ECR
I-1335 . . . 143, 144

C-265/06 Commission v Portugal [2008]
I-2245 . . . 295

C-268/06 Impact v Minister for
Agriculture and Food and Others [2008]
ECR I-2483 . . . 180

C-275/06 Promusicae 2008 I-00271 . . . 103

C-300/06 Voss (Ursula) v Land Berlin [2007]
ECR I-10573 . . . 412

C-308/06 Intertanko [2008] ECR I-4057 . . . 177

C-309/06 Marks & Spencer plc v Customs and
    Excise Commissioners [2008] STC 1408;
    [2008] 2 CMLR 42 . . . 120, 121
C-404/06 Quelle AG v Bundesverband
    der Verbraucherzentralen und
    Verbraucherverbände [2008]
    ECRI-2685 . . . 180
C-460/06 Paquay v Société d'Architectes Hoet +
    Minne SPRL [2008] 1 CMLR 12; [2008] ICR
    420 . . . 423
C-506/06 Mayr v Backerei und Konditorei
    Gerhard Flockner OHG [2008] All ER (EC)
    613; [2008] 2 CMLR 27 . . . 423
C-33/07 Jipa [2008] ECR I-5157 . . . 332
C-47/07 P Masdar (UK) v Commission [2008]
    ECR I-9761 . . . 244
C-77/07 Commission v France [2007] ECR
    I-158 . . . 220
C-118/07 Commission v Finland [2009] ECR
    I-10889 . . . 143, 144
C-158/07 Förster v IB-Groep [2008] ECR
    I-8507 . . . 311, 342
C-370/07 Commission v Council [2009] ECR
    I-8917 . . . 125
C-550/07 P Akzo Nobel Chemicals v
    Commission [2010] ECR I-8301 . . . 118, 389
C-555/07 Kükükdeveci [2010] ECR I-365 . . . 116,
    174, 175, 180, 181, 182, 433
C-8/08 T-Mobile [2009] ECR I-4529 . . . 365
C-22 and 23/08 Vatsouras and Koupatantze v
    ARGE Nürnberg [2009] ECR I-4585 . . . 342
C-40/08 Asturcom v Rodriguez Noguiera [2009]
    ECR I-9579 . . . 206
C-47/08 Commission v Belgium [2011] ECR
    I-4105 . . . 333
C-50/08 Commission v France [2011] ECR
    4195 . . . 333
C-52/08 Commission v Portugal [2011] ECR
    4275 . . . 333
C-53/08 Commission v Luxembourg [2011] ECR
    I-4309 . . . 333
C-54/08 Commission v Austria [2011] ECR
    I-4355 . . . 333
C-61/08 Commission v Germany [2011] ECR
    I-4399 . . . 333
C-58/08 Vodafone and others [2010] ECR
    I-4999 . . . 88, 89, 90
C-73/08 Bressol [2010] ECR I-2735 . . . 335
C-97/08 AKZO Nobel v Commission [2009]
    ECR I-8237 . . . 362
C-101/08 Audiolux SA v GBL [2009] ECR
    I-9823 . . . 95, 105
C-118/08 Transportes Urbanos y Servicios
    Generales [2010] ECR I-635 . . . 166,
    205, 206
C-127/08 Metock et al [2008] ECR
    I-6241 . . . 320, 345
C-135/08 Rottmann [2010] ECR I-1499 . . . 305, 337
C-154/08 Commission v Spain [2009] ECR
    I-187 . . . 188, 200, 214

C-438/08 Commission v Portugal [2009] ECR
    I-10219 . . . 333
C-28/09 Commission v Austria [2011] ECR
    I-13525 . . . 288, 294
C-34/09 Zambrano v ONEM [2011] ECR
    I-1177 . . . 345, 346
C-104/09 Roca Alvaraz [2010] ECR
    I-08661 . . . 421
C-145/09 Land Baden-Württemberg v
    Tsakouridis [2010] ECR I-11979 . . . 332
C-161/09 Skoma-Lux [2007] ECR I-10841 . . . 107
C-208/09 Ilonka Sayn-Wittgenstein v
    Landeshauptmann von Wien . . . 349
C-236/09 Test-Achats [2011] 2 CMLR
    38 . . . 103, 431
C-399/09 Landtová [2011] ECR I-415 . . . 163
C-434/09 McCarthy (Shirley) v Secretary of
    State for the Home Department, not yet
    reported . . . 346
C-149/10 Chatzi [2010] ECR I-8489 . . . 116, 399
C-188 and 189/10 Melki and Abdeli [2010] ECR
    I-5667 . . . 162, 208
C-411/10 and C-493/10 NS v Secretary of State
    for the Home Department and ME v Refugee
    Applications Commissioner [2012] 2 CMLR
    9 . . . 103
C-364/10 Hungary v Slovak Republic
    ECLI:EU:C:2012:630 . . . 221
C-411/10, 493/10 ME v Refugee Applications
    Commissioner [2012] 2 CMLR 9 . . . 103
C-424–5/10 Ziolkowski and Szeja [2011] ECR
    I-14035 . . . 322
C-617/10 Fransson, Judgment of 26 February
    2013 (OJ (2013) C280) . . . 104
C-171/11 Fra.bo SpA v DVGW . . . 274, 278
C-237 and 238/11 French Republic v European
    Parliament Judgment of the Court (Third
    Chamber) of 13 December 2012 . . . 55
C-256/11 Dereci [2011] ECR I-11315 . . . 346
C-356–7/11 O, S & L ECLI:EU:C:2012:
    776 . . . 346
C-399/11 Melloni, Judgment of 26 February
    2013, not yet reported . . . 104, 142
C-583/11 P Inuit v EP & Council . . . 230, 231
C-176/12 Association de Médiation Sociale
    (AMS) (C-176/12) ECLI:EU:C:2014:2 . . . 173
C-274/12 P Telefónica v Commission , judgment
    of 19 December 2013, not yet reported . . . 232
C-284/12 Deutsche Lufthansa and Frankfurt-
    Hahn Airport [2013] ECR I-755 . . . 387
C-293/12 and C-594/12 Digital Rights Ireland
    et al, Judgment of 16 May 2014, not yet
    reported . . . 159
C-306/12 Spedition Welter [2013] ECR
    I-650 . . . 180
C-370/12 Pringle v Ireland [2012] ECR I-756 . . . 60
C-258/13 Sociedade Agricola
    ECLI:EU:C:2013:810 . . . 104
C-413/14 P Intel v Commission [2014] ECR I-547
    and appeal pending . . . 251, 379, 381, 390

General Court/Court of First Instance

T-30/89 Hilti A G v Commission [1990] ECR
II-163; [1990] 4 CMLR 16 . . . 117, 389

T-51/89 Tetra Pak Rausing SA v Commission
[1990] ECR II-309; [1991] 4 CMLR
334 . . . 251, 379, 380, 390, 393

T-68 and 77–8/89 Re: Italian Flat Glass [1992]
ECR II-1403 . . . 368, 375

T-79/89 BASF AG v Commission [1992] ECR
II-315; [1992] 4 CMLR 357 . . . 225

T-138/89 BBV v Commission [1992] ECR
II-2181 . . . 227

T-83/91 Tetra Pak International SA v
Commission [1994] ECR II-755 . . . 350

T-447-9/93 Associazione Italiana Tecnico
Economica del Cemento (AITEC) v
Commission [1995] ECR II-1971 . . . 230

T-585/93 Greenpeace International v
Commission [1995] ECR II-2205 . . . 231

T-194/94 Carvel [1995] ECR II-2765; [1995] 3
CMLR 359 . . . 73

T-374–5/94 European Night Services [1998] ECR
II-3141 . . . 370

T-105/95 WWF UK (World Wide Fund for Nature)
v Commission [1997] ECR II-313 . . . 216

T-175/95 Swedish Journalists [1998] ECR
II-2289 . . . 73

T-47/96 SDDDA v Commission [1996] ECR
II-1559 . . . 213

T-102/96 Gencor v Commission [1999] ECR
II-753 . . . 395

T-113/96 Dubois v Commission [1998] ECR
II-125 . . . 240

T-122/96 Federolio v Commission [1997] ECR
II-1559 . . . 230

T-62/98 Volkswagen AG v Commission [2000]
ECR II-2707 . . . 251

T-112/98 Mannesmannröhren-Werke AG v
Commission [2001] ECR II-729 . . . 121

T-166/98 Cantina v Commission [2004] ECR
II-3991 . . . 244

T-112/99 Metropole Television v Commission
[2001] ECR II-2459 . . . 368

T-191/99 Petrie [2001] ECR II-3677 . . . 216

T-219/99 Virgin/British Airways [2003] ECR
II-5917 . . . 379

T-342/99 Airtours plc v Commission [2004]
ECR II-1785 . . . 379, 396

T-69/00 FIAMM v Council of the European
Union [2005] ECR II-5393; [2006] 2 CMLR
9 . . . 244, 247, 248

T-67/01 JCB v Commission [2004] ECR
II-0049 . . . 374

T-177/01 Jego-Quere & Cie SA v Commission
[2004] ECR I-3425; [2004] 2 CMLR 12 . . . 235

T-168/02 IFAW v Commission [2004] ECR
II-4135 . . . 74

T-237/02 Technische Glaswerke Ilmenau v
Commission [2006] ECR II-5131 . . . 74

T-212/03 My Travel Group plc v Commission
[2008] ECR II-1967 . . . 246

T-279/03 Galileo International Technology
and Others v Commission [2006] ECR
II-1291 . . . 248

T-391/03 & T-700/04 Franchet et al v
Commission [2006] ECR II-2023 . . . 74

T-16/04 Arcelor [2010] ECR II-211 . . . 244, 247

T-201/04 Microsoft Corp v Commission [2007]
ECR II-3601 . . . 379, 380

T-376/04 Polyelectrolyte Producers Group
v Council and Commission [2005] ECR
II-3007 . . . 240

T-425, 444, 450, and 456/04 France v
Commission . . . 384

T-49/07 Sofiane Fahas v Council of the
European Union [2010] ECR II-5555 . . . 230

T-299/08 Elf Aquitaine v Commission [2011]
ECR II-2149 . . . 362

T-56/09 and T-73/09 Saint-Gobain Glass France
SA and Others v European Commission
(2014) ECLI:EU:T:2014:160 . . . 251, 390

T-286/09 Intel v Commission, not yet
reported . . . 379, 381, 390

T-18/10 Inuit, not yet reported . . . 230, 231

T-262/10 Microban [2011] ECR
II-7697 . . . 231, 232

T-380/11 Souliotis v Commission
ECLI:EU:T:2013:420 . . . 232

Table of National Legislation

Belgium

Constitution
  Art 25a . . . 155
Loi sur le Travail . . . 291

Czech Republic

Constitution . . . 38, 162–3

Denmark

Constitution . . . 164
  s 20 . . . 164
  s 20(2) . . . 163

France

Code de Travail . . . 291
Constitution
  Art 55 . . . 160, 161
  Art 88 . . . 161, 162
Maritime Code . . . 212

Germany

Accession Act to Maastricht Treaty 1992 . . . 157
Grundgesetz . . . 117, 142, 155–9, 420
  Art 1 . . . 112
  Art 2.1 . . . 141
  Art 12 . . . 158
  Art 14 . . . 141, 158
  Art 23 . . . 155
  Art 24 . . . 155, 156
  Art 25 . . . 155
  Art 100–I . . . 158
  Art 101 . . . 117, 156
  Art 101(1) . . . 157
  Arts 102–104 . . . 117
Transformation Act . . . 158–9

Hungary

Constitution . . . 164

Ireland

Constitutional Amendment no 27 . . . 321
Constitution . . . 164, 345
  Art 15(4.2) . . . 164
  Art 29(4) . . . 164
  Art 29(4.10) . . . 164
  Art 40(3.3) . . . 164

Italy

Constitution . . . 105, 141
  Art 11 . . . 159, 160
Electricity Industry Nationalization Act . . . 139

Poland

Constitution
  Art 90 . . . 165

Spain

Civil Code . . . 179
Constitution . . . 142
  Art 93 . . . 166

Sweden

Law on Alcohol
  Ch 4(2)(1) . . . 283

UK Primary Legislation

Criminal Law Act 1977 . . . 148
Equal Pay Act 1970 . . . 151
European Communities Act 1972 . . . 147–53
  s 1 . . . 147
  s 2(1) . . . 148–53
  s 2(2) . . . 148
  s 2(4) . . . 148–53
  s 3 . . . 149
  s 3(1) . . . 148
  s 3(2) . . . 148
  Sch 2 . . . 148

European Union Act 2011 . . . 12, 100, 153–4
   s 2 . . . 154
   s 4(1) . . . 154
   s 4(4) . . . 154
   ss 5–8 . . . 154
   s 18 . . . 154
Human Rights Act 1998 . . . 146
Merchant Shipping Act 1988 . . . 148, 151
Sex Discrimination Act 1975
   s 6(4) . . . 150

UK Secondary Legislation

Transfer of Undertakings (Protection of
   Employment) Regulations 2006 (TUPE)
   (SI 2006/246) . . . 151
Civil Procedure Rules 1998 (SI 1998/3132)
   Pt 68 . . . 193
Equal Pay (Equal Value Amendment)
   Regulations 1983 (SI 1983/1794) . . . 413

Table of International Legislation

Cotonou Agreement (2000) . . . 106

EEA Treaty . . . 18
European Convention on Human Rights . . . 5,
  47, 52, 63, 83, 102, 103, 111, 112, 113–15, 117,
  146, 332, 340, 416
  Art 6 . . . 103, 113, 117, 121, 207, 416, 427
  Art 7 . . . 113
  Art 8 . . . 103, 114, 344, 345, 349
  Art 13 . . . 103, 113, 117, 207

Protocol 1
  Art 1 . . . 112

Lomé Convention . . . 106

UN Charter
  Art 105 . . . 144
UN Convention on the Law of the Sea . . . 177

Yaounde Convention . . . 106

Table of EU Treaties

Accession Treaty 2003 . . . 19
Amsterdam Treaty . . . 3, 11, 28, 32, 33–5, 36, 49, 73, 87, 93, 96, 97, 99, 101, 116, 125, 126, 128, 130, 163, 172, 256, 276, 401, 403, 429, 430
   Art B . . . 32

Budgetary Treaty 1975 . . . 59, 67, 68

Charter of Fundamental Rights of the European Union . . . 12, 37, 38, 98, 101–4, 173, 233, 235, 332
   Chapters I–VI . . . 102
   Arts 20–23 . . . 402
   Art 20 . . . 116, 399
   Art 21 . . . 402
   Art 27 . . . 173
   Art 47 . . . 207
   Art 51 . . . 102
   Art 51(1) . . . 173
   Art 52(1)–(5) . . . 103
   Art 53 . . . 142
Charter of Fundamental Social Rights of Workers *see* Social Chapter
Constitutional Treaty . . . 1, 15, 29, 36–9, 51, 52, 53, 57, 71, 73, 76–8, 90, 100, 101, 107, 123, 126, 132, 134, 135, 138, 165, 166, 208, 262, 432
   Preamble . . . 432
   Art I-2 . . . 432
   Art I-6 . . . 138, 143, 166

EC Treaty 1993 . . . 9, 14, 34, 38, 74, 81, 83, 90, 91, 99, 101, 111, 113, 116, 125, 126, 138, 144, 145, 211, 266, 300, 334, 337, 339, 349, 352, 399, 402
   Preamble . . . 256, 300
   Title IV . . . 34
   Art 2 . . . 95, 111, 256, 359, 360
   Art 3 (now Art 8 TFEU) . . . 64, 111, 256, 398
   Art 3(1)(f) . . . 360
   Art 3(1)(q) (now Art 6 TFEU) . . . 339, 340
   Art 4 . . . 256
   Art 5 (now Art 5 TEU) . . . 32, 88
   Art 6 (now Art 18 TFEU) . . . 95
   Art 7 (now Art 13 TFEU) . . . 319
   Art 10 (now Art 4(3) TEU) . . . 64, 95, 111, 141, 144, 145, 173, 181, 185, 207, 256
   Art 11 . . . 34
   Art 12 (now Art 18 TFEU) . . . 64, 111, 173, 204, 256, 260, 307, 310, 323, 335, 338, 340, 345, 349, 398, 399
   Art 13 (now Art 19 TFEU) . . . 112, 398, 416, 430
   Art 17 (now Art 20 TFEU) . . . 310, 321, 340, 345, 349

Art 18 (now Art 21 TFEU) . . . 307, 335, 338, 342, 345, 349
Art 18(1) . . . 339
Arts 19–21 . . . 338
Art 25 (now Art 30 TFEU) . . . 121, 270, 282, 249
Art 28 (now Art 34 TFEU) . . . 256, 274, 276, 277, 278, 280, 282, 283, 285, 287, 288, 290, 291, 292, 293, 294
Art 29 (now Art 35 TFEU) . . . 274, 278, 283, 287
Art 30 (now Art 36 TFEU) . . . 256, 268, 277, 278, 279, 280, 282, 283, 287, 293
Art 34 . . . 111
Art 34(2) (now Art 40(2) TFEU) . . . 244, 245, 398
Art 39 (now Art 45 TFEU) . . . 111, 302, 307, 308, 310, 317, 318, 341, 398
Art 39(1) (now Art 45 TFEU) . . . 333
Art 39(2) (now Art 45(2) TFEU) . . . 111
Art 40 (now Art 46 TFEU) . . . 314
Art 43 (now Art 49 TFEU) . . . 111, 313, 322, 325, 398
Art 43(2) . . . 233
Art 44 (now Art 50 TFEU) . . . 322
Art 47 (now Art 53 TFEU) . . . 314
Art 49 (now Art 56 TFEU) . . . 164, 208, 322, 325, 343
Art 50 (now Art 57 TFEU) . . . 334, 398
Art 52 (now Art 59 TFEU) . . . 314, 322
Art 53 (now Art 60 TFEU) . . . 314
Art 80 . . . 126
Art 81 (now Art 101 TFEU) . . . 123, 187, 362, 365, 366, 369, 370, 371, 372, 373, 374, 382, 391, 392, 393
Art 81(1) . . . 364, 365, 367, 368, 369, 371
Art 81(2) . . . 373
Art 81(3) . . . 369, 371, 372
Art 82 (now Art 102 TFEU) . . . 123, 362, 372, 375, 378, 380, 381, 382, 392, 393
Art 85 (now Art 105 TFEU) . . . 363
Art 86 . . . 399
Art 90 (now Art 110 TFEU) . . . 270, 271, 272, 399
Art 90(2) (now Art 110(2) TFEU) . . . 272
Art 95 (now Art 114 TFEU) . . . 82, 88, 259, 261, 262
Art 100a . . . 124, 125
Art 118a (now Art 154 TFEU) . . . 428
Art 119 (now Art 157 TFEU) . . . 149, 406, 414, 427
Art 126(1) . . . 199
Art 130s . . . 124, 125

Art 131 (now Art 205 TFEU) . . . 23, 24

Art 132 (now Art 206 TFEU) . . . 23

Art 133 (now Art 207 TFEU) . . . 23

Art 137 (now Art 153 TFEU) . . . 399

Arts 138–139 (now Arts 154–155 TFEU) . . . 134

Art 141 (now Art 157 TFEU) . . . 111, 399, 401,
    405, 407, 408, 409, 416, 426, 428

Art 141(3) . . . 415

Art 141(4) . . . 424

Art 149(2) (now Art 165 TFEU) . . . 339, 341

Art 152 (now Art 168 TFEU) . . . 88

Art 174(4) (now Art 191 TFEU) . . . 86

Art 175 (now Art 192 TFEU) . . . 126

Art 191 (now Art 224 TFEU) . . . 56

Art 202 (now Art 16 TEU) . . . 132

Art 211 (now Art 17 TEU) . . . 107, 132, 133

Art 221 (now Art 251 TFEU) . . . 61

Art 225a (now Art 257 TFEU) . . . 66

Art 226 (now Art 258 TFEU) . . . 184, 186,
    219, 224

Art 227 (now Art 259 TFEU) . . . 221

Art 228 (now Art 260 TFEU) . . . 219

Art 230 (now Art 263 TFEU) . . . 59, 109,
    193, 200, 224, 225, 227, 233, 235, 236, 241,
    250, 371

Art 231 (now Art 264 TFEU) . . . 225, 234

Art 232 (now Art 265 TFEU) . . . 59, 237, 239

Art 234 (now Art 267 TFEU) . . . 66, 151, 156,
    160, 166, 190, 193, 194, 196, 197, 235, 236,
    251, 320, 391

Art 241 (now Art 277 TFEU) . . . 236

Art 243 (now Art 279 TFEU) . . . 203

Art 249 (now Art 288 TFEU) . . . 107, 181,
    185, 224

Art 255 (now Art 15 TFEU) . . . 73

Art 272 (now Art 313 TFEU) . . . 69

Art 273 (now Art 315 TFEU) . . . 69

Art 281 . . . 23

Art 287 (now Art 339 TFEU) . . . 242

Art 288 (now Art 340 TFEU) . . . 200, 241, 244

Art 300 (now Art 218 TFEU) . . . 232

Art 308 (now Art 352 TFEU) . . . 83, 429

EEA Treaty . . . 18, 63

EEC Treaty . . . 6, 9, 12, 13, 14, 15, 25, 29, 30, 32,
    84, 139, 152, 161, 294, 305, 334, 400

Art 2 . . . 360

Art 3 . . . 239

Art 5 (now Art 4(3) TEU) . . . 139, 179

Art 6 (now Art 18 TFEU) . . . 334

Art 7 (now Art 18 TFEU) . . . 95, 139, 173, 334

Art 12 (now Art 30 TFEU) . . . 172, 265

Art 30 . . . 256, 291

Art 36 . . . 256, 279, 280, 281

Art 37 . . . 139

Art 43 . . . 124

Art 48 (now Art 45 TFEU) . . . 347

Art 48(3) . . . 347

Art 49 (now Art 45 TFEU) . . . 348

Art 52 (now 49 TFEU) . . . 323

Art 54 . . . 57

Art 59 (now Art 56 TFEU) . . . 324, 325,
    334, 352

Art 60 (now Art 57 TFEU) . . . 334

Art 61 . . . 239

Art 74 . . . 239

Art 75 . . . 239

Art 84 . . . 239

Art 85 (now Art 101 TFEU) . . . 360, 382, 387

Art 86 (now Art 102 TFEU) . . . 360, 382, 387

Art 90 . . . 160

Art 95 (now Art 114 TFEU) . . . 172

Art 97 . . . 172, 163

Art 100 . . . 124, 125

Art 118 . . . 84

Art 118a . . . 125

Art 119 (now Art 157 TFEU) . . . 83, 173, 401,
    404, 406, 407, 408, 411, 413, 430, 433

Art 128 (now Art 166 TFEU) . . . 334

Art 137 . . . 57

Art 169 (now Art 258 TFEU) . . . 172

Art 173 . . . 223, 250

Art 177 . . . 170

Art 184 . . . 250

Art 189 (now Art 288 TFEU) . . . 139

Art 235 (now Art 352 TFEU) . . . 57, 83,
    125, 414

Art 274 . . . 133

EURATOM Treaty (European Atomic Energy
    Community) . . . 8, 14, 23, 25, 99

European Coal and Steel Community Treaty
    1951 (ECSC) . . . 7, 9, 13, 23, 25, 99

Art 33 . . . 233

Lisbon Treaty 2007 . . . 1, 3, 8, 11, 14, 15, 23, 25,
    28, 29, 32, 34, 35, 36, 38–40, 42, 43, 44, 45, 47,
    48, 49, 50, 51, 52, 53, 55, 57, 58, 59, 60, 66, 67,
    69, 72, 73, 74, 76, 77, 80, 81, 82, 85, 86, 87, 90,
    91, 93, 96, 97, 99, 100, 101, 105, 106, 107, 109,
    110, 114, 123, 125, 126, 127, 128, 130, 131, 132,
    133, 135, 138, 158–9, 162, 163, 164, 165, 166,
    189, 202, 208, 219, 220, 223, 224, 226, 227, 230,
    231, 256, 259, 262, 304, 337, 338, 352, 399, 401,
    407, 432

Protocol 21 . . . 12

Protocol 36 on Transitional
    Provisions . . . 50, 51

Art 3 . . . 50

Luxembourg Accords . . . 24, 25, 47, 48, 115, 240

Merger Treaty 1965 . . . 8, 24, 95

Nice Treaty 2001 . . . 11, 28, 35–6, 37, 49, 51, 59,
    60, 66, 73, 93, 96, 97, 99, 125, 130, 165, 226

Schengen Agreement 1985 . . . 33, 34, 75, 267,
    350, 353

Single European Act (SEA) . . . 11, 17, 28–31, 39,
    49, 57, 66, 81, 86, 93, 94, 97, 99, 101, 131, 163,
    165, 259, 352, 402

Preamble . . . 29

Art 2 . . . 53
Art 6 . . . 54
Social Chapter . . . 402
Statute of the Court of Justice . . . 35, 61
    Art 2 . . . 61
    Art 16 . . . 60
    Art 20 . . . 61, 62
    Art 50 . . . 66
    Art 62a . . . 61
    Protocol
        Art 23a . . . 196, 217
    Rules of Procedure . . . 61, 62, 190
        Art 50 . . . 225
        Art 51 . . . 225
        Art 99 . . . 192, 198, 202
        Art 101 . . . 193
        Art 104a . . . 202
        Art 104b . . . 202
        Arts 105–114 . . . 196

Treaty for a Constitution for Europe *see*
    Constitutional Treaty
Treaty Establishing the European Community
    see EC Treaty 1993
Treaty Establishing the European Economic
    Community *see* EEC Treaty
Treaty on European Union (TEU Maastricht
    numbering) . . . 3, 11, 23, 28, 31–3, 42, 49, 57,
    67, 73, 77, 90, 93, 95, 97, 125, 157, 163, 164, 259,
    365, 402
    Art 1 . . . 32
    Art 6 . . . 36
    Art 7 . . . 36
    Arts 11–45 . . . 32
    Arts 23–46 . . . 8
    Art 42 . . . 8
    Arts 43 et seq . . . 34
    Art 47 . . . 125
    Art 48 . . . 33
    Art B . . . 32
    Declaration No 2 on Nationality . . . 304, 337
Treaty on European Union (TEU) (post-Lisbon
    numbering) . . . 14, 22, 23, 38, 46, 59, 61, 63,
    67, 74, 86, 93, 94, 97, 99, 100, 101, 110, 125, 126,
    131, 155, 157, 164, 211, 219, 224, 351, 352
    Preamble . . . 94
    Art 1 . . . 86
    Art 2 . . . 22, 72, 76, 94, 112, 398, 401, 432
    Arts 3–6 . . . 64
    Art 3 . . . 79, 94, 112, 256, 359, 398, 401
    Art 3(2) . . . 83, 302
    Art 3(3) . . . 83
    Art 3(5) . . . 23, 83
    Art 4 . . . 79, 86, 90, 256
    Art 4(1) . . . 79
    Art 4(3) . . . 94, 95, 138, 139, 141, 173, 179, 181,
        185, 207, 211, 212, 359
    Art 5 . . . 32, 79, 86, 89, 90, 91, 104, 120
    Art 5(1) . . . 79, 86, 91
    Art 5(2) . . . 79, 89, 232

Art 5(3) . . . 86, 91
Art 6 . . . 36, 76, 83, 112, 114
Art 6(1) . . . 100, 103
Art 6(2) . . . 52, 114
Art 6(3) . . . 114
Art 7 . . . 36, 131
Art 8 . . . 22, 23
Art 9 . . . 338
Arts 10–12 . . . 72
Art 10 . . . 72, 86
Art 11 . . . 72, 127, 338
Art 12 . . . 86, 87, 127, 135
Art 13 . . . 42, 53, 67, 86, 226, 237
Art 13(2) . . . 79
Art 13(4) . . . 42
Art 14 . . . 54, 58
Art 14(1) . . . 57
Art 14(2) . . . 53
Art 15 . . . 42, 53
Art 15(2)–(3) . . . 53
Art 15(6) . . . 54
Art 16 . . . 47, 50, 51
Art 16(3) . . . 48
Art 16(4) . . . 50, 51
Art 16(8) . . . 48, 74
Art 16(9) . . . 48
Art 17 . . . 43, 46, 211
Art 17(2) . . . 46, 127
Art 17(3) . . . 44, 45
Art 17(5) . . . 43, 53
Art 17(6) . . . 45, 58
Art 17(7) . . . 44, 58
Art 17(8) . . . 45, 58
Art 18 . . . 44, 53, 54, 256
Art 19 . . . 62, 104
Art 19(1) . . . 60, 208, 235
Art 19(3) . . . 62
Art 20 . . . 34, 35
Art 20(4) . . . 22
Art 21 . . . 23, 24
Art 22 . . . 24
Arts 23–46 . . . 24, 117
Art 23 . . . 24
Art 24(1) . . . 75
Art 27 . . . 54
Art 27(2) . . . 52
Art 29 . . . 126
Art 38 . . . 68
Art 40 . . . 63
Art 46 . . . 154
Art 47 . . . 23
Art 48 . . . 38, 72, 91, 100, 131, 135, 154
Art 49 . . . 22, 57, 72, 76, 131
Art 50 . . . 131
Art 51 . . . 87, 100, 359
Art 114 . . . 88
Art 263 . . . 105
Art 294 . . . 47
Art 340 . . . 105
Protocol no 1 . . . 87

Protocol no 2 . . . 88, 89, 407
Protocol no 6 . . . 55
Protocol no 17 . . . 164
Protocol no 27 . . . 359
Protocol no 33 . . . 407, 408
Declaration no 1 . . . 101, 103, 432
Declaration no 2 . . . 114
Declaration no 7 . . . 50, 51
Declaration no 17 . . . 138, 143
Declaration no 18 . . . 91
Declaration no 24 . . . 23, 91
Declaration no 38 . . . 60
Declaration no 41 . . . 83
Declaration no 42 . . . 83, 91
Declaration no 52 . . . 15, 39, 77
Declaration no 53 . . . 38, 102
Treaty on the Functioning of the European
    Union (TFEU) . . . 2, 9, 23, 38, 49, 63, 74, 79,
    93, 94, 99, 100, 111, 125, 180, 239, 251, 281,
    351, 387
Preamble . . . 359
Title V . . . 196
Arts 2–6 . . . 79, 90
Art 2 . . . 80, 93
Art 2(1) . . . 79
Art 2(3) . . . 80
Art 2(4) . . . 24, 80
Art 2(5) . . . 80
Art 3 . . . 23, 80, 91, 93, 256, 257, 359
Art 3(1)(b) . . . 359, 360
Art 3(2) . . . 23, 85
Art 4 . . . 80, 91, 256
Art 4(2) . . . 259
Art 6 . . . 80, 91, 339, 341
Art 8 . . . 398, 401, 432
Art 10 . . . 398, 432
Art 11 . . . 46, 122
Art 13(2) . . . 232
Art 15 . . . 73
Art 18 . . . 64, 95, 105, 116, 138, 139, 173, 204,
    212, 256, 260, 302, 303, 307, 310, 319, 323,
    334, 335, 338, 340, 345, 349, 398, 399
Art 19 . . . 48, 112, 116, 130, 302, 398, 402, 416,
    430, 432, 433
Art 19(1) . . . 189
Art 19(2) . . . 131
Art 20 . . . 102, 302, 321, 337, 338, 340,
    345, 349
Art 20(2) . . . 302, 338
Art 21 . . . 102, 302, 307, 310, 335, 337, 338,
    339, 342, 345, 349, 353
Art 21(1) . . . 339
Art 22 . . . 102, 302, 338, 340
Art 23 . . . 102, 302, 338
Art 24 . . . 102, 302, 338
Art 25 . . . 46, 102, 338
Art 26 . . . 82, 131, 256, 258, 300, 302
Art 27 . . . 256
Art 28 . . . 256, 258, 259, 264, 265
Art 28(1) . . . 257

Art 29 . . . 256, 258, 259, 264
Art 30 . . . 121, 172, 256, 258, 259, 264, 265,
    268, 269, 270, 281
Art 31 . . . 139, 256, 257, 258, 259, 264,
    268, 269
Art 32 . . . 256, 258, 259, 268, 269
Art 33 . . . 259
Art 34 . . . 214, 256, 259, 260, 274–97
Art 34(2) . . . 243
Art 35 . . . 256, 259, 268, 274, 278, 282, 287
Art 36 . . . 256, 259, 260, 268, 274, 275, 277,
    278–82, 284, 285, 287, 288, 289, 290, 292–4,
    296, 297
Art 37 . . . 259
Art 40(2) . . . 116, 244, 245, 357, 398
Art 42 . . . 368
Art 45 . . . 79, 259, 261, 302, 305, 307, 308, 310,
    314, 317, 318, 319, 332, 333, 337, 341, 347,
    348, 398
Art 45(1) . . . 302
Art 45(2) . . . 116
Art 45(3) . . . 131, 302, 314, 330
Art 45(3)(d) . . . 321
Art 45(4) . . . 301, 303, 332
Art 46 . . . 79, 127, 259, 261, 302, 305, 314
Art 47 . . . 105, 259, 302, 305
Art 48 . . . 124, 131, 259, 302, 395
Art 48(7) . . . 131
Art 49 . . . 259, 302, 303, 305, 311, 312, 313,
    314, 322, 323, 324, 325, 327, 398
Art 50 . . . 259, 302, 305, 311, 322
Art 51 . . . 75, 259, 302, 305, 311, 333
Art 52 . . . 259, 302, 305, 311, 330
Art 53 . . . 259, 302, 305, 311, 314
Art 54 . . . 259, 302, 305, 311, 312
Art 55 . . . 259, 302, 305, 311
Art 56 . . . 164, 208, 259, 302, 303, 305, 311,
    314, 322, 323, 324, 325, 327, 334, 343,
    351, 398
Art 57 . . . 259, 302, 305, 311, 312, 322, 334
Art 57(d) . . . 311
Art 58 . . . 259, 302, 305, 311
Art 59 . . . 123, 259, 302, 305, 311, 314, 322
Art 60 . . . 259, 302, 305, 311
Art 61 . . . 259, 302, 305, 311
Art 62 . . . 259, 302, 305, 311, 330
Arts 63–66 . . . 259
Art 67 . . . 352
Art 67(2) . . . 352
Arts 68–75 . . . 352
Arts 77–80 . . . 351, 352
Art 81 . . . 131
Art 101 . . . 187, 227, 359, 360, 364, 361–73,
    379, 381–92
Art 101(1) . . . 361, 366, 368–78, 382
Art 101(2) . . . 361, 370
Art 101(3) . . . 361, 368, 371–4, 391, 394
Art 102 . . . 227, 360, 361, 362, 374–83, 387,
    388, 389, 392, 393, 394
Art 103 . . . 360, 387

Art 103(2)(a) . . . 63
Art 105 . . . 43, 360, 387
Art 105(3) . . . 133
Art 106 . . . 399
Art 106(3) . . . 131, 133
Arts 107–114 . . . 196
Art 107 . . . 360, 383, 384, 385
Art 107(2) . . . 384
Art 107(3) . . . 384
Art 108 . . . 108, 383, 385–7
Art 108(2) . . . 212, 384, 386
Art 108(3) . . . 384, 385
Art 109 . . . 383, 385–7
Art 110 . . . 160, 172, 256, 264, 268, 269, 270,
    271, 272, 399
Art 110(1) . . . 270, 271, 272
Art 110(2) . . . 268, 270, 271, 272
Art 113 . . . 52, 82
Art 114 . . . 52, 82, 88, 124, 256, 259, 261, 262
Art 114(9) . . . 212
Art 115 . . . 52, 82, 83, 124, 256, 261
Art 118 . . . 127
Art 126 . . . 130
Art 134 . . . 68
Art 149 . . . 84
Arts 151–169 . . . 96
Art 151 . . . 401
Art 153 . . . 68, 84, 131, 399, 401
Art 154 . . . 134, 428
Art 155 . . . 134
Art 157 . . . 52, 112, 116, 149, 150, 173, 399,
    400, 401, 403–14, 417, 424, 426, 427, 428,
    429, 432, 433
Art 157(1) . . . 403
Art 157(2) . . . 403, 404
Art 157(3) . . . 415
Art 157(4) . . . 401, 424, 425
Art 165 . . . 68, 127, 339, 341
Art 166 . . . 68, 334
Art 167 . . . 68
Art 168 . . . 68, 88
Art 168(5) . . . 84, 89
Art 173 . . . 68
Art 191 . . . 86, 281
Art 192 . . . 126, 130, 131
Art 195 . . . 127
Pt 4 (Arts 198–204) . . . 24
Pt 5 (Arts 205–222) . . . 24
Art 205 . . . 23, 24
Art 206 . . . 23, 24, 264
Art 207 . . . 23, 24, 46, 85, 105, 131, 257, 264
Art 207(3) . . . 25
Art 207(4) . . . 25
Art 216 . . . 105
Art 216(1) . . . 85
Art 217 . . . 106, 131
Art 218 . . . 46, 57, 64, 106, 131, 232
Art 218(8) . . . 115
Art 218(11) . . . 63
Art 220 . . . 106

Pt 6 (Arts 223–287) . . . 43
Arts 223–234 . . . 54, 132
Art 223 . . . 130
Art 223(1) . . . 55
Art 224 . . . 56
Art 225 . . . 46, 58
Art 226 . . . 58
Art 227 . . . 59, 338
Art 228 . . . 59, 338
Art 230 . . . 58
Art 233 . . . 58
Art 234 . . . 58
Art 235(1) . . . 53
Art 236 . . . 48
Arts 237–243 . . . 47
Art 238 . . . 49, 50, 51
Art 238(3) . . . 51
Art 238(4) . . . 49
Art 240 . . . 52
Art 240(2) . . . 52
Art 241 . . . 46
Arts 244–250 . . . 43
Art 244 . . . 44, 53
Art 245 . . . 44
Art 247 . . . 45
Art 250 . . . 47
Art 251 . . . 61
Art 252 . . . 130
Art 253 . . . 60
Art 254 . . . 60, 66
Art 255 . . . 60
Arts 256–279 . . . 62
Art 256 . . . 66, 66, 202
Art 257 . . . 60, 66, 202
Art 258 . . . 46, 63, 96, 172, 184, 186, 200, 203,
    211–220, 221, 222, 224, 249, 280
Art 259 . . . 63, 96, 211, 220, 221
Art 260 . . . 63, 96, 186, 211, 219, 220
Art 260(2) . . . 219
Art 261 . . . 219, 251, 390
Art 263 . . . 46, 59, 60, 63, 66, 67, 88, 95, 96,
    109, 110, 111, 193, 194, 200, 211, 215, 222,
    223, 224, 226, 227, 230, 231, 233, 235, 236,
    237, 238, 240, 241, 243, 249, 250, 371,
    387, 390
Art 263(2) . . . 232
Art 263(4) . . . 226
Art 263(6) . . . 225
Art 264 . . . 63, 201, 225, 233, 234
Art 264(2) . . . 233
Art 265 . . . 59, 63, 96, 111, 211, 237, 238,
    239, 240
Art 265(1) . . . 237
Art 265(2) . . . 238
Art 265(3) . . . 237
Art 266 . . . 234, 239
Art 266(1) . . . 239
Art 267 . . . 63, 64, 65, 66, 96, 151, 156, 160,
    166, 167, 170–208, 234, 235, 236, 249, 251,
    330, 391

Art 267(2) . . . 195
Art 267(3) . . . 195, 197
Art 268 . . . 63, 211, 239, 240, 241
Art 270 . . . 63, 211
Art 272 . . . 64
Art 273 . . . 221
Art 275 . . . 63, 189
Art 276 . . . 63
Art 277 . . . 64, 96, 236, 249, 250
Art 278 . . . 211, 218
Art 279 . . . 203, 211, 218
Art 280 . . . 109, 111
Arts 282–287 . . . 67
Art 288 . . . 106, 107, 108, 109, 110, 122, 123, 138,
   139, 171, 174, 175, 180, 181, 185, 224, 225, 231
Art 288(1) . . . 43
Art 288(2) . . . 186
Art 289 . . . 47, 57, 107, 127, 132, 231
Art 289(2) . . . 130, 231
Art 289(3) . . . 130
Art 289(4) . . . 130
Art 290 . . . 43, 46, 47, 57, 107, 109, 132,
   133, 231
Art 290(2) . . . 132
Art 291 . . . 43, 46, 109, 197, 132, 133, 231
Art 294 . . . 57, 124, 127, 128
Art 295 . . . 109, 123
Art 296 . . . 84, 91, 107, 110, 126, 233
Art 297 . . . 107, 108, 110, 175
Art 300 . . . 67
Arts 301–304 . . . 68
Arts 305–307 . . . 68
Art 308 . . . 68
Art 311 . . . 131
Art 312 . . . 131
Arts 313–316 . . . 69
Arts 314–319 . . . 46
Art 314 . . . 48, 59

Art 315 . . . 59, 69
Art 319 . . . 67
Arts 326–331 . . . 35
Art 332 . . . 130
Arts 333–334 . . . 34
Art 339 . . . 242
Art 340 . . . 96, 187, 200, 211, 236, 237, 239,
   240, 241, 244, 246, 249
Art 340(2) . . . 63, 93, 239, 240, 241, 243
Art 344 . . . 115, 138, 220
Art 345 . . . 282
Arts 346–348 . . . 212
Art 349 . . . 384
Art 351 . . . 143
Art 352 . . . 52, 83, 91, 125, 131, 154, 261, 359,
   414, 429
Art 352(2) . . . 83
Art 352(4) . . . 83
Annex II . . . 24
Protocol no 2 . . . 88
Protocol no 3
   Art 9 . . . 60
Protocol no 4 . . . 66
Protocol no 6 . . . 55
Protocol no 27 . . . 359
Protocol no 33 . . . 407, 408
Declaration no 1 . . . 101, 103, 432
Declaration no 2 . . . 114
Declaration no 7 . . . 50, 51
Declaration no 17 . . . 138, 143
Declaration no 18 . . . 91
Declaration no 24 . . . 91
Declaration no 38 . . . 60
Declaration no 41 . . . 83
Declaration no 42 . . . 83, 91
Declaration no 52 . . . 15, 39, 77
Declaration no 53 . . . 38, 102
Treaty of Rome *see* EEC Treaty

Table of EU Secondary Legislation

Directives

Dir 64/221 (Repealed) on the Right of Citizens of the Union and their Family Members to Move and Reside Freely within the Territory of the Member States . . . 161, 314,
  Art 1 . . . 334
  Art 3 . . . 174
  Art 8 . . . 330
  Art 9 . . . 330
Dir 68/151 . . . 179
Dir 68/360 (repealed) Relating to the Right of Workers to Leave One Member State and Enter the Territory of Another . . . 308, 309, 314, 315
  Art 3 . . . 344
  Art 6 . . . 316
  Art 10 . . . 345
Dir 70/50 (OJ Special Edn 1970 I L13/29) on the Abolition of Measures which have an Effect Equivalent to Quantitative Restrictions on Imports . . . 257, 276, 295
  Preamble . . . 275
  Art 2 . . . 276
  Art 2(3)(f) . . . 287
  Art 3 . . . 284, 276
Dir 73/148 (repealed) . . . 314
  Art 8 . . . 345
Dir 75/34 (repealed) . . . 314
Dir 75/117 (repealed) Equal Pay Directive . . . 402, 403, 408, 413
  Art 1 . . . 408, 413
  Art 6 . . . 414
Dir 76/207 (repealed) Equal Treatment Directive . . . 52, 83, 150, 402, 403, 409, 414, 415, 418, 421, 423, 427, 428, 429
  Art 1 . . . 415, 421
  Art 1a . . . 415
  Art 2 . . . 421
  Art 2(1) . . . 421, 422
  Art 2(2) . . . 419
  Art 2(3) . . . 418, 419, 421
  Art 2(4) . . . 424, 425, 426
  Art 2(6) . . . 415
  Art 3 . . . 417, 419
  Art 3(1) . . . 418, 422
  Art 5 . . . 417, 419
  Art 5(1) . . . 418, 419, 421, 422
  Art 6 . . . 179, 427
  Art 9(2) . . . 419
Dir 77/187 Business Transfer Directive . . . 151
Dir 77/249 (OJ 1977 L78/17) Mutual recognition of professional qualifications (Lawyers) . . . 326, 327
  Art 4(1) . . . 327
  Art 4(2) . . . 327
  Art 4(4) . . . 327
  Art 5 . . . 327, 328
Dir 77/388 Sixth VAT Directive . . . 99
Dir 79/7 (OJ 1979 L6/24) Social Security Directive . . . 402, 406, 419, 427–8
  Art 4(1) . . . 416, 429
  Art 7 . . . 81, 405, 406, 418, 428
  Art 7a . . . 406
Dir 80/987 . . . 184
Dir 81/389 (Animal protection) . . . 267, 268
Dir 83/189 (Technical standards) . . . 182, 183, 263, 288
Dir 83/643 on the Facilitation of Physical Inspections and Administrative Formalities in Respect of the Carriage of Goods between Member States
  Art 5 . . . 267
Dir 85/337 . . . 184
Dir 85/384 (OJ 1985 L223/15) . . . 26, 322
Dir 86/378 (repealed) Occupational Pensions Directive . . . 402, 407, 427, 428
Dir 86/613 (OJ 1986 L359/86) on equal treatment of the self-employed and protection of self-employed women during pregnancy and motherhood . . . 403
Dir 89/48 (OJ 1989 L19/16) Mutual Recognition of Diplomas Directive . . . 328
  Art 4(1)(b) . . . 328
Dir 89/987 for the protection of employees in the event of insolvency of the employer . . . 187
Dir 90/364 (repealed) Free Movement Directive . . . 336
Dir 90/365 (repealed) Free Movement Directive . . . 336
Dir 90/366 on the residence of students . . . 234
Dir 91/156 (OJ 1991 L78/32) Waste Directive . . . 124
Dir 92/85 (OJ 1992 L348/1) Pregnancy and Maternity Directive . . . 402, 403, 420, 421, 423, 428
  Art 8 . . . 420
  Art 9 . . . 428
  Art 10 . . . 420, 422, 423, 428
Dir 93/96 (repealed) Free Movement Directive . . . 336
Dir 96/34 (repealed) Parental Leave . . . 402, 421
Dir 97/80 (repealed) Burden of Proof in Cases of Discrimination based on Sex . . . 402, 414
Dir 97/81 (OJ 1998 L14/9) Part-time Workers Directive . . . 123, 306, 402, 409, 412
Dir 98/5 (OJ 1998 L77/36) Mutual recognition of professional qualifications (Lawyers) . . . 326, 328

Dir 98/23 (OJ 1998 L131/10) on the Framework
    Agreement on Part-time Work . . . 429
Dir 98/24 (OJ 1998 L131/11) on the protection of
    the health and safety of workers . . . 263
Dir 98/34 (OJ 1889 L204/37) replacing 83/189
    Technical standards . . . 183, 257, 288
Dir 99/70 (OJ 1999 L175/43) Fixed-term Work
    Directive . . . 181
Dir 2000/43 (OJ 2000 L180/22) Racial Equality
    Directive . . . 116, 260, 351, 409
    Art 2 . . . 304
Dir 2000/78 (OJ 2000 L3030/16) Framework
    Employment Directive . . . 116, 175, 181, 260,
    409, 416
    Art 2 . . . 304
    Art 6 . . . 175, 180
Dir 2002/14 (OJ 2002 L80/79) on Employee
    Consultation Recital 17 . . . 87
Dir 2002/73 . . . 427
Dir 2003/33 (OJ 2003 L152/16) . . . 262
Dir 2003/86 (OJ 2003 L251/12) on the Right to
    Family Reunification . . . 346, 351
Dir 2003/109 (OJ 2004 L16/44) concerning the
    Status of Third-country Nationals who are
    Long-term Residents . . . 351
Dir 2004/38 (OJ 2004 L158/77) on the Right
    of Citizens of the Union and their Family
    Members to Move and Reside Freely within
    the Territory of the Member States . . . 108,
    299, 302, 303, 308, 314, 315, 317–21, 334, 336,
    345, 346
    Preamble . . . 327
    Art 2 . . . 318, 319
    Art 3 . . . 319
    Arts 4–14 . . . 314
    Art 4 . . . 315
    Art 5 . . . 315
    Art 6 . . . 315
    Art 7 . . . 309, 315
    Art 7(1)(b) . . . 336
    Art 7(3) . . . 309
    Art 7(3)(d) . . . 310
    Art 8 . . . 316
    Art 8(4) . . . 316
    Art 11 . . . 316
    Art 12 . . . 321
    Art 13 . . . 320, 321
    Art 14 . . . 309, 316, 321, 336
    Art 14(4)(b) . . . 315
    Art 15 . . . 316
    Art 16 . . . 322
    Art 17 . . . 322
    Art 18 . . . 322
    Art 22 . . . 316, 347
    Art 23 . . . 320
    Art 24 . . . 315, 317, 342
    Art 24(1) . . . 315
    Art 24(2) . . . 315
    Art 25 . . . 316
    Art 27 . . . 330, 331, 332, 337

Art 27(2) . . . 332
Art 28 . . . 330, 332, 337
Art 28(3) . . . 330
Art 29 . . . 332, 337
Art 30 . . . 329
Art 30(3) . . . 329
Art 31 . . . 329, 330
Art 32 . . . 331, 332
Art 35 . . . 345
Dir 2004/113 (OJ 2004 L373/37) Equal
    Treatment between Men and Women in
    Access to and the Supply of Goods and
    Services . . . 116, 403, 430–1
    Art 5(1) . . . 431
    Art 5(2) . . . 431
Dir 2004/114 (OJ 2004 L375/12) on the
    Conditions of Admission of Third- country
    Nationals for the Purposes of Studies . . . 351
Dir 2005/36 (OJ 2005 L255/22) Mutual
    Recognition Directive . . . 326
    Art 1 . . . 326
    Art 2 . . . 326
    Art 15 . . . 326
    Art 21 . . . 326
Dir 2006/54 (OJ 2006 L204/23) Consolidating
    Equal Treatment Directive . . . 260, 402, 403,
    408, 409, 414, 415, 417, 420, 424, 426, 428, 429
    Recital 3 . . . 417
    Recital 10 . . . 410
    Recital 36 . . . 87
    Art 1 . . . 414
    Art 2 . . . 304, 403
    Art 2(1) . . . 408
    Art 2(1)(a) . . . 410
    Art 2(1)(b) . . . 410
    Art 2(2)(c) . . . 420
    Art 3 . . . 424
    Art 4 . . . 408, 413, 414
    Art 14 . . . 417, 418
    Art 14(1) . . . 415, 417
    Art 14(2) . . . 415, 419
    Art 15 . . . 420
    Art 17 . . . 414, 426
    Art 17(1) . . . 414
    Art 18 . . . 414, 426
    Art 19 . . . 414
    Arts 20–22 . . . 427
    Art 23 . . . 414, 415, 417, 426, 427
    Art 24 . . . 414
    Art 28(1) . . . 420
    Art 30 . . . 427
    Art 33 . . . 213
Dir 2006/123 (OJ 2006 L376/36) Services
    Directive . . . 299, 326, 336
    Art 1(2) . . . 327
    Art 1(3) . . . 327
    Art 2(1) . . . 327
    Art 2(2a–1) . . . 327
    Art 2(3) . . . 327
    Art 3(1) . . . 327

Arts 9–27 . . . 327
Dir 2009/50 (OJ 2009 L155/17) . . . 351
Dir 2010/18 (OJ 2010 L68/13) parental
   leave . . . 402, 403
Dir 2010/41 (OJ 2010 L180/1) on equal
   treatment between self-employed men and
   women . . . 403, 429
Dir 2014/104 (OJ 2014 L349/1) anti-trust
   damages actions . . . 391

Regulations

Reg 15/61 (JO 1961 1073) . . . 301
Reg 17 of 6 February 1962 . . . 230, 239, 372, 387,
   388, 393
   Art 8 . . . 373, 387
Reg 38/64 (JO 1964 965) . . . 301
Reg 1612/68 (repealed) on Freedom of
   Movement for Workers within the
   Community . . . 303, 310, 314, 317, 319, 339,
   343, 344, 345, 348
   Art 7 . . . 317, 319
   Art 7(1) . . . 317
   Art 7(2) . . . 307, 308, 318, 338, 341
   Art 7(3) . . . 309
   Art 10 . . . 319, 320, 344, 349
   Art 11 . . . 320
   Art 12 . . . 320, 321, 344
Reg 1251/70 (repealed) on the Rights of
   Residence after Retirement or Incapacity of
   Workers . . . 302, 314
Reg 1408/71 on the Application of Social
   Security Schemes to Employed Persons, to
   Self-employed Persons and to Members of
   their Families Moving within the Community
   Art 69 . . . 308
Reg 4064/89 Merger Regulations . . . 382, 393–5
Reg 404/93 (OJ 1993 L47/1) as Regards the
   Requirements for Communications in the
   Banana Sector . . . 157
Reg 182/2011 (Comitology) . . . 43, 46, 133
Reg 1049/2001 (OJ 2001 L145/43)
   Regarding Public Access to European
   Parliament . . . 73, 121
   Art 4(1)–(3) . . . 74
   Art 4(5) . . . 73
Reg 1091/2001 (OJ 2001 L150/4) . . . 351
Reg 1/2003 (OJ 2003 L1/1) Competition
   Regulation . . . 46, 63, 123, 227, 251, 360,
   371, 387–92
   Arts 1–16 . . . 388
   Art 10 . . . 372
   Art 17 . . . 388
   Art 18 . . . 388
   Art 18(3) . . . 388
   Arts 19–21 . . . 388
   Art 23 . . . 388, 389, 390
   Art 23(1) . . . 389
   Art 23(2)(a) . . . 390

Arts 24–26 . . . 388
Art 27 . . . 118, 388, 389
Art 28 . . . 118, 388, 389
Reg 139/2004 (OJ 2004 L24/1) Merger
   Regulation . . . 251, 375, 394
   Art 2(2)–(3) . . . 394
   Art 3 . . . 394
   Art 4(1) . . . 395
   Art 6 . . . 395
   Art 7(1) . . . 395
   Art 7(5) . . . 395
   Art 8(5) . . . 395
   Art 10(1) . . . 395
   Art 10(3) . . . 395
   Art 13 . . . 396
   Art 14 . . . 396
   Art 14(1) . . . 395
   Art 14(2) . . . 396
   Art 15 . . . 396
   Art 21(1)–(2) . . . 395
Reg 772/2004 (OJ 2004 L123/18) technology
   transfer agreements . . . 373
Reg 168/2007 (OJ 2007 L53/1) . . . 115
Reg 717/2007 (OJ 2007 L171/32) . . . 89
Reg 764/2008 (OJ 2008 L218/21) Laying down
   Procedures relating to the Application of
   Certain National Technical Rules to Products
   Lawfully Marketed in Another Member
   State . . . 257, 284
Reg 330/2010 (OJ 2010 L102/1) vertical
   agreements and concerted
   practices . . . 373, 374
   Arts 1–5 . . . 374
Reg 461/2010 (OJ 2010 L129/52) distribution
   agreements in respect of motor
   vehicles . . . 373
Reg 1217/2010 (OJ 2010 L335/36) research and
   development agreements . . . 373
Reg 1218/2010 (OJ 2010 L335/43) specialization
   agreements . . . 373
Reg 182/2011 (OJ 2011 L55/13) comitology . . . 43,
   46, 133
Reg 492/2011 (OJ 2011 L141/1) . . . 303, 307, 310,
   314, 317–322, 311
   Arts 1–5 . . . 314
   Art 1 . . . 315
   Art 2 . . . 315
   Art 3(1) . . . 315
   Art 5 . . . 317
   Art 7 . . . 317, 318
   Art 7(1) . . . 317
   Art 7(2) . . . 317, 318, 319, 321
   Art 7(3) . . . 318
   Art 8 . . . 317
   Art 9 . . . 317, 318
   Art 10 . . . 320, 321
Reg 887/2013 replacing Annexes II and III to
   Regulation (EU) No 211/2011 of the European
   Parliament and of the Council on the citizens'
   initiative (OJ 2013 L247/11) . . . 46

Reg 216/2013 on the electronic publication of the
    Official Journal of the European Union (OJ
    2013 L69/1) . . . 225
Reg 1407/2013 on the application of Arts 107 and
    108 of the Treaty on the Functioning of the
    European Union to *de minimis* aid (OJ 2013
    L352/1) . . . 385

Recommendations

Recommendation July 1962 (1962) JO
    (2118) . . . 301
Recommendation 2011/696 (OJ 2011
    L275/38) . . . 110
Recommendation 2012 (OJ 2012 C338) . . . 191

Commission Notices

Notice on the Definition of the Relevant Market
    (OJ 1997 C372/5) . . . 366, 376, 377

Notice on Agreements of Minor Importance
    (OJ 1997 C372/13) . . . 370
Notice on Agreements of Minor Importance
    (OJ 2001 C368/11) . . . 365, 370
Notice on the Handling of Complaints by the
    Commission (OJ 2004 C101/05) . . . 391
Notice on Informal Guidance Relating to
    Novel Questions Concerning Arts 81 and
    82 of the EC Treaty that Arise in Individual
    Cases (Guidance Letters) (OJ 2004
    C101/78) . . . 371
Notice on the Conduct of Settlement Procedures
    in View of the Adoption of Decisions
    Pursuant to Article 7 and Article 23 of
    Council Regulation No 1/2003 in Cartel Cases
    (OJ 2008 C167/01) . . . 390
Notice on the Enforcement of State Aid
    Law by National Courts (OJ 2009
    C85/1) . . . 387
Notice on Best Practices in Proceedings
    Concerning Articles 101 and 102 TFEU
    (OJ 2011 C308/6) . . . 389

Table of Decisions

European Decisions

Decision 70/243 (OJ 1975 L94/19) . . . 68
Decision 78/516 Unitel . . . 361
Decision 80/334 Fabbrica Pisana . . . 388
Decision 87/373 (OJ 1987 L197/33) Comitology
    Decision . . . 133
Decision 88/591 (OJ 1988 L319/1) . . . 29
Decision 93/731 (OJ 1993 L340/43) . . . 73
Decision 94/90 (OJ 1994 L46/58) . . . 73
Decision 95/3052 (OJ 1995 L321/1) on exchange
    of information about national measures dero-
    gating from the principle of free movement of
    goods . . . 284, 364
Decision 98/273 Volkswagen . . . 251, 390
Decision 2000/527 (OJ 2000 L212/09) . . . 73
Decision 2002/772 (OJ 2002 L283/1) . . . 55
Decision 2003/2 Hoffmann-La Roche . . . 390
Decision 2003/80/JHA Framework
    Decision . . . 125
Decision 2004/752 (OJ 2004 L333/7) . . . 66
Decision 2007/5 (OJ 2007 L1/11) . . . 48
Decision 2008/203 (OJ 2008 L63/14) . . . 116
Decision 2009/881 (OJ 2009 L315/50) on the
    exercise of the Presidency . . . 48

Decision 2009/908 (OJ 2009 L322/28) on the
    exercise of the presidency and conduct of
    meetings . . . 48
Decision 2011/695 (OJ 2011 L275/29) on
    the Terms of Reference of the Hearing
    Officer . . . 389
Decision 2013/336 (OJ 2013 L179/92) . . . 60
Decision AOIP v Beyrard [1976]
    1 CMLR D14 . . . 361
Decision AROW v BNIC OJ 1982 L379/1;
    [1983] 2 CMLR 240 . . . 363
Decision Hennessy/Henkel [1981] 1 CMLR
    601 . . . 366
Decision Kodak [1970] CMLR D9 . . . 361
Decision Polypropylene Cartel
    Community v ICI [1988]
    4 CMLR 347 . . . 361

French Constitutional Court Decisions

Decision 2004/496 of 10 June 2004 . . . 162
Decision 2006/540 . . . 162
Decision 2007/560 . . . 162

Table of Opinions

Opinion of July 1962 (1962) JO (2118) . . . 301
1/75 [1975] ECR 1355 . . . 80
1/76 [1977] ECR 741 . . . 24
1/91 [1991] ECR I-6079 . . . 76
1/94 [1994] ECR I-5267 . . . 24, 78, 85, 107
2/94 [1996] ECR I-1759 . . . 83, 114
1/96 [1996] ECR I-1759 . . . 52

Council Legal Service Opinion, Council
    Document 11197/07 (JUR260) of 22 June
    2007 . . . 143
1/09 [2011] ECR I-1137 . . . 142
2/13 (http://curia.europa.eu/juris/liste.
    jsf?num=C-2/13) . . . 63, 83, 114

Abbreviations

ACP	African, Caribbean, and Pacific
AFSJ	Area of Freedom, Security and Justice
AG	Advocate General
BRICS	Brazil, Russia, India, China and South Africa
CAP	Common Agricultural Policy
CCP	Common Commercial Policy
CCT	Common Customs Tariff
CFI	Court of First Instance (now General Court)
CFP	Common Fishing Policy
CFSP	Common Foreign and Security Policy
CHEE(s)	charge(s) having equivalent effect
CJEU	Court of Justice of the European Union
CMLR	Common Market Law Reports
CML Rev	Common Market Law Review
CoJ	Court of Justice
CoR	Committee of the Regions
COREPER	Committee of Permanent Representatives
CRD	Citizens' Rights Directive (2004/38)
DG	Directorate General
EAW	European Arrest Warrant
EC	(1) European Community/ies; (2) Treaty Establishing the European Community
ECA	European Communities Act 1972
ECB	European Central Bank
ECHR	European Convention on Human Rights
ECR	European Court Reports
ECSC	European Coal and Steel Community
ECtHR	European Court of Human Rights
ECI	European Citizens' Initiative
ECU	European currency unit
EDA	European Defence Agency
EDC	European Defence Community
EEA	European Economic Area
EEC	(1) European Economic Community; (2) Treaty Establishing the European Economic Community

EESC	European Economic and Social Committee (formally ECOSOC)
EFTA	European Free Trade Association
EIB	European Investment Bank
EMS	European Monetary System
EMU	economic and monetary union
ENP	European Neighbourhood Policy
EOC	Equal Opportunities Commission (UK)
EP	European Parliament
EPC	(1) European Political Community; (2) European political cooperation
ERTA	European Road Transport Agreement
ESCB	European System of Central Banks
ESDP	European Security and Defence Policy
EU	European Union
EURATOM	European Atomic Energy Community
FCC	Federal Constitutional Court (Germany)
FYR	former Yugoslav Republic
GATT	General Agreement on Tariffs and Trade
GDP	gross domestic product
ICJ	International Court of Justice
IGC	intergovernmental conference
IP	Intellectual Property
IVF	*in vitro* fertilization
JHA	Justice and Home Affairs
MEP	Member of the European Parliament
MP	Member of Parliament
NATO	North Atlantic Treaty Organization
NGO	non-governmental organisation
OECD	Organisation for Economic Co-operation and Development
OEEC	Organisation for European Economic Co-operation
OJ	Official Journal
OMC	open method of coordination
OSCE	Organization for Security and Co-operation in Europe
PJCC	Provision on Police and Judicial Cooperation in Criminal Matters
QMV	qualified majority voting
SAP	Social Action Programme
SDA	Sex Discrimination Act 1975
SEA	Single European Act
SI	statutory instrument
TCN	third-country national
TEU	Treaty on European Union (Maastricht Treaty)

TFEU	Treaty on the Functioning of the European Union
TRIPs	Agreement on Trade-related Aspects of Intellectual Property Rights
TUPE	Transfer of Undertakings (Protection of Employment) Regulations 2006
UN	United Nations
VAT	value added tax
WEU	Western European Union
WHO	World Health Organization
WTO	World Trade Organization

PART I

Introduction to the Institutional and Procedural Law of the European Union

The first 'half' of this book considers the topics that may well be covered in one or two introductory or first-year courses in universities depending on how the teaching of EU law is organized. Trends in course structure can change over the years, but if there are introductory courses in the first year, then Part I will be particularly suitable for them, while Part II on the substantive law will be more suitable for second or final-year courses.

Following the entry into force on 1 December 2009 of the 2007 Lisbon Treaty, numerous changes have been made to the content of this book and notably to the institutional law contained in Chapters 1–4.

The chapters in Part I set the scene for understanding the substantive law discussed in Part II: without Part I, very many things in Part II will not make much sense. The chapters in this part of the book look at the historical roots of the European Communities as they developed into the present-day European Union. Chapter 1 considers essentially the rationale for the EU, why it was established, what it is, and some of the difficulties encountered along that path to the present day. In particular, at the end of the chapter, there is a discussion of the failed Constitutional Treaty, which was abandoned after the electorates in France and the Netherlands rejected it and the attempts to revive it were discontinued. The discussion of its replacement, the Lisbon Treaty, includes the rejection of the treaty by the Irish electorate in June 2008, the second Irish referendum on that treaty, and its eventual entry into force in 2009. Having established why the Union was formed, Chapter 2 considers *what* was formed—that is, what it consists of—by looking at the institutions set up to run the Union. The chapter further investigates their powers and duties, and their interaction with each other; it also introduces the European Court of Justice, and its role and jurisdiction in adjudicating EU law.

Chapter 3 then moves on to consider how the Union and its institutions are empowered or enabled to operate, by looking at the transfer of powers, and how those powers are divided and controlled. This chapter also includes a discussion of the constitutional basis of the Union.

Chapter 4 turns to the legal system that enables the Union to fulfil its goals and operate, and which binds it all together, including the various sources and forms of law that make up that legal system and how those laws are made by the institutions considered in Chapter 2. Finally, at the end of the chapter, the very dynamic interrelationship of the institutions in the law-making processes is highlighted.

Chapter 5 deals with the consequences of the establishment of this body of EU law; it thus looks directly at the supremacy of EU law from both the point of view of the Union as understood by the Court of Justice of the European Union and the point of view of a number of the member states.

Chapters 6 and 7 divide between them the procedural law of the EU by considering the jurisdiction of the Court of Justice, and the system of remedies as provided by the Treaty and significantly developed by the Court of Justice. Chapter 6 considers how the Court of Justice ensures that the laws made and other sources of EU law are effective and useful, through the extensive development of individual remedies. As a bridge to Chapter 7 concerning the procedural actions against member states and institutions, Chapter 6 includes a consideration of the Art 267 preliminary ruling procedure of the Treaty on the Functioning of the European Union. This procedure was the vehicle by which individual remedies were developed by the Court of Justice.

The book then turns to substantive law in Part II, an introduction to which is given at the beginning of that Part.

Whether EU law is studied in two or more courses or all in one course, it can be observed that many of the cases that appear in Part I are ones that have arisen in an action in one of the substantive law topics. *Van Gend en Loos*, for example, which first established direct effects, is a case concerned with customs duties and free movement of goods in the common market; *Von Colson*, establishing indirect effects, arises from a sex discrimination case; and *Factortame*, concerned with nationality discrimination, supremacy, and national procedural rules, is a case based essentially on the right of establishment from the substantive area of the free movement of persons. EU law and the book abound with many more examples. Studying both parts together very often reinforces the study and understanding of each one.

1

The History and Constitutional Basis of the European Union

1.1 Introduction

Any study of European Union (EU) law and its predecessor, European Community (EC) law, must be preceded by the study and understanding of the history and development of the Union. Without it, you will probably be somewhat confused. It will be exceedingly difficult to understand just why the Union is so complex and so strangely constructed. You will not understand why the law-making procedures and forms of law have been subject to so many changes and remain so complex, especially now following the Lisbon Treaty changes to qualified majority voting in Council. You will not appreciate why there are such concepts as 'direct effects' and 'subsidiarity', and why there is a huge body of further reading on such strange subjects as 'comitology'. In any subject, merely learning the rules does not help you to understand the purpose for which they were enacted and the reasons that led to the need for them in the first place. This is even more the case with the EU. Many of the laws, whilst clearly aimed at specific topics such as ensuring the free movement of goods or persons, or requiring the equality of treatment of different groups, or regulating the recognition of a profession in the member states, are a compromise of different perspectives. In the EU, these perspectives arise from different nations, different cultural understandings, different histories, and different social and economic backgrounds and systems; hence the treaties, and laws that have been produced under the treaties, are often achieved only as a compromise of these different elements. On their own, the individual rules may not make a great deal of sense; with an understanding of their history and development, hopefully, they might make a lot more sense.

This chapter tries to set the context and provide an understanding of the historical basis of the Union, before looking in detail at its constitutional base.

A brief mention will be made here in respect of the terms 'European Union' and 'European Community', because their use can be confusing. The term 'European Union' was brought in by the Treaty on European Union (TEU, also known and referred to as the 'Maastricht Treaty'), and describes the extension by the member states into additional policies and areas of cooperation. At that time, the EU consisted of three pillars comprising the existing Communities (the three original treaties), a Common Foreign and Security Policy (CFSP), and, following the reorganization by the Treaty of Amsterdam, a third pillar called Provisions on Judicial and Police Cooperation in Criminal Matters. Following the entry into force of the 2007 Lisbon Treaty, the three-pillar structure was effectively broken up. The CFSP has been kept in the EU Treaty, and the freedom, security, and justice matters, which were in the third pillar, are now organized in a title of the Treaty on the Functioning of the EU. At present, most undergraduate EU law courses, and indeed books, are not likely to consider these aspects of EU law in any depth, if at all.

1.2 **The Motives for European Integration**

Even a cursory glance at European history will reveal what a chaotic, despotic, border-changing, bone-crunching, blood-spilling time we have had over the centuries. The most horrific of the series of wars is, of course, World War II during which some 55 million souls worldwide, but mostly in Europe, lost their lives. There have been centuries of invasions, occupations, and dictatorial rule in most, if not all, of the countries of Europe at some stage. Of course, since World War II we do not gas, maim, butcher, torture, or murder people in the biblical proportions as before, but even post-World War II we have seen some pretty nasty regimes imposing their will against peoples and countries in Europe, and further conflicts between European nations and peoples. As a result, since 1945 an estimated additional 900,000 people have died in Europe, which is incredible—more so because some of these events are not long in the past, but much more recent. In the 1990s, the Balkans, especially in Croatia and Kosovo, became the latest to be added to the list of European killing fields.[1] With this firmly in mind, it should come as no surprise that the strong reaction after World War II to this death and destruction was a very important and motivating factor in the moves to create a more peaceful and stable European environment in which countries would be able to develop and prosper without resorting to the obliteration or subjugation of others. It is too easy, in the present period of relative peace and stability, to understate this motive. Of course, there are reasons underlying the violence, and featuring large, as Ward clearly sets out in the first pages of his critical introduction to EU law,[2] is the desire to make Europe one; to homogenize Europe; to unify Europe; and in pursuit of this goal, for one country or ethnic group to impose its culture or religion or government on others. Unfortunately, most of these attempts have been neither peaceful nor voluntarily accepted on the part of the subjects on the receiving end of such unwelcome attention and, over the ages, these attempts have affected the majority of the citizens of Europe. Generally, the attempts to unite, from the Romans to World War II, have led to wholesale loss of life—even attempted genocide and that ghastly modern euphemism for the same, 'ethnic cleansing'. It is therefore this bleak, but simple and understandable, backdrop that led to an increased desire to do something to stop the cycle of death and destruction. Whilst there had been ideas and discussions to unite European nations over the centuries, particularly following World War I, it was only after World War II that these desires and expressions found substance.

As a recognition of this, the EU won the 2012 Nobel Peace Prize, which is something quite remarkable although not universally appreciated.[3] The reasons given by the Nobel Peace Prize Committee Secretary for the award are the reasons which have been highlighted in previous editions of this book as those motivating European integration in the first place and contributing to the developing integration of Europe. The initial impetus was the desire to establish and maintain peace, but to continue to remain relevant, especially to new generations; the EU had to and still has to establish new legitimacies. To some extent the additional reasons given for the Peace Prize award recognize and

---

[1] For the full catalogue of such events, refer to the chilling *Historical Atlas of the 20th Century: Wars, Massacres and Atrocities of the Twentieth Century*, available at **http://users.erols.com/mwhite28/war-1900.htm**.

[2] I. Ward, *A Critical Introduction to European Law*, 3rd edn, Cambridge University Press, Cambridge, 2009.

[3] To see but one of many comments portraying a range of views go to **http://www.guardian.co.uk/world/2012/oct/12/nobel-peace-prize-2012-live**.

acknowledge those new legitimacies, but in view of the present day resurgence of nation-alism in many countries and the large degree of apathy and even antipathy towards the EU, the EU still needs to do more to justify itself.[4]

1.3 The Founding of the European Communities

The period following World War II saw a number of moves towards the integration of European nation states although, admittedly, some of these find their roots in the inter-war period. However, post-1945, political and economic cooperation and develop-ment between nations was regarded as crucial to replace the economic competition that was viewed as a major factor in the outbreak of wars between European nation states. Some of these moves were taking place within a worldwide effort for greater political cooperation between nation states, the most notable being the establishment of the United Nations in 1945 and the Council of Europe in 1949. The Council of Europe must not be confused with the EU institutions, the Council (of Ministers) and the European Council, despite similarity of name. Arguably, the most notable achievement of the Council of Europe is the establishment of the European Convention for the Protection of Human Rights and Fundamental Freedoms (ECHR) and its enforcement machinery, notably the Committee of Ministers and Court of Human Rights (ECtHR), based in Strasbourg.[5]

There were also inherently economically motivated steps towards international cooperation that resulted in the establishment of such organizations as the International Monetary Fund (IMF), the General Agreement on Tariffs and Trade (GATT), and, most notably, the Marshall Plan, which funded the establishment of the Organisation for European Economic Co-operation (OEEC), and the later Organisation for Economic Co-operation and Development (OECD), designed initially to finance the post-war reconstruction of Europe.

When we come to the European Communities, which were the forerunners of the EU that we have today, their purposes are not so distinctly discernible. As remains the case today, even before the foundation of the Communities there was a conflict of opinion between those who wished to see European integration take the form of a much more involved model, such as a federal model, and those who wished merely to see a purely economic form of integration, such as a free trade area. The first steps were, predictably, a modest compromise of the political, economic, and social desires of various parties. The scene was set by the address by Winston Churchill at the University of Zürich in September 1946, and his call to build 'a kind of United States of Europe' and in particular, for the time, the brave call for a partnership between France and Germany. However, even within that speech Churchill and Britain did not envisage a role as a key participant and instead envisaged Britain outside any general European integration, in the same way as the USA and the Soviet Union, merely observing and assisting a European state to rise from the ashes of the destruction of World War II.

At the time, a further and developing factor, which considerably influenced the desire on the part of the European nations to cooperate, was the deteriorating relations between the former Allied powers. It was not long after the Americans, the British, and

---

[4] The Nobel Peace Prize Committee secretary Geir Lundestad advised that the EU was awarded the prize for its 'accumulated record over more than six decades' and that the prize was deserved for the peace and reconciliation brought about in the EU and support of democracy and human rights. The further individu-ally cited reasons will be highlighted in turn and summarized later in the chapter.

[5] http://www.coe.int/.

the Russians had met victoriously in the streets of Berlin in 1945 that understandings between those countries broke down and they became increasingly suspicious of each other. Winston Churchill had described in March 1946, in Fulton, Missouri, the situation of increasing Soviet influence and control over Eastern Europe, in a phrase that was taken up generally, as a kind of 'iron curtain'[6] that had descended between Western and Eastern Europe. The general situation came to be described as the 'Cold War', and lasted in lesser and greater states of tension until the collapse of communism in Europe in 1989–90. The prospect of reuniting the divided eastern and western occupied zones of Germany after the war disappeared in the late 1940s with this 'cold war' development and, instead, the two separated entities of West and East Germany were established. With this increased fear of the domination of Europe by the Soviet Union and possible expansion, combined with possible Soviet influence and control over the countries of Western Europe, the tension mounted in the late 1940s and throughout the 1950s. At its worst, in the 1960s, the Cold War threatened the nuclear annihilation of the opposing parties and much of the world. It therefore became increasingly important that the countries of Western Europe integrate amongst themselves to form a bulwark against further Soviet expansion. The Cold War was thus a clear and real catalyst for West European integration. And, finally, it should not be forgotten that, following the end of World War II, there were considerable food shortages in Europe leading to hunger and, in some parts, even starvation. This too was a motivation for integration to ensure the peaceful and uninterrupted ability to grow and produce sufficient food in Europe to feed its populations, and goes a long way towards explaining the importance given to the Common Agricultural Policy (CAP) in the negotiations and establishment of the Treaty Establishing the European Economic Community (the EEC Treaty). Food security and economic security were regarded as indispensable for political security.

1.3.1 **The Schuman Plan (1950)**

The climate was certainly ready to consider a greater form of integration in Europe and the first direct impetus for the Communities came in the form of the plan proposed in May 1950 by French Foreign Minister Robert Schuman,[7] based on the research and plans of Jean Monnet, a French government official, to link the French and German coal and steel industries.[8] These industries would be taken out of the hands of the nation states and put under the control of a supranational body. This would not only help economic recovery, but also remove the disastrous competition between the two states. It was aimed to make future war not only unthinkable, but also materially impossible, because it put

---

[6] 'From Stettin in the Baltic to Trieste in the Adriatic, an iron curtain has descended across the Continent': http://www.winstonchurchill.org/learn/biography/in-opposition/qiron-curtainq-fulton-missouri-1946 and http://www.earthstation1.com/pgs/churchill/des-ChurchillZurichSummer46-UnitedStatesOfEurope. mp3.html. Note, however, that the origin of this phrase can be reliably traced to Joseph Goebbels, the German Third Reich Propaganda Minister, written in an open letter to the Allies entitled 'Das Jahr 2000' and published in *Das Reich*, 25 February 1945, pp 1–2, which was a prediction on how Europe would look in the year 2000 following an Allied–Soviet victory over Germany.

[7] An appreciation of Robert Schuman's personal history helps to explain why he received Jean Monnet's plan so readily. Schuman fought in both world wars, but for the Germans in World War I and for the French in World War II, because he lived on the border between the two countries, meaning that, when the border was moved following World War I, his nationality was altered.

[8] This reconciliation of France and Germany after World War II is the first of the five achievements of the EU which was cited as justifying the award of the Peace Prize.

control over coal and steel production, vital then for the production of armaments and thus the capability of waging war in the hands of a supranational authority and not the individual member states. The plan was open for other European countries to join in its discussions. The UK, though, was reluctant to involve itself, even in the negotiations, sending only observers. The plan was readily accepted by Germany under Chancellor Adenauer. Belgium, the Netherlands, and Luxembourg, the 'Benelux' nations, which had already moved ahead with their customs union, also saw the benefits to be gained from membership and this form of integration. Italy also considered it to be in its economic interest to join and, perhaps more importantly, believed that such integration would help to act as a defence against the perceived threat in that country from increased internal communist support and a possible seizure of power. Thus six nations went ahead to sign the European Coal and Steel Community Treaty (ECSC) in Paris in 1951, which entered into force on 1 January 1952.

This first form of integration was thus both politically and economically motivated. It was also a mix of both intergovernmental and supranational integration (which terms are considered in Section 1.5.1), because the institutions set up included both the High Authority (to become the European Commission), which was a supranational body, and a Council of Ministers of representative government ministers from the member states. Whilst the Community established did not fulfil the wishes of Monnet, who was a federalist,[9] he was appointed the first President of the High Authority and the degree of integration that it achieved was, without any doubt, a very important and indispensable first step from which further integration could follow. Indeed, it was assumed by some—the so-called neo-functionalists—that further integration would be inevitable.[10]

It was not long before the next proposals for greater integration were put forward.

1.3.2 The Proposed European Defence Community and European Political Community

The Schuman Plan that formed the basis of the ECSC was not the only proposal for integration being discussed and negotiated at the time. Monnet put forward a proposal (the Pleven Plan) for a European Defence Community (EDC) in 1952. In addition, because it was argued to be politically and practically necessary, in support of that, a European Political Community (EPC) was also proposed in 1953 to oversee political control and foreign policy for the EDC. The proposals and the negotiations proved to be complex and drawn out because they were surrounded by other political considerations, such as the expansion of communism in South East Asia and concerns about rearmament of West Germany. Both of these proposals, with hindsight, were perhaps far too ambitious for the time and thus premature. They faced opposition from both outside the ECSC, the UK in particular, and within the Community, most notably and fundamentally from France, which, after some prevarication, failed to ratify the EDC in the National Assembly. Even today, the prospect of a common European army and political union is far too radical; with hindsight, then, the EDC was simply unrealistic—even though the other five countries had agreed to it.

Since 1955, however, there has been a limited defence arrangement with the Western European Union (WEU), which was established to fill the vacuum of the collapsed EDC.

---

[9] For a complete biography, refer to F. Duchene, *Jean Monnet: The First Statesman of Interdependence*, W. W. Norton & Co., London, 1996.

[10] This will be considered at Section 1.5.1.

The WEU was taken under EU auspices by the Treaty of European Union (1992) and worked closely with the North Atlantic Treaty Organization (NATO) but has now been wound up as the EU slowly assumed competences in these areas.[11] Prompted by the Balkan wars in the 1990s, movement was subsequently made towards establishing an effective European Security and Defence Policy (ESDP) that was formally set up in 1999 and led to the establishment, not long afterwards, of the EU Rapid Reaction Force. Defence cooperation now takes place under the umbrella of the European Defence Agency (EDA),[12] which was established in 2004 by a Joint Action of the Council of Ministers in order 'to support the Member States in their effort to improve European defence capabilities in the field of crisis management and to sustain the ESDP as it stands now and develops in the future'. With the exception of Denmark, all present EU member states participate in the EDA but as further details are beyond the remit of this book, refer to the web addresses cited in the footnote for further details.

The Lisbon Treaty has established a framework for a common defence policy, whilst confirming the commitments of those EU member states that are members of NATO to that organization (see Art 42 TEU).

An extensive chapter on CFSP is now to be found in Arts 23–46 TEU.

1.3.3 Progress Nevertheless

It might have been thought that the unfortunate failure to agree the EDC would have put paid to any further attempts at European integration and it was, without doubt, a blow to the European federalists. Rather than jeopardize any such attempts, however, it appeared to strengthen the resolve of some of the original six member states to take matters further. Once again, Jean Monnet was centrally involved. He had resigned as President of the ECSC High Authority in order to promote European integration.[13] Working in particular with the Benelux nations, it was proposed that rather than leave the integration to two industries, the nations should integrate the whole of their economies. Following the Messina Intergovernmental Conference (IGC) in 1955, the Spaak Report (named after Belgium's prime minister) was prepared to consider the establishment of an Economic Community, and an Atomic Energy Community for energy and the peaceful use of nuclear power. There were also additional external catalysts for such further moves, including the Algerian war of independence, the Soviet suppression of the 1956 Hungarian Uprising, and the Suez Canal climb-down,[14] which served to highlight the real politics at play in the world in the 1950s and the precarious position of individual nation states in Europe, which no longer wielded the influence that they did prior to World War II. All of this assisted in bringing the European treaties' negotiations to a much quicker and more successful conclusion. Thus, in 1957, the Treaties of Rome were agreed by the same six nations, establishing the European Economic Community (EEC) and the European Atomic Energy Community (EURATOM).

At first, all three Communities each had their own institutions, but shared a Court of Justice and a common Parliamentary Assembly. The separate institutions were merged

---

[11] http://www.weu.int/.

[12] See http://www.eda.europa.eu/.

[13] As the founder and leading member of the Action Committee for the United States of Europe.

[14] This was the joint invasion by British and French forces to regain control of the Suez Canal after it had been forcibly nationalized by President Nasser of Egypt. Britain and France were forced to give way in the face of growing world and US pressure.

under the treaty establishing a single Council and a single Commission of the European Communities (the Merger Treaty) in 1965, which entered into force in 1967 and the provisions of which have been incorporated into the present treaties. Due to the range of subject matters and policies covered, the EEC Treaty was the most important. The ECSC Treaty, established for 50 years only, expired in 2002. The Treaty Establishing the European Community (or EC Treaty, now essentially the Treaty on the Functioning of the European Union, or TFEU) took over the obligations and responsibilities arising under the ECSC Treaty.

1.4 The Relationship of the UK with the European Communities and Union

1.4.1 The Early Relationship

As noted earlier, in the late 1940s and early 1950s, the UK was also initially keen to see a united Europe, but without its direct participation. It had, at the time, a historical legacy that involved quite different economic and social ties, including the Empire and Commonwealth and the Atlantic alliance, both of which featured strongly in the recently won World War II. These ties of security and common language are often overlooked, but played no small part in the attitude of Britain to European integration in the immediate post-war years. Britain also regarded its status as remaining a world power, its sovereignty, and independence might be compromised by membership. As well as the offer to participate in the ECSC negotiations, Britain was also invited to participate in the EEC and EURATOM negotiations. However, it played no significant or indeed useful part, and withdrew after minimal participation.[15] Instead, with Austria, Switzerland, and other nations, the UK embarked on the path of establishing the European Free Trade Association (EFTA) in 1958, which involved no supranational or political aims of economic integration and was intended merely to set up a free trade area for goods.

It was not long, however, before a change of heart and policy took place, in what could be regarded as a tacit admission of error. Within months of the entry into force of the EEC Treaty, the Macmillan Conservative government led the UK application for associate membership and, very shortly after that, on 9 August 1961, an application for full membership. The reasons for previously not joining had been undermined. Amongst the changes were the demise of the UK's previous world-power status, the fact that direct links with most of the world had been weakened by the economic demise of the UK, the Suez climb-down, and the continuing conversion of the Empire into a Commonwealth of independent states. Trade patterns were also shifting towards Europe, and the Atlantic alliance was less prominent—and pointedly so after the disagreement as to how to handle the Suez crisis. More than anything, Britain had observed the much faster economic progress made by the six and this provoked the desire for membership. Whether Britain was ever interested in the entire Community package is not clear. Britain had now, however, to bargain from the outside, and its applications both for associate and full membership were steadfastly and consistently rejected by French President Charles de Gaulle, including the 1967 second UK application by the Wilson Labour government. De Gaulle's opposition to the potentially distorting influence of the UK in the Community was clearly

---

[15] In the post-war period the UK had undergone a period of nationalization of key industries including coal and steel, therefore the plan to relinquish state control of these industries was another reason that the proposals were not considered in the UK's best interests at the time.

expressed at the time and included the fear of too much influence or indeed domination by the USA.[16]

1.4.2 From Membership Acceptance to Date

In 1970, following the resignation and withdrawal from politics of de Gaulle in France, the entry application by the Conservative Prime Minister Edward Heath was successful. Thus, the UK joined in 1973, as did Ireland and Denmark, mainly because of their trade dependency with the UK. However, soon afterwards the UK sought to renegotiate entry terms and held a referendum on membership. The timing of the 1973 entry was, in fact, unfortunate. Instead of the UK being able to participate equally in the post-war boom and recovery, the world economy and that of Europe had received a severe setback, and Britain, along with the rest of the Western world, became the hostage of massive oil price increases. Instead of a period of economic prosperity, the 1970s witnessed high inflation and economic stagnation (sometimes termed 'stagflation'). To aggravate matters still further, the high and arguably inequitable level of the British contribution to the European budget became the focus of attention. It did not take long before disquiet with the terms of entry arose. It seems that the UK paid too high a price to join the club and that budget wrangles, which both then and in the future were to polarize opinion both in Europe and the UK, were inevitable. The pattern of trade in the UK, which initially favoured imports from Commonwealth non-EEC countries, coupled with having to pay the higher EEC CAP-regulated food prices, meant that British contributions were extremely high and simply added to the then severe UK domestic economic problems.

To recap for a moment, in the context of the UK entry, the Community was spawned in the aftermath of World War II. For membership, the original states exchanged some sovereignty and monetary contribution for security, the stability of democratic nationhood, and economic progress. It is argued that Britain did not need the first two, and the third proved illusory in the 1970s and 1980s. Hence when, in 1974, a new government was elected in the UK, a renegotiation of the terms of entry was started. This was climaxed by the clear-cut (over 67 per cent in favour) approval of the British public in the then unprecedented 1975 referendum that not only *post facto* approved membership, but also the renegotiated terms—and specifically the revised budget contributions. However, it was only a partial cure for the level of contributions and this dispute was later reopened by the UK Prime Minister Margaret Thatcher, and budget contributions still feature as a contentious issue between the UK, the other member states, and the EU every time an EU budget plan is negotiated. Its effect was, however, to cast the UK firmly in the role of the reluctant partner and of troublemaker in Europe. Viewed politically, the UK had decided to cast its lot with the Communities, aware that some loss of sovereignty was involved, and that a potentially high monetary contribution was required. One side of the bargain was not, as with other member states, the security of nationhood or the stamp of approval and stability of the democratic political system that membership gave. The fact that the UK had won the war and had centuries of stability meant that these were so well secured in the UK that the European Communities could never seriously be considered for these advantages, or to keep the peace, which Britain had secured by victory in the last war, albeit with considerable help. The other side of the bargain was to share in the spoils of European economic progress. Given the changing circumstances, this proved to be a

---

[16] First rejection: **http://europa.eu/about-eu/eu-history/1960-1969/1963/index_en.htm**; second rejection: **http://news.bbc.co.uk/onthisday/hi/dates/stories/november/27/newsid_4187000/4187714.stm**.

dubious economic gain. No wonder that there was a feeling by some, which still remains, that membership had sold Britain short.

In the 1980s, the first part of the decade was occupied with further wrangles over the British budget contribution and reluctance to reform the Communities that hindered progress on other matters in the Community, and which did not engender relaxed relations with Britain's EC partners. It was surprising that then Conservative Prime Minister Thatcher signed the Single European Act (SEA), which saw the first major reform of the original treaties, because of the steps contained within it for further integration and some democratization of the Communities. Indeed, it was regarded later as an error by Mrs Thatcher,[17] who was most probably lured into agreeing to the SEA by the promise of the liberalized trade advantages of the single market, which will be considered in Section 1.6.7.

The budget contributions have remained a long-running point of disagreement. During the negotiations for the second major reform of the Communities—and in particular economic and monetary union introduced by the Treaty of European Union in Maastricht—Britain demonstrated once again just how out of line it was with its other partners. The UK opted out of the Social Policy Chapter, whereas all other member states agreed to this. The TEU agreed at Maastricht also provided a process and timetable for moving towards economic and monetary union. The UK negotiated another opt-out here in respect of the decision whether to join the final stage, in which a single currency would be established. Exacerbating the poor relationship with the other European partners was the fact that John Major's Conservative government (1992–97) was so clearly and publicly split on the issue of Europe that almost any decision that was needed on the Communities was one that was close to impossible to achieve. Hence, the idea that any progress could be made by all of the then 15 member states of the Communities was an unrealistic idea. Thankfully, that abysmal state of affairs did not continue beyond 1997. The change of government in the UK on 1 May 1997 also saw an immediate change in the relationship with Europe. In 1997, whilst the delayed negotiations for the TEU were still ongoing, the new Labour government announced its intention to sign up to the Social Chapter, which was carried through soon afterwards, and generally to take a more positive participatory role in Europe. The UK opposition to economic and monetary union seemed to have been removed, at least in principle, although 18 years on, the likelihood that the UK will actually join is very unlikely. This is very much an issue which has been affected by the severe economic crises in Greece, Spain, and other countries and which has undermined the euro, although in 2014, a slow recovery was taking place.[18]

The negotiations for the Amsterdam and Nice Treaties, the Convention and IGC for the Constitution for Europe, the expansion to 28 states by 2013, and the changing political relationships between the leading EU states (notably France, Germany, and the UK) have led to a far more complex Union now than previously. Inevitably, in an EU that now has a membership of 28 states, each individual state will have less prominence. However, France, Germany, and the UK remain the largest and most economically powerful three states in the Union; each of them can still play a leading role in EU affairs, both positive and negative. The UK's attitude remains somewhat ambivalent, on the one hand expressing itself to be at the heart of Europe and on the other showing a reluctance to commit as deeply as other member states. In 2007, in the negotiations for the 2007 Lisbon Treaty,

---

[17] I. Ward, *A Critical Introduction to European Law*, 3rd edn, Cambridge University Press, Cambridge, 2009, p 108.

[18] The end of 2014 and beginning of 2015, however, saw that progress disappear and with the election in Greece of an anti-austerity government, the economic prospects at the time of writing look far from clear, although Spain, which also suffered greatly, appears to be making a slow recovery.

further opt-outs were secured by the UK government, in particular from the Charter of Fundamental Rights, which will not apply internally in the UK, and opt-outs from full participation in the Area of Freedom, Security and Justice (Protocol 21) and the Schengen area.[19] A change of government in 2010 had not changed things and it seems that the UK is no less a reluctant partner in 2015 than it has been for a number of decades previously, despite having had the most pro-European of the major UK parties in the coalition government to 2015. In particular, three developments serve to highlight and confirm this renewed lack of enthusiasm for the EU. The first is the enactment of the European Union Act 2011, which introduces measures to ensure that any future transfer of competences or treaty amendments must be subject to a ministerial statement in the House of Commons as to their impact and whether they require a further transfer of competences or powers. If that is the case, then either an Act of Parliament would be required to allow the transfer, or if the treaty proposals were substantial and not, for example, only approving the accession of a new member state, then a referendum would first be required in which, of course, a majority would have to approve the changes for them to be ratified.

The second development was the stance taken by David Cameron, the UK coalition government prime minister, in Brussels in December 2011 by refusing to participate in the economic and fiscal treaty proposals, wielding in effect the UK veto and blocking a new treaty between all 27 (at the time) member states. The long-term political consequences have yet to be felt, but it is clear that the UK is in a far less influential position in the EU than it has been for a long time. This position has been further undermined by the position taken by the Cameron-led UK government in the collapsed 2012 EU budget negotiations.[20] The third is the promise, after being elected to a Conservative majority government in 2015, to re-negotiate terms and hold a referendum on EU membership by 2017. The UK's present self-distancing, even before any negotiations or referendum and France's present quietness, leave only one leading EU member state and that is Germany. Whether this is a healthy or positive outcome for the EU is not clear.[21]

1.5 The Basic Objectives and Nature of the European Union

Whilst the formal aims of the Union can readily be seen by looking at the preambles to the treaties, there is a deeper underlying debate about the overall goal of the Communities and now Union. The stated general aims include the creation of the common market, which was to be achieved by abolishing obstacles to the freedom of movement of all the factors of production: namely, goods, workers, providers of services, and capital. The original EEC Treaty also provided for the abolition of customs duties between the member states and the

---

[19] Although purely internal application of the EU rights' Charter was never intended, with the Charter impacting only on matters within the scope of activity of the EU itself and its application in the member states but not to member state activity itself. These topics are further considered in Sections 1.6.8 and 1.6.9 and in Chapter 4, Section 4.4.4.

[20] However right the UK and Cameron may be, it is the poor standing in the EU that prevents the UK from building a larger coalition of states sharing the same views as the UK. Alternatively, it could be argued that, in view of European history, the cost of the EU is cheaper than the cost of war. On the budget negotiations refer to http://www.bbc.co.uk/news/world-europe-20457065.

[21] For various debates around these themes see http://www.euromove.org.uk/index.php?id=6330, http://esharp.eu/big-debates/the-uk-and-europe/131-separation-or-divorce-for-the-uk-and-the-eu/ and http://www.bbc.co.uk/news/uk-politics-26515129. At the time of writing, there was only speculation as to what might be achieved. See amongst many comments: http://www.bbc.com/news/world-europe-32660871. There will clearly be a lot of TV and press coverage over the coming months and years.

application of a common customs tariff to imports from third countries. There were to be common policies in the spheres of agriculture and transport, and a system ensuring that competition in the common market would not be distorted by the activities of cartels or market monopolists. An embryonic social policy and regional policy also appeared. Apart from these formally set-out objectives, there has been a debate older than the Communities themselves as to whether there was a grand or master plan for the integration of Europe. Even if it were not originally clear that the 'pooling of resources', as then termed, by a transfer of sovereign powers meant that the Communities would take over in certain agreed areas, this was made clear not long afterwards by the Court of Justice of the European Union (CoJ) in its landmark decisions in *Van Gend en Loos* and *Costa v ENEL*.[22] The debate has continued over whether the Communities were supposed to integrate only in the specific areas, as originally set out in the ECSC and the then EEC Treaty, and arguably confined largely to free trade, or whether something more dynamic was intended. Many terms have been used to describe these developments. It was originally considered that, because there was success in certain policies, this would automatically lead to a spillover from one area to another to lead to increasing integration. This is termed 'functional integration', or 'neo-functionalism'. Others have described this as 'creeping federalism'. In fact, it was considered that, in order for the original policies to work properly, there had to be continuing integration, otherwise the whole project would probably first stagnate, and then roll backwards to collapse. Thus, sector-by-sector integration and the process of European union were regarded as an inexorable process. For example, the setting of common trade tariffs and the establishment of the common market for the free circulation of goods would require and lead to exchange rates being stabilized to ensure that production factors and costs in the member states were broadly equal. This, in turn, requires monetary union to be established to ensure that exchange rates do not drift apart, and this requires full economic union to be achieved, so that the value of different components of the common currency is not changed by different economic and fiscal policies in different countries. Obviously, then, the fiscal policies must be integrated and this economic integration would require that the political integration would have to follow in order to provide stable and consistent policy control over the economic conditions applying in the Community, and now Union. According to this view, federalism, in some form, would thus seem to be the probable outcome of this process. Such an outcome is a vehemently contested one and it is argued that the failure to result in federalism and the periodic resort to national self-interest by some states is evidence that neo-functionalism is not a given in EU development. Equally though, it is not entirely discredited and, as will be considered further in Section 1.6, the spillovers from widening to deepening and vice versa can also be regarded in the light of neo-functionalism.

Before discussing this further, a number of other terms that will be used need to be defined both now and in Section 1.5.1 following:

- A *free trade area* involves the removal of all customs and tariffs between members, but is usually regulated by the unanimous agreement of all members.

- A *customs union* involves a free internal area and a common policy on tariffs of all the member states and third-party states.

- A *common market* includes the previous two points, plus the free movement of all factors of production.

- An *economic union* also includes the establishment of a common economic policy and fiscal policy.

---

[22] This will be fully explored in Chapter 3.

1.5.1 **Intergovernmentalism, Supranationalism, and Federalism**

The following terms are employed to describe the form of integration undertaken by the EU:

- *Intergovernmentalism* is the hitherto traditional way in which international organizations work, the decisions of which require unanimity and are rarely enforceable; if enforceable, they are usually only so between the signatory states and not the citizens of those states.

- *Supranationalism* describes the fact that the decision-making is made at a new and higher level than that of the member states themselves and that such decisions replace or override national rules.

The term *federalism* itself is a rather flexible term, in that it can refer to a fairly wide band of integration models. But essentially, for the purposes of this discussion, it means that there would also be a form of political integration whereby the member states would transfer sovereign powers to the federation, which would control the activities of the members from the centre. There are plenty of examples of states set up on a federal basis, including the USA, Germany, Canada, Australia, Switzerland, and Belgium. Certain local issues are still regulated by the constituent states, such as education, culture, and land management, but most economic and political power is transferred to the centre including, most notably, defence and trade.

Finally the term *multilevel governance* needs to be outlined as another term which seeks to explain the dynamic and evolving nature of the EU, given that no one of the above three terms on their own, or indeed together, accurately explain its nature. In particular as the arguments about the consequences of the increasing competences of the EU evolved, so too did the realization that the EU was governed at a number of levels. This will also be explored by the discussions of competences, subsidiarity, and the increasing role of national parliaments in Chapter 3. So overall, in deciding the policies and the details of putting those policies into action, the regional authorities, the national parliaments, the states, and the institutions of the EU are involved, hence multilevel governance.

1.5.2 **Progress to a Federal Europe?**

Is federalism the goal of European integration? Only a few persons have argued openly for this degree of integration, although some of the founding fathers of the Community—Monnet, Schuman, and Spaak—had expected that sector-by-sector functional integration would lead slowly to ever greater degrees of federalism. It is also arguable that an agenda of federalism has been buried under the euphemism 'a closer', or 'ever closer', union and that, to make the progress to the possible ultimate destination of the Union more acceptable, these terms have been used in the EEC Treaty (which became the EC Treaty in 1993) and in the TEU. The latest version, that is, 'to continue the process of creating an ever closer union', can be found in the preamble to the TEU, as amended by the Lisbon Treaty. It is, though, unclear, and arguably deliberately so, whether these refer to federalism or something short of that. The original plans put forward by Monnet for the ECSC may have been much more federal in nature and openly so, particularly because, as planned, the Community was to be governed by a supranational High Authority only, but it was at the insistence of the member states that the original ECSC was also governed by a Council of Ministers, clearly intergovernmental, and by a Parliamentary Assembly. This mixed model was followed in both the EURATOM and EEC Treaties. Therefore, while the Union and some of its institutions do operate on the supranational level, it does not signify an inevitable move to federalism. Only as future developments unravel will its final destination become clearer.

The Constitutional Treaty, which was ultimately abandoned in June 2007, was seen, particularly by some states, as a very distinct further step in the direction of a federal Europe—hence the resistance in particular to the term 'Constitution for Europe', which appeared to imbue the EU with the appearance of a federal state or some form of statehood. With hindsight a single treaty named the Consolidated EU and EEC Treaty or something similar might have been better employed. The 2007 Lisbon Treaty removed the term 'Constitution' and the other more symbolic references in the treaty to a flag and an anthem, etc. and can be regarded as a softer form of the Constitutional Treaty.[23] Hence the debate is not stale and continues, as the EU and member states continue getting ever closer, but without spelling out where they might ultimately be going. Whilst the euro crises may have brought calls from some states for even greater economic and political integration, it has produced the opposite effect in other member states, notably the UK; hence, more than ever, there is no single opinion of all member states on where the EU should be going in the future, in terms of the degree of integration.

Despite the failure of the EDC and EPC proposals for significant further integration in the mid-1950s, the ECSC remained successful and was joined in 1957 by the other two communities. EURATOM was not particularly successful, because it was originally designed under the assumption that there would be extreme difficulty in the energy market, but that proved not to be the case as the world energy market stabilized itself considerably in the late 1950s (although with current future energy concerns, it may find more relevance). The EEC proved immediately to be a success under the leadership of the first EEC Commission President, the German Walter Hallstein. It was far more political in outlook, despite the contrary view of de Gaulle as to how the Communities should be organized and governed. It is particularly noteworthy in view of the failure of the original member states to agree on the EDC and EPC. The success of the EEC seemed to give support to the neo-functionalist view that success in one sector would lead inevitably to success in other sectors and assist the process of European integration. Indeed, the success in the area of the common customs tariff appeared to work as envisaged by the neo-functionalists/federalists and led to spillover into other areas, in particular to further pressure for the reform of the CAP. This form of functionalism was adopted deliberately by the High Authority and the EEC Commission as the way in which to achieve further progress with European integration, and these bodies put forward a linked package deal of reforms for the Communities. However, such reforms were quickly thwarted by a boycott of the Community institutions by de Gaulle in 1965[24] and his fierce defence of state nationalism. Previous signs of the stance to be adopted by de Gaulle had already been seen by his unilateral veto of British entry to the Communities in 1963, despite the fact that entry negotiations had been ongoing for two years. Since those days, and despite periods of stagnation, the Union has moved on with numerous treaty revisions and most recently the 2007 Lisbon Treaty. These developments will be considered in the following sections and returned to at the end of the chapter in respect of the Lisbon Treaty.

---

[23] Although some of the member states appear to like those elements: see Declaration 52 attached to the treaties.

[24] This is further considered in Section 1.6.6.2 and Chapter 2, Section 2.3.3.4.

1.6 The Widening and Deepening of the Communities and Union

This section concerns the parallel developments of the Communities by which they have increased not only in terms of the number of member states and external interfaces with the outside world, but also the extent to which the member states have gone in integrating economically, socially, and politically within the Communities and now Union.

In 1969, a fresh start for the Communities appeared to take place. Whilst in itself it did not lead to massive or immediate change, it did allow for a new agenda for change to be constructed. As much as anything, it was allowed to happen because of the resignation of de Gaulle as French president and his disappearance from the European political scene. The member states held a summit in The Hague in 1969, to try to get the Communities moving again after the setbacks they had suffered. Notable were the 1963 and 1965 crises caused by de Gaulle: the former being the first of the rejections of UK membership; and the latter, the boycott of the European institutions. The 1969 Hague Summit set as its goals the completion, widening, and deepening of the Communities.

Although the completion of the common market, which should have been fully achieved by 1969, took considerably longer and actually had to wait until 1992, the widening and deepening of the Communities were processes that were always going to be ongoing. The terms 'widening' and 'deepening' are the ones that were used then and still survive in Union jargon, describing its development in two ways:

- *Widening* refers primarily to the process of the expansion of the Union to include new member states, but can also apply to the extension of the EU into new policy areas and in developing new sectors for integration.

- *Deepening* refers to the degree of integration that takes place. By this is meant the extent to which integration is intergovernmental or supranational—but deepening could also apply to integration in new policy areas, because it would consider the extent to which the Union has encroached into areas of the member states' competences previously held exclusively.

So, to some extent, the terms are overlapping and the same development can be argued to fit into both categories. At a fairly simple level, though, they refer in turn to the quantitative and qualitative changes over the years.

1.6.1 The Widening of the Union

The Paris IGC of 1972 finally paved the way for the first expansion of the member states, which took place in 1973 when the UK, Ireland, and Denmark joined. Were it not for de Gaulle, this would have happened sooner and might have been better for the Community if it had. Norway was also to have joined at this time, but a referendum of the Norwegian electorate on the eve of membership resulted in a majority against and Norway failed to become a member—not for the last time.

A second expansion took place in 1981, when Greece joined, and a third in 1986 after protracted negotiation periods for Spain and Portugal. Whilst none of these three countries were economically in a strong position in relation to the existing member states, and in view of this were regarded by some as unfit for membership, politically their acceptance into the Communities without delay was regarded as crucial. This was considered both to support the recently emerged democracies in all of these countries after varying periods of authoritarian or dictatorial right-wing rule, and to act as a counterforce to any possible violent reaction to the left and possible establishment of governments sympathetic to Moscow or a return to authoritarianism.[25] The Cold War still featured prominently in this period of history, hence entry was facilitated sooner than the economic conditions might have permitted.

A smaller automatic expansion took place in 1990, with the unification of West and East Germany as the first tangible change to result from the fall of the communist regimes in the Soviet Union and East European countries. It woke up the institutions to the possibility of a number of the former East European states seeking membership and prompted a longer-term evaluation of the conditions required of aspirant member states which, in turn, led to a set of criteria being agreed at the Copenhagen Summit in June 1993. The requirements included the need for stable government and institutions guaranteeing democracy, the rule of law, human rights, and the protection of minorities. Economically, applicant states would have to have a functioning market economy and the ability to cope with life in the single market. The applicants would have to accept the *acquis communautaire*[26] in its entirety, including the overall political, economic, social, and monetary aims of the Union—no easy task, even for the present member states.

The next and fourth enlargement took place sooner than expected as a result of the changes in Eastern Europe and the economic success facilitated by the SEA, discussed in Section 1.6.7.

1.6.2 **The European Economic Area and the 1995 Expansion**

After observing in the late 1980s the economic benefits of the SEA enjoyed by the member states of the then Communities, other European states, most of which had cooperation or association agreements with the Communities and were members of the EFTA, started to make overtures for greater cooperation and some for possible membership. Initially, further expansion was not favoured by the Commission of the European Communities, because it was thought that it would stifle plans for deeper integration of the then existing member states, in particular, progress on the single market and possible further progress to economic and monetary union. Additionally, prior to the collapse of communism in Europe in the late 1980s, for varying reasons, some of the EFTA member states were uncertain about the appropriateness of full membership. Hence, a lesser form of integration was proposed by the European Commission, in which the participants could benefit from the advantages of the single market and the competition policy, but not be involved in the other economic or political aspects of the Communities, including decision-making. This offer was open to all the then existing members of the EFTA. However, the negotiations for this new form of cooperation were very drawn-out and subject to considerable delays during their course. They were also taking place against the backdrop of the collapse of communism in Eastern Europe. One of the consequences of

---

[25] Support for new democracies in Greece, Portugal, and Spain in the 1980s is the second of the five achievements of the EU which was cited as justifying the award of the Nobel Peace Prize.

[26] *Acquis communautaire* is the term used to describe the accumulated body of EU law, including treaties, secondary legislation, and judicial developments. There was an exhibition in Brussels (2004) that graphically displayed the EU's *acquis communautaire*. It ran to over 80,000 pages and took up approximately 8 metres when stretched out in display cases in the exhibition! Actually, according to the Commission's own figures, at the end of 2002, the number of pages of binding legislation in the OJ was 97,000 and further provided in 2011 that the *acquis* of the EU consisted of 8,862 regulations and 1,885 directives in addition to the primary law (the treaties). See **http://ec.europa.eu/eu_law/infringements/infringements_annual_report_29_en.htm** (COM (2011) 588 final).

this was that the previous objections or difficulties that might be raised by Eastern-bloc countries and the Soviet Union in particular, that full membership of militarily neutral countries of the Communities (namely, Austria, Finland, and Sweden) would not be compatible with their status as neutral countries, were significantly undermined, if not completely negated. Regardless, in October 1991, the EFTA member states of Austria, Finland, Iceland, Liechtenstein, Norway, Sweden, and Switzerland signed an agreement with the EEC on the creation of the European Economic Area (EEA). The agreement reached was that the EFTA members were not represented in the Community institutions and would take no part in the decision-making processes of the Community. They would be subject to all Community law relating to the single market, as defined by the Court of Justice. However, an additional problem was encountered whilst negotiations were being finalized and shortly before the treaty was to come into force on 1 January 1993. The Swiss electorate rejected membership of the EEA in a referendum in December 1992, which caused considerable political and legal difficulties because Liechtenstein, with which Switzerland has a monetary union, had agreed to join. The remaining six EFTA states went on to sign the agreement in March 1993 and it came into force on 1 July 1993. It was soon clear, though, that, as far as business confidence was concerned, full membership of the EU was the condition that attracted investment and not membership of the EEA. Indeed, both the concept and the consequences of the EEA might not, in any case, have been fully understood by outside interests. Hence, almost before the ink had dried on the signatures to the EEA Treaty, Austria, Finland, Norway, and Sweden applied for full membership of the European Communities. In view of the fact that most of the bargaining had already been done for the EEA, entry terms were easily and rapidly decided, and the four applications were quickly accepted. On 1 January 1995, therefore, the Community was joined by Austria, Finland, and Sweden, bringing the number of member states to 15. The Norwegian electorate once again, though, chose to reject membership in a referendum held in December 1994 and again Norway failed to join the Communities. The entry of the three former EFTA members meant that Iceland, Norway, and Liechtenstein are the only remaining EFTA members of the EEA, and one of these has a membership application pending. Iceland's membership is presently on hold at the request of the Icelandic government since May 2013. Switzerland remains outside both the EC and the EEA but remains a member of EFTA. Its application for full membership, lodged in 1992, was put on hold following the EEA rejection and this remains the case today. A special series of bilateral agreements have been negotiated with Switzerland instead, covering many, if not most, aspects of the EEA.[27]

1.6.3 The 2004 and 2007 Expansions

The expansion that took place on 1 May 2004 was the largest in the history of the EU; ten new states joined, namely the Czech Republic, Cyprus, Estonia, Hungary, Latvia, Lithuania, Malta, Poland, Slovakia, and Slovenia.

Despite the fact that the negotiations were rather oddly conducted, with some states being given priority, this manner of proceeding was changed and discussions proceeded on the basis of a 'big bang' of ten new states entering at the same time. As a result, the overall time taken to resolve terms of entry was surprisingly quick considering the number

---

[27] Although its refusal to accept Croatian migrants and generally limit EU inward migration in breach of its free Movement of Persons Agreement has brought reaction from the EU affecting the free movement of students and the opening of the Swiss electricity market. Further measures may be taken in the future: see http://www.swissinfo.ch/eng/swiss-confirm-eu-s-key-decision-on-free-movement/40521130.

of states involved, and their differing economic and social circumstances. The haste was fuelled by the political events unfolding in the world, in particular by the break-up of the Soviet Union and the bloody fragmentation of the Republic of Yugoslavia. For reasons that had similarly prompted the rapid entries of Greece, Spain, and Portugal in the 1980s, which were also regarded as premature due to the economic weakness of those countries, the ten new countries were brought into the fold much quicker than the economic conditions alone would have permitted, because of the political desire to lock these countries into a Western liberal-democratic club of nations. Hence, the Eastern expansion took over the agenda and Commission time.[28] The accession agreements with all the member states were concluded and the entry terms settled for the Treaty of Accession, which was signed in Athens on 16 April 2003. The ten new member states duly joined on 1 May 2004, with celebrations across Europe—albeit low-key in some member states such as the UK.

After the successful conclusion to the accession negotiations in December 2004, a favourable Commission Opinion in February 2005, and the conclusion of the Accession Treaty in April 2005, in September 2006 the EU Commission expressed its view that Bulgaria and Romania were ready for accession as originally planned in the Accession Treaty. Entry into the Union of these two countries took place on 1 January 2007, but equally subject to criticisms that entry for these countries was also economically premature and that other issues such as corruption had not been satisfactorily tackled prior to membership. For similar reasons as previous expansions regarded as premature, the politics of new-member entry prevailed. It is easier also to encourage and enforce change from within, rather than for the EU to impose pressure externally on non-member states. On 1 July 2013 Croatia became the twenty-eighth member state but just three days before entry amended the law on the European Arrest Warrant (EAW) to effectively give immunity from prosecution to an ex secret police chief and 20 others suspected of an assassination in Germany. That decision has now been reversed but was not the best of membership starts, with the Commission threatening sanctions on its newest member state within days of EU membership.

1.6.4 **Future Widening**

At present, there are six countries that are official candidate states: Iceland, the former Yugoslav Republic (FYR) of Macedonia, Turkey, Montenegro, Serbia, and Albania.

With regard to Turkey, the Commission recommended on 6 October 2004 that the EU should open entry negotiations; in December 2004, the Brussels European Council Summit approved this position, with 3 October 2005 seeing the start of entry negotiations. Without doubt, these negotiations are the most controversial in the history of the Union, mainly because of the recognition of Cyprus and the predominantly Muslim population of Turkey, but also in view of the human rights record of Turkey, and the fact that, quite simply, geographically most of the Turkish land mass lies in Asia and not in Europe. Its economic situation is also regarded as problematic as is its failure to recognize fully and politically an existing member state, Cyprus. However, it may be argued that Turkish membership is exactly what the EU should come to terms with: the creation of a multi-ethnic, multicultural, and multi-religious Union.[29] Albeit slowly, accession negotiations have been ongoing

---

[28] Support for former communist states in the 1990s is the third of the five achievements of the EU which was cited as justifying the award of the Nobel Peace Prize.

[29] Support for the modernization of Turkey is the fourth of the five achievements of the EU which was cited as justifying the award of the Nobel Peace Prize. The latest position with regard to Turkish membership can be found at **http://ec.europa.eu/enlargement/candidate-countries/turkey/index_en.htm** or **http://ec.europa. eu/enlargement/countries/detailed-country-information/turkey/index_en.htm**. For a balanced view of

since 2005 to discuss various topic chapters—13 so far from 35 now identified—all of which have to be agreed before an Accession Treaty can be finalized. In view of the fact that Turkey has not added Cyprus to the customs union with the EU, the Council of the EU has decided that no new chapters will be commenced and the existing ones will not be provisionally closed. In 2012, there was an initiative to re-launch negotiations to break the stalemate that had arisen.[30] Once accessions negotiations are successfully achieved, candidate countries become known as acceding states. There is no fixed timetable for the negotiations, Accession Treaty, or entry, and the process is expected to take at least ten years, especially as some member states have expressed strong doubts about the wisdom of this expansion, in particular Austria, France, and Germany. The entry of Turkey remains both contentious and a long way off.

The FYR of Macedonia made an application to join in March 2004 and was considered as of 16 December 2005 to be a candidate country. Entry negotiations had been recommended in October 2009 but have not yet commenced. Its name remains a problem which has to be resolved.[31]

Following Iceland's change of opinion about EU membership, which was prompted by its financial crises in 2007–8, events moved quite quickly at first, also assisted by present EEA membership. In July 2009, it applied for full membership; entry negotiations were recommended in June 2010 and commenced in July 2010. At the start of 2013, 11 chapters had been provisionally closed with a further 16 open and being negotiated. However, in the same year, Iceland requested its application be put on hold and that remains the case at the time of writing.

Montenegro applied for membership in 2009 and was granted candidate status in December 2010. Access negotiations commenced in June 2012. Serbia was granted candidate status on 1 March 2012[32] but negotiations will not commence until Serbia's relations with Kosovo have been normalized.

Albania was granted official candidate status on 27 June 2014 but entry negotiations have not commenced. Clearly its relations with other Balkans states have to be normalized and formalized before membership can be granted, especially under the 'good neighbour' requirement of new states, briefly considered in Section 1.4.6.1. The process too may take a long time.[33]

As to other possible members, the rest of the Balkan states[34] are considered to be potential candidate countries. Thus, the countries of Bosnia-Herzegovina and Kosovo have all been formally recognized by the EU as eligible for future EU membership, but only if they prove themselves to the satisfaction of the EU and existing member states to be fit for membership.[35]

all of the challenges to Turkish membership, see K. Dervis et al, *The European Transformation of Modern Turkey*, Centre for European Policy Studies, Brussels, 2004.

[30] At the time of writing (January 2015) things remain at a standstill.

[31] For the latest refer to **http://ec.europa.eu/enlargement/countries/detailed-country-information/fyrom/index_en.htm**.

[32] For further details on Montenegro and Serbia refer to **http://ec.europa.eu/enlargement/countries/detailed-country-information/montenegro/index_en.htm**.

[33] **http://ec.europa.eu/enlargement/countries/detailed-country-information/albania/index_en.htm**

[34] Peace-building in the Western Balkans is the final of the five achievements of the EU which was cited as justifying the award of the Nobel Peace Prize. For the full statement of the Peace Prize Committee go to **http://www.nobelprize.org/nobel_prizes/peace/laureates/2012/press.html**.

[35] For full details of this process and the requirements, see **http://ec.europa.eu/enlargement/the-policy/countries-on-the-road-to-membership/index_en.htm**, **http://ec.europa.eu/enlargement/countries/check-current-status/index_en.htm**, and **http://ec.europa.eu/enlargement/potential-candidates/index_en.htm**.

Less likely as possible future candidate states, in the short to medium term, are the states of the former Soviet Union that border the EU, because of the political controversy and impact on relations with Russia—and while it is to be noted that some of those countries (notably the Ukraine) have expressed their desire for future membership, this opinion appears to vary internally in the Ukraine and the conflict which developed in 2014 will curtail this process regardless of how pro-EU the legitimate Ukrainian government happens to be.[36]

One or two other countries have previously made applications, but have either withdrawn them or put them on hold. Norway has twice concluded entry negotiations only for entry to be rejected by the Norwegian electorate at the eleventh hour both times. At present, it has no application pending but the possibility of future membership remains on the political agenda, although recent opinion polls show mixed results in favour of full membership.[37]

The rejection by the Swiss of membership of the EEA in 1992 also led to the suspension of its application for full membership. Even though Swiss governments have expressed the view that Switzerland will eventually apply for full membership, that aim has been severely dented on two occasions now following referenda.[38] The first was a categorical rejection by the Swiss electorate of even starting entry negotiations for EU membership in a private initiative referendum in March 2001, in which 77 per cent of those voting said 'no'. Secondly, the Swiss voted to restrict Croatian migrant entry and to control immigration generally including that from the EU despite the fact that there was a free movement of persons agreement with the EU.[39] There are, then, presently no plans to reactivate the dormant application by Switzerland, although significant governmental and other elements consider membership of the EU as necessary and indeed inevitable, if not today, then at some stage in the future.[40]

An exhibition in Brussels in October 2004 presented some, not entirely serious but also in view of developments not too far wide of the mark in some respects, prophecies for the future, including the following:

> In 2010, the EU will expand to include Albania, Armenia, Belarus, Bosnia and Herzegovina, Georgia, Macedonia, Moldova, Montenegro, Serbia, and the Ukraine. Following this, in 2015, the EU will take in Morocco, Algeria, Egypt, Tunisia, Libya, Jordan, Israel, Palestine and change its name from the EU to simply 'The Union'.

Moving from fantasy to reality, the fact that the EU is opening accession negotiations with Turkey invites a final consideration in respect of further widening and enlargement. What is the limit? The answer to this is as much driven by the answer to the question: what is Europe, politically and geographically? Already, two Mediterranean island states have pushed the geographical border of the EU further. Cyprus lies closer to the Middle East and is nearer to Asia than Europe, and Malta is not much further away from Africa than it

---

[36] See http://ec.europa.eu/external_relations/ukraine/index_en.htm; for a press opinion on the issue, see http://www.signandsight.com/features/1708.html. For a background study, see inter alia: http://rt.com/tags/ukraine/ or http://www.washingtonpost.com/blogs/worldviews/wp/2014/01/30/9-questions-about-ukraine-you-were-too-embarrassed-to-ask/.

[37] For further details, see http://eeas.europa.eu/norway/index_en.htm, http://www.euractiv.com/enlargement/norwegians-eu-membership-ahead-g-news-529950.

[38] See the Swiss sites for their Volksabstimmungen: http://www.swissvotes.ch/ although this is not up to date. Similar is http://www.atlas.bfs.admin.ch/maps/12/map/mapIdOnly/0_de.html.

[39] The vote was approved by 50.3% on a turn-out of 56.6%: see http://www.bfs.admin.ch/bfs/portal/de/index/themen/17/03/blank/key/2014/013.html.

[40] For further details, see http://eeas.europa.eu/switzerland/index_en.htm.

is from other parts of Europe. Indeed, there are existing parts of some member states that are clearly beyond any usual definition of Europe. The Canaries (Spain) lie off the west coast of Africa; French Guyana is in South America; the Azores and Madeira (Portugal) are in the middle of the Atlantic; and the French islands of Guadeloupe, Martinique, and Reunion lie in the Caribbean. Greenland was part of the EU until it was granted home rule from Denmark in 1979 and left the EU in 1985.

In fact, there are not many European states left to apply, depending on the definition given to 'Europe'—only Norway, Liechtenstein, the smaller states of Andorra, Monaco, and perhaps parts of the former Soviet Union, such as Ukraine, Belarus, and Moldova, but no mention of these countries is made in the present enlargement strategy. An application to join by Morocco in 1987 was rejected, though on the geographical ground that Morocco was in Africa and could not be considered as coming within Europe. There is also perhaps now the more focused question of whether the present citizens of the EU want a bigger Europe. At the time of writing, there appears to be more resistance to than support for further expansion.[41]

1.6.4.1 Accession Preconditions

Regardless of which new state is a candidate, under Art 20(4) TEU, all new states are required to accept and adopt the entire body of EU law, the *acquis communautaire*,[42] as contained in the treaties, protocols, declarations, conventions, agreements with third countries, secondary legislation, and the judgments of the Court of Justice. Since the TEU, the criteria for membership have been much more clearly spelled out. Article 49 TEU provides that 'Any European State which respects the values referred to in Article 2 and is committed to promoting them may apply to become a member of the Union.'

These principles are human dignity, freedom, democracy, equality, the rule of law, and respect for human rights, including the rights of persons belonging to minorities outlined in Art 2 TEU. In addition, potential member states will be required to satisfy a number of criteria that have been revised over the years from those provided at Copenhagen in 1993 and later refined at the time when possible applications of the newly emergent democracies in Eastern Europe were anticipated. The criteria were essentially a refinement of previous practice and have been further refined in subsequent summit meetings since the 1999 Helsinki European Council Summit added a form of 'good neighbour' requirement for entrant states, that disputes with neighbouring countries be resolved before entry, and expressed in Art 8 TEU.[43] It might have been a good idea, but the most visible case requiring the application of that policy was Cyprus. However, the Greek and Turkish parts of the island were not able to resolve their differences fully prior to the entry of Cyprus to the EU on 1 May 2004. Thus, although the whole island of Cyprus is in the EU, EU law is applied only in the southern Greek half of the island despite the fact that a referendum vote in Cyprus to reunite the island was approved by the Turkish side, but rejected by the Greek Cypriot electorate. Note, though, that Turkish Cypriots are citizens of a member state, the Republic of Cyprus, even though they live in the northern part of Cyprus; therefore their personal rights as EU citizens are not affected. Potential border disputes existing between Estonia and Latvia and the Russian Federation were also not resolved

---

[41] For the EU's overall enlargement strategy and progress, see http://ec.europa.eu/enlargement/ or http://ec.europa.eu/enlargement/countries/strategy-and-progress-report/index_en.htm.

[42] See n 26 and http://ec.europa.eu/enlargement/policy/conditions-membership/chapters-of-the-acquis/index_en.htm.

[43] See the EU Neighbourhood policy website: http://ec.europa.eu/enlargement/neighbourhood/overview/index_en.htm.

prior to accession, and a dispute between Slovenia and Croatia is yet to be resolved. The Helsinki Summit also marked a realization that the Copenhagen criteria could not be strictly applied and that some flexibility had to be exercised. The Laeken European Council Summit in December 2001 also emphasized that membership was dependent on candidate countries ensuring that their judicial institutions were capable of meeting the requirements of EU membership. The applicability of the criteria for deciding whether an eligible candidate can become an admissible one was confirmed at the Copenhagen Summit, which took place in December 2002, and in relation to Turkish membership the member states emphasized the need to meet the political criteria.

1.6.5 **The EU and the World: External Relations**

The EU has diverse roles to play in the world orders. Not surprisingly given the more limited original political scope of the Communities at the outset, trade relations with the rest of the world featured most prominently, but not exclusively. However, these roles and obligations in the area of external relations were spread over the various treaties, making an overview difficult to obtain. Also the competences to undertake external relations were granted in different terms under the three original treaties. For example, the ECSC Treaty expressly granted the legal capacity to make external agreements generally in pursuit of the objectives of the treaty; the EURATOM (EAEC) Treaty also allowed for general agreements to be concluded; and the EC Treaty (Art 281) provided that the European Community had been given legal personality and was provided with powers to conclude specific types of agreements only, such as commercial agreements under the common customs tariff (ex Arts 131–3 EC, now Arts 205–7 TFEU) or the association agreements. The original Treaty on European Union did not, though, possess legal personality. This has now been corrected by the Lisbon Treaty and Art 47 TEU provides that 'The Union shall have legal personality', which thus allows the EU to participate in international actions and agreements across all areas of external relations. The member states did, however, add a declaration (Declaration No 24) to make it clear that this does not mean that a new general power has been provided to the Union and that it continues to be constrained in its competences by the existing grant of powers to the Union by the member states. The Lisbon Treaty has also gone a long way in rationalizing and ordering external relations in the treaties, and the range of external relations and activities has now been better coordinated between the TEU and TFEU. Given the breadth of this very wide and far-ranging subject, which is not usually treated in any depth in EU courses, this section will simply outline the range of external activities undertaken by the EU and make brief mention of the commercial activities.[44]

The external relations of the EU are set out in general in the TEU and in more detail in the TFEU. Listed under the competences in Art 3 TFEU is the exclusive competence under Art 3(2) of the Union to conclude international agreement if provided for with the treaties or necessary to enable the Union to exercise its internal competence. Article 3(5) TEU refers to the Union's relations with the wider world and Art 8 TEU sets out the basics of the European Neighbourhood Policy (see Section 1.6.4.1 above and n 43). Article 21 TEU outlines the general provisions on the range of external involvements of the EU and, in particular, the CFSP. Article 21 also provides a series of guiding principles by

---

[44] For a more detailed look at the range of external relations conducted by the EU, refer to **http://ec.europa.eu/policies/external_relations_foreign_affairs_en.htm.**

which all external policies and actions shall be pursued, including democracy, the rule of law, and respect for fundamental, human, and equality rights.

The European Council is now formally confirmed in the role of formulating and pursuing external action (Art 22 TEU) and shall take decisions on either a proposal from the Council, or jointly from the High Representative[45] and Commission in the areas of their prime interest.

Outside the general tidying up of external relations and their placement within the TFEU is the area of CFSP, which remains in the TEU (Arts 23–46), although oddly Art 2(4) TFEU provides the basic competence for the Union in this area. Hence, the TEU contains all the foreign policy aspects and the TFEU everything else. Article 23 TEU and Art 205 TFEU respectively subject the EU in those areas to the principles contained in Art 21 TEU. Association agreements for countries and territories that have special relations with some of the member states are covered by Part Four of the treaty, Arts 198 et seq TFEU, and the countries are listed in Annex II attached to the TFEU. Part Five of the TFEU (Arts 205–22), entitled 'External Action by the EU', groups together the major planks of EU external action in a series of titles. Article 205 TFEU provides generally that international actions shall be guided by the principles set out in Art 21 TEU.

1.6.5.1 Commercial Activities

In view of the increasing share of world trade that the Union has, it is no wonder that external relations in this area are very important. Even at the start of the Communities, part of the role envisaged was to contribute to the harmonious development of world trade and the liberalization of international trade. From the start, therefore, the Community was given the competence to forge economic ties with the outside world (ex Art 131 EC). Particularly under the common customs tariff, where it was clear that this could only sensibly be done by the EU as a whole, the EU has slowly assumed the competences to negotiate on behalf of the member states, including representing the EU in the important trade institutions set up in the world and committing them to the GATT and World Trade Organization (WTO) negotiations. The EU now participates in the WTO on behalf of the member states and has been recognized as replacing the authority of the formal members, which are the individual member states, as far as the competence of the EU over the Common Commercial Policy (CCP) is concerned.[46] Such activity has been challenged in the past, but the capacity to enter into international commitments was approved by the Court of Justice: for example, in Case 22/70 *Commission v Council (ERTA)* and in Opinion 1/76.[47] The CoJ further outlined this position in its Opinion 1/94, which held that where the Community has internal exclusive competence in a matter, this is transferred into powers to negotiate exclusively with non-member countries externally and extends to where, although not exclusive, the EU has achieved complete harmonization of a particular area.

The CCP is now contained in Arts 206–7 TFEU, which cover the customs union and the common external tariff for goods entering the EU from outside the EU, now including commercial aspects of intellectual property. Although this is an exclusive competence of the Union, if international agreements are needed in pursuit of this policy, the process by

---

[45] A section on the High Representative can be found in Chapter 2, Section 2.4.2.

[46] For further details, see Y. Devuyst, *The European Union Transformed: Community Method and Institutional Evolution from the Schuman Plan to the Constitution for Europe*, Peter Lang, Brussels, 2005, pp 133–40.

[47] Case 22/70 *Commission v Council* [1971] ECR 263, [1971] CMLR 335, and Opinion 1/76 [1977] ECR 741; see also comments on these cases in Chapter 3.

which they may be negotiated can be carefully controlled by the Council of the Union. The Council grants the initial power to open negotiations and appoints a special committee to which the Commission should report on the state of negotiations. Depending on the subject matter, set out in Art 207(3) and (4) TFEU, the Council will either act by qualified majority or unanimity.

1.6.6 The Deepening of the Union

This section charts the increasing degree of integration entered into by the member states, starting with the original treaties establishing the Communities and following this to the present position after the Lisbon Treaty amendments.

1.6.6.1 The Primary Treaties and Early Amendments

The first and fundamental movement on the path of integration was, of course, the ECSC Treaty, now expired, which was soon followed by the agreement and ratification of the EEC and EURATOM Treaties. It was clear at the time of negotiation that a transfer of sovereign powers from the member states to the Community to be established was involved, particularly in the climate of the time and the clear federalist intentions of the main protagonists of the plan, Schuman and Monnet.

The only amendments that were made to the primary treaties for the first two decades were minor ones brought about, first, by the decision to merge the institutions of the three Communities and, secondly, by the accession treaties required for the new member states. Prior to the Merger Treaty of 1965, each of the Communities had its own Council and High Authority/Commission; however, the Court of Justice and the Parliamentary Assembly had both been shared by all three Communities from the outset. The merger of the institutions was a practical step to provide common coordination and to cut out a duplication of effort and resources. The first accession treaties for Denmark, Ireland, and the UK dealt specifically with the details of accession of the new member states or merely made the changes to the treaties considered necessary for it to continue working in the same way as previously, but with adjustments to reflect the increase in member states and the composition of the institutions: for example, Council voting numbers and Commission membership. The fundamental constitutional core of the Communities and how they worked remained untouched until 1986.

1.6.6.2 The 1960s and the Luxembourg Accords

Initially, the Communities were very successful in achieving the aims set out and promoting economic growth in the member states in contrast with countries such as the UK. The dismantling of customs duties was achieved by the original six member states before the target date set down in the EEC Treaty. Additionally, competition policy was seen to be working and the CAP was clearly successful in terms of guaranteeing production. It was, however, the subject of criticism because its price-support mechanisms led, over time, to the massive overproduction and stockpiling of commodities such as milk, butter, sugar, and wine, which not only cost the Community a great deal of money to dispose of, but also incurred political ill-favour worldwide because developing world agricultural products had no chance of entering the heavily protected European Community market.

However, following this initial period of success and achievement, any chance of either further expansion or deeper integration was stifled. The brake on such progress was most effectively applied to the Commission and the Communities in 1965 by French President de Gaulle's boycotting of the Community institutions, which caused damage that lasted for decades. In 1965, the Commission proposed that the Communities move to a system of own resources and that the Council move to majority voting, which was no more than as originally envisaged by the Treaty of Rome. It was further proposed that the Parliamentary Assembly should have some control over the expenditure of the Communities. These proposals were categorically opposed and vetoed by de Gaulle who, when the other member states were not opposed, adopted a policy of non-attendance at the Community institutions by the French representatives, which became known as 'the institutions boycott' or the 'empty chair' policy. All progress, indeed, all business, in the Communities simply halted. The compromise agreement to break the deadlock was the infamous Luxembourg Accords—in essence, an agreement to disagree. This basically provided that where the member states were not able to agree a proposal and where a vital national interest of any member state was at stake, discussions, according to the French, should continue until agreement was reached but ultimately as all six member states did not agree, the reality was that a member state could veto the proposal in Council. There was no definition of a vital interest, so member states were left to define a vital interest themselves. Thus, until the political demise of de Gaulle, the planned moves for deeper integration were prevented.

1.6.6.3 Stagnation and 'Eurosclerosis'

The whole unfortunate episode surrounding the Luxembourg Accords resulted in stagnation in the decision-making process for many years. It led to the long, slow, painful period of the Communities that has become known as the period of 'Eurosclerosis', which lasted from 1966 until the mid-1980s. The basic problem was the near inability of the member states to reach decisions on legislation and widespread dissatisfaction at the slow pace at which the goals of the EEC were being achieved. Whilst a lot of the blame can be laid at the door of the French boycott and the Luxembourg Accords, the ability to reach decisions was made much more difficult by the doubling of the member states between 1973 and 1985. Trying to obtain the unanimous agreement of first 6, then 9, then 10, and then all 12 members proved at times to be simply impossible. Amongst the main concerns were the time taken by the Community institutions to make new laws and the amount of work with which the Council was faced, partly because particular provisions were presented many times as the Commission made amendments to make them acceptable to all member states. A notorious example exists of a directive that did nothing more controversial than harmonize the training requirements for architects,[48] but which took the institutions 17 years to agree and finally enact. Further concerns related to the lack of representative democracy in the decision-making process of the Community and the delays experienced by litigants in the Court of Justice. It was clear to everyone that changes had to happen. Whilst it was true that some adjustments had been made in the form of amendments to the original treaties, these were of a limited nature. More significantly, but restricted to a specific process, was the increase in powers of the European Parliament in the budgetary process by the Budgetary Treaties of 1970 and 1975. Otherwise, little further progress had been achieved in this period.

1.6.6.4 Revival Attempts

In 1969, following the resignation of de Gaulle and the change of government in West Germany to a Social Democrat-led one, a summit of the heads of government was arranged in The Hague expressly to re-launch European integration. The 1969 Hague Summit established the system of European political cooperation (EPC), but it was

---

[48] Directive 85/384 (OJ 1985 L223/15).

deliberately intergovernmental in nature and sat outside the formal treaty set-up. As such, it can be regarded as another move away from supranationalism and the neo-functionalists' dream of progress on European integration. It was also unfortunate, but the reforms and the re-launching of the Communities envisaged at The Hague were severely disrupted by the world economic situation that grew steadily worse in the early 1970s. The Middle East wars and ensuing oil crises led to very high inflation and stagnation in the world economies, and to the unwinding of the first attempt at some sort of monetary union, namely economic and monetary union (EMU), which bound European currencies into a flexible relationship with one another and established the European monetary unit.[49] The year 1973 also saw the entry of three new member states, two of which—the UK and Denmark—were even then the least federal-minded member states in the European Communities. There were nevertheless further attempts to revive the flagging fortunes of the Communities. A further summit in Paris in 1974 led to the formalization of the previously informal European Council summit meetings to provide an overriding political guide to the Communities. This, however, tended to strengthen further the intergovernmental hand of control over the Communities rather than to provoke deeper integration. The Paris Summit also, for the first time, allowed the Commission a role in the summitry, something pressed for by the then new Commission President Roy Jenkins. The summit also made the decision that the European Parliament should be directly elected as from 1978, although this could not take place until 1979 due to difficulties in the UK in preparing the legislation. Finally, the European Monetary System (EMS) was established in 1978, despite the collapse of the previous attempt (the EMU). The EMS proved to be stable and, with the establishment of the European currency unit (ECU), became the precursor to monetary union and the euro.

These limited successes, however, did little to counter the generally prevailing malaise that hung over the Communities and institutions. This was not helped by the attitude and activities of certain member states. Even when de Gaulle disappeared from the international scene, in 1979, new UK Prime Minister Thatcher appeared to take up the baton of intergovernmentalism and the bolstering of purely national interests. Whilst the UK may well have had a case in arguing for a more equitable budget contribution, and neither Mrs Thatcher nor indeed anyone else has gone as far as de Gaulle in disrupting the work of the Communities, her negotiating style and public pronouncements left much to be desired. These budget wrangles and sheer lack of progress generally in the Community dragged on seemingly endlessly into the mid-1980s. The stagnation and intergovernmentalism not only thwarted any moves to more federalism, but also engendered a period of national protectionism that itself was threatening to undermine some of the basic goals of the European Communities already achieved—notably the common market itself, which was simply not being completed as envisaged and, if anything, was becoming more fragmented. It was abundantly clear and understood that reform, and, indeed, radical reform, of the Community and institutions was necessary.

Numerous reports and studies were conducted by the different Community institutions and, additionally, many external reports had been commissioned over the years that had all recommended changes. A number of areas in which improvements were required had already been identified by those reports in the lifetime of the Communities.[50] The

---

[49] This was not a currency like the present day euro, but an accounting unit based on the average of the basket of member currencies.

[50] Amongst them were: the Vedel Report of 1972, with proposals by the Commission to strengthen the powers of the European Parliament; the Tindemans Report on 'European Union' of 1976; the Report of the Three Wise Men of 1979; the Spierenburg Report of 1979; the Columbo/Genscher Initiative of 1981; and the Stuttgart European Council of 1983, which made a 'Solemn Declaration' that there should be greater

fact that there were so many of these speaks volumes for their effectiveness (or, more accurately, *in*effectiveness) in tackling the deep-rooted problems of European stagnation. However, whilst individually they did not provide a solution, collectively all of them, especially the latter ones, helped finally to establish and develop the climate for the eventual changes brought about by amendment and in particular by the SEA, which led in turn to the TEU, the Treaties of Amsterdam and Nice, and the Treaty for a Constitution for Europe and its replacement, the 2007 Lisbon Treaty. In 1985, a sufficient head of steam had built up for the member states to accept, albeit some reluctantly, that the necessary changes were ones that could only effectively be undertaken by treaty revision. It was finally accepted that the founding treaties should be substantively amended.

1.6.6.5 The Contrasting Positive Role Played by the Court of Justice

An observation that needs to be made at this stage, but which will be repeated in Chapters 2 and 4, is that whilst the Community institutions were busily going nowhere on the path to European integration, the Court of Justice appeared not to be affected by the 'Eurosclerosis' and had, from a very early date, adopted a very supranational tone in its judgments, with the far-reaching decisions on direct effects and supremacy in Case 26/62 *Van Gend en Loos* and Case 6/64 *Costa v ENEL*. These judgments contributed greatly not only in terms of building a separate Community and now EU legal system, but also by enhancing the supranational status of the new European legal order and constitutionality of the Communities.

1.6.7 The First Radical Change: The Single European Act

The SEA was the first significant amendment of the primary treaties. It is an important watershed in the historical development of the Union and is not to be underestimated in its importance, although it was at the time, not only by external observers and commentators, but also the heads of state and government who signed up to it. It is sometimes difficult to grasp its importance because it is the first of a series of package-deal changes to the treaties that not only add new areas of competence, but also simultaneously make various institutional changes and policy amendments.

The situation in the middle of the 1980s was that both the stagnation of the Communities and the lack of international competitiveness of Europe in relation to US and Japanese industrial and commercial progress had been clearly recognized. These concerns were taken up by Commission President Jacques Delors, who brought a package of reforms to the member states based on the Dooge Committee report, together with a new report prepared by the British Vice-President of the Commission, Lord Cockfield, dealing with the measures considered necessary for the completion of the single market. Whilst there remained opposition to any significant institutional changes recommended, especially by the UK, the single market completion was the carrot that brought the Eurosceptic governments on board, particularly the UK and Germany, as the proposals were hailed as a shining example of trade liberalization. Whilst the other member states were undoubtedly also interested in the trade and economic aspects of the reforms proposed, the smaller states in particular had a greater desire to see the institutional reforms recommended. All of these matters were put on the agenda for the 1985 IGC, itself initially opposed by

European integration towards a European Union. There was also the prescient European Parliament publication *Draft Treaty of the European Parliament Establishing the European Union* of 1984 and, finally, the Dooge Committee set up by the Fontainebleau Summit of 1984.

the UK. The single-market reforms were linked to the institutional changes and it is fair to say that the far-reaching political consequences of these were seriously downplayed by the EC Commission. It was also true that the far more radical changes proposed by the European Parliament a year or so earlier in its draft Constitution had caused a lot more consternation in and opposition by the member states. The European Parliament proposals were not ones that could be accepted by the Council at the time, hence the SEA proposals, which put the primary focus on market liberalization and were far more modest and much more acceptable to the member states. Even the title underplays the significance of the matter. An 'Act' suggests something less than a new treaty. It suggests secondary status rather than primary treaty material. So, in 1985, the draft SEA was put to and debated at the IGC. It was agreed by the ten member states in December 1985 and came into force in the EEC in May 1987, after signature and ratification by all 12 states (Portugal and Spain having joined the Communities in January 1986).

The SEA amended the EEC Treaty in several important respects and whilst the changes were not massive in themselves, they proved to be a catalyst to further European integration. Apart from the proposals to complete the internal market, perhaps most important was the change to the legislative process affecting ten treaty Articles and generally the extension of the Community's competence and concern in new policy areas. The SEA also introduced provisions that made it possible to make changes to the judicial structure in the future by supplementing the Court of Justice with an extension that was regarded as being vital to cope with the significant increases in the number of cases reaching the Court and the increased delay being caused as a result. The decision, in 1988, on the establishment of a Court of First Instance of the European Communities (CFI) was the result,[51] with the CFI being set up in October 1988.

Before considering in further detail the changes brought about by the SEA, it needs to be stressed here generally what was being done by the SEA. It was the first substantive amendment of the original treaties. Although this has happened on a number of occasions since then and thus has the appearance of being something that can easily be done, at the time it was, without doubt, a significant development. For most, if not all, of the states, especially the UK, signing up to and joining the Communities in the first place was a massive and historic commitment. Changing that original deal was not something to be taken lightly, and could even be regarded as being as important as the recent attempts to reform the EU by the abandoned Constitutional Treaty and its replacement, the 2007 Lisbon Treaty. The very substance of the original treaties was being altered and, in order to amend a treaty, another treaty is needed; so, despite its name, the SEA is a true amending treaty agreed by the member states. The preamble to the SEA states that it is 'a step towards European Union'.

1.6.7.1 The Internal Market and '1992'

In 1985, the Commission had identified 279 areas in which directives or other provisions were considered necessary to complete the internal market. The SEA set a new date of 31 December 1992 for the completion of the internal common market, which had been delayed previously by the member states. This programme proved to be a success not only in itself, because the member states did get on with enacting the needed legislation, but also because it gave a clear signal to European business that 'Europe meant business', a catchphrase that was employed at the time. By the end of October 1992, 282 directives had been proposed and drafted, and by the end of December 1992 all but 18 had been

---

[51] Decision 88/591 (OJ 1988 L319/1).

adopted by the Council. The system of QMV in the Council, for the completion of the internal market was highly instrumental in this success. Company mergers and investment increased dramatically and considerable economic progress was made in these years. It was the promise of economic gains to be made that had convinced the member states to accept the other proposals agreed in the SEA and, as it turned out, proved by and large to be true, although the exact amount of economic benefit to be gained might have been forecast on the high side.[52]

1.6.7.2 SEA Institutional and Policy Changes

The SEA also made formal the existence of the European Council of Heads of State and Government, which was originally established as European political cooperation (EPC). The SEA reintroduced and extended QMV in the Council; introduced the cooperation procedure in law-making, which provided the European Parliament with more than just a consultative role for the first time; paved the way for the CFI; and increased Commission powers—all of which are further considered in Chapter 2.

The SEA also added economic and social cooperation under which the European Regional Development Fund was established. This was designed to help to redress regional imbalances between various areas of the Communities by financing infrastructure developments. It also set up the Social Fund to finance employment initiatives and the European Investment Bank, which operates as a commercial bank lending money to finance projects in the promotion of which the Community has an interest.

Further new policy areas were added to the EEC Treaty, including research and technology (Arts 163–73), which set out the framework for the pursuit of research and development cooperation, and environmental protection, under Art 174(1), and introduced the objective of, and initial measures towards, monetary union.

1.6.7.3 Evaluation of the SEA

Whilst the SEA had its critics and was condemned by some parties,[53] its success lay not in what it actually changed, although there was considerable progress with the internal market; its true success lay in its longer-term influence in reinvigorating integration. It is certainly the case that it did not represent a radical shift to supranational or federal integration. In contrast to the original treaties, the member states were the ones constructing the agenda for it and not the federalist visionaries of the immediate post-war period. Also, in view of the preceding 15–20 years that had seen a complete stand-still on any such progress, it is not surprising that the changes introduced by the SEA can be regarded as modest and even disappointing. There is a saying that 'an inch is better than a mile, in the right direction'. To view the limited, mainly intergovernmental changes brought by the SEA as a backward step on the integration road misses the point somewhat. It represented forward movement at a time of massive political conservatism in Europe, and perhaps as important was the fact that, for the first time, the original primary treaties had been substantively amended. The original legal and constitutional base was shown not to be cast in stone and thus set for all time to come. It could be altered—and not just once, but as many times as deemed necessary. The SEA allowed that to happen and, after a 20-year

---

[52] *Completing the Internal Market*, White Paper from the Commission to the European Council (Milan, 28–9 June 1985), COM (85) 310, 14 June 1985 and the later Cecchini Report, which forecasted the cost of non-Europe to be €200 billion. See P. Cecchini et al, *The European Challenge 1992: The Benefits of a Single Market*, Wildwood House, Aldershot, 1998.

[53] I. Ward, *A Critical Introduction to European Law*, 3rd edn, Cambridge University Press, Cambridge, 2009, p 8.

delay, it did introduce real majority voting in the Council of Ministers with clear and obvious benefits, albeit within limited fields. It allowed the member states to get comfortable with QMV and thus prepared the ground for the future use of majority voting which was incrementally introduced into many other areas.

The success of the SEA and the benefit to the Communities was also observed, externally at that time, as other European states on the outside of the Communities were able to witness the increase in investment from beyond Europe into the EC and, indeed, away from their own countries. They wanted in and initially plans were made to accommodate them in association agreements with the European Communities and, in an extended form of these, the EEA, as noted in Section 1.6.2. It led much more quickly than originally envisaged to the further widening of the Communities, also noted earlier.

1.6.7.4 Post-SEA

It was realized very soon after the signing of the SEA that it was only part of the answer and further institutional changes were advocated, largely by the Commission. As a result, even before the deadline of 1992 had passed, plans were being put forward by Commission President Delors for further treaty reform, especially on economic and monetary union and social policy. A further IGC was planned and set up to debate the adoption of common monetary and fiscal policies. The UK opposed both this further proposal for integration and that the IGC should debate it at all.

However, external political events were moving rapidly in the world. UK Prime Minister Thatcher was deposed by her own party as Conservative leader, and, thus, as UK prime minister. Along with the 'Iron Lady',[54] the 'Iron Curtain' was also being dismantled, changing the political situation in Europe radically and leading very quickly to German reunification. The IGC planned for 1991, to discuss and provide for greater economic integration, was supplemented by a parallel second IGC as it was considered necessary that political decision-making should also be integrated in order to lock in any decisions reached on monetary union. Otherwise, it was feared that any gains or decisions reached for monetary and economic union would be lost if the political decisions supporting them could still be taken independently by each member state. This, in turn, would lead to a drifting apart of the economic conditions in the member states. This is a clear example of functionalist integration in action, in which integration in one area demands or inevitably leads to integration in another area in order to prevent the first area from unravelling.

The parallel IGCs commenced work in December 1990 but, like the later EEA negotiations, they were also subject to delays as a result of the considerable political, social, and economic change taking place across Europe at that time.

1.6.8 The Maastricht Treaty on European Union

The single treaty that was drafted following the two IGCs and eventually accepted by the member states, however, considerably complicated the constitutional base of the Communities and Union because it not only amended the existing treaties, but it also added another treaty to remain in force alongside the existing treaties. It also proved to be a huge compromise, with opt-outs in a number of matters for some of the member states. It is also criticized for its complex three-pillar construction established to govern the

---

[54] One of the nicknames given to Margaret Thatcher, allegedly by the Soviet *Red Star* and *TASS* party newspapers.

Communities and the various policies of the Union, involving a mix of intergovernmental and supranational elements.[55]

The main changes introduced by the treaty were the timetable and convergence criteria to move to a single economy and monetary union, complete with a single currency.[56] It provided more political cooperation, especially in the areas of foreign policy, security, home affairs, and justice (Arts 11–45 old TEU). The EEC Treaty name was changed to 'European Community (EC)' to represent the changes that had taken place and the huge expansion in the range of topics and policies covered by the treaty. A new overall term, the 'European Union', was introduced under Art 1 TEU, and described the extension by the member states into additional policies and areas of cooperation. The Union, as constituted by the TEU, comprised three pillars: the then existing Communities (the three original treaties), a CFSP, and cooperation in the fields of Justice and Home Affairs (JHA). The TEU also started a trend that was continued at Amsterdam in the attachment to the treaties of numerous protocols and declarations that help, in many cases, to define further some provisions of the treaties themselves and to outline the reservations of some member states. Justifiably, these have been criticized for making Community and EU law too opaque and too splintered.

Apart from the complexity of the new constitutional base, a large part of the problem facing European governments when trying to sell this treaty at home was that the European public had not been taken on board during the period of negotiation. Whilst there was some lip service paid to the idea of European citizenship and what this meant for the personal right of free movement of Union citizens, which was really only given teeth later by the Court of Justice, the European public had largely been left out of the reform process. There were further minor improvements for the European Parliament in the law-making process, but the TEU also represented a backward step as far as progress towards deeper integration was concerned. The other two pillars, as first established, were intergovernmental in nature, with decisions having to be taken unanimously by the member states. Very little had been done to increase the democratic credentials of the Communities: in fact, the powers of the Council were left largely untouched, even strengthened, in respect of the two new pillars, whereas the European Parliament had virtually no say.

The treaty did contain an expression of commitment to the rule of law and democracy but failed to provide for any significant democratic accountability of the EU and the rule of law itself. There was also an attempt to define the relationship between the Union and the member states by the introduction of the term 'subsidiarity' that was written in the new treaty (Art B) and which was further defined in Art 5 EC (now 5 TEU). It was supposed to delineate the respective powers of the Union and the member states, but instead has merely confused them and, as such, is regarded as somewhat reflective of the ambivalence of the member states at the time.[57]

The TEU was also supposed to redress concerns about the democratic deficit in the Communities by increasing the power of the European Parliament through the

---

[55] In particular, see D. Curtin, 'The Constitutional Structure of the Union: A Europe of Bits and Pieces' (1993) 30 CML Rev 17. This form of amendment was seen again later by the way in which the 2007 Lisbon Treaty also amended the existing treaties. See also the Online Resource Centre at **www.oxfordtextbooks. co.uk/orc/foster5e/**.

[56] The eurozone, **http://www.eurozone.europa.eu/**, of which there are 19 members. Despite the severe eurozone economic difficulties in 2012–13, Latvia became the eighteenth member on 1 January 2014 and Lithuania became the nineteenth member on 1 January 2015 (**http://www.consilium.europa.eu/en/ policies/joining-euro-area/latest-country-to-join-euro-area/**).

[57] Subsidiarity is discussed in further detail in Chapter 3. See also I. Ward, *A Critical Introduction to European Law*, 3rd edn, Cambridge University Press, Cambridge, 2009, p 47.

introduction of the co-decision procedure to a limited number of treaty Articles. This had the effect of increasing, once again, the range and complexity of law-making procedures in the Community, which are considered in detail in Chapter 4.

The TEU also brought into the Union structure the Schengen Agreement of 1985 on free movement and security measures, relating to such free movement in the area of the member states which had signed up to it, but not including the UK, Ireland, and Denmark.

The TEU was agreed by the member states in February 1992 and was due to come into force on 1 January 1993; however, the process was thrown into confusion by its rejection by a slim Danish majority in a referendum. As a result, further compromises had to be found in order to appease the Danish electorate. The Edinburgh Summit in December 1992 agreed to allow Denmark various protocols and declarations to opt out of participation in Stage III of EMU, the single currency, and the defence arrangements of Maastricht, whilst not actually changing the treaty itself. It came into force in November 1993, but this treaty creation was clearly an unhappy experience that the European leaders promised was going to be handled better next time. However, there was little time in which to learn the lessons from Maastricht, because the next time was just around the corner. Already in 1992, with the visible political changes in Europe, further expansion had been contemplated, so the Copenhagen Summit laid down criteria that would have to be met by aspiring member states (noted earlier in Section 1.6.4.1).

Whilst politically the TEU was also supposed to be an attempt to tidy up the constitutional base of the Communities, the end result was far from this goal. All in all, the revised constitutional base was far too fragmented, with the establishment of a three-pillared Union and the numerous protocols and declarations allowing various member state opt-outs and positions. Furthermore, the Union that was established was only an 'ever closer one'. It was not the federal union originally mooted and which suggested far greater integration than the reality that was agreed by the member states; hence, the end-product was more intergovernmental cooperation.

The TEU and the aftermath also led to new jargon in the Community political and legal order, which was the result of the new complex shape of the Union and the difficulties in getting the treaty ratified in all member states, and reflected the frustrations of some member states not being happy about the more reluctant states. Hence, the terms 'European architecture' to describe the new three-pillar structure and 'variable geometry' to describe the way in which a central core of states might integrate deeper. This is also described by the term 'multi-speed Europe'.

1.6.9 **The Amsterdam Intergovernmental Conference and Treaty**

As a part of the agreement for the TEU and specified in the treaty itself in Art 48, a timetable was pre-planned for the further revision of the treaties by providing that another IGC be constituted in 1996 with a view to signing another amending treaty in Amsterdam in 1997. The objectives were to reform the institutional structure for enlargement, to consider the role of the individual in relation to the Union, to revise social policy, and to review the intergovernmental pillars. However, due to the delays in ratifying the TEU, the agenda was increasingly hijacked by new items. The political landscape of the Union had changed greatly in a very short time. One of the few things on which enough member states were agreed was the opening up of entry negotiations with the new democracies of Eastern Europe. Hence, the focus of attention soon shifted to further institutional reform for the next, much larger expansion of the Union. The focus thus became narrowly concentrated on the size of the Commission, the European Parliament, QMV, and the rotation of the presidency of the Council of Ministers. The negotiations were highly problematic; the UK government was even seeking to reopen previous treaties, curb the powers of the Court of Justice, and reverse some decisions not favoured by the UK. Hence, in this climate, the IGC dragged on into early 1997. This might have been deliberate, because the UK general election had been set for 1 May 1997 and the Labour Party looked to be in a strong position to win. Labour did win and there was a new UK government, which quickly removed some of the objections that the Conservative Party had raised in the negotiations, and offered a promise to opt in to the social policy. As a result, final negotiations were soon wrapped up and the treaty was concluded in Amsterdam in June 1997. It was signed by all member states at a late-night summit in October 1997 and, following a slow but less troublesome ratification by all member states, entered into force on 1 May 1999.

1.6.9.1 The Treaty of Amsterdam

The Treaty of Amsterdam did introduce some changes, some of which have further complicated the structure of the Union and the treaties. A clear failure was the lack of significant institutional reform, which had become the main focus for the IGC and supposedly indispensable for future expansion.

What could be agreed, following the landslide Labour victory in the UK, was that the Agreement on Social Policy, previously lying outside the treaty structure, was accepted by all 15 member states and therefore a Chapter on Social Policy could be incorporated into the EC Treaty. A new section on employment was introduced which provided, as one of the first examples of a more open method of coordination (see Chapter 4, Section 4.7), that the member states can develop cooperative ventures to combat unemployment. It was agreed that the EU would incorporate the Schengen Agreement on the elimination of all border controls for 12 states in a new Title IV in the EC Treaty, but not for the UK, Ireland, or Denmark, which secured opt-outs in this area. The Court of Justice and the European Parliament were also given a greater role in the JHA pillar, now renamed the 'Provision on Police and Judicial Cooperation in Criminal Matters' (PJCC).

The institutional reforms were far more modest. The proposals to extend QMV in Council were severely restricted notably by Germany, amongst others. However, the variety of legislative procedures, which were getting out of hand, was slightly reduced and the European Parliament's powers were modestly increased by the moderately extended use of the co-decision procedure. The number of Commissioners was capped at 20, although subsequent IGCs and enlargement reopened this issue along with other institutional matters, considered in detail later and in Chapter 2.

The various changes were consolidated within both the EC and EU Treaties and, unhelpfully, these were renumbered as a result—something that has done little to promote the clarity of Union law. The treaties were renumbered again following the entry into force of the Lisbon Treaty. Regrettably, the Treaty of Amsterdam added even more protocols, thus making even more obscure an overall picture of EC and EU law. The Treaty of Amsterdam, according to some, did very little; others regard it as a needed consolidation of European political union, although the tangible benefits and progress are hard to discern. Additionally, the Treaty of Amsterdam seemed to throw a spanner in the works of further integration by the replacement of further supranational integration with the possibility of allowing some member states to cooperate further, without all member states having to do so. It introduced Art 11 into the EC Treaty, and into the TEU a section (Arts 43 et seq, now Art 20 TEU) on 'closer cooperation' that allows any number of member states that so wish to integrate in other areas. This seemed to make the fragmentation of the Communities even more possible and to allow for the possibility that the body of Community law known as the *acquis communautaire*, which applies in all member states in the same way, could be undermined as different combinations of member states go their own way with particular policies. Thus far, this has not been taken advantage of, but it has been further defined and regulated, albeit rather untidily, by the Lisbon Treaty (Art 20 TEU and Arts 326–34 TFEU), but with no minimum number of states required.

The Treaty of Amsterdam, as finally agreed, proved to be far from the solution needed for preparing for enlargement, consolidating the political union and establishing a firm basis for European governance. It did too little to restore public faith and confidence in the Union. As a result of the fact that Amsterdam failed to resolve the institutional reforms considered essential for the next big enlargement of the EU, there was so much left over that had to be addressed before enlargement could take place that yet another IGC was deemed necessary and was called to deal with the leftovers.

1.6.10 **The Nice Intergovernmental Conference and Treaty**

The IGC was convened in February 2000 with the more tightly drawn objectives of institutional change ahead of enlargement. The summit in December 2000 proved to be the most difficult and drawn-out thus far. It was finally agreed at 5.00 am on 11 December 2000, prompting some of the heads of state to declare at the end that 'such an IGC and Council should not be allowed to happen again'.[58] The member states wrangled mainly over the extension of QMV and voting weights in Council, and the conclusions reached were neither conclusive nor satisfactory, despite the various statements of success following the summit. The size of the Commission was also a contentious issue. QMV was extended to 27 more treaty Articles, but not in as many areas as proposed by the Commission because of the various red lines drawn by countries which, cumulatively, significantly reduced the extension.

The discussions were also drawn-out because of the arguments over the combinations of country votes to get a qualified majority or a blocking minority, and even qualifications on a majority were devised defining a minimum number of states and/or a percentage (62 per cent) of population of the EU required. In particular, the big three member states, France, Germany, and the UK, were fighting to keep their level of influence against the wishes of many of the smaller states, and whilst agreement was reached at Nice on the voting formula, it was very much an imperfect one as was soon shown to be the case. The co-decision procedure was extended again for the European Parliament and the ultimate maximum size of the Commission was also postponed again.

The Treaty of Nice was signed by the member states in February 2001, but did not enter into force until 1 February 2003, because of its rejection by a single member state once again. This time, the Irish electorate decided to show its Eurosceptic credentials and, in June 2001, voted against ratification of the Treaty of Nice, on a 35 per cent turn-out of the electorate. When the government was returned to power with an increased majority, a second referendum was organized which resulted in a far more positive endorsement of the treaty by the Irish electorate (about 63 per cent in favour). At the same time, the Irish introduced a second question that asked for approval for future moves on integration to be put to a referendum only if the Irish Parliament considers that the changes are so great as to necessitate an amendment to the Constitution. Ireland did, however, in 2008, put the Lisbon Treaty to a referendum and rejected it, as considered further in Section 1.6.12.

---

[58] See the comments in particular by Tony Blair and French President Jacques Chirac: **http://news.bbc. co.uk/1/hi/not_in_website/syndication/monitoring/media_reports/1065523.stm.**

The Nice Treaty did not bring about any further radical change to the Union, but further defined certain policies previously adopted and made other adjustments in preparation for the 'big bang' expansion of the Union with ten additional members.

One policy that was tightened was the 'closer cooperation' provision introduced by the Treaty of Amsterdam, so that there was a minimum requirement of eight states for those which wished to pursue this cooperation and, more importantly, they were required to adhere to the *acquis communautaire*. Note, though, that the requirement for a minimum of eight states has not been retained by the Lisbon Treaty.

It was agreed that a Charter of Fundamental Human Rights should be included within the Union, although the member states did not, or could not, agree that it should formally be a part of the treaty or of the Union, so it was not therefore legally binding within the legal order. The Union was still committed to the respect for and observation of human rights and fundamental freedoms (Art 6 TEU) and, in any case, the Court of Justice had already built up a considerable body of case law upholding fundamental rights in the Community legal order. The Nice Treaty also introduced a provision designed to do something about the situation in which there was a clear risk of a serious breach by a member state of one of the respected principles of liberty, democracy, respect for human rights and fundamental freedoms, and the rule of law contained in Art 6 TEU. This change was provoked as a result of the lack of anything originally contained within the treaties to deal with such a situation when this very prospect looked threatening. At the start of 2000, an Austrian government was formed containing the right-wing Freedom Party (FPÖ) led by Jörg Haider, who has been known over the years for making inflammatory racist statements. Whether there was a real threat or not, the inclusion of this party in the government of one of the member states of the EU was not appreciated by the other member states, which took political sanctions against Austria and sent an expert there to assess the situation. None of the moves were authorized, though, by any provision in the treaties. Now, Art 7 TEU provides that a risk of breach can be determined and recommendations to deal with the situation can be agreed by a majority decision, including suspension of voting rights of the member state concerned.

The Nice Council Summit provided, finally, a 'Declaration on the Future of the Union' that was to address a number of issues for the next IGC, which was planned for 2003. These were to include a better definition and understanding of 'subsidiarity', to determine the status of the Charter, and to simplify the treaties (a final admission of the complexity of the treaties as they have accumulated, and indeed even been added to, by the agreements at Nice). Other issues to be addressed were the use of so many protocols and declarations, and how national parliaments feed their legitimacy into the Union. It also provided that a Convention on the Future of Europe be established to draft a 'Constitutional' Treaty for the EU.

To that end, the Laeken Summit was held in December 2001 to set up formally and prepare the agenda for the Convention. It laid out in a declaration the goals for making the EU more democratic, transparent, and efficient. In particular, attention would be paid to the governance of the Union, institutional preparations for the forthcoming expansion, the division of competences, and democratic participation in decision-making processes of the Union.[59]

---

[59] See the presidency conclusions of the Laeken Summit at **http://ue.eu.int/ueDocs/cms_Data/docs/ pressData/en/ec/68827.pdf**; and on the division of competences, see Chapter 3, Section 3.5.

1.6.11 **The Constitutional Treaty for Europe**

Whilst, strictly considered this whole topic should be regarded as historical interest only, an appreciation of this tortured period in the EU's history and development is helpful to understand the position in which the EU finds itself now.

A Constitutional Convention was set up in March 2002, headed by a praesidium of 12 members and led by Valerie Giscard d'Estaing, the former French president. It consisted of representatives of the heads of state and government of the 15 member states and the 13 candidate countries, 30 representatives of the national parliaments and 26 from the candidate countries, 16 Members of the European Parliament (MEPs), and two members from the Commission. It was intended to involve the peoples of Europe, and be a new and different way of preparing change in comparison with the usual government-only IGCs. It was charged with looking at how the EU related to its citizens (and vice versa), how competences should be divided between the Union and the constituent states, and, within the Union, how competences were shared between the institutions. It was also to look at the question of democratic legitimacy. The Convention presented a Constitutional Treaty to the European Council in Greece on 18 July 2003, and the draft Constitutional Treaty was presented to the Heads of State and Government Summit in December 2003.

Whilst the vast majority of changes were accepted by all member states, they could not agree on voting figures in Council, and the summit broke down on this point. The failure, at the time, was the most public and notable failure in the history of the Union. The recriminations started immediately afterwards and the finger of blame pointed most notably at the large states of Poland, Germany, France, Spain, Italy, and the UK. Ironically, agreement had been reached on every other issue but, by not reaching agreement on this last matter and instead walking away and abandoning the attempt to agree, everything in the draft Constitutional Treaty was potentially up for renegotiation and further disagreement in the future. What was agreed included: transferring power to the EU on 15 new policy domains; transferring 40 Article bases from unanimity to QMV; making the Charter of Fundamental Rights legally binding; giving the EU the status of a legal person to negotiate international agreements for all member countries; creating a common EU foreign minister to lead a joint foreign ministry with ambassadors, a fixed president for the Council, and qualified majority voting for the election of all high-positioned officials; commencing the project of a common EU defence; and entitling the next treaty 'Constitution', with the express statement that it should have primacy over the national constitutions. In all, it would have been no mean feat, but in December 2003, it was a failure.

After the failed Rome Summit, ten new member states joined on 1 May 2004, on the basis of the Nice Treaty. This event, and the low turn-out in the European Parliament elections in early June 2004, seemed to refocus the attention of the member states on reaching agreement on the Constitution, which was finally signed in October 2004 by the member states in Rome and handed over to each of the member states to ratify by parliamentary approval or referendum, or both, according to the constitutional or legal requirements of each state.

After 14 member states had ratified, the process of ratification was interrupted by the rejection of the treaty by the electorates of France and Holland in June 2005. It was agreed that there should be a period of reflection, but that the ratification process should continue. In the meantime, therefore, the Treaty of Nice and any protocols and declarations on transitional measures remained in force.

1.6.12 **The 2007 Lisbon Treaty**

Following the two-year period of reflection about the Constitutional Treaty, the member states returned to considering the next move in Brussels in June 2007. The Constitutional Treaty was officially abandoned and an agreement was reached for a new amending treaty, called then the 'Reform Treaty', but now most commonly referred to as the 'Lisbon Treaty', which did not replace the existing treaties, but instead amended them. A new IGC was convened in July 2007 to hammer out the details. Many of the features agreed for the Constitutional Treaty were incorporated into the Lisbon Treaty, which was agreed in December 2007. Unfortunately, however, the amendment of the then existing treaties was considerable.

The main changes can be summarized as follows.

- The TEU was turned more into an overview treaty and the EC Treaty was renamed the 'Treaty on the Functioning of the European Union (TFEU)' dealing with substantive issues; both, however, still concern the institutions. The Union obtained legal personality and the term 'Community' was replaced throughout by 'Union'.

- The proposed Union Minister for Foreign Affairs is called instead the 'High Representative of the Union for Foreign Affairs and Security Policy'.

- The European Council was made an official institution with a president appointed for a term of office of two and a half years to replace the six-month rotating presidency. The rotation of the Council presidency remains six-monthly. Both were envisaged by the Constitutional Treaty.

- The Lisbon Treaty retained the simplified procedure by which the treaty can be revised in new Art 48 TEU.

- The Charter on Fundamental Rights became legally binding, but with an opt-out for the UK and Poland on the application of the Charter in purely domestic situations, and by a later political deal also for the Czech Republic.[60]

Hence, far from consolidating the treaty, protocols, and declarations, the European leaders have made the constitutional architecture of the Union even more complicated and fragmented. The treaty was signed in Lisbon on 13 December 2007 by all 27 member states and was planned to enter into force on 1 January 2009, provided that all member states ratified it. However, that ratification process was thrown into confusion by the rejection by the Irish electorate.

At the Brussels Summit in December 2008, in exchange for agreement by Ireland to hold a second referendum, EU leaders agreed to provide legal guarantees relating to Ireland's taxation policies, its military neutrality, and ethical issues. More controversially, they also agreed that each state should maintain one Commissioner each, keeping the present total at 27, with the hope that the Irish electorate would subsequently agree to ratify the treaty. These agreements were formalized in an agreement at the June 2009 European Council Summit.[61] Following the positive vote in favour of the Lisbon Treaty at the beginning of October 2009, Ireland and Poland ratified the treaty, followed by the Czech Republic, after securing an exemption from the Charter of Fundamental Rights, noted earlier, and after hearing from the Czech Constitutional Court that the treaty did not conflict with the Czech Constitution. The treaty then, after such a long delay, quickly

---

[60] Now contained in Declaration 53 attached to the treaties, although it has to be stated it was never intended to apply in purely domestic situations, only those concerned with EU matters.

[61] **http://www.consilium.europa.eu/uedocs/cms_data/docs/pressdata/en/ec/108622.pdf.** Now officialized in the 2013 Irish protocol attached to the treaties, OJ 2013 L60/131.

entered into force on 1 December 2009 and the many changes that it brought in are noted in this text in the following chapters.

1.7 Future Developments and Conclusions

The two most immediate concerns are ones that continue the themes already identified earlier—that is, the further widening and deepening of the Union. The further widening of the Union has already been considered in detail, but does represent a serious challenge for the cohesion of the Union—particularly in respect to the attitudes already voiced about possible Turkish membership. The process of further deepening is also continuing following the entry into force of the Lisbon Treaty. Does this mean that we are any nearer a true federal union? Of course, as noted earlier, there is not a single and fixed view of what is a 'federal state'; rather, there are many, but the question is whether the EU displays enough of the characteristics of a state that is federally organized to be considered one. And if not now, then just how much more is necessary and to what extent, if any, was the Lisbon Treaty a step in this direction?

At present, the EU enjoys the transfer of considerable powers from the member states, its own institutions and law-making powers, an internal market, a division of powers and competences, the supremacy of EU law, its own binding catalogue of fundamental rights, its own parliament, and also some of the more symbolic external trappings of statehood, such as a currency, a flag, an anthem, and a national day (although these have been removed from the treaties under the Lisbon Treaty).[62] It has a citizenship,[63] but no *demos*; that is, no coherent European population that identifies itself with an embryonic European state.

It has been shown that the path to European unity is not straight and wide, and is far from certain. It is not planned in advance and any plans that are put in place can easily be hijacked by rapidly evolving European and world political events, such as oil price increases, world economic crises, currency collapses, the collapse of communism in Europe, the terrorist attacks of 11 September 2001, and more recently the world-wide banking crisis leading to the continuing euro difficulties. The widening and deepening of the EU, whilst considered under separate headings, are inextricably linked matters. The Union has been deepened in order to cope with forthcoming planned widenings (for example, the first expansion) and deepenings have prompted subsequent widenings (as with the SEA prompting the EFTA expansion). Expansion reveals difficulties that have to be addressed at the next opportunity, which has to be an IGC set up to discuss measures either to deepen the Union or to widen it. Whilst the 25 member states were able to agree on the Constitutional Treaty, they were not able to ratify it and, following the rejection by the Irish of the Lisbon Treaty, that too was in doubt for a while. The Union of 28, and possibly more in the future, will play an increasingly important role in world affairs, not only economically, but also politically, and if for no other reason than because of its economic size. It needs to adapt to do this and, internally also, it still needs to address the issues of governance and democracy—not dealt with properly to date.

However, European integration was regarded from the beginning as a process and not an end in itself. The Constitutional Treaty and its replacement, the Lisbon Treaty, have

---

[62] Note, though, that 16 member states agreed Declaration 52 attached to the treaties that the flag, anthem, motto, euro, and Europe Day would continue as symbols to express the community of the people in the EU and their allegiance to it.

[63] To be explored in Chapter 9.

been regarded as both an example of further deeper integration, because they represent a far more comprehensive ordering of the Union and member states, and also as a brake on further unwelcome integration, because of their clearer delineation of competences. The Lisbon Treaty makes matters clearer and sets discernible boundaries on the exercise of Union power. It remains an unfolding story and the end is not yet written, but quite what the end is will no doubt also continue to be the subject of considerable debate.[64]

Further Reading

Books

BACHE, I. et al *Politics in the European Union*, 4th edn, Oxford University Press, Oxford, 2014.

BLAIR, A. *The European Union since 1945*, Pearson Longman, Harlow, 2005.

CINI, M. and BORRAGAN, N. *European Union Politics*, 3rd edn, Oxford University Press, Oxford, 2009.

CRAIG, P. *The Lisbon Treaty: Law, Politics and Treaty Reform*, Oxford University Press, Oxford, 2010.

DEVUYST, Y. *The European Union Transformed: Community Method and Institutional Evolution from the Schuman Plan to the Constitution for Europe*, rev'd and updated edn, Peter Lang, Brussels, 2006.

DUCHENE, F. *Jean Monnet: The First Statesman of Interdependence*, W. W. Norton & Co., New York, 1996.

EECKHOUT, P. *EU External Relations Law*, 2nd edn, Oxford University Press, Oxford, 2011.

HILLION, C. (ed) *EU Enlargement: A Legal Approach*, Hart Publishing, Oxford, 2004.

NICHOLLS, A. 'Britain and the EC: The Historical Background' in S. Bulmer et al (eds) *The UK and EC Membership*, Pinter Press, London, 1992.

PRECHAL, S. *Reconciling the Deepening and Widening of the European Union*, Cambridge University Press, Cambridge, 2008.

ROSAS, A. and ARMATI, L. *EU Constitutional Law: An Introduction*, Hart Publishing, Oxford, 2010.

SCHÜTZE, R. *European Constitutional Law*, Cambridge University Press, Cambridge, 2012.

SZYSZCZAK, E. and CYGAN, A. *Understanding EU Law*, 2nd edn, Sweet & Maxwell, London, 2008.

TATHAM, A. *Enlargement of the European Union*, Kluwer Law International, London, 2009.

WALL, S. *A Stranger in Europe: Britain and the EU from Thatcher to Blair*, Oxford University Press, Oxford, 2008.

WARD, I. *A Critical Introduction to European Law*, 3rd edn, Cambridge University Press, Cambridge, 2009 (in particular chs 1, 2, and 7).

Articles

BARRETT, G. '"The King is Dead, Long Live the King": The Recasting by the Treaty of Lisbon of the Provisions of the Constitutional Treaty Concerning National Parliaments' (2008) 33 EL Rev 66.

---

[64] A final footnote needs to be added here that in view of the new 2015 UK Conservative Government's promise to re-negotiate membership and hold a referendum on membership by 2017, this will inevitably cause a long period of further uncertainty about the EU and its future.

DREISSEN, B. 'Delegated Legislation after the Treaty of Lisbon: An Analysis of Article 290 TFEU' (2010) 35 EL Rev 837.

DOUGAN, M. 'The Treaty of Lisbon 2007: Winning Minds, Not Hearts' (2008) 45 CML Rev 17.

MAJONE, G. 'Unity in Diversity: European Integration and the Enlargement Process' (2008) 33 EL Rev 457.

MARTINICO, G. 'Dating Cinderella: On Subsidiarity as a Political Safeguard of Federalism in the European Union' (2011) 17 EPL 649.

SCICLUNA, N. 'When Failure Isn't Failure: European Union Constitutionalism after the Lisbon Treaty' (2012) 50 JCMS 441.

Web-based Materials

http://europa.eu/index_en.htm
The European Union website

http://europa.eu/pol/enlarg/index_en.htm
On enlargement of the EU

http://eiop.or.at/eiop/
The European Integration Online Papers website

http://www.fedtrust.co.uk
The Federal Trust for education and research

http://www.federalunion.org.uk
The Federal Union

2

The Union Institutions

2.1 Introduction: The Institutional Framework

The original institutional set-up that was established over 50 years ago has been, in the best of European Union traditions, changed, expanded, and complicated quite considerably since.

The first Community, the European Coal and Steel Community (ECSC), now no longer in existence, set the institutional scene by establishing a mix of supranational and intergovernmental institutions, although the original intention of the founding fathers was to have only the supranational element of the High Authority and not the governmental Council of Ministers. The tripartite system of the Council of Ministers, the Commission (then called the 'High Authority'), and the European Parliament (then called the 'Assembly') was established at that time, and became the institutional foundation that has since been added to and refined considerably. A notable feature has been the changes to law-making which originally consisted of a proposal made by the Commission, which was simply decided upon by the Council of Ministers. The European Parliament, as the forum in which to discuss and debate proposals, would, in a limited number of instances, deliver an opinion on the proposed legislation and thus also play a limited role within this process. Additionally, there is now an overall policy steering body, the European Council, which is a full EU institution following the Lisbon Treaty, and additional consultative bodies (the European Economic and Social Committee (EESC) and the Committee of the Regions (CoR)) to gather together public interest group and regional opinions in order to feed these into the decision-making process. All of these aspects will be considered in this chapter, commencing with a consideration of each of the institutions in turn.

Each of the original three Communities, as first established, had its own set of institutions (a Council of Ministers and a Commission) sharing a common Court of Justice and a Parliamentary Assembly. In 1965, the separate Council and Commission for each Community were merged, and a unitary set of four 'official' institutions was established to serve all three Communities. These were first expanded to five, as the result of the TEU adding the Court of Auditors to the list of principal institutions, and then to seven with the Lisbon Treaty adding the European Council and the European Central Bank (ECB).[1]

Presently, Art 13 TEU states that the Union's institutions shall be: the European Parliament; the European Council; the Council; the Commission; the Court of Justice of the European Union (CoJ); the ECB; and the Court of Auditors. Article 13 TEU requires that each institution shall keep within the limits of the powers conferred on it in the treaties. Article 13(4) provides for two advisory bodies: the EESC and CoR. These are part of a secondary group of bodies completing the institutional structure, and include the Committee of Permanent Representatives (COREPER),

---

[1] See Art 13 TEU for the new list and Art 15 TEU in particular for the European Council.

the European Investment Bank (EIB), and the European System of Central Banks (ESCB). In addition, as the activities and competences of the EU have expanded, there are a large number of supplementary agencies and bodies to oversee those various activities.[2]

The detailed provisions governing the institutions are set out in Part Six of the TFEU, Arts 223–87.

2.2 The Commission

The Commission (otherwise known as the 'European Commission') fulfils the role of an executive administration for the Union and was given the sole right as the proposer of legislation under the original treaties. This remains the case and makes the Commission more powerful than simply a civil service bureaucracy carrying out the will of an elected government. While it is not to be confused with a government itself, it is able to formulate policy within the parameters of the agreed policy areas contained in the treaties and to make proposals for legislation to realize this. The real power of initiative is, however, somewhat compromised by the overall policy formulation and guidance provided by the Council of Ministers and the European Council which, after the entry into force of the Lisbon Treaty, has been provided with a much more formal role in the institutional management of the Union. The Commission also has its own powers of decision generally to be inferred from Art 17 TEU and Art 288(1) TFEU, providing the institutions with law-making powers, and specifically under the competition law policy (Art 105 TFEU). Further, it is able to exercise powers and enact administrative legislation under powers delegated to it by the Council of Ministers,[3] which will be considered in further detail in Section 2.2.3.

2.2.1 Composition of the Commission

The composition, tasks, and functions of the Commission are determined by Arts 17 TEU and 244–50 TFEU.

As the Union itself has increased in membership, so too has the Commission, and whilst it used to be the case that the larger states had two Commissioners each, it became increasingly clear from the 1995 expansion, which saw an increase to 20 Commissioners, that if the Commission were to become too large it would not assist effective management. On a more practical level, there were simply not enough subject matters for an effective and realistic division of work into 20 or more portfolios, and it was agreed during the 2004 accession negotiation discussions that the number of Commissioners should be reduced to less than the number of states, which was originally formally agreed by the Lisbon Treaty in 2007. Realizing the reform aspirations, as with many needed reforms in the Union, has been more difficult than anticipated and, following the deal struck for the second Irish referendum in 2009, this remains the case. It had been agreed that, when the Lisbon Treaty came into force, Art 17 TEU would specify that the number of Commissioners should be reduced to two-thirds of the number of member states as from 1 November 2014. However, as noted, the deal struck with Ireland retains one Commissioner for each state, and under the existing powers granted by Art 17(5) (1st sentence) TEU to the

---

[2] See http://europa.eu/about-eu/agencies/index_en.htm and/or http://europa.eu/epso/success/recru/contacts/agencies_list_cast_en.pdf.

[3] Governed by Arts 290 and 291 TFEU and Regulation 182/2011 (OJ 2011 L55/13).

European Council and Art 244 TFEU, the number of Commissioners can be changed but presently remains at one per state.[4]

The Commissioners, although proposed appointments by the member states, are required to be completely independent in the performance of their duties and not to take or seek instructions from any government or any other body (Art 17(3) TEU and Art 245 TFEU). The Commissioners are often though regarded as each member state's representatives in Brussels but, to counterbalance this view, another view suggests that after a while in Brussels, a member state's Commissioner has a tendency to 'go native'—that is, to adopt a much more Union, rather than national, perspective on things.

In statistics from 2005, the Commission was assisted by about 25,000 staff, and following the 2004 and 2007 expansions of the Union, this figure rose to around 38,000.[5] It is asserted by the Union itself that this is fewer than in most medium-sized city councils in Europe. The Commission, then, is simply not a massive bureaucracy. In the member states there are hundreds of thousands of civil servants, with some single departments employing far more than the entire European Commission.[6] Part of the reason for the much lower numbers in the EU is that most of the work covered or generated by EU legislation is, in fact, carried out by the national agencies—particularly in respect of the Common Agricultural Policy (CAP).

2.2.2 Appointment and Removal

Under rules amended by the Lisbon Treaty, first, the Commission President is proposed by qualified majority voting (QMV) by the European Council under Art 17(7) TEU and is then subject to approval by the European Parliament by majority vote. Such proposals and appointment of the President normally go through unopposed; however in 2014, the UK and Hungary opposed the appointment of Jean-Claude Juncker, the former Luxembourg prime minister, who was nevertheless appointed under a majority vote 26–2. Secondly, the High Representative, who will automatically be one of the Vice-Presidents of the Commission[7] is appointed by QMV of the European Council (Art 18 TEU). Then, the Commission President Elect, with the member states in Council, further nominates the other Commissioners who are subject en bloc to the approval of the European Parliament but then appointed formally by the European Council.[8] This makes the rejection of a single Commissioner Designate technically, although not practically, impossible, as was seen in 2004 and 2014. The European Parliament objected in 2004 to the Italian Commissioner nomination because of his genuinely held, but incongruous, views on homosexuality and the role of women. Commission President Designate Barroso decided not to submit to the Commission for approval in fear of a probable rejection of the entire Commission and

---

[4] Agreement reached at the European Council Summit of 11–12 December 2008. Refer to Document 17271/1/08, http://www.consilium.europa.eu/ueDocs/cms_Data/docs/pressData/fr/ec/104669.pdf, the 2013 Irish Protocol OJ 2013 L60/131, and the decision in OJ 2013 L165/98.

[5] The figure given on the Commission website in 2015, however, puts that figure as 23,000 employed in the central Brussels departments (DGs). Refer to http://ec.europa.eu/about/index_en.htm.

[6] To test this assertion, the author looked at Cardiff, a medium-sized European city, which has about 25,000 staff working directly for the council, plus those who work in the Welsh Assembly in Cardiff and in the many independent agencies undertaking council work, making a total of about 35,000. In the UK, the Office for National Statistics reported in October 2013 a figure of 448,835 direct government civil servants in the UK: http://www.statistics.gov.uk, in particular http://www.ons.gov.uk/ons/taxonomy/index.html?nscl=Government#tab-data-tables.

[7] Considered also in Section 2.4.2.

[8] See the diagram in the Online Resource Centre for this book: www.oxfordtextbooks.co.uk/orc/foster5e/.

instead reshuffled the proposed Commission, with a replaced nomination for Italy, which was then approved by the European Parliament and appointed by the Council. In 2014, each of the Commissioners designated were questioned by the European Parliament (EP) about the portfolio they had been proposed for. As a result, the Hungarian nominee was not approved for the portfolio originally proposed but was accepted for different one. The Slovenian nominee though was rejected outright and a new nominee had to be proposed and approved.[9]

The term of office for all Commissioners is a renewable period of five years (Art 17(3) TEU). There are seven Vice-Presidents in the Juncker Commission (2014–19). The number of Vice-Presidents is no longer specified by the treaty.

The Commission can be removed by a vote of censure by the European Parliament, but only collectively (Art 17(8) TEU and Art 245 TFEU), and until the replacement Commission is appointed in its entirety, the old Commission stays in office. The High Representative, though, is only required to resign as a Commissioner and not as the High Representative. The en-bloc removal is something of a blunt instrument if the objection is to the activities of only one Commissioner; there is, though, the procedure under Art 247 TFEU for the Court of Justice, on an application of the Council or the Commission (but not the European Parliament), to retire a Commissioner compulsorily for serious misconduct or if he or she no longer fulfils the conditions required for the performance of his or her duties. Censure of the entire Commission was threatened in 1999 following a damning report of an independent committee of experts appointed by the European Parliament that exposed serious fraud, cronyism, and incompetence on the part of individual Commissioners. Whilst it did not come to a vote of censure, it forced the resignation of the entire Santer Commission on 15 March 1999 as the only way in which to oust the culpable Commissioners.[10] A new Commission was approved by the European Parliament in September 1999 under the presidency of Prodi, who required from the individual Commissioners a promise to resign on demand, thus increasing the power of the President within the Commission. The Lisbon Treaty has retained this method of mass expulsion, but provides in a new Art 17(6) TEU that a member of the Commission shall resign if the Commission President so requests—a new power given to the President, as yet untested, but which would seem to obviate the need for a mass dismissal by censure if only one or more Commissioners should be removed. Indeed, the prospect of this may have assisted the Maltese Commissioner, involved in a public scandal, in deciding to resign in 2012.[11] Hence it would seem that, in future, the EP need only to threaten to dismiss the entire Commission if the Council or Commission President fail to remove a Commissioner in breach. Commissioners proposed mid-term are appointed by the Council after consulting the EP and obtaining the agreement of the Commission President.

---

[9] A very good overview of the whole process can be found at http://www.elections2014.eu/en/news-room/content/20141017STO74416/html/EP-votes-on-the-new-European-Commission. For a blow-by-blow account of the appointment see http://www.europeanvoice.com/tag/theneweuropeancommission 2014-19/.

[10] In a follow-up to this, Case C-432/04 *Commission v Edith Cresson* confirmed not only that Commissioner Cresson had breached her duties as a Commissioner, but also that the Court of Justice had an independent discretionary right to hear such actions, free from any influence of national courts. The Belgian criminal courts, however, had cleared Cresson of any criminal wrongdoing.

[11] See inter alia the Commission press release: http://europa.eu/rapid/press-release_MEMO-12-788_en.htm and EU Observer report: https://euobserver.com/institutional/117887.

2.2.3 **Tasks and Duties**

Article 17 TEU contains within a single Article a general view of the duties of the Commission—that is, that it shall promote the general interest of the Union and take appropriate initiatives to that end. From that flow a number of duties and functions, as follows:

(a) It must ensure that the provisions of the treaties and the measures taken by the institutions under them are applied. The Commission is described as the 'guardian', or 'watchdog', of the Communities, because it is given the task of prosecuting breaches of the treaty by member states under Art 258 TFEU, other institutions under Art 263 TFEU, and individuals under various provisions of the treaties and secondary legislation, such as Regulation 1/2003 in respect of competition policy.

(b) It formulates and proposes legislative initiatives on matters dealt with in the treaties, if it expressly so provides or if the Commission considers it necessary. Here, the Commission is acting as the initiator of legislation and has the sole right to do so (Art 17(2) TEU), although it may now be requested to submit legislative proposals by either the Council (Art 241 TFEU) or the European Parliament (Art 225 TFEU). The TEU now also provides for a European Citizens' Initiative (ECI) whereby if at least one million citizens from at least seven member states come together, they may request the Commission to submit a proposal (see Arts 11 and 24 TFEU).[12] Whilst a number (28 to November 2014) have been rejected as not coming within the criteria or failing on procedural grounds, others are in progress or have been accepted.[13] There are no guarantees that even if the ECI is accepted, any such legislative proposals will be adopted by the Commission, and even if they are, they may not be approved by the Council or the European Parliament.

(c) The Commission has limited powers of independent decision-making by participation in the shaping of measures taken by the Council of Ministers and by the European Parliament in the manner provided for in the treaties.

(d) It has powers under the delegated legislation procedure conferred on it by the Council of Ministers and European Parliament subject to the possibility of a veto or an approval procedure by the Council or European Parliament (Art 290 TFEU). Article 291 TFEU now governs other instances of the Commission's power to implement legislation which are subject to a revised system of supervisory committees.[14]

(e) The Commission also manages the Union's annual budget.[15]

(f) The Commission also has powers and duties in representing the EU externally.[16]

The Commission is regarded as the most supranational institution of the EU, due largely to its independence from direct national influences. Its decision-making process, under

---

[12] ECIs are now regulated in detail by Regulation 887/2013 and have been available since 1 April 2012. See also the webpage **http://ec.europa.eu/citizens-initiative/public/welcome** and the guide to ECIs **http://ec.europa.eu/citizens-initiative/files/guide-eci-en.pdf**. Clear statistics though are missing as yet from the website.

[13] The Right2Water appears to be the most successful to date, causing the Commission to remove a proposed regulation of water supply from a Concessions Directive: see **http://ec.europa.eu/citizens-initiative/public/welcome** and **http://www.right2water.eu/**.

[14] Implementing powers are regulated by Regulation 182/2011, which provides for supervision by a range of advisory and examination committees, known collectively as 'comitology'.

[15] See Arts 314–19 TFEU for its budgetary duties.   [16] Articles 207 and 218 TFEU.

Art 250 TFEU, provides that the Commission can decide matters collectively by a majority. All members of the Commission are expected to abide collectively by Commission decisions.

Commission activity is most pronounced in the field of competition policy and in the management of the CAP and Common Commercial Policy (CCP), because of the high degree of day-to-day decision-making necessary. It is also very much involved in representing the Union in international organizations such as the General Agreement on Tariffs and Trade (GATT) and the World Trade Organization (WTO), and in concluding international agreements on behalf of the Union, such as the association agreements with various countries.[17]

2.3 The Council (of Ministers) of the European Union

Unfortunately, the Council of Ministers has undergone a few name changes; it is presently known simply as 'the Council', having previously been called 'the Council of Ministers'. Following the Lisbon Treaty, it is to be called officially the 'Council of the Union'. Furthermore, unhelpfully, there is also the European Council, considered in Section 2.4 and now also a main institution, with which it should not be confused.[18] The Council was in the past the main legislative organ of the Union, but with the increased participation of the EP, law-making is increasingly becoming an equal partnership. Its tasks, composition, and functions are outlined in Art 16 TEU and Arts 237–43 TFEU and throughout the treaties. It consists of representative ministers of the member states, depending on the subject matter under discussion. Thus, different configurations of the Council take place, with the foreign ministers attending the General Affairs Council, for example, and agriculture or finance ministers attending the specialist Councils. In total, following the Lisbon Treaty reforms, there are ten different Council configurations, with the General Affairs Council coordinating the work of the other Council configurations, with the exception of the Foreign Affairs Council which is coordinated by the High Representative's Office and chaired by the High Representative.[19]

2.3.1 Functions and Powers

Article 16 TEU imposes on the Council the general requirement to carry out policy-making and coordinating functions, as laid down in the treaties, as well as exercising legislative and budgetary functions jointly with the European Parliament. Article 290 TFEU confers upon it the power to take decisions and to delegate to the Commission. Following the Lisbon Treaty reforms, the Council decides on the adoption of legislative proposals predominantly now by the co-decision procedure, which is that contained within the 'ordinary legislative procedure' (Art 289 TFEU), which provides the European Parliament with an equal say but a final right of veto, as outlined under Art 294 TFEU, considered in Section 2.3.3 on legislative procedures and in Chapter 4. The Council, along with the

---

[17] Which were noted in Chapter 1.

[18] It should also not be confused with the 'Council of Europe', the overall governing body of the European Convention on Human rights: **http://www.coe.int/web/portal/home**.

[19] Art 16 TEU itself just refers to two configurations, the General and Foreign Affairs Councils, but for a full list, see **http://www.consilium.europa.eu/council/council-configurations?lang=en** or OJ (2010) L263/12.

European Parliament, is also responsible for the adoption of the annual budget (Art 314 TFEU).

2.3.2 The Presidency of the Council

The Council is chaired by a presidency that is held by each of the member states in turn for a period of six months only, as determined by Arts 16(9) TEU and 236 TFEU and Council Decision 2007/5.[20] Thus ministers, or the head of government or state, chair the Council meetings or summit for a period of six months. The term 'troika' is used in conjunction with the Council to describe the situation in which, to provide continuity in policy, the current president and both the previous and succeeding presidents act in conjunction, particularly in the pursuit of international relations. The Lisbon Treaty provides that the Foreign Affairs Council is chaired by the High Representative (Art 16(9) TEU).

2.3.3 Role and Voting in the Legislative Procedures

As a result of the numerous institutional reforms over the years, the Council's role in deciding on and enacting secondary legislation is slowly being matched by the EP, distinctly so in the ordinary legislative procedure, but not in the special legislative procedures. Quite how, and with whom the Council acts depends on the particular treaty provision under which legislation is enacted—that is, on the legal base. As was outlined in Chapter 1, in broad terms, the political institutional balance has seen a number of movements over the decades, mostly in favour of a power shift from the Council to the European Parliament in the law-making process. However, it is not only the European Parliament that participates with the Council, and it may have to consult the EESC and/or the CoR. In considering its participation with the European Parliament alone, there are different procedures for law-making, as will be explained in detail later. When legislating, the Council is obliged now to meet in public (Art 16(8) TEU).

2.3.3.1 Forms of Voting

There are different forms of decision-making within the Council itself; that is, ways in which it takes decisions or votes. In contrast to the previous treaty provision on voting, the new Art 16(3) TEU is a much more accurate reflection of both law and practice. Article 16(3) provides that the Council shall act by a qualified majority except where the treaties provide otherwise. Following the Lisbon Treaty reforms, QMV is by far the most common method of voting, although it would be usual practice for the Council President to attempt to gain the consensus of all member states before proceeding to take a formal decision. A requirement of unanimity is now much rarer.

2.3.3.2 Unanimity

Turning to the methods themselves, unanimity is clear: all member states must agree, which means all 28 from the year 2013. This is where the member states can wield a veto: see, for example, when acting under Art 19 TFEU requiring unanimity on the part of the Council to enact measures outlawing different forms of discrimination. The more that voting is done on this basis, the less that potentially and probably will get done, hence a move to more majority voting is crucial. Member states that abstain do not prevent the others

---

[20] OJ 2007 L1/11. See also Decision 2009/881 (OJ 2009 L315/50) and Decision 2009/908 (OJ 2009 L322/28) on the exercise of the presidency and conduct of meetings.

from agreeing a measure unanimously, which is then binding on all (Art 238(4) TFEU). Unanimity is still used in a considerable number of treaty Articles (almost 40), especially following the Lisbon Treaty amendments, which brought within the treaties structure areas of law previously lying purely within the intergovernmental EU Treaty, such as Common Foreign and Security Policy (CFSP), and policing. It is also retained for taxation and some matters in the areas of the environment and employment.

2.3.3.3 Simple Majority Voting

Simple majority voting, whereby a measure is enacted by an arithmetic majority—for example, by 15 states with 13 against—is quite rare and is required for only eight Articles of the TFEU, concerned mainly with the setting up of advisory committees and the institutions.

Article 238 TFEU defines this requirement as follows: 'Where it is required to act by a simple majority, the Council shall act by a majority of its component members.'

2.3.3.4 Qualified Majority Voting

In 1965, the Council was due to move from unanimity to QMV for certain subject areas of the treaty. This was objected to by French President de Gaulle and the ensuing dispute led eventually to a boycott of the institutions by the French members. It was only resolved when a compromise, called the 'Luxembourg Accords' or 'Luxembourg Compromise', was reached.[21] This was essentially an agreement to disagree, but provided that, were a member state to identify a very important national interest, all of the member states should try to reach a unanimous decision rather than overrule that member. The six member states could not, however, agree on the consequence of a failure to agree. The conclusion, which was certainly that of the French and generally accepted, was that an objecting member state effectively had a veto over the decision. The legal position of the Accords was uncertain, but despite the provision in the treaty for majority voting and QMV, the Council denied itself this ability for many years. Successive enlargements and the difficulties in reaching a consensus led the Council to realize that it could no longer make progress using only unanimity. Thus, particularly after the treaty revisions of the Single European Act (SEA) and the TEU, the Council has moved slowly, but significantly, to using QMV in more and more areas (on 12 occasions with the SEA and 30 more with the TEU)—so much so, in fact, that the continued validity of the Luxembourg Accords had been brought into doubt. The Amsterdam and Nice Treaties extended the use of QMV in another 47 instances and Lisbon by another 44 instances.[22] Unanimous voting will be retained for a few matters, particularly measures considered necessary to fulfil certain EU aims, but for which express powers have not been foreseen. Unanimity has been retained for the areas of CFSP and defence policies, taxation, social security matters, and appointments to some of the institutions.

More use of QMV is necessary because it allows votes to be taken by majorities. The possible alternative—that is, to take decisions by simple majority—is not a real alternative because it is not politically acceptable for most member states. Thus, the use of QMV enhances both democracy and efficiency in law-making in the EU where otherwise decisions would be extremely difficult to reach in a Council of 28 possible vetoes. It also may

---

[21] Considered in Section 1.6.6.2.

[22] The Council website states that it is used now in 85 policy areas: **http://www.consilium.europa.eu/en/ council-eu/decision-making/**.

be argued to encourage debate as objecting member states cannot simply fall back on a veto but must seek to persuade other states to object by argument.

2.3.3.5 How QMV Works

The voting figures and procedure for QMV are contained not just in the Treaties (Art 16 TEU & Art 238 TFEU) but also in Protocol 36 on Transitional Provisions, Title II and further qualified by Declaration 7 on Arts 16(4) and (5), both attached to the treaties. Each member state has a block number of votes crudely in proportion to the size of the population and economic power but, instead of a simple majority of states or votes being able to secure a decision, a certain majority of votes has to be achieved from the combination of the blocks of votes of the member states.[23] The qualified majority is now 260 votes (73.86 per cent) from a possible total of 352. Thus, a blocking minority of 92 votes will prevent a proposal from being passed. If voting on a proposal that has been introduced by the Council, other institution, or member state rather than the Commission, an additional requirement is imposed that a minimum of 72 per cent of the member states must have voted in favour and that if a member state so requests, the total must represent a minimum of 65 per cent of the EU population.[24]

The actual numbers of votes per state has always been a matter of contention and particularly so for the larger states. Prior to the reforms adopted at Nice, at the extreme, Germany, with a population of approximately 81 million, had ten votes in comparison with Luxembourg, with a population of about 600,000, which had two votes. This was clearly disproportionate. Prior to the last enlargement, it was noted that with a greater number of states, a blocking minority would be harder to achieve because it required more votes and thus more countries. At the same time, though, it was noted that as the number of states increased, the relative share of influence of the large states decreased, despite their high share of the population. It is worth noting that four countries—Germany, France, the UK, and Italy—had just over 57 per cent of the EU-25 population and approximately 53 per cent in the EU-28; therefore, if voting were undertaken by simple majority based directly on population, it would mean that the four large states could dictate to the other 24 states. However, because such behaviour would not be acceptable to the small and medium-sized states, various compromises have been made to the voting rules—at first, informal, and then institutionalized and retained with some elaboration in the Lisbon Treaty. The compromises seek to achieve a balance between facilitating decision-making, but nevertheless providing that a sizeable minority of states can block decisions. Hence, the reform of QMV became a hotly contended issue, with the debate first concentrating on the number of votes per member state, and then on the additional requirements based on the number of states voting and the populations of those states.

To go back to basics for a moment, the idea is that the number of Council votes per country should in some way, even if very crudely, represent the population and the gross domestic product (GDP) of the countries or, to put it another way, the political and economic clout. This is tinged with the fear of domination of Europe by a few large states over the wishes of numerous smaller states. Hence, the votes for each country for a qualified majority were deliberately biased for the protection of smaller states and to ensure more of

---

[23] France, Germany, Italy, UK—29; Poland, Spain—27; Romania—14; Netherlands—13; Belgium, Czech Republic, Greece, Hungary, Portugal—12; Austria, Bulgaria, Sweden—10; Croatia, Denmark, Finland, Ireland, Lithuania, Slovakia—7; Cyprus, Estonia, Latvia, Luxembourg, Slovenia—4; and Malta—3. TOTAL—352; QM is 260 (= 73.86%).

[24] See Art 3 of Protocol 36, in N. Foster (ed), *EU Treaties and Legislation*, latest edn, Oxford University Press, Oxford.

a consensus. The Treaty of Nice went some way towards addressing the over-representation of the smaller states by giving the larger member states a higher proportion of votes, but still disproportionate compared to the smaller states. However, it was not accepted without further condition because this change meant that a smaller combination of larger states could outvote the small states—something with which the smaller member states were not happy, hence further compromises had been devised for the Treaty of Nice. Even with the Nice reforms, Malta—the smallest state with a population of about 390,000, but three votes in Council—has a voting power far in excess of its population in comparison with Germany, with 82 million population and 29 votes. However, as soon as Nice was agreed, it became clear that Germany and other states were not happy with the voting figures. It was agreed, however, not to reopen the agreement reached at Nice, which had been—almost literally—a nightmare to achieve.[25]

The next opportunity to address this was not far away: the European Council Summit to discuss and agree the draft Constitutional Treaty, as proposed by the Convention on the Future of Europe. However, it became clear that without changing the actual number of votes, as agreed in Nice, any possibility of addressing the continuing concerns about the imbalance of votes could only be done through further tinkering with the proportions of states required to vote in favour of a proposal and/or the proportion of the population of the EU as a whole that should be required to support a qualified majority vote.

Following the entry into force of the Lisbon Treaty, QMV will operate as follows. The voting figures remain the same but the support of a specified majority of member states and percentage of the EU population is required. These will be governed by Art 16 TEU, Art 238 TFEU, Protocol 36 on Transitional Provisions, and Declaration No 7 attached to the treaties.

From 1 November 2014, the situation outlined in Art 16(4) TEU is as follows.

- Between 2014–17, the rules under the new treaties require that a qualified majority must comprise at least 55 per cent of Council members comprising at least 16 states and 65 per cent population. Where the Council does not act on a proposal from the Commission or from the High Representative of the Union for Foreign Affairs and Security Policy, the qualified majority needs to be 72 per cent of the members of the Council. However, the Declaration[26] insists that if states having either at least 75 per cent of population or 75 per cent of the blocking votes oppose that, then these rules do not apply and discussions must continue. The blocking minority must also achieve a threshold of four states (Art 16(4) TEU) to prevent a small minority of large member states from blocking a proposal representing at least 35 per cent of the EU population plus one state (Art 238(3) TFEU).

- From 1 April 2017, when a single state can no longer ask that a population requirement be imposed, the requirements to oppose are reduced to 55 per cent of population or sufficient member states that constitute a blocking minority; in which case they can also ask the Council to continue discussions.

The end result is, of course, another example of the political power and numbers games that the member states find so important, but it does mean that the EU attempts to make law-making more democratic, transparent, and efficient have been hindered. Instead, the process has become far from transparent and easy to understand. One needs to have in mind both treaties (Art 16 TEU and Art 238 TFEU), and Protocol 36 and Declaration No 7,

---

[25] See the discussion in Chapter 1, Section 1.6.10.
[26] N. Foster (ed), *EU Treaties and Legislation*, latest edn, Oxford University Press, Oxford.

to see the full picture on QMV in Council—a genuinely deplorable situation. Of course, most legislative decisions will be reached either by consensus being achieved or by a clear majority, but the exception-riddled rule on QMV makes it exceedingly difficult to gain a clear understanding of how QMV or indeed any voting in Council actually happens.

2.3.4 Council General Law-making Powers

Apart from voting that is specified in particular Articles throughout the treaty, the Council also has general powers to enact legislation. Article 113 TFEU empowers the Council of Ministers, acting unanimously, to adopt provisions for the harmonization of legislation concerning turnover taxes, excise duties, and other forms of indirect taxes—value added tax (VAT)—to the extent that such harmonization is necessary to ensure the functioning and establishment of the internal market. Article 114 TFEU provides that the Council shall act by a qualified majority on a proposal that has as its object the establishment and functioning of the internal market. Article 115 TFEU, as an exception to Art 114, provides for the approximation of laws not catered for by any of the specific parts of the treaty and requires unanimity by the Council.

Article 352 TFEU is the most general of law-making powers and provides that the Council may enact measures to attain the objectives of the Union. This general power has been used extensively by the Council, particularly for measures not originally sanctioned elsewhere, such as in 1976 to support the enactment of the Equal Treatment Directive (76/207), which went much further than old Art 119 (now Art 157 TFEU), which was concerned narrowly with equal pay matters only. It was used often to enact environmental measures before the treaty was amended to include a Title on Environment. However, its proposed use to accede to the European Convention on Human Rights (ECHR) was prevented by the Court of Justice, which stated, in Opinion 1/96, that it could not be used as the basis for acceding to the ECHR. The overuse of the general powers, referred to as 'competence creep', has been criticized and resisted by the member states. It was addressed both in the Constitutional Treaty and Lisbon Treaty, by more clearly establishing the division of competences (considered further in Chapter 3). The power for the Union to accede to the ECHR is now specifically provided for in the amended Art 6(2) TEU.

2.3.5 The Committee of Permanent Representatives (COREPER) and the Council Secretariat

The Council is not a unitary or permanent body, as noted earlier, and in all configurations meets only on about 90 occasions per year. Hence, then, it requires assistance to deal with the workload and to provide preparation for, and some continuity between, meetings. This help comes in two forms.

COREPER consists of representatives of the member states, who may be part of the ambassadorial delegation or other civil servants on secondment. It is now formally established within Arts 16(7) and 240 TFEU. This body was brought in to reduce the workload of the Council, to balance the result of the delegation of decision-making power to the Commission, and to sift the Commission proposals. It also oversees and, to a lesser extent, controls the numerous management committees that were set up to supervise the delegation of power to the Commission and which are considered further later.

Article 240(2) TFEU also provides for a permanent Council General Secretariat to undertake much of the more mundane work of the Council, such as organization of, and preparation for, meetings. It will also help the new High Representative in the new External Action Service (Art 27(2) TEU).

2.4 **The European Council**

The European Council, which the Lisbon Treaty established as a formal institution of the Union, arose from the summit meetings of the heads of state and government of the member states, who met from time to time to discuss matters outside the formal scope of the Community treaties and to provide impetus for the Community (and now Union) or act in response to international crises. After this informal start, Art 2 SEA placed the European Council on a legal basis and formalized European Political Cooperation in the areas of foreign policy consultation and cooperation, and monetary cooperation. These moves have been further formalized and brought into the EU framework by Arts 13 and 15 TEU. The European Council now comprises the 28 heads of state and government in addition to the new European President and the President of the European Commission (Art 15(2) TEU), the latter two of whom do not have voting rights (Art 235(1) TFEU). The new High Representative for Foreign Affairs and the Foreign Minister may also participate in its meetings, but also without voting rights.

Article 15 TEU provides that the European Council shall give the Union the necessary impetus for its development and shall define its general political direction and priorities. Note, though, that legislative functions are specifically excluded. It, therefore, enjoys a much broader role than the Council of Ministers, which is restricted to matters included in the treaties.

The European Council will meet at least twice every six months and member states' ministers may also take part, as may an assistant to the Commission President (Art 15(3) TEU). It will meet every time in Brussels in a purpose-built headquarters rather than, as before, in the member state holding the Council presidency.

Previously, decision-making was entirely by consensus whereas now, in certain areas, as provided by the treaty and as noted in this volume, it also decides by QMV. One of the most notable instances of this, which is also one of the most—if not *the* most—notable institutional changes introduced, is the establishment of the new position of the European President, which will be considered separately in the section following. It appoints the High Representative by qualified majority (Art 18 TEU) and decides on the composition of the European Parliament and the membership, both by unanimity (Art 14(2) TEU and Arts 17(5) TEU and 244 TFEU, respectively).

The European Council has been criticized for being a purely intergovernmental organization and for presenting a distinctly intergovernmental attitude at the top of the Union institutional hierarchy. Whilst it has, at times, provided the necessary political will and impetus to achieve very notable goals, such as economic union and the euro, it is feared that trying to achieve the agreement of 28 heads of state or government will prove very demanding. It is regarded, post-Lisbon, as having gained in status and power, not least because of the continuity of leadership and thus direction provided by the more permanent and independent President.

2.4.1 **The European Council President**

New to the Union, brought forward from the Constitutional Treaty to the Lisbon Treaty is the creation of a President for the European Council, known already as the 'European President'. Election to the post is by the European Council by qualified majority for a period of two-and-a-half years, renewable once. Herman Van Rompey was the first European Council President elected, who stood down as premier of Belgium to comply with the requirement of independence (Art 15(6) TEU). He was re-elected unopposed by the European Council for a second term on 1 March 2012 with a term of office ending 30 November 2014. The Former Polish Prime Minister Donald Tusk was elected unanimously as his successor.[27]

The President is provided with the tasks of chairing the European Council and driving forward and organizing its work in cooperation with the Commission and General Affairs Council. He or she shall seek to obtain consensus by the European Council and report to the European Parliament after each of the meetings (Art 15(6) TEU). He or she shall also oversee the external representation of the Union, without prejudice to the powers of the High Representative.

2.4.2 The High Representative of the Union for Foreign Affairs and Security Policy

The High Representative[28] is, first of all, chosen from amongst the Commissioners, then elected by the European Council by qualified majority, and then automatically becomes a Commission Vice-President (Art 18 TEU). The High Representative conducts the CFSP, chairs Council foreign affairs meetings, leads the Commission in external relations, and is assisted by an external action service set up for this purpose (Art 27 TEU).

2.5 The European Parliament

As originally conceived and constituted, the European Parliament was called the 'Assembly', and consisted of members nominated by and largely from the member states' parliaments. It was arguably more aptly named at that time because it was not a true legislative body capable of law-making in its own right and consisted of only one chamber. However, the term 'Parliament' was used by its members from 1962,[29] and with more authority following the direct election of its 518 members for the first time in 1979. The term arguably carries more prestige and very arguably attracts greater respect from the public. Consequently, Art 6 SEA provided legal recognition of the Assembly's decision to call itself the 'European Parliament', which is clearly confirmed by Art 14 TEU. The European Parliament is governed by Art 14 TEU and Arts 223–34 TFEU, and has enjoyed significant incremental increases in its powers and functions with each new amending treaty.

One of the biggest problems with which the European Parliament has to contend, through no fault of its own, is the requirement that it still meet in plenary session in Strasbourg, but also meet in Brussels and have the Secretariat based in Luxembourg, whilst its members commute back and forth from their national constituencies. Its seat was supposed to have been settled a long time ago, but none of the countries involved is willing to lose the presence of the European Parliament despite the massive increase in costs in which this results and, worse, the inefficiency engendered due to the waste of time and resources. Case law has been generated by this vexed issue in which the European Parliament understandably argues for a permanent presence in Brussels to join the Commission, the Council, and now the European Council, whereas France notably, also for understandable reasons, argues for

---

[27] http://www.european-council.europa.eu/the-president/biography?lang=en.
[28] http://eeas.europa.eu/high-representative-about/index_en.htm.
[29] Resolution of 30 March 1962 (OJ 1962 C1045).

maintaining Strasbourg as the plenary home of the European Parliament. Thus far, France has succeeded even when the European Parliament tried only to reduce by one and not abolish the plenary sessions, as the rulings of the Court of Justice probably represent the official treaty and protocols position.[30] The European Parliament therefore appears destined to be in transit between the plenary sessions in Strasbourg, additional sessions in Brussels, and its Secretariat in Luxembourg. See now Protocol 6 attached to the treaties by the Lisbon Treaty. In 2012, MEPs voted 432–218 for a single seat and also voted to merge plenary sessions in 2012 and 2013 to reduce the number of times they would have to travel and thus reduce all the associated travelling costs. This was challenged successfully again by France.[31]

2.5.1 Membership

Following a number of previous attempts made at the time of previous treaty amendments, the number of MEPs has finally settled at 750 plus the President thus 751.[32] MEPs are elected to serve the electorate in constituencies and are organized into cross-border political groupings, rather than member states, with the total number per state crudely in proportion to population. Further possible expansions will almost certainly cause the issue of membership to be reopened.

2.5.1.1 Elections and Political Parties

Article 223(1) TFEU requires a common system of election to be set up for the election for the European Parliament. While all member states now, including the UK, have used proportional representation voting systems, this is still not a common election, and although the same period of Thursday to the weekend is used, the actual polling days differ across member states according to election-day traditions—for example, the UK prefers a Thursday, whereas other member states have always used a Saturday or Sunday as polling day.[33]

Two cases have marginally increased the franchised electorate of the European Parliament. In Case C-145/04 *Spain v UK*, the Court of Justice condoned the extension of voting rights in European Parliament elections beyond the EU citizens resident in Gibraltar to third-country Commonwealth nationals also lawfully resident there, despite the fact that they did not have UK nationality and thus did not have EU citizenship. The CoJ looked instead for close links of those residents with Gibraltar. In Case C-300/04 *Eman and Sevinger*, the Court of Justice confirmed that Dutch nationals living in the overseas territory of Aruba also had the right to vote in European Parliament elections despite not living in the Netherlands. Whilst the CoJ acknowledged that a refusal to grant voting rights was permissible if objectively justified, in the case the Dutch authorities had failed to justify the different treatment, in that Dutch nationals in the Netherlands could vote and Dutch nationals in Aruba could not. Hence, denial of voting rights was a

---

[30] See Case 108/83 *Luxembourg v European Parliament* [1984] ECR 1945, Case 358/85 *France v European Parliament (Re Brussels Meetings)* [1986] ECR 2149, Case 51/86 *France v European Parliament (Re Meetings Facilities)* [1988] ECR 4821, and Case C-345/95 *France v European Parliament* [1997] ECR I-5215.

[31] In the case brought by France and supported by Luxembourg, the CoJ agreed with the opinion of the AG that the existing law required a continuation of 12 separate sessions in Strasbourg per year and annulled the merged sessions planned for 2013: Cases C-237–8/11 [2012] ECR I-796. There is also a website in support of the single-seat European Parliament: http://www.singleseat.eu/index.html and http://www.singleseat.eu/resources/Single+Seat+ECJ+PRESSER.PDF.

[32] Refer to http://www.elections2014.eu/en/. Latest figures: http://www.europarl.europa.eu/meps/en/crosstable.html.

[33] Now permitted by Decision 2002/772 concerning the election of the MEPs by direct universal suffrage (OJ 2002 L283/1).

Table 2.1 Membership of EP political groupings

Group	Membership
Group of the European People's Party (Christian Democrats) and European Democrats (PPE-DE)	219 (None in the UK since the Conservative Party withdrew and joined the European Conservatives and reformist grouping)
Progressive Alliance of Socialists and Democrats in the European Parliament (S&D)	190 (20 in the UK)
European Conservatives and Reformists	72 (21 in the UK)
Alliance of Liberals and Democrats for Europe (ALDE)	69 (1 in the UK)
European United Left–Nordic Green Left (GUE/NGL)	52 (1 in the UK)
The Greens/European Free Alliance	50 (6 in the UK)
Europe of Freedom and Direct Democracy Group (EFDD)	47 (23 in the UK)
Non-attached members (NI)	52 (1 in the UK)
Total	754

breach of the principle of equal treatment. In both cases, the number of persons affected was relatively small.

Once elected, MEPs sit in transnational political groupings, recognized under Art 224 TFEU (ex Art 191 EC), although there is a strong national element and organization within these, particularly as a result of national political party discipline. There are seven distinct groups plus a final group for those members not wishing to be aligned to any of the specific groups and which have the European and UK membership shown in Table 2.1.

2.5.2 **Functions and Powers**

Apart from the obvious function of a parliament, which is that of a discussion and debate forum, the European Parliament has a number of other powers and functions. The main role that it currently enjoys is that of providing democratic legitimacy to the EU, which clearly suffers from lack of popular support—as evidenced so dramatically in the last few years by the rejections of new treaties by the Dutch, French, and Irish electorates in referenda. The European Parliament is the only directly democratically elected and thus endorsed institution, although the extent to which it can be said to provide a clear and obvious link between the citizens of the massive constituencies and the EU is difficult to assess. Turn-out at the 2014 EP election was *c*.42 per cent which is low and much lower than for previous EP elections, but some national general elections in Europe have registered similar low turn-outs recently.[34] So whilst

---

[34] E.g. Lithuania, Poland, Romania, and Switzerland all registered less than 50% in General elections. For full details, see **http://epp.eurostat.ec.europa.eu/portal/page/portal/product_details/dataset?p_product_code=TSDGO310.**

a higher turn-out would be desirable politically, the fact that citizens choose not to exercise their right to vote is only a very poor argument for questioning its legitimacy. However, as will be seen in some of the other roles that it plays, it is approachable by the ordinary citizen.

2.5.2.1 Legislative Powers

Before the SEA was negotiated, as far as legislative participation was concerned, the European Parliament had advisory and consultative powers only. Old Art 137 EEC provided that the Assembly shall 'exercise the advisory and supervisory powers which are conferred on it by this Treaty'. The treaty specified only 17 instances in which the European Parliament had to be consulted before a decision could be adopted by the Council.[35] Its participation in the legislative process has been increased by successive treaty amendments. The present authorization for the European Parliament's law-making role is Art 14(1) TEU, which empowers it to exercise legislative and budgetary functions jointly with the Council. It was the TEU that gave the European Parliament its most extensive role in the legislative process by introducing the co-decision procedure, which has become the most widely used procedure. It is considered in Chapter 4. The Lisbon Treaty extended it very considerably, although not as far as in the draft Constitutional Treaty. It is referred to now as the 'ordinary legislative procedure' (see Arts 289 and 294 TFEU) and it can be observed that the procedure has been extended in line with the extension of QMV in the Council of Ministers, hence the change of name. The successive extensions to the European Parliament's legislative role undoubtedly impact on the debate about the term 'democratic deficit' and whether that term can correctly still be used to cast doubt on the democratically legitimized participation of the EP in the law-making process in the EU? The ordinary legislative procedure now accounts for about 90 per cent of law-making and today the EP has effectively equal participation in this process. Neither the Council nor EP can force their view on the other partner in the process.

Finally, the European Parliament has a power of consent, which is a prerequisite for the accession of new member states, or the entry of the Union into international and association agreements (Art 49 TEU and Art 218 TFEU),[36] and a new power of veto over delegated non-legislative Acts (Art 290 TFEU). This new power answers the criticism that the European Parliament had been left out of the procedure when decision-making powers are delegated by the Council to the Commission and avoids some of the complexity of the previous comitology procedures, noted at Section 2.2.3.

2.5.2.2 Control and Supervision of the Executive

The European Parliament has, through various treaty amendments, gained revised powers of appointment and removal of the Commission, as well as a role of the scrutiny of the work of the Commission and EU generally.

2.5.2.2.1 Appointment

Previously the President of the Commission nominated by the member states was approved by the European Parliament and the whole Commission, as nominated by the member states in conjunction with the President of the Commission, was subject to the

---

[35] See e.g. old Arts 54 and 235 of the EEC Treaty.

[36] Which was withheld from the proposed Anti-Counterfeiting Trade Agreement with the USA in 2012. See http://www.europarl.europa.eu/pdfs/news/expert/infopress/20120703IPR48247/20120703 IPR48247_en.pdf.

approval of the European Parliament (see Art 14 TEU). As noted in Section 2.2.2, politically the EP has been able to amend this so that in effect it can approve or disapprove of Commissioners one by one and force their withdrawal if not approved by it. Under the new Art 17(7) TEU, a new appointment procedure was introduced. The European Council, acting by a qualified majority, shall propose to the European Parliament a candidate for President of the Commission, who shall be elected by the European Parliament by a majority of its members. Then the Council, by common accord with the President Elect, shall adopt the list of the other persons whom it proposes for appointment as members of the Commission. Finally, the President, the High Representative of the Union for Foreign Affairs and Security Policy, and the other members of the Commission shall, after submitting individually to a questions hearing,[37] be subject as a body to a vote of consent by the European Parliament and appointed by the European Council, acting by a qualified majority.

2.5.2.2.2 Censure and/or Removal

At least on paper, the European Parliament's most powerful weapon would seem to be its power to censure the Commission—which means, in effect, to require it to resign from office. Article 17(8) TEU and Art 234 TFEU provide that a two-thirds vote of the majority of the members is needed, but the Commission is required to resign in its entirety. The censure motion cannot be used against individual Commissioners, which is regarded as unfortunate. For example, in 1999, under the Santer Commission, certain Commissioners were accused of financial improprieties and fraud. A censure motion against the entire Commission failed, but following the very critical report of a committee of independent experts set up by the European Parliament and Commission, the entire Commission resigned without a further vote of censure taking place. Whilst the end result was that which was required—that is, that certain Commissioners were removed from office—the result is criticized because the particular Commissioners were able to hide behind the collective resignation and not be singled out. Until the new Commissioners are approved, the censured Commissioners remain in office. So far, no motions of censure have been adopted.[38] This right continues under the new Art 17(8) TEU, as amended by the Lisbon Treaty. The Commission President can, though, require an individual Commissioner to resign under Art 17(6) TEU and could perhaps be persuaded by the European Parliament to take that action.

Other powers of scrutiny now available to the European Parliament include: the ability to set up a committee of inquiry to investigate the alleged contravention or maladministration in the implementation of EU law, formalized in the treaty structure now by Art 226 TFEU; the ability to question, orally or in writing, the Commission under Art 230 TFEU; and the right to discuss the Commission's annual general reports under Art 233 TFEU. The European Parliament is also entitled to request the Commission to submit proposals that the European Parliament considers necessary for the implementation of the treaties (Art 225 TFEU), although the Commission is not obliged to do anything about such a submission except to inform the European Parliament of the reasons for not submitting a proposal (Art 225 TFEU).

---

[37] See e.g. **http://www.elections2014.eu/en/new-commission** or go to the EP News page at **http://www. europarl.europa.eu/news/en** and search from there for detailed information on the hearings process.

[38] The latest one, at the time of writing, was held on 27 November 2014 to discuss any possible involvement of new Commission President Juncker in Luxembourg tax avoidance schemes. The motion was not approved. See **http://www.europarl.europa.eu/ep-live/en/plenary/video?date=24-11-2014**.

Other supervisory functions and powers of the European Parliament include, under Art 227 TFEU, the right of Union citizens to petition the European Parliament and the right for Union citizens to complain to a parliamentary commissioner, otherwise known as an Ombudsman, about the maladministration of the Union institutions—with the exception of the judicial activities of the Union Courts (Art 228 TFEU). Individuals, legal or natural, may complain either directly or through an MEP, provided that the matter has not been the subject of legal proceedings. The investigations terminate with the issue of a report to the European Parliament, the institutions concerned, and the complainant. The Ombudsman also reports annually to the EP on the general running and performance of the administration.

2.5.2.3 Budgetary Powers

From the 1970s, the European Parliament had been given budgetary powers and under the Budgetary Treaty of 1975, the European Parliament was given the power to reject the budget entirely, which it did in 1979 and 1984 (see Art 314 TFEU), and on occasion subsequently. The 1979 rejection was partly in response to the increase in democratic legitimacy that the European Parliament gained as a result of being directly elected in that year for the first time. However, rejection is not so drastic as it sounds because, if the budget is rejected, the so-called 'one-twelfth rule' comes into operation which means that, until the new budget is approved, the Commission can spend per month up to one-twelfth of the previous year's head of expenditure (Art 315 TFEU). In order to try to avoid future disruptive budget rejections, from 1988 various inter-institutional agreements have been agreed by the institutions[39] to improve the functions on the budgetary procedure and on financial planning. Thus, the European Parliament now discharges the Commission's implementation of the budget on an annual basis, although this has become a more political event and an opportunity to hold the Commission to account.

Following the Lisbon Treaty, the Council and European Parliament enjoy full parity in adopting the budget, and the distinction between compulsory and non-compulsory expenditure has been removed (Arts 314–15 TFEU).

2.5.2.4 Right to Litigate

Although the European Parliament was not originally named as one of the privileged applicants for the purposes of taking actions under Arts 263 and 265 TFEU, the Court of Justice held in Case 13/83 *European Parliament v Council (Transport Policy)* that it was able to bring an action against the other institutions for failure to act under then Art 232 EC (now Art 265 TFEU), and whilst originally it was held not to have a general right of challenge under Art 230 EC (now Art 263 TFEU), in Case 302/87 *European Parliament v Council (Comitology)* it was held to have the right to take action to protect its own prerogative powers (*European Parliament v Council (Chernobyl)*).[40] Acts that have legally binding consequences on the European Parliament can also be challenged under Art 263 TFEU (see Case 294/83 *Les Verts v European Parliament* and Case 34/86 *Council v European Parliament (Budgetary Procedure)*). The TEU also amended Arts 230 and 232 EC (now Arts 263 and 265 TFEU) to specify that the acts or omissions of the European Parliament can be challenged under the usual conditions, and the Treaty of Nice provided express confirmation in Art 230 (now Art 263 TFEU) that the European Parliament is one of the

---

[39] In the version: Agreement of 6 May 2006 (OJ 2006 C139/1), amended five times, not substantively to 2012. The new budget 2014–21 (**http://ec.europa.eu/budget/index_en.cfm**) may require a new agreement.

[40] See also in this respect, Case C-295/80 *European Parliament v Council (Students Residence Directive)*.

privileged applicants able itself to challenge acts of the other institutions and other agencies and bodies of the EU without any restriction in its *locus standi*.

2.6 The Court of Justice of the European Union

The Court of Justice (CoJ), once a single body institution, now comprises the Court of Justice, the General Court (formerly the Court of First Instance (CFI)) and, since the Treaty of Nice, specialized courts (previously known as 'judicial panels'), one of which, entitled the Civil Service Tribunal (Arts 19(1) TEU and 257 TFEU), has been created and is considered in Section 2.6.6. The Court of Justice is a free-standing independent Union Court and it is not in a hierarchical relationship with the national courts as in a system of appeal. Article 19(1) TEU outlines the general functions of the Court of Justice, which are to ensure that, in the interpretation and application of the treaties, the law is observed and, since Lisbon, to provide remedies sufficient to ensure effective legal protection in the fields covered by Union law. The second general duty was added by the Lisbon Treaty and arguably would seem to allow the CoJ to expand rights not previously directly sanctioned by the treaties. It may, thus, be possible to make it easier for individuals to challenge Union acts under Art 263 TFEU, which is an issue that will be covered in Chapter 7.

2.6.1 Composition and Organization

The Court of Justice presently consists of 28 judges and nine Advocates General (AGs), nominated and appointed by unanimous agreement of the governments of the member states.[41] It was agreed at the Intergovernmental Conference (IGC) for the Lisbon Treaty that a declaration (Declaration No 38) be attached to the treaties to accommodate an increase of three AGs if requested by the Court of Justice. That request has been made and one of the three permitted additional AGs has taken up office. The second paragraph of the Declaration provides:

> In that case, the Conference agrees that Poland will, as is already the case for Germany, France, Italy, Spain and the United Kingdom, have a permanent Advocate-General and no longer take part in the rotation system, while the existing rotation system will involve the rotation of five Advocates-General instead of three.[42]

Under Arts 253–4 TFEU, the judges must be chosen from persons whose independence is beyond doubt and who possess either the qualifications necessary for appointment to the highest judicial office in their own countries or recognized juridical competence, which includes academic lawyers, of whom the appointment to the highest courts is a tradition in a number of countries. The Lisbon Treaty provides that the appointment of judges in future takes account of the opinion of an advisory panel comprising former members of the Court of Justice (Art 255 TFEU).[43]

The CoJ can sit as a full court,[44] a grand chamber of 15 judges to hear cases involving either member states or Community institutions,[45] or in chambers (of which there are ten) of three or five judges.

---

[41] These are partially replaced, according to Art 9 of Protocol 3 on the Court of Justice, every three years.

[42] See Council Decision 2013/336 (OJ 2013 L179/92) which will, with effect from 7 October 2015, increase the total number of AGs to 11 and thus fulfil entirely Declaration No 38.

[43] That panel has now been appointed under Art 255 TFEU (OJ 2014 L41/18).

[44] Exceedingly rare, see Case C-370/12 *Pringle v Ireland*, judgment of 27 November 2012, [2012] ECR I-756; see the case note in 50 CML Rev 2013, 805–48.

[45] See Art 16 of the Statute of the Court of Justice for details: N. Foster (ed), *EU Treaties and Legislation*, latest edn, Oxford University Press, Oxford.

The TEU introduced an amended Art 221 EC (now Art 251 TFEU), which reduces the occasions on which the CoJ may need to sit in plenary session—now, when a member state or a Union institution, as a party to an action, requests plenary jurisdiction.

2.6.2 **Procedure**

The Court of Justice is faced with a large of number of cases that can arise ad hoc from any of the member states in one of the now 24 official languages acceptable to the CoJ, but the CoJ operates internally in French as its only working language. The procedure of the CoJ is governed by a protocol containing the Statute of the Court of Justice and by its Rules of Procedure.[46] As a new international court, its rules were based initially on the rules of procedure of the International Court of Justice (ICJ) in The Hague and generally reflect civilian law procedure, with the emphasis on written proceedings rather than oral, as is the case in the UK and other common law systems.

There are essentially four stages to proceedings: first, written proceedings;[47] secondly, investigation and preparatory work on the case; then, oral proceedings, including the AG's opinion, which can be omitted in certain circumstances, as noted later; and finally judgment, which follows deliberation in secret in French. Judgments of the Court of Justice are delivered in a single ruling and Art 2 of the Statute of the Court provides that, before taking up judicial office, each judge shall, in open court, take an oath to preserve the secrecy of the CoJ's deliberations.

Arguments in favour of the single opinion of the CoJ are that it supports the authority of the EU Court and the EU legal system. It helps to build up a new common European law and to avoid reliance on the laws of particular states. It also provides for more authoritative decision-making for the future.

Arguments against are that it often results in terse and cryptic judgments, with little evidence of reasoning; that it stifles true legal argument; and that it may inhibit judges and the development of law. To some extent, these criticisms may be countered by the existence and role of AGs, which is to assist the CoJ by giving an opinion, in complete independence and impartiality, on the legal issues of a case, which will be examined in depth, and critically to review the jurisprudence of the CoJ on the subject. Although the opinion of the AG is not binding on the CoJ, it carries weight and adds to the development of EU law. Thus, an opinion of the AG acts like a first instance decision subject to an automatic and instant appeal. AGs can adopt a public view or the parties' views, but cannot be bound to present any particular view. It is no longer a mandatory requirement that the opinion of the AG be heard before every judgment is given. According to Art 20 of the Statute of the Court of Justice, the CoJ may decide in a case that raises no new point of law, after hearing the view of the AG, that the case be determined without a submission from the AG. It was estimated by the Court of Justice that about 30 per cent of the cases in 2004 and 50 per cent in 2010 were decided without an opinion of an AG.[48] Note now that the procedure expedited under Art 62a of the Statute, and Art 104 of the Rules of Procedure, omits that part of the procedure comprising the chance to reply and rejoinder the original application and defence in a case, and interventions may be refused by the President in order to render a judgment in much less than six months in a case and even as quickly as just over two months.

---

[46] N. Foster (ed), *EU Treaties and Legislation*, latest edn, Oxford University Press, Oxford.

[47] These can be filed online via the e-Curia website (**http://curia.europa.eu/**).

[48] Refer also to the 2012 Annual Report of the Court of Justice, available at **http://curia.europa.eu/jcms/jcms/Jo2_7032/**.

2.6.2.1 **The Form of Judgments**

The report is drafted first of all in the language of the case, which is chosen by the parties or the defending member state from the present 24 official languages.[49] The internal working documents of the CoJ and its deliberations are, however, conducted in French, which is its working language. The full report, as required by the Rules of Procedure of the Court, comprises a brief summary of judgment, followed by the report for the hearing drawn up by the Judge Rapporteur containing the facts and procedure, and a summary of the arguments of the parties.

The next part of the report contains the opinion of the AG, although this does not form an official part of the report. The final part contains the reasons or grounds for the judgment presented in numbered paragraphs and, finally, the usually very succinct single ruling of the CoJ.

2.6.2.2 **The Reporting of Cases**

There is only one official set of reports of cases emanating from the Court of Justice and the General Court. These are the European Court Reports, which are cited as 'ECR' and preceded by the year of publication. These are published in all of the official languages. These are divided into Part I, containing the judgments of the Court of Justice, Part II containing the judgments of the General Court, and ECR-SC containing staff cases, which are no longer automatically translated into all the official languages. Until 2003, all cases were published, but thereafter a selective publication policy was adopted whereby, under Art 20 of the Statute of the Court of Justice, cases can be decided without an AG opinion and not subsequently published in paper form, although they will always be available electronically. However, publication of cases in these reports is severely delayed by two to three years, largely as a result of the translation requirements into the official languages, and alternative reports must be consulted if the full written text is required.[50]

The principal alternative that reports cases very soon after judgment is the series the Common Market Law Reports, cited as 'CMLR'.[51] This provides reports in English of not only the judgments of the EU Courts, but also of cases from the national courts of member states that have considered or applied important points of EU law or that have demonstrated the attitude of the national courts to such EU concepts as supremacy or direct effects.

2.6.3 **Jurisdiction**

Article 19 TEU provides that the Court of Justice, including the General Court and the specialized courts, each within their jurisdiction, shall ensure that, in the interpretation and application of the treaties, the law is observed. The CoJ's factual jurisdiction is then determined by Art 19(3) TEU and Arts 256–79 TFEU. The CoJ's geographic jurisdiction is limited by the treaties to the area of the member states, but a judgment of the CoJ can have consequences and effects outside the geographic area—for example, in Case 48/69 *ICI v Commission (Dyestuffs)* in which the ICI head office, then outside the territory of the Community, was fined through subsidiaries based in the EEC.

---

[49] http://ec.europa.eu/languages/policy/linguistic-diversity/official-languages-eu_en.htm.

[50] Summaries of cases can also be found in the Official Journal, now official in the electronic version only, and full cases can be found on the Curia website (http://curia.europa.eu/).

[51] http://www.sweetandmaxwell.co.uk/Catalogue/ProductDetails.aspx?productid=7212&recordid=500 but usually available through University Westlaw database subscriptions.

In addition, the CoJ has jurisdiction under the EEA Treaty to provide interpretations on disputed rules made thereunder; under Art 218(11) TFEU, the other institutions and the member states may obtain the opinion of the Court of Justice on the compatibility of proposed international agreements and treaties with the TEU and TFEU. The latest of these (Opinion 2/13[52]) was the rejection of the compatibility of the Draft Agreement of the EU to accede to the ECHR. For further detail see Chapter 4, Section 4.6.2.

Article 275 TFEU excludes the jurisdiction of the CoJ on matters decided under the CFSP, except those relating to compliance monitoring under Art 40 TEU and Art 263 TFEU. Article 276 TFEU excludes jurisdiction over police and law enforcement agency operations or actions.

The CoJ's jurisdiction can be divided in a number of ways, which can be helpful in understanding what it does. One way is to look at the broad types of action available under Union law and adjudicated by the CoJ. This also considers the parties to the actions. Here, three main categories can be established: one includes the actions taken against the member states such as under Art 258 TFEU; another, actions concerned with the review of acts of the Union institutions or damages actions such as under Art 263 or Art 340 TFEU; and a third consists of preliminary rulings under Art 267 TFEU. Certain other aspects of the CoJ's work, such as interim measures and appeals from the General Court, stand outside such a division and have to be considered separately. One can also consider the way in which the CoJ is acting: for example, as a constitutional court, when considering the powers of the institutions and member states or the relations between them. It acts as an administrative court in cases of judicial review of acts of the institutions. It acts as an appeal court in hearing cases from the General Court. It also acts to determine the scale of fines against those offending competition law and also the member states when they breach EU law obligations, and as such therefore acts as a kind of administrative criminal law court. Finally, it acts as an advisory court when providing rulings to national courts in response to preliminary ruling references.

The jurisdiction can also be divided into the following two, much more commonly found, classifications:

(a) *direct judicial control*, whereby the CoJ interprets a rule and applies it to decide the case itself

(b) *indirect judicial control*, whereby the CoJ interprets and rules on the validity of provisions not the subject of an action before the CoJ. This jurisdiction is mainly concerned with the rulings on the request of national courts.

2.6.3.1 Direct Actions

Direct actions are also termed the 'contentious jurisdiction' of the CoJ under which the CoJ upholds the lawful exercise of the EU legislative and executive powers in actions against the Union institutions under Arts 263–5 TFEU, concerning the judicial review of legally binding acts. The CoJ also upholds compliance of the Union obligations by the member states via Arts 258–60 TFEU, and conformity with EU law by individuals via various treaty Articles and secondary legislation, such as Art 103(2)(a) TFEU and Regulation 1/2003 concerned with competition policy. Articles 268 and 340(2) TFEU confer non-contractual (delictual) jurisdiction, and Art 270 TFEU gives the Court of Justice jurisdiction over staff cases, now handed over to a specialized Civil Service Tribunal court (formerly judicial panel) with limited appeal rights, considered in Section 2.6.6.

---

[52] http://curia.europa.eu/juris/liste.jsf?num=C-2/13.

The CoJ has a preventative judicial control intended to block the conclusion of an envisaged agreement by the EU with a third state or international organization considered incompatible with the TFEU under Art 218. It can also be called upon to adjudicate in contractual disputes between Union institutions and contractual partners, if called on to do so under an arbitration clause in the contract (Art 272 TFEU). Finally, under Art 277 TFEU, the CoJ hears indirect challenges to EU legislation by individuals in proceedings already taking place before it.

2.6.3.2 Indirect Actions

Indirect judicial control is exercised by the preliminary ruling proceeding of Art 267 TFEU, whereby references are made from the courts of the member states for judicial rulings by the Court of Justice.

The actions mentioned will be considered in further detail in Chapters 6 and 7.

2.6.4 Methodology: Interpretation and Precedent

A consideration of the methodology of the work of the CoJ is helpful in understanding the very pro-integrationist stance, also referred to as the CoJ's 'judicial activism', that it has often adopted in judgments and how this has helped to build a new European legal order.

2.6.4.1 Interpretation

The EU treaties and some of the secondary legislation are framework measures that often require considerable amplification and interpretation. This has given a wide scope to the Court of Justice to engage in expansive interpretation of the texts. The CoJ has taken a very proactive role at times in European integration, often to the consternation of some of the member states. Notable judgments are those concerned with what are now fundamental decisions of the CoJ, including direct effects, supremacy, and the liability of the member states. In these respects, the cases of *Van Gend en Loos, Costa v ENEL*, and *Factortame* (Spanish fishermen and the UK) are very good examples.

Whilst there have been criticisms voiced over the years of this activism, if it were not for the lead given by the CoJ in certain fundamental questions of EU law jurisprudence, the EU legal system would not have obtained the coherency or strength that it has today and, as a result, the EU itself would be less secure. The CoJ has, as a result, been highly instrumental in European integration and in confirming the constitutional basis of the Union.[53]

The style of interpretation is described as teleological or far-seeing or forward-looking, in that the CoJ tries to determine, in light of the aims and objective of the treaties and legislation, what was intended and what result would assist those goals. The Court of Justice often refers to the 'spirit of the Treaty', the Community (now Union) project itself, the preamble, and to general provisions of the treaty—notably Arts 2, 3, 10, and 12 EC (now Arts 3–6 TEU and Art 18 TFEU)—in order to help it to reach a particular conclusion. As such, then, these represent a form of contextual approach, taking many things into account to justify a judgment. For example, see [71]–[75] of the judgment in Case 26/62 *Van Gend en Loos*, in which virtually all of these justifications are covered in reaching the conclusion that EC law was capable of giving rise to direct effects, despite there being no express words to that end in the Treaty itself.

---

[53] For brief, but informed, discussion on the critique and support of the Court's judicial activism, see I. Ward, *A Critical Introduction to European Law*, 3rd edn, Cambridge University Press, Cambridge, 2009, pp 97–101, and S. Douglas-Scott, *Constitutional Law of the European Union*, Longman, Harlow, 2002, pp 210–23.

The CoJ often refers to the concept of *effet utile*, or the 'useful effect' of EU law, which would be undermined if a particular provision were not interpreted in a much more expansive way, more in line with the objectives of the treaty rather than the actual words used. See, for example, Cases C-6 and 9/90 *Francovich et al v Italy*, in which the establishment of liability on the part of member states could never have been derived from a literal reading of the treaty or secondary law. These EU methods of interpretation are applied in addition to the usual array found in the member states' legal systems, including the logical, literal, and purposive means of interpretation, although any strict use of such methods has often been rejected by the CoJ as unsuitable in the EU context. See, for example, Case 6/60 *Humblet* and Case C-70/88 *Chernobyl*, in which direct use of the literal and historical intent methods, respectively, were rejected.

2.6.4.2 Precedent

While there is no formal system of precedent, the Court of Justice, just like courts in civil law jurisdictions, tries to maintain consistency in its judgments. Past decisions are often cited in court and do therefore carry some persuasive, rather than any formal, authority. In particular, whilst all rulings of the CoJ are binding within the case itself, certain decisions are regarded as forming a sort of precedent for the national courts—for example, the early decision in Cases 28–30/62 *Da Costa* that references need not be made to the Court of Justice where the materially identical question had already been answered by the CoJ, in the recently heard case *Van Gend en Loos*. Furthermore, leading cases in Community law, such as *Van Gend en Loos* and *Costa v ENEL*, have acquired a higher and more authoritative status than other cases—dealing, for example, with an interpretation of one of the common customs tariff classifications or some such other mundane item of EU secondary legislation. And this is so much so that this difference in status has now been more formally recognized by the decision no longer to publish all cases in the official series of Court reports, the ECR. Those from the chambers of three are not to be published, nor are rulings from chambers of five in which there has been no opinion of the AG, but this does not include Art 267 TFEU preliminary rulings.[54]

There are instances, though, in which the Courts use the terminology of precedent: see, for example, Case C-310/97 P *Commission v Assidomän*, in which the CoJ mentions *ratio decidendi* at [54], and both identifies previous precedents and distinguishes past cases relied on by one of the parties (at [54]–[62]); judicial review cases often refer back to the leading Case 25/62 *Plaumann v Commission*. In Case C-263/02 P *Commission v Jego-Quere*, the *Plaumann* test was held virtually to dictate the result in subsequent cases. Hence, unofficially, the system of case law developed by the Court of Justice increasingly seems to resemble a true case law system relying on precedents to take the law forward to new cases. It must also be made clear, though, that the CoJ will not be constrained by previous case law it if considers a change in the law to be required: for example, see Case C-267/91 *Keck*, which expressly sought to explain a previous ruling (Case 120/78 *Cassis de Dijon*).

2.6.5 The General Court

The first measure to tackle the growing caseload and thus length of proceedings before the Court of Justice, was the setting up of a Court of First Instance (CFI) in 1986 by the

---

[54] They will, however, be available electronically in the language of the case via the Court of Justice website: http://curia.europa.eu/jcms/jcms/j_6/.

SEA (now governed by Art 256 TFEU). The CFI commenced operation on 1 September 1989 and was renamed by the Lisbon Treaty as the General Court. It presently has 28 members, one of whom may act as an AG where considered necessary in complex cases (Art 254 TFEU) but this is very rarely utilized. The General Court is divided into chambers of three and five judges, but can sit in Grand Chamber or full court. More recently, Art 50 of the Statute of the Court of Justice has allowed for a single judge to hear cases in the General Court.

The jurisdiction was initially limited, but has been slowly expanded to any area of jurisdiction and, from 2004, also includes direct actions for Art 263 TFEU annulment applications brought by natural and legal persons, but not by the member states or the Union institutions. It has also been extended to include Art 267 TFEU preliminary references unless there is a risk to the unity of EU law, in which case the case should be referred to the Court of Justice by the General Court but this jurisdiction has not been exercised to date. Article 256 TFEU allows for future changes of jurisdiction of the General Court to be made by amendment of the Protocol on the Court of Justice rather than by treaty amendment.

The General Court also has jurisdiction to hear appeals from the specialized courts. Appeals from the General Court may be made on points of law only to the Court of Justice. Three grounds are given:

(a) lack of competence by the court

(b) breach of procedure

(c) the infringement of a Union provision or rule of law by the General Court or an error in the interpretation or application of law.

After years of increasing caseloads and growing back-logs, the expansion of the EU and Court of Justice in 2004—which saw a large influx of new judges but, at least at first, few new cases from the new member states—combined with the increased jurisdiction of the General Court, enabled the CoJ to make inroads into the back-log. In 1998, there were over 1,000 cases pending before the Court of Justice. In 2003, this figure stood at 974 and, in 2004, it was reduced to 840.[55] With these figures, the length of proceedings that had increased over the years also changed for the better, with Art 234 EC (now Art 267 TFEU) references, direct actions, and appeals all showing reductions in length, and markedly so in 2009–11 from 25.5 to 16.1 months, 24.7 to 16.7 months, and 28.7 to 14.3 months respectively.

2.6.6 Specialized Courts

The Treaty of Nice provided for the establishment of judicial panels (now specialized courts) attached to the CFI (now General Court) to relieve that Court of some of its caseload (Art 225a EC, now Art 257 TFEU). These specialized courts will operate as first instance courts, with appeal to the General Court. The first decision under the new power was taken by the Council of Ministers in November 2004[56] and an EU Civil Service Tribunal[57] comprising seven judges has been established to hear staff cases with

---

[55] For full details, see p 4 of the Annual Report of the Court of Justice: **http://curia.europa.eu/jcms/jcms/Jo2_11035/rapports-annuels**.

[56] Decision 2004/752 (OJ 2004 L333/7).

[57] Which is the title given to it by the Court of Justice rather than specialized court. See **http://curia.europa.eu/jcms/jcms/T5_5230/**.

an appeal, on law only, to the General Court and exceptional review by the Court of Justice. Staff cases were an apparently not inconsiderable load on the CoJ. The possibility of establishing more panels for specialist subjects remains and a tribunal/specialized court for patent cases appears possible but not immediately.

2.6.7 The European Central Bank

The ECB[58] was set up under the TEU to achieve price stability in the Union and is responsible for monetary policy regulating eurozone interest rates and the euro. Following the entry into force of the Lisbon Treaty, it became a full institution of the EU and is governed by Art 13 TEU, Arts 282–4 TFEU, and Protocol 4 attached to the treaties. It also cooperates with the national central banks in the ESCB.

2.6.8 The Court of Auditors

Although the Court of Auditors[59] was made a full institution by the TEU and is regulated under Art 13 TEU and Arts 285–7 TFEU, it is not one usually covered in any detail in textbooks and will be mentioned here only briefly.

The Court of Auditors was established under the 1975 Budgetary Treaty and audits the expenditure of the institutions for legality and sound financial management. It produces an annual report that is forwarded to the European Parliament to debate and to provide the Commission with a discharge if the expenditure is correct (Art 319 TFEU)—which it has not been for a number of years. There is though no follow-up procedure by which either the Council or EP respond to its dissatisfaction and demand or require changes be made. The amended Art 263 TFEU provides that the Court of Auditors can take action to protect its prerogatives in judicial review actions against acts of the main legislative institutions.

2.7 The Union's Advisory Bodies

The following bodies are not full institutions named in Art 13 TEU, but are advisory bodies established by Art 300 TFEU and intended to assist the main institutions.

2.7.1 The European Economic and Social Committee

The EESC[60] (previously also known under the acronym 'ECOSOC'[61]) was introduced to serve in an advisory role to represent various sectional interests and must be consulted for the adoption of certain legislation as determined by the treaty, although, once received, its opinion may be ignored by the Council. However, failure to consult would open up the legislation enacted to annulment, by analogy with the European Parliament in Cases 138–9/79 *Roquette and Maizena v Council*. Its members are appointed in a personal capacity along national lines by the Council voting by QMV and are drawn from

---

[58] https://www.ecb.europa.eu/home/html/index.en.html.

[59] http://www.eca.europa.eu/en/Pages/ecadefault.aspx.

[60] http://www.eesc.europa.eu/?i=portal.en.home.

[61] Which is the same abbreviation of a Committee of the same name of the General Assembly of the United Nations (http://www.un.org/en/ecosoc/) so the presumption is that at least part of the reason for the name change, if not the principal reason, was to avoid confusion with the UN body.

various sections of society to provide a wide-ranging array of views on legislative proposals. The EESC is also able to give opinions on its own initiative without invitation from the Council, Commission, or the European Parliament, and is governed by Arts 301–4 TFEU.

2.7.2 The Committee of the Regions

A much later Union body, the CoR[62] was established by the TEU, and is also an advisory body set up to represent regional and local bodies and to meet the criticisms that the Union fails to recognize regional interests, particularly those of federal states. Usually, only the central or national bodies of federal states were formally represented in the Union institutional set-up—namely, the Council of Ministers, which draws its members from the state governments.

The CoR must be consulted for the enactment of certain legislation, such as Arts 153, 165–8, and 173 TFEU, and is governed by Arts 305–7 TFEU. In the UK, membership is drawn from local authorities and the devolved governments in Scotland, Wales, and Northern Ireland.[63]

2.8 Other Union Bodies

Note that there is also a European Investment Bank[64] (Art 308 TFEU) to channel funding into European projects, an Economic and Financial Committee to advise the Council and Commission on internal market coordination matters under Art 134 TFEU, and a Political and Security Committee to advise to the Council and the Foreign Minister on international situations under Art 38 TEU.[65]

2.9 Union Financing

This final section of the chapter considers an activity in which the three main institutions participate; that is, how the Union is financed and how the budget is drawn up and approved.

As a result of the delay to the introduction of the system of own resources by the objections of French President de Gaulle in 1965–6, a system of Community own resources and a revised budgetary procedure were not introduced until 1970,[66] when the European Parliament was given the last word on non-compulsory expenditure. This regime was amended by the Budgetary Treaty of 1975.[67]

'Own resources' means that the Community (now Union) can rely on certain incomes that have been designated Union income. These include agricultural levies, duties received under the Common Customs Tariff (CCT), and a percentage on the revenues from VAT as agreed by the member states (currently set at 1.6 per cent of the rate used for VAT assessment). This system became self-sufficient as from 1 January 1980.

---

[62] http://cor.europa.eu/en/Pages/home.aspx.

[63] Full details of the selection criteria and process for all member states can be found at http://www.cor.europa.eu/inca2006/ui/ViewDocument.aspx?siteid=default&contentID=543a f8a8-3b1e-4b51-81a5-4195651ae0ea.

[64] http://www.eib.org/.

[65] Full lists of other institutions, bodies, and agencies can be found at these websites: http://europa.eu/about-eu/institutions-bodies/ and http://europa.eu/about-eu/agencies/index_en.htm.

[66] Decision 70/243 (OJ 1975 L94/19).   [67] OJ 1975 L359/1.

The procedure for determining expenditure and the annual budget is governed by Arts 313–16 TFEU (ex Arts 272–3 EC).

2.9.1 The Budgetary Procedure

The Commission proposes the first draft of the budget and the maximum increase for non-compulsory expenditure, and forwards it to the Council which prepares the draft budget by a qualified majority. The draft is then sent to the European Parliament, which can approve it within 45 days, in which case it will be adopted, or can amend by a majority any part of it following the entry into force of the Lisbon Treaty. The draft is then returned to the Council. In the case of disagreement, a conciliation committee is constituted of equal members of the Council, or its representatives and MEPs, to agree a joint text, failing which the budget is deemed rejected and the Commission must submit a new draft. See Arts 313–316 TFEU.

If the stalemate continues into a new financial year, the one-twelfth rule automatically applies until the dispute is resolved, whereby the Commission is provided with one-twelfth of the previous year's money per month (Art 315 TFEU).

The European Parliament's powers have thus considerably increased under the Lisbon Treaty.

2.10 Chapter Summary

As can be seen, the institutional set-up of the EU is now considerable and sophisticated. It has seen a considerable number of changes over the decades to cope with the numerous changes imposed on the EU both externally and internally, in particular the cumulative expansions of the EU, to remedy particular issues such as the democratic deficit, efficiency in law-making, participation of wider interests and national parliaments, and to be better able to react to world events and present a common EU position in the world. The latter though, understandably in a Union now of 28 member states, is a long way from being perfected, if it ever will. The institutional evolution is though another witness of the dynamic and changing nature of the entity which is the European Union.

Further Reading

Books

ARNULL, A. *The European Union and its Court of Justice*, Oxford University Press, Oxford, 2006.

BURROWS, N. and GREAVES, R. *The Advocate General and EC Law*, Oxford University Press, Oxford, 2007.

CORBETT, R., JACOBS, F. and SHACKLETON, M. *The European Parliament*, 8th edn, John Harper, London, 2011.

DEVUYST, Y. *The European Union Transformed: Community Method and Institutional Evolution from the Schuman Plan to the Constitution for Europe*, rev'd and updated edn, Peter Lang, Brussels, 2006.

EARNSHAW, D. and JUDGE, D. *The European Parliament*, 2nd edn, Palgrave, Basingstoke, 2008.

HAYES-RENSHAW, F. and WALLACE, H. *The Council of Ministers*, 2nd edn, Palgrave, Basingstoke, 2006.

WARD, I. *A Critical Introduction to European Law*, 3rd edn, Cambridge University Press, Cambridge, 2009.

Articles

BARENTS, R. 'The Court of Justice after the Treaty of Lisbon' (2010) 47 CML Rev 706.

DAVIES, G. 'Subsidiarity: The Wrong Idea, in the Wrong Place, at the Wrong Time' (2006) 43 CML Rev 63.

DE WAELE, H. and BROEKSTEEG, H. 'The Semi-permanent European Council Presidency: Some Reflections on the Law and Early Practice' (2012) 49 CML Rev 1039.

LAVRANOS, N. 'The New Specialised Courts within the European Judicial System' (2002) 30 EL Rev 261.

MOBERG, A. 'The Nice Treaty and Voting Rules in the Council' (2002) 40(2) JCMS 259–82.

PEERS, S. 'Towards a New Form of EU Law? The Use of EU Institutions outside the EU Legal Framework' (2013) 9 ECL Rev 37.

SOLANKE, I. '"Stop the ECJ?": An Empirical Analysis of Activism at the Court' (2011) 17 EL Rev 764.

TIMMERMANS, C. 'The European Union's Judicial System' (2004) 41 CML Rev 393.

Web-based Materials

http://www.european-council.europa.eu/home-page.aspx
The European Council

http://www.consilium.europa.eu/homepage?lang=en
The Council (of Ministers)

http://ec.europa.eu/index_en.htm
The European Commission

http://ec.europa.eu/commission/2014-2019/president_en
The Juncker Commission

http://www.europarl.europa.eu/parliament.do?language=en
The European Parliament

http://curia.europa.eu/
The Court of Justice

http://www.eesc.europa.eu/index_en.asp
The European Economic and Social Committee

http://cor.europa.eu/en/Pages/home.aspx
The Committee of the Regions

The EU has websites on the ordinary legislative procedure (including a very good flow chart):

http://eur-lex.europa.eu/browse/summaries.html
http://www.europarl.europa.eu/aboutparliament/en/0080a6d3d8/
Ordinary-legislative-procedure.html (with a flow chart)

3

The Empowerment of the Union: Transfer, Division, and Control of Powers

3.1 Introduction

The nature of the European Union was not set out clearly when it was first established, involving as it did a mix of intergovernmental and supranational elements and it has developed considerably since then to become a very complex entity. As a result, many questions have been raised about the Union and its relationship with the member states. How democratic is it? Is it moving towards a federal set-up of some sort? Whilst demanding constitutionality of new member states, to what extent does the Union itself conform to the constitutional standards regarded as imperative for modern democracies? To a large extent, these questions were taken on following the Laeken Summit by the Convention on the Future of Europe. This prepared the Constitutional Treaty that was agreed by the member states in 2004, although subsequently abandoned in 2007 following its rejection by the electorates in France and the Netherlands. This chapter attempts to explore this multifaceted and increasingly intricate relationship between the Union and the member states. It commences with the transfer of sovereign powers and democratic legitimacy of the Union, and, connected to this, the establishment of constitutionalism within the Union.

The second section will consider the division and control of competences between the Union and the member states and also, in this context, the principles of subsidiarity and proportionality, which are the political solutions to the very emotive questions about how power is shared between the Union and the member states. Subsidiarity is a way of deciding how to determine where the line between Union and member states' competences should be drawn. Even after the division of competences has been decided, which determines whether it is the EU or the member states who have the right to act and thus enact legislation in certain areas, there remains the question of the status of those acts produced under the Union competence and whether they take priority over national law. This means the issue of supremacy, which will be considered fully in Chapter 5.

3.2 The Transfer of Sovereign Powers

When the European Communities were first set up, as catalogued in Chapter 1, it was done in cognizance of the fact that, in order to be able to achieve the goals set for it, the member states had to pool their resources in the new entity or, in other words, had to transfer some of their sovereign rights to the Communities and their institutions in order for them to do their work. This was later made plain by the European Court of Justice in the seminal *Van Gend en Loos* case, but with the proviso that the power transfer, or transfer of sovereignty, was done within limited fields only and was not a general transfer of power. A general transfer would include the ability to decide its own competences and is often described in German as *Kompetenz-Kompetenz*—the ability to redefine competences without reference to any other or outside body. In similar terms, the term 'omnipotence', as employed in the Dicean discussion about parliamentary sovereignty in the UK, conveys the same conceptual meaning. This was certainly not the case with the transfers of powers by the member states to the Communities and Union.[1] The power that the Union possesses is there by virtue of its transfer by the member states. However, the Communities and now Union are not static entities; rather, they have developed considerably since first being established and the competences have grown also with the complexity of the Union. Each successive treaty amendment has transferred further powers to the Union, with a corresponding loss of sovereignty in those areas as agreed by the member states. How these powers are divided and employed is considered in Section 3.5. First, however, we shall explore democracy as one of the requirements of constitutionality, which, following the entry into force of the Lisbon Treaty, is now an express and therefore much more prominent basic value of the Union—see new Arts 10–12 TEU.

3.3 Democracy in the Union

3.3.1 The Democratic Credentials of the Union

Article 2 TEU requires that the Union is founded on democracy, amongst other values; Article 10 TEU states that the EU is founded on representative democracy; and Art 11 TEU provides for a participatory democracy. Under Art 49 TEU, any potential new member state needs to comply with those principles. It is not, however, clear whether the Union itself fully corresponds to them. As first established, there was certainly very little democratic input. The European Parliament has though been directly elected since 1979 and the latest increase in its powers by the Lisbon Treaty further corrects the original imbalance of power with the Council of Ministers in favour of the EP, as is considered in Chapters 2 and 4. It can also be argued further that the individual ministers from the member states who constitute the Council are part of and represent nationally elected bodies, and therefore provide the Council with indirect democracy. They are not, however, directly accountable to the European citizens. In addition, they can only indirectly pursue a national mandate in the Council negotiations and under qualified majority voting (QMV) they can be outvoted. Furthermore, the European Council plays an increasing role in policy formulation and overall steering of the Union, in particular now very formally following its elevation to a full EU institution by the Lisbon Treaty. It too though enjoys indirect democracy as it is made up of elected heads of state and government. The Commission still has the right of initiative of legislation and, although the European Parliament and, in the limited circumstances outlined in Art 289(4), other EU bodies can ask the Commission to propose law, they cannot insist that it does so. Although the Commission is not elected, its appointment can only take place following the agreement of the European Council (indirectly democratic) and approval of the EP (directly democratic), so that too is imbued with a level of democratic legitimacy. The European

---

[1] But some movement in this direction may be argued to exist now following the introduction by the Lisbon Treaty of the self-revising ability under new Art 48 TEU.

Parliament, as a result of cumulative improvements, has modest increasing parliamentary control over the legislature and executive, taking part in the latter's appointment and being able to question both. All these aspects mean that the accusation of democratic deficit that is levelled at the Union is a much weaker one today and in fact compares well with some of the member states whose democratic credentials are incomplete.[2] At the Laeken Summit in December 2001, the member states called for more democracy and laid down principles calling for more openness and transparency in the Union.

3.3.2 **Transparency and Open Governance**

The lack of previous openness and transparency, particularly in the Council of Ministers' decision-making processes, is regarded as one of the reasons for European voter apathy in the European Parliament elections and is itself symptomatic of the alleged democratic deficit in the Union. This was recognized increasingly as a result of the initial Danish rejection of the TEU and later with the Irish rejection of the Nice Treaty in the early 1990s, the Dutch and French rejections of the Constitutional Treaty in 2005, and the further Irish rejection of the Lisbon Treaty in 2008. Some steps, though, have been taken to tackle the problem and to provide for more open governance, although a lot of distrust among the European electorates of the EU and its main institutions remains, as can be witnessed by the low voting turn-out in the 2009 and even lower in the 2014 European Parliament elections. Voting patterns have also changed and there is considerable support for Eurosceptic parties.[3]

Specific measures to increase openness include two decisions[4] which were enacted to provide access to Commission and Council documents, but which allowed the institutions to subject those rights to their own internal rules. The Court of First Instance (CFI) and the Court of Justice were, however, able to define ever more expansive individual rights stemming from the decisions. In Case T-194/94 *Carvel*, the right of access was held to be an individually enforceable right. Case T-175/95 (the *Swedish Journalists* case) opened up access to Council documents from the third pillar to public scrutiny. The case caused the Council to create restrictions to access in its Decision 2000/527.[5] Case C-353/99 P *Heidi Hautala v Council* appeared to establish a right to information in the face of the weakness of the actual rights contained in the decisions. However, the member states did agree at Amsterdam to a new Art 255 EC (now Art 15 TFEU) to provide a treaty right of access to documents, the details of which were to be determined by subsequent legislation. After much wrangling, a new EU measure, Regulation 1049/2001,[6] was adopted, which while containing various exceptions to access to the documents held by the Council, the Commission, and the European Parliament, was regarded as a positive step forward in creating a more open form of decision-making in the Union.

It has, since its enactment, been the subject of many challenges before the Court of Justice to try to determine the extent of the exceptions to access to documents. In the leading case, Case C-64/05 P *Sweden v Commission*, Art 4(5) of the Regulation, which provides an exception to the main principle that documents should be disclosed when any member state from which a document originated requests in advance that it be withheld,

---

[2] E.g. the UK which has two-thirds of the legislature unelected!

[3] See the figures for the transnational European Parliament groupings provided in the table in Chapter 2, Section 2.5.1.1 and the further references to the election results in that section. Note though also that some individual states have experienced even lower electorate turn-outs than the EP.

[4] Decision 93/731 (OJ 1993 L340/43) and Decision 94/90 (OJ 1994 L46/58).

[5] OJ 2000 L212/09.   [6] OJ 2001 L145/43.

was challenged as to its scope. Previously, it had been held that the exception did indeed protect documents arising from the member states.[7] Because many of the working documents of the institutions do arise from the member states, all of these would be potentially protected if the member states were so to desire. In the Case C-64/05 P *Sweden v Commission* appeal case, the Court of Justice held that this exception, which amounted in effect to a blanket veto, was incompatible with the spirit of transparency contained within the regulation and the specific obligation to disclose. If the reason not to disclose was not one of those listed in Art 4(1)–(3), then disclosure would be presumed unless the member state were able to provide special reasons for not disclosing it. Another exception in Art 4(2) provides that the institutions may refuse disclosure of documents that are concerned with inspections, investigations, and audits unless there is an overriding public interest in disclosure. This was held by the CFI (now the General Court) not to apply to those inspections, investigations, and audits that had been completed.[8] Only rarely in ongoing proceedings would disclosure be approved, although blanket refusals remain unacceptable.[9]

The case law on transparency is thus creeping towards a clearer understanding of the limits and understanding of it for all parties.

Finally, introduced by the Lisbon Treaty, is the requirement that the Council meet in public when deliberating and voting on draft legislative acts (Art 16(8) TEU).[10]

3.4 The Constitutional Basis of the Union

3.4.1 The Community and Union Treaties

Within the usual understanding of international law norms, treaties are only agreements between signatory member states. They do nothing other than obligate the states to comply with the terms of the agreement, which are usually limited to distinct subject areas, such as free trade in goods. In contrast, the previous EC and EU Treaties (now TFEU and TEU) provide the Union with certain characteristics that go much further than a simple international agreement. They provide for their own institutional set-up, exclusive competences in some areas, and their own law-making powers to enable them to enact regulations, directives, and decisions that are binding in the member states. Laws are enacted by the Union's own set of institutions, including the participation in that process by a directly elected European Parliament, thus involving a distinct political input. However, the member states in the Council of Ministers remain in the driving seat as far as an overall view of the legislative processes is concerned and, following the Lisbon Treaty, the European Council is confirmed as the political driving force of the EU, situated as an official main institution at the apex of the institutional set-up. Very significant in this new order is that some of the secondary legislation that can be enacted, are self-executing laws that are directly applicable in the member states. Furthermore, the process for enacting that legislation is increasingly by (qualified) majority voting, which means that member

---

[7] See Case T-168/02 *IFAW v Commission* [2004] ECR II-4135.

[8] In Cases T-391/03 and T-700/04 *Franchet et al v Commission* [2006] ECR II-2023.

[9] See Case T-237/02 *Technische Glaswerke Ilmenau v Commission* [2006] ECR II-5131. See also the more recent Cases C-39/05 and C-52/05 *Sweden & Turco v Council* [2008] ECR I-4723, in which the Court of Justice held that reliance on the exceptions of Art 4 must be reasoned and explained, along with how specifically the documents requested cannot be revealed despite any overriding public interest argument.

[10] The Article states that the Council shall divide its business into two parts dealing with legislative acts and non-legislative activities, with the presumption that the latter can be considered behind closed doors, the equivalent of non-reserved and reserved business common to many meetings.

states can be overruled, yet the law still applies and is binding in all member states. The Union and member states are required also to uphold the express commitments to the rule of law and fundamental rights. There is a supreme or constitutional court, the Court of Justice, to adjudicate on disputes between the constituent bodies. Furthermore, the agreements reached are not static ones, although there was little change for the first 20 years of life of the Communities; the Communities and now the Union have developed as the treaties have progressively been amended and expanded. Thus, the competences of both the Communities and now Union, and the internal institutions, have been increased considerably.

Much of this is in keeping with expectations of what would normally appear in a constitutional document. Indeed, the status of the treaties as a constitutional framework was not long in doubt in the view of the Court of Justice, which confirmed in its leading judgments of Case 26/62 *Van Gend en Loos* and Case 6/64 *Costa v ENEL* that the Community treaties went beyond the usual intergovernmental treaties and agreements between sovereign states, and had in fact created a new legal order.

On the side of caution for a moment, there are also certain attributes of the Communities and now Union that do not comply with constitutionalism or statehood. There is no overall competence of the Union to decide its own competence, as noted earlier. The member states remain those that decide whether the competences of the Union should be increased. The Union has only an incomplete external competence: there is no single body that makes law and represents the Union externally, as would the government of a federal state;[11] and, extremely importantly, there is no coherent identity held by the people of Europe.[12] So, whilst there are some features of constitutionalism, the Union is far from constituting a federal or confederal state. For the moment, after considering the important, but sometimes overlooked, protocols, the further question of how constitutionalism is being developed within the Union will be considered—in particular in respect of the division of competences and subsidiarity.

3.4.1.1 Protocols

A particular complication to the body of constitutional law is the addition of numerous protocols the status of which is declared in Art 51 TEU to be an integral part of treaty law. Protocols are instruments that have been used increasingly in the Union legal order. They are agreements of the member states that have been reached usually at the same intergovernmental conference (IGC) when substantial treaty amendments have been agreed but which, for varying reasons, have not been incorporated into the main body of the treaties. They often provide further definition to principles outlined in the treaties, such as the protocol on subsidiarity—but all too often they contain some of the most controversial decisions reached by the member states, such as the old protocol on social policy from 1992, which was not agreed by all member states, or important decisions on enlargement or the institutions, or the relationship of the national parliaments to the Union. Protocols dealt with the opt-outs from various stages of the integration process, such as monetary union for the UK, or the opt-outs of the Schengen Agreement for the UK, Ireland, and Denmark. There are protocols on what the member states and EU institutions must understand from a Court of Justice judgment: for example, in the *Barber* case of 1990[13] that sought to prevent the retroactive effect of a Court judgment so

---

[11] Although the creation of the High Representative to coordinate all external relations of the EU (under Art 24(1) TEU) can be regarded as a step in this direction.

[12] Allied to this—or, as argued by some, the root of this—is that there is no single identifiable European people, or *demos* as it is termed.

[13] Which is considered in Chapter 11.

as to limit the exposure of businesses and the insurance industry to back-dated claims for equal pay. Others are of a more technical nature and contain, for example, detailed rules on the Court of Justice or the European Central Bank (ECB).[14]

Each of the treaty amendments have added protocols to the body of the constitutional law of the Union, including the latest, the 2007 Lisbon Treaty. Because they are the equivalent, and have the status, of treaty law and may alter either directly or impliedly the treaty provision, they amend the constitutional base of the Union. This is not very helpful, because there are now so many protocols on all sorts of matters that gaining an overall view of the constitutional and legal basis of the Union has become, if not impossible, then extremely difficult. The abandoned Constitutional Treaty was supposed to tidy up the law base of the Union, but only consolidated numerous protocols instead, which was the same approach taken by the Lisbon Treaty, which merely consolidated the protocols attached to the various treaties into one set of 37 protocols.[15]

3.4.1.2 Insistence of Constitutionality

A further element of a constitution is the requirement to be constitutional itself. Articles 2, 6, and 49 TEU require the Union itself, and present and future member states, to respect certain principles including liberty, democracy, human rights and fundamental freedoms, and the rule of law.

In providing a basic level for the governance of the EU, the treaties, in the view of the Court of Justice in cases including *Les Verts*[16] and in its Opinion on the European Economic Area (EEA),[17] represented the constitutional framework of the Communities (now EU). In *Les Verts*, the CoJ held that the European Community is based 'on the rule of law, inasmuch as neither its member states nor its institutions can avoid a review of the question whether the measures adopted by them are in conformity with the basic constitutional charter, the Treaty'.[18]

As such, then, a constitutional framework already exists without any further need or without actually changing anything; however, the Constitutional Treaty would certainly have contained all of the elements of constitutionality. All of the basic principles and rules were present in Part I in typical constitutional manner. These included the outline of competences, the principles of representative and participatory democracy, rules regulating the entry and exit of member states, and the range of values now contained in Art 6 TEU. Whilst these have been retained within the treaties under the Lisbon Treaty, it remains unclear whether this makes the EU any more federal or supranational than it was under the previous treaties, there are supporters and arguments on both sides.

3.4.2 The Abandoned Constitutional Treaty

Although this treaty was abandoned in 2007 following its rejection by the electorates of Holland and France, because of its importance in the development of the Union and especially concern about constitutionality, it needs to be considered here. In the run-up to the 2004 IGC, which debated the results of the Convention on the Future of Europe and

---

[14] http://eur-lex.europa.eu/collection/eu-law/treaties-other.html#TableOther.
[15] 38 now with the 2013 Irish Protocol: OJ 2013 L60/131.
[16] Case 294/83 *Parti Ecologiste 'Les Verts' v European Parliament* [1986] ECR 1339.
[17] Opinion 1/91 (Draft Opinion on the EEA) [1991] ECR I-6079.
[18] See also now the *Kadi* case [2008] ECR I-6351, which clearly demonstrates the respect of the rule of law and human rights in the EU by the Court of Justice. This case is considered in further detail in Chapters 4 and 5.

the new forthcoming treaty, there was a lot of discussion about the meaning of the title given to the results of the work carried out by the Convention and in particular one word within that title. The word that was picked over, discussed, defined, and analysed was 'constitution' within the overall title then of 'Draft Treaty establishing a Constitution for Europe'. As much attention was given to this word as was given to the word 'federal' when the TEU was being debated in Maastricht. Both words, it seems, for some parties including certain member states, are highly emotive words because of the political connotations and consequences attached to them. 'Federal' was so emotive that it was dropped in favour of the euphemism 'ever closer union' which was accepted and written into the TEU. The term 'constitution' in this later debate was also regarded as a highly sensitive word, but was, surprisingly, accepted far more readily by the member states. It seems the 'C' word was not as offensive as the 'F' word but, in the aftermath period of reflection following the rejection by France and the Netherlands, even this term fell out of favour and was removed from the Lisbon Treaty reforms, along with the other symbols that represent statehood, such as references to the Union flag, anthem, or Union day. Hence, even the debate about whether a single constitutional document is needed for the EU is something that has been taken off the burner entirely.[19]

A constitution is, according to the *Oxford English Dictionary*, 'a body of fundamental principles according to which a State or other organization is governed', within which fairly simple definition lies some of the difficulty pounced upon by both sides of the argument. As a body of fundamental principles, a constitution sets outs the range of powers, duties, and obligations of the constituent parts of the organization—that is, the governing or central body and its members. On the one hand, some argued that a constitution was something enjoyed by as humble an organization as a local allotment association or a local political social club, and therefore nothing to be feared. On the other hand, a view was put forward that a constitution is something so closely connected with states and statecraft that, in the European context, it actually meant the establishment of or progress towards the 'dreaded' European superstate—or some sort of acknowledgement at least that the EU was a true state and not simply a collective of sovereign member states. In other words, the term 'constitution' in this context could only mean elevating the EU to some form of statehood or federal state and therefore was to be avoided at all costs.

Leaving aside the further consequences of the adoption of this term for the moment, it is clear that it can apply to a range of organizations and obviously includes states. The question might then be posed, in relation to the EU, whether as an organization, of whatever type, it should and does have a constitution.

We need first, then, to consider whether the EU *should* have a constitution. If we mean a body of fundamental principles to regulate both the internal and external affairs of the organization, the answer must be 'yes'. It makes sense that an organization, and particularly one so large and so complex as the EU, definitely *should* have a constitution.

Secondly, it is a simple question to ask 'Does the Union have a set of fundamental principles or rules or laws?' The answer is, again, 'yes'—in the form of the treaties, as amended and extended. The subsequent question is then begged: 'Do these amount to a constitution?' This is where we need to look deeper. Presently, these are not termed a 'constitution', but this does not mean to say that there is not a constitutional order in the EU. The UK, for

---

[19] Note though that 16 member states agreed in Declaration 52 attached to the treaties 'that the flag with a circle of twelve golden stars on a blue background, the anthem based on the "Ode to Joy" from the Ninth Symphony by Ludwig van Beethoven, the motto "United in diversity", the euro as the currency of the European Union and Europe Day on 9 May will for them continue as symbols to express the sense of community of the people in the European Union and their allegiance to it'.

example, has survived many centuries without having a constitution as such.[20] The discussion of 'constitutionalism' in the Union, however, is not only about whether there is, or is not, something called a 'constitution', but it is also very much connected to the debates surrounding the governance of the EU and the transfer of power to the Union from the member states. Having transferred powers and thus competences from the member states to the Union by and within the treaties, the focus is on how these competences or powers are divided between the member states and the Union, and exercised by the institutions of the Union. This, in turn, involves discussion of further principles regulating this division and exercise of power—namely, 'subsidiarity' and proportionality and other alternative means, as will be discussed in turn in the following sections.

3.5 Competences, their Division, and Subsidiarity

Allied to the topics of the transfer of member states' sovereign powers and the supremacy of EU law are the issues of competences, their division, and the principles of subsidiarity and proportionality—tools by which the most appropriate division of competences can be determined.

Van Gend en Loos clearly showed that the transfer of sovereign powers from and by the member states to the Community was the very empowerment of the Community itself. This transfer provides the competence for the Community (EU) to make its own laws although at the time, as was stated by the Court of Justice, this was in limited fields. The original treaties, though—and indeed those still applicable—do not provide a clear-cut expression of the relationship between the law of the EU (namely, the law created under the treaties by the institutions) and the national or domestic laws of the member states. There was no rule to say, in the event of conflict between rules covering the same subject matter, which should take priority. Neither did the original treaties make any expression as to their own status; that is, were they constitutional rules or just another international treaty between member states?

Whilst the question of supremacy was quickly and clearly settled by the CoJ, at least from the Community (EU) standpoint (discussed in Chapter 5), the matter of competence is not so easily dealt with. In order for EU law to be supreme, the EU must possess the competence to act in the first place. If it does not have the competence to act in a certain way or to create certain new laws then, logically, such laws cannot take priority over member states' national law. This interlinked relationship between supremacy and competence can be observed in Case 22/70 Commission v Council (ERTA) (at [30]–[31]) and in Opinion 1/94, in which it was held that if the Community (EU) has competence, then the member states cannot act contrary to it—which is another way of expressing EU law supremacy.

3.5.1 The Conferral and Division of Competences

One of the most fundamental elements of a constitutional order is the vertical division of competence or power between the constituent elements and the central element of the organization in question. In the EU constitutional order, the law-making powers of the Union and its ability to take independent action were originally provided by a transfer of sovereign powers from the member states when either, as original member

---

[20] That is, as a single and complete document.

states, they created the Communities or, as later entrants, they joined the Community (EU). This transfer or, as can otherwise equally be expressed, this conferral of competences was expressly acknowledged by the Court of Justice in *Van Gend en Loos* and is essentially the legitimization of Community action, but it is to be stressed, once again, that this transfer is only within the areas agreed by the member states. This is expressed now in Art 1 TFEU.[21] On the face of it, any transfer of power and competences should, in theory, be a clear-cut process whereby any exercise of these powers by the Union institutions can only be within the terms granted by the member states and contained in the treaties. In other words, there should be nothing done by the EU institutions that is not expressly permitted by the treaties. This, in EU law jargon, is called 'attributed competence'. The other side of this particular coin is that what is attributed to the Union by the member states is consequentially removed from member states' competence—that is, the member states no longer have competence in the fields transferred.[22]

3.5.2 **Exclusive, Concurrent, and Complimentary Competences**

The range of actions of the Union can be seen in Art 3 TEU and Arts 2–6 TFEU, which set out in general terms the objectives and activities of the Union, but do not specifically detail any one of them. This is left to specific titles and chapters in the TFEU. Where the treaty specifies an object, it invariably provides a power to achieve that object: for example, Arts 45 and 46 TFEU set out respectively the objective and power of achieving the free movement of workers in the EU.

If the division—also termed allocation—of competences and those that were exclusively the Union's were clearly set out, there would be no particular difficulty. Unfortunately, in the beginning, the division of competences was not clearly set out, largely because the initial treaties were much more limited in scope, so this was less of a concern. A further unique dynamic of the EU, in contrast with traditional international organizations, is that the Communities (and now Union) were not intended to be a static one-off creation, but to be a long-term and evolving creation. Indeed, as discussed in Chapter 1, the founding intentions were that integration in one area was expected to spread to other areas and powers would be needed to regulate those new areas. In addition, the Community and now Union would have to react to events in the world as they unfolded and affected it. Hence, it was anticipated that the competences of the Communities and now Union equally needed to be dynamic and evolving, and not static. This meant that the EU would also have to be reactive and have the competences capable of expansion and reaction.

It is necessary, therefore, to consider what the competences were, how they developed in the EU legal order, how the member states considered and reacted to this, and what measures were taken to control the competence creep—that is, the gradual loss or transfer of competences away from the member states that they and their citizens considered was and is taking place.

---

[21] '1. This Treaty organises the functioning of the Union and determines the areas of, delimitation of, and arrangements for exercising its competences.'

[22] See Art 2(1) TFEU and Arts 4 and 5 TEU. Article 4(1): '1. In accordance with Article 5, competences not conferred upon the Union in the Treaties remain with the Member States.' Article 5(1) and (2): '1. The limits of Union competences are governed by the principle of conferral. The use of Union competences is governed by the principles of subsidiarity and proportionality. 2. Under the principle of conferral, the Union shall act only within the limits of the competences conferred upon it by the Member States in the Treaties to attain the objectives set out therein.'

Competences not conferred upon the Union in the treaties remain with the member states. Furthermore, each of the institutions is bound to act within the limits of the powers conferred on them (Art 13(2) TEU).

The Union enjoys exclusive competences in a few areas only, such as for certain aspects of the common customs duties, commercial policy to third countries (as upheld by the Court of Justice in its Opinion 1/75), and parts of the Common Fishing Policy (CFP). The division of competences is set out in Art 2 and exclusive competences listed in Art 3 TFEU, and include also competition policy for the internal market and monetary policy for the eurozone.

In other areas, the dividing line is not so clear and competence is concurrent—also termed 'shared' or 'non-exclusive' competence—between the member states and the EU.

Article 4 TFEU provides:

1. The Union shall share competence with the Member States where the Treaties confer on it a competence which does not relate to the areas referred to in Articles 3 and 6.

2. Shared competence between the Union and the Member States applies in the following principal areas:

   (a) internal market;

   (b) social policy, for the aspects defined in this Treaty;

   (c) economic, social and territorial cohesion;

   (d) agriculture and fisheries, excluding the conservation of marine biological resources;

   (e) environment;

   (f) consumer protection;

   (g) transport;

   (h) trans-European networks;

   (i) energy;

   (j) area of freedom, security and justice;

   (k) common safety concerns in public health matters, for the aspects defined in this Treaty.

In addition now, as introduced by the Lisbon Treaty (Art 2 TFEU), are co-ordinated and complementary competences for the Union to support member state action.[23] Article 2(4) provides that the EU also has the competence to pursue a common foreign and security policy.

Finally, there are areas of law over which powers have not been transferred to the Union and over which the member states retain their own exclusive competence.

It is in the area of shared competences that most difficulties arise, because it can be unclear whether the Union or the member states enjoy the competence for a particular action. Furthermore, the degree of sharing also alters according to the subject matter. For example, in areas such as the internal market, as soon as the Union acts under its

---

[23] Article 2(3) and (5) TFEU outline these. The Union can assist member states in coordinating their economies. Article 6 provides that:

The Union shall have competence to carry out actions to support, coordinate or supplement the actions of the Member States. The areas of such action shall, at European level, be:
(a) protection and improvement of human health;
(b) industry;
(c) culture;
(d) tourism;
(e) education, vocational training, youth and sport;
(f) civil protection;
(g) administrative cooperation.

competence, it assumes exclusive power to act and the member states are then deprived of the power to act in conflict. If the Union chooses not to act, the member states retain the power to act. Thus, where it does act, it takes over competence. This is known as 'pre-emption'. A good example can be seen in the area of the free movement of goods, which will be considered in Chapter 8. The Court of Justice held, in one of its most famous and leading cases,[24] that only where the Community had not acted could the member states act independently and, even then, if concerned with a general area that was otherwise regulated by the EC, the member states could act only within prescribed limits. As a result, there can be a genuine grey area between what is sanctioned and what is not; namely, what is within the Union competence and what is still within the member state competence.

This is a matter that has troubled the Communities and Union time and again, particularly as it became clear from the progressive judgments of the Court of Justice that the EU has taken over from the member states in some areas to which the member states were not sure they had agreed or, indeed, to which they had thought that they had *not* agreed, or thought that they had excluded from EU competence. For example, in Case C-262/88 *Barber*, pension payments were held to be pay and therefore within the equal pay competence, and not therefore a matter of state competence and exclusive regulation, as was previously considered to be the case because of its assumed connection with state pension policy (a matter still within the exclusive competence of the member states according to Directive 79/7).[25] Hence, there was a reaction by some of the member states that considered that the Commission and Community were extending their competences by stealth, and not with the agreement of the member states.

The next sections consider how competences could be, and were, extended and what measures were subsequently developed by the member states to control or limit this expansion or creep of competences. These notably include subsidiarity, restrictive drafting, and proportionality.

3.5.3 **Extension of Competences**

Under traditional international law understanding, the only way in which to add any competences to a created international organization is by treaty amendment. Whilst treaty amendment has taken place in the EU, it is only one of three ways in which the competences of the Union can be extended.

The first—that is, treaty amendment—is deliberate and clear-cut. The fields of Union competence have expanded greatly as a result of the member states assigning additional competences to the Union, with successive treaty changes, such as the adding of a chapter on environmental policy to the EC Treaty by the Single European Act (SEA) or monetary Union by the Maastricht Treaty. The Lisbon Treaty also contains the agreement of the member states to extend areas of Union competence further into intellectual property rights, sport, tourism, and civil protection, amongst others.

---

[24] Case 120/78 *Rewe-Zentral AG v Bundesmonopolverwaltung für Branntwein (Cassis de Dijon)* [1978] ECR 649, [1979] 3 CMLR 494. The member states, though, have tried to limit this pre-emption by Protocol 25 on the exercise of shared competence to specific acts and not whole areas.

[25] Art 7 of the directive (OJ 1979 L6/24):

  1. This Directive shall be without prejudice to the right of Member States to exclude from its scope:
    (a) the determination of pensionable age for the purposes of granting old-age and retirement pensions and the possible consequences thereof for other benefits;...

The second and third ways are not express, and were those which led to the use of the term 'competence creep' to describe the manner in which the Union's and institutions' competences have advanced incrementally. This increase is effected by both general and implied powers that have been employed by the institutions, including the Commission, but these have often been subject to the review of the Court of Justice, highlighting that this too is a dynamic and evolving area of EU law. The difficulties experienced in this area were, in fact, specifically taken on in the Lisbon Treaty.

3.5.4 Residual Powers

The second way in which competences have been extended is via the so-termed 'residual' law-making powers that include both specific and general variants.

3.5.4.1 Specific Residual Powers

The specific variants are those that grant subsidiary law-making powers to complete goals in specific areas such as Arts 114 and 115 TFEU, which provide for measures for the completion of the internal market and for the approximation of laws affecting the establishment or functioning of the internal market.

Article 114 TFEU provides that, to achieve the objectives of the internal market, set out in Art 26 TFEU, where powers are not otherwise provided by the treaty, action can be taken by QMV. In other words, action can be taken outside the express and exclusive grant of powers to the Union by a majority and not by the agreement of all member states.

Article 115 TFEU is an exception to the powers granted in Art 114, which is a general power to enact harmonizing legislation. It contains safety measures, however, so that member states and institutions do not go too far: the Council must act by unanimity and must consult the European Parliament.

These Articles should not be used, however, where other Articles would be more suitable. See, for example, Case C-376/98 *Germany v European Parliament and Council (Tobacco Advertising I)*, in which Art 95 EC (now Art 114 TFEU) was held to be inappropriate and thus lacking the competence to enact a measure aimed more at the protection of health, rather than at completing the internal market. However, in Case C-210/03 *R v Secretary of State for Health, ex p Swedish Match*, the Court of Justice held that if obstacles to trade emerge, the Commission can intervene to harmonize even if the internal market is not the prime motive—in that case, concerned with the banning of a type of snuff. In Case C-377/98 *Netherlands v European Parliament and Council (Biotechnology Directive)*, the CoJ held that Art 95 EC (now Art 114 TFEU) can be used in an area dealing with intellectual property, even though the directive provided that the member states could restrict patents and thus free movement of goods on the grounds of public morality. And, finally, in the second *Tobacco Advertising* case, C-380/03 *Germany v European Parliament and Council*, Art 95 EC (now Art 114 TFEU) could be used to enact a directive restricting the advertising of tobacco products, where differences in the national laws relating to this advertising would have the effect of creating obstacles to free trade; the Community directive was thus necessary to harmonize the internal market to allow it to function properly.

Note also in this context, Art 113 TFEU which provides a residual specific power for the Council, acting unanimously and consulting the EP and EESC, to adopt harmonizing legislation in the areas of turn-over taxes, excise duties, and indirect taxes where necessary to ensure the establishment and functioning of the internal market and to avoid distortion of competition.

3.5.4.2 General Residual Powers

The general variant is Art 352 TFEU, the residual law-making power, and now known as the 'flexibility clause', which provides that where doing so in furtherance of any of the objectives of the treaties and where no specific power exists, the Union may act by means of the Council after obtaining the consent of the European Parliament. Article 352(2) TFEU requires the Commission also to draw such proposals to the attention of the national parliaments in accordance with the subsidiarity principle, considered in Section 3.5.6.

Article 352(4) TFEU does not permit harmonization of member states' laws or apply to the areas of Common Foreign and Security Policy (CFSP). It is also subject to Declaration Nos 41 and 42, also considered at the end of this section, restricting the objectives to which Art 352 TFEU applies to those contained in Art 3(2), (3), and (5) TEU. It remains to be seen whether the Court of Justice will regard Art 352 TFEU as being so constrained.

Because these are general powers, they have led to problems regarding exactly how far they sanction EU activity in the face of member states' activity. However, they have been generously interpreted by the CoJ. Article 308 EC (now Art 352 TFEU) was used as the treaty base for the original Equal Treatment Directive 76/207 because, at the time, the relevant treaty base (then Art 119 EEC) only extended as far as equal pay. Article 308 EC was also used quite extensively to introduce legislation concerned with environmental matters where there was not, at the time, a treaty Article base available.

A limit to such use was found when the Court of Justice held, in its Opinion 2/94 of 1996, that Art 235 EEC (as Art 308 was then, now Art 352 TFEU) could not be used to accede to the European Convention on Human Rights (ECHR) because of the profound constitutional impact that it would have on the Community and the member states, which was neither envisaged nor, indeed, sanctioned by the EC Treaty.[26] Furthermore, the use of Art 308 EC would be improper if a specific treaty base were shown to exist (see Case 8/73 *HZA Bremerhafen v Massey-Ferguson*) and which should, therefore, have been used instead. More recently, in Cases C-402/05 P and C-415/05 *Kadi v Council*, a challenge to the use of Art 308 EC (now Art 352 TEU) was made following freezing the assets of persons whom the United Nations (UN) considered to be related to terrorists following the 9/11 attacks. It was argued that this was beyond the competence of the EU, but it was not accepted by the CoJ, which linked the economic action of the Council to the common market—a link that seems somewhat tenuous. It would seem, therefore, that even very weak links to the Union and its activities will suffice to justify the use of Art 352 TFEU. Article 352 TFEU can also be used in pursuit of the objectives of the Union now, as opposed previously to only the EC, so its potential scope for use is much wider. This is countered by the requirement that measures taken under this Article will be subject to the same procedure as that required for the monitoring of subsidiarity, requiring consultation of the national parliaments, and still restricts the European Parliament's role, but now to consent rather than only consultation. Measures cannot be used to harmonize national laws in areas in which harmonization is excluded by the treaties or in pursuit of CFSP objectives.

However, increases in the competences of the EU outside express treaty sanction have been increasingly criticized and challenged in general democratic terms. Even if using either Art 115 or Art 352 TFEU requiring unanimity of all member states in the Council

---

[26] Note that even where there is an express treaty commitment to accede to the ECHR now (Art 6 TEU), the draft agreement to facilitate that was held by the Court of Justice in Opinion 2/13 not to conform with the overall requirements of the EU legal order. See Chapter 4 for further details.

of Ministers, national parliaments are being by-passed and the change is being effected without any formal treaty amendment process. Hence, there have been challenges to some proposed and completed Community (EU) actions by the member states in Council before the Court of Justice (see Case 242/87 *Council v Commission (Erasmus)*), and by a series of amendments to the treaties to try to curb this development and drafting the legal bases restrictively, so that the Commission cannot use the base for further legislative intervention. See, for example, Art 149 TFEU, under the Employment Title, or Art 168(5) TFEU, which provides for 'incentive measures designed to protect and improve human health, excluding any harmonization of the laws and regulations of the member states'—in other words, the EU can take action, provided that it does not interfere with the existing laws in the member states. See also now the new requirement in Art 296 TFEU as a further means by which competence creep may be halted. Article 296 provides that, 'When considering draft legislative acts, the [European Parliament] and the Council shall refrain from adopting acts not provided for by the relevant legislative procedure in the area in question'.

Further attempts, outside specific treaty Article amendments, to try to delineate or make clearer that area of grey and to define the division of competences, are the introduction of the principles of subsidiarity and proportionality. These were designed to address the concerns of the member states about how competence is being exercised, albeit without much clear success so far.

3.5.5 Implied Powers

The exercise of implied powers is the third method of competence expansion. This was recognized by the Court of Justice in cases dealing with both internal and external powers of the Commission where there are no express powers in the treaty. Powers are nevertheless required to achieve an EU goal and are thus implied to meet the general objectives set out in the treaties. This development is also referred to as 'parallelism'.

3.5.5.1 Internal

The Court of Justice supported implied powers in the Community legal order as early as Case 8/55 *Fedechar* and interpreted them expansively in Cases 281, 283–5, and 287/85 *Commission v Germany (Migration Policy)*, in which Art 118 EEC (now Art 153 TFEU) provided for cooperation between member states in a social field and was employed by the Commission to enact a decision requiring the member states to supply information. When the decision was challenged, the CoJ held that where an Article of the EEC Treaty confers a specific task on the Commission, it must be accepted, if that provision is not to be rendered wholly ineffective, that it confers on the Commission necessarily and per se the powers that are indispensable in order to carry out that task, such as the gathering of information.

3.5.5.2 Impact on External Competences

In Case 22/70 *Commission v Council (ERTA)*, the then six member states had negotiated independently a road transport agreement with other non-EC states that was then adopted by resolution of the Council, but subsequently challenged by the Commission because there was a previous Community act regulating this area. The Court of Justice held that the authority of the Community to conclude international agreements arises not only from express conferment, but also impliedly from other treaty provisions providing express internal competences in the same area. Thus, where the internal powers have been acted upon, the member states are prevented from acting externally in those areas—particularly where such action would impact on the internal policy. Thus, the Union alone is in the position to carry out the contractual obligations towards third countries. In the particular case, because the member states' negotiations were the continuance of agreements reached originally before the internal policy was formulated, it was held that the member states within the Council were entitled to act.[27]

However, a ruling by the Court of Justice did set some limits on implied powers. Opinion 1/94 concerned the competence of the Community or member states within the Community to conclude the General Agreement on Trade in Services (GATS) and Agreement on Trade-related Aspects of Intellectual Property Rights (TRIPs) of the World Trade Organization (WTO) talks. The Court of Justice held that implied powers operate only between the member states and the Community, and not the Commission and the Council, hence whilst there was joint competence in these areas, there was not an exclusive Community competence. That Opinion has effectively been overruled in Case C-414/11 *Daiichi Sankyo*[28] as far as the Union's involvement in Intellectual Property Agreements is concerned, due to the Amendment of Art 207 TFEU which specifically refers to the commercial aspects of intellectual property agreements. That then just serves to reinforce the earlier case law that the Union's external powers to act will be implied where not already express. See also Cases 467–9/98 *Commission v Finland (Air Transport)*, in which it was confirmed that where the Community has acted in pursuit of exclusive internal powers that it possesses, any action by the member states in adopting an international agreement (bilateral agreements with the USA) affecting the common Community rules was an unlawful intrusion on Community competence. There was no express power to regulate air transport with consequences outside the EU; however that power was nevertheless implied in view of the impact on the internal exclusive power if member states were to go it alone.

Following the entry of the Lisbon Treaty, Art 3(2) TFEU effectively puts into statutory form and, indeed, strengthens the position reached already in the jurisprudence of the Court of Justice by providing:

> The Union shall also have exclusive competence for the conclusion of an international agreement when its conclusion is provided for in a legislative act of the Union or is necessary to enable the Union to exercise its internal competence, or in so far as its conclusion may affect common rules or alter their scope.

This is effectively repeated in the Title on International Agreements, Art 216 (1) TFEU:

> 1. The Union may conclude an agreement with one or more third countries or international organisations where the Treaties so provide or where the conclusion of an agreement is necessary in order to achieve, within the framework of the Union's policies, one of the objectives referred to in the Treaties, or is provided for in a legally binding Union act or is likely to affect common rules or alter their scope.

It remains to be seen if the member states will react to the exercise of external powers taken under these provisions and whether the EU Institutions and CoJ will treat them as providing the same powers.

---

[27] The case then is rather ironic in that it was the member states (albeit within the Council) which helped develop this particular form of competence creep by legitimizing the action taken as Community action, not expressly granted though by the treaties, something about which the member states were in future to complain.

[28] [2013] ECR I-520.

3.5.6 **The Principle of Subsidiarity**

Subsidiarity requires decisions to be taken at the most appropriate level, whether that is at the level of the Union or the level of the member states. Thus, the desire to regulate activities within the Union should not insist on action at the Union level when it is not necessary. While there was arguably always the view that legal measures that were taken centrally by the Union institutions should be taken only where necessary and that, if such measures were not suitable, member states were allowed to regulate matters individually, this understanding did not find formal expression in any EU provision. There are implied examples of its use, such as the discretion given to the member states to meet the requirements of a directive, or the principles of mutual recognition and the rule of reason established by the Court of Justice in the *Cassis de Dijon* case[29] but, as originally established, the Communities had no express statement of this principle.

The principle of subsidiarity made its first express appearance in the Community legal order in 1986 when introduced by the treaty amendments made by the SEA. At that time, however, it was introduced specifically in respect of environmental measures under old Art 174(4) EC (now Art 191 TFEU) only. Essentially, it provided that the Community should take action only where objectives could be better attained at the Community level than the level of individual member states. It was introduced generally into the Community legal order by the TEU and is now to be found in Art 1 TEU, which provides that decisions are to be taken openly and as closely as possible to the citizen. Article 5(1) TEU then provides, 'The use of Union competences is governed by the principles of subsidiarity and proportionality', and further provides in Art 5(3) TEU that:

> in areas which do not fall within its exclusive competence, the Union shall act, only if and in so far as the objectives of the proposed action cannot be sufficiently achieved by the member states, either at central level or at regional and local level, but can rather, by reason of the scale or effects of the proposed action, be better achieved at Union level.

Article 5 TEU also encapsulates the principle of conferral, which was also expressly included by the Lisbon Treaty in new Arts 4 and 5 TEU, providing that the EU can act only to the extent that competences have been conferred on it to do so. The exact meaning of Art 5(3) TEU is, however, far from clear, particularly regarding where the line might be drawn between the competence of the Union and the competences of the member states. Thus, the general introduction of these concepts has not proved to be the instant fix desired by the member states, let alone a concept that is readily understandable, or indeed translatable, into a clear-cut process by which it is decided whether Union action is appropriate and thus lawful within the terms of the concept. It seems to suggest that decision-taking that might be accumulated in the centre, namely by the institutions, but which is not actually necessary at this level, should instead be taken by the member states. Decisions, in short, should be taken closer to the people, which is the formulation of the principle contained in the statement made in Art 1 TEU. Thus it needs to be shown that EU actions are necessary, in that the member states are unable to achieve the same objectives, and that there are greater benefits to be achieved at the Union level. In support of Art 5 TEU are Art 10 TEU which requires decisions to be taken as openly and as closely as possible to the citizen and Art 13 TEU, which requires that each institution act within the limits of the power conferred on it.

The difficulties with this principle thus remain who decides when to apply it and whether it has been observed in the decision-making process. If the matter is one within

---

[29] The rule of reason and the principle of mutual recognition are discussed in Chapter 7.

the exclusive competence of the Union, subsidiarity does not apply. The problem is, though, as noted earlier, that 'exclusivity' itself is not a clear-cut term. The practice has arisen now that, in order to justify taking the action, the Commission needs to outline why it has competence to take the particular action, and does so in the preamble and recitals to proposed legislation[30]—although it may be argued that this has become more of a cant by the Commission than clear justification.[31]

It may therefore give rise to considerable litigation to determine whether it has been adhered to correctly. Whilst the principle itself was not disturbed by the Treaty of Amsterdam, that treaty did add a protocol as an attempt to clarify its meaning, which has since been amended and expanded by the Lisbon Treaty.[32] It requires the Commission to consult widely before formally proposing legislation and, in an amendment brought in by the Lisbon Treaty, its draft legislative acts shall be forwarded to the national parliaments at the same time as they are to the European Parliament and Council. Indeed, the protocol has been tightened up in its latest version, under which the Commission must accompany drafts with detailed statements as to how the proposal complies with the principles of subsidiarity and proportionality, and provide evidential support to demonstrate that Union action is required and the general and financial impact of the proposed legislation.

Articles 6 and 7 further outline the national parliaments' ability to object to the proposal and the procedure by which those objections are further considered by the Union institutions in the legislative processes, along with that the Commission must issue a reasoned opinion if it wishes to maintain the proposal for further consideration in the legislative process.[33] All in all, it is quite a convoluted process, the extensive details of which will not therefore be rehearsed here and the principle remains difficult to be precise about. In addition to the requirement in Art 12 TEU,[34] there is also Protocol (No 1) on the Role of National Parliaments, which also outlines how national Parliaments, when considering draft EU legislation, should determine whether the principle of subsidiarity has been complied with.

---

[30] See e.g. Directive 2002/14 on employee consultation, recital 17 (N. Foster (ed), *EU Treaties and Legislation*, latest edn, Oxford University Press, Oxford).

[31] See e.g. recital 36 from Directive 2006/54: 'Since the objectives of this Directive cannot be sufficiently achieved by the Member States and can therefore be better achieved at Community level, the Community may adopt measures in accordance with the principle of subsidiarity as set out in Article 5 of the Treaty. In accordance with the principle of proportionality, as set out in that Article, this Directive does not go beyond what is necessary in order to achieve those objectives.'

[32] Protocol (No 2) on the Application of the Principles of Subsidiarity and Proportionality (N. Foster, *EU Treaties and Legislation*, latest edn, Oxford University Press, Oxford). Note that, under Art 51 TEU, protocols enjoy treaty status.

[33] National parliaments have eight weeks to comment, each having two votes, and if votes amounting to one-third of the total votes object, the Commission is 'yellow carded' and is required to reconsider its proposal. This happened in 2012 when the Commission proposal for a Posted Workers Directive was objected to. The Commission subsequently amended the proposal but it has yet to gain the approval of the Council and the EP. If consequently a majority of the member states' parliaments consider subsidiarity to have been breached, an orange card is raised which the Commission has to rebut by reasoned opinion which is forwarded to the EP and Council to vote on.

[34] Article 12 TEU provides that:

National Parliaments contribute actively to the good functioning of the Union:

(a) through being informed by the institutions of the Union and having draft legislative acts of the Union forwarded to them in accordance with the Protocol on the role of national Parliaments in the European Union;

(b) by seeing to it that the principle of subsidiarity is respected in accordance with the procedures provided for in the Protocol on the application of the principles of subsidiarity and proportionality...

As a last resort—previously impliedly, but now expressly stated under Art 8 of Protocol 2—legislative acts may be challenged under Art 263 TFEU for infringing the principle. Some of these challenges are considered in the next section.

Whilst no new challenges have yet reached the Court of Justice focused specifically on the amended protocol, challenges from before the changes took place have been made.

3.5.6.1 Challenges for Non-compliance with the Principle

Non-compliance with the subsidiarity principle is a ground for annulment under an Art 263 TFEU judicial review action before the Court of Justice, as is made clear by Protocol 2, noted earlier. However, even though there had been actions to challenge EU legislation for a breach of the principle in the past, there has been limited judicial guidance on its true value. This is no surprise given the obscurity of the principle, which involves the balancing of economic and political priorities—principles that the CoJ is reluctant to second-guess.

In Case C-84/94 *UK v Council (Working Time Directive)* and Case C-377/98 *Netherlands v European Parliament and Council (Biotechnology Directive)* arguments raised by the member states in the cases that subsidiarity had not been observed were rejected by the Court of Justice. In *UK v Council (Working Time Directive)*, the CoJ dismissed this part of the action with little discussion merely to confirm that the Council had a clear power to act on working hours as an issue of the health and safety of workers. In other words, if it had the competence to act, it could act. However, in Case C-376/98 *Germany v European Parliament and Council (Tobacco Advertising Ban Directive)*, the harmonizing Directive 98/43 banning most forms of tobacco advertising was enacted under Art 95 EC (now Art 114 TFEU) as an internal market measure. This was challenged by Germany, arguing that the measure was more closely allied to a public health measure and thus should have been enacted under Art 152 EC (now Art 168 TFEU), which expressly prohibits harmonizing legislation. The Court of Justice held that measures under (the then) Art 95 EC must have the primary object of improving conditions for the establishment or functioning of the internal market, and that other Articles of the treaty may not be used as a legal basis in order to circumvent the express exclusion of harmonization. It held further that to construe the internal market Article as meaning that it vests in the Community (EU) legislature a general power to regulate the internal market would be incompatible with the principle embodied in (the then) Art 5 EC that the powers of the Community are limited to those specifically conferred upon it. The CoJ thus held that the measure did little to enhance the internal market and annulled it entirely. The CoJ also indicated that in cases in which there was no specific competence covering the subject matter of the measure the internal market-base Art 95 EC (now Art 114 TEU) could be used.

The judgment is not a clear endorsement that subsidiarity is a clearly justiciable issue; rather, it is another confirmation that where an incorrect legal base is used, this provides grounds for the annulment of the measure based on it.[35] The judgment is regarded as a reply to national courts, in particular, the German Federal Constitutional Court,[36] which might have been minded to take EU law into its own hands, by showing that the Court of Justice is prepared to police incursions into the member states' competences by the EU's institutions. Cases C-154–5/04 *Alliance for Natural Health* provide another view of the CoJ that arguments based on a possible breach of subsidiarity will not allow it to interfere with decisions that are the result of the exercise of legislative discretion. In Case C-58/08

---

[35] See, for further details on the legal base, Section 4.8.1 in Chapter 4.
[36] This is considered in Chapter 5, Section 5.5.2 concerned with EU law reception in Germany.

Vodafone and ors decided in 2010, the Court of Justice did not interfere with the Roaming Regulation 717/2007 (OJ 2007 L171/32) on the basis of either subsidiarity or proportionality. It was argued that roaming charges should be capped only by each individual country and not by EU action. The Court of Justice held that the power to act had been conferred on the EU and that the need for Union action to maintain the smooth functioning of the internal market and competition was clear. The exercise of the discretion by the EU legislature had not been disproportionate.

It would seem that if a measure is enacted which is clearly and genuinely concerned with the internal market, and thus which can only effectively be regulated on an EU-wide basis by the EU, it will be extremely difficult for this to be challenged on the ground of a breach of subsidiarity. Almost inevitably, the CoJ will be given further opportunities to come up with clearer and workable definitions of its meaning. It is possible that the principle of subsidiarity will also join the ranks of general principles of EU law, although it is one introduced deliberately by the member states rather than created or introduced by the Court of Justice.

As a final thought on subsidiarity, one cannot help thinking that, whatever its true value, it is not directly concerned with the rights of the citizens, but rather with the division of power between the member states and the Union. Quite where a decision is taken, providing it is taken, has little import for the citizens and more for the member states.

3.5.7 **Restrictive Drafting**

Legal bases have been drafted restrictively so that the Commission cannot use the base for further legislative intervention.

See, for example, Article 168(5) TFEU, which provides for action to promote cooperation in public health matters, but 'excluding any harmonization of the laws and regulations of the member states'. In other words, the Union can take action provided that it does not interfere with the existing laws in the member states. Another method, in addition to specific treaty Article amendments to control the extension and exercise of competences, is the introduction of the principles of subsidiarity and proportionality, which now find formal treaty expression. These are designed to address the concerns of the member states about how implied competences were being employed by the Commission, albeit without much clear success thus far.

3.5.8 **Proportionality**

Proportionality, apart from being a legal principle in its own right and often employed by individuals in challenges to Union action, is also contained in Art 5 TEU and is linked to the subsidiarity principle, in that both are concerned with the control and exercise of powers by the institutions; however, unlike subsidiarity, proportionality also applies to matters of exclusive EU competence.

The treaty definition of 'proportionality' under Art 5(2) TEU provides that: 'Under the principle of proportionality, the content and form of Union action shall not exceed what is necessary to achieve the objectives of the Treaties.'

Like subsidiarity, it too is subject to Protocol 2, and Union acts are open to possible challenges if breaching proportionality. Draft legislation must also state how it complies with the principle of proportionality. It was, for example, raised in Case 84/94 *UK v Council (Working Time Directive)* by the UK under the argument that the restrictions imposed on working time were not minimum requirements, but were excessive—that is, disproportionate. This view was rejected by the Court of Justice on the ground that unless there had been a manifest error or misuse of powers, the Council must be allowed to exercise its discretion in law-making involving social policy choices.

The extent to which proportionality can be employed to challenge Union law in an action to annul a harmonization measure dealing with food supplements was shown to be limited. In Cases C-154–5/04 *Alliance for Natural Health*, the CoJ expressed the view that arguments based on a possible breach of proportionality will not allow it to interfere with decisions that are the result of the exercise of legislative discretion. Legality can be affected only as a result of the legislative act being manifestly inappropriate.

This was confirmed in similar terms in the follow-up case, Case C-344/04 *R v Department of Transport, ex p International Air Transport Association and European Low Fares Airline Association*, at [80]:

> With regard to judicial review of the conditions referred to in the previous paragraph, the Community legislature must be allowed a broad discretion in areas which involve political, economic and social choices on its part, and in which it is called upon to undertake complex assessments. Consequently, the legality of a measure adopted in those fields can be affected only if the measure is manifestly inappropriate having regard to the objective which the competent institution is seeking to pursue.

However, in Case C-310/04 *Spain v Council (Spanish Cotton Subsidies)*,[37] the CoJ held that the Council in legislating had failed to take into account all the relevant matters and in particular labour costs, and had thus as a consequence not complied with the principle of proportionality. The case remains as a rare example of success in pleading proportionality and in the *Vodafone* case, considered also earlier in respect of subsidiarity, proportionality was also tested and satisfied in that no others means was considered to be available to the Commission to ensure there was no distortion in the functioning of, nor to competition in, the internal market, other than the reduction in roaming charges.

3.5.9 The Lisbon Treaty and the Division and Control of Competences

The concerns about the lack of democratic accountability, transparency, and clear-cut division of competences in the Union, and that the Union is taking over far more power from the member states than is desirable or necessary, to some degree led to the rejection of the Constitutional Treaty by the electorates in France and the Netherlands in 2005. This is ironic, in that the rejections and the subsequent shelving of the Constitutional Treaty at the time delayed progress in providing a clearer, constitutional, treaty basis for the division of power, because the Constitutional Treaty contained Articles that were intended to address these very issues (although it may be argued that they did so imperfectly, albeit along the right lines). Apart from repeating the principle of subsidiarity, the Constitutional Treaty set out, for the first time in the EU, a far clearer division of competences. These were carried over into the Lisbon Treaty almost unaltered but, as with many of the amendments, the changes made to both the TEU and the previous EC Treaty were more complicated than they needed to be. Hence, the new Arts 4 and 5 TEU provide the principles of competence, fidelity, conferral, subsidiarity, and proportionality, and new Arts 2–6 TFEU provide further details about the categories and areas of Union competence and the division of competences first provided by the Constitutional Treaty.

---

[37] [2006] ECR I-7285.

Article 5(1) TEU provides that the limits of Union competences are governed by the principle of conferral, and that the use of Union competences is governed by the principles of subsidiarity and proportionality. Article 5 TEU goes on to outline that 'conferral' means that the Union shall act within the limits of the competences conferred upon it by the member states in the Constitution to attain the objectives set out in the Constitution, and makes clear that competences not conferred upon the Union in the Constitution remain with the member states. Furthermore, the principle of subsidiarity was restated in Art 5(3), which also relies on a protocol for further definition, the Articles of which also provide a procedure whereby the national parliaments can police the use of subsidiarity and address the Commission if they feel that it has been breached.

Article 3 TFEU sets out the exclusive competences, for example the customs duties, in which the member states are not able to act at all; Art 4 TFEU sets out the areas of concurrent or shared competences, whereby the member states may only act if the EU has not yet acted or has ceased to act; and Art 6 TFEU provides competences for the EU to act in support of the member states' own actions only.

Finally, in the attempt to counter competence creep, the Lisbon Treaty has introduced a requirement in Article 296 TFEU that relates to the competence and legal base issues, and states that: 'When considering draft legislative acts, the EP and the Council shall refrain from adopting acts not provided for by the relevant legislative procedure in the area in question.' Furthermore, Protocol 25 on shared competences and three declarations attached to the treaties also address these issues. Protocol 25 states that 'when the Union has taken action in a certain area, the scope of this exercise of competence only covers those elements governed by the Union act in question and therefore does not cover the whole area'. A revised declaration (No 18) on competences confirms the respective rights of the member states and Union, the latter represented by the Commission in these matters. Declaration Nos 24 and 42 are also pertinent here in that they seek to prevent further competence creep arising from the conferral of legal personality on the EU as a whole and the use of the general law-making power under Art 352 TFEU. The revisions made by the Lisbon Treaty also allow for a reduction in the competences of the EU under Art 48 TEU and for the ordinary revision procedure by member states (or EP or Commission) submitting a proposal to the Council which is then submitted to the European Council and notified to national Parliaments. This has not happened yet.

The next chapter will consider how the powers which have been transferred to the EU are used by the Union in terms of the forms of secondary laws that can be enacted by them and, allied to that and to this chapter, the choice of legal base for EU secondary law. First, though, the range of sources of EU law will be considered.

Further Reading

Books

CRAIG, P. *The Lisbon Treaty: Law, Politics and Treaty Reform*, Oxford University Press, Oxford, 2010.

HIX, S. *The Political System of the European Union*, 2nd edn, Macmillan, Basingstoke, 2005.

KONSTANTINIDES, T. *Division of Powers in European Union Law: The Delimitation of Internal Competences between the EU and the Member States*, Kluwer Law International, London, 2009.

LENAERTS, K. and VAN NUFFEL, P. *Constitutional Law of the European Union*, 2nd edn, Sweet & Maxwell, London, 2004.

Articles

ALBI, A. and VAN ELSUWEGE, P. 'The EU Constitution, National Constitutions and Sovereignty: An Assessment of a European Constitutional Order' (2004) 29 EL Rev 741.

BECK, G. 'The Problem of Kompetenz-Kompetenz: A Conflict between Right and Right Where There Is No Praetor' (2005) 30 EL Rev 42.

CRAIG, P. 'Constitutions, Constitutionalism and the European Union' (2001) 7 ELJ 125.

CRAIG, P. 'Competence, Clarity, Conferral, Containment and Consideration' (2004) 29 EL Rev 323.

CYGAN, A. 'Democracy and Accountability in the European Union: The View from the House of Commons' (2003) 66 MLR 384.

CYGAN, A. 'The Parliamentarisation of EU Decision-making? The Impact of the Treaty of Lisbon on National Parliaments' (2011) 36 EL Rev 480.

DASHWOOD, A. 'The Relationship between the Member States and the European Union/ European Community' (2004) 41 CML Rev 355–81.

DAVIES. G. 'Subsidiarity: The Wrong Idea, in the Wrong Place, at the Wrong Time' (2006) 43 CML Rev 63.

FABBRINI, F. and GRANAT, K. 'Yellow Card but No Foul: The Roles of the National Parliaments under the Subsidiarity Protocol and the Commission Proposal for an EU Regulation on the Right to Strike' (2013) 50 CML Rev 115.

HARBO, T.-I. 'The Function of the Proportionality Principle in EU Law' (2010) 16 ELJ 158.

HORSLEY, T. 'Subsidiarity and the European Court of Justice: Missing Pieces in the Subsidiarity Puzzle' (2012) 50 JCMS 267.

KUMM, M. 'The Jurisprudence of Constitutional Conflict: Constitutional Supremacy in Europe before and after the Constitutional Treaty' (2005) 11 ELJ 262–307.

KUMM, M. 'Constitutionalising Subsidiarity in Integrated Markets: The Case of Tobacco Regulation in the European Union' (2006) 12 ELJ 503.

OLIVER, P. 'The French Constitution and the Treaty of Maastricht' (1994) 43 ICLQ 1.

WEATHERILL, S. 'Better Competence Monitoring' (2005) 30 EL Rev 23–41.

WEATHERILL, S. 'Competence Creep and Competence Control' (2005) 24 YEL 1.

4

EU Law: Sources, Forms, and Law-making

4.1 Introduction

This chapter starts by taking an overall view of the EU legal order, the different forms of EU law, and the variety of sources of law contributing to this legal order. In addition, the rules known as 'soft law' are also briefly considered. Following this, the ways or processes by which the binding EU secondary laws are made are considered, and, finally, alternative decision-making and law-making developments are reviewed.

4.2 The EU Legal System

The Treaty on European Union and the Treaty on the Functioning of the European Union, as amended, are the principal sources of law for the Union. As will be clear from the opening chapters, the treaties and EU law are not static bodies of law, but are amended from time to time as the member states agree, as can clearly be seen by the changes introduced by the Single European Act (SEA), the Maastricht Treaty (TEU), the Treaties of Amsterdam and Nice, and, most importantly of all now, the Lisbon Treaty. In establishing the basic format of the Communities at the time of their founding, legal models were sought on which to build the legal system for the Communities. At that time, there were no member states from common law jurisdictions; it is therefore to be expected that the Community and now EU legal system would broadly resemble a civil law system, and in particular follow legal structures found in the French and German legal systems. For example, much of the procedure of the courts is based on French administrative law, as are actions for damages under Art 340(2) TFEU. In turn, looking over the longer-term development of EU law, this has been influenced by both the legal structures and the principles of law in the member states and, in turn, EU law has influenced the development of law in the member states.[1]

Thus, the construction of the EU legal order proceeded by means of the establishment of framework treaties providing broad principles and aims, which reflected the way in which civil law countries approached legislative enactment with codified law. They commence with general abstract principles, such as the preamble and Arts 2 and 3 TFEU. This approach has been strengthened by the latest amendments and rearrangement of the treaties and the material in them. The TEU has been made into a general overview treaty,

---

[1] E.g. refer to Lord Irvine of Lairg, 'The Influence of Europe on Public Law in the United Kingdom' in B.S. Markesinis (ed), *The Coming Together of the Common Law and the Civil Law: The Clifford Chance Millennium Lectures*, Hart Publishing, Oxford, 2000, pp 24–5.

providing the broad basis for the former Treaty Establishing the European Community, which has become, as it is inelegantly titled, the Treaty on the Functioning of the European Union. This is the treaty that provides the details of the overall policies set out in the TEU. It too, though, retains its general introduction and Articles.

The TEU also has a general preamble, and Arts 2 and 3 providing a list of objectives including, for example, under Art 3(4) that 'The Union shall establish an economic and monetary Union whose currency is the euro'. The TEU also includes something else with which lawyers from civil law countries are quite familiar—that is, a form of 'good-faith' clause. Article 4(3) TEU imposes an obligation on the member states both to act positively to achieve the goals of the treaty and not to act in any way that would jeopardize those aims.[2]

The rest of the TFEU, although putting the broad aims into greater detail, nevertheless provides merely an outline for the areas of law that the member states agreed should be integrated. It provides, for example, the basic legal regime for the free movement of goods and workers, competition law, and agriculture. Some sections are more detailed than others, and whereas free movement of goods has required little secondary legislation, competition law and agriculture have been subject to considerable legislative addition. Thus, for the most part, the treaties require completion by detailed regulations and directives. The areas agreed by the member states can be and have been added to: for example, environmental and consumer protection by the SEA, and new policy areas introduced by the TEU, notably economic and monetary union, and health and safety and industry policies.

Apart from the secondary legislation needed to put into effect the goals of the various policies, any gaps and ambiguities in the legislation and interpretation of the treaty and secondary legislation are resolved by the Court of Justice and, as a result, a body of case law has slowly arisen, itself relying on a variety of internal and external sources, such as general principles and fundamental rights. These latter sources will also be considered within this chapter. Further, making up the overall array of sources, are various international treaties and provisions of international law which are binding or have effect in the EU legal system.

4.2.1 **The Style of the EU Legal System**

Before moving on to consider the individual elements of the EU legal system, it is worthwhile considering how the legal system is intended to work. Like the civil law systems, the EU legal system is a 'deductive' system; therefore, the approach adopted to the application of the law is from the general to the particular. This means starting with general principles of the treaty or code and becoming increasingly particular, through more specific treaty Articles and secondary legislation and, where necessary or helpful, by the use of case law. The common law approach, in contrast, involves the gradual development and build-up of rules of law from the particular situations or cases to establish a general rule. The cases give rise to a general principle of law that is then applied in future cases. This system is known as 'inductive reasoning'. Where deductive reasoning is applied to resolving legal disputes, the result in a particular case is achieved by working from the general to the particular.

As will be demonstrated in the following chapters, the interpretation techniques of the CoJ also follow the approach of taking into account the general aims to help to decide in particular cases. The CoJ will often make reference to the preamble and general

---

[2] This is also referred to as the principle of solidarity and the solidarity Article/clause.

provisions of the treaty to justify a particular decision, and will apply law in the scope of the treaty as a whole, in light of the basic aims and objectives of the treaty and not only the specific legislation. For example, Art 2 EC was referred to in Case 7/75 *Mrs and Mrs F v The Belgian State* concerning social security, and Art 3 EC in Case 6/72 *Europemballage and Continental Can v Commission* and Case 14/83 *Von Colson*, which was very strongly argued on the basis of Art 10 EC (now Art 4(3) TEU). More recently the *Francovich* case (6 and 9/90) was also argued strongly on the basis on Art 10 EC to establish, for the first time under Community (EU) law, state liability for the failure of the member state to implement a directive. Then, any secondary legislation on the topic can be considered and, finally, the Court of Justice may refer to the relevant case law on the interpretation and application of the treaty or other legislative provisions.

Article 18 TFEU,[3] the general prohibition of discrimination on the ground of nationality, is also relevant to all areas of EU law and used as a general tool of the Court of Justice to reach just results on particular occasions that might not otherwise have been reached by the application of more specific provisions. For example, it has been used to extend the equality-of-law requirement in respect of vocational training and fees into more mainstream education, as can be seen in Cases 24/86 *Blaizot*, 263/86 *Humbel*, 39/86 *Lair*, and 293/83 *Gravier*, amongst others.

4.2.2 **The Classification of the Elements of EU Law**

EU law can be divided broadly into three main components: institutional law, procedural law, and substantive law.

4.2.2.1 **Institutional Law**

Institutional law is in essence, and is sometimes called, the 'constitutional law' of the EU, and concerns the structure or constitution of the Union, the regulation of the main institutions and other bodies of the Union, the sources of EU law, and the special concepts of EU law, including supremacy and direct effects. Institutional law also concerns the relationship of the institutions between themselves, the relationship of the Union with the member states, and its external relations with other countries and international organizations. The institutions are the bodies responsible for the legislative and budgetary processes and, as their relationship alters in time due to treaty amendment, disputes arise over the boundaries of the powers and duties of the institutions, and their relationship to one another, which give rise to increasing case law.

As in other areas of EU law, the role of the Court of Justice has been fundamental to the development of the Union. The CoJ has been called upon many times to adjudicate inter-institutional disputes, and those between institutions and member states. It is becoming increasingly involved as the institutions seek to protect their powers or legally to extend them: for example, the CoJ has assisted the European Parliament in pressing for and gaining increased litigation rights to reflect its democratic power in the EU, now formally recognized by treaty amendment (Art 263 TFEU). Generally, also, the CoJ has been instrumental in the development of the legal system because of this judicial activism—and not without criticism at times. Its pronouncements on the status and effects of the provisions of EU law have resulted in the establishment and development of ground-breaking, and now fundamental, leading principles of EU law, including direct

---

[3] Which was old Art 6 and before that Art 7 EEC, which are the numbers found in old case law. Article 18 TFEU, as it now is, is also considered in Chapter 11.

effects, supremacy, and state liability. The institutional law is an expanding area of EU law, as exemplified by the changes wrought by the numerous treaty amendments and, in particular most recently, by the Lisbon Treaty, which have expanded the areas of competence and altered the power relationships in the Union—for example, by providing the European Parliament with greater legislative power and establishing the European Council as a full institution, and creating a new President of the European Council.

4.2.2.2 Procedural Law

Procedural law is sometimes referred to as the 'administrative law' of the Union and largely involves judicial review or judicial control in the Union. It is concerned with the various actions that can be taken by the institutions, member states, and natural and legal persons under rules provided by the TFEU (see Arts 258–60, 263, 265, 267, 277, and 340 TFEU). These actions, then, are mainly concerned with the enforcement of rights against the EU institutions, the member states, and individuals. Procedural law covers a range of remedies: indirect actions involving the national courts and direct actions at the level of the Union, both of which will be considered in Chapters 6 and 7.

Procedural law is thus concerned with the details of actions before the Courts, all of which must be based on a specific provision within the treaties or on a principle of law developed by the Court of Justice. The CoJ is often at its most restrictive in this area—for example, by restraining the right or ability of individuals to challenge acts of the Union by a fairly strict interpretation of the rights provided in the treaty Articles. The admissibility barriers that have to be overcome by individuals for actions under Arts 263, 265, and 277 TFEU are considerable, and will be considered in Chapter 7. Cases referred to the CoJ from the national courts are received for the most part much more favourably.

4.2.2.3 Substantive Law

Substantive law involves the legal rules established to carry out the broad policy areas of law agreed under the EU treaties, and can be distinguished from the law relating to the institutions and the procedural law of the EU. The substantive law is largely secondary law, and takes effect predominantly in the member states and not at the Union level, despite its primary base in treaty Articles. The substantive law of the EU is also described as 'economic law', or the 'law of the economy of the EU', and even as 'EU private law'. However, this is not a particularly meaningful label, because the concept of economic law varies from state to state and between political systems. Additionally, this simplistic tag may not explain the attitude of the Union, as expressed by the Court of Justice, to the substantive law of the EU, and suggests that it is only concerned with the economic considerations of the Union and not wider concerns that may be relevant. The Union is quite clearly—as demonstrated by the preambles and opening Articles to the treaties, particularly as amended by the Treaties of Amsterdam, Nice, and Lisbon—concerned with far more than the setting up of a regulatory framework for limited aspects of the economies dealing only with free-trade rules. Examples that reflect purely economic integration or cooperation would be agreements between the European Free Trade Association (EFTA) and General Agreement on Tariffs and Trade (GATT) countries, which want only the economic trade rules. Latterly, many more social concerns and policies are being given voice in the Union legal order and treaties: see, for example, the much-expanded titles on social policy, education, culture, and public health in the TFEU (Arts 151–69). Further evidence can be found in the statements made by the CoJ that the Community places social concerns above economic considerations (for example, in Case C-324/96 *Deutsche Telekom v Vick*).

There is a large and increasing number of areas of substantive law that now arises from the EU treaties and subsequent intergovernmental agreements. The number has been increased by the SEA, the TEU, and the Amsterdam, Nice and Lisbon Treaties. The substantive law chapters following, however, will deal with four topics only, all of which were within the original policies of the Community, although to a different extent, social provision being at the time very limited. Those included are the free movement of goods, the free movement of workers and persons, competition law, and equality law. Due to the expansion of this area and the necessary space constraints imposed on textbooks, this text, however, will concentrate only on the sex discrimination aspects of equality law.

The first two, at least, are centrally concerned with the achievement of the economic goals of the Union, but it has been the subject of argument as to whether the concerns, and thus law, in these areas have been promulgated only for economic ends, or whether there are other wider social concerns and aims of the Union. The general question to be asked is whether there was also an intention for these laws to achieve social aims or whether it is only because these economic laws were seen to impact so strongly on the social level in the member states that this view may now be taken. The Court of Justice has, for a long time, referred to the support that must be given to the four freedoms of the Union that it regards as fundamental elements, or cornerstones, of the Union and will do its best to uphold them. It will interpret the EU rules of law generously—that is, wherever possible, it will try to uphold the EU rules in the face of national legislation. The exceptions or derogations allowed to the member states in some of the provisions are interpreted narrowly against the member states. The aim is to give the greatest possible effect to EU rights and less scope to member state derogations which, if allowed free rein, would undermine the aims of the Union. (See, for example, a case from the area of the free movement of goods, Case 40/82 *Commission v UK*, concerned with a justification by the UK for restricting the import of turkeys into the UK, just before Christmas, on protection-of-health grounds.)

4.3 **The Sources and Forms of EU Law**

What should be mentioned again, at the outset of this particular section of the book, is the term *acquis communautaire*, which might (or more probably *will*) be encountered in EU law studies, and which was considered also in Chapters 1 and 2. This refers to—or is a way of describing—the whole body of EU law that has been built up over the years (now decades), which comprises all the sources of law considered in this chapter. It is more likely to be heard in connection with the entry of new member states, which are now, without negotiation, required to accept in total the *acquis communautaire*. It has been estimated that this amounts now to about 80,000 pages of legal text.[4] The treaties, the protocols, declarations, secondary legislation, international agreements, and the case law and development of legal principles by the Court of Justice all contribute to the *acquis communautaire*.

Whilst no formal hierarchy of laws is set out in the treaties, some clarification has been provided by reforms introduced by the Lisbon Treaty (see Figure 4.1). The treaties remain

---

[4] In September 2004, an exhibition in Brussels to demonstrate the EU to visitors featured a display of the *acquis communautaire* that allegedly ran, when spread out, to over 80,000 pages and over 8 metres: see the Joint Presidency/Commission press announcement 'The Image of Europe' (8 Sept 2004), General Affairs and External Relations. In 2011, the Commission estimated the *acquis* to consist of 8,862 regulations and 1,885 directives in addition to the primary law (the treaties). See **http://ec.europa.eu/eu_law/infringements/infringements_annual_report_29_en.htm**, COM (2011) 588 final.

Figure 4.1 Hierarchy of sources of EU law

clearly at the apex of the hierarchy and with them now the EU Charter of Fundamental Rights but in second place, traditionally occupied by EU secondary law (legislative acts), are general principles and fundamental rights which were previously considered to be lower in the hierarchy.[5] However, it is to be noted, but unfortunately not without some confusion, that some general principles and fundamental rights are also part of primary law as they may be contained in either the treaties or in the Charter of Fundamental Rights. They are however accorded this ranking because they may not only lead to the annulment of secondary and other lower-ranking legal rules but also may be used to interpret provisions of primary law, but not their annulment. Then follow international treaties which are ranked above the final major category, secondary EU law, which has its own three-part hierarchy, considered in Section 4.5.2.[6] Finally, we need to consider the jurisprudence or case law of the Court of Justice. It is not universally acknowledged as a formal source of law, which is a bit surprising as it is through the case law of the Court of Justice that some of the leading and strongest general principles have been recognized or introduced into the EU legal order, such as supremacy, direct effects, equality, and very many of the general principles considered already in either the first- or second-ranking category of sources. As a result of this somewhat schizoid and boundary-crossing classification, general principles will be introduced in rank order in Section 4.4.5 but the details of the general principles themselves will be considered with the rest of the case law of the Court of Justice in Section 4.6.4.

---

[5] This elevating of the status of general principles is supported, to some extent, by the comments of the Court of Justice itself in Case C-101/08 *Audiolux SA v GBL* [2009] ECR I-9823. See also e.g. P. Craig and G. de Búrca, *EU Law: Text, Cases, and Materials*, 5th edn, Oxford University Press, Oxford, 2011, p 103. The hierarchy is also confirmed now in EU documentation as in this paper issued by the European Parliament: **http:///www.europarl.europa.eu/ftu/pdf/en/FTU_1.2.1.pdf**.

[6] For the sake of consistency of introduction of these topics in further detail, the treaties and treaty-based sources of law will be considered first followed by international treaties and then general principles and human rights.

4.4 **Primary EU Law**

4.4.1 **The Treaties**

The primary source of law in the Union comes from the treaties, with two main treaties now of equal standing: the TEU and the TFEU. Two other original founding treaties, the European Coal and Steel Treaty (ECSC), which is no longer in force, and the European Atomic Energy Treaty (EURATOM), have been supplemented considerably by a number of treaties agreed by the member states. These include the Merger Treaty and the various acts of accession providing details for the entry into the Communities and Union of new member states. However, the most important additional treaties are the SEA, the TEU, the Treaty of Amsterdam, and the Treaty of Nice, which have cumulatively amended the original treaties considerably in comparison with their scope. The Lisbon Treaty of 2009 is the last, and for the moment the most fundamental, amendment of the treaties.

All the treaties of the Union are drawn up in all the official languages of the Union, which are equally authentic. Any difficulties that arise from the fact that different meanings may, despite all attempts, arise between languages is usually overcome by the Court of Justice applying the teleological interpretation of the spirit of the provision rather than the letter. A comparison of a number of language versions may be necessary in order to discern the true meaning of a particular provision.[7]

The special nature of these treaties is encapsulated within the concept of direct applicability, which means that, on the accession of a member state to the Union, all the provisions of the treaties automatically become part of the generally binding law of the member state, which is applicable not only to the member states but also to the citizens of that country. This form of law is also known as 'self-executing law', a term previously recognized in international law to describe the way in which some provisions of law have legal validity in the member states, in that a member state need take no further action to incorporate or transform the treaty into the national legal order once it has ratified the treaty, although some member states, such as the UK and Germany, may need an introductory Act to mark the presence of the treaty formally (but even then would not reproduce the text of the treaty into a national Act). It does not rely on the way in which the member state has incorporated it for its validity. The early case of Case 26/62 *Van Gend en Loos* is confirmation of the deeper impact of this directly applicable Community (EU) law, because the Court of Justice made it clear that Community law is also the legal concern of individuals and not only the member states.

The treaties are framework treaties in that they lay down broad guidelines for the pursuit of certain agreed aims and objectives. They do not provide extensive details for the implementation of these policies, which is left for the most part to secondary legislation of the Union or, failing that, to the Court of Justice which will rule on what was intended by the treaty provision. For example, although the old EC Treaty broadly provided that workers should be guaranteed freedom of movement in the Communities, it did not define—nor, indeed, did any secondary legislation define—what was meant by 'worker'. It was thus up to the CoJ to provide definitions of what it considered should be included in the definition of 'worker' in the EU context (see Chapter 9 for details).

---

[7] See e.g. Case C-106/89 *Marleasing SA v La Comercial Internacional de Alimentacion SA* and Case C-149/97 *Institute of the Motor Industry v Customs and Excise Commissioners*, in which the different language versions of the Sixth VAT Directive were discussed.

The scope of the treaties has expanded considerably since the establishment of the EEC in 1957, and now covers wide areas of the economic and social life of the member states, including economic and monetary policy, judicial and police cooperation, culture and tourism, humanitarian aid, and foreign policy, amongst many others, although not all to the same level of integration and Union control. The Lisbon Treaty did not actually add to these areas of Union influence, but merely strengthened EU action in some existing areas, such as external relations, and security and defence policies. It did, however, attach the catalogue of human rights as a binding part of the Union law. Unlike the changes proposed by the Constitutional Treaty, the Lisbon Treaty did not replace the existing treaties, but amended them quite considerably under the overall term 'European Union', with 'European Community' being removed. Two main treaties thus exist but the previous pillar structure has been removed—albeit with a residual self-standing Common Foreign and Security Policy (CFSP) remaining within the TEU and not in the renamed TFEU (which contains all the remaining sectors of EU competence).

Treaty amendment is usually achieved by the signing and ratifying of an amending treaty after discussion and agreement of the member states in an intergovernmental conference (IGC), as outlined in Chapter 1. The Lisbon Treaty has amended the procedure by which the treaties are amended by providing now in Art 48 TEU for both an ordinary and a simplified revision procedure. Under the ordinary procedure, proposals for amendment may come from any member state, the European Parliament, or the Commission which submit it to the Council which, in turn, notifies the European Council and the national parliaments. If the European Council, having consulted the European Parliament and Commission, considers it should be taken forward, it will convene a Convention, attended by representatives from the national parliaments, heads of state or government, European Parliament, and the Commission, which shall adopt by consensus a recommendation which will be discussed at an IGC and further agreement, signing, and ratification takes place in the usual form. Alternatively, the European Council may decide by simple majority, with the consent of the European Parliament, that the changes do not justify a Convention and may then proceed directly to an IGC. The simplified revision procedure, which applies only to Part Three of the TFEU, policies, and internal actions, allows for the European Council to decide unanimously after consultation with the European Parliament and Commission on treaty amendments which are then subject to ratification in the usual way by the member states.[8]

4.4.2 The Protocols Attached to the Treaties

As noted in Chapter 1, the two main treaties have been amended on a number of occasions, often significantly, but even with the additional amended treaties they do not represent the entirety of primary EU law. Following an unfortunate practice of limited beginnings, each successive IGC has negotiated and subsequently added what now amounts to a complex range of protocols to the treaties.[9] Article 51 TEU declares these protocols to be an integral part of the respective treaties.

What this means in practice is unclear, but it is generally understood in international law terms that protocols are a lesser, but no less binding, version of an international treaty agreement. They are used to provide interpretation for Articles of treaties and are often

---

[8] Note that the UK has now introduced the European Union Act 2011 which subjects any major changes or changes of competences to a referendum. Further details are considered in Chapter 5.

[9] **http://euobs.com/?aid=13235&rk=1**. The Lisbon Treaty attaches 37 protocols and 65 declarations to the existing treaties.

employed to provide agreed regulation of more technical matters. In the EU legal system, they possess treaty status, although the value of this status has not yet been questioned before the Court of Justice. What is clear is that the treaty constitutional basis has become increasingly complex. Whilst some steps have been attempted to consolidate them, if anything so far this has tended to make life even more complex—for example, the renumbering of the EC and TEU Treaty Articles by the Amsterdam and Lisbon Treaties. One of the aims in drafting the Constitutional Treaty was that this matter would be looked at and, as with the treaties themselves, be considerably simplified. However, all that happened was that the protocols attached to various treaties were consolidated and attached as a list of protocols to the Constitutional Treaty which was, of course, abandoned in the end. The 2007 Lisbon Treaty is a kind of halfway house in its approach to constitutional and treaty reform. Whilst it does provide an amended framework of laws for the relations between the member states and the Union, it does so by extensively amending the existing treaties, attaching to them a consolidated collection of 37 protocols, now 38 with the Irish Protocol of 2013.

4.4.3 **Declarations**

In addition, attached to each subsequent amending treaty has been a list of declarations of the member states, sometimes by all member states but mainly by only a few member states—or even only one member state—that make a unilateral declaration on a particular matter: for example, the Declaration by Austria and Luxembourg on credit institutions, which was attached to the Amsterdam Treaty. The Lisbon Treaty has added yet more, so that this unfortunate aspect of the EU legislative base has been made worse and not better. There are now 65 declarations attached to the treaties. These declarations need to be noted because, like the protocols, they may alter our view or perception of the meaning or application of a treaty provision; however, unlike the protocols, they enjoy no express treaty status and thus their actual status is uncertain.[10] However, the Lisbon Treaty has attached the Charter of Fundamental Rights to the treaties in the form of a declaration that states that the Charter has legally binding force.

4.4.4 **The EU Charter of Fundamental Rights**

To the primary law source must now be added the EU Fundamental Rights Charter.[11] When first established in 2001, the Charter had no legally binding effect on the member states but following the Lisbon Treaty it was attached to the treaties and has treaty status (Art 6(1) TEU). This status is further confirmed by the member states in Declaration 1 attached to the treaties.[12] It was not intended to replicate the rights contained within the

[10] See, for an early look at this: A.G. Toth, 'The Legal Status of the Declarations Annexed to the Single European Act' (1986) 23 CML Rev 803. Without making any clear-cut express statement as to the status, the Court of Justice held, in Case C-192/99 *Ex p Manjit Kaur v Secretary of State for the Home Department*, that in order to determine UK nationality, it was necessary to refer to the 1982 Declaration attached to the treaties, thus acknowledging a legal effect of the instrument without expressly declaring it to be binding on the member states. Further judicial advice on the value of declarations has been received in Case C-354/04P *Gestoras* in as much as no legal binding effect was accorded to them by the Court of Justice.

[11] Reproduced in full in N. Foster (ed), *EU Treaties and Legislation*, latest edn, Oxford University Press, Oxford.

[12] '1. Declaration concerning the Charter of Fundamental Rights of the European Union. The Charter of Fundamental Rights of the European Union, which has legally binding force, confirms the fundamental rights guaranteed by the European Convention for the Protection of Human Rights and Fundamental Freedoms and as they result from the constitutional traditions common to the Member States. The Charter

European Convention on Human Rights (ECHR) but to provide a set of rights relevant to the EU brought together largely from the existing case law of the Court of Justice, the constitutions of the member states, and international conventions from the Council of Europe including the ECHR, the UN, and the International Labour Organization (ILO). It nevertheless overlaps with some of the rights provided in the ECHR. It is divided into six chapters covering dignity, freedoms, equality, solidarity, citizens' rights, justice, and a seventh chapter on general provisions, the so-called horizontal Articles. Some of the provisions within the dignity chapter may not seem relevant for the EU, such as freedom from slavery and execution,[13] unless the scope of EU law in police and criminal matters extends very significantly over the years. There are exceptions to the scope of its application internally within Poland and the UK, agreed in Protocol 30, and in the Czech Republic by Declaration 53.

The freedoms and equality rights are to be expected and for the most part lend themselves well to the EU context.[14] The workers' rights, though, in the solidarity chapter,[15] which also includes general social and economic rights, are more in line with policy areas now catered for to some extent in the EU legal order. This chapter also contains environmental protections but which are expressed only in general terms and rely on other provisions of EU law to provide the details of the rights. The fifth chapter contains the citizens' rights,[16] which are restricted to EU citizens and which for the most part reproduce the rights contained in Arts 20–5 TFEU, although the right of access to documents is also included. The final substantive rights chapter, justice, contains rights of natural justice and procedural law rights,[17] many of which had already featured in the jurisprudence of the Court of Justice.

The seventh chapter contains the general rights of to whom and how the Charter applies. Article 51 of the Charter defines the scope of the application of the Charter as addressed to the institutions and bodies of the Union only when they are applying EU law and not extending to the member states when not implementing EU law. Furthermore,

---

does not extend the field of application of Union law beyond the powers of the Union or establish any new power or task for the Union, or modify powers and tasks as defined by the treaties.'

[13] Chapter I: dignity (human dignity, the right to life, the right to the integrity of the person, prohibition of torture and inhuman or degrading treatment or punishment, prohibition of slavery and forced labour).

[14] Chapter II: freedoms (the right to liberty and security, respect for private and family life, protection of personal data, the right to marry and found a family, freedom of thought, conscience, and religion, freedom of expression and information, freedom of assembly and association, freedom of the arts and sciences, the right to education, freedom to choose an occupation and the right to engage in work, freedom to conduct a business, the right to property, the right to asylum, protection in the event of removal, expulsion, or extradition).

Chapter III: equality (equality before the law, non-discrimination, cultural, religious, and linguistic diversity, equality between men and women, the rights of the child, the rights of the elderly, integration of persons with disabilities).

[15] Chapter IV: solidarity (workers' right to information and consultation within the undertaking, the right of collective bargaining and action, the right of access to placement services, protection in the event of unjustified dismissal, fair and just working conditions, prohibition of child labour and protection of young people at work, family and professional life, social security and social assistance, health care, access to services of general economic interest, environmental protection, consumer protection).

[16] Chapter V: citizens' rights (the right to vote and stand as a candidate at elections to the European Parliament and at municipal elections, the right to good administration, the right of access to documents, European Ombudsman, the right to petition, freedom of movement and residence, diplomatic and consular protection).

[17] Chapter VI: justice (the right to an effective remedy and a fair trial, presumption of innocence and the right of defence, principles of legality and proportionality of criminal offences and penalties, the right not to be tried or punished twice in criminal proceedings for the same criminal offence).

the Charter does not extend the field of application of EU law nor modify its powers and tasks, a proviso that is repeated in Declaration No 1 attached to the treaties.

Article 52(1) contains a derogation clause, similar to those found in the ECHR[18] in that derogations will only be permitted if they are provided for by law, meet the essential rights contained in the Articles, are proportionate, and are only acceptable if they are necessary and genuinely meet objectives of general interest or the need to protect the rights and freedoms of others. As with the provisions of the ECHR, a court faced with conflicting rights will have to balance the rights of those rights-holders but this is something the Court of Justice has already been doing with cases involving a claim to the protection of fundamental rights.[19]

Article 52(2)–(4) and Art 53 essentially provide rules of conflict in the event of clashes with the protection regimes of the EU treaties, the member states, and the ECHR.

Article 52(5) suggests that there is a distinction between rights, actionable without further ado before the courts, and principles which are declared to be enforceable only via implementing legislation and are justiciable only as persuasive interpretations. We are not informed definitively, though, which of the Articles contain rights and which contain principles although some help is provided by the explanation and commentaries to the report.[20]

Article 6(1) TEU provides that the Union recognizes the rights in the EU Charter of Fundamental Rights as having the same legal status as the treaties, The Charter was considered prior to its elevation to binding status in the EU by the CoJ in Case C-540/03 *European Parliament v Council (Family Reunion Directive)*. The CoJ made reference both to the fact that the Charter was not a legally binding instrument at that time, and to the fact that the Family Reunion Directive was enacted in compliance with both Art 8 ECHR and the Charter. There was, then, some oblique recognition of the Charter without going as far as to apply it either directly or indirectly. The CoJ can now do so without difficulty.[21] Much case law has already made mention of the Charter, with a 2011 report by the Commission stating that 42 rulings in 2011 referred to the Charter, up from 27 in 2010.[22]

Notable rulings include the *Test-Achats* case,[23] in which the CoJ invalidated a derogation in EU gender equality legislation that enables insurers to differentiate between men and women in individuals' premiums and benefits which was found to be incompatible with sex equality also contained within the Charter. In the *Dublin Regulation* case,[24] the member state responsible for the assessment of an asylum seeker, who first entered the EU through Greece before seeking asylum in the UK, was determined. The Court of Justice stressed that member states are under the obligation to respect the Charter when they

---

[18] See e.g. Article 8(2): http://www.echr.coe.int/Documents/Convention_ENG.pdf.

[19] See e.g. *Hauer v Rhineland Pfalz*, noted in Section 4.3.5.

[20] There have been two extensive documents of explanation and commentary on what the Charter and rights provide: http://www.europarl.europa.eu/charter/pdf/04473_en.pdf but in an updated version in OJ 2007 C303/17; commentary: http://ec.europa.eu/justice/fundamental-rights/files/networkcommentaryfinal_en.pdf.

[21] Further cases have followed in which the Court of Justice cites the Charter amongst other rights instruments in support of its general arguments within the cases. See Case C-432/05 *Unibet*, in which the Union's own catalogue of fundamental rights was mentioned in support of Arts 6 and 13 ECHR, Case C-275/06 *Promusiciae*, and Case C-411/10 *NS v Home Office* [2012] 2 CMLR 9.

[22] See the 2011 report on the application of the EU Charter: http://ec.europa.eu/justice/fundamental-rights/files/charter-brochure-report_en.pdf.

[23] Case C-236/09 *Test-Achats* [2011] ECR I-773 but see information note by the Commission to insurance companies on the judgment (OJ 2012 C11/01).

[24] Joined Cases C-411/10 and C-493/10 *NS v Secretary of State for the Home Department and ME v Refugee Applications Commissioner* [2012] 2 CMLR 9.

establish the responsibility for examining an asylum application. In particular, member states must not transfer an asylum seeker to another member state if they cannot be unaware that systemic deficiencies in the asylum procedure and reception conditions may amount to substantial grounds for believing that person would face a real risk of being subjected to inhuman or degrading treatment. This case also considered Protocol 30 and whether that had the effect of exempting the UK from the application of the Charter. The Court of Justice held that the Protocol was not an 'opt-out' but a document clarifying the interpretation of the Charter and that the case, in fact, involved EU law in the shape of the Dublin Convention which was established to determine which EU member state should be responsible for determining asylum applications. The status was therefore not relevant in that case. In Case C-617/10 *Fransson*,[25] Article 51 and the scope of the application of the Charter were considered by the CoJ. The Court held that when member states are putting into effect the requirements of EU directives, the national law transposing them was also subject to the Charter; hence the conclusion is that the Article provides not just a narrow understanding on the scope of EU law but also its implementation in the member states.

The Charter was also obliquely raised in case C-399/11 *Melloni*[26] in which a national court asked if Art 53 of the Charter allowed national courts to apply stricter standards than provided by EU law in the event of difference. The CoJ, relying on previous case law on supremacy held that not to be the case. In Case C-258/13, *Sociedade Agricola*, the Court of Justice made it quite clear that where a case did not involve EU law but just national law, the Charter would not apply and could not be relied on, which was the expected interpretation and indeed, as far as the member states are concerned, the hoped-for interpretation.

It is without doubt that the Charter will be a rich source of jurisprudence to come.

4.4.5 General Principles and Other Fundamental Rights

General principles are those principles of law which are adopted from a wide variety of external sources, some of which though have now been given primary status because they have been incorporated within the treaties or the Charter of EU Fundamental Rights, for example the principles of subsidiarity and proportionality in Art 5 TEU, which were considered in Chapter 3, or the general right to equality in Art 20 of the Charter. Apart from those codified deliberately into primary law, general principles have mainly been introduced into the EU legal order by the Court of Justice. They are employed to assist the Court to interpret and assess the EU's own laws including treaty provisions and to provide guidance on the application of EU law. They may also be pleaded or relied on by parties challenging EU law or the actions of EU institutions and additionally the actions of the member states in the application of EU law. Apart from the general justifications, outlined earlier, there are three particular treaty Articles which also justify the introduction of general principles. Article 19 TEU provides that the Court of Justice shall ensure that, in the interpretation and application of the treaties, the law is observed. It is a general guideline set by the treaty for the functioning of the Court of Justice. This is taken to mean law from outside the treaty rather than some duplicated reference back to the treaty. The

---

[25] Judgment of 26 February 2013 (OJ (2013) C280)).

[26] Judgment of 26 February 2013, not yet reported. See the case note in (2013) 50 CML Rev 1083. This case will also be considered in Chapter 5.

Article has thus been employed to justify the introduction of very many different general principles of law, most notably human rights.

Two Articles of the treaty specifically mandate the Court to take account of general principles of law. Article 263 TEU refers to the infringement of any rule of law relating to the application of the treaty as one of the grounds for an action for the challenge to the validity of EU law and Article 340 TEU, concerned with damages claims against the Union institutions, allows the consideration of claims on the basis of the general principles of the laws of the member states. Whilst these last two are specific to the claims raised under those treaty Articles, they do, however, serve to reinforce the Court of Justice's claim that it can rely on general principles as a source of law in the EU legal order. The sources of general principles are the national legal systems, in particular the constitutions of member states and the many rules of natural justice, found in a majority of the member states. Others have been developed from the treaty, for example Article 18 TFEU involving the prohibition of discrimination on the grounds of nationality, which has been one of the foundations for a general principle of equality and non-discrimination.

Whilst some are clearly of higher rank, others are not, and rather than trying to conduct an exercise of sorting and ranking them all, which may well just reflect my view on where they should be treated, I will merely note a few prominent examples here. The equality rights, various fundamental rights and principles of legal certainty and non-retroactivity stand out as prominent examples and are considered in Section 4.6.4 on the case law contribution of the Court of Justice.

The process of recognition of the status of general principles was considered by the CoJ in Case C-101/08 *Audiolux SA v GBL* [2009] ECR I-9823. It held that in order to be recognized as a general principle, a principle of law has to possess a general and comprehensive character which is naturally inherent in general principles. It refused to recognize an 'equal treatment protection of minority shareholders' principle from company law because of the limited and specific nature of it.

4.5 Secondary Sources of EU Law

4.5.1 International Agreements, Treaties, and Conventions

Within the treaties, there are provisions that empower the Council and the Commission to conduct external relations, the agreements of which are binding on both the Union and the member states (Art 216 TFEU) and, as such, then form a further true source of EU law. This is possible because, following the Lisbon Treaty (Art 47 TFEU), the entire Union has legal personality (it is a legal person capable of entering into formally binding agreements). It is usually represented by the European Commission in negotiations in coordination with the High Representative of the Union for Foreign Affairs and Security Policy, who is responsible for negotiating agreements relating to the CFSP.

The express treaty-making powers of the Union can be found in three principal treaty Articles and the types of agreement that can be concluded fall into three main types. Article 207 TFEU provides that EU commercial and trade policy is conducted by the Commission under the authority of the Council. Under this provision, the EU acts as a single actor, while the European Commission negotiates trade agreements and represents European interests on behalf of the 28 member states. The Council concludes the agreements and can thus bind the member states to agreements ranging from bilateral trade agreements with individual countries to the multiparty GATT and World Trade Organization (WTO) agreements—although, as seen later, much of the subject matter of the GATT and WTO agreements falls outside the express and exclusive competence of the Community. However, confirmation that particular provisions of the GATT can be binding on the Community was confirmed by the Court of Justice in Cases 21–4/72 *International Fruit*.

Article 217 TFEU provides for the conclusion of association agreements with non-member states that can be regarded as either a precursor to membership or as an agreement in its own right without any view to future membership of the EU. These can be concluded by the Council, with the assent of the European Parliament, with either individual third countries or within more extensive multinational agreements to govern, amongst other things, various aspects of the trade relations between them. The most important agreements are the agreement on the European Economic Area (EEA),[27] the association agreements with candidate member states, the bilateral agreements with Switzerland and the Mediterranean countries, and the preferential treatment agreements that have been concluded with the Mediterranean countries. Furthermore, there are the very comprehensive Yaounde and Lomé Conventions, and the Cotonou Agreement (2000)[28] with the African, Caribbean, and Pacific (ACP) countries, all of which provide binding rules for the Community.[29] For example, in Case 181/73 *Haegemann v Belgium*, provisions of the association agreement between the Community and Greece were held to be binding on the member states even though such agreements were not envisaged by Art 249 EC (now Art 288 TFEU). A more recent example is Case C-265/03 *Simutenkov*, which concerned rights provided under the EC–Russian Federation partnership agreement and the rights of a Russian football player employed by the Spanish club Deportivo Tenerife. In a similar manner to the *Bosman* ruling, the number of players that could be fielded from non-EEA countries was restricted in national competitions. The judgment followed the *Bosman* ruling with the interpretation by the Court of Justice that the partnership agreement contained directly enforceable free movement rights.

Finally, and more generally, the treaty provides, under Art 218 TFEU, a power for the conclusion of international agreements with non-member states in matters covered by areas of the treaty not specifically catered for by the other two treaty-making-power Articles. In furtherance of this, Art 220 TFEU requires the Commission to maintain appropriate relations with international organizations such as the United Nations (UN), the Council of Europe, and the Organisation for Economic Co-operation and Development (OECD). The Union is to be represented by the Commission and the new High Representative. In many of these areas, however, the Union must act with the member states, because the subject matters of the agreements often straddle matters coming both within Union competence and outside Union competence. These agreements, and international agreements entered into by the member states alone, can still bind the Union, as confirmed in Cases 21–4/72 *International Fruit Company*, for example, in which the Court of Justice held that the Community is bound by the provisions of the GATT concluded by the member states prior to membership of, or prior to the assumption of responsibility for the agreement by, the Community. The direct effects of these agreements will be considered in Chapter 6.

Following the Lisbon Treaty, the Union, rather than only the EC previously, has legal personality and will have a right to conclude international agreements over a wider range of topics than previously, such as UN conferences, international finance and trade conferences, and more widely in the WTO. In this case, the EU would not be subject

---

[27] See Chapter 1, Section 1.6.2.   [28] OJ 2000 L317/3.

[29] For a comprehensive review of international agreements entered into by the EU and its member states, see N. Lavranos, *Decisions of International Organizations and European Law*, University of Amsterdam, Amsterdam, 2004.

to the limitations outlined in Opinion 1/94,[30] which constrained the Commission's ability to negotiate without the member states in the field of services in the WTO. In addition, the new High Representative is responsible for negotiating agreements relating to the CFSP.

4.5.2 **EU Secondary Legislation**

In the EU, secondary legislation arises entirely subject to the authority, higher rank, and procedures provided for in the treaties. Article 288 TFEU provides the means by which the Union institutions are able to enact various forms of secondary legislation, which are also a source of law for the UK and other member states, and are binding on them. The acts of secondary legislation presently consist of regulations, directives, and decisions. Although the Constitutional Treaty had envisaged a radical shake-up to the forms of secondary legislation, this was toned down in the Lisbon Treaty, which did not change this aspect but did introduce a distinction in Arts 288, 289, 290, and 297 TFEU between legislative and non-legislative acts. It introduced a clear hierarchy of secondary law consisting of the legislative acts of the law-makers and the non-legislative acts, which are the delegated and implementing administrative acts enacted by the Commission and other Union bodies under the authority of enacted legislative acts. Delegated acts (Art 290 TFEU) are non-legislative acts which supplement or amend non-essential elements of the legislative act. The power to adopt this type of act can be delegated to the Commission by the European Parliament or the Council. Implementing acts (Art 291 TFEU) are commonly adopted by the Commission under its implementing powers but, in certain cases, the Council may also adopt implementing acts.[31] Articles 288 and 297 TFEU make it clear that both legislative and non-legislative acts can be in the form of regulations, directives, and decisions.[32]

All EU secondary legislation is published in the Official Journal (OJ), which, as its name suggests, is the official publication of the Union and is published in two main parts, with a supplement. The 'L' series (legislation) contains the binding legislative acts. The 'C' series (information and notices) contains a very wide range of documents that are not binding as such, and includes notices, draft legislative acts, press releases, job advertisements, and all other non-legally binding publications, with the exception of public procurement notices, which are published in the 'S' series supplement. The OJ was, until 1 July 2013, officially authentic only in its printed form,[33] from 1 July 2013 though only in its electronic form. The printed version can be found still in libraries and official documentation centres.[34]

---

[30] [1994] ECR I-5267, referred to in Chapter 1, Section 1.6.5.1.

[31] These are considered in further detail in Section 4.10.

[32] The Lisbon Treaty does not change the list of legislative acts that can be adopted under the new Art 288 TFEU (old 249 EC), but does provide in Art 290 TFEU for non-legislative acts that can be adopted under delegated powers of the Commission, which are, in effect, the administrative acts that it could previously adopt under Art 211 EC, so really this is a change in name only. The choice of which particular act to adopt may be determined by the legal base specifying whether regulation, directive, or decision, but where this is not the case, which is more frequent, Art 296 TFEU provides that the institutions shall select it on a case-by-case basis.

[33] As confirmed by the Court of Justice in Case C-161/09 *Skoma-Lux* [2007] ECR I-10841.

[34] It can be located in most university libraries, but is most easily accessed at **http://eur-lex.europa.eu/JOIndex.do?ihmlang=en**.

4.5.2.1 Regulations

Regulations are defined in Art 288 TFEU: 'A regulation shall have general application. It shall be binding in its entirety and directly applicable in all member states.' They are general provisions of legislation applicable to the entire Union, member states, institutions, and individuals, rather than to specific individuals or groups. Regulations are detailed forms of law, so that the law in all member states is exactly the same. As far as implementation is concerned, like treaty provisions, regulations are directly applicable or self-executing. This is the mode of incorporation of law that is generally or universally binding. Regulations become legally valid in the member states without any need for implementation on the date specified or on the twentieth day after publication in the OJ (see Art 297 TFEU). It was held in Case 39/72 *Commission v Italy* that member states cannot subject the regulation to any implementing measures other than those required by the act itself. There may, however, be circumstances in which the member states are required to provide supporting measures to ensure the effectiveness of the regulation, as in Case 128/78 *Commission v UK (Re: Tachographs)*, in which administrative rules had to be introduced concerning enforcement and the sanctions for failure to install tachographs in lorry cabs. The regulation required supportive enforcement.

4.5.2.2 Directives

Directives are also defined in Art 288 TFEU: 'A directive shall be binding as to the result to be achieved, upon each member state to which it is addressed, but shall leave to the national authorities the choice of form and methods.' Directives are binding on those to whom they are addressed and can be targeted if desired to specific member states, although in practice they are addressed to all member states. Directives set out aims that must be achieved, but leave the choice of the form and method of implementation to the member states. This was done to ease the way in which national law could be harmonized in line with EU law and to give the member states a wider area of discretion to do this. If, for example, a member state considers that the existing national law is already in conformity with the requirements of a new directive, then it need not do anything, apart from the requirement now in most, if not all, directives that the member state inform the Commission of measures taken to implement the directive. The Commission monitors this and failure to notify may prompt the Commission to open infringement proceedings for non-implementation.

Directives enter into force either on the date specified or 20 days after publication, which is rare (see Art 297 TFEU). Member states are given a period in which to implement directives, which can range from one year to five or more, depending on the complexity of the subject matter and the urgency for the legislation (although two years is usual). Some directives, especially if consolidating and adding rules to an existing area of EU law, may contain more than one entry-into-force date to take account of the law that should have already been enacted and the new provisions for which the member states are given a further implementation period (see, for example, Directive 2004/38[35] in the area of free movement of persons).

Directives are not directly applicable in the sense of being automatic and general in application, and giving rights without further implementation; however, directives have been held to give rise to directly enforceable rights in specific circumstances and if certain criteria are satisfied, for example where they have not been implemented at all or where

---

[35] OJ 2004 L158/77.

they have been incorrectly implemented. This judicial development will be considered in Chapter 6 and in Section 6.3.3 on direct effects.

4.5.2.3 Decisions

Decisions were defined by Lisbon in Art 288 TFEU: 'A decision shall be binding in its entirety. A decision which specifies those to whom it is addressed shall be binding only on them.' Decisions are specific, binding, and enforceable acts of law that are addressed to member states or to specific individuals, for example in the area of competition law determining the actions of and agreements between companies to be either in conformity or in conflict with EU competition law rules. The change appears to give formal recognition to the very many 'one-off', in EU jargon '*sui generis*' acts, which have legal effects and can be challenged using Art 263 TFEU. Most case law previously arose from challenges to decisions by individuals in the areas of competition law and agricultural policy.

4.5.2.4 Delegated and Implementing Legislation

The Commission is empowered to create non-legislative but nevertheless binding acts, which may be in the form of regulations, directives, or decisions, under the delegated and implementing powers granted respectively by Art 290 and 291 TFEU, considered in Section 4.10.

4.5.2.5 Other Acts Producing Binding Legal Effects

Article 288 TFEU is not exhaustive of the legally binding acts that can be created by the institutions, and the Court of Justice has held that it can review all measures taken by the institutions that are designed to produce legal effects, whatever their nature and form. Thus, such acts need not stem from the specific acts listed in Art 288 TFEU and are often termed *sui generis*, meaning literally 'in a class of its own', or 'unique'. Hence, then, the establishment of another class of binding law in the EU legal order, some examples of which could easily be classified under other headings—especially the contribution of the CoJ. See, for example, Cases 8–11/66 *Noordwijks Cement Accord*, in which a Commission letter not formally labelled as a regulation, directive, or decision could nevertheless be challenged under Art 263 TFEU (ex Art 230 EC), which is the action to challenge the validity of binding acts of EU law, because the letter had led to a change in the legal status of applicant companies, rendering them subject to competition law liability where they had been previously immune. See also Case 22/70 *Commission v Council (ERTA)*, in which a decision of the member states outside the Council of Ministers was nevertheless held to be a reviewable act of the Community. Even a press release has been found to have legal effects in Case C-106/96 *UK v Commission* and was consequently annulled for lacking a legal base. (These are considered in further detail in Chapter 7, Section 7.4 on Art 263 TFEU.)

Article 295 TFEU now puts on a statutory basis the inter-institutional agreements that have for a long time played a role in establishing the ground rules for the European Parliament, Council, and Commission to work together, in particular in areas such as delegated powers or better law-making. These may now be made formally binding under Art 295 TFEU instead of being part of a hazy area of soft law, considered in Section 4.7.

Finally, the rulings of the Court of Justice may be counted amongst the binding sources of EU law, and are covered in Section 4.6. Article 280 TFEU provides that these rulings are enforceable.

4.5.2.6 Recommendations and Opinions

Whilst, expressly under Art 288 TFEU, recommendations and opinions do not have any binding force, it was established in Case 322/88 *Grimaldi* that, despite this, national courts are required to take recommendations into account when interpreting national law based on EU law. Recommendations, in particular, often provide a gloss on a regulation or directive, or extend its scope of application. See, for example, the randomly selected Commission Recommendation 2011/696 of 18 October 2011 on the definition of nanomaterial.[36]

4.5.2.7 Procedural Requirements

Article 296 TFEU requires that the binding acts of institutions shall state the reasons on which they are based and shall refer to any proposals or opinions that were required to be obtained. In practice, this means the treaty base must be cited also. Failure by the institutions to comply with these requirements will give rise to grounds for judicial review and possible annulment of the measure under Art 263 TFEU. For example, it was held in Case C-325/91 *France v Commission* that there was a requirement to state the treaty base, without which the measure is void. The Lisbon Treaty has introduced a new requirement in Art 296 TFEU, which relates to the competence and legal base issues. It states that, 'When considering draft legislative acts, the European Parliament and the Council shall refrain from adopting acts not provided for by the relevant legislative procedure in the area in question.' This is another attempt to curb the competence creep and/or use of the incorrect legal base.

Article 297 TFEU provides the rules concerning the publication of the various acts, regulations, directives, and decisions adopted under Art 251, which must be signed by the presidents of the European Parliament and the Council, and published in the OJ. Directives addressed to all member states must also be published. They become valid on the specified date, in the absence of which on the twentieth day following publication. Otherwise, directives and decisions take effect on the date of notification given in the acts, and these are also published in the OJ.

The Lisbon Treaty clarified the position of legislative and non-legislative acts—that is, of the administrative types of act, which are considered further in Section 4.6 on delegated powers. The revision reduced the very many different, less formal, types of act that have been developed over the years and those specifically introduced under the TEU. The non-legislative, delegated acts must be signed by the president of the institution that adopted them and shall also be published in the OJ.

4.6 The Court of Justice's Contribution

When the European Communities were established, the legal system was to be found only in the written medium within the treaties and the limited secondary EC legislation that existed at the time. Initially, there seemed to be little room for an additional and non-legislative source of law. However, because the treaties are largely framework treaties, they require substantial supplement. Whilst much of this is provided by the secondary legislation of the EU, both this secondary legislation and the founding and primary treaties' Articles often need to be interpreted. There is, then, much scope for activity on the part of the Court of Justice. Furthermore, as with all legal systems, codified or written

---

[36] Recommendation 2011/696 (OJ L275/38).

law cannot possibly cater for all economic and social developments that can take place, and the judges must at times either adapt existing rules to fit the situation or introduce new rules to settle the matter judiciously. The CoJ has determined that, for example, the EC Treaty (now TFEU) and secondary legislation must be interpreted and applied according to the scheme of the treaty as a whole, and in light of the broad principles of the preamble and Arts 2, 3, 10, and 12 of the former EC Treaty, to achieve the result required.[37] The resulting case law or jurisprudence has grown from a wide variety of law. It is not restricted in origin to the crude judicial interpretation of words or phrases from Community and now EU legislative provisions. Instead, the CoJ has cast its net of judicial interpretation much wider and signalled a clear departure from reliance on the treaties only, or indeed on international law, by the development of some of the most fundamental doctrines and principles of Community and now EU law. These include direct effects, supremacy, state liability, and the development of general principles of EU law, and the application of outside general principles, fundamental rights, and procedural rules. This law, as developed by the Court of Justice in cases before it, is quite clearly an EU source of law and indeed a highly influential one. In some instances, it has been directly influential in bringing about treaty changes well before the formal treaty amendment of such provisions by the member states (see, for example, Arts 263 and 265 TFEU, and the extension of judicial review rights to the European Parliament). The decisions of the CoJ are binding on the member states not only where the CoJ decides strictly on the basis of the treaties or secondary law, but also where it decides on the basis of legal rules that it has observed and used as inspiration from outside the EU, or in order to develop a new EU rule itself. To back up this position, Art 280 TFEU provides that judgments shall be enforceable.

In developing EU law, the CoJ has been able to rely on and simultaneously develop general principles and fundamental rights within the legal order that have been used both to assist it in the interpretation and application of EU law, and by parties engaging in litigation involving EU law, to assist them in challenging EU law or the actions of Union institutions and, additionally, the actions of the member states in the application of EU law. These additional sources of law are sometimes classified into broad groupings. Whilst this is probably not particularly useful because of the diversity of principles and the degree of overlap, presenting them in this way may, however, aid accessibility. They can therefore be divided into three groups concerned with: human or fundamental rights; equality principles; and, finally, those relating to general procedural rights. It must be stressed, however, that the categories are far from watertight and that there is considerable overlap.

4.6.1 **Human or Fundamental Rights**

Originally, there was no catalogue of rights in the Community treaties and fundamental rights provision was completely absent from any of the treaties (although some isolated Articles provided rights that either coincided with general principles or helped in the development of general principles of Community and now EU law). Now there is the EU Charter and when or if the EU accedes to the Council of Europe, the ECHR will also apply; however, it is still worthwhile looking at the development of fundamental rights in the EU legal order and considering some of those rights. The EC Treaty contained a number of such Articles: Art 2 (concerned with social protection, the standard of living, and quality of life); Arts 3 and 39 (dealing with the free movement of persons); Arts 12, 34, and 39(2) (concerned with discrimination); Art 43 (social security); and Art 141 (equal

---

[37] See also Chapter 2, Section 2.6.4.

pay). More recently, Art 13 (now Art 19 TFEU) was added, which provides a general ability to prohibit discrimination across a range of issues and which has led to the enactment of directives to tackle specific forms of discrimination.[38] Similar Articles with enhanced provision are now to be found in Arts 2, 3, and 6 TEU and Arts 8–10, 18, 19, 40, 45, 153, and 157 TFEU. When the Communities were first established, there was no specific and binding set of obligations imposed by the treaty on the Community institutions to guarantee individual rights of citizens. This initial apparent lack of commitment to human rights was, in turn, reflected in the early decisions of the Court of Justice when faced with arguments or pleas raised by litigants based on basic or human rights. Hence, the early case law of the CoJ presents the view of a Community unsympathetic to the fundamental human rights of individuals. (See Case 1/58 *Stork v High Authority* and Case 40/64 *Sgarlata v Commission*, in which arguments based on individual rights were clearly rejected in favour of upholding Community law.) This position can be contrasted with the then six member states' positions regarding human rights. Following World War II, West European nations were more than ever ideologically committed to the concept of protecting human rights. The German and Italian Constitutions were rewritten, with very strong commitments to basic rights contained within a rights catalogue. By 1955, all the original members of the EEC except France had ratified the ECHR. The Community and Court were thus morally, if not legally, obliged to observe fundamental human rights—especially those contained in the constitutions of the member states. Thus, the CoJ could not maintain its unsympathetic stance and adopted, from the late 1960s, a new response that was seen clearly in Case 26/69 *Stauder v City of Ulm*. A German citizen protested that his fundamental right of human dignity, protected by Art 1 of the German *Grundgesetz* (its Basic Law, or Constitution), was being infringed by having his name on the coupon when claiming reduced-price butter released by the Community. The CoJ held that the Community did not require his name, and Community law itself had not prejudiced his fundamental rights, which enabled the Court to express the opinion that such rights were nevertheless 'enshrined in the general principles of Community law and protected by the Court'.[39]

After the French ratification of the ECHR in 1974, the Court of Justice referred also to the ECHR as an example of the member states' commitment to fundamental rights.

Encouragement came also from the Joint Declaration by Community Institutions on Fundamental Rights, 5 April 1977, which stressed the importance of national constitutions and the ECHR. Hence, for the first time, in Case 44/79 *Hauer v Land Rheinland-Pfalz*, the CoJ considered in some detail a provision (Art 1 of Protocol 1) of the ECHR to help it to decide the case. Although it recognized the right of property in the case, its use was subject to overriding Community interests. Thus, despite recognition of the fundamental rights, in the early days, cases were resolved usually on the basis of either Community law applying or the rights being subject to limitations mainly of the Community interest.

In a number of cases, the CoJ reaffirmed its statement that fundamental rights form part of the general principles based on constitutional traditions of member states. For example, Case 11/70 *Internationale Handelsgesellschaft* showed the potential for conflict and ultimate harm to the Community legal order if the Community were to fail to uphold human rights provisions. No self-respecting legal system in Europe could ignore, or be seen to be ignoring, such ideologically important rights as these and, in that case, the

---

[38] See Chapter 11 for details.

[39] See the more recent Case C-36/02 *Omega*, in which the Court of Justice confirms recognition of the right to human dignity.

CoJ gave a guarantee that members states' constitutions will not be infringed despite the superiority of Community law, because of the commitment of the Community to human rights and the fact that they form part of the Community legal order. In Case 63/83 *R v Kirk*, a fine imposed on a fishing boat captain by a UK court, which was based on a national UK statutory order, was held to infringe the principle of non-retroactivity, because the order was supposedly validated by later Community legislation. The CoJ held that such an action violated the principle of non-retroactivity of criminal law enshrined in Art 7 ECHR and now a principle of Community law. Non-retroactivity was also confirmed as a principle of Community law in *Kolpinghuis Nijmegan*, considered further in Section 4.3.7.4. In Case 222/86 *UNECTEF v Heylens et al*, the CoJ was able to refer to Arts 6 and 13 ECHR to support the right to judicial review and the right to be heard in support of a claim for an additional right: the right to free access to employment. In Case 5/88 *Wachauf*, the CoJ extended its support of fundamental rights by holding that the actions of member states in implementing Community measures must also comply with the requirements of human rights provisions.

A very strong support for the respect for human rights in the EU legal order can be found in Joined Cases C-402/05 P and C-415/05 P *Kadi and Al Barakaat*[40] concerned with the translation into EU regulations of UN measures against the support of terrorism, namely the freezing of assets of persons listed by the UN as suspected of being involved. The applicants Kadi and Al Barakaat challenged the regulation which carried and was the cause of the alleged infringements of human rights, including the right to be heard and the right to an effective remedy, in an appeal to the Court of Justice from the CFI.[41] The Court of Justice made clear that neither the member states nor the EU institutions can avoid review of the conformity of their acts with the basic constitutional charter, the EC Treaty, which established a complete system of legal remedies and procedures designed to enable the Court of Justice to review the legality of acts of the institutions. Furthermore, a guarantee of fundamental rights forms an integral part of the EU legal order and their respect is a condition of the lawfulness of EU acts and that, as constitutional principles of the EU, this status could not be affected by any international agreement or the fact that EU acts were based on an international obligation. The Court held that a review of the validity of any Community measure in light of fundamental rights must be considered to be the expression, in a Community based on the rule of law, of a constitutional guarantee stemming from the EC Treaty as an autonomous legal system.[42] The resolution and thus the regulation were held patently to breach the right to be heard and to an effective remedy in the inclusion of the applicants names in the list without recourse to any form of judicial review. The Court of Justice acknowledged that security interests may justify the secret compilation of the list but would not exclude a judicial review of the lawfulness after publication. Therefore, as far as the applicants were concerned, the regulation was annulled.

4.6.2 The EU and the ECHR

As can be seen from the case law, the ECHR is increasingly referred to by the CoJ in support of its judgments. See, for example, the cases from the area of the free movement of persons including Case C-413/99 *Baumbast*, Case C-459/99 *MRAX*, and Case C-109/01

---

[40] [2008] ECR I-6351.

[41] This case is also considered in Chapter 5 with regard to the status of international law and EU law.

[42] See Judgment at paras 281–4, 292, 296, and 316.

Akrich, all of which featured Art 8 ECHR, the right to family life, and are considered further in Chapter 9. The elevated status given to the ECHR by the Court of Justice has now been reflected in a greater status within the treaty base and has been strengthened even further following the entry into force of the Lisbon Treaty. Article 6(3) TEU continues to oblige the EU to a broad general commitment to respect the Articles of the ECHR and those human rights common to constitutional traditions of the member states as general principles of EU law.

The new Art 6 TEU also settles years of debate as to whether the EU should or could accede to the ECHR. In 1996, the Court of Justice gave Opinion 2/94 that, under the treaties at the time, the Union did not have the power to accede. Now that the EU has its own catalogue of rights, in the form of the Fundamental Rights Charter, it might be argued that membership is more acceptable—but, conversely, with its own catalogue of rights there might be no further need for either debate of or accession to the ECHR. However, the new Art 6(2) TEU clearly provides that the Union shall accede to the ECHR and declares in any event that those rights contained in the ECHR shall constitute general principles of the Union's law. This may seem now to be superfluous in view of the introduction of the EU's own catalogue of rights, however, Protocol No 8 requires the accession agreement to ensure the preservation of the special characteristics of Union law and not to affect the competences or powers of the Union or institutions. Furthermore, Declaration No 2 specifically notes that dialogue between the CoJ and the European Court of Human Rights (ECtHR) should both continue and be reinforced when the EU accedes to the Convention.[43]

A considerable amount of work has been put into drafting an accession agreement in view of the rather complex consequences of the EU as a non-state entity joining and being subject to the ECHR. Ultimately though following accession, the laws and actions of the EU will be subject to the review of the Court of Human Rights in Strasbourg, which is a considerable step for the Union to have made. The draft agreement has now been finalized[44] but before any further progress can be made towards actual accession, the CoJ was asked whether it considered the Agreement to be compatible with the treaties.[45]

The main features of the agreement as submitted for the opinion of the CoJ are as follows.[46] Decisions of the Court of Human Rights will be binding on the EU, including the CoJ. The agreement will become part of EU law and be legally regarded in the legal order in the same way and status of other international agreements.[47] Article 3 of the draft agreement would introduce to the Convention a co-respondent procedure to cater for circumstances whereby both the EU and one or more member states were the subject of proceedings instigated initially against only one of them. The EU or one or more member states may then be called to join the proceedings as a co-respondent. This will cover situations where

---

[43] '2. Declaration on Article 6(2) of the Treaty on European Union. The Conference agrees that the Union's accession to the European Convention for the Protection of Human Rights and Fundamental Freedoms should be arranged in such a way as to preserve the specific features of Union law. In this connection, the Conference notes the existence of a regular dialogue between the Court of Justice of the European Union and the European Court of Human Rights; such dialogue could be reinforced when the Union accedes to that Convention.' (Whilst accession is being pursued, no date has been set.)

[44] To be found at this Council of Europe site: **http://www.coe.int/t/dghl/standardsetting/hrpolicy/ Accession/default_en.asp**

[45] Opinion 2/13 application notice OJ 2013 C260/19, 07.09.2013. Judgment **http://curia.europa.eu/juris/ liste.jsf?num=C-2/13**.

[46] Which will be considered only in overview, whereas details can be found in the agreement and the cited literature at the end of this chapter.

[47] As considered in Section 4.5.1.

it may be unclear to the applicant whether the EU, which enacted an Act or a member state, which implemented it, is responsible when that act is alleged to have breached the applicant's rights. In addition to the existing principle of the exhaustion of local remedies,[48] which means cases must be brought to the CoJ first before access to the machinery of Strasbourg is permitted, the Agreement supports this with a prior involvement procedure. This provides that before any review by the Strasbourg Court may take place both the national courts and EU courts must be allowed to review an applicant's complaint first. If the EU courts were not given this right, a case from a member state involving EU law or action may by-pass the CoJ and adjudicate on EU law contrary to the autonomy of EU law, a principle which the EU negotiators required to be observed. The EU will have its own judge at the Court in Strasbourg, members of the EP will be entitled to participate in the Parliamentary Assembly of the Council of Europe, and, whilst the EU will not become a member of the Council of Europe or its Committee of Ministers, the EU will be consulted on matters discussed and decided by the Strasbourg Committee of Ministers.

However before any further progress could have been made to actual accession, the CoJ was asked whether it considered the agreement to be compatible with the treaties. It decided in December 2014 that the agreement was not compatible with the EU Treaties for the following reasons taken from the 258-paragraph Opinion.[49] The CoJ considered that the agreement was liable to adversely affect the specific characteristics and the autonomy of EU law in so far as it does not ensure sufficient coordination between the ECHR and EU legal orders. Further, it is liable to affect Article 344 TFEU, which requires member states not to submit disputes under EU law to any other forum, in so far as the Accession Treaty does not preclude the possibility of disputes between Member States or between Member States and the EU concerning the application of the ECHR being brought before the ECtHR. It also held that it does not lay down arrangements for the operation of the co-respondent mechanism and the procedure for the prior involvement of the Court of Justice that enable the specific characteristics of the EU and EU law to be preserved. Finally, in this comment on it, it fails to have regard to the specific characteristics of EU law with regard to the judicial review of acts, actions, or omissions on the part of the EU in CFSP matters in that it entrusts the judicial review of some of those acts, actions, or omissions exclusively to a non-EU body.

So presently, quite a bit more work remains to be done in amending the agreement and then re-negotiating those amendments with the Council of Europe and its 48 member states, 28 of which though are EU member states. It was never going to be easy.

Article 218(8) TFEU provides that when accession is to be approved, the Council shall act unanimously and the member states separately by their constitutional requirements. Following that, all the 48 member states of the Council of Europe must also agree, hence accession will not be taking place very quickly.

4.6.2.1 European Union Agency for Fundamental Rights

A much more practical development is the establishment of a European Union Agency for Fundamental Rights[50] to collect information and data, to provide advice to the EU

---

[48] Whereby applicant parties are required to pursue their claims in their domestic courts first before being permitted to bring a complaint action before the Commission and Court of Human Rights in Strasbourg.

[49] http://curia.europa.eu/juris/liste.jsf?num=C-2/13.

[50] Created by Regulation 168/2007, available at http://eur-lex.europa.eu/LexUriServ/LexUriServ.do?uri=CELEX:32007R0168:EN:NOT, and see http://fra.europa.eu/fra/index.php and http://ec.europa.eu/justice_home/fsj/rights/fsj_rights_agency_en.htm.

and its member states, and to promote dialogue with civil society to raise public awareness of fundamental rights. It takes further the work of the European Monitoring Centre
on Racism and Xenophobia (EUMC), which it succeeds, and is able to give opinions on
legislative proposals at the request of the European Commission, European Parliament,
or Council—although the regulation is silent as to how these opinions are to be treated
by the institutions once received. The Agency will also be given certain thematic areas
to investigate and on which to report, set by the member states under a multi-annual
framework.[51]

4.6.3 Equality and Non-discrimination

The prohibition of discrimination is catered for in the treaties under a number of
Articles: Art 18 TFEU, the non-discrimination on the grounds of nationality Article; Art
157 TFEU, relating to sex discrimination; Art 40(2) TFEU, in respect of the Common
Agricultural Policy (CAP); and Art 45(2) TFEU, for the free movement of workers. It
is also a general principle recognized by the Court of Justice. It applies in all areas of
EU law, especially to the fundamental freedoms. For example, in Cases 75 and 117/82
Razzouk and Beydoun v Commission, the CoJ held that a Commission decision, which
discriminated between men and women in relation to a certain pension payment, should
be annulled as being contrary to the fundamental right of equal treatment of sexes. The
principle was applied in Case 114/76 *Bergman v Grows-Farm (Skimmed-milk Powder)*,
wherein the CoJ held that a scheme to force animal-feed producers to incorporate
skimmed-milk powder in animal feed discriminated against non-dairy farmers. It was
also applied to religious discrimination in Case 130/75 *Prais v Council*, although on the
facts involving a Community competition for a post held on a Jewish religious festival, the
Council was held not to have breached the general principle of equality. It was nevertheless held by the CoJ that, wherever possible, Community employees and citizens should
have the general principle of non-discrimination in respect of religious freedom upheld
in their favour. The *Mangold* case, Case C-144/04, allowed the CoJ to uphold the principle
of non-discrimination as a general principle to be applied in the absence of specific rights
or where any such rights existing should not be directly enforceable in the case due, for
example, to a lack of direct effects.[52]

The Union has moved further towards the development of a general principle of equality or at least non-discrimination on a range of issues, by an amendment made originally to the EC Treaty by the Treaty of Amsterdam. Article 19 TFEU now provides that
the Council may take appropriate action to combat discrimination based on sex, racial
or ethnic origin, religion or belief, disability, age, or sexual orientation, and directives
have now been issued under this Article.[53] The existence and value of a general principle
of equal treatment has been acknowledged and confirmed by the Court of Justice in a
number of cases, including, for example, Case C-149/10 *Chatzi*, in which the Court held
that the principle of equal treatment is one of the general principles of EU law and is
now affirmed by Article 20 of the EU Charter of Fundamental Rights. In that case, it was
applied to support the right to parental leave on an equal basis.

---

[51] See Decision 2008/203 (OJ 2008 L63/14), available at **http://eur-lex.europa.eu/LexUriServ/
LexUriServ.do?uri=OJ:L:2008:063:0014:0015:EN:PDF**.

[52] Direct effects will be considered fully in Chapter 6. See also Case C-555/07 *Kükükdeveci* [2010]
ECR I-365.

[53] See e.g. Directives 2000/43 (OJ 2000 L180/22), 2000/78 (OJ 2000 L3030/16), and 2004/113 (OJ 2004
L373/37), which will be considered briefly in Chapter 11.

4.6.4 **General Principles of Procedural Law and Natural Justice**

A number of principles are closely associated with the administrative law principles found in many of the member states, but may also be classified under the rules of natural justice and due process. These can be found in differing forms in the member states' legal systems: for example, as common law rules in the UK, or as a part of the Constitution in Germany or contained with the ECHR.[54] Judicial review, confidentiality/legal privilege, legal certainty, non-retroactivity, legitimate expectation, and proportionality have been selected here as broad categories of general principles that have been identified and applied by the Court of Justice.

4.6.4.1 **The Right to Judicial Review**

A general right to have administrative decisions reviewed by a court exists, which also includes a number of consequential rights, such as the duty of authorities to give reasons for their decisions. The Court of Justice bases its view on the constitutions of the member states and notably on Art 6 ECHR, dealing with a fair and public hearing, and Art 13 ECHR, which requires the provision of an effective judicial remedy. See Case 222/84 *Johnston v Chief Constable of the RUC* and Case 222/86 *UNECTEF v Heylens*, in which latter case the CoJ had already determined that free access to employment was a fundamental right that should be respected in the Community. It thus becomes essential that there be a remedy of a judicial nature against any decision of a national authority refusing the benefit of that right. The *UNECTEF* case established that the duty to give reasons was a general principle to be recognized in the Community legal order. In Case 17/74 *Transocean Marine Paints Association v Commission*, the principle of the right to a fair hearing (under the Latin maxim *audi alterem partem*) was introduced by the Advocate General (AG). He argued that, in the absence of being allowed to present its view on the condition imposed in a decision, the Commission's decision would be in breach of a general principle of law clearly applicable in the UK and other legal systems. This was upheld by the CoJ.

The CoJ also held in Cases 33 and 59/79 *Kuhner* that where a person's rights were affected, they must be given the opportunity to make their views known and the right to be heard must be upheld as a general principle of good administration.

The extension of these considerations, and in particular about the right to judicial review in respect of intergovernmental acts of the member states under the former third pillar, was considered in Cases C-355/04 P *Segi v Council* and C-303/05 *Advocaten voor de Wereld*. The CoJ held that the third pillar provided less extensive rights of review, in particular of common positions and framework decisions; nevertheless, where these instruments affected the rights of individuals, fundamental rights law was to apply to both Community institutions and member states implementing Union law. In both cases, however, no breaches were held to have taken place.[55]

4.6.4.2 **Confidentiality/Legal Privilege**

In Case 155/79 *AM & S v Commission*, a company refused to hand over certain documents during a raid by Commission officials under the rules on competition law, on the ground that if it were to do so, the principle of legal privilege would be breached. The Court of Justice held that the principle was recognized in the Community legal order, provided that it was in relation to, or preparation for, a client's defence—but it must be between a party and an independent lawyer. Supporting and extending this principle are Cases

---

[54] See Arts 101–4 of the German Constitution, the *Grundgesetz*.
[55] Note now the former third pillar has been subsumed into the TEU, Arts 23–46.

136/79 *National Panasonic* and T-30/89 *Hilti.*[56] The *Hilti* case decided that the privilege extends also to the in-house lawyer's reports of the independent lawyer's findings but not to the work of the in-house lawyer per se. In Case C-36/92 P *Samenwerkende*, a refusal to hand over documents considered to be confidential was held to be unjustified in light of the existing protections in Community law under which the Commission is required to notify undertakings of the documents that it intends to release to the national authorities and thus give the undertakings the chance to seek judicial review to protect those documents. As such, the refusal to supply would be unjustified. In the end, the General Court (previously the Court of First Instance) and Court of Justice must be the arbiters of what is privileged. The principle of professional secrecy does not apply to allow a company to protect documents from the Commission, but to ensure that information received by the Commission in an investigation is not disclosed to competitors.[57]

4.6.4.3 Legal Certainty

The basic concept underlying legal certainty incorporates a number of ideas concerned with the boundary between legality and illegality or lawfulness and unlawfulness, which should be marked clearly in advance. Additionally, the existence of sanctions or punishment for the breach of the rule or overstepping the boundary should also be reasonably ascertainable, not in terms of the exact punishment, but at least in relation to the type and scope or range of punishments applicable. As such, the principle of proportionality is included in this category. Textbook and writers' considerations of EU law differ in their classification of general principles, and proportionality may thus be classified as a distinct and separate principle. The different treatment accorded to it is not really important; the point is that it is nevertheless recognized as a general principle by the CoJ and is often quoted in cases to defeat the arguments of the member state or the Commission in justifying action or behaviour that has affected the rights of others (mainly individuals in the EU context). Legal certainty, thus, includes the underlying concepts of legitimate expectations, protection of vested rights, proportionality, and non-retroactivity.

Legal certainty was first acknowledged by the Court of Justice in Case 43/75 *Defrenne v Sabena (No 2)* and later confirmed in Case 262/88 *Barber v Guardian Royal Exchange* to support the CoJ's argument that the judgment could not be retroactively effective, although there is an argument to suggest that if a treaty Article is held to be directly effective, as in the *Sabena* case, it must have been so from the outset of the Community and not from the date of judgment of the CoJ; however, for understandable pragmatic reasons, such as the massive and unexpected additional costs for most if not all employers, the ruling was not retrospective.

Allied to legal certainty is the concept of *res judicata*, which embodies the principle that once appeal time limits have expired a judgment becomes definitive and beyond challenge. It was expressly confirmed in Case C-224/01 *Köbler.*[58]

4.6.4.4 Non-retroactivity

The non-retroactivity principle is seen in its purest form in Case 63/83 *R v Kent Kirk* and Case 262/88 *Barber*, and is firmly established as a general principle of EU law. Law should not retroactively impose punishments nor be the legal base for punishments, particularly with regard to criminal sanctions, nor should it be the basis for a change

---

[56] And more recently again C-550/07 P *Akzo Nobel Chemicals v Commission* [2010] ECR I-8301.

[57] Refer to Arts 27 and 28 of Regulation 1/2003 (OJ 2003 L1/1) and Cases 209/15 and 218/78 *Dow Benelux, Van Landewyck*, 53/85 *AKZO*, and C-550/07 P *AKZO*.

[58] [2003] ECR I-10239; this case in also considered in Chapter 6.

in legal status or administrative sanctions. Case 80/86 *Public Prosecutor v Kolpinghuis Nijmegan* is also a very good example of the principle being cited by the CoJ in defence of the rights of the individual. In this case, it was used to protect the company from being prosecuted by the Dutch authorities on the strength of retroactive Community law validating national law, where the Netherlands had failed to implement the directive correctly into national law.

Civil or non-criminal law retroactivity may also occur when a person's actual rights or expected rights are altered, redefined, or totally removed: see, for example, Case 106–7/63 *Töpfer v Commission* dealing with the retroactive validation of import licence refusals by the German authorities. The principle of non-retroactivity may take on more subtle forms in civil law applications to remove the difficulties created by the alteration or withdrawal of rights by EU legal measures. These cases also involve the next principle, in that the plea is very often that the legitimate expectations of the individual have been infringed by the EU measure about which he or she is complaining. Particularly where the Commission is trying to regulate a very difficult market in goods, provided that the legitimate expectations of the parties affected have been respected, then a measure that is retroactive in effect may be upheld. See Case 98/78 *Racke v HZA Mainz* concerned with the regulation of the wine market and in particular with compensatory charges on wine imports at a time when the Community was then overproducing with the result being massive surpluses—the so-called 'wine lake'.

4.6.4.5 Legitimate Expectation or Vested Rights

The legitimate expectations of affected parties must be observed, especially when they predate an EU provision affecting their rights, hence there is some degree of overlap with non-retroactivity. In Case 88/76 *Sugar Export v Commission*, a regulation was enacted by the Commission on 30 June 1976 that removed the right of Sugar Export to cancel licences previously granted when refunds payable on sugar exports, to reduce the overproduction and surplus of sugar in the Community, dropped in value. The date of entry into force was set as 1 July, but the regulation was not published until 2 July 1976. Sugar Export applied for a cancellation on 1 July 1976, but was at first refused by the Commission. The CoJ interpreted the regulation as coming into force on 2 July 1976 and held that, whilst there was no intention of retroactivity, the rights vested in the applicant, applicable as on 1 July 1976, must be protected.

The principle was confirmed by the CoJ in Case 112/77 *Töpfer v Commission* under similar factual circumstances dealing with the sudden removal of the right to cancel an export licence. In Case 81/72 *Commission v Council (Staff Salaries)*, the principle was employed in different circumstances when the Council adopted a three-year experimental period for a system of staff salary payments, but changed this after only nine months. Despite the view that the Council could not bind itself as such, the CoJ held that the employees had a reasonable or legitimate expectation that the Council would abide by its decision.

4.6.4.6 Proportionality

The principle of proportionality embodies the concept that the punishment should fit the crime and not go further, or must be reasonable in the circumstances, and puts the question to the relevant authority of whether the same result could have been achieved by other methods or means less harmful to the party concerned. So, in the EU context, it means that individuals should not be affected by actions beyond that effect necessary in the public or Union interest, and any fines or punishment must be in proportion to the seriousness of the breach. It occurs frequently throughout all areas of EU law and especially in relation to the internal market. It was invoked in Cases 11/70 *Internationale*

Handelsgesellschaft, 36/75 *Rutili*, and 159/79 *R v Pieck* in respect of the free movement of persons, and in Case 178/84 *Commission v Germany (Beer Purity)* in relation to the free movement of goods. A good example is Case 181/84 *R v Intervention Board for Agricultural Produce, ex p Man*, in which a company was required to give a security deposit to the Intervention Board when seeking a licence to export sugar outside the Community. The applicant was late, but only by four hours, in completing the relevant paperwork. The Board, acting under a Community regulation, declared the entire deposit of over £1.5m to be forfeit. The CoJ held that the automatic forfeit of the entire deposit in the event of any failure was too drastic in view of the function of the system of export licences—that is, it was disproportionate to the aims.

The principle of proportionality has now been given statutory recognition under Art 5 TEU to apply to relations between the Union and the member states in ensuring that any action at the Union level must be in proportion to the aims of the EU and not go beyond those strict aims (see Chapter 3 for further details). Article 5 TEU provides that 'the content and form of Union action shall not exceed what is necessary to achieve the objectives of the Treaties'.[59]

4.6.4.7 Unjustified Enrichment

Unjustified enrichment is an area of law that falls between contract and tort law in common law terms, and is referred to as 'quasi-contract'. In simple terms, it provides an actionable right to recover property or money that another party has obtained unfairly, or without lawful means or right. There have now been a few cases in the EU legal order that have considered this principle and, although not covered extensively in EU law courses, it is something of which it is worth being aware. The Court of Justice has recognized the principle of unjust enrichment in a number of rulings, which often arise in connection with the payment of taxes and duties that have been levied erroneously, as in Case C-309/06 *M&S* (see later in this section), and/or breach of Community law, as in Cases C-192–218/95 *Comateb et al* (see later in this section) and Case C-147/01 *Weber's Wine World*, which involved duties levied on the alcohol by Austria, and where these duties have been passed on to the ultimate consumer or purchaser. Member states have argued that a refund of taxes would lead to unjust enrichment, because the companies had passed on the increased costs and would probably not pass on any refunds to their customers.

In 1973, in C-309/06 *M&S*, chocolate-covered tea-cakes sold by Marks & Spencer were designated as 'biscuits' by UK tax authorities and therefore value added tax (VAT) was charged on them at the standard rate. However, in the mid-1990s, the tax authorities realized their mistake and re-designated the tea-cakes as 'cakes'. Cakes are zero-rated for VAT purposes and M&S therefore attempted to recover the VAT previously paid. In their defence, the Commissioners of Customs & Excise argued that any repayment should be capped (at 10 per cent), because the VAT had been passed on to M&S's customers in the price of the tea-cakes and therefore would result in M&S being unjustly enriched. The House of Lords referred the following questions to the Court of Justice for preliminary ruling:

1. Is there a right, derived from principles of Community law, to refund wrongfully paid VAT?

2. If so, can the right to repayment of wrongfully paid VAT be restricted on the basis of unjust enrichment?

---

[59] In this context, the principle of subsidiarity may also be regarded as one of the emerging general principles of EU law, but one that, given its coverage in Chapter 3, Section 3.5, will not be covered here.

The CoJ answered the first question in the affirmative—that is, that a right to repayment of wrongfully paid tax derives from the principle of fiscal neutrality. In response to the second question, the CoJ held that the application of an unjust enrichment defence against a claim was not contrary to Community law, but that the unjust enrichment defence should be regarded as an exception to the right of repayment of wrongfully paid tax and therefore should be interpreted strictly 'following an economic analysis in which all relevant circumstances are taken into account'.

In *Comateb et al*, which was similar to the *M&S* case, the wrongfully paid duty (in this instance, French 'dock dues') had previously been held to be a charge having an equivalent effect to a customs duty and thus contrary to Art 25 EC (now 30 TFEU) (in Case C-163/90 *Legros*). Thus 27 companies (including Comateb) sought to recover the dock dues from the French Department of Customs and Indirect Taxes, although French regulations stated that a party could not recover charges if those charges had been 'passed on to the purchaser'. The Court of Justice held that a member state may object to repayment to the trader of a national charge levied in breach of Community law only where it is established that the charge has been borne in its entirety by someone other than the trader and that reimbursement to the trader would amount to its unjust enrichment. It is for the national courts to determine, in light of the facts in each case, whether those conditions have been satisfied. If the charge has been passed on only in part, it is for the national authorities to reimburse to the trader the sum not passed on. The fact that a legal obligation exists to incorporate the charge in the cost price does not mean that it can be assumed that the entire charge has been passed on, even when failure to comply with that obligation would involve a penalty.

Unjust enrichment as a general principle is thus taking its place in the EU legal order.

4.6.5 **Summary**

The category of general principles is already a wide one and potentially capable of great expansion. Indeed, in keeping with a system of law in which case law is regarded as important and can supply legal principles that become general principles to be applied in future cases, other new principles, in addition to those considered earlier, can arise. Amongst those knocking on the door of more widespread recognition is 'transparency'. Although the Court of Justice has been equivocal about the status of this as a possible general principle,[60] its actual status in the legal system has nevertheless been endorsed by statutory intervention: first by a number of decisions, but now by Regulation 1049/2001.[61] This provides a right of access to Union documents.

Another example of a potential general principle is 'good faith', which received support as a general principle of EU law in Case 366/95 *Steff-houlberg Export*, concerned with the recovery of exports refunds that had been found to have been unduly paid. The export company was not responsible for the breach of rules and had acted in good faith. Under national law, and also in view of the time elapsed, the refunds should not be recoverable. The CoJ held this to be the position under EC law also. Other contenders include:

- the right not to incriminate oneself, which arises out of criminal law and is contained in Art 6 ECHR[62]

---

[60] See Case C-58/94 *Netherlands v Council* and Case C-353/99P *Hautala v Council*.

[61] OJ 2001 L145/43.

[62] In the EU this was supported in Case C-60/92 *Otto BV* and by the General Court in Case T-112/98 but with the proviso that rather than Art 6 ECHR being directly available in EU law, less concerned with criminal law, an equivalent in EU law nevertheless existed. Its scope, though, in EU law, is not yet clear.

- environmental protection, now expressed in Art 11 TFEU, which has featured in a number of cases, particularly in the area of the free movement of goods, as a principle which will justify limits on free movement.[63]

4.7 'Soft Law'

'Soft law' is a concept that is already recognized in national legal systems, and which relates mainly to guidelines and rules of conduct. It has also developed within the EU system and encapsulates various rules of conduct that are not legally binding or enforceable in a court, or where failure to comply with them would not necessarily lead to a certain and specific sanction. Nevertheless, a number of forms of soft law have developed in the EU, including a very early example, the Luxembourg Accords, which were considered in Chapter 1.

Soft law includes all those rules or guidelines that aid the interpretation or assist in the application of enforceable EU law, or which influence the political behaviour of the member states and the institutions. There are also forms of soft law that have relevance for legal and natural persons.

Some forms of soft law are more clearly evident in the EU legal system than others: for example, recommendations and opinions, which are mentioned in Art 288 TFEU, which states quite clearly that they have no binding force, although they can have a form of persuasive authority for the member states in interpreting and applying national law, as was noted by the Court of Justice in C-322/88 *Grimaldi v Fonds des Maladies Professionelles*. Also a form of soft law are all the general principles and fundamental rights that are not strictly legally binding or directly legally enforceable in the EU legal order, unless where expressly stated by the CoJ, but which are nevertheless highly persuasive rules in line with which the Union and its institutions should behave.

There are various forms of communication from the Commission that have been held to have a quasi-legal status, including: guidelines in policy areas;[64] Commission notices, especially in the area of competition policy, for example the minor agreements notice;[65] various procedures and opinions which were reached under the second and third pillars of the Maastricht Treaty; and sometimes even press statements. Whilst not binding, they are nevertheless highly influential on the Court of Justice, but it remains the case that there is no clear-cut view of their validity.[66] Whilst soft law may be regarded as extremely helpful and might help to 'grease the axles of the EU law machine' by helping it to run more smoothly, it is not without its difficulties, particularly as any rules that are not benign—that is, those that alter the legal or factual position of an individual or by their nature dictate behaviour—are, for the most part, beyond legal question or challenge. As such, they would seem to infringe the general principle of legal certainty and democratic answerability. Consider, as an

---

[63] See e.g. Case C-463/01 *Commission v Germany* or Case C-302/86 *Commission v Denmark (Disposable Beer Cans)*.

[64] See e.g. a guideline taken completely at random from the Europa website: 'Communication from the Commission: Science and Technology—The Key to Europe's Future: Guidelines for Future European Union Policy to Support Research', COM (2004) 353(01).

[65] Refer to OJ 2001 C368/13.

[66] Refer to L. Senden, *Soft Law in European Community Law*, Hart Publishing, Oxford, 2004.

example, the difficulties and discussion with regard to the legal validity of comfort letters in competition law.[67] As a result of the change to the competition law procedure and notification rules, this long-standing practice has been scrapped, but a new form of non-legally binding notice has been brought in by Regulation 1/2003, known as a 'guidance notice', but which should be used in very limited circumstances only.[68] Because notification is no longer an automatic requirement, it is hoped that such letters will now be a rare event.

The inter-institutional agreements, which could previously be classified as a form of soft law, have now been provided with a statutory base under Art 295 TFEU, noted briefly in Section 4.5.2.5.

Finally, a development that may also be considered in this context, although the final product may end up in binding legislation, is the open method of coordination (OMC) in decision-making, considered briefly in Section 4.11. This can be regarded as having some of the features of soft law, in that the rules are contrived by methods other than the legislative procedures laid down in Arts 288 et seq TFEU and are thus beyond the legal redresses provided for in the treaties, but which rules do, however, result in standard forms of EU law that are then able to be subject to challenge.[69]

4.8 The Participation of the Institutions in the Legislative Processes

The first part of this chapter concerned the various forms of law to be found in the EU legal order. This next section deals with how the binding secondary law of the EU is enacted. These forms of law now constitute the vast bulk of EU law, and their enactment has unfortunately become rather complex over the years, involving principally three institutions, but—according to the process required, of which there are many—often more of the Union bodies. The Lisbon Treaty did though make good progress in rationalizing the legislative processes, although the Constitutional Treaty would have gone further.

First, though, an allied issue needs to be addressed in order to provide a complete picture and to explain what determines which particular process should be employed in any given circumstance.

4.8.1 The Legal Base for Legislative Proposals

Articles of the treaties that empower the EU institutions to enact further legislation to carry out the policies of that title or chapter provide the key to the legislative procedure that must be used to enact the laws and are, thus, the legal base for further legislation in pursuit of that policy. The treaty Articles either provide details of the procedure themselves (for example, Art 59 TFEU, which provides that 'the European Parliament and Council, acting in accordance with the ordinary legislative procedure and after

---

[67] In particular, Case 99/79 *SA Lancome v ETOS BV* (the *Perfumes* case). See also Chapter 10, Section 10.5.

[68] See the notice, Informal Guidance Relating to Novel Questions Concerning Arts 81 and 82 EC Treaty that Arise in Individual Cases (Guidance Letters), OJ 2001 C101/78. See also Chapter 10, Section 10.5.

[69] See e.g. Directive 97/81 on Part-time Work (OJ 1998 L14/9). For further information on this topic refer to K. Armstrong, *Governing Social Inclusion: The Law and Politics of EU Co-ordination*, Oxford University Press, Oxford, 2010 or M. Büchs, *New Governance in European Social Policy: The Open Method of Coordination*, Palgrave Macmillan, Basingstoke, 2007.

consulting the Economic and Social Committee and the European Parliament, shall issue Directives') or refer to another treaty Article for the procedure to be used, as in Art 48 TFEU, which refers to the ordinary legislative procedure outlined in Art 294 TFEU. The original treaty Article is known, then, as the legal base which determines the participants in the procedure and the level of their participation. Law-making always involves the Commission and Council plus the European Parliament, and sometimes, as noted earlier, the Economic and Social Committee (EESC) or the Committee of the Regions (CoR).

The treaty base is, then, fundamental to the relative powers and ability of the other institutions to affect the content of EU law. For example, the use of qualified majority voting (QMV) in the Council of Ministers is extremely important to the Commission, which stands a greater chance of having proposals accepted by a majority rather than by all member states in Council. Minority or marginal views can thus be ignored rather than taken into account at the draft stages. The legal base is also vital to the level of participation of the European Parliament in the legislative process, namely, whether it is merely consulted or gives its consent, or whether co-decision is used, in which case the European Parliament has more power. For example, measures in support of the single market under Art 114 TFEU require QMV rather than unanimity in the Council. As indicated, because this makes life easier for the Commission, the Commission tries to exploit this by introducing as much legislation as possible under Art 114 TFEU, whereas the Council has argued that the proposals should have as their legal base other Articles requiring unanimity (for example, Art 115 TFEU concerned directly with approximating legislation for the common market). From another perspective, a single member state that objects to a particular measure would be likely to wish to veto it and would therefore want unanimity voting in Council to have that chance; it would object to the Council deciding to adopt the measure under a legal base requiring QMV. For the most part, the particular treaty legal base is clear, in that the subject matter of the proposal is clearly within the subject matter of a specific treaty Article and, therefore, base. However, the subject matter may straddle different treaty subject areas and thus lend itself to more than one treaty base. Hence, there is sufficient ground for differences of opinion as to which is the correct treaty base to use, and the institutions and member states have often fought over this. In particular, the European Parliament has not refrained from challenging the Council for use of the incorrect legal base and has brought a number of cases before the Court of Justice.

An early example—and one likely to be in materials books—is Case 68/86 *UK v Council (Hormones)*, which concerned a directive banning growth-producing hormones, based on old Art 43 EEC concerned with measures in support of the CAP, which required a qualified majority only. This was objected to by the UK, which argued that it should have been based on the old Art 100 EEC, a single-market measure that required unanimity. The question raised was whether this was free movement, as argued by the UK, thus a single-market measure, or really to do with agricultural policy, in which case, the treaty Article under that section would be the most appropriate. The Court of Justice held that the CAP Article was the appropriate one, because it lent itself more to the subject matter concerned. Similarly, in Case C-155/91 *Commission v Council (Waste Directive)*, the Waste Directive 91/156, adopted by the Council under old Art 130s EC (an environment-measure legal base, then requiring unanimity), was challenged by the Commission on the basis that old Art 100a EC concerned with the internal market, requiring majority voting only, should have been used as the legal base. On this occasion, the CoJ disagreed and held that the protection of the environment, as stated in the directive, was the real reason and not the free movement of waste. Therefore, the challenge by the Commission was rejected. The issue was not so much the right to move waste around, but the promotion of the most efficient way of dealing with waste to protect the environment by removing any prevention of movement to the most efficient operators or disposers of waste.

A further case concerned the adoption by the Council in June 1993 of a directive specifying a minimum working week, albeit with the ability of workers to work longer voluntarily. The UK, which was opposed to this, was unable to veto the proposal, because it was introduced under the health and safety of workers provision under the old Art 118a EEC requiring a qualified majority in the Council. In Case C-84/94 *UK v Council*, the UK formally requested that the Court of Justice annul the directive, arguing that it would have been more appropriate to base the measure on old Art 235 EEC (now Art 352 TFEU) or old Art 100 EEC, either of which would have required unanimity on the part of the Council, thus allowing the UK the chance to veto the measure before its possible enactment. The CoJ was, however, satisfied with the choice of Art 118a EEC, as a health and safety of workers matter.

A final case here in which to focus on the issues raised earlier is Case C-300/89 *Commission v Council (Titanium Dioxide Directive)*. The Council adopted a directive on the basis of old Art 130s EC as an environmental measure that then required unanimity in Council and only consultation of the European Parliament, despite the protests of the European Parliament at the time. The Commission argued that it should have been adopted using Art 100a EC as a single-market measure, which then required QMV and the cooperation procedure instead. Whilst the CoJ acknowledged that both could be a valid base, the use of Art 130s instead of Art 100a deprived the European Parliament of its greater role in the legislative process. Even if both were used, as suggested by the Council, it would still have to decide unanimously and be able therefore to overrule any objections of the European Parliament.

What emerges from this case law is that the view of the Court of Justice is essentially that, in the interests of the democratic process, law-making, which now involves the European Parliament, demands that, where two legal bases are available requiring differing procedures, the one allowing the European Parliament the greater role must be used so as not to deprive it and the EU of its democratic right, unless it can be shown the matter is primarily more concerned with a particular treaty base.

In view of the simplification of the legislative procedures by the Treaties of Amsterdam and Nice and especially now by the Lisbon Treaty, many more treaty subject areas have moved under what is now termed the ordinary legislative procedure (previously known as the co-decision procedure) in favour of the European Parliament. As such, there is increasingly less room for a dispute as to the correct legal base, therefore less scope for argument and less possibility for court action in the future.[70]

However, legal base considerations did spill over into a consideration of measures in subject matters that straddled the old EC and EU Treaties and, thus, the first and third pillars because of the different law-making procedures. Whilst this strict division no longer exists following the Lisbon Treaty, the CFSP is still contained within the TEU and is subject to unanimity on the part of the Council. Hence, there is still scope for argument on issues that potentially overlap the TEU and TFEU competences, in relation to which the considerations rehearsed in the following cases are still instructive. For example, Case C-176/03 *Commission v Council* concerned whether Framework Decision 2003/80/JHA, which provided for criminal sanctions to protect the environment enacted under old Art 47 TEU under the third pillar requiring unanimity, should have been enacted under

---

[70] Your course may include other cases which consider the legal base such as Case C-370/07 *Commission v Council* [2009] ECR I-8917, Case C-94/03 *Commission v Council* [2006] ECR I-1

Art 175 EC (now 192 TFEU). The Court of Justice held that, in deciding whether a base in the TEU or in the EC Treaty was more appropriate, it should not consider the aims and content of the legislation, but whether in fact it fell within EC competences, in which case the EC Treaty base was the appropriate one. The case concerned criminal fines for environmental pollution, the criminal aspect falling within the EU Treaty, but the main policy on the environment secured in the EC Treaty. In view of much concern by the member states, the CoJ sought to clarify this in a later case. In Case C-440/05, a framework directive dealing with fines for ship pollution was adopted under Art 29 TEU, and was challenged by the European Parliament and Commission, which argued that it should have been adopted under the transport policy within Art 80 EC. The CoJ held that the subject matter was more in line with the EC Treaty and that, as stated in Art 29 TEU, in cases of conflict, the EC Treaty should take precedence and thus it should provide the legal base. However, it was clear that the EC Treaty provided no rights as to the type and level of fines that could be levied, which could only be done under the procedure provided by the TEU, which splits the decision-making process into policy under the EC Treaty, but criminal measures to ensure compliance with the policy under the TEU.

Following the Lisbon Treaty, the problem may also be alleviated to some extent, in that both treaties expressly state in Art 1 that they shall have equal status; as a result, the emphasis for the CoJ may well shift back to deciding the most appropriate legal base according to the aims and content of the proposal.[71] A warning to observe the correct legal base is also now provided in Art 296 TFEU, which provides: 'When considering draft legislative acts, the [European Parliament] and the Council shall refrain from adopting acts not provided for by the relevant legislative procedure in the area in question.'

4.9 Law-making Principles and Procedures

A number of factors have influenced, first, the establishment of the particular law-making procedures and, secondly, their expansion and evolution. These are charted from the relatively straightforward beginnings via a period of numerous and complex forms and procedures, but now have been rationalized considerably by the Lisbon Treaty. The issues provoking such change include the democratic deficit of the law-making procedure overall, the expansions in the number of member states, voting arrangements in the Council, and the establishment of the two intergovernmental pillars by the TEU and their removal by the Lisbon Treaty. As a result, there have been numerous treaty amendments both increasing and complicating the legislative procedures. Whilst the Treaty of Amsterdam made an attempt to rein in the prolixity and complexity of these procedures, it is the Lisbon Treaty that has gone furthest—although unfortunately not to the extent proposed by the Constitutional Treaty, as will be made apparent later.

---

[71] The cases concerned with competence overlap with legal base cases and are considered in Chapter 3—in particular, see Case C-376/98 *Germany v European Parliament and Council (Tobacco Advertising Ban Directive)*. See further e.g. two more recent cases in which the appropriateness of the chosen legal base was challenged. In Case C-210/03 *R v Secretary of State for Health, ex p Swedish Match*, the Court of Justice held that if obstacles to trade emerge, the Commission can intervene to harmonize even if the internal market is not the prime motive. That case concerned the banning of a type of snuff. In the second *Tobacco Advertising* case, C-380/03 *Germany v European Parliament and Council*, Art 95 could be used to enact a directive restricting the advertising of tobacco products, where differences in national laws relating to this advertising would have the effect of creating obstacles to free trade; thus the Community directive was held necessary to harmonize the internal market to allow it to function properly.

Three institutions principally are involved in law-making. However, it is worth noting that before law-making even commences, the overall policy is decided by the member states during both treaty negotiation and amendment, and on an ongoing basis by the European Council in making recommendations and requesting actions by the main institutions—notably the Council of Ministers and the Commission.

4.9.1 The Law-making Procedures

There are now, after the entry into force of the Lisbon Treaty, essentially three law-making procedures in the EU, plus the delegated law-making power of the Commission. Even before the Lisbon Treaty, one clear, leading law-making procedure had emerged and is now repackaged as the ordinary legislative procedure. The three now are: the ordinary legislative procedure; the/a special legislative procedure; and the consent (formerly known as 'assent') procedure. All law-making procedures start with the Commission (Art 17 (2) TEU), which puts policy into effect by means of preparing and proposing legislative instruments, although following the entry into force of the Lisbon Treaty, suggestions and recommendations for legislative acts may also come from the European Parliament, the European Council, the member states, the European Central Bank (ECB), the Court of Justice, the European Investment Bank (EIB), national parliaments, and EU citizens (see Arts 11–12 TEU and Art 289 TFEU). The Council and European Parliament then dispose of these legislative proposals—that is, they decide the final shape and enact the legislation. The actual detail of each procedure varies according to the way in which the Council votes and the different forms of participation of the European Parliament. Additionally, for some procedures other institutions are involved, most notably the EESC and the CoR.

The institutions involved overall and the extent to which they are involved are determined by the treaty. First of all, Arts 289 TFEU et seq provide the details of a number of procedures that are available to enact community legislation. Which particular process is employed depends on the subject matter for which legislation is required and then, in turn, the treaty Article(s) that govern those matters. In other words, legislation is enacted under a particular procedure prescribed in the legal base, noted earlier, which is the treaty Article covering the subject matter of the legislation under consideration. For example, Art 46 TFEU, which empowers legislation to be enacted for the free movement of workers, requires the ordinary legislative procedure (Art 294 TFEU).[72]

In addition to the procedures themselves, we need to consider why they have become so convoluted and the consequences of this, although it is not necessary to learn the fine details and points of each and every legislative process. This, apart from being tedious, is not very productive and, like many sets of rules, will simply change over time.

4.9.1.1 The Ordinary Legislative Procedure

Article 289 TFEU has been amended over the years to provide that the European Parliament acts more extensively with the Council and Commission in the legislative process, notably by the introduction of the co-decision procedure[73] and to provide for its renaming as the ordinary legislative procedure, detailed in Art 294 TFEU. It provides for the enhanced participation of the European Parliament to the extent that, ultimately, it can reject a legislative proposal at a second reading. The European Parliament cannot

---

[72] A complete list of the legal bases requiring co-decision under the ordinary legislative procedure can be found at **http://ec.europa.eu/codecision/docs/legal_bases_en.pdf**. See Arts 118, 165, and 195 TFEU.

[73] See the Commission pages on the co-decision procedure: **http://www.europarl.europa.eu/aboutparliament/en/20150201PVL00004/Legislative-powers**.

impose its own will on the content of a legislative proposal but it would be equally true to say that the Council cannot impose its will on the content of a legislative proposal against the wishes of the European Parliament. Note that, in this procedure, the Council votes by QMV. The following description takes into account the amendments made to the procedure by the Treaties of Amsterdam and Lisbon, which ironed out some of the initial teething troubles and delays originally experienced in the operation of the procedure.[74] The description has been marked with reference numbers that relate to Figure 4.2, as amended in light of the Lisbon Treaty.

The main stages of this procedure are that the Commission proposal [1], taking into account the opinions of the national parliaments [1A] and other bodies where specified [1B], is forwarded simultaneously to the European Parliament for its opinion and the Council for consideration. The European Parliament can, at first reading [2], either approve the proposal or amend the proposal by a simple majority or (although not strictly allowed under the procedure detailed in Art 294 TFEU) reject or substantially amend the proposal, in which case the proposal is returned to the Commission for an amended proposal [3]. The Council, at first reading [4], can either, within three months, approve those amendments by a qualified majority [5], in which case the act can be adopted [6], or if there have been no amendments [7], simply adopt the act by a qualified majority [8]. This often involves considerable exchanges of views between the three institutions to reach an agreement at first reading, but, where successful, disposes with the need to spend time on the rest of the procedure. Instead, the provision can be enacted without further ado. Otherwise, the Council adopts a common position [9] on which the Commission comments [10].

The proposal then goes to the second reading by the European Parliament [11], which can, within three months and with a possible one-month extension, either approve the common position or, for whatever reason, do nothing within the time limit [12], in which case the act is deemed to have been adopted [13]. If, however, the European Parliament rejects, by an absolute majority, the common position [14], the act is deemed not to have been accepted [15]—that is, the proposal will not become law and the procedure ends. The European Parliament, however, may propose amendments to the common position [16], which are forwarded to the Commission for comment [17] and the Council for a second reading [18].

At second reading [18], the Council may, within three months plus a month's extension, approve the European Parliament's amendments by a qualified majority or unanimously if the Commission has issued a negative opinion [19], in which case the act is adopted as amended [20]. If, on the other hand, the Council does not accept the amended common position [21], the matter is referred, within six weeks, to a conciliation committee to attempt to achieve a compromise, also within six weeks with a possible two-week extension [22 and 23]. The committee comprises members of the Council, with an equal number of Members of the European Parliament (MEPs) and the Commissioner responsible.

If a joint text is approved by the committee [24], the Council, by qualified majority (unless the treaty base requires unanimity), and the European Parliament, by a simple majority, may adopt the provision together within six weeks [25] and the act is adopted [26]. If, however, there is no approval of the joint text [27], or no agreement by the conciliation committee on a joint text within the time limit in the first place [29], then in both cases the procedure comes to an end and the act is deemed not to have been adopted [28 and 30].

---

[74] See a complete step-by-step explanation by the Commission: **http://www.europarl.europa.eu/ aboutparliament/en/20150201PVL00004/Legislative-powers**.

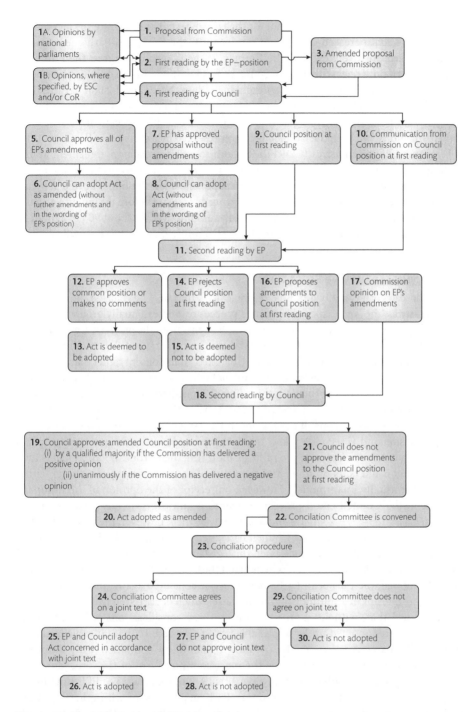

Figure 4.2 The ordinary legislative procedure

Source: Flow chart of the co-decision procedure reproduced with grateful acknowledgement under the general authorization of the European Commission; see **http://www.europarl.europa.eu/aboutparliament/en/20150201PVL00004/Legislative-powers**.

As you can see, this procedure is not for the faint-hearted and, despite the fact that its powers have been increased clearly and significantly, the European Parliament cannot enforce its own positive view over the Council; if the two cannot agree, the European Parliament can only reject the proposal—but in fact has done this on only very few occasions. The procedure was extended by the Amsterdam, Nice, and Lisbon Treaties into many new areas, and is now by far the most frequently employed legislative procedure in the treaty. The procedure is, though, also supplemented by a joint agreement[75] of the three main institutions, but with the Council being represented by a member of the Committee of Permanent Representatives (COREPER), both to seek to reach an agreement at first reading and to conduct tripartite discussions at all stages in order to eradicate differences and find agreement. Despite its complexity on paper, most legislation is enacted at points 6 or 8 in Figure 4.2, i.e. relatively soon in the procedure. Even before taking into account the changes introduced by the Lisbon Treaty, it was employed in about 90 per cent of all secondary law enactment. It is calculated by the Commission that the treaties provide 83 instances of the use of this procedure.

4.9.1.2 Special Legislative Procedures

The second category is really a bundle of procedures that may be referred to in the treaties variously as 'the', or 'a', special legislative procedure, and essentially groups together a number of procedures that differ in one or more elements from the ordinary legislative procedure (Art 289(2)–(4) TFEU). Instead of QMV, the Council may vote by unanimity, or the European Parliament may simply be consulted or asked for its consent rather than allowed to co-decide. Other bodies, such as the EESC, CoR, or ECB, may also be included in the process.

The procedure often incorporates the original consultation procedure, which originally featured in a limited number of treaty Articles (17) only and provided that the Council was required to consult the European Parliament as to its opinion before coming to a decision on EU secondary law. Under this procedure, the Commission proposes legislation that it deems necessary to fulfil a Union aim, the European Parliament is then consulted and it offers its opinion, and the Council then decides on the matter, either by QMV but usually unanimously. However, on receipt of the opinion of the European Parliament, the Council could proceed to ignore it and override any view that it has given. In Cases 138–9/79 *Roquette and Maizena v Council*, however, the Court of Justice annulled a regulation because the Council had failed to consult or obtain the opinion of the European Parliament before it passed the legislation. Furthermore, in Case C-65/93 *European Parliament v Council* it was held that if the Commission proposal has been substantially altered, the European Parliament must be consulted again, and that failure to do so will also result in annulment of the measure, which occurred in this case.

It is argued that, without express authority, these considerations will continue to apply to measures adopted under a special legislative procedure that fails to consult the European Parliament when required. Council unanimity combined with European Parliament consultation appears to be the most common form of this procedure. For examples of special legislative procedure, see Arts 19, 126, 192, and 332 TFEU (unanimity of Council and consultation of the European Parliament alone or with others), Art 252 TFEU (unanimity of Council and a consenting European Parliament), or Art 223 TFEU (under which the European Parliament takes the lead and consults the Commission, plus obtains the consent of the Council). The Council can legislate alone on a Commission

---

[75] Joint declaration on practical arrangements for the co-decision procedure (OJ 2007 C145/02), reproduced in N. Foster, *EU Treaties and Legislation*, latest edn, Oxford University Press, Oxford.

proposal under Art 26 TFEU regulating the Common Customs Tariff, Art 108 TFEU in respect of aid grants, and Art 207 TFEU on matters within the common commercial policy. Apart from its delegated powers of legislating, considered in Section 3.7, the Commission can also legislate alone under Art 45(3) TFEU on workers' rights to remain and under Art 106(3) TFEU on member states' grants to companies.

4.9.1.3 **The Consent Procedure**

The consent (previously known as the 'assent') procedure was introduced by the SEA and extended under the TEU and Lisbon Treaty, so that the European Parliament's consent is required by the Council in respect of membership applications to the EU, the Union's membership of international agreements and organizations, and association agreements with third countries (Arts 49 and 50 TEU and Arts 218 and 217 TFEU). In the event of disagreement, the European Parliament effectively has a right of veto in that, without its consent, the proposal cannot be adopted; there are, however, no formal mechanisms built in by which a dialogue between the two institutions can be initiated in the event of a disagreement on any aspect or an entire agreement. In reality, though, any such dispute would have been subject to debate and discussion behind the scenes.

Assent is also employed to confirm serious and persistent breaches by a member state (Art 7 TEU), to approve the budget (Arts 311–12 TFEU), to approve anti-discrimination legislation (Art 19(2) TFEU), for the flexibility clause (Art 352 TFEU), and also in establishing a procedure for the revision of the treaties (Art 48 TEU). The procedure is not subject to time limits.

4.9.1.4 *Passerelle* **Provisions**

It is possible without treaty amendment, under Art 48 (7) to change the legislative procedure required in specific instances from a special legislative procedure to an ordinary by a so-called '*passerelle*' provision. To do so though, requires a special procedure itself of unanimity in the European Council and consent by a majority of the component members of the EP. However, national parliaments must be given six months to consider this and a single member state can veto any such proposal. There are special '*passerelle*' possibilities in Arts 81, 153 and 192 TFEU.[76]

4.9.2 **Why so Many Changes to the Legislative Procedures?**

As noted earlier, first the increase, then the decrease in the decision-making procedures are the product of a number of developments in the EU: the democratic deficit; the various expansions of member states; voting arrangements in the Council for the member states; movement and expansion of the EU into new policy areas; and as a response to the international regulation of pan-European or even global problems, such as the environment or business regulation. One of the unfortunate consequences of the increase in procedures is that it had led to legal disputes between the member states and institutions, and between the institutions themselves, about whether the correct legal procedure and legal base have been used and not, for the most part, concerned with the substance of the final legislative act. Many cases were more concerned with the degree of power wielded by the European Parliament or individual states on the Council. As a result, the procedures have become complicated and difficult to understand without close study.

---

[76] http://en.euabc.com/word/777.

The desire to reform the procedures has so far found only limited success. The draft Constitutional Treaty for Europe proposed that the co-decision route become the only procedure; the member states, however, insisted on retaining a revised form of the consultation procedure requiring Council unanimity in a number of areas such as tax, some aspects of social and environmental policy, some bases of the CFSP, and justice and home affairs (JHA) issues. This was carried forward by the Lisbon Treaty as the special legislative procedure under Art 289 TFEU. Whilst it can involve the European Parliament legislating with the participation of the Council, this is only for matters directly concerning the European Parliament (Arts 223–34 TFEU); otherwise, where used, it is the Council acting unanimously with the consent of the European Parliament. The co-decision procedure, renamed the 'ordinary legislative procedure', will apply to economic and monetary union, and has replaced consultation for the CAP and the Common Commercial Policy (CCP), aspects of external relations, the free movement of third-country nationals (TCNs), and the area of freedom, security, and justice, previously one of the intergovernmental pillars. The areas retaining consultation and unanimity on the part of the Council are not inconsiderable, and the examples here are not exhaustive.

4.10 The Delegation of Powers

Prior to the Lisbon Treaty, Arts 202 and 211 EC authorized the delegation of powers to the Commission. Delegation of powers is now regulated by Art 290 TFEU whereas Art 291 TFEU regulates implementing powers.

In order for day-to-day decision-making to be effective, in most, if not all, democratic systems of government, some form of executive action is required, either to implement or complete legislative acts, or to be used in respect of detailed, technical issues not requiring the debate or input of the main legislators.

Delegation can be in the form of wide discretionary powers and include legislative, as well as administrative, forms of secondary legislation. Delegation may, however, be subjected to confirmation or limits or rules laid down by the delegating authority, or the delegating authority may retain the right to rescind the decision. This latter right is usually subject to a time limit by which the delegating authority must act. In the EU legal order, a system of committees was set up to supervise the exercise of delegated power, whereby the Council retained control over the delegated power. This set-up and system has now been amended by the Lisbon Treaty in that Art 290 TFEU provides the power for the Council and European Parliament to delegate powers to the Commission to enact non-legislative acts of general application, the objectives, content, scope, and duration of which must be expressly defined in the empowering legislative act. Furthermore, Art 290(2) TFEU provides that the empowering act may either provide for the European Parliament or Council to revoke the delegation or only enter into force if no objection has been expressed by the European Parliament or Council within a period set in the empowering act. This replaces part of the Committee structures set up in the past to oversee delegated and implementing powers exercised by the Commission, in terms of the regulatory committees.[77] The

---

[77] This system of management committees were known collectively as 'Comitology'. An overview of the changes can be found in Council press release 6378/11, 14 February 2011, available online at **http://www. consilium.europa.eu/uedocs/cms_data/docs/pressdata/EN/genaff/119270.pdf**. See also the Common Understanding Memorandum 8753/11 of 10 April 2011.

previous form of delegation and management committees had been considered by the Court of Justice as early as 1958. In Case 9/56 *Meroni v High Authority*, the CoJ stressed the necessity of preserving the balance of powers in the institutional structure of the Communities, as envisaged by the treaties, and which would therefore not allow the delegation of discretionary powers involving policy decisions. In Case 25/70 *Köster*, the delegation of power to the Commission within the management committee procedure was challenged on the ground that the procedure disturbed the institutional balance of the Community contrary to the treaty and undermined the independence of the Commission. The CoJ observed that the management committee could not take decisions itself, but merely provided options for implementation, and therefore the power balance was not disturbed. Thus, provided that the empowering legislation is adopted by the procedures envisaged by the treaty, the details can be delegated to the Commission. The CoJ held further, in Case 23/75 *Rey Soda*, that implementing powers under old Art 211 EC must be interpreted widely, especially under the CAP, in relation to which actions must often be taken on a day-to-day basis and discretion is necessary to cope with changing circumstances.

In Case 16/88 *Commission v Council (Re: Management Committee Procedure)* concerning the Commission's power of implementation under old Art 274 EEC, the Council delegated power to conclude certain contracts to the Commission subject to a management committee procedure. The Commission argued that implementation under old Art 274 concerning budgetary procedure was not subject to management committees. The CoJ held that, because it was also legislative in character, it was validly subject to the management committee procedures. It was argued that, since the formalization of the comitology procedures, too much power had been given to the committees and is consequently lost from the Commission and European Parliament. The European Parliament attempted to challenge the committee management structure in the Comitology Decision (Case 302/87 *European Parliament v Council*), particularly because the Council failed to state in which circumstances particular procedures would apply, but the challenge failed due to inadmissibility, at that time, of the direct challenge by the European Parliament. These criticisms were fed into the revisions undertaken by the Lisbon Treaty which resulted in the new systems established by Art 290 TFEU, considered earlier and Art 291 TFEU, considered next.

Article 291 TFEU now provides that powers may be conferred on the Commission to adopt implementing measures when uniform conditions for implementing legally binding Union Acts are needed. These are then subject to a revised comitology procedure outlined in Regulation 182/2011 (OJ 2011 L55/13). This provides now for two forms of committee comprising advisory, which are similar to those set up by the old Comitology Decision, and examination committees, which are the equivalent of the previous management and regulatory procedures.[78]

In other specific circumstances, the Commission has further powers of its own: under Art 45(3)d to draw up implementing regulations on the rights of workers to remain in member states after work has finished, under Art 105(3) TFEU concerned with competition law exemptions, and under Art 106(3) TFEU (concerned with state aids).

---

[78] See the Council Factsheet: **http://www.consilium.europa.eu/uedocs/cms_data/docs/pressdata/EN/ genaff/119516.pdf.**

4.11 The Community Method, the Open Method of Communication, and Governance Issues

There has certainly been considerable discussion about the way in which the EU is gov-erned, not in so much detail perhaps in the standard textbooks, but sufficient for it to be included in this text, so that at least an understanding of these terms is achieved and a consideration of their main aspects provided. Whilst there have been numerous minor changes and additions to the institutional structure, the most important issues remain the same. Essentially, these all relate to how the Communities and now Union should be run. There are also individual topics that reoccur within this overall theme, including the relative democratic weakness of the European Parliament or lack of any other direct democratic input, the way in which the Council wields its decision-making powers, and the lack of open government in the EU institutions.

For the most part, decision-making remains within the same institutional form of governance—itself changed little since the beginning of the Communities. This is known as the 'Community method' and includes the process of the transfer of power from the member states, the institutional set-up, and decision-making in the EU, as described earlier. The tensions between the intergovernmental and supranational elements of the Communities' form of governance, the limited democratic input, and the lack of openness and citizen participation have led to moves to address these concerns by the introduction of alternative methods of policy coordination and governance for the EU. In particular is the development of the OMC, which had its roots in the social dialogue procedure by which Community-wide standards were agreed when the Social Policy Chapter lay out-side the treaty set-up. After consultation and discussion by and between the social and other interest groups most directly concerned with the policy, any ensuing agreements that were reached under that policy would be enforceable at the EU level. After the change of UK government in 1997, following previous resistance to this method, the social dia-logue method was imported into the EC Treaty under Arts 138–9 EC (now Arts 154–5 TFEU) and extended to a wider social policy field.

The advantage of OMC is that it is regarded as a less painful method of making pro-gress in such areas of shared competence, or of supporting or coordinating competence, of the EU because hard law measures would generally require unanimity by the now 28 member states. Hard law measures are thus difficult to achieve or prove too difficult for some states, which might or would veto any legislative proposals in Council in matters of national sensitivity, such as tax. OMC, though, has not been widely used and is not with-out criticism. The Community (Union) method remains the most preferred and used. Despite the optimism shown for OMC at the Lisbon Summit in 2000 and the Convention on the Future for Europe that produced the draft Constitutional Treaty, the final treaty that emerged largely ignored OMC. The Lisbon Treaty has done nothing to change this. The use of OMC is criticized as representing a retreat from firm legal commitments to achieve a more social Europe, or as a downgrading or abandoning of fixed legislative policies on social and employment matters, replacing them instead with the uncertain soft law options of dubious value and validity. OMC may also be seen as undermining the democratic input into the legislative process of the European Parliament—an input that has been so hard fought over so many years—and, as a result, it is hard to see a role for the European Parliament without seriously compromising OMC or unnecessarily duplicat-ing effort and input, thus making the democratic involvement process very inefficient. A union of 28 member states certainly poses more challenges than did the original union of only six and OMC is regarded as not being very workable, without significant change, for an enlarged EU.[79]

A good example of soft law input is the practice of the Commission when issuing communications following a leading judgment, or series of judgments, of the Court of Justice. By doing so, the Commission advises how it considers the judgment should operate in practice and it seeks to shape member states' behaviour without recourse to legislative enactments to do so.[80]

4.12 Law-making: Getting the Balance Right

As outlined earlier, there are a number of dynamics taking place in the policy-making and law-making procedures of the EU. The most notable remains the balance between the direct democratic legitimacy of the European Parliament in the face of the previous legislative superiority of the Council. The problem is that increasing the input and power of the European Parliament, whilst it would increase democratic participation, albeit indirectly, might jeopardize the present level of efficiency of the law-making process. Whilst it is far from perfect at the moment, it does seem to have achieved a relatively happy medium of getting most things done and in view of the changes introduced by the Lisbon Treaty and the fact that most legislation is now enacted as a joint act of the European Parliament and the Council, a lot of those criticisms have been met. A further increase in the power of the European Parliament truly to rival that of the Council might have the knock-on effect of creating a conflict between the two institutions, which may result in stalling the law-making processes; if nothing were ever to get done as a consequence, it would hardly be a useful democratic input. So, if too much participation by the European Parliament would lead to a slowing down of the legislative processes, should efficiency be sacrificed for the sake of democracy? Conversely, of the present state of affairs, one could pose the question 'Should democracy be sacrificed for the sake of efficiency?'

Under the Constitutional Treaty, and introduced by the Lisbon Treaty, there is more involvement of national parliaments to check that subsidiarity is conformed with (new Art 12 TEU), take a view on accession applications, oversee legislative proposals, and be kept informed about policy initiatives in the same way as the European Parliament, especially in the matters covered by the old third pillar dealing with justice affairs. National parliaments have also been given a formal role (new Art 48 TEU) in any future treaty amendment proposals. The difficulty with these proposals is that the national parliaments may also become a rival for power with the European Parliament and may also reduce efficiency in the law-making processes if the views of 28 (or more) national parliaments have to be obtained before progress can be made.

Turning to the alternative, OMC also has its alleged advantages of increased participation, openness, and flexibility, but it is also fraught with danger in that decisions made under it may be beyond legal challenge. It also increases the power of the Commission and member states without any reference to, and probably at the expense of, the European Parliament and, if expanded, the EESC and the CoR.

---

[79] See D. Hodson and I. Maher, 'The Open Method as a New Mode of Governance: The Case of Soft Economic Policy Co-ordination' (2001) 39 JCMS 719, 721–2; and S. de la Rosa, 'The Open Method of Coordination in the New Member States: Perspectives for Its Use as a Tool of Soft Law' (2005) 11 ELJ 618.

[80] The best example is the issue of Commission Practice Note on import prohibitions following the leading Case 120/78 *Cassis de Dijon*. There are numerous other examples, especially in the area of competition law.

In a union of 28 or more member states, and given the complicated institutional structure, it should come as no surprise that there are tensions at the centre of, and considerable changes in, the relations between the principal actors in trying to get right the balance of power—particularly as the main institutions compete with one another for the exercise of that power. To struggle to address the democratic credentials is a large part of that struggle, but, as outlined in Chapter 1, the Union is not a static, but very dynamic enterprise, continually evolving.

Further Reading

Books

ARMSTRONG, K. *Governing Social Inclusion: The Law and Politics of EU Co-ordination*, Oxford University Press, Oxford, 2010.

BERNITZ, U., NERGELIUS, J., and CARDNER, C. *General Principles of EC Law in a Process of Development*, Kluwer Law International, London, 2008.

BIRKINSHAW, B. *The European Legal Order after Lisbon*, Kluwer Law International, London, 2010.

GRAGL, P. *The Accession of the European Union to the European Convention on Human Rights*, Hart Publishing, Oxford, 2013.

PEERS, S. and WARD A. (eds) *The EU Charter of Fundamental Rights: Politics, Law and Policy*, Hart Publishing, Oxford, 2004.

PEERS, S. et al (eds) *The EU Charter of Fundamental Rights: A Commentary*, Hart Publishing, Oxford, 2014.

PRINSSEN, J.M. and SCHRAUWEN, A. (eds) *Direct Effect: Rethinking a Classic of EC Legal Doctrine*, Europa Law Publishing, Groningen, 2002.

SENDEN, L. *Soft Law in European Community Law*, Hart Publishing, Oxford, 2004.

TRIDIMAS, T. *The General Principles of EC Law*, 2nd edn, Oxford University Press, Oxford, 2006.

Articles

ARNULL, A. 'From Charter to Constitution and Beyond: Fundamental Rights in the New European Union' [2003] Public Law 774.

BARRATA, R. 'Accession of the EU to the ECHR: The Rationale for the ECJ's Prior Involvement Mechanism' (2013) 50 CML Rev 1305.

BAST, J. 'New Categories of Acts after the Lisbon Reform: Dynamics of Parliamentarisation in EU Law' (2012) 49 CML Rev 885.

BERGHE, F. VAN DER 'The EU and Issues of Human Rights Protection: Some Solutions to More Acute Problems?' (2009) 46 CML Rev 1035.

BOER, N. DE 'Addressing Rights Divergences under the Charter: *Melloni*' (Case Note on Case C-399/11) (2013) 50 CML Rev 1038.

BORRAS, S. and GREVE, B. 'Special Issue: The Open Method of Co-ordination in the European Union' (2004) 11(2) Journal of European Public Policy 185–208.

BÚRCA, G. DE 'The Constitutional Challenge of New Governance in the European Union' (2003) 28 EL Rev 814–40.

CRAIG, P. 'Delegated Acts, Implementing Acts and the New Comitology Regulation' (2011) 36 EL Rev 671.

DICKSON, J. 'Directives in EU Legal Systems: Whose Norms Are They Anyway? (2011) 17 ELJ 190.

LEEUW, M.E. DE 'Openness in the Legislative Process of the European Union' (2007) 32 EL Rev 295.

DOUGLAS-SCOTT, S. 'The European Union and Human Rights after the Treaties of Lisbon' (2011) 11 HRL Rev 645.

DRIESSEN, B. 'Delegated Legislation after the Treaty of Lisbon: An Analysis of Article 290 TFEU' (2010) 35 EL Rev 837.

GRAGL, P. 'A Giant Leap for European Human Rights? The Final Agreement on the European Union's Accession to the European Convention on Human Rights' (2014) 51 CMLR 13.

HOFMANN, H. 'Legislation, Delegation and Implementation under the Treaty of Lisbon: Typology Meets Reality' (2009) 15 ELJ 482.

IGLESIAS SANCHEZ, S. 'The Court and the Charter: The Impact of the Entry into Force of the Lisbon Treaty on the ECJ's Approach to Fundamental Rights' (2012) 49 CML Rev 1565.

JACOBS, F. 'Human Rights in the EU: The Role of the ECJ' (2001) 26 EL Rev 331.

LANG, J. 'Checks and Balances in the European Union: The Institutional Structure and the "Community Method"' (2006) 46 CML Rev 127.

LECZYKIEWICZ, D. 'Horizontal Application of the Charter of Fundamental Rights' (2013) 38 EL Rev 479.

LENAERTS, K. 'Exploring the Limits of the Charter of Fundamental Rights' (2012) 8 ECLR 375.

PAPADOPOULOS, T. 'Criticising the Horizontal Direct Effect of the EU General Principle of Equality' (2011) 4 EHRLR 437.

PEERS, S. 'Supremacy, Equality and Human Rights' (2010) 35 EL Rev 849.

PEERS, S. and COSTA, M. 'Accountability for Delegated and Implementing Acts after the Treaty of Lisbon' (2012) 18 ELJ 427.

SARMIENTO, D. 'Who's Afraid of the Charter? The Court of Justice, National Courts and the New Framework of Fundamental Rights Protection in Europe' (2013) 50 CML Rev 1267.

Web-based Materials

http://ec.europa.eu/social/main.jsp?catId=329&langId=en
The Commission website on social dialogue

Webpages on the ordinary legislative procedure:

http://europa.eu/legislation_summaries/institutional_affairs/treaties/lisbon_treaty/
ai0016_en.htm
http://www.europarl.europa.eu/aboutparliament/en/0080a6d3d8/
Ordinary-legislative-procedure.html (with a flow chart)

5

The Supremacy of EU Law

5.1 The Supremacy of EU Law

The supremacy or priority of EU law can be considered from two perspectives: first, from the point of view of the Union and, secondly, from that of the member states. As with the doctrine of direct effects considered in Chapter 6, it is through the decisions and interpretation of the Court of Justice that the reasons and logic for the supremacy of EU law have been developed.

5.2 The View of the Court of Justice

There is, despite the reforms introduced by the Lisbon Treaty and the inclusion of an express statement in the abandoned Constitutional Treaty, still no express declaration or specific legal base for the supremacy of EU law in the treaties. It can be argued that some of the Articles of the treaties impliedly require primacy: for example, Art 4(3) TEU, the fidelity or good-faith clause;[1] Art 18 TFEU, the general prohibition of discrimination on the grounds of nationality; Art 288 TFEU, the direct applicability of regulations; and Art 344 TFEU, the reservation of EU and not national dispute resolution for matters coming within the scope of the treaties. In the absence of an initial express statement written into the treaties,[2] another route was needed to establish this supremacy of EU law over national law. (Note that the 2007 Lisbon Treaty has side-stepped a direct expression of supremacy, by adding a declaration (Declaration No 17), which instead supports supremacy by upholding the case law of the Court of Justice on supremacy and referring to the Opinion of the Council Legal Service that confirmed the same conclusion.) However, from the outset, the Communities included their own supreme Court of Justice, which is the equivalent of a constitutional court, to adjudicate on disputes between the institutions of the Union, and between the member states and the institutions. Without an express treaty statement of priority, the CoJ took the lead in providing basic constitutional principles on which the new legal order was based.

The CoJ's view on supremacy is quite straightforward. In the first pronouncement dealing with this, *Van Gend en Loos*, it held that the member states had limited their sovereignty, albeit within limited fields as agreed in the EC Treaty, and held that individuals in the Community could uphold rights under Community law in the national courts and in the face of conflicting national law. From its case law—notably, Case 26/62 *Van Gend en*

---

[1] Which, in various other texts dealing with EU law, is also called the solidarity clause and the principle of cooperation—the latter by the Court of Justice in Case C-221/89 *Factortame (No 2)*.

[2] That is, before the express acknowledgement of supremacy by the member states in the Constitutional Treaty, Art I-6, which was removed in the Lisbon Treaty, but will be considered further later in this chapter.

Loos, Case 6/64 *Costa v ENEL*, and Case 106/77 *Simmenthal*—it is clear that Community and now EU law is clearly regarded by the Court of Justice as an autonomous legal order that is related to international law and national law, but which is nevertheless distinct from them and thus subject to its own logic in relation to supremacy over the law of the member states. It was not long, though, before this supremacy over national law was stated expressly by the CoJ in *Costa v ENEL* in 1964.

The *Van Gend en Loos* case, already considered in Chapter 3 as the leading case in the development of the doctrine of direct effects, substantially prepared the ground for the CoJ to develop its argument for supremacy of Community law in *Costa v ENEL*. *Van Gend en Loos* was instrumental in affirming the CoJ's jurisdiction in interpreting Community legal provisions, the object of which is to ensure uniform interpretation in the member states, and established direct effect of Community law in the national legal orders. The CoJ held that 'the Community constitutes a new legal order of International law for the benefit of which the States have limited their sovereign rights, albeit in limited fields, and the subjects of which comprise not only member states but also their nationals'.

Further elaboration of the new legal order in *Van Gend en Loos* was then given in Case 6/64 *Flaminio Costa v ENEL*. This case primarily concerned the claim for payment of an electricity bill of a very low value (then approximately £1). In 1962, the Italian government passed an Act to nationalize the electricity industry; the newly nationalized industry sent out bills to recover debts previously outstanding. Mr Costa claimed that the action was in conflict with Art 37 EEC (now Art 31 TFEU) concerned with state monopolies and refused to pay his bill. The case, however, also raised the wider issue of whether a national court should refer to the Court of Justice if it considers that Community law may be applicable or, in the view of the Italian government, simply apply the subsequent national law.

In addressing this question, the CoJ again stressed the autonomous legal order of Community law:

> By contrast with ordinary international treaties the EEC Treaty has created its own legal system which became an integral part of the legal systems of the member states and which their courts are bound to apply. By creating a Community of unlimited duration, having its own institutions, its own personality, its own legal capacity, and more particularly real powers stemming from a limitation of sovereignty or a transfer of powers from the states to the Community the member states have limited their sovereign rights and have created a body of law to bind their nationals and themselves.

The CoJ also established that Community (EU) law takes priority over all conflicting provisions of national law, whether passed before or after the Community (EU) measure in question:

> The integration into the laws of each Member State of provisions which derive from the Community, and more generally, the terms and spirit of the Treaty, make it impossible for the states, as a corollary, to accord precedence to a unilateral and subsequent measure over a legal system accepted by them on the basis of reciprocity. Such a measure cannot therefore be inconsistent with that legal system.

As additional justifications, the Court of Justice also invoked the use of some of the general provisions of the EEC Treaty: old Art 5 (now Art 4(3) TEU), the requirement to ensure the attainment of the objectives of the treaty, and old Art 7 EEC (now Art 18 TFEU), the prohibition of discrimination—both of which would be breached if subsequent national legislation were to have precedence; and old Art 189 EEC (now Art 288 TFEU), regarding the binding and direct application of regulations, which would be meaningless if subsequent national legislation were able to prevail.

The CoJ summed up its position:

> It follows . . . that the law stemming from the treaty, an independent source of law, could not because of its special and original nature, be overridden by domestic legal provisions, however framed, without being deprived of its character as Community law and without the legal basis of the Community itself being called into question.

Therefore, the conclusion must be that EU law must be supreme over subsequent national law.

In Case 106/77 *Simmenthal*, the CoJ ruled that:

> A national court which is called upon, within the limits of its jurisdiction, to apply provisions of Community law, is under a duty to give full effect to those provisions, if necessary of its own motion to set aside any conflicting provisions of national legislation, even if adopted subsequently.

The CoJ ruled that directly effective provisions of Community law preclude the valid adoption of new legislative measures to the extent that they would be incompatible with Community provisions. Any inconsistent national legislation recognized by national legislatures as having legal effect would deny the effectiveness of the obligations undertaken by the member state and imperil the existence of the Community. This case is considered further in Section 5.2.1 in respect of constitutional practice.

Therefore the voluntary limitation of sovereignty, and the need for an effective and uniform Community (EU) law, requires supremacy. To give effect to subsequent national law over and above the Community (EU) legal system that member states have accepted would be inconsistent.

In Case C-213/89 *Factortame (No 1)*, the Court of Justice, building on the principle laid down in *Simmenthal* that a provision of EC law must be implemented as effectively as possible, held that a national court must suspend national legislation that may be incompatible with EC law until a final determination on its compatibility has been made. Thus, national rules that prevented a national court from issuing an interim injunction suspending the application of a national statute during a dispute whilst considering the existence of alleged rights under Community law are to be set aside. It was later held in Case C-221/89 *Factortame (No 2)* that the UK law did, in fact, breach Community law.

Finally, in this context, it is worth mentioning the consequence of a member state not giving primacy to EU law when it should do so, in which case liability on the part of the state will be incurred. This principle was first established by the CoJ in *Francovich*, and later confirmed in *Factortame III* and other cases.[3]

So far, the national legislation considered has been so-called 'ordinary' national legislation—that is, municipal law—and the CoJ has maintained a consistent position on supremacy, including the supremacy of secondary EU law over 'ordinary' national legislation. But what about provisions of a member state's constitution? It is in this respect that the most serious conflicts between the views of the national judiciaries and the CoJ have arisen.

5.2.1 Supremacy and Member State Constitutional Law

The Court of Justice's view in respect of national constitutional law differs little from that in respect of 'ordinary' national law and can be seen in Case 11/70 *Internationale*

---

[3] Discussed in Chapter 6.

Handelsgesellschaft. This case concerned the claim that Community levies were contrary to the German Constitution (Arts 2.1 and 14 *Grundgesetz*) and thus, as far as the national court was concerned, inapplicable. On referral, the Court of Justice held that national courts do not possess the power to review Community law. The important question arising from the case was whether the Court of Justice was in a position to declare supremacy over national constitutional law and so, in effect, review that law. In doing so, it would effectively deny the ability of national courts to overcome the fact that there is a clear distinction or separation of the national and EU law legal systems, otherwise known as the 'autonomy of jurisdictions', but nevertheless do so itself. In other words, national courts would not be able to question the supremacy of EU law, but the CoJ would be able to determine that national constitutional law was, or is, not in conformity with EU law—something clearly of great concern to national supreme courts.

The second case arises from a conflict between the Italian Constitution and Community law. In Italy, constitutional practice existed that the power to disregard or declare invalid a provision of national law was the sole right of the Italian Constitutional Court. In Case 106/77 *Simmenthal*, a lower court was faced with inconsistency between a Community law provision and a national provision. The national court was aware that a reference to the Italian Constitutional Court would have the effect of subrogating Community law to national legal practice, inconsistently with existent Community case law on the matter, as was evident from the earlier Case 6/64 *Costa v ENEL*; however, disregarding the national law was contrary to Italian constitutional requirements. The Italian magistrate referred to both courts, but asked the Court of Justice whether subsequent national measures that conflict with Community law must be disregarded without waiting until those measures are set aside by legislative or other constitutional means.

The CoJ first declared that the doctrine of direct effects of Community legislation was not dependent on any national constitutional provisions, but a source of rights in itself. Therefore national courts must give full effect to those rights, including a refusal to apply conflicting national legislation. The CoJ also ruled that directly effective provisions of Community law also preclude the valid adoption of new legislative measures to the extent that they would be incompatible with Community provisions. The national court should therefore disregard the inconsistent national law. The CoJ established that if there were no violation of Community fundamental rights, the Community measures would be acceptable and there should be no reference to national constitutions to test their validity. It held:

> The law stemming from the treaty, an independent source of law, cannot because of its very nature be overridden by rules of national law, however framed, without being deprived of its character as Community law. Therefore the validity of a Community measure or its effect within a Member State cannot be affected by allegations that it runs counter to either fundamental rights as formulated by the Constitution of that State or the principles of a national constitutional structure.

The Court of Justice has not been so expressly forthright since *Simmenthal*. The conclusion following this case is that any inconsistent national legislation recognized by national legislatures as having legal effect would, in the CoJ's view, deny the effectiveness of the obligations undertaken by the member states and, in particular, the good-faith clause, Art 10 EC (now Art 4(3) TEU), and thus imperil the very foundations of the Community (EU). In its widest interpretation, the judgment holds that 'Inconsistent national measures of any sort which are introduced by member states are effectively invalid from their adoption'. However, if the same national law were also applicable to purely domestic situations, there is not a requirement to set it aside and it remains valid in that circumstance. It must not though apply to situations governed by EU law. See Cases C-10–22/97 *IN.CO.GE.'90.*

The stance taken by the Court of Justice is in sharp contrast to the initial stance by some of the member states' courts. Indeed, *Internationale Handelsgesellschaft* produced a head-on clash between the CoJ and the German Federal Constitutional Court and German Constitution, which will be further reviewed from the German perspective in Section 5.5.2.

Case C-213/89 *Factortame (No 1)* is another confirmation that national constitutional practices or rules—in this case, the doctrine of parliamentary sovereignty in the UK—must not be allowed to stand in the way of an EU law right. It was previously the position in the UK under the doctrine of parliamentary sovereignty that the courts had no power to set aside, or not apply, an Act of Parliament. The CoJ held[4] that, even though the Community law rule was still in dispute, the national procedure should be changed so as not to possibly interfere with the full effectiveness of the Community law right. This case is also a witness to EU law incursion into national procedure, which will be taken up further in Chapter 6.

Case C-399/11 *Melloni*[5] provided yet another opportunity for the CoJ to re-confirm its uncompromising position on the supremacy of EU law even over national constitutions. This was notwithstanding an interpretation of Article 53 of the EU Charter of Fundamental rights which seemed to suggest that where the standards of national constitutions are higher than EU standards, then the national standard should prevail. The case concerned the European Arrest Warrant (Framework Decision 2002/84) and the arguably higher standard offered by the Spanish Constitution for its application. The CoJ made clear that the primacy of EU law cannot be undermined even by national constitutional law but that any application of national law can only be done in the light of the interpretation of the Charter by the CoJ and when the primacy and unity effectiveness of EU is not compromised. The measure in question was held by the CoJ to conform with EU fundamental rights and was thus applicable without reference to national standards.

The CoJ is, therefore, clear that EU law is supreme over all types of national law. The cases mentioned here are only the leading cases on supremacy—that is, those that expressly declare EU law primacy. Many other cases imply EU law supremacy: for example, all cases that declare direct effects presuppose supremacy. If EU law were not supreme over national law, especially subsequent law, then direct effects would be denied. Conversely, if direct effects were denied where they fulfil the criteria, supremacy would therefore also be denied because national law would be seen to prevail.

A related but slightly different expression by the CoJ of how the autonomy should be protected is its Opinion 1/09.[6] The CoJ was asked for an opinion on whether a proposed non-EU independent Patent Court (serving 38 EU and non-EU states) to be set up outside of the treaty was compatible with the treaty. It was to apply and interpret EU law and could make references to the CoJ. The CoJ held that it would not be compatible as it would undermine the uniformity of the autonomous EU legal system both within the member states and in the EU legal order itself. Consequently the member states were not able to establish that court.

In summary, the EU view on supremacy is that, because of its unique nature, EU law denies the member states the right to resolve conflicts of law by reference to their own

---

[4] See [17]–[23] of the judgment.

[5] Judgment of 26th February 2013, not yet reported (OJ (2013) L114/12).

[6] Opinion 1/09 on the Creation of a European Patents Court [2011] ECR I-1137.

rules or constitutional provisions. EU law obtains its supremacy through the transfer of state power and sovereignty to the Union by the member states in those areas agreed. The member states have provided the Union with legislative powers to enable it to perform its tasks. There would be no point in such a transfer of power if the member states were able to annul or suspend the effect of EU law by later national law or provisions of the constitutions. If that were allowed to be the case, the existence of the EU legal order and the Union itself would be called into question. A precondition of the existence and functioning of the Union is the uniform and consistent application of EU law in all the member states. It can only achieve such an effect if it takes precedence over national law. Therefore, the legal and logical consequences of this is the fact that any provision of national law that conflicts with EU law, regardless of the date of enactment or rank, must be invalid.

The Constitutional Treaty had provided an express statement of supremacy (Art I-6), although without expressly stating that it would be supreme over the member states' constitutions. When that treaty was abandoned, however, the member states used the opportunity to tone down significantly the clear statement previously made, but without denying this supremacy. Hence, supremacy is now dealt with in a declaration (Declaration No 17), which refers obliquely to the well-settled case law that established the supremacy of EU law and further by a reference in an annex to the final act of the treaty citing the opinion of the Council Legal Service on primacy.[7]

On the other hand, it can be argued that, whatever the form of acknowledgement, supremacy has been expressly stated by the member states and is thus not something easily resisted anymore; some of the supreme courts in some member states have, however, been more reluctant to give way to EU law supremacy. We will have to wait for new cases reaching those courts to see if that situation continues and, in respect of the new member states, whether it applies in those also. For the moment, the following sections of this chapter will consider how EU law has been received in some of the member states thus far.

5.2.2 **Supremacy and International Law**

The relationship between EU law and provisions of international law has been considered by the Court of Justice.[8] In the event of a collision between a provision of international law and EU law, which should take priority? These agreements now are essentially governed by Art 351 TFEU which provides:

> The rights and obligations arising from agreements concluded before 1 January 1958 or, for acceding States, before the date of their accession, between one or more Member States on the one hand, and one or more third countries on the other, shall not be affected by the provisions of the Treaties.

---

[7] Which reads:
It results from the case-law of the European Court of Justice that primacy of EC law is a cornerstone principle of Community law. According to the CJEU, this principle is inherent to the specific nature of the European Community. At the time of the first judgment of this established case law (*Costa/ENEL*, 15 July 1964, Case 6/64) there was no mention of primacy in the treaty. It is still the case today. The fact that the principle of primacy will not be included in the future treaty shall not in any way change the existence of the principle and the existing case-law of the European Court of Justice.
[Council Legal Service Opinion, Council Document 11197/07 (JUR260) of 22 June 2007]

[8] E.g. Case C-162/96 *Racke v Hauptzollamt Mainz* [1998] ECR I-3655, the *BITs* cases: Cases 205/06, C-249/06, and C-118/07, and Case C-84/98 *Commission v Portugal*.

To the extent that such agreements are not compatible with the Treaties, the Member State or States concerned shall take all appropriate steps to eliminate the incompatibilities established.

This means that supremacy of EU law does not apply to agreements made before accession to the EU. However agreements made, or those modified to the extent that the CoJ would regard them as new agreements after accession, are subject to the general rule of EU law supremacy, that where they are inconsistent with EU law they should give way to EU law.

An example of a modified agreement can be found in Case C-466/98 *Commission v UK* which concerned the 'open sky' agreements with the USA concluded originally by the UK under the Bermuda I Agreement in 1946 but modified extensively under the Bermuda II Agreement in 1977. When challenged by the Commission, the CoJ held that the modified agreement was essentially a new agreement and thus not covered by Art 351. Any inconsistencies would therefore be subject to EU law. In the *Bilateral Investment Treaties (BITs)* cases, Cases 205/06, C-249/06, and C-118/07, the CoJ held that the application of the EU Treaties did not disturb the duties member states owed to third countries under agreements entered into previously but that the EU itself was not so bound. Member states, though, are required, in the case of conflict to do all they can to eliminate inconsistencies. If they cannot, they should then denounce the prior agreement, as held by the CoJ in Case C-84/98, *Commission v Portugal*. In Case C-324/93 *Evans Medical*, though, the CoJ held that provisions of an agreement which were contrary to EU rules on the matter may still be applied where third parties rely on them and are still required to perform duties arising from them.

5.2.2.1 UN Resolutions

Joined Cases C-402/05 P and C-415/05 P *Kadi and Al Barakaat*[9] concerned the translation into EU regulations of United Nations (UN) measures against the support of terrorism, namely the freezing of assets of persons listed by the UN as suspected of being involved. The applicants Kadi and Al Barakaat could not, of course, challenge the UN resolution itself and the UN resolution was not under review or challengeable before the Court of Justice. They did challenge the regulation which put into effect the UN resolution and was the cause of the alleged infringements of human rights, including the right to be heard and the right to an effective remedy, in an appeal to the Court of Justice from the CFI (now the General Court).[10] The issue for this chapter is whether the Court of Justice had the right to review or was precluded from reviewing a regulation intended to put into effect a UN resolution, something which, according to Art 105 of the UN Charter, is excluded.

The CFI and the Court of Justice both stated that the Community is based on the rule of law and that therefore its acts are subject to judicial review, but according to the CFI such a review was restricted due to the international origin of the relevant acts. In contrast, the Court of Justice made clear that neither the member states nor the EU institutions can avoid review of the conformity of their acts with the basic constitutional charter, the EC Treaty, which established a complete system of legal remedies and procedures designed to enable the Court of Justice to review the legality of acts of the institutions. Furthermore, a guarantee of fundamental rights forms an integral part of the Community legal order and respect for these rights is a condition of the lawfulness of Community acts and, as constitutional principles of the EU, this status could not be affected by any international

---

[9] [2008] ECR I-6351.
[10] They also challenged on the ground that the EU did not have the competence to enact such a regulation, an issue which will not be pursued here. Also the human rights aspect is considered in Chapter 4.

agreement or the fact that EU acts were based on an international obligation. A review of the validity of any Community measure in light of fundamental rights must be considered to be the expression, in a Community based on the rule of law, of a constitutional guarantee stemming from the EC Treaty as an autonomous legal system.[11] The Court of Justice, therefore, could review the Union measures and thus indirectly the UN resolution. The resolution and thus the regulation were held patently to breach the right to be heard and to an effective remedy in the inclusion of the applicants' names in the list without recourse to any form of judicial review. The Court of Justice acknowledged that security interests may justify the secret compilation of the list but would not exclude a judicial review of the lawfulness after publication. Therefore, as far as applicants were concerned, the regulation was annulled.

Hence, then, the overall conclusion is that EU law in the Union takes priority over conflicting international law even in the case of UN provisions.

5.3 EU Law in the Member States

With 28 member states now, it would occupy far too much space to look at the reception of EU law in all of them; therefore only a sample of states has been chosen, commencing with the UK. Before this is undertaken, it needs to be considered how international law was traditionally received into national legal systems.

5.3.1 Theories of Incorporation of International Law: Monism and Dualism

The method of incorporation of international law into the member states' legal systems and EU law is determined initially by the particular outlook that a state has in respect of the validity of such law. There are two prevailing theories of the incorporation of external law into national legal systems that are applicable in the context of the initial incorporation of the Community and now EU treaties into the member state legal systems: monism and dualism.

Monism basically assumes that international law and national law form part of a single system or hierarchy of laws; therefore the acceptance of international law would not require formal incorporation by legislative transformation, but after treaty agreement and assent or ratification, it would be self-executing. In other words, it would be directly applicable within the state. So, all that is required by such a state to achieve this is the assent to, or ratification of, an international treaty. It does not, however, determine where on the single hierarchy the international law should be placed and this leaves open difficulties of whether, in individual states, it takes priority over all law, or only over municipal or, otherwise expressed, ordinary, national law and not constitutional law. France is a good example of a monist state and will be considered in Section 5.5.4.

Dualism, on the other hand, regards international law and national law as fundamentally different systems of law that exist alongside each other. In order to overcome the barrier existing between the two systems, legislation is required to transform rules of international law into the national legal system before it can have any binding effect within the state in such circumstances. It is for the member states to determine where the international law is then placed within the national hierarchy of laws. The UK and

---

[11] See Judgment at paras 281–4, 292, 296, and 316.

Germany are examples of dualist states, and are states that will be considered first in looking at the reception of EU law into the member states.

5.4 EU Law in the UK

The UK was not one of the original and founding member states of the Communities. It had a number of difficulties to overcome in order to accommodate the duties of membership of the EEC in 1973. It had to accept all the previous Community legislation passed: not only the treaties, but also the regulations, directives, and the judicial legal developments of this established new legal order. This is known in EU jargon as the acceptance of the *acquis communautaire*.[12] It had, on the other hand, time to adjust for this. Being a later entrant state, the UK could see in advance the legal and constitutional problems that would arise as a result of membership. It could see the judicial developments of direct effects and the supremacy of EU law, and take account of them before entry—so there were no excuses for failure to do so or, indeed, the acceptance of these leading principles of EU law. The particular difficulties faced by the UK legal system at the time in accommodating EC membership and EC law were those of the largely unwritten constitution, the dualist approach to international law, and the doctrine of parliamentary sovereignty.

5.4.1 The 'Unwritten' Constitution

The UK does not have a single codified constitutional document; instead, the UK Constitution is made up of a number of written and unwritten elements, although most of it is now in written form. Furthermore, there is no concept or form of entrenchment of particular parts of either the Constitution itself, or of any of the special or other parts of the Constitution that are regarded as particularly important, including Acts of Parliament, all of which can be removed by simple repeal by the same or any future Parliament. This has the consequence that even if a particular political action or legal action is so important and envisaged as very long term, if not permanent, it is very difficult, if not impossible, under UK constitutional law, to entrench this. It makes it effectively impossible to alter the UK Constitution with any certainty. Thus, any transfer of power to the Union under traditional constitutional thinking could not be regarded as permanent and could, at least theoretically, always be reversed by a subsequent Act of Parliament.

5.4.2 The Dualist Approach to International Law

International treaties are a prerogative of the Crown, as represented by the government in Parliament in the UK, and the courts have no jurisdiction in respect of the validity of such treaties, although they can provide persuasive arguments for the interpretation of national law. In order to apply expressly in the UK legal order, a provision of an international treaty must be enacted by the UK Parliament as an act of national legislation. It has to be converted into domestic law before it can have any binding effect within the UK.[13] This particular approach to international law provoked the question of how to convert the original three EC treaties into national law without transforming every provision into an

---

[12] A concept that has also been considered in Chapters 1 and 4.

[13] A good example of this is how the ECHR had to be converted into the Human Rights Act 1988 before it had binding effects within the UK courts for individuals.

Act of Parliament, which would have been contrary to the treaties. Furthermore, it was necessary to ensure that the treaties or any of their provisions were not simply overruled by the implied repeal of subsequent Acts of Parliament. As it stood, the dualist approach, if followed, would not have recognized the supremacy of Community law.

5.4.3 **The Doctrine of Parliamentary Supremacy**

Formally, the doctrine of UK 'parliamentary sovereignty' means that there are no legal limitations on the UK Parliament and that it has the right to make or unmake any law whatsoever. Further, no person or body is recognized as having a right to override or set aside the legislation of Parliament. The doctrine also implies that, as such, it is impossible to bind future parliaments. Subsequent Acts can either expressly or impliedly override a prior Act. There is no constitutional role for UK courts, which therefore cannot review the validity of Acts passed by Parliament. The courts must enforce and apply Acts of Parliament equally and without question.[14]

One of the problems in considering this doctrine of parliamentary sovereignty is the nature of the concept itself. It is not a rigid constitutional enactment and is really only a constitutional convention that was built up over centuries, refined by eminent jurists to the position stated by Dicey in the latter half of the nineteenth century, and confirmed by the courts. As a convention, it is subject to the erosion of time to reflect the changing circumstances in which it must be employed. Even Dicey conceded that this was not an absolute convention and that there were political, if not legal, limits to it. The fact that there has been considerable comment and publicity about the attack on parliamentary sovereignty as a consequence of Community and Union membership misconceives the status of this particular parliamentary convention. Further consideration here is beyond the scope of this volume.[15] It posed, however, a distinct problem for the UK and, until relatively recently, also for the courts in considering whether, in a situation of conflict, EU law or a national statute should take priority.

5.4.4 **UK Entry and the European Communities Act 1972**

The European Communities Act (ECA) 1972 was the Act of Parliament that facilitated UK entry into the Communities. Both entry to the EC and Community law implementation in the UK initially focuses on how the ECA observes and takes account of then such well-established Community law concepts as direct effect and supremacy, and the difficulties noted earlier in respect of dualism and sovereignty. In contrast with the earlier practice of incorporation of international treaties, the ECA did not reproduce the whole of the treaties or subsequent secondary legislation as Acts of Parliament. If this were done, the words of any future Act that conflicted with EU law obligations could override the prior treaty. Instead, the Community treaties were adopted by a simple assent. Section 1 of the Act future-proofs the Act by allowing for subsequent EC and EU treaties to be regarded in the same way as the original treaties. The Act thus impliedly recognizes the unique new legal system and is regarded now as a special form of UK legislation.[16]

---

[14] See the UK case of *BRB v Picken* [1974] AC 765.

[15] For a full consideration of this topic, refer to T. Allen, 'The Limits of Parliamentary Sovereignty' (1986) PL 614–29; J.D.B. Mitchell, 'What Happened to the Constitution on 1 January 1973?' (1980) Cambrian L Rev 69; H.W.R. Wade, 'Sovereignty and the European Communities' (1972) 88 LQR 1; H.W.R. Wade, 'What Has Happened to the Sovereignty of Parliament?' (1991) 107 LQR 1–4.

[16] See now the High Court judgment in *Thorburn v Sunderland City Council* [2002] 1 CMLR 50.

Section 2(1) of the ECA recognizes the legal validity and direct applicability of Community (EU) treaties and regulations already in existence in the EU legal order, and provides that all such future Community legal provisions shall also be recognized as such. It also recognizes the doctrine of direct effect. It provides:

> All such rights, powers, liabilities, obligations and restrictions from time to time created or arising under the Treaties, and all such remedies and procedures from time to time provided for by or under the Treaties, as in accordance with the Treaties are without further enactment to be given legal effect or used in the United Kingdom shall be recognized and available in law, and be enforced, allowed and followed accordingly.

It is somewhat convoluted, but the subsection recognizes the doctrine of direct effect and allows for future developments by the Court of Justice. This is termed in the Act as 'enforceable Community right…and similar expressions'. Thus, those rights or duties that are, as a matter of Community (EU) law, directly applicable or effective are to be given legal effect in the UK.

Section 2(2) allows for the implementation of other EU obligations that are not automatically applicable in the UK, via forms of UK secondary legislation such as Orders in Council or statutory instruments (SIs). The power that the executive has to make secondary legislation is subject to the limits in Schedule 2 to the Act, in respect of the imposing or creation of taxation, the introduction of retrospective legislation, sub-delegation, and the introduction of new criminal offences with more than a two-year period of imprisonment as penalty, or a higher value limit of more than Level 5 on the fine scale.[17]

Section 2(4) is the subsection that recognizes the supremacy of Community (EU) law and therefore also concerns sovereignty:

> Any such provision…and any enactment passed or to be passed [that is any secondary legislation and Act of Parliament which has been passed previously or may be passed in the future]…shall be construed and have effect subject to the foregoing provisions of this section.

This is a reference to the entire section and in particular s 2(1), and means that any future Act of Parliament must be construed in such a way as to give effect to the enforceable EU rights in existence. This is achieved by denying effectiveness to any national legislation passed later that is in conflict and this is, in turn, controlled by directions to the courts concerned with the application or construction of legislation. The courts are required to interpret any future Act to be consistent with EU law or, in effect, to be subordinate where inconsistency arises. This view was clearly confirmed by the House of Lords in *Factortame* when it held that s 2(4) should be understood as if 'a section were incorporated into the Merchant Shipping Act which enacted that the provisions with regard to the registration of British fishing vessels were to be "without prejudice to the directly enforceable Community rights of nationals of any member states of the EEC"'.[18]

Section 3(1) then instructs the courts to refer questions on the interpretation and hence the supremacy of Community (EU) law to the Court of Justice if the UK courts cannot solve the problem themselves by reference to previous Court rulings. This follows the *Costa v ENEL* ruling and is backed up by ECA, s 3(2), which requires the courts to follow judicially decisions of the Court of Justice on any question of Community (EU) law. This would include direct effects and supremacy, although it does not expressly say so.

---

[17] As last amended by the Criminal Law Act 1977, to £100 per day but these figures are subject to periodic revision.

[18] *R v Secretary of State for Transport, ex p Factortame and ors (No 1)* [1990] 2 AC 85, 140.

It is suggested, then, that the combination of s 2(1) and (4), with the control of s 3(1) and (2), achieves the essential requirements of the recognition of direct effects and the supremacy of EU law for past and future UK legislation.

5.4.4.1 The ECA and Parliamentary Sovereignty

The view of how the ECA has affected parliamentary sovereignty is determined by what the Act actually achieves. There are two main positions in respect of this. Either s 2(4) acts as a rule of construction or it attempts a form of entrenchment, whereby it modifies the doctrine of parliamentary sovereignty. As a rule of construction, it commands the courts to interpret national law to comply with EU law. The earlier decisions on Community law by courts in England and Wales considered that this should apply only where the national legislation is reasonably capable of such construction: see, for example, the cases of *Macarthys v Smith* and *Garland v British Rail & Engineering Ltd*,[19] considered in the following section. However, this view is being modified because it is regarded as too restrictive a view of what is achieved by the ECA—see *Factortame*, in the following section. The alternative of limited entrenchment means that it allows the courts to apply EU law directly over national law, regardless of the actual words. This enables the courts to ignore any implied repeal or unintentional inconsistency of future Acts of Parliament and thus arguably modifies the doctrine of parliamentary sovereignty in that one Parliament has been seen to bind a future one. Express inconsistency remains a problem even under this interpretation, but how EU law is received in the member states is as much dependent on the national judiciary as it is on the national parliaments, so a consideration of its reception in the courts is vital.

5.4.5 Judicial Reception of Community and EU Law in the UK

Where there is a conflict between an earlier UK law with later EU law, there is no difficulty; the doctrines of parliamentary supremacy and the supremacy of EU law will produce the same result. An example is Case 83/78 *Pigs Marketing Board (Northern Ireland) v Redmond* from 1979, in which the Community Agricultural Policy (CAP) rule on the organization of the market was seen to prevail over national law.

The difficulty arises when there is a conflict between a later UK law and an earlier EU law provision. In such a case, are the words within the ECA to be taken as a rule of interpretation or a question of entrenchment, which effectively involves the modification of doctrine of parliamentary supremacy by ss 2(1), 2(4), and 3 ECA?

The most important of the earlier cases are *Macarthy's v Smith* and *Garland*, the first concerning a clash between s 6 of the Sex Discrimination Act (SDA) 1975 and Art 119 EC (now Art 157 TFEU), in which the Court of Appeal clearly held:

> It is important now to declare and it must be made plain. The provisions of Article 119 take priority over anything in our English Statute on Equal Pay which is inconsistent with Article 119. That priority is given by our own law, by the ECA itself. Community law is now part of our law and whenever there is any inconsistency Community law has priority.

However, Lord Denning, speaking *obiter*, thought that, with regard to an express or intentional repudiation of the treaty by Parliament or Parliament's expressly acting inconsistently, the courts would be bound to follow the express and clear intent of Parliament to repudiate

---

[19] *Macarthys Ltd v Smith* [1979] 3 All ER 325 and *Garland v British Rail & Engineering Ltd* [1982] ICR 420 (HL).

the treaty or a section of it by the subsequent Act. That not being the case, though, Community (EU) law takes priority according to the Court of Appeal. This case has survived the years, and even the subsequent cases of the House of Lords concerned with the relationship between EU and national law have not removed it from our consideration, because even though Denning's words are merely *obiter*, they remain the only clear statement by a superior court about what might happen in the event of an express statement by Parliament of the intention to conflict with EU law.

In *Garland v BREL*, the first important statement from the House of Lords, Mrs Garland had complained that the practice of allowing the families of male ex-employees of BREL concessionary rail travel facilities after retirement, but not the families of female ex-employees, was discriminatory. Under s 6(4) SDA, provisions in relation to retirement were exempted from the rules on sex discrimination and Mrs Garland's claim failed initially. Previous UK case law[20] had determined that s 6(4) SDA be given a wide interpretation so as to discount anything to do with, or connected to, retirement and therefore discrimination in such circumstances was lawful. Article 141 (now Art 157 TFEU) and Directive 76/207, however, made no such exception regarding retirement, and therefore UK and Community law were regarded by the House of Lords as inconsistent. The House of Lords asked the Court of Justice to give a ruling on the interpretation of Art 141 (now Art 157 TFEU) to determine if it covered conditions in retirement. The CoJ held that it did so. Upon return to the House of Lords, the Lords considered themselves bound, in view of the Court of Justice ruling and the ECA, to interpret the SDA in such a way as to be consistent with the UK obligations under Community law. Whilst the House of Lords stated that the case was no occasion to pronounce on any further effects of the ECA, it nevertheless did state *obiter* that UK courts should interpret UK law to be consistent no matter how wide a departure from the prima facie meaning it was. The case therefore very much follows the line that s 2(4) ECA allows courts to construe subsequent statutes quite widely in order to give consistency to EU law and, clearly therefore, may amount to a rule of construction.

In *Duke v GEC Reliance*, brought at roughly the same time as the *Marshall* case, Mrs Duke was required to retire at the age of 60, earlier than men who could retire at the age of 65. Section 6(4) SDA was applied to render the discrimination lawful. The House considered the *Marshall* ruling, in which the Equal Treatment Directive was held to apply to retirement itself and to have direct effects but, because this concerned a private-sector employer, the House of Lords rightly concluded that the directive itself could not be enforced against individuals and thus it had no horizontal direct effects. Therefore a head-on clash between the Community law directive and a UK statute took place, with the directive being later in time. The post-accession statute was inconsistent with a subsequent Community obligation, and thus too late for any intention of Parliament to comply with the directive to be contained within the provisions of the national law. Consequently, the House of Lords held that there was no enforceable Community right to which the provisions of the English SDA would be required to give way by virtue of s 2(4) ECA, and that s 2(4) cannot apply to construe a UK statute to enforce Community directives against individuals. In the view of the House of Lords in the case, it could only apply to directly applicable Community law. The House of Lords held that s 2(4) refers to s 2(1), which only refers to directly effective Community law or directly applicable law; therefore it was not appropriate. Mrs Duke was defeated by the House of Lords, as was the view of s 2(4) even as a rule of construction. This case was not followed by the House of Lords, and

---

[20] One of which is *Roberts v Cleveland Area Health Authority* [1979] 2 All ER 1163, [1979] ICR 558.

now Supreme Court, in later cases and, clearly in view of Case 152/84 *Marshall*, a reference should have been made by the House of Lords to the Court of Justice under Art 234 EC (now Art 267 TFEU).

Pickstone v Freemans plc involved a generous interpretation of the 1983 UK regulations, which amended the Equal Pay Act 1970, to read consistently with Community law obligations. This was largely based on the intention of Parliament in passing the regulations to ensure that national law complied with the Community directive, but also in line with Court of Justice rulings. Section 2(4) was used to justify the CoJ's interpretation of national law, but only insofar as it was reasonably possible. The case of *Litster v Forth Dry Dock & Engineering Co Ltd* concerned the rights of employees on the transfer of the undertaking of a business. A number of employees were claiming unfair dismissal after a ship-repairing company was transferred between owners. The relevant law is the Transfer of Undertakings (Protection of Employment) Regulations 2006 (TUPE), but purported to implement the obligations contained in EEC Council Directive 77/187, but the national regulations were considered to be somewhat ambiguous. The directive could not give rise to direct effects because it involved an attempt to enforce it against a private employer. The House of Lords could not, therefore, achieve a satisfactory result in keeping with the European directive and the case law of the Court of Justice by a literal attempt; therefore it concluded that it must use the Community legislation to construe the later UK legislation contrary to its literal meaning and imply additional words to achieve consistency with the purpose of the directive. Here, s 2(4) was clearly being used as a rule of construction—and quite a generous one.

R v Secretary of State for Transport, ex p Factortame Ltd is a particularly important statement of the view of the House of Lords on the supremacy of EU law. You may find the series of litigation in the *Factortame* cases very confusing, particularly since the case numbers are not always used consistently. To try to clarify the matter, the facts and procedure of the case are as follows.

The UK wanted to protect the British fishing quotas under the European quota system and passed the Merchant Shipping Act in 1988, aimed at stopping the practice of quota-hopping by Spanish-owned vessels registered in the UK, by requiring that a minimum percentage of the directors of a company owning fishing vessels registered in the UK be British nationals. The company and vessel owners sought an interim injunction against the Crown not to apply a disputed national regulation issued under that Act. This was granted in the main action on merits by the Queen's Bench divisional court, which decided, rather slowly, to refer the substantive issue to the Court of Justice, which case was given the docket number C-221/89. This is *Factortame (No 2)*.

The Crown appealed against the injunction, raising a procedural point, and a further line of cases commenced that was appealed up to the House of Lords, which also made a reference to the Court of Justice. This time the procedural action was subject to a much faster process, so that it was received earlier by the CoJ than the substantive law case; hence it was given the docket number C-213/89 which is why it is *Factortame (No 1)*.

Upon the return of the procedural aspect from the Court of Justice, which essentially held that the national court should grant interim relief, the House of Lords held that if a national rule precludes the national court from granting an interim relief, so that there is the chance that the court could determine whether there is a conflict between national law and Community law without irreparable harm being done, the national court must set aside that rule. If the injunction against the Crown were not granted, the Spanish fishing companies would most probably go out of business whilst waiting for the CJEU to decide the substantive issues; for that referral to be returned to the Queen's Bench Division and decided actually took two years and seven months. Although the substantive point of

Community (EU) law in relation to the UK law had not been decided at that stage, the House of Lords nevertheless considered that if Community law rights were found to be directly enforceable in favour of the appellants, those rights would prevail over the inconsistent national legislation, even if later. The court held:

> This [s 2(4)] has precisely the same effect as if a section were incorporated into the national statute . . . which in terms enacted that the provisions . . . [of an Act] . . . were to be without prejudice to the directly enforceable Community rights of nationals of any member state of the EEC.

Lord Bridge commented on the view that the earlier decisions in favour of Community law were an attack on parliamentary sovereignty:

> If the supremacy within the European Community of Community law over the national law of member states was not always inherent in the EEC Treaty it was certainly well established in the jurisprudence of the Court of Justice long before the United Kingdom joined the Community. Thus, whatever limitation of its sovereignty Parliament accepted when it enacted the European Communities Act 1972 was entirely voluntary. Under the terms of the Act of 1972 it has always been clear that it was the duty of a United Kingdom court, when delivering final judgment, to override any rule of national law found to be in conflict with any directly enforceable rule of Community law. Thus, there is nothing in any way novel in according supremacy to rules of Community law in those areas to which they apply and to insist that, in the protection of rights under Community law, national courts must not be inhibited by rules of national law from granting interim relief in appropriate cases is no more than a logical recognition of that supremacy.

Factortame (No 2) dealing with the substantive matter was decided in the High Court as predicted, in favour of Community law.

As a result of this case, the view of s 2(4) ECA is that it is a direct rule to give priority, rather than a rule of construction that requires there to be national law to construe. It would also seem to suggest that, as far as the Supreme Court is now concerned, entry to the Communities and s 2(4) ECA have led to the modification of the doctrine of parliamentary sovereignty, and EU law in the areas agreed by treaty is now supreme over national law. Whether this overrides the dictum in *Macarthy's v Smith* is open to question. It remains open for Parliament expressly to repeal the Act or pass legislation expressly in breach of EU law obligations. Politically, however, this is extremely unlikely, although the recent European Union Act 2011 may yet have a bearing on this debate, considered in the following section.

The series of *Factortame* cases is extremely important for a number of reasons in EU law, in particular from the point of view of supremacy over national law and constitutional doctrine, and should be most carefully studied.[21] The *Factortame* case returned to the High Court—*Factortame (No 3)*—on whether damages would be payable. It was held that the legislative failure of the UK government would give rise to liability provided that damage and cause were established. This was appealed to the Court of Appeal, which confirmed the decision of the High Court and finally, in October 1999, to the House of Lords, which held that the government had manifestly and gravely disregarded the limits on its discretion, and that the breach of Community law was sufficiently serious to entitle the applicants to damages for losses directly caused by the breach. Subsequently, the House of Lords confirmed in Case C-9/91 *R v Secretary of State for Employment, ex p EOC*

---

[21] An overview of the main elements of the litigation has been placed in the Online Resource Centre, available at **www.oxfordtextbooks.co.uk/orc/foster5e/**.

the conclusion reached in *Factortame* and held that, in judicial review proceedings, UK courts could declare an Act of Parliament to be incompatible with EC law, although this does not extend to being able to annul the UK Act of Parliament, nor indeed command a government to repeal the Act or compel or command a minister to change the law.

So whilst judicially, in the UK, EU law supremacy appears to be an accepted and settled matter, this does not prevent cases reaching the courts on this topic. The most prominent are the *Metric Martyrs* cases,[22] in which an argument was raised that a later UK Act, the 1985 Weights and Measures Act, had impliedly repealed the 1972 ECA and that UK law should then take precedence over EC law. The High Court rejected this view, making the comment that the ECA had acquired a 'constitutional quality' that prevented implied repeal. The case appears to confirm the view that there has been a kind of entrenchment introduced that does amend our view of parliamentary sovereignty in the UK.

Finally, in a 2005 case, *Jackson*,[23] Lord Steyn acknowledged that the supremacy of Parliament remained a general principle of the UK Constitution, but that it was a common law principle established by the judges in a different era. This suggests that it is viewed as a doctrine that might need qualification by the courts in future. In respect of the ECA, in the same case Lord Hope suggested that even an intentional or express repudiation of EU law might not be followed by the new Supreme Court. In other words this was left open. It is though, in practice, the effect of s 2(1) when read with s 2(4) ECA. These judgments make constitutional legal sense in holding that common law could amend or even overturn such a well-established and fundamental constitutional rule as parliamentary sovereignty. After all, it was the courts and common law which created and elevated the status of this rule in the first place.

The conclusion for the UK is that it has clearly and unambiguously accepted the supremacy of EU law even over UK Acts of Parliament and over constitutional practice. Whether this is four-square on the basis of the logic of EU law as provided by the Court of Justice and not by reference to the UK's ECA remains unclear. The case law points to both conclusions, but the UK seems to have gone further than some of the other member states. Certainly, the *Factortame* litigation and the conclusion at its end that, in matters of EU law, the UK courts are able not to apply UK Acts of Parliament does introduce a form of constitutional review by the courts, hitherto not the case in the UK, and therefore does impact and undermine the doctrine of parliamentary sovereignty, at least as far as EU law is concerned.

5.4.6 **The European Union Act 2011**

We must now move from the courts and the conclusion that they had, by and large, accepted the supremacy of EU law, and go back to the UK Parliament because of the enactment by the 2010 UK coalition government of a quite radical Act concerning the relationship between the UK and the EU. The European Union Act 2011 puts in place a series of conditions on future UK acceptance of new EU powers or even some amendments to existing competences and powers. It may well have been influenced by the types of reservation that will be seen in the courts of some of the other member states featured in subsequent sections, notably Germany and Italy. Whilst not directly pronouncing on

---

[22] See *Thorburn v Sunderland City Council* (n 14), [60]–[67] and the case note by Boyron (2002) 27(6) EL Rev 771–9.

[23] *Jackson v AG* [2006] AC 262, 302–4.

supremacy, it will question any open acceptance of new treaty changes and most other treaty amendments.

Section 2 deals with treaty revisions under the Art 48 TEU ordinary revision procedure. Such revisions are made subject to a UK procedure, which requires that there be both an Act of Parliament supporting the revision and positive approval in a national referendum. The same will apply to the simplified revision procedure governed by Art 46 TEU unless an exemption provided under s 4(4) of the Act applies, such as the accession of new member states, changes that do not apply to the UK (such as those that apply to the eurozone), or the codification of existing laws and practice. There is a further exemption under s 4(1) if the change is deemed to be not significant for the UK, but that is to be decided by the minister (under s 5). If the minister determines that the change involves a transfer of power or competence, then a referendum is seemingly inevitable. It is to be noted, though, that s 4 appears to tie the minister's hand quite considerably: because the reasons for requiring an Act and referendum have been so extensively stated in s 4 itself, it would appear that very little, if indeed any, change will escape. It depends, of course, on just how strictly or not the sections are interpreted, first by the minister, then by the courts, if disputes come before them. Section 6 provides that the same approval regime applies to changes to treaty voting rules and the procedures for enacting EU secondary legislation under the so-called *Passerelle* provisions.[24] Section 7 provides that certain new specific decisions of EU law cannot be accepted by a minister unless approved by an Act of Parliament. In similar terms, under s 8, any new EU secondary legislation proposed under Art 352 TFEU cannot be accepted by a minister in Council unless approved first by an Act of Parliament. Finally, s 18 has been termed a 'sovereignty clause', but appears to restate the provision under the ECA that EU law should be applicable, but equally to state that this is only so because that Act allows it. Section 18 provides that directly applicable or directly effective EU law (that is, the rights, powers, liabilities, obligations, restrictions, remedies, and procedures referred to in s 2(1) ECA) falls to be recognized and available in law in the UK only by virtue of that Act or where it is required to be recognized and available in law by virtue of any other Act. It ignores, though, the judicial developments and interpretation of the ECA, so at this stage it is difficult to predict how, if it ever is considered by the courts, they will interpret it or whether it will make any change to the existing case law interpretations.

The Act may well lead to greater scrutiny of proposed changes to EU laws, but at what cost? If the procedures set out in the Act are carried out to the letter and for almost any proposed change, then the UK ministers and Parliament will become very engaged in considering EU matters, which will impact considerably on the use of parliamentary time. Further, if Acts of Parliament and referenda are subsequently necessary, the cost and organization of such will not only involve the expenditure of huge sums of money, but also the whole process in the UK of approving or rejecting proposed EU amendments will be considerably extended. It may well be that there will be a lot of rejections, thus progress on EU matters for the whole Union of 28 member states may be stalled or completely blocked. Presently, however, it is too early to predict how it might work in practice or be received, or indeed if it will actually ever be invoked but, as ever, the passage of time will tell.

---

[24] *Passerelle* provisions are those Articles that may be changed in terms of voting requirements and specifically from unanimous to qualified majority voting by Art 46 TEU.

5.5 Reception of EU Law in Other Member States

A majority of member states have not experienced any problems so far, although there is always room judicially for this position to change. Whilst it would be beyond this particular volume to conduct a tour of all the member states, it will be enlightening to have a brief look at some other countries—especially some of the member states that were later entrants, in order to see if there is a theme emerging as regards reception of EU law, and particularly with regard to the attitude to the supremacy of EU law and, in particular, over national constitutional law.

5.5.1 **Belgium**

In Belgium, the Constitution was amended under Art 25a to allow for the transfer of powers to institutions governed by international law. However, because Belgium was a dualist country, later laws would prevail over earlier ones, including international treaties, if simply converted into national law. Furthermore, as in the UK, the courts in Belgium have no role in respect of judging the validity of international agreements; however, they accepted Community law supremacy in its own right as if it were a monist country and not by dependence on a Belgium statute—see *Minister for Economic Affairs v SA Fromagerie 'Le Ski'*,[25] in which it was held that, in the case of conflict between national law and the directly effective law of an international treaty, the latter would prevail, even if earlier in time. Its position since that early case has not changed.

5.5.2 **Germany**

5.5.2.1 **The German Constitution (*Grundgesetz*)**

In Germany, in contrast, difficulties were experienced especially in respect of the relationship between fundamental rights provision in the *Grundgesetz* and that in the Community and EU legal order. Traditionally, Germany adopted the dualist approach to the reception of international law, whereby some form of transformation or adoption of international law was necessary in order for it to have any direct application in the state. There had to be a process of incorporation by statute and, once incorporated, a law would simply rank as with other *Gesetze* (Acts of the German Parliament). If a later law were in conflict with an earlier law, the later law would prevail. Articles 24 and 25 of the *Grundgesetz* provide for the peaceful cooperation of the German state with international organizations. Article 24 *Grundgesetz* allows for membership of international organizations and a transfer of powers to them, and was used to establish membership of the European Communities. Although Art 25 declares general rules of public international law to be an integral part of federal law and to take precedence over national law, it is silent as to the effect of international law on German constitutional law. In order to cater specifically for further European integration, particularly into new areas as proposed in the TEU, and to take account of the increasing concern about possible infringements of the *Grundgesetz*, a new Art 23 *Grundgesetz* (and known as the Europa Artikel) was added and amendments were made to other key provisions. Article 23 provides that sovereign powers can be transferred to the EU provided that the transfer has the approval of both Houses of the German Parliament: the Bundestag and Bundesrat. Joint approval was

---

[25] [1972] CMLR 330.

also required for the ratification of the EU Treaty and is further required for any future changes affecting the contents of the *Grundgesetz*.

5.5.2.2 The Reaction of the German Courts

Previously, German courts had been divided as to the effect of Community primary law and secondary law and, at times, had refused to make a reference in cases of doubt or non-acceptance, thus denying the parties to the case the chance to see whether EEC law would have affected the outcome of the case.[26] The most important court in Germany is the Federal Constitutional Court (FCC) because of its constitutional position in the German state.

In the *Internationale Handelsgesellschaft* case (BVerfGE 37, 271), known in Germany as '*Solange I*', the FCC held that as long as the recognition of human rights in the EEC had not progressed as far as those provided for by the *Grundgesetz*, German courts retained the right to refer questions on the constitutionality of secondary Community law to the FCC, with the possible result that Community law might be ignored if it did not have sufficient regard for basic rights. This position has been modified with subsequent rulings by the FCC. In the *Wünsche Handelsgesellschaft* decision (BVerfGE 73, 339), known as '*Solange II*', the FCC has accepted that Community recognition and safeguards of fundamental rights through the case law of the Court of Justice are now sufficient and of a comparable nature to those provided for by the *Grundgesetz*. Thus, as long as EU law ensures the effective provision of fundamental rights, the FCC will not review EU law in light of the rights provisions of the Constitution. The FCC also stated that it would not be prepared to accept constitutional complaints against Community law from lower courts on this basis. It is argued that a reservation of supremacy is still inherent in the ruling. The basis for the decision is not, however, the inherent supremacy of EU law, but rather the fact that Art 24 *Grundgesetz* allowed a transfer of powers to the EU and that the subsequent accession act obliges the German courts to accept the supremacy of EU law. The decision by the FCC in *Solange II* also held that the Court of Justice was a statutory court within the meaning of Art 101 *Grundgesetz* and individuals have the right to have access to statutory courts. This effectively means that German courts can no longer refuse to make references in last instance to the CJEU, as had happened in the case of *Kloppenburg*,[27] in which the Federal Tax Court had denied the direct effects of directives and refused a reference to the Court of Justice. The FCC held in *Re: VAT Exemption*,[28] the follow-up to the *Kloppenburg* case, and in the separate case of *Re: Patented Feedstuffs*,[29] that German courts which are courts of last instance in terms of Art 234 EC (now Art 267 TFEU) would be in breach of the German Constitution if they were to fail to refer to the Court of Justice when necessary. The earlier judgment of the Federal Tax Court was consequently annulled. Therefore, German courts of last instance are obliged to make a reference where a dispute as to interpretation or application of EU law exists. Applications to the FCC to question the constitutionality of EU legislation have now been declared to be inadmissible, because the FCC considered that such acts are not acts of German public authorities within the scope of the *Grundgesetz* and cannot thus be complained of to the FCC.[30] Following these cases, there would seem to be no procedural difficulty in getting

---

[26] See e.g. Decision of the Federal Constitutional Court BVerfGE 22, 293.
[27] Bundesfinanzhof 25 April 1985, NJW 1988, 1459, [1988] 3 CMLR 1.
[28] NJW 1988, 2173, [1989] 1 CMLR 113.   [29] NJW 1988, 1456, [1989] 2 CMLR 902.
[30] See BVerfGE 58, 1, 27, known as the '*Eurocontrol I*' decision, and the judgment of 12 May 1990, NJW 1990, 974 concerning the enactment of the Cigarette Packet Warnings Directive (OJ 1989 C124/5). For further details, see BVerfG 12 May 1989, NJW 974, G. Nicolaysen in (1989) 24 EuR 215–25 and W.H. Roth, 'The Application of Community Law in West Germany: 1980–1990' (1991) 28 CML Rev 137–82, 144.

EU law rights at least considered in the proper forum in Germany. Any court that refuses either to follow a previous ruling of the Court of Justice or which refuses to make an Art 234 ruling may be subject to the review of the FCC for a breach of Art 101(1) *Grundgesetz*.

The German Accession Act to the Maastricht Treaty on European Union was passed by the German Parliament in December 1992. However, as a result of considerable criticism that there had been no real debate on the TEU in Germany and that a referendum had not been held to test public opinion on further integration, and as a consequence of the general perception in Germany that the EU was assuming competences to which it did not have the right, constitutional complaints were made to the FCC. In its judgment in *Brunner et al v The Federal Republic of Germany*, the FCC considered the changes to the Constitution, the constitutionality of the TEU, and generally the relationship between the EC and the German Constitution. Whilst it held that the transfer of powers was compatible with the principles of the *Grundgesetz*, future extensive transfers could not be made without the approval of the German Parliament, and the FCC would reserve to itself a right to review the compatibility of EC law fundamental rights provisions and the range of rights exercised by the EC with the German Constitution. It further commented that, if the EU institutions acted in ways not clearly sanctioned by the treaties, any resulting EU legislative acts would not be binding on the German legal order. As such then, the judgment appeared to back-track on previous judgments, although this final comment was not based on any existing intrusion into national competences by the TEU or by the EU. As such then its validity is dubious.

After the Maastricht judgment, the relationship between the Court of Justice and the FCC remains unclear. Even though the FCC claims that fundamental rights will be protected and upheld by a relationship of cooperation between both courts, it does not clearly explain how this protection will work in practice. It seems that the FCC has accepted the standard of basic rights protection provided by the CoJ, but reserves a right to review EU acts that would evidently infringe basic rights under the *Grundgesetz* if the Court of Justice does not offer protection. So far, this has been a theoretical case.

The lengthy series of cases originating from Germany challenging the EU banana regime preference of African, Caribbean, and Pacific (ACP) states, and not the South American countries traditionally supplying Germany, which became known as the 'banana battle', certainly raised the issue again, but did not culminate in a decision defining when exactly the FCC is willing to use its reserved power to review EU acts.

In 1993, an EC regulation[31] on the banana market, which was aimed at benefiting bananas imported from the ACP countries, placed quotas and duties on the import of other bananas—mainly those from Latin American countries (and referred to as *Dollarbananen*). Consequently, it was subject to a number of challenges, and in Cases C-465–6/93 *Atlanta Fruchthandelsgesellschaft I & II*, the Federal Tax Court initially upheld German law on the ground of basic rights violations over the Community rules; however, the basis for challenging the regulation was dismissed by the Court of Justice. Subsequently, the *Banana Market Regulations* case[32] came before the FCC to consider the possible breach of the *Grundgesetz* by an import company in Germany. The company had, for several years, imported about 100,000 tonnes of these bananas per annum, but was allowed an import quota of only 150 tonnes under a preferential duty for 1994 according to the new regulation. Special circumstances in favour of the company had not been taken into account. The company challenged the quota, and implicitly the regulation,

---

[31] Regulation 404/93 (OJ 1993 L47/1).
[32] *Bananenmarktverordnung* of 7 June 2000, BVerfG–2 BvL 1–97.

before the Administrative Court (VG) in Frankfurt am Main, asking for interim measures. Together with other importers in a similar situation, it claimed a breach of its basic rights to carry commercial activity, to property, and to exercise a profession (Arts 12 and 14 *Grundgesetz*), because the new quota was about to ruin its business.

The Administrative Court referred the EC regulation to the FCC according to Art 100-I *Grundgesetz* in order to decide on its compatibility with basic rights under the Constitution. According to the *Solange II* decision, such a submission is inadmissible as long as the Community legal order provides a sufficient protection of basic rights, which has generally been accepted. However, in this case, the Frankfurt Administrative Court argued that recent Court of Justice case law showed a less effective protection of individuals' basic rights, especially when weighing individual rights against Community measures of the Common Agricultural Policy (CAP). It was noted that the CoJ had already upheld the validity of the EC regulation on bananas in a previous case, when Germany had challenged it because of alleged violations of World Trade Organization (WTO) law and basic rights.[33]

After having granted the interim measures to avert the company's financial ruin,[34] the FCC finally decided that the complaint concerning the main procedure was inadmissible.

It held that the plaintiff had failed to show a decline of the standard of protection of basic rights in Court of Justice case law. It also pointed out subsequent amendments to the regulation, as well as the CoJ's decision of 1996[35] requiring the Commission to provide for transitory hardship clauses and that several parts of the regulation that had contradicted WTO law had to be partly revised. After a more conciliatory judgment by the CoJ in Cases C-364–5/95 *T Port GmbH & Co v Hauptzollamt Hamburg-Jonas*, the FCC had also toned down its language and held that, as in previous cases, it was satisfied that the level of human rights protection in the EU was sufficient so as not to engage the need for review by the FCC itself, and hence a further challenge before it to the EC regulation was rejected as inadmissible.[36]

Turning to the highest German court in civil and criminal matters, the German Supreme Court (Bundesgerichtshof) ruling accepted the principle of state liability on the part of the German state for a legislative breach of Community law in Case C-46/93 *Brasserie du Pêcheur v Federal Republic of Germany*. However, the CoJ held that the breach, which was the prohibition of the use of additives in brewing beer contrary to EC free movement of goods rules, had not been sufficiently serious to impose liability.

Sometimes, the Court of Justice and German courts do see eye to eye. In Case C-36/02 *Omega Spielhallen v Bonn*, the German constitutional right to human dignity was pleaded by the German authorities and was upheld by the CoJ in the face of a claim to rely on the fundamental freedom to provide services in respect of a simulated laser combat game, which was successfully restricted.

The decision of the FCC (Case 2BvE 2/08 Lisbon Judgment) indirectly deals with EU matters, because the focus is on the constitutional compatibility of German legislation that dealt with the Lisbon Treaty. Following the agreement on the Lisbon Treaty on further integration of the EU by the member states, the German Bundestag and Bundesrat passed the transformation Act and an accompanying law, extending and strengthening the rights of the Bundestag and the Bundesrat in European matters. This latter law was

---

[33] Case C-280/93 *Germany v Council* [1994] ECR I-4973.   [34] BVerfG (1995) EuZW 126.

[35] Case C-68/95 *T Port GmbH & Co v Bundesanstalt für Landwirtschaft* [1996] ECR I-6065.

[36] As noted by the BVerfG, 2 BvL 1–97, [68]. For further discussion, see also H.-W. Arndt, *Europarecht*, 4th edn, C.F. Müller, Heidelberg, 1999, pp 77–80; T. Oppermann, *Europarecht*, 2nd edn, Beck, Munich, 1999, pp 571–3; T. Stein, '*Bananen*: Split?' (1998) EuZW 261 et seq.

challenged before the FCC by German Members of Parliament. The court decided that the Lisbon Treaty and its transformation Act were compatible with the Constitution, but that the accompanying Act strengthening the rights of the Bundestag and Bundesrat was not. It held that European integration could not be achieved by means that abolished the member states' discretion to organize or establish economic, cultural, and social conditions of life. In this respect, constitutional organs such as the Bundestag and Bundesrat had a responsibility to integrate. Thus the participation rights of these two organs within negotiations at European level had to be elaborated in a much clearer way than had been the case in the challenged statute. In the case, the issues were as much how the German constitutional procedure coped with EU integration as with its reserved power of review over the constitutionality of EU in Germany.

Subsequently, there has been a ruling by the FCC in the *Honeywell* case[37] which steps back to some degree from the Lisbon Judgment by declaring that review should only take place where sufficiently qualified. This means essentially only in the most obvious and manifest cases of EU law breaching member states' competences. In any event, such a review can take place only after the Court of Justice has been given the chance to review the case via a preliminary ruling reference and only by the FCC and no other court in Germany.

The FCC has made clear that it retains its competence to review any EU acts in order to ensure that they do not exceed the limits of what EU organs have been authorized to do by the member states and has thus, even in this latest case, confirmed the line taken already in the Maastricht Treaty case, albeit subject to the qualifications now that any breach by the EU must be manifest and that the Court of Justice first be given the chance to adjudicate on the matter.[38] Thus whilst jurisprudentially possible, it is unlikely as a result of this latest case that the FCC will of its own accord preemptively strike down EU law in favour of German national law. Although in the *Data Retention Directive* case[39] the reverse took place when the FCC annulled a German statute which, according to the FCC, had not respected the Basic Law when transposing an EU directive. Until a new national statute was enacted, Germany was technically in breach of its obligation to implement EU law and facing prosecution by the EU Commission.[40] However, the particular directive was later annulled by the CoJ.[41] It remains to be seen if this prosecution is pursued.

5.5.3 Italy

In Italy, the position both constitutionally and judicially was, and is, very similar to that of Germany, whereby both had new constitutions set up after World War II, with strong provision for fundamental rights. Both states allowed a transfer of power to international organizations, but were silent as to the effect on constitutional law. Article 11 of the Italian

---

[37] Judgment of the FCC Second Senate of 6 July 2010 (2 BvR 2261/06) BVerfGE 126, 286, available at **http://www.bundesverfassungsgericht.de/entscheidungen/rs20100706_2bvr266106en.html**.

[38] The FCC has been further asked in three constitutional complaints (2 BvR 987/10, 2 BvR 1485/10, and 2 BvR 1099/10) about the constitutional legality of the Eurozone bail-out packages. Whilst the complaints were dismissed as unfounded, the FCC did stress the requirement of a separate approval each time by the Bundestag and that the executive must give the Bundestag sufficient notice and time to consider any approvals prior to the Federal government taking a binding decision. See **http://www.bundesverfassungsgericht.de/pressemitteilungen/bvg11-055en.html**.

[39] Judgment BVerfGE 125, 260.

[40] **http://europa.eu/rapid/press-release_IP-12-530_en.htm**.

[41] Joined Cases C-293/12 and C-594/12 *Digital Rights Ireland et al*, Judgment of 16 May 2014, not yet reported. See **http://curia.europa.eu/juris/documents.jsf?num=C-293/12**.

Constitution provides for the limitation of national sovereignty in favour of international arrangements to secure peace and justice between nations.

As in Germany, the focus in Italy is on its Constitutional Court. Given that two of the leading EU cases on supremacy, *Costa v ENEL* and *Simmenthal*, arose from Italy, it should certainly have been clear to the Italian Constitutional Court what was expected of it. Again, there has been a mixed reaction, also along the lines of the German Federal Constitutional Court.

Despite a previous, less enthusiastic response to Community law in the case of *Frontini v Ministero delle Finanze*, in *Granital v Amministrazione delle Finanze*[42] the supremacy of Community law was accepted both on the basis of an interpretation of Art 11 of the Italian Constitution, allowing for the limitation of sovereignty in favour of international organizations, and by reason of Court of Justice case law. The case did, however, make the reservation that Italian law should be cast aside only where directly applicable Community law exists—similar, in effect, to the judgment of the House of Lords in the *Duke* case. A later decision in *Fragd v Amministrazione delle Finanze*[43] suggests that the Italian Constitutional Court is still prepared to review EU law in light of the fundamental rights provisions in the Italian Constitution if EU law is regarded as not respecting these rights. This stance was confirmed in *Admenta*,[44] in which the Italian state council held that fundamental rights as protected by Italian law could not be reviewed in light of EU law and were therefore to be reviewed exclusively in light of Italian constitutional law. Thus far, this remains the situation in Italy, with the possibility for outright rejection of EU law supremacy.

5.5.4 **France**

The system of French courts is divided into two hierarchies, each with its own appeal courts and final appeal, and, in addition, the Constitutional Court (Conseil constitutionnel). They have had, however, significantly different attitudes to EU law, despite the fact that both are subject to Art 55 of the French Constitution, which is monist and gives international law a rank above municipal law, but is silent as to the effect on the Constitution. This is the point that has led to discrepancies between hierarchies.

5.5.4.1 **The French Courts of Ordinary Jurisdiction**

The French courts of ordinary jurisdiction have felt no hesitation in making Art 234 EC (now Art 267 TFEU) references to the Court of Justice and giving supremacy to EU law on the basis of Art 55 of the Constitution. The French Supreme Court of Ordinary Jurisdiction (Cour de cassation) has, in fact, gone further and found for the supremacy of EU law without direct reference to Art 55 of the Constitution, and more on the basis of the inherent supremacy and direct effects of EU law itself as in the *Café Vabre* case,[45] in which Art 90 EEC (now Art 110 TFEU) was held to prevail over a subsequent national statute. These rulings have been consistently followed by the lower courts and reference to either Art 55 of the Constitution or even the decisions mentioned earlier is rarely made: for example, *Garage Dehus Sarl v Bouche Distribution*.

---

[42] *Granital SpA v Amministrazione delle Finanze*, Judgment of 8 June 1984 [1984] 1 Giui It 1521, noted by Gaja (1984) 21 CML Rev 756–72.

[43] *Fragd v Amministrazione delle Finanze* [1985] ECR 1605, noted by Gaja (1990) 27 CML Rev 93.

[44] *Admenta v Federfarma* [2006] 2 CMLR 47.

[45] *Café Vabre* [1975] 2 CMLR, 336, noted in (1975) 16 CML Rev 367.

5.5.4.2 **French Public Courts**

The French administrative courts deal with complaints by citizens against any acts of the state administration. The Supreme Administrative Court (Conseil d'État) has from time to time completely denied the supremacy of EU law or the need to make reference to the Court of Justice, relying heavily on the French principle of law, *acte clair*. This states that where a provision of law is clear, there is no need to refer to a higher court; rather, it is simply to be applied. The leading case is *Minister of the Interior v Cohn-Bendit*,[46] in which Daniel Cohn-Bendit ('Danny the Red') was deported from France in 1968 and in 1975 requested re-entry, but was refused. He claimed that the refusal was contrary to Directive 64/221, previously declared directly effective by the Court of Justice in the *Van Duyn* case. The Conseil d'État held that individuals could not directly rely on directives to challenge an administrative act and declined to follow previous Court rulings or to make a reference itself. The judgment in the *Cohn-Bendit* case has been followed by the same court and lower courts.

Two cases have, though, demonstrated a much more cooperative attitude on the part of the French administrative courts. These are, first, *Nicolo*,[47] in which the Conseil d'État reviewed the supremacy of international law, including EEC Treaty Articles, and held the latter to take precedence over subsequent national law, largely on the basis of Art 55 of the Constitution. The submissions of the government commissioner were instructive in his use and observation of the decisions from the courts of other member states, and their acceptance of Community law supremacy. Secondly, in *Boisdet*,[48] incompatible national law was declared invalid in the face of a Community regulation. In doing so, the Conseil d'État followed the Court of Justice case law. In *Perreux* (2009)[49] though the French court effectively reversed previous decisions by holding that an EC directive can be relied upon to challenge a French administrative act. The cases of *Rothmans & Philip Morris Tobacco and Arizona Tobacco*[50] decided that not only are EC directives to be given priority over national law, even where the directive predates the French statute, but also that an award of damages against the French authorities can be made where damage is suffered as a consequence of non-compliance with EC law, clearly following the lead of the CoJ in the *Francovich* case.

Previously receiving no direct mention in the French Constitution, the EC and EU are now referred to in a new Art 88. This was introduced as a result of the Conseil constitutionnel ruling that the move into new policy areas under the TEU would be incompatible with the Constitution. As a result of the change to Art 88 of the Constitution, the French Constitutional Court declared that it will no longer review Community law in light of the Constitution, save in relation to express elements, which is taken to mean those protecting fundamental rights. However, Art 88, as with Art 55, the original validation of Community membership and Community law within the French legal order, still requires reciprocity. This means that, in order for any international treaty, and also now the EU treaties, to be upheld and complied with in France, they must be upheld reciprocally by the other party or parties. Failure to comply by another party under the customary international law understanding of this principle would mean that France would itself no longer be obliged to comply with the treaty or the part of it not complied with thus

---

[46] *Minister of the Interior v Cohn-Bendit*, Decision of the Conseil d'État, 22 December 1979, 8 *Dalloz* 1979, see also [1980] 1 CMLR 543.

[47] [1990] 1 CMLR 173.　　[48] [1990] 1 CMLR 3.

[49] 30 October 2009, Conseil d'État, No 298348: http://www.legifrance.gouv.fr/affichJuriAdmin.do?idT exte=CETATEXT000021219388.

[50] [1993] 1 CMLR 93.

retaining, in principle, a distinct reservation on its recognition of supremacy in a way similar to the German Federal Constitutional Court.

Clearly, in a Union of 28 states, this is not very practical and more likely to engender chaos. In any event, reciprocity was expressly excluded as a defence to a breach of Community (EU) law in Cases 90–1/63 *Commission v Belgium and Luxembourg* and Case C-146/89 *Commission v UK (Fishing Limits)*.[51]

However, despite the change to the Constitution and the rules being more sympathetic to the supremacy of EU law, cases taking a less cooperative position are still being decided by the Conseil d'État. In conclusion, the French recognition of supremacy of EU law arises as much, if not more, from the French Constitution as from the inherent supremacy of EU law but not extending to supremacy over the Constitution itself.

5.5.4.3 The French Constitutional Court (Conseil constitutionnel)

As noted in the previous section, following the change to Art 88 of the Constitution, the French Constitutional Court has declared (Decision 2004/496 of 10 June 2004) that it will no longer review EU law in light of the Constitution, save in relation to express elements, which is taken to mean those protecting fundamental rights—thus retaining, in principle, a distinct reservation on its recognition of supremacy in a way similar to the German Federal Constitutional Court. In a further case (Decision 2006/540), the Conseil constitutionnel held that in relation to implementing EU directives, a constitutional requirement under Art 88 of the French Constitution, an implementing law can only be found to be unconstitutional if it is clearly incompatible with the directive. The Lisbon Treaty was also questioned before the Conseil constitutionnel (Decision 2007/560) which held that whilst it introduced nothing new, it could not be subjected to constitutional review; however, if treaty clauses did impact on French national sovereign competences, then constitutional revision would be required. The assumption from the decision is that if the revisions were not made, then the new treaty competences would offend the existing French Constitution thus, in effect, subrogating EU law to the French Constitution.

French constitutional procedural law involving the Conseil constitutionnel was considered by the Court of Justice in Cases C-188–9/10 *Melki and Abdeli*. The rule that national courts must refer first to the Conseil constitutionnel any questions of constitutionality including that of EU law, appeared to undermine the rights of parties to make preliminary ruling references to the Court of Justice under Art 267 TFEU. The Court held, though, that the rule did not offend EU law provided that national courts remained free nevertheless to refer to the Court of Justice and to disapply any national law they considered to be contrary to EU law.

5.5.5 The Czech Republic

The Czech Republic, even though a later entrant state, is also regarded as one of the EU's more sceptical members. Previously, in a case in 2004, the Czech Constitutional Court annulled national government instruments on the grounds that the Czech government did not have the competence to issue them, because the sector was one in which the competence had been transferred to the EU. However, in line with the German *Brunner* judgment, discussed earlier, it qualified this transfer by stating that the transferred powers could be exercised by the EU only in conformity with the requirements of the Czech Constitution and constitutionality in the Czech Republic.[52] In a case heard soon afterwards, measures

---

[51] See also Chapter 7, Section 7.2.2.5, on defences to Commission enforcement actions.
[52] See Judgment of Czech Constitutional Court (Sugar quotas), Pl. ÚS 50/04, of 8 March 2006.

adopted under the EU third pillar dealing with the European arrest warrant caused the Czech Constitutional Court even more difficulties because, in its view, even the Court of Justice had difficulties with determining how national courts should accord primacy to third-pillar acts and whether framework decisions do, in fact, take primacy over national laws, although provided that the EU maintained a sufficient level of fundamental rights protection, it would not further review EU laws.[53] The Czech Constitutional Court has also been asked to review the compatibility of the Lisbon Treaty with the Czech Constitution. Whilst it held that it was compatible, it expressed views that the powers transferred to the EU and the division between national and EU competences should be made much clearer and in similar vein to other constitutional courts, notably the German FCC, it commented that a transfer of overall competence (*Kompetenz-Kompetenz*) would be in breach of the constitutional sovereignty of the Czech Republic.[54] In a second judgment on the Lisbon Treaty, this time dealing with the delay by the Czech president in ratifying the treaty, the court held that there should not be undue delay, save only for constitutional challenges, but that the decision on the ultimate transfer of powers was one for the Czech Parliament and not the Czech Court.[55]

Finally, and most significantly in 2012,[56] the Czech Constitutional Court declared *ultra vires* a previous ruling of the CoJ[57] concerned with nationality discrimination in pension payments between Czech and Slovaks. That ruling has led to an amendment of national law which the Czech Court held to be incompatible with the Czech Constitution which allowed a discrimination as part of the political settlement of the dissolution of Czechoslovakia. The long-term consequences, if any, of this rebuff have yet to reveal themselves.

5.5.6 **Denmark**

The Danish Constitution, s 20(2), allows for the delegation of powers to international authorities by statute adopted by a five-sixths parliamentary majority, or a simple majority in a popular vote if the former is not reached or not chosen by the Parliament, which has largely been the case in Denmark.[58]

In line with the rather Eurosceptic view of a good part of the electorate of Denmark, its Supreme Court has also taken a less positive view of supremacy. The Danish Acts for the Maastricht Treaty on European Union were challenged in *Carlsen et al v Prime Minister*

---

[53] See Judgment of Czech Constitutional Court, Pl. ÚS 60/04, of 3 May 2006.

[54] Judgment of Czech Constitutional Court, Pl. ÚS 19/08, of 26 November 2008.

[55] Judgment of Czech Constitutional Court, Pl. ÚS 29/09, at **http://www.usoud.cz/en/decisions/?tx_ ttnews[tt_news]=466&cHash=eedba7ca14d226b879ccaf91a6dcb2**. See also the case note on a Czech court decision to annul the EU Act and make a reference to the CoJ (Case C-253/12, pending): (2012) 49 CML Rev 1475.

[56] Judgment of Czech Constitutional Court, Pl. ÚS 5/12 (2012). See J. Komerek, 'Czech Constitutional Court Playing with Matches: The Czech Constitutional Court Declares a Judgment of the Court of Justice of the EU Ultra Vires; Judgment of 31 January 2012, Pl. ÚS 5/12, Slovak Pensions XVII' (2012) 8 EU Const, p 323.

[57] In Case C-399/09 *Landtová* [2011] ECR I-415. See the case note by R. Zbíral (2012) in 49 CML Rev (2012) 1475.

[58] In 1986, 56.2% voted for and 43.8% against the Single European Act; in 1992, 49.3% voted for and 50.7% against the Maastricht Treaty; in 1993, 56.8% voted in favour and 43.2% against the Maastricht Treaty, with the opt-outs agreed in Edinburgh (including defence policy, the third phase of economic and monetary union and a common currency, Union citizenship and in the judicial field); in 1998, 55.1% voted for and 44.9% against the Amsterdam Treaty; and in 2000, 53.1% voted against and 46.9% for Denmark joining the single European currency, the euro, which of course then it did not join. In contrast, Denmark ratified the Lisbon Treaty, without a prior referendum, by way of consent of the Danish Parliament under Art 19 of the Constitution.

Rasmussen[59] as providing too much power to the EC institutions and going beyond the transfer of powers authorized by the Danish Constitution, s 20. The Danish Supreme Court held that ratification of the TEU did not violate the Danish Constitution and that the transfer of powers under s 20 was wide enough for the EU to act, including its perceived need to act under the general residual power of Art 308.[60] However, two provisos were laid down: that power to adopt measures contrary to the Constitution cannot be delegated to international organizations; and that the national courts retain the power to review EU law in this light and to hold it inapplicable in the event of conflict—essentially, the same reservations as expressed by the German, Italian, and Irish constitutional courts. This decision and the earlier position were confirmed in 2013 in Case 199/2012 of 20 February 2013 in respect of the ratification of the Lisbon Treaty.[61]

5.5.7 Hungary

The Hungarian Constitutional Court[62] has struck down a national law, which was required by a Commission regulation, on the ground that it had retroactive effects. The reasoning of the court reveals that this was considered to be an entirely domestic issue and not therefore a challenge to Community law, although, in strict terms, a reference should have been made to the Court of Justice as the source of the retroactive provision was in fact the EU regulation. This issue was not, though, raised in the case. In a judgment in 2010[63] also on the constitutionality of the Lisbon Treaty, the Hungarian Constitutional Court held that the Lisbon Treaty was not a threat to the Constitution or sovereignty of the Hungarian state.

5.5.8 Ireland

The Irish Constitution has been amended to allow for EC and EU membership (Art 29(4)). The Irish courts have the power to strike down national laws that are repugnant to the Constitution, but it is not stated whether this applies to EU law (Art 15(4.2)). However, the Constitution provides that nothing in the Constitution can disturb the primacy of Community (EU) law (Art 29(4.10)), putting it effectively beyond judicial review.

A case that struck at the heart of the religious and moral underpinning of the Constitution caused some difficulty. In Case C-159/90 *Society for the Protection of Unborn Children Ireland Ltd v Grogan*, in which advertising information about abortion services in another member state was challenged on the ground of the illegality of abortions in Ireland, the Irish Supreme Court held that the advertising could be prohibited. The Court of Justice, when confronted with the argument that the provision of information was a service within the meaning of Art 49 EC (now Art 56 TFEU), held that it was not an economic activity and thus outside EC law, thus removing the chance of a head-on clash with the Irish Constitution. As a result, though, Protocol 17 was attached to the TEU, which provides that:

> Nothing in the Treaty on European Union, or in the Treaties establishing the European Communities, or in the Treaties or Acts modifying or supplementing those Treaties, shall affect the application in Ireland of Article 40.3.3 of the Constitution of Ireland.

---

[59] Case I 361/1997 *Carlsen v Prime Minister Rasmussen*, 6/4/1998, [1999] ECR I-49, [1999] 3 CMLR 854.
[60] See J.H. Danielsen, 'One of Many National Constraints on European Integration: Section 20 of the Danish Constitution' (2010) 16 EPL 181.
[61] Danish Supreme Court, Case 199/2012, Decision of 20 February 2013 and see the extended case note: H.P. Olsen (2013) 50 CML Rev 1489.
[62] Judgment 17-2004 AB, available at **http://www.mkab.hu/index.php?id=home_en**.
[63] Lisbon Judgment (143/2010) (VII.14.) AB).

More significant is the *Crotty v An Taoiseach* case, which concerned a direct challenge to Ireland signing up to the Single European Act (SEA). Following its consideration of what the Irish Constitution actually permitted, the Irish Supreme Court held that the constitutional provision would not cover any further transfers of sovereignty and thus use of that power by the Community unless approved of in a constitutional amendment. Thus every new EU treaty, including therefore the now abandoned Constitutional Treaty, which introduced significant changes, must be approved by an amendment to the Irish Constitution and that must be done following approval in a referendum.[64]

5.5.9 **Poland**

In Poland, Art 90 of the Constitution provides for the transfer of powers to international organizations, but does not state then the hierarchy of such powers once transferred. A challenge had been made to Polish accession to the EU as being contrary to the Polish Constitution. Whilst the Polish Constitutional Court ruled that accession was in line with the Constitution, the judgment revealed some deep-seated resistance to the automatic acceptance of EU law supremacy. It was prepared to accept sympathetic interpretations of Polish law, but not to the extent that a contrary result was reached, particularly in the area of the individual rights and freedoms protection contained in the Constitution. In other words, when it comes to a clash involving rights protected by the Polish Constitution, Polish law and not EU law would prevail. This judgment[65] is certainly in line with, and probably goes further than, the German *Brunner* judgment, noted earlier. A 2005 case on the European Arrest Warrant[66] highlighted the view of the Polish Constitutional Court that it has the right to declare EU law is *ultra vires* when in conflict with the Polish Constitution. In the case though, as with the German FCC, noted at the end of Section 5.5.2.2, it was the national implementing law that was found to be in conflict with the Constitution and further, the Polish Parliament was to be given time to amend the Constitution. The Lisbon Treaty has also been considered by the Polish Constitutional Court[67] where the supremacy of Polish law over EU law was upheld. The court considered that competences transferred did not constitute permanent limitations on Polish sovereignty but merely a representation of that sovereignty at the EU level.

This court, with the Czech Constitutional Court, appears to have gone the furthest in the denial of EU law supremacy.

---

[64] As was seen in Chapter 1, this process has led now to the Irish electorate rejecting an amending treaty on two occasions (Nice in 2001 and Lisbon in 2008), although in both instances, a second vote approved them, after negotiations between Ireland, the EU, and the other member states secured concessions or amendments favoured by Ireland.

[65] A summary of the judgment is available at **http://www.trybunal.gov.pl/eng/summaries/documents/ K_18_04_GB.pdf**. In particular, see [14] and [15] of the reasoning. See also the case comment K. Kowalik-Bańczyk, 'Should We Polish it Up? The Polish Constitutional Tribunal and the Idea of Supremacy of EU Law' (2005) 6 German Law Journal 1355. For an overall view of the legal preparation for Polish EU membership, see A. Lazowski, 'Adaptation of the Polish Legal System to European Union Law: Selected Aspects', Sussex European Institute Working Paper No 45, available at **http://www.sussex.ac.uk/sei/documents/wp45.pdf**. Generally, the Constitutional Court can be viewed online at **http://www.trybunal.gov. pl/eng/**.

[66] Judgment K 18/04 of 11 May 2005.

[67] **http://www.trybunal.gov.pl/eng/summaries/documents/K_32_09_EN.pdf**.

5.5.10 **Spain**

Whilst previously having made clear its acceptance of EU law supremacy according to the Spanish Constitution, Art 93,[68] the Spanish Constitutional Court was faced head-on with the question of the supremacy of EU law when asked by the Spanish government to provide an opinion on the compatibility of aspects of the Constitutional Treaty with the Spanish Constitution. In particular, Art I-6, that Union law shall take priority over national law, was raised, along with questions about the legal basis (Art 93 Spanish Constitution) of the accession and provision for fundamental rights protection. The case in fact preceded the Spanish referendum on membership and the judgment is very much in line with the German *Brunner* case, in that—whilst accession and the Constitutional Treaty, since abandoned, were held to be acceptable under the Spanish Constitution without further amendment—the Spanish Constitutional Court reserved the right to judge Community law in light of its own constitutional protection of rights.[69]

In 2004, there was a Spanish Constitutional Court ruling that involved a failure to request an Art 234 EC (now Art 267 TFEU) ruling that was considered as a violation of the fundamental right to effective judicial protection.[70]

The Court of Justice considered, in Case C-118/08 *Transportes Urbanos y Servicios Generales*,[71] a Spanish domestic procedural rule which required the exhaustion of domestic remedies before an applicant would be allowed to bring an action for damages against the Spanish state for a breach of EU law. This was not, however, a requirement when taking an action for a breach of national constitutional law. It was held by the Court thus to be a breach of the EU principle of equivalence.[72]

5.6 **Summary on Reception: Sufficient Evidence of an Emerging Trend?**

The tentative conclusion is that a consensus appears to be emerging from the national and constitutional courts that EU law supremacy is accepted only insofar as it does not infringe the individual rights protection of the national constitutions, in which case the constitutional courts will exercise their reserved rights over national constitutions to uphold them over inconsistent EU law or to review EU law in light of their own constitutions. Only a few states appear to be accepting EU law unconditionally, such as Belgium and the UK, which may be because their constitutions are more flexible, at least from the view of the judges. The flurry of cases considering the Lisbon Treaty do, though, seem to confirm the trend that the constitutional courts will regard any transfer of competences which leads to EU laws which appear to impinge on the national constitutions or sovereignty as inferior to them. Also, whilst always clear (from the *Van Gend en Loos* and *Costa v ENEL* cases) that competences are only transferred in limited fields, the constitutional courts are making it quite clear that no overall transfer of competences has taken place. Further direct rejections of supremacy are probably avoidable if the Court of Justice is allowed to defuse any possible conflict before the case reaches a constitutional court,

---

[68] See, in particular, Judgment 132/1989.

[69] For a full discussion of Tribunal Constitucional Opinion 1/2004, refer to F. Castillo de la Torre, 'Tribunal Constitucional (Spanish Constitutional Court), Opinion 1/2004 of 13 December 2004, on the Treaty Establishing a Constitution for Europe' (2005) 42 CML Rev 1169–202.

[70] Judgment 58/2004 of the Constitutional Court, which is noted in (2005) 42 CML Rev 535.

[71] [2010] ECR I-635.   [72] This is considered in Chapter 6, Section 6.6.

providing the question of conflict is first referred to the CoJ via the Art 267 TFEU pre-liminary ruling procedure. In view of the number of constitutional courts that appear to be reserving a power of review or even going so far, as with the Czech Court, as to hold a Court of Justice ruling as *ultra vires*, this is something that the member states, the Union, and the Court of Justice need to be taking seriously—perhaps in (another?) protocol dealing with judicial cooperation. The apparent, less wholesome, reception in the new member states may, however, have more to do with the fact that such newly emergent democracies are jealous of their newly won rights and freedoms, and are not prepared to cede them without careful review.

Further Reading

Books

ALBI, A. *EU Enlargement and the Constitutions of Central and Eastern Europe*, Cambridge University Press, Cambridge, 2005.

ALTER, K.J. *Establishing the Supremacy of European Law: The Making of an International Rule of Law in Europe*, Oxford University Press, Oxford, 2002.

BULMER, S. and LEQUESNE, C. *The Member States of the European Union*, Oxford University Press, Oxford, 2005.

CRAIG, P. 'Britain in the European Union' in J. Jowell and D. Oliver (eds) *The Changing Constitution*, 6th edn, Oxford University Press, Oxford, 2007.

Articles

ALONSO GARCIA, R. 'The Spanish Constitution and the European Constitution: The Script for a Virtual Collision and Other Observations on the Principle of Primacy' (2005) 6(6) German Law Journal 1001–24, also available at http://www.germanlawjournal.com/pdf/Vol06No06/PDF_Vol_06_No_06_Developments_1001–1024_Garcia.pdf.

AVBELJ, M. 'Supremacy or Primacy of EU Law: (Why) Does it Matter?' (2010) 17 ELJ 744.

BECK, G. 'The Problem of Kompetenz-Kompetenz: A Conflict Between Right and Right Where There Is No Praetor' (2005) 30 EL Rev 42.

BOGDANDY, A. VON et al 'Reverse Solange: Protecting the Essence of Fundamental Rights against Member States' (2012) 49 CML Rev 489.

BURSENS, P. 'Why Denmark and Belgium Have Different Implementation Records: On Transposition Laggards and Leaders in the EU' (2002) 25(2) Scandinavian Political Studies 173–95.

CHARPY, C. 'The Status of (Secondary) Community Law in the French Internal Order' (2007) 3 EU Const 436.

CRAIG, P. 'Sovereignty of the United Kingdom Parliament after *Factortame*' (1991) 9 YEL 221–55.

CYGAN, A. 'Democracy and Accountability in the European Union: The View from the House of Commons' (2003) 66 MLR 384.

DASHWOOD, A. 'The Relationship between the Member States and the European Union/ European Community' (2004) 41 CML Rev 355–81.

DANIELSEN, J. 'One of Many National Constraints on European Integration: Section 20 of the Danish Constitution' (2010) 16 EPL 181.

DUTHEIL DE LA ROCHERE, J. '*Conseil Constitutionnel* (French Constitutional Court) Decision No. 2004/496' (2005) 42 CML Rev 859.

FAHEY, E. 'A Constitutional Crisis in a Teacup: The Supremacy of EC Law in Ireland' (2009) 15 EPL 515.

FOSTER, N. 'The German Constitution and EC Membership' [1994] Public Law 392–408.

GAJA, G. 'New Developments in a Continuing Story: The Relationship between EC Law and Italian Law' (1990) 27 CML Rev 83.

GIEGERICH, T., 'The German Federal Constitutional Court's Misguided Attempts to Guard the European Guardians in Luxembourg and Strasbourg' (2013) 1232 Der Staat im Recht, 49.

HØEGH, K. 'The Danish Maastricht Judgment' (1999) 24 EL Rev 80.

HOFFMEISTER, F. 'German *Bundesverfassungsgericht: Alcan*, Decision of 17 February 2000; Constitutional Review of EC Regulation on Bananas, Decision of 7 June 2000' (2001) 38 CML Rev 791.

HOFFMEISTER, F. 'Constitutional Implications of EU Membership: A View from the Commission' (2007) 3 CYELP 59–97.

HOGAN, G. 'The Nice Treaty and the Irish Constitution' (2001) 7 EPL 565.

KALEDA, S. 'Immediate Effect of Community Law in the New Member States: Is There a Place for a Consistent Doctrine?' (2004) 10 ELJ 102.

KOKOTT, J. AND SOBOTTA, C. 'The Kadi Case—Constitutional Core Values and International Law—Finding the Balance?' (2012) 23 EJIL 1015.

KOMEREK, J. 'Playing with Matches: The Czech Constitutional Court Declares a Judgment of the Court of Justice of the EU Ultra Vires' (2012) 8 ECL Rev 323.

KOMEREK, J. 'The Place of Constitutional Courts in the EU' (2013) 9 ECL Rev 420.

KOWALIK-BANCZYK, K. 'Polish Constitutional Tribunal and the Idea of Supremacy of EU Law' (2005) 6 German LJ 1355.

KUMM, M. 'The Jurisprudence of Constitutional Conflict: Constitutional Supremacy in Europe before and after the Constitutional Treaty' (2005) 11 ELJ 299.

LAZOWSKI, A. 'Half Full and Half Empty Glass: The Application of EU Law in Poland (2004–10)' (2011) 48 CML Rev 503.

MASTENBROEK, E. 'Surviving the Deadline: The Transposition of EU Directives in the Netherlands' (2003) 4 European Union Politics 371–95.

MEHDI, R. 'French Supreme Courts and European Union Law: Between Historical Compromise and Accepted Loyalty' (2011) 48 CML Rev 439.

PAYANDEH, M. 'Constitutional Review of EU Law after Honeywell: Contextualizing the Relationship between the German Constitutional Court and the EU Court of Justice' (2011) 48 CML Rev 9.

PLIAKOS, A. and ANAGNOSTARAS, G. 'Who Is the Ultimate Arbiter? The Battle over Judicial Supremacy in EU Law' (2011) 36 EL Rev 109.

RICHARDS, C. 'The Supremacy of Community Law before the French Constitutional Court' (2006) 31 EL Rev 499.

ROSS, M. 'Effectiveness in European Legal Order(s): Beyond Supremacy to Constitutional Proportionality' (2006) 31 EL Rev 476.

SCHMID, C. 'All Bark and No Bite: Notes on the Federal Constitutional Court's "Banana Decision"' (2001) 7 ELJ 95.

THOMSON, R. 'Same Effects in Different Worlds: The Transposition of EU Directives' (2009) 16(1) Journal of European Public Policy 1–18.

USHER, J.L. 'The Reception of General Principles of Community Law in the United Kingdom' (2005) 16 EBLR 489.

ZIEGLER, K.S. 'Strengthening the Rule of Law, but Fragmenting International Law: The *Kadi* Decision of the Court of Justice from the Perspective of Human Rights' (2009) 9(2) HRL Rev 288–305.

6

Ensuring EU Laws
Are Effective: Remedies
and Art 267 TFEU

6.1 Introduction

This chapter brings together a number of related matters for consideration. They are all indirectly linked to the preliminary ruling procedure under Art 267 TFEU, which was the vehicle by which the leading principles and remedies in EU law were developed by the Court of Justice, in particular the means by which EU law could be enforced by individuals via the national courts, rather than by the Commission, other institutions, or member states in direct actions before the CoJ, which will be considered in Chapter 7. Article 177 EEC (now 267 TFEU) facilitated the establishment of a system of so-called 'dual vigilance' for the enforcement of EU law. The individual remedies developed include direct effects, indirect effects, and state liability as the most important. The system of remedies has developed so extensively that it has also made inroads into national procedural law as a reaction to the impact that those rules can have on the equal application of EU law rights across the member states. These aspects will be considered at the end of this chapter, which will commence with a brief introduction to Art 267 TFEU, followed by a consideration of the range of individual remedies developed, and then a full consideration of Art 267 TFEU.

6.2 An Introduction to Art 267 TFEU

The preliminary ruling procedure, which is also referred to as the 'Art 267 TFEU reference', provides the link, or bridge, between the national legal systems and the EU legal system. Under Art 267 TFEU, the courts of the member states can seek a ruling from the Court of Justice on the interpretation of all forms of EU law, including international treaties, and on the validity and interpretation of EU secondary legislation.

The details of the Art 267 TFEU procedure will be considered after looking at the remedies established by the Court of Justice, commencing with direct effect and its distinction from direct applicability.

6.3 Direct Applicability and Direct Effects

6.3.1 Definitions and the Distinction between Directly Applicable and Direct Effects

These two elements of the EU legal system and the distinction between them are fundamental to the study and understanding of the nature of EU law. The doctrine of direct effects is a judicial development of the Court of Justice. It is connected to, and very often confused with, direct applicability; however, there are fundamental differences between the two concepts. Direct effects plays a central role in the EU legal order because of its link with the application and enforcement of EU law in the courts of the national legal systems, and is therefore very much related to the supremacy of EU law. Unfortunately, the terminology of the CoJ and many of the national courts has not always been consistent. This has added greatly to the difficulty in understanding these concepts. More often in the past than now, the courts did not use the term 'direct effects' but would describe a provision of EU law as 'directly applicable', but only in the sense that the provision gave rise to rights enforceable by individuals before the national courts.

Thankfully, such confusing use of terms is less frequent these days. The term 'direct effects' was sometimes considered to be a sub-concept of direct applicability, or direct applicability was considered a prerequisite for direct effects. The Court of Justice has spoken of regulations that are directly applicable but which, by their very nature, can have direct effect in Case 131/79 *Santillo*, which suggests that this is automatically the case. In Case 9/70 *Grad*, the CoJ stated that the ability of an individual to invoke a decision before a national court leads to the same result as would be achieved by a directly applicable provision of a regulation—again, as if to suggest that the concepts are the same, and hence the confusion and the need for clarification.[1]

6.3.2 **Direct Applicability**

'Direct applicability', a term previously recognized in international law, should be used to describe the way in which some provisions of EU have legal validity in the member states. It is therefore a mode of incorporation of law that is generally or universally binding. The term 'self-executing' is also often used to describe such law, in that the legal provision itself establishes its validity in the host state. In the EU, 'directly applicable' is specifically mentioned in Art 288 TFEU in relation to regulations that shall have general application and are directly applicable. The member states are obliged not to transform EU regulations into national legislation, except where necessary under the regulation: see Cases 39/72 *Commission v Italy (Slaughtering Cows)* and 128/78 *Commission v UK (Tachographs)*, because there are occasions on which implementing legislation is required to make an EU regime effective—in the latter case, to provide sanctions against the lorry operators who failed to install tachographs in lorry cabs. The regulation simply made the fitting of tachographs compulsory.

The term 'direct applicability' applies also in respect of treaty Articles, because these also satisfy the criteria of directly applicable law by their automatic validity in the member states following the ratification of an EU treaty. The treaty Articles themselves are not actually transformed into national law and they are generally binding, in that they also obligate individuals and not only the member states.

6.3.3 **Direct Effects**

'Direct effects' is the term given to judicial enforcement of rights arising from provisions of EU law that can be upheld in favour of individuals in the courts of the member states.

---

[1] Of the earliest articles on the subject, those that the author considers to be clear and succinct are: L. Brinkhorst in a case note on the *Grad* and *SACE* decisions (1971) 8 CML Rev 380–92; J.A. Winter, 'Direct Applicability and Direct Effect: Two Distinct and Different Concepts in Community Law' (1972) 9 CML Rev 425; and A. Easson, 'The Direct Effect of EEC Directives' (1979) 28 ICLQ 319–53.

Provided that certain criteria are satisfied (considered in the following section), an EU law provision will give rise to a right that is enforceable by individuals in the national courts. Whereas direct applicability applies only to regulations and treaty Articles, direct effects have been declared by the Court of Justice in a series of cases in respect of treaty Articles, regulations, directives, decisions, fundamental rights, general principles, and provisions of international agreements to which the Union is a signatory.

6.3.3.1 Treaty Articles

The first and leading case in which this doctrine was established as a leading principle of EU law is Case 26/62 *Van Gend en Loos*, which concerned the imposition of a customs tariff by the Dutch authorities allegedly contrary to Community law, old Art 12 EEC (now Art 30 TFEU), which provided that 'member states shall refrain from introducing between themselves any new customs duties on imports or exports or any charges having equivalent effect, and from increasing those which they already apply in their trade with each other'. The defendant customs authority argued that, because the treaty Article was addressed to the member state, it could not be enforced by individuals against the state. In support of this view, the Belgian, German, and Dutch governments, and even the Advocate General (AG), argued that the correct way in which to enforce the treaty obligation was by formal action by the Commission (under Art 169 EEC, now Art 258 TFEU) or by another member state, but not by individuals. The Court of Justice rejected this view and held that the Community had been endowed with sovereign rights, the exercise of which affects not only member states, but also their citizens, and that Community law was capable of conferring rights on individuals that become part of their legal heritage and enforceable by them before the national courts. It held that the provision (old Art 12 EEC) was suited by its nature to produce direct effects.

To be capable of direct effects that are enforceable in the national courts, a treaty provision must satisfy the criteria established by the Court of Justice. It must:

(a) be clear and precise

(b) be unconditional (for example, as to time limits)

(c) not require implementing measures to be taken by member states or Community (now EU) institutions

(d) not leave discretion to member states or Community (now EU) institutions.[2]

The CoJ, thus, not only enabled private parties to defend their rights arising from EU law in the face of inconsistent or contrary national law, but also added to the system of enforcement of EU law by empowering individuals to take action that would result in enforcement in situations in which a member state had failed to comply with EU law and in which the Commission had not taken any action. This is regarded as particularly helpful, because private individuals have clear reasons of self-interest to bring actions and, because there are so many of them who may be affected by EU law, the vigilance of EU law is much more widespread and effective.

Case 48/65 *Alfons Lütticke GmbH v Hauptzollamt Saarlouis* is an early demonstration of the difference between Articles of the treaty that could give rise to direct effects and those that could not. The case declared that old Art 95 EEC (now Art 110 TFEU) satisfied the criteria so as to give rise to direct effects, but that Art 97 did not.[3] Old Art 95 provided

---

[2] These criteria are not rigidly applied as set out here, but flexibly and providing a provision generally meets those requirements, it will most likely be declared to have direct effects.

[3] Art 97 was repealed by the Treaty of Amsterdam.

that 'No Member State shall impose, directly or indirectly . . . any internal taxation of any kind' and old Art 97 provided that 'member states . . . may, in the case of internal taxation . . . establish average rates'. The Court of Justice ruled that Art 95 had created direct effects, but that, since member states had a discretion to decide whether to levy an average rate of tax, Art 97 did not produce direct effects.

Since these early cases, direct effects have been found to arise from many treaty Articles,[4] which often obligate not only organs of the state as in a vertical relationship, but other individuals, in particular, in the EU context, employers. It was confirmed by the Court of Justice that employers are obligated to comply with the requirements of a treaty Article and that other individuals may enforce corresponding rights directly against the obligated party who has failed to comply with EU law. The first case to confirm this was Case 43/75 *Defrenne v Sabena (No 2)*, in which the rights of an air hostess for equal pay guaranteed under Art 119 EEC (now Art 157 TFEU) were upheld against the employing airline Sabena, which was in breach of the obligation. This ability to enforce rights against other individual legal entities is termed 'horizontal direct effects' because it applies on the horizontal axis between two individuals.

Article 12 EC (now Art 18 TFEU), the general prohibition of discrimination clause imposed on the member states, was found to be capable of horizontal direct effects in Case 36/74 *Walrave and Koch*,[5] but Art 10 EC (now Art 4(3) TEU), the good-faith clause imposing a general obligation on the member states to act in conformity with and not against Community interests, was held in Case 44/84 *Hurd v Jones* not to give rise to direct effects, although this Article has subsequently been highly influential in helping the Court of Justice to develop other means of enforcing EU law, including indirect effects and state liability, as considered later.

Provisions of the accession treaties have also been held to give rise to direct effects: see, for example, Case C-113/89 *Rush Portuguesa v Office National d'Immigration*, which detailed the rights to which non-Community workers were entitled whilst working outside their EC country of immigration in another host member state.

6.3.3.2 Fundamental Rights Charter

Whilst waiting for the view of the CoJ on whether provisions within the EU Charter of Fundamental Rights can produce direct effects, the Charter itself provides that it is not generally applicable in that it applies to obligate the EU and the member states only. It is not therefore to be regarded in the same way as the treaties and regulations which obligate everyone (see Art 51(1) of the Charter). The decision in Case C-176/12 *Association de Mediation Sociale (AMS)* would certainly seem to support that view. In that case the CoJ held that despite the French private body not complying with either a directive or Art 27 of the EU Charter of Fundamental Rights, neither could give rise to horizontal effects between private parties. It may be though, that the particular right which may fall under consideration may already be covered in existing treaty rights or indeed in general principles, which themselves have been declared to be directly effective. The *AMS* case though should not be read to dictate the result in any forthcoming cases considering the Charter, particularly if it involved a state authority in a vertical relationship.

---

[4] Although very dated now, L. Collins provided a list of those treaty Articles that had been considered by the Court of Justice for direct effects in *European Community Law in the United Kingdom*, 4th edn, Butterworths, London, 1990, pp 122–6.

[5] Indeed, in Case C-92/92 *Phil Collins v Imtrat*, Art 18 TFEU (Art 7 EEC as it was) was upheld as being directly effective on its own without connection to any other treaty Article.

6.3.3.3 **General Principles**

More recent case law, in particular from the area of discrimination law, has indicated that general principles may also give rise to vertical and horizontal direct effects. As this is a new and developing area of law, Cases C-144/04 *Mangold* and C-555/07 *Kükükdeveci* and others are considered in Section 6.3.4.3.

6.3.3.4 **Regulations**

While regulations are clearly directly applicable by reason of Art 288 TFEU and can therefore also obligate other individuals, they are not necessarily directly effective. The question of whether they can also give rise to direct effects also depends on whether they satisfy the same criteria as for treaty Articles as laid down in the *Van Gend en Loos* case. The leading case for regulations is Case 93/71 *Leonesio v Italian Ministry of Agriculture*, in which Italian farmers were able to enforce a regulation against the Italian state providing for compensation payments that had been subject to delays by the Italian authorities. The Court of Justice held that the regulation should not be subject to delays and was immediately enforceable in the national courts.

Given that regulations are also generally applicable in that they apply to everyone and not only provide rights, but are also capable of imposing obligations on everyone, it should not be a surprise that they are capable of giving rise to direct effects horizontally also. For example, in Case C-253/00 *Munoz v Frumar Ltd*, the Court of Justice upheld the right of one individual trader to rely on the rights provided by a regulation in a civil action against another individual not complying with the regulation.

6.3.3.5 **Directives**

Directives have caused particular problems for the Court of Justice. At first, they were thought, as a general rule, not to be precise enough to give rise to direct effects because they were not directly applicable and only obligated the member states to achieve an end result. Arguably, because they often provide a wide margin of discretion, they were considered incapable by their very nature of fulfilling the *Van Gend en Loos* criteria. However, Case 9/70 *Grad*, discussed in the following section, considered and allowed for the possibility that direct effects could arise from other non-directly applicable forms of EU law outside treaty Articles and regulations and Case 41/74 *Van Duyn v Home Office* confirmed that directives could give rise to direct effects, provided that they also satisfy the same criteria. The provisions of the directive would have to contain a clear and precise obligation, which they can and often do. In this case, Art 3 of Directive 64/221 was held to give rise to rights directly enforceable against the state before the national courts by Miss Van Duyn. In other words, the discretion for directives is not in what should be achieved but how it should be achieved. The obligation or requirement is not discretional, but quite how it is achieved in each member state is.

A further aspect of directives that might have caused difficulty was that directives usually allow the member states a period of time in which to implement them—two years being fairly common—which was considered in Case 148/78 *Publico Ministero v Ratti*. This concerned the prosecution of Mr Ratti by the Italian authorities for breaches of national law concerning product labelling. Although Mr Ratti had complied with two Community product-labelling directives, the period for implementation of one of the two directives had not expired. The Court of Justice held that he could rely on the one for which the time period had expired, provided that it satisfied the requirements of clarity and precision, among others, but not the directive the implementation period of which had not expired. Although not expressly or directly contradicting the ruling with regard to time limits in *Ratti*, a series of cases commencing with Case C-144/04 *Mangold* provide that in certain circumstances the time limit for the implementation of a directive may be unimportant. This is where in addition to the specific rights contained within the directive—in the *Mangold* case this was Directive 2000/78 and the prohibition of age discrimination—there is also a general principle prohibiting discrimination. Mangold suffered age discrimination but the directive's implementation period had not expired; the Court of Justice, however, held that the discrimination also breached the general principle prohibiting discrimination and this could not be undermined by the unexpired transposition period of a directive. The directive was argued to provide a more exact setting in which the pre-existing general principle could be interpreted and applied. The argument in the case was that both a strict application of Art 6 of Directive 2000/78 and the application of the general principle would have had the same result. However, if relying on the directive only, this would have caused problems because of the non-expiry of the implementation period; thus the directive was incapable of producing direct effects. In order to get over those difficulties, it was better to use the general principle. This position was confirmed in Case C-555/07 *Kükükdeveci*. Both cases are considered further in Section 6.3.4.3.

Case 51/76 *Verbond* concerned the situation in which a directive had been implemented, but the implementation was not faithful to the requirements of the directive. The Court of Justice held that to deny the rights of individuals in such circumstances would be to weaken the effectiveness of Community obligations and that, as a result, individuals helped to ensure that member states kept within the realms of the discretion granted to them. Thus, with a body of case law emerging, it became clear that there was no difficulty in enforcing a directive against the member states, which are obligated to achieve the end result required by the provisions of the directive.[6]

6.3.3.5.1 *The Question of Horizontal Direct Effects of Directives*

For a considerable time, however, the question of whether directives could be held to give rise to horizontal direct effects, and thus be enforceable against other individuals, received no answer from the Court of Justice. At the time, arguments against horizontal effects were that directives did not have to be published and this would have offended against legal certainty. Furthermore, directives are addressed to and obligate member states and not individuals, and therefore the latter should not be bound by them. By making them enforceable potentially against everyone, the CoJ would blur the distinction between them and regulations, because they would resemble directly applicable law—something not intended under the scheme now found in Art 288 TFEU.

Arguments for the horizontal direct effects of directives are that Community (EU) law should be equally actionable against the state and other individuals to ensure uniform consistency throughout the Union, and to avoid giving rise to two categories of right. The discretion for directives is not in what should be achieved but how it should be achieved; thus the obligation or requirement is not discretional, but quite how it is achieved in each member state is. Furthermore, treaty Articles are also addressed to member states, but can nevertheless obligate individuals. Directives, whilst not initially compulsorily publishable, invariably were published and indeed now *must* be published (see Art 297 TFEU).

The CoJ finally decided this issue in Case 152/84 *Marshall v Southampton Area Health Authority*, saying that directives could only be enforced against the state, or arms of the

---

[6] In this respect also Case C-62/00 *Marks & Spencer*, in which M&S were able to rely on a VAT Directive which although implemented, was not implemented faithfully when it came to the accurate imposition of tax rates to products, resulting in the overpayment of taxes. M&S were able to reclaim despite an attempt by the UK authorities to limit claims. This case is also considered in Section 6.5.7.4.

state, and not against individuals, although the case itself concerned vertical direct effects, because the health authority was held to be part of the state. The decision, however, led to a whole host of problems, because of the distinction that was created between the ability to enforce rights against private as opposed to public employers. The result of this decision is that the scope of the concept of a 'public service' as opposed to a 'private body' became crucial. This can be seen in the later UK case of *Duke v Reliance*[7] in which, on similar facts to those of *Marshall*, Mrs Duke lost her claim for compensation for being forced to retire earlier than men. Two further decisions in Case 222/84 *Johnston v RUC* and Case C-188/89 *Foster v British Gas* showed that, although the concept was wide enough to include national law, national enforcement agencies, and nationalized industries, and included any form of state control or authority, a distinction between public sector and private sector rights nevertheless remains. This is considered in further detail later.

Case 8/81 *Becker* confirmed the restriction of the direct effects of directives to the vertical axis, but highlighted the further benefits of direct effects for the EU legal order. It made clear that directly effective EU law also operates in a wider sense as a standard by which national law is, in effect, considered by the Court of Justice to see if it meets the standard of EU law, rather than simply providing a narrower individual right only. Whilst the CoJ has no formal right to review the compatibility of national law, direct effect does allow it to state that there is an incompatibility on the part of the national law with the directly effective standard contained in the EU law. The *Becker* case thus prepared the ground for the establishment of indirect effect, considered in Section 6.3.4.2.

6.3.3.6 Decisions

In Case 9/70 *Grad v Finanzamt Traunstein*, the CoJ held that it would be contrary to the binding nature of Community law if the provisions of a decision were not able to be invoked by individuals. They must also satisfy the criteria and can only be enforced against those obligated. In *Grad*, a decision addressed to the German state concerned with the harmonization of tax regimes was held to give rise to effects that could be enforced by an individual affected by it.

6.3.3.7 International Agreements

Although there is no statement in the EU treaties that international agreements entered into by the Union or by the member states within the Union are generally binding or can give rise to direct effects, the Court of Justice has held that they may also give rise to direct effects, provided that they satisfy the criteria previously established. Agreements such as association agreements, between the Union and a single state or even a number of states, lend themselves more easily to producing direct effects due to the more limited nature and scope of the agreements than is the case with the more complex multilateral agreements, the subject matter of which may well go beyond the jurisdictional scope of the treaties. For example, provisions of the EEC–Portugal Association, parts of the EEC–Morocco Agreement, and provisions of the Yaounde Convention Agreement were held to be directly effective in Case 104/81 *Kupferberg*, Case 87/75 *Bresciani*, and Case C-18/90 *Kziber* respectively. In contrast, provisions of more complex agreements, such as the General Agreement on Tariffs and Trade (GATT), which are mixed agreements involving both the competences of the EU and the member states, have not shown themselves to the Court of Justice to be so amenable to direct effects. In Cases 21–4/72 *International Fruit*, the CoJ held that the provisions in question were not directly effective because they were

---

[7] [1988] AC 618.

held to be too flexible and too easily subject to change by political negotiation, rather than clearly applicable in a strict and reasonably foreseeable way by the courts. More recently, in line with the transition from the GATT to the World Trade Organization (WTO), the CoJ has appeared to soften its stance and expressed the possibility in Case C-280/93 *Germany v Commission* that the GATT provisions may have direct effects, but only where the Community intended to implement a particular GATT provision or expressly referred to it in a Community act. For example, in Case 70/87 *Fediol*, a reference in a Community regulation to a commercial practice identified in the GATT was held to allow the CoJ to interpret the Community act according to the GATT rule. It was, however, emphasized by the CoJ in Case C-149/96 *Portugal v Council* that the WTO rules do not give rise to direct effects. The CoJ did not wish to tie the hands of the Community by confirming binding rules of law for the Community when those same rules are not considered to be rigidly binding by other parties. The WTO and GATT regimes are not based on binding and immediately enforceable rules, but on rules the breach of which leads first to further negotiation and even the sanctioning of reciprocal action being taken by the offended state on completely different goods.

Rules emanating from the United Nations (UN) have also been considered by the Court of Justice. Whilst such rules, as pre-existing obligations of all the member states which are members of the UN, are thus to be respected by the EU, they appear not likely to give rise to direct effects. Thus, they join those rules from the WTO and GATT which are not in the view of the Court of Justice capable of providing individuals with directly effective rights. In Case C-308/06 *Intertanko*,[8] the Court of Justice held that because the UN Convention on the Law of the Sea did not create rights for individuals it could not be used by the CoJ to determine the validity an EU act alleged to be in breach of the Convention. In the UN asset-freezing sanctions cases (Cases C-402/05 P and C-415/05 P *Kadi and Al Barakaat*), the Court of Justice annulled a regulation which put into effect UN resolutions for breaching EU human rights standards and in doing so made it quite clear that the international obligations could not dictate the outcome in the EU legal order, a constitutionally autonomous international legal order.

Thus, it cannot be said that there is a presumption in favour of international agreements having direct effects; it depends on their nature and whether they intend to provide rights for individuals.

6.3.4 Overcoming the Lack of Horizontal Direct Effect for Directives

6.3.4.1 Extending the Definition of 'the State'

One way in which to get over the unfortunate results of the *Marshall* ruling, which led to differences in treatment between state and private employees, is to expand the concept of 'public sector' to include more employers, and thus more individuals capable of enforcing their rights vertically in the national courts through direct effects. In Case C-188/89 *Foster v British Gas*, the House of Lords referred to the Court of Justice the critical question of what was meant by 'state authority'. In *Marshall*, the health authority was clearly regarded as a part of the state; *Foster v British Gas* involved, at that time, a nationalized, but independently run, organization. It was later privatized. The CoJ held that emanations of the state against which direct effects were available were those bodies that provided a public service under the control of the state and to which for that purpose were granted special powers. Direct effects are then available against such bodies. However, although

---

[8] [2008] ECR I-4057.

the case showed that the concept was wide enough to include nationalized industries and includes any form of state control or authority, a distinction nevertheless remains between 'public', however widely framed, and 'private' employers. So, it may be concluded that expanding the scope of what is meant by an 'emanation of the state' will broaden the concept and protect more people, but this still does not get to the heart of the matter. It still allows a variation as between public and private employees and, because there are inevitably different situations in each of the member states as regards the public and private sectors, there will also be a difference in the rights of individuals between the member states because of the different extent and understandings of the state. Thus, because of this distinction, a different result can occur in each member state where national concepts of what is within the control of the state may differ.

The difficulties and limits to this approach are demonstrated in the UK case *Doughty v Rolls Royce plc*, in which the Court of Appeal considered that the nationalized Rolls Royce was not a public body for the purposes of the claim to direct effects in the case, because it was not providing a public service and was not subject to special powers. Whilst the result in *Rolls Royce* is almost certainly correct, it can be seen that privatization of once nationalized companies might also affect the rights of individuals. If decided today, *Foster v British Gas* would arguably have a different outcome. In a case concerned with the concept of the state, Case C-157/02 *Rieser Internationale Transporte GmbH v Autobahnen-und Schnellstraßen Finanzierungs AG*, the Court of Justice held:

> When contracts are concluded with road users, the provisions of a directive capable of having direct effect may be relied upon against a legal person governed by private law where the State has entrusted to that legal person the task of levying tolls for the use of public road networks and where it has direct or indirect control of that legal person. The state was the sole shareholder of the company and had actual and effective overall control over both budgets and its activities.

This means that private companies undertaking a public duty come within the scope of the *Foster* ruling.[9]

There remains, however, no uniformity, and, indeed, no certainty, as to the application of EU law between public and private employers within member states and between member states. Certain individuals are thus denied rights that employees in the public sector can enforce in the face of non-compliance by member states. It further has to be borne in mind that the state has contracted in most, if not all, member states as state monopoly industries are broken up for the purposes of competition and inevitably privatized. This means more employees are placed into the horizontal relationship and not able to avail themselves of the direct effects of directives. Widening the concept is essentially swimming against a very powerful tide. The result of this is that the scope of the concept of public service, as opposed to a private body, remains a crucial, but sometimes artificial, distinction.

6.3.4.2 Indirect Effects

To some extent, Case 8/81 *Becker*, noted earlier, and its acknowledgement of a wider concept of direct effect as a standard by which national law is, in effect, reviewed by the Court of Justice, had already pointed EU law in the direction that it was about to follow in the next development. Case 14/83 *Von Colson* provided a solution where national law was not in tune with Community law and direct effects were not really a solution that

---

[9] And further supported now by Cases C-53/04 *Marrosu and Sardino* and C-180/04 *Vassallo*.

the CoJ could have employed in the case itself. The ruling offers an alternative for individuals defeated by the lack of horizontal direct effects. The case concerned Art 6 of the Equal Treatment Directive (76/207) and a claim against a public employer for the lack of adequate compensation when discriminated against. At the same time, Case 79/83 *Harz v Tradex* was also heard by the CoJ, which involved a similar claim against a private employer. Rather than highlight the unfortunate results of the lack of horizontal direct effects of directives against the private, but not the public, employer, the CoJ concentrated on old Art 5 EEC (now Art 4(3) TEU), which requires member states to comply with Community obligations. The CoJ held that this requirement applies to all authorities of member states, including the courts, which are obliged therefore to interpret national law in such a way as to ensure that the obligations of a directive are obeyed, regardless of whether the national law was based on any particular directive. The effectiveness of this depends on the willingness or ability of the member states' courts to interpret national law, if it exists, to achieve the correct result.

However, the CoJ held in Case 80/86 *Public Prosecutor v Kolpinghuis Nijmegen BF* that the principle could not be applied by a member state to retroactively sanction the prosecution of a Dutch firm for stocking adulterated mineral water in breach of a Community directive the implementation period of which had expired, but which had not been implemented by the Netherlands. The decision is consistent with *Marshall*, in that directives cannot impose obligations on individuals. Thus, the sympathetic interpretation of EU law directives required by *Von Colson* could not be used in breach of the general principles including legal certainty and non-retroactivity.

The lack of national law to interpret, however, has caused problems in furthering the principle enunciated in *Von Colson*. The next case required further advice from the CoJ to achieve a just result consistent with its decision in *Marshall*. Case C-106/89 *Marleasing* concerned Directive 68/151, which had not been implemented in Spain, but which would have determined the outcome of the case. The Spanish courts wanted to know whether the directive could nevertheless be directly upheld against an individual by another individual. Whilst the Court of Justice reaffirmed that directives do not give rise to effects between individuals, it also stressed that it was up to the courts to achieve the result required by the directive by the interpretation of national law, whether the national law post-dated or pre-dated the directive. The relevant national law, the Spanish Civil Code, pre-dated it, but had to be interpreted in a way clearly not covered by it to conform with the later unimplemented directive. Such retroactive interpretation will cause severe difficulties where there is a clear conflict between the national law and an EU directive, as was the case in the UK House of Lords case *Duke v GEC Reliance Systems*, in which the House of Lords refused to interpret pre-existing UK law in light of the later Equal Treatment Directive, in spite of the decision in *Marshall*. This difficulty was highlighted before the CoJ in Case C-334/92 *Wagner Miret*, which also involved Spanish legislation pre-dating a Community directive, but which involved head-on incompatibility. The CoJ this time acknowledged the unsuitability of the *Von Colson* sympathetic interpretation in all cases, and in Case C-168/95 *Criminal Proceedings against Luciano Arcaro*, the CoJ acknowledged that the limits of the *Von Colson* principle would be overreached if there were a retroactive interpretation of national law in light of the directive, which would have determined the criminal liability of an individual. This confirmed the limitation recognized in the *Kolpinghuis* case.

Cases C-397–401/01 *Pfeiffer v Rotes Kreuz*, concerned the meaning of 'working time' from the directive of the same name in view of a number of pre-existing work time definitions in Germany. The Court of Justice, in considering how far national courts can go in applying *Von Colson*, confirmed that national courts are bound to interpret national law as far as possible in light of the directive to achieve the result sought by a directive. They should also give full effectiveness to EU law, taking into account national law as a whole, as opposed to looking narrowly at a particular national implementing provision. However, as was emphasized in Cases C-268/06 *Impact* and C-555/07 *Kükükdeveci v Swedex*, a national court is not expected to interpret national law contrary to the clear meaning (*contra legem*) although in Case C-404/06 *Quelle AG*, it was held that such a difficulty facing the national court does not prevent the Court of Justice from nevertheless ruling that national law should in fact be interpreted according to an EU provision.[10]

From time to time, the AG has tried to persuade the CoJ to take a further step and declare for horizontal direct effects of a directive, as in Case C-91/92 *Faccini Dori*, but the CoJ has declined to follow this advice. It reasoned that whilst there was a case for vertical direct effects to stop states relying on their own wrongs, recognition of horizontal direct effects would blur the distinction between regulations and directives contrary to the treaty. Instead, as it did also in Case C-334/93 *Wagner Miret*, the CoJ expressed the view that if member states are unable to construe national law to be read in conformity, which is a distinct possibility as a result of the court being either incapable or unwilling to do so, it must be assumed that member states nevertheless intend to comply with their Community law obligations. Thus, if there is a breach, member states must compensate any loss incurred as a result of that breach according to the principles established in *Francovich*, considered in Section 6.4. In other words, the failure to succeed under *Von Colson* should not unfairly extinguish all remedies available to individuals because of the state's failure to comply with EU law.

6.3.4.3 General Principles and Direct Effects

There are now cases which suggest directives can nevertheless be influenced by a general principle to dictate the result of a case between two individuals and thus give an appearance of horizontal direct effects. Case C-144/04 *Mangold*[11] concerns a German law that made it easier to offer fixed-term contracts to those over the age of 52 and thus made it easier to end the employment relationship at the end of a fixed-term contract. This was an attempt to make the employment of older persons more attractive; that is, it was designed in a roundabout way to help the employment chances for older workers. However, it was challenged as contrary to the general directive prohibiting discrimination on the grounds of age, the implementation period of which directive had not, at the time of the case, expired. The CoJ held that the German legislation had, indeed, gone too far and was contrary to the prohibition of discrimination on the ground of age. The case thus appeared to provide for the horizontal direct effects of a directive and, more surprisingly, it did so even before the period of expiry of the transposition period had ended. However, note that the CoJ held that the principle of law breached by the member state was the general principle of the prohibition of discrimination. According to the CoJ, this could not be undermined by the unexpired transposition period of a directive, which provided a more exact setting in which the pre-existing general principle could be interpreted and applied. The argument was that both a strict application of Art 6 of Directive 2000/78 and the application of the general principle would have had the same result. However, if relying on the directive only, this would have caused problems because of the non-expiry of the implementation period. Therefore, in order to get over those difficulties, it was better to

---

[10] A later offering from the CoJ in support of the earlier case law is Case C-306/12 *Spedition Welter* [2013] ECR I-650, which provides the updated reasoning of the Court that the requirement that national courts read national law in conformity with EU law is inherent in the system of the TFEU.

[11] Also considered in Chapter 11, Section 11.10.1.4.

use the general principle. In other words, the use of a general principle got around the fact that the directive, according to the past case law (notably the *Ratti* case), was incapable of producing direct effects due to the fact that the obligations contained in it were not yet due. The end result, as far as the Court of Justice is concerned, is that it remains the case that horizontal direct effect of directives is not recognized.

Another take on the case is that it suggests that the general principles may give rise to horizontal direct effects, but this judgment requires further confirmation and does not apply to directives.[12]

The further Case C-212/04 *Adeneler v ELOG*[13] does provide some clarification of the judgment in *Mangold*. The case concerned the Fixed-term Work Directive (1999/70), which was due to be implemented by July 2002 but which had not been implemented by Greece, and Greek employees whose then current fixed-term contracts had ended. New fixed-term contracts, according to the directive, were only to be allowed if objectively justified. A Greek court wished to know when the obligation under the directive should be used to interpret national law by national courts. The Court of Justice held that the general obligation (of the sort established in *Mangold*) arose only following the implementation period, but would apply regardless of whether the directive was capable or, indeed, incapable of direct effects for any reason. Thus far, this case takes things no further than the *Ratti* and *Von Colson* cases, noted earlier. However, the CoJ went on to hold that, in the period between publication of the directive and the expiry of the implementation period, member states were nevertheless constrained (under Arts 10 and 249 EC, now Art 4(3) TEU and Art 288 TFEU) from taking any measures that would compromise attaining the requirements of the directive. This means that they should not, prior to the expiry of the implementation period, interpret national law in a manner that might compromise the objectives of the directive when the implementation period has then expired.[14] This would seem almost to mean that, effective from the publication date and not the expiry date, the directive's objectives must be complied with, thus tearing up one of the remaining differences between regulations and directives. The national court's required interpretation would also apply to other individuals, but this is only the same as indirect effects, except at the earlier stage. In further support now of the influence of a general principle is Case C-555/07 *Kükükdeveci* which involved a dispute as to a notice period between an employee and a private employer. German law precluded periods of employment completed while the employee was under the age of 25 from counting towards the notice period. Ms Kükükdeveci had been dismissed with only one calendar month's notice, instead of at least four months' notice, as a consequence of the German law which she argued was contrary to EU law. Directive 2000/78 was also applicable to this case, as in the *Mangold* case noted earlier, to prohibit age discrimination and should have been implemented in Germany at the material time, but it had not been and, in any case, would not give rise to horizontal direct effects. The preliminary ruling question was, essentially, on what provision of law could Kükükdeveci rely? The Court of Justice held that the general principle of EU law prohibiting discrimination on the grounds of age, as expressed in Directive 2000/78, applies to preclude national law from discriminating as in the case itself. The CoJ held that the directive merely gives expression to the principle of equal treatment in employment and the principle of non-discrimination on grounds of age as general principles of EU law. Thus, the general principle applies directly between parties,

---

[12] The *Mangold* case has been supported by the AG in Case C-227/04 *Lindorfer v Council*, but not by the Court of Justice, so beware of using this case as support to read more into *Mangold* than exists.
[13] [2006] ECR I-6057.   [14] See in particular [120]–[123] of the judgment.

but not the directive, which merely provides a specific application of the general principle. The question which will have to wait for subsequent case law is whether it is better to have the general principle give rise to horizontal direct effects or the directive, bearing in mind that the general principle finds no clear expression anywhere in the treaties or secondary legislation. In view of the status of general principles in the hierarchy of sources of EU law, that is probably the correct result, although the consensus appears to be arising that this is only possible where the general principles are backed up by specific expressions of those rights in directives as in the *Mangold* and *Kükükdeveci* cases, and not in their own right. In any case, they too must pass the criteria established in *Van Gend en Loos*.

The final category of cases that appear in some way to circumvent the inconsistencies produced by the ruling in *Marshall* is admittedly of less importance and much more limited in scope, and may well be a category that will not attract new cases; that being so, it may well disappear altogether at some stage. For the moment, though, it does warrant brief consideration.

6.3.4.4 Incidental Horizontal Direct Effect

Although the opinion of the AG in Case C-91/92 *Faccini Dori* that horizontal direct effects of directives should be recognized by the Court of Justice was rejected, the CoJ has nevertheless given judgment in a few cases now that, on their face, appear to allow horizontal direct effects. The cases involve a directive that has influenced the outcome involving private parties, but in an incidental rather than a direct way and without imposing a strict obligation on any of the individual parties. The directive is pleaded not to exert rights directly, but to overcome what would otherwise be the application of incompatible national law in a way that is detrimental to one of their interests. These cases also support, and are supported by, the wider view of direct effects put forward in Case 8/81 *Becker*, as a means by which national law is, in effect, reviewed by the CoJ to see if it meets the standard of EU law, rather than as providing an individual right to assert an EU law-based right against another party.

In the leading case in this line, Case C-194/94 *CIA Security International SA v Signalson SA and Securitel SPRL*,[15] it was claimed that CIA had breached the national technical standard for alarm systems. CIA pleaded the inapplicability of the national standard because of the failure of the state to notify it to the Commission, as required by Directive 83/189. The Court of Justice accepted this argument, which meant that CIA could in effect rely on the Notification Directive to remove an obligation to meet the national standard that would otherwise have been imposed under national law. The directive relied on imposed no obligation on the other party, only on the state; therefore there is no question here of horizontal direct effects of a directive. It is true that the other party, which had alleged that CIA had not met the standard, was affected in that its allegation was legally unfounded and that it lost the action as a result. However, the national standard could only be rendered lawful by the state complying with the directive, thus it remained the state's obligation to ensure that its law was in compliance with EU law and not an individual's. It has been noted that, following this case, the number of notifications of technical standards by the member states increased significantly, thus supporting the free movement of goods regime.[16]

The next case does not follow the trend set by the first ones for good policy grounds. In Case C-226/97 *Lemmens*, Lemmens was prosecuted for drink-driving, the evidence

---

[15] More extensive details of this case can be found in C. Barnard, *The Substantive Law of the EU*, 3rd edn, Oxford University Press, Oxford, 2010, pp 127–35.

[16] Ibid, p 126.

having been obtained by use of a breath-analysis machine, the standards of which had not been notified to the Commission, as required under Directive 83/189. Lemmens sought to argue the inadmissibility of that evidence for his conviction based on the failure of the state to notify the standard and was thus in line with the *CIA* case, which held that a party need not have to rely on a national standard that has not been notified, that his prosecution should not stand. However, the CoJ held that whilst the failure to notify the standard may have hindered the marketing of such machines and as a result the free movement of goods, it did not render unlawful the use of the product as far as national prosecutions for establishing criminal wrongdoing and could not therefore aid the defendant in his claim.

In Case C-443/98 *Unilever Italia SpA v Central Foods SpA*, the principle established in the earlier cases was extended to contractual relations between two individual parties. The Italian state had adopted a food standard before waiting for clearance under the Community Standards Directive requirements. Unilever's supply of olive oil, which did not comply with the Italian standard, was rejected by the purchaser, Central Foods. In an action for payment, Unilever questioned the Italian legislation. The Court of Justice held that the Italian law should not apply, and that the case was no different in principle from the *CIA* case and did not create horizontal direct effects.[17] No obligation had been placed on an individual; it was merely that unnotified national standards could not apply regardless of the possible consequence on the contractual relations and liability between the two parties.[18]

In looking overall at this case law development, the Court of Justice makes it clear that the cases do not establish the horizontal direct effect of directives. For the most part, the cases are mainly narrowly restricted to the application of Directive 83/189 and its replacement Directive 98/34, requiring the notification of technical standards although, as the case law has revealed, this is not the only directive involved. More to the point is that the Technical Standards Directive essentially involves the direct relationship between the member states and the Commission and not, as with most other directives, an obligation on the member states which directly impacts on the relations between individuals and the state or between individuals. The following analysis may therefore represent the position reached. Directives are being interpreted to determine the validity of national law which may affect the legal position of private parties involved in cases. However, any such effect only amounts to preventing reliance on national law that does not conform with EU law, hence the view that the effect, as far as the private parties are concerned, is incidental only. The real or underlying purpose of the CoJ's willingness to uphold the provisions of the directive or, regarded from the other side, not to allow the application of non-conforming national law, is merely then to enforce the public law obligations of the state rather than directly to affect the contractual relations between parties; although, as can be seen in the cases, those relations are affected by obligations imposed on the member states by a directive. Viewed another way, in estoppel terms, parties may rely on the directive as a shield to estop another party from relying on national law that would otherwise harm their interests; they are not using it as a sword to attack the other party. And viewed in a third way, it could be said that incidental effects and indirect effects are both part of the broader view of direct effects in Case 8/81 *Becker* that the national laws should not be allowed to apply where not in compliance with EU law.

[17] Go to the Online Resource Centre for a pictorial representation of this case: **www.oxfordtextbooks. co.uk/orc/foster5e/**.

[18] The Unilever case was approved in Case C-159/00 *Sapod Audic v Eco-Emballages SA* [2002] ECR I-5031. This latter case though highlighted two aspects: that any question of damages arising from a contract being held as breached or unenforceable, was a matter for national law, providing they were not less favourable than those available in purely domestic law cases. We will consider this latter aspect further in Section 6.6.

An equally limited case law development which produces a similar third-party impact arising from the enforcement of a directive is Case C-201/02 *Wells v Secretary of State for Transport*.[19] As in the cases noted previously, a directive does not provide a direct right between individuals but serves to provide a right against another party, in this case a state, which nevertheless has an impact on another individual. Directive 85/337 requires states to carry out environmental impact assessments when authorizing quarrying. The UK had failed to do so and was challenged by Wells. The UK argued that if it now had to carry out the assessment, the quarry owners would have to stop operations, and thus be adversely impacted. The Court of Justice held that such adverse repercussions on a third party do not justify denying an individual the right to invoke the directive against the member state.[20]

These cases also serve to highlight the fact that legal difficulties between individuals or an impact on an individual can be caused by the failure of a member state to comply with an EU law directive. In such circumstances, where a failure adversely and directly affects an individual, there has already been a further judicial remedy provided by the Court of Justice that holds the state liable in damages to compensate the individual for any loss sustained. This is considered next.

6.4 State Liability: The Principle in *Francovich*

State liability is the term given to the action first raised and accepted by the Court of Justice in Cases C-6 and 9/90 *Francovich*, which allows an action by an individual against a member state when the member state has failed to comply with EU law obligations and that has resulted in damage or loss to the individual. The *Francovich* case has provided an alternative, therefore, to both Commission actions against member states to enforce EU law and the difficulties generated by the lack of horizontal direct effects of directives, or indeed the entire absence of direct effects where the EU law provision fails to satisfy the *Van Gend en Loos* criteria. Instead, the state is held liable for its failure, which results in damage to an individual.

The *Francovich* case concerned a claim by Italian nationals against the state for a guaranteed redundancy payment granted by Directive 80/987, which had not been implemented by Italy, or alternatively for damages incurred as a result of the state failing to implement the directive in time. Francovich and other workers were made redundant when the company employing them became insolvent. The company itself had made no payments and, as a result of the insolvency, no action was possible against the company. The Court of Justice had held already, following Art 226 EC (now Art 258 TFEU) proceedings in Case 22/87 *Commission v Italy*, that Italy had breached its obligations by its failure to implement the directive; however, this could not help Francovich and his co-workers, because the purpose of Art 226 is to establish a breach of EC law on the part of a member state and not to provide an individual remedy. The CoJ held that the directive was not capable of direct effects because of the discretion granted to the member states as to the result to be achieved, in particular which authority was to be responsible for setting up a compensation agency. In addition, and part of the problem for the national court in the first place, there was no national law to interpret in conformity with the directive; instead,

---

[19] [2004] ECR I-723.

[20] The quarry owners would be perfectly entitled to seek compensation from the state if they could attribute any losses they suffered to the failure of the state to act in accordance with the requirements of the directive.

relying heavily on the fundamental doctrines of EU law of direct effects and supremacy as outlined in *Van Gend en Loos, Costa v ENEL, Simmenthal*, and *Factortame*, the CoJ determined that the duty of the member states to ensure the full application and enforcement under Arts 10 and 249 EC (now Art 4(3) TEU and Art 288 TFEU), if breached, would give rise to liability. The CoJ rejected the defence that the liability of the state was only a matter for the national laws. It held that the protection of individuals under EU law would be weakened if they were unable to claim damages for loss caused by a member state's failure to comply. It considered, therefore, that the principle was inherent in the scheme of the treaty that member states should make good any damage caused to individuals that was the consequence of a breach of EU law. The CoJ held, though, that the claim required the directive to contain an individual right, which could be determined by the provisions of the directive itself, and that there must be a link between the breach and the damage caused.

The decision in *Francovich* provides individuals with a remedy that stems not from the provision of EU law directly, but from the breach by the member state of the general obligations in Arts 10 and 249 EC (now Art 4(3) TEU and Art 288 TFEU) to comply with EU law. Hence, the case adds a remedy for individuals to fill the gap left where EU provisions have not been implemented by member states or are held not to be directly effective, or because directives are effective only on the vertical and not horizontal axis. Damages are consequently to be assessed in accordance with national procedural rules, subject, however, to overriding EU law principles, which will be considered in the final section of this chapter. The ruling has been described by Bebr as the 'ultimate consequence' of *Van Gend en Loos*.[21] Its focus once again is an individual remedy in the national courts.

The possibility of individuals obtaining damages from member states which breach EU law has mitigated the difficulties caused by directives not having horizontal direct effects, when otherwise they might go away empty-handed. It may have helped the Court of Justice in the 1994 judgment in Case C-91/92 *Faccini Dori v Recreb Srl* to confirm its continued opposition to horizontal direct effects. Whilst stressing the need for national courts to interpret national law wherever possible to comply with directives, the CoJ pointed out that, in circumstances in which the states had caused damage by non-implementation of EU law, the state would be subject to a liability to compensate any loss in line with the principle established in the *Francovich* case.

6.4.1 **The Principle of State Liability Developed**

Since those cases, the Court of Justice has had the opportunity to develop the law, starting with Joined Cases C-46/93 *Brasserie du Pêcheur v Federal Republic of Germany* and *Factortame (No 3)*. *Factortame* concerned the breach of a treaty Article rather than the failure to comply with a directive, but this was held by the CoJ to be no bar to incurring liability. The result of this case law is that the principle of state liability is applicable to all domestic acts and omissions, legislative, executive, and judicial, which are in breach of EU law, directly effective or not, and in principle by all three arms of state.[22] There was, however, a new focus on the seriousness of the breach. *Factortame (No 3)* introduced the revised criteria that if the state is facing choices comparable to the institutions when law-making, which essentially involves conducting a balancing act of many interests, the

---

[21] G. Bebr, 'Case Note on *Francovich*' (1992) 29 CML Rev 557.

[22] The position of national courts will be considered in Section 6.4.2.2. Case C-424/97 *Haim* also makes it clear that liability can result from a breach by any public body which breaches EU law, not just the central organs of state.

seriousness of the breach also must be analogous to that applied to the EU institutions for damage caused unlawfully by legislative acts under Art 288(2) TFEU. This is known as the 'Shöppenstedt formula' (after Case 5/71 *Zuckerfabrik Shöppenstedt*). In order for liability to arise on the part of the member state, there must have been a sufficiently serious breach of a rule of law designed for the protection of individuals. This is the standard applied to damage caused by a legislative act rather than from administrative action. As such, it is a higher standard because, according to the CoJ, the creation of legislative acts involves choices of economic policy and is thus far more difficult to achieve.

The 'sufficiently serious' requirement was further elaborated by the Court of Justice in *Factortame (No 3)*. It suggested that this would be satisfied where a member state had manifestly and gravely disregarded the limits of its discretion. The factors that should be taken into account by the national court assessing this are:

- the clarity and precision of the rule breached
- the measure of discretion
- whether the infringement and damage were intentional or involuntary
- whether the error in law was excusable or inexcusable
- whether there was any contribution to the problem by the EU institutions
- whether any incompatible national law was being maintained.

The cases also confirmed that liability can occur without having to establish a breach by the member state following an Art 226 EC (now Art 258 TFEU) action by the Commission. However, in cases in which the infringement is not yet clear, this could be problematic. If proven, damages arise from the date of the infringement and not from the date of proving the infringement, unlike the Art 260 TFEU penalty which we shall look at in the next chapter.

Both at the Union level and at the state level, further case law has been provoked that helps to determine how serious a breach is required for member states to incur liability. At the Union level, it has proved to be extremely difficult to succeed in damages against the Union institutions.[23] The Court of Justice initially has taken a similar approach in Case C-392/93 *R v HM Treasury, ex p British Telecom plc*. In this case, the UK government successfully argued that its incorrect implementation of a directive was due to a misunderstanding of what the directive required. The CoJ agreed that the directive was capable of more than one interpretation and as there was not a sufficiently serious breach of EU law, no liability arose. Likewise, in Case C-319/96 *Brinkmann*, the incorrect application of a tax classification by Denmark, although financially damaging to a company, was not deemed sufficiently serious to incur liability because it was a mistake in the interpretation of the directive that was made also by other states. These cases show that where discretion is introduced by the possibility of a range of interpretations of the requirements of the EU law, the threshold of liability will be significantly higher and thus more difficult to achieve.

These cases comply with the analysis at the Union level; the higher degree of discretion enjoyed by the institutions in deciding on the appropriate rules raises the bar in proving a sufficiently serious breach to establish liability. Hence, where there is discretion on the part of the member state in deciding exactly what action is necessary to implement the EU law obligation or where there is an excusable error in interpretation, then the

---

[23] According to the AG in the *Factortame* case, up to 1995, only eight awards had been made ([1996] ECR 1029, 1101).

standard of fault for liability will be raised. In line with this view, where the obligation is much clearer and the breach much more obvious, liability will be easier to impose, as in *Francovich* and *Factortame*, noted earlier, and Cases C-5/94 *Hedley Lomas*, C-178/94 *Dillenkofer*, and C-140/97 *Rechberger*, in which liability was established basically on the grounds of straightforward infringements of Community law. Case C-278/05 *Robins* confirms this position, in that the lower the degree of discretion on the part of the member state and the clearer the requirements of the directive, the higher the chance that the member state would incur liability for a mere breach. Conversely, the more ambiguous or unclear a provision of EU law, the more discretion would be enjoyed by the member state in implementing this and the breach would correspondingly have to be much more serious before the member state would incur liability. In the *Robins* case, the argument hinged on the minimum level of protection required under Directive 89/987 for the protection of employees in the event of insolvency of the employer. It was argued that the requirement was imprecise and that this was a view shared by a number of member states. The CoJ accepted the argument and held that, in view of the discretion to interpret the imprecise duty, the UK was not liable.

Case C-352/98 P *Bergaderm* indicates an approach of the Court of Justice to align the rules on the finding of liability for both member states and the Union institutions to that of showing that either manifestly and gravely disregarded the limits of their discretion. On the one hand, in the case of member states where little or no discretion exists, that means that a mere breach will suffice; on the other hand, it may be easier in future for individuals to obtain compensation from Union institutions for mere infringements that have not involved a great deal of discretion on the part of the institution.[24]

In cases in which liability does arise, the determination of the degree of seriousness of the breach, and thus the level of damages to be awarded, if any, remains a question of national procedural law, provided that remedies are not excessively difficult to obtain in the national legal systems and that damages, where applicable, are an adequate remedy. (For further details on the impact on national procedural law of EU law rights, see Section 6.6.)

6.4.2 **The Extension of the *Francovich* State-liability Principle**

The principle of state liability has been extended in two ways: first, to the private sphere, in which it has been seen to determine liability in disputes between two private parties; and, secondly, to the courts of the member states.

6.4.2.1 **Private Parties**

Case C-453/99 *Courage Ltd v Crehan* involved a dispute between two private parties involving a claim that a breach of competition law Art 81 EC (now Art 101 TFEU) by another private party caused loss to the applicant. Building on the foundation cases of *Van Gend en Loos, Costa v ENEL*, and *Francovich*, the Court of Justice reasoned that the extension of the principle of state liability was required by the new legal order for the effective protection of rights that would be undermined if it were not open to any individual to claim damages for loss caused to him by a contract or by conduct liable to restrict or distort competition. *Francovich* liability therefore has been extended to determine liability between private parties where one has caused loss to the other by a breach of EU law.[25]

---

[24] This will be considered further in Chapter 7 (damages actions under Art 340 TFEU).

[25] This has since been followed up in Cases C-295–8/04 *Manfredi*, making it clear that individuals must be able to obtain full compensation as a result of loss caused by a breach of EU competition rules.

6.4.2.2 **National Courts**

Case C-224/01 *Köbler* extends state liability to breaches of EU law rights by the judiciary, which the state would have to compensate. Whilst previous case law under *Francovich* has indicated that the Court of Justice holds the view that state liability is applicable to all branches of government, there was some reticence that this might apply to the judicial branch, given the respect for the independence of the judiciary accorded in representative liberal democracies.[26] However, in Case C-224/01 *Gerhard Köbler v Republic of Austria*, the CoJ held that the state may also, potentially at least, be liable for the breaches of Community law by the national courts provided that they were manifest and sufficiently serious.[27] It was held in the particular case, however, that the breach complained of was not serious enough despite the opinion of AG Leger that the error of Community law made by the Austria Administrative Court was not an excusable error.

The *Köbler* decision has, though, since been approved by the Court of Justice in Case C-173/03 *Traghetti del Mediterraneo SpA v Italy*. In this case, it was alleged that a company had been forced into liquidation as a result of errors in the interpretation of Community law undertaken by the Supreme Court in Italy and that the chance to correct those errors was denied by that court because it did not make a reference to the Court of Justice. In a further action by the administrator of the company, the CoJ held that it could not rule out that 'manifest errors' by a national court would lead to compensation under the principle of state liability. However, it was up to the national courts to decide in each case. The consequence of this slight extension of liability is that liability for damage caused by courts is not limited, as in *Köbler*, to 'intentional fault and serious misconduct' in cases in which that standard would have excluded liability for 'manifest infringement'. In other words, it extends liability to those instances in which national courts have manifestly infringed the law in their interpretation, thus causing damage. The CoJ has also ruled, in Case C-212/04 *Adeneler*, that the obligation the member states have to refrain from making laws that would compromise the aims of a directive also applies to the national courts. The courts of the member states must, therefore, refrain from interpreting domestic law in a manner which might seriously compromise the aim sought. Since that case the CoJ has held in Case C-154/08 *Commission v Spain* that the incorrect interpretation made by a supreme court and the failure to make an Art 267 reference will render the member state liable. The reluctance to go this further step appears thus to have been overcome.[28]

6.5 Article 267 TFEU: The Preliminary Ruling Procedure

As was outlined in the introduction, Art 267 TFEU sets out the preliminary reference procedure by which the courts of the member states can refer questions to the Court of Justice on matters of EU law.

Article 267 TFEU has as its purpose the uniform interpretation and application of EU law in all the member states, and contributes to legal certainty by ensuring that EU law means the same thing in each and every member state—even more important now with

---

[26] See H. Toner, 'Thinking the Unthinkable? State Liability for Judicial Acts' (1997) 17 YEL 165.

[27] The logic of the conclusion confirms that Art 258 actions against member states apply to all parts of the state, all of which may trigger liability. The Court of Justice regards, arguably correctly so, each member state as a single entity, therefore it is not possible to absolve one part of the state, even those constitutionally independent, thus the national courts, from liability if they are responsible for a breach of EU law. See Chapter 7, Section 7.2.1 for the Art 258 action.

[28] This case is also considered in Chapter 7, Section 7.2.1.3.

a Union of 28 member states. It was designed to work with the cooperation of national courts by providing the means whereby national courts would not give their own interpretations to EU law or decide themselves on its validity. The intended relationship was of equality and cooperation, rather than hierarchy or an appeal system, so the CoJ should provide only guidelines and not direct the national courts. It provides for the sharing of jurisdiction over EU law between the Court of Justice and the national courts. The main task of the CoJ is therefore to interpret and rule on the validity of EU law, so that a national court can reach a conclusion on a case involving EU law. The national courts' role in the process is to determine the facts of a case, ask a question of the Court of Justice when one arises, and later to apply the ruling to the facts of the case. The Court of Justice should not concern itself with the application of the ruling that it has made or advise the national court how to apply the ruling. It is to be noted that, within the national courts, it is the right of the national court to decide whether to refer a question and not an individual right of appeal. The role of the national courts post-Lisbon has been bolstered by the provision of Art 19(1) TFEU that 'Member States shall provide remedies sufficient to ensure effective legal protection in the fields covered by Union law'.

The Lisbon Treaty has amended the previous version of this Article to make it clear that the CoJ can interpret all acts of not only the main institutions, but also all bodies, offices, and agencies of the Union. It has also extended the Court of Justice's jurisdiction to provide preliminary rulings for the area of freedom, security and justice, previously excluded under one of the Maastricht Treaty pillars. Furthermore Art 267 TFEU has been provided with an urgent procedure in paragraph 4, which along with the expedited procedure is considered in Section 6.5.5.1. Article 267 jurisdiction though is excluded from the Common Foreign and Security Policy (Art 275 TFEU).

Article 267 TFEU was the instrument that allowed the CoJ to develop the doctrines of direct effects and supremacy, vital for the development of the system of remedies under EU law that have been so helpful to individuals: for example, in getting around the restrictions placed on them by the strict *locus standi* requirements of the direct actions, or where the Commission has been slow in ensuring that the member states comply with their obligations. Having created such doctrines, the CoJ receives numerous questions specifically asking whether a particular provision has direct effects.[29]

A number of details of this procedure need to be considered to gain a true picture of how this works including: the questions that may or may not be referred; the timing of a question; whether there is discretion or an obligation on any of the national courts to refer; and the effects of a ruling by the Court of Justice on both the EU legal order and the national legal order.

First of all, this section will look at the issue of which national bodies can make references that will be accepted by the CoJ.

6.5.1 **Which Law-adjudicating Bodies Can Refer?**

The Court of Justice has accepted references from a varied number of bodies that are not courts in the strict sense, but which nevertheless decide legal issues based on EU law, including administrative tribunals, arbitration panels, and insurance officers. The determination of what is an acceptable court or tribunal is a question for the CoJ and is not dependent on national concepts. Certain criteria have now been established by which it

---

[29] Article 267 references make up the bulk of the case law heard by the Court of Justice: 404 cases from 632 in total in 2012.

may reasonably be determined whether a particular body may refer to the CoJ for guidance under Art 267 TFEU. For example, it was clear from *Van Gend en Loos* that not only judicial, but also administrative, tribunals were acceptable. Whilst the majority of fora in the member states deciding legal matters pose no problem, it is those bodies that lie either partially or entirely outside the state legal system that raise the question of whether they are suitable for the purposes of Art 267 TFEU. The following cases have helped to define the scope of acceptable bodies.

In Case 61/65 *Vaassen*, a reference was received from the arbitration tribunal of a private mine employees' social security fund. The Court of Justice held that the facts that the powers to nominate members, and to give approval to both the panel itself and rules changes, were in the hands of a government minister, and that the panel was a permanent body operating under national law and rules of procedure qualified it as a court or tribunal in the eyes of Community law. Case 246/80 *Broekmeulen v HRC* concerns a reference made by the Appeal Committee of the Dutch Medical Professions Organization. This was held by the CoJ to be acceptable because it was approved by, and had the assistance and considerable involvement of, the Dutch public authorities, its decisions were arrived at after full legal procedure, the decisions affected the right to work under Community law and were final, and there was no appeal to Dutch courts. However, in the next cases jurisdiction was refused. In Case 138/80 *Borker*, a reference from the Paris Bar Association Council on the right of a French lawyer to appear as of right before German courts was refused on the ground that there was no lawsuit in progress and the Bar Council was not therefore acting as a court or tribunal called upon to give judgment in proceedings intended to lead to a decision of a judicial nature. In Case 102/81 *Nordsee v Nordstern*, a reference from a privately appointed arbitration body was refused despite the fact that the arbitrator's decision based on law, including Community law, was binding. The CoJ held that because there was no involvement of national authorities in the process, there was not a sufficiently close link to the national organization of legal remedies and thus the arbitrator could not be regarded as a court or tribunal for Art 234 EC (now 267 TFEU). Jurisdiction was also refused in Case C-24/92 *Corbiau v Administration des Contributions* because a reference had been made from the Office of the Director of Taxation, a fiscal body that acted in both an administrative and judicial capacity and thus lacked sufficient independence to be regarded as a court or tribunal for the purposes of Art 234 EC (now Art 267 TFEU).

Case C-54/96 *Dorsch* is particularly instructive, because the CoJ took an opportunity to spell out the criteria to be taken into account in deciding whether the body is an acceptable one, including: whether the body is established by law; whether it is permanent; whether its jurisdiction is compulsory; whether its procedure is *inter partes* ('between two parties', i.e. adversarial); whether it applies rules of law; whether it is independent; and whether the decision rendered is of a judicial nature.

A refusal was made in Case C-53/03 *Syfait v GlaxoSmithKline*, in which a question raised by a national competition law authority was refused on the grounds that it was too closely connected to the state. It was closely supervised by a minister and thus its members' independence was compromised and, further, its authority could be assumed by the EU Commission under Community competition law rules.

In view of this case law, it would seem that it is not critical to acceptance if the body is private or there is not an appeal from its decision. A strong indicator is the level of involvement by national authorities. Whether all these criteria will be strictly applied in all cases in the future is uncertain. This is because the lack of an appeal in a case may lead to instances in which the national body itself has to interpret EU law without guidance if the CoJ is unwilling to accept jurisdiction, something that must be less than desirable from an EU point of view.

There is now a reformulated set of guidelines issued by the Court of Justice on most aspects of preliminary ruling references that briefly mentions the originating courts.[30]

6.5.2 **The Question Referred: Relevance and Admissibility**

This section covers a number of connected issues all relating to whether the question raised by the member state body is one that is either relevant or not, or is an admissible question as far as the Court of Justice is concerned. To a degree, the response to some of the questions sent to the CoJ by member state courts has varied according to the increasing caseload of the CoJ. Where relevant and admissible, the content and form of the question must also be decided, and this will also be considered. Any question should, of course, relate to a matter of EU law and questions should relate to either the interpretation of EU law or, in the case of secondary EU law, its validity also.

Article 267 TFEU itself contains little by way of guidance, except to provide that if the member state court or tribunal considers that a decision on a question of EU law is necessary to enable it to give judgment, it may or shall request a ruling from the Court of Justice. The relationship or partnership that is supposed to hallmark this procedure requires that, once requested, a ruling be given by the CoJ to complete the EU side of the procedure. Unfortunately, this is not always as clear-cut in practice and questions arise as to who decides whether a preliminary ruling is necessary: the parties to the case, the national court, or the Court of Justice. According to the letter of the Art 267 TFEU procedure, it is for the national court to decide to refer a question. The drafters of the treaty did not envisage this system providing a remedy for individuals; however, it is often assumed that references will be made on the initiative of one of the parties. The national courts themselves are not obliged to refer. In Case C-344/04 *IATA*, the Court of Justice held that a national court is not obliged to refer a question of validity on the argument of one of the parties unless the court itself is sure that a good case for invalidity has been made.

This analysis continues to be the stated view of the Court of Justice, as provided in Case C-236/02 *J Slob v Productschap Zuivel*, in which the CoJ held:

> It should be stated at the outset that it is for the national court alone to determine the subject matter of the questions which it wishes to refer to the Court. The Court cannot, at the request of one party to the main proceedings, examine questions which have not been submitted to it by the national court.

The initial approach of the CoJ was very welcoming, and it was happy to correct improperly framed references and accept them. In Case 16/65 *Schwarze v EVGF*, a national court requested a ruling on the interpretation of Community law and the validity of national law in conflict. The CoJ concluded that it was concerned more with the validity of a Community act and was therefore able to answer. It has consistently refused to rule on the validity of national laws; however, it has often reformatted such a question in order to give an answer to the underlying reason for the reference; that is, whether the EU law conflicts with the national law and should take priority. A further exception exists in respect of questions about national law, where the national law is directly and unconditionally based on or refers to EU law and is binding on the national court. See Joined Cases C-297/88 and C-197/89 *Dzodzi*, and Case C-346/93 *Kleinwort Benson* in which it was held that such references would be accepted providing that the relationship between

---

[30] Information note on reference from national courts for a preliminary ruling, updated and reissued as Recommendation 2012 (OJ 2012 C338), which will be reproduced in N. Foster (ed), *EU Treaties and Legislation*, latest edn, Oxford University Press, Oxford.

EU law and national law was direct and unconditional and the resulting law was binding on the national court.

Turning to further case law, the first of which should by now be familiar, according to the Court of Justice in Case 26/62 *Van Gend en Loos*, the finding by a national court that it needs to refer is not to be questioned by the Court of Justice. This position was confirmed in Case 6/64 *Costa v ENEL*, in which the CoJ held that it is a decision of the national court alone whether a decision on the question is necessary for it to give judgment. Furthermore, in Case 106/77 *Simmenthal*, the CoJ has declared that it was unable to review the facts of the case presented to it; that is, it will not go behind the national decision. However, as the number of cases and back-log increased in the 1980s and 1990s,[31] the CoJ was seen to be less willing to accept all references and has, from time to time, declined to give a ruling on questions referred to it on the grounds that no real question arises, or that such references are an abuse or misuse of Art 267 TFEU. This is not to say, however, that it has operated a crude quota to cut down references, because the number of cases that were regarded as irrelevant or inadmissible is minimal.[32]

Confirmation that it is the court making the reference that engages or disengages the Court of Justice's involvement is Case C-210/06 *Cartesio Oktató és Szolgáltató*, which involved a procedural appeal against an order to refer to the Court of Justice from a court in Hungary whereby the higher appeal court may approve the request to withdraw the reference. The Court of Justice held that it would continue to hear the case unless withdrawn by the court making the reference and not the appeal court. The Court of Justice made clear that the appeal procedure against the order was a matter of national law, but the Court of Justice itself would not take direct cognizance of that appeal decision.

6.5.2.1 Lack of Relevance, Clarity, or Basic Information

In Case 93/78 *Mattheus*, a disputed contract's continuation was determinable by the entry of Spain, Portugal, and Greece to the Community. When a reference was made to help to resolve the disputed contract, the Court of Justice held that this was a matter to be determined by the member states and the potential new states, and it refused jurisdiction. The question raised must be one that is justiciable before the courts and one raised by the court and not by the contractual agreement of the parties. The CoJ has also held that facts and issues must be sufficiently clearly defined, in Case C-320/90 *Telemarsicabruzzo SpA*. In Case C-83/91 *Meilicke v ADV/ORGA*, the CoJ held that the questions raised could not be answered by reference to the limited information provided in the file, in which case the CoJ would be exceeding its jurisdiction in answering what was really a hypothetical question.

A formal ground for refusing a judgment is provided following a change to the rules of procedure in 1991 and now contained in Art 99 of the 2012 Rules, whereby the CoJ was given the authority to dispose of a case in which the question is manifestly identical to one already answered, but only, however, if the CoJ consults and circulates the observations

---

[31] Preliminary rulings before the Court of Justice: 1961—1; 1965—7; 1969—17; 1973—61; 1977—84; 1981—108; 1985—139; 1989—139; 1993—204; 1998—264; 2004—249; 2007—265. Taken from the general website entry page for judicial statistics of the Court of Justice: **http://curia.europa.eu/jcms/jcms/Jo2_7032/**.

[32] Judge David Edwards, 'The Preliminary Reference Procedure: Constraints and Remedies', paper delivered at the CCBE/College of Europe Colloquium, 'Revising the European Union's Judicial System, Assessing the Possible Solutions, Revising the Preliminary Ruling Mechanism', Bruges, 19–20 November 1999, p 5, estimated that only 27 cases had been rejected since the 1980 *Foglia* case in the nine years up to 1999.

of all parties first. This is so procedurally cumbersome that the course of action is rarely employed. The CoJ has, however, issued guidelines in 1996, updated to 2012,[33] to the national courts to help them to decide whether a reference should be made. The CoJ's view is that it is up to the member states' courts to determine if they need a ruling and that the Court of Justice should answer such questions, however formed. References generally, though, should be clear and succinct, but sufficiently complete to give the CoJ a clear understanding of the factual and legal context of the main proceedings. National courts should explain why an interpretation is necessary in their view to enable them to give judgment. After another change to the rules of procedure, the CoJ may now, after hearing from the AG, seek clarification from the referring court if the question or issue is unclear (Art 101 2012 Rules of Procedure).[34]

6.5.2.2 No Genuine Dispute or an Abuse of the Procedure

The two *Foglia v Novello* cases are of special importance. Case 104/79 *Foglia v Novello (No 1)* concerned a contract for wine between a French buyer, Novello, and an Italian supplier, Foglia. Clauses stipulated that the buyer and the carrier (Danzas) should not be responsible for French import duties, which were contrary to Community law. These were, however, charged on the French border and subsequently reimbursed by Foglia. Foglia sought to recover from Mrs Novello, who denied responsibility to pay them on the basis that they were illegally charged by the French authorities. The Italian judge made a reference to the Court of Justice asking whether the French tax was compatible with the treaty. The CoJ rejected the reference on the grounds that there was no genuine dispute between the parties and that the action had simply been concocted to challenge French legislation. The CoJ considered this to be an abuse of the Art 234 EC (now Art 267 TFEU) procedure, particularly because there were remedies available to dispute the tax before the French courts. However, not satisfied by this, the Italian judge made a further reference, *Foglia v Novello (No 2)*, in which he specifically pointed out that the previous case marked a radical change in the attitude of the Court of Justice to a national court's decision to refer. He asked the CoJ to give guidelines on the respective powers and functions of the CoJ and the referring court. The CoJ held that its role was not to give abstract or advisory opinions under Art 234 EC, but to contribute to actual decisions, and that although discretion is given to the national courts, the limits of that discretion are determinable only by reference to Community law.

Whilst *Foglia* may be regarded as a rarity, it is not alone, as is witnessed by Case C-318/00 *Bacardi-Martini v Newcastle United*, in which a French law prohibiting the advertising of alcohol was at the centre of a dispute between Newcastle United and the advertisers, the products of which had been advertised at the home game of Newcastle, but unlawfully broadcast in France. The Court of Justice dismissed the reference after seeking clarification from the English High Court as to why Community law would have a bearing on the case, in that another member state's law was in question but where English law was applicable to the case. The CoJ concluded that it did not have sufficient material to make a ruling.

A refusal of jurisdiction on the grounds of it being an abuse of the procedure took place also in Case C-188/92 *TWD Textilwerke*. A Commission decision addressed to Germany was not challenged within the two-month time limit under Art 230 EC (now Art 263

---

[33] An updated version of which can be found at OJ 2012 C338/1. An earlier version of the guidelines was introduced into the UK Rules of Procedure 'Practice Direction for the Court of Appeal', 14 January 1999 and Civil Procedure Rules, Pt 68: **http://www.dca.gov.uk/civil/procrules_fin/contents/parts/part68.htm**.

[34] N. Foster (ed), *EU Treaties and Legislation*, latest edn, Oxford University Press, Oxford.

TFEU) for a direct challenge, but instead via the national court. The CoJ held this to be an abuse of the procedure for not acting within the time limit, despite the consequence that this seems to go against the promotion of Art 267 TFEU as a vehicle for realizing individual rights in the face of the continued strict application of *locus standi* requirements under Art 263 TFEU, considered in the next chapter.

6.5.2.3 References Nevertheless Accepted

The decision in *Foglia v Novello* has been cited as authority to the Court of Justice in subsequent cases. In Case 46/80 *Vinal v Orbat*, which involved Italian law in Italy, the government claimed that the case was not admissible because it was just an excuse to challenge national law under Art 234 EC (now Art 267 TFEU). The CoJ, after obtaining further information from the parties and assuring itself that there was a genuine underlying dispute, accepted the reference. The CoJ however also accepted a reference in Case C-412/93 *Leclerc-Siplec* despite the fact that it was clear that the parties had concocted a dispute; it was to challenge French law in a French court. Thus the different treatment from the *Foglia* case was that it was the national law being challenged in the same member state's courts rather than the law of another member state. The CoJ is though also concerned with whether the dispute giving rise to the reference is genuine or not, but not necessarily rejecting a reference if it is not. The combination of a concocted dispute and the law of another member state would appear to be fatal.

In Case 14/86 *Pretore di Salo v X*, there were no actual proceedings between two parties (namely, not *inter partes*)—something regarded previously as one of the criteria needed to be classed as a court for the purposes of Art 267 TFEU. The case involved investigative proceedings only of an Italian magistrate to determine whether a criminal offence might have been committed by a person or persons unknown in the case in which a river had been found to be seriously polluted. Nevertheless, when a question of a possible breach of Community law was referred to the CoJ by the magistrate, it was held to be admissible. The CoJ held that it was up to the national court to decide if a reference was necessary to help it. If there had been a breach of EU law, it was worth pursuing the matter further, if not, then there would be no case to answer. In Joined Cases C-297/88 and C-197/89 *Dzodzi v Belgium* and C-28/95 *Leur-Bloem*, the CoJ has given rulings in what were essentially purely internal matters involving the application of free movement of persons rules to nationals undertaking no cross-border movement, where the national decision was based on Community law. The CoJ considered that if it did not do so, Community law might be interpreted differently when the member states applied it in an internal situation; therefore, for the sake of uniformity, the reference was accepted.

Finally, we have Case C-150/88 *Eau de Cologne v Provide*, concerning a contractual payment dispute before a German Court, in which an Italian law at the root of the problem was brought into question. The reference from the German court was accepted by the CoJ as it held that the case differed from the earlier *Foglia* litigation, involving, as it did, a genuine dispute. This would seem to indicate that the matter of a non-national law is, in fact, justiciable before the Court of Justice. It remains to be seen if that is a settled point.

6.5.2.4 The Question Referred: Overall View

Although these cases, and others like them,[35] would appear to be contradictory, the case of *Foglia v Novello* must be viewed on its own merits that the Court of Justice did not wish

---

[35] Refer to S. Douglas-Scott, *Constitutional Law of the European Union*, Longman, Harlow, 2002, pp 234–342, or to T. Tridimas, 'Knocking on Heaven's Door: Fragmentation and Defiance in the Preliminary Reference Procedure' (2003) 40 CML Rev 9.

to encourage national courts to challenge the validity of laws of other member states, especially when there existed the possibility of proceedings in the French courts to challenge the French law and from which an Art 234 EC (now Art 267 TFEU) reference could be launched if deemed necessary by the French judge. Otherwise, the CoJ may decline to take a case under Art 267 TFEU in a number of situations: where the question referred is hypothetical; where it is not relevant to the substance of the dispute; where the question is not sufficiently clear for any meaningful legal response; and where the facts are insufficiently clear for the application of the legal rules. The decision to refer is now assisted by the provision of the Court of Justice Guidelines updated to 2012. An order for a reference should include:

- a statement of the facts essential to a full understanding of the legal significance of the main proceedings
- an exposition of the applicable national law
- a statement of reasons for the reference
- a summary of the main arguments of the parties.

The cases highlight that a combination of involving non-national law with a contrived dispute will almost certainly be fatal to the chances of the reference whereas the presence of just one of those factors, not necessarily, as was seen in Case C-150/88 *Eau de Cologne v Provide*.

The cooperation between national courts and the Court of Justice still exists, but the CoJ no longer simply accepts anything put before it. It has begun to exercise more positive control over its own jurisdiction in the manner similar to superior national courts. This approach is reflected in the case law arising from Art 267(2) and (3) TFEU, considered in the following sections.

6.5.3 A Discretion or Obligation to Refer?

Whether there is a discretion or obligation to refer a question, once raised, depends first on which sentence of Art 267 TFEU applies. Article 267(2) TFEU[36] states that any court may refer if it considers it necessary to reach a decision in the case, whereas Art 267(3) TFEU states that courts against the decision of which there is no judicial remedy shall bring the matter before the Court of Justice.

6.5.4 The Discretion of Lower Courts

Courts not falling within Art 267(3) TFEU are not obliged to refer, but have a wide discretion to refer at any stage of the proceedings and in any sort of proceedings: see Cases 13/61 *De Geus v Bosch* and 28/62 *Da Costa en Schaake*. Part of the reasoning for this rule is that an aggrieved party can appeal to a higher court if necessary. In Cases 146 and 166/73 *Rheinmühlen-Düsseldorf*, the CoJ made it quite clear that any national court that considers that a ruling on Community law will help it to decide an issue has the discretion to decide regardless of any national rules of precedent or referral. This was confirmed by the CoJ in Case C-312/93 *Peterbroeck Van Campenhout v Belgium*, in which the Court of Justice held that a national procedural rule, which prevented a

---

[36] Here, the figures in brackets refer to the paragraphs; although they are not actually labelled as such in the treaty, it is, however, how they have been referred to over the years.

national court from raising a matter of EC law of its own motion concerning the compatibility of a national law with EC law, was itself contrary to Community law and that national courts must set aside rules of national law preventing the Art 234 EC (now Art 267 TFEU) procedure from being followed. Case C-213/89 *Factortame (No 1)* also confirms this point that national law rules of any status must not prevent Community law from applying.[37]

6.5.5 The Timing of the Reference

In principle, national courts can refer at any stage of the proceedings and in any sort of proceedings, as has already been noted in Cases 13/61 *De Geus*, 93/78 *Mattheus v Doego*, and 14/86 *Pretore di Salo*. In Cases 36/80 and 76/80 *Irish Creamery Milk Suppliers*, the Court of Justice advised that the optimum time would be when facts have been established and any questions involving national law only had been settled. The CoJ has also provided extrajudicial guidelines about when a reference should be made if considered necessary. Points 18 and 19 of the 2012 Guidelines also recommend that the facts and legal context should be established, and both parties' views heard, before the reference is sent.

6.5.5.1 Urgent and Expedited References

Allied to the topic of the timing of the reference are two special procedures, which have been developed by the CoJ to amend the Article 267 procedure in special circumstances. These are the accelerated or expedited procedure and the urgent procedure that are provided for under Article 23a of the Protocol on the Statute of the Court of Justice and detailed further in Articles 105–6 and 107–14, respectively, in the Rules of Procedure of the Court of Justice.

Under the expedited or accelerated procedure, a national court may request that this procedure be utilized where it is a matter of exceptional urgency and the case will be listed immediately, giving the parties 15 days to submit observations. The President of the Court will decide on a proposal from the Judge-Rapporteur, after hearing the AG. From its introduction in 2008 to 2012, 25 applications were not granted, but in the same period, eight were granted. These cases were heard between two and four months from application. The urgent preliminary ruling procedure relates specifically to the area of freedom, security, and justice (now Title V TFEU) and was introduced to deal quickly with cases involving the detention of persons.

The details of the urgent procedure are now set out in Arts 107–14 TFEU and Decision 2008/79.[38]

In this route, the written procedure can be omitted or undertaken electronically. From 2008 to 2012, eight were rejected and 16 were heard, with a length of proceedings of between 1.9 and 2.5 months. Whilst it is useful to know that these procedures exist, it is unlikely that you will need to know the details.

None of which impinges on the ultimate discretion of national courts provided by Art 267 TFEU, which can decide when to refer and which criteria are necessary to decide this question.

---

[37] The inroads that the Art 234 EC (now Art 267 TFEU) procedure has made into national procedural law will be considered further in Section 6.6.

[38] For further information on these procedures refer also to the latest Annual Report of the Court of Justice, see **http://curia.europa.eu/jcms/jcms/Jo2_7000/**.

6.5.6 **Courts of Last Instance**

In this category, an initial problem exists in deciding which courts are 'courts of last instance' for the purpose of Art 267(3) TFEU. The case law of the Court of Justice makes it clear that the relevant court is the highest court for the case, rather than the highest court in the member state. In Case 6/64 *Costa v ENEL*, there was no right of appeal from the Italian magistrates' court because the sum of money involved was so small. The CoJ held that national courts against the decisions of which there is no judicial remedy must refer a question of Community law to the Court of Justice. In most instances, this is an adequate answer, and Art 267(3) TFEU should apply to those proceedings that deny an appeal or judicial review and thus become last instance. However, the situation in member states may not be so easy to determine: for example, in the UK it is possible, and it has happened, that the Court of Appeal and the House of Lords (now the UK Supreme Court) Appeal Committee can refuse leave to appeal in a case that has been decided by the Court of Appeal. This has the result that the lower of the two courts then becomes the court of last instance and results in a denial of the consideration of EU law to an applicant, because the case itself has closed and cannot then be referred. This was the case in *Magnavision v General Optical Council (No 2)*, in which the issue of Community law was raised in the first case under this name, but was neither considered nor referred, nor was an appeal to the House of Lords allowed. The applicant then applied to the High Court, stating that the previous refusal meant that the High Court became the court of last instance for the purposes of Art 234 EC (now Art 267 TFEU). This application was also refused on the grounds that the case had been closed and the High Court also refused to refer this question to the Court of Justice, thus denying a consideration of Community law points.

The same situation occurred when the Court of Appeal and the House of Lords refused leave to appeal in the case of *Chiron Corporation v Murex Diagnostics Ltd (No 8)*, which meant that the Court of Appeal became the last-instance court. Once again, it was too late for a reference to be lodged, because the case had been decided and appeals are only considered once the case has finished—a point expressly acknowledged by the House of Lords Appeal Committee in the case. The Court of Justice had also recognized this problem in the Swedish Case 99/00 *Criminal proceedings against Lyckeskog* and had suggested that, in such circumstances, the Supreme Court considering the appeal should consider whether a reference was necessary. In order both to overcome the unfortunate earlier UK position and to take account of the *Lyckeskog* case, a change of the UK appeal procedure was deemed necessary and put into place.[39]

6.5.7 **Avoiding the Obligation to Refer: The Development of Precedent and *Acte Clair***

Whilst Art 267(3) TFEU provides the general rule that final courts must refer, over the years the increase in cases being referred has been seen to have led to a more circumspect consideration by the Court of Justice as to the appropriateness of a reference and, in two

---

[39] The House of Lords (now called the Supreme Court) Appeal Committee made a recommendation that was adopted as an exception to the rule that no reason be given for the refusal to grant leave to appeal. In cases in which it is contended that Community law may have a bearing, the Appeal Committee will give the reason why it considers the matter comes within the reasons of the *CILFIT* case and thus obviates the need for a reference. If a reference is considered necessary, the House of Lords (now Supreme Court) will make one before deciding whether an appeal can be made. See the Practice Directions in Civil Appeals, 34, January 2006: http://www.publications.parliament.uk/pa/ld199697/ldinfo/ld08judg/bluebook/bluebk-1.htm#34.

cases spanning a period of 20 years, the CoJ has outlined the circumstances in which it is not necessary to make a reference. This has arguably created a form of precedent in the EU legal order, and may have introduced changes to the relationship between the national courts and the Court of Justice. The CoJ has held that it is no longer necessary to make a reference where the provision in question has already been interpreted by the CoJ, or the correct application is so obvious as to leave no scope for any reasonable doubt and thus no question of EU law arises to be decided.

6.5.7.1 There Is a Previous Ruling on the Point

Cases 28-30/62 *Da Costa* raised the same question as had previously been asked in the *Van Gend en Loos* case. The CoJ referred to its previous judgment in *Van Gend en Loos* as the basis for deciding the issue and advised that a materially identical question would, if the national court wished, excuse the obligation to refer. (See also now the 2012 Rules of Procedure of the CoJ, Art 99, which confirms the position stated in *Da Costa*.)[40]

6.5.7.2 The Answer Is Obvious (*Acte Clair*)

The judgment by the Court of Justice in Case 283/81 *CILFIT* expanded the decision of *Da Costa*. In *CILFIT*, the Italian Supreme Court asked the Court of Justice directly in what circumstances it need not refer. The CoJ replied that, in addition to the reason given in *Da Costa*, a court might not refer if the correct application, but not interpretation, may be so obvious as to leave no scope for any reasonable doubt that the question raised will be solved. This was argued by many writers[41] to have positively introduced into the EU legal system the French law doctrine of *acte clair*, by which the national court need not make a reference if it considers the answer to the question on EU law obvious. Whilst to a degree this is true, it is not an entirely accurate representation of the judgment. The judgment in *CILFIT* is more restrictive than a straightforward application of *acte clair*. The CoJ qualified it by stating that the national court must be convinced that the matter is equally obvious to courts of other member states, that it is sure that language differences will not result in inconsistent decisions in member states, and that Community law must be applied in light of the application of it as a whole with regard to the objectives of the Community. These criteria would be extremely difficult, if not actually impossible, to fulfil if followed to the letter—especially now in a Union of 28 member states[42]—but were arguably provided so as to maintain an appearance of the bridge of equality between the EU and national legal systems. The 2012 Recommendations, Point 12, are clear in listing as an exception to the requirement to submit the ground that 'the correct interpretation of the rule of law in question is obvious', although the restrictive interpretation of it from the *CILFIT* case remains.

6.5.7.3 Questions of Validity

A question of the validity of secondary EU law must be referred to the Court of Justice by courts of last instance but note that the validity of primary law including the treaties,

---

[40] See also Point 12 of the Art 267 TFEU Guidelines, which makes the same point. E.g. in 2012, 36 cases were ordered to be removed from the Register.

[41] See, among many: C. Barnard and E. Sharpston, 'The Changing Face of Art 177 References' (1997) 34 CML Rev 1113; D. O'Keeffe, 'Is the Spirit of Art 177 under Attack?' (1998) EL Rev 509; H. Rasmussen, 'The European Court's *Acte Clair* Strategy in *CILFIT*' (1984) 9 EL Rev 242.

[42] The court or judge would have to speak all 24 official languages to the extent of understanding the legal systems of 28 countries plus EU law. Does such a person exist?

protocols and EU Rights Charter cannot be questioned.[43] In Case 314/85 *Firma Foto-Frost v Hauptzollamt Lübeck-Ost*, the CoJ held that national courts could not decide for themselves that Community law provisions were invalid because of the danger that otherwise uniform Community laws would be declared invalid in some member states but not in others. If this question were raised and an answer not possible from previous judgments, then national courts would be obliged to refer the question to the Court of Justice. If an appeal is still possible under national rules, this could still be done as an alternative. This point has been written into the Court of Justice Guidelines, Points 15–17. However, in Case 66/80 *ICC*, which involved the questioning of a Community provision already held to be declared invalid by the CoJ in a previous case, the CoJ makes it patently clear that, although such a judgment is addressed primarily to the court that requests the original ruling, it can and should be relied on by other national courts before which the matter arises, thus obviating a need to refer the same question again.

Latterly, the point has been confirmed in Case C-461/03 *Schul* that only the Court of Justice has the authority to declare EU law to be invalid and further, in Case C-344/04 *IATA*, that a national court is not obliged to refer a question of validity on the argument of one of the parties unless the court itself is sure that a good case for invalidity has been made.

6.5.7.4 Failure to Refer by National Courts

To some extent, the fears that *acte clair* will be abused by national courts have been realized in some cases that have come to light. In *R v London Boroughs' Transport Committee*,[44] decided in 1992, the House of Lords refused to refer a question to the Court of Justice, claiming that EC law was obvious, which, on the facts, appeared arguable. In 1998, a Greek court, the Council of State, itself interpreted EC law (then Art 126(1) EC) in the case of *Katsarou v Greek State*[45] against the interests of an applicant seeking mutual recognition of qualifications as *acte clair* and thus, as far as the Greek court was concerned, removing any obligation to refer. These cases may result in injustice to the litigants affected, at best the possibility of getting the EU law point heard is denied. This denial of rights may be the price to be paid now for having a more flexible arrangement under Art 267 TFEU, an aspect which is considered at the end of this section. In Case C-62/00 *Marks & Spencer plc*, the Court of Appeal in the UK considered that individuals could rely on the direct effect of sufficiently precise and unconditional Community law provisions only if, and insofar as, the provision had not been properly implemented in national law. If a directive had been properly implemented, as in the present case, it could not be relied on. However, the Court of Justice held that it would be inconsistent with the legal order of the Community if individuals were able to rely on a directive that had been incorrectly implemented, but not able to rely on it where the national authorities applied the correctly implemented legislation in a way that was actually incompatible with the directive.[46]

---

[43] It may be that general principles considered to be of primary status may also be beyond questioning their validity. See Chapter 4 and the hierarchy and status of the sources of EU law, Section 4.3.

[44] [1991] 1 WLR 828.

[45] Judgment 3457/1998 of 25 September 1998, *Armenopoulus* 1999, 125, as cited in T. Tridimas, 'Knocking on Heaven's Door: Fragmentation and Defiance in the Preliminary Reference Procedure' (2003) 40 CML Rev 9.

[46] On paper all was well but the implementing law was either interpreted incorrectly or applied in a way which failed to comply with the original directive.

Even an attempt to obtain a remedy where a reference was denied has thus far not been successful. In Austria, in Case C-224/01 *Köbler*, the Austrian Supreme Administrative Court had decided a point of Community law itself, claiming it to be clear after withdrawing a reference to the Court of Justice seeking a ruling on the same point. The applicant in the case then sought damages from the Austrian state for the loss that he had suffered as a result of the decision in the first case, which he claimed to be contrary to Community law. On a reference in the second case, the Court of Justice held that the Community law point was *not* clear and that the Austrian court was *not* entitled to take the view that the matter was clear. However, the Austrian court's infringement for the purposes of the state liability action was not sufficiently serious for the Court of Justice and Köbler lost his claim, although making it clear that a state could be held liable for an incorrect judgment where the breach was sufficiently serious. The Court of Justice did, however, state that the Austrian court, from which there was no appeal, should have made a reference and should have applied it. Generally, the Court of Justice held that courts of last instance must make references in order to prevent rights conferred on individuals by EU law being infringed. As such, the judgment may represent a refinement of the *acte clair* principle in the EU legal order by removing its availability to courts of last instance. Confirmation of this is needed, though, from the CoJ before this can be stated with certainty, because it was in last-instance courts that it was first applied.

A gloss on *Köbler* has been provided by the Court of Justice in Case C-173/03 *Traghetti del Mediterraneo SpA v Italy*. In the case, it was alleged that a company had been forced into liquidation as a result of the errors in the interpretation of Community law undertaken by the Supreme Court in Italy and that the chance to correct those errors was denied by that court, which did not make a reference to the Court of Justice. In a further action by the administrator of the company, the CoJ held that it could not rule out that 'manifest errors' by a national court would lead to compensation under the principle of state liability. However, it was up to the national courts to decide in each case. In other words, it extends liability to where national courts have manifestly infringed the law in their interpretation, which has caused damage; however, as yet no applicant has succeeded in obtaining damages in these circumstances. An alternative corrective action against courts of last instance which err in interpretation and fail to refer a question to the CoJ, might be an enforcement action by the Commission under Art 258 TFEU, similar to Case C-154/08 *Commission v Spain* (See Chapter 7, Section 7.2.1.3).

6.5.8 The Effect of an Art 267 TFEU Ruling

6.5.8.1 The Effect on the Court of Justice

In strict terms, in the absence of a system of binding precedent in the EU legal order, a ruling by the Court of Justice is binding and effective in that case only, and there is no further binding effect on the CoJ. However, although it is not restrained by any doctrine of precedent, the CoJ tends to follow previous decisions to maintain consistency and will cite previous judgments, or parts of a judgment, as a basis for a current decision. (For example, see the cases relating to the definition of the term 'worker' in Chapter 9 on the free movement of persons.) In this way, a development and build-up of legal principles as in common law countries does take place.

In other circumstances, the CoJ has been known to overrule previous decisions without much commotion when it feels that the situation warrants it. Under the Art 340 TFEU actions for damages section, Case 25/62 *Plaumann* and the later overruling Case 4/69 *Lütticke* decided that an Art 288 EC (now Art 340 TFEU) action could be mounted as an independent action and not only if preceded by an Art 230 EC (now Art 263 TFEU) action to annul. The *Plaumann* case was later confirmed as remaining the present state of the law in Cases C-50/00 *UPA* and C-263/02 P *Commission v Jégo-Quéré*.

6.5.8.2 The Effect on the National Courts

An Art 267 TFEU ruling is a mandatory judgment and not an advisory opinion, and, as held in Cases 28/62 *Da Costa* and later in Case 69/85 *Wünsche*, is fully binding on the national court. A ruling of the Court of Justice is then to be treated in each member state according to how its own system of law regards authoritative judgments. As far as the UK is concerned, national courts are bound under treaty obligations to apply the ruling received from the Court of Justice to the facts of the case; and where that national court is the Supreme Court (formerly the House of Lords), the ruling is consequentially binding on all lower courts (see Case 12/81 *Garland v BREL*).

The 2012 Recommendations, Point 35, provide that the Court of Justice wishes to see how its judgment has been applied in the national proceedings, and would welcome a copy of the national court's final decision.

From the UK, there is now an informative case in which the national court judge refused to apply the ruling of the Court of Justice because he considered the CoJ to have rendered an unacceptable ruling in making findings of fact in a case concerned with trademark infringement of football merchandise. However, Case C-206/01 *Arsenal FC v Matthew Reed* was overruled on appeal by the Court of Appeal and the ruling of the Court of Justice was applied conscientiously.[47]

There have been times where the Court of Justice, by analogy with Art 264 TFEU, which provides the power to determine that effects of a regulation may be regarded as definitive, has limited the temporal effect of a judgment, especially when the result of a judgment would have given rise to previously unforeseen extensive and probably harmful economic consequences. For example, in Cases 43/75 *Defrenne (No 2)* and C-262/88 *Barber*, the judgments were held not to be retroactive, but only effective from the date of judgment, or for claims already commenced, because they would unexpectedly have imposed on employers potentially substantial pay-outs for numerous backdated claims based on the rulings.[48]

On validity, as noted earlier, the CoJ held in Case 66/80 *ICC* that although a declaration of invalidity was directly addressed to the referring court only, it was sufficient reason for another court to regard the declaration as generally binding; however, the discretion to refer remains.

In Case C-453/00 *Kühne & Heitz*, the CoJ appears to be making a demand that all national authorities, including the national courts, regard its interpretative rulings as applicable in all of their activities. It did so on the grounds that general principles, especially legal certainty, demanded that this form of precedent should apply. It is difficult to argue anything else in light of the supremacy of EU law.[49]

6.5.9 The Evolution of Art 267 TFEU References

Article 267 TFEU has allowed the Court of Justice to develop a system of remedies, including direct effects, indirect effects, and state liability, which can be secured in the member states' courts so that future cases need not be referred to the CoJ. The increase in

---

[47] See A. Arnull, 'Case Note on *Arsenal Football Club plc v Matthew Reed*' (2003) 40 CML Rev 753–69; and G. Davies, 'Of Rules and Referees: *Arsenal Football Club plc v Matthew Reed*' (2003) 28 EL Rev 408–17.

[48] Both of these rulings will be considered in further detail in Chapter 11.

[49] The implications for national procedural rules is considered in Section 6.6.

cases and increasing case back-log is argued to have led to a change in attitude on the part of the CoJ, and it is now less willing to accept all references without question. It has, in a limited number of cases, provided the national courts with the grounds for not making a reference when, under a strict reading of the treaty, a reference would be required.

As a result of the development of this system of remedies and judicial devices to avoid references, a form of precedent (the *Da Costa* case) means that a Court of Justice ruling now has a far more general importance than only to the parties in a single case and appears to have placed the CoJ at the apex of the systems of national courts. Inevitably, this also appears to have changed the nature of the relationship from a symbiotic or horizontal one to more of a vertical or hierarchical relationship, although some might describe the original understanding of a relationship of equals and cooperation as somewhat illusory.[50] These developments have then given rise to what is described as a form of conscious, or deliberate, sectoral delegation of responsibility[51] over EU law to the national courts, which then also become enforcers of EU law in their own right in cases in which there exists a Court of Justice precedent on which to rely. Hence, a more hierarchical relationship than was ever intended by the drafters of the treaty or the member states has ensued.

This view is supported by the change to the CoJ's Rules of Procedure (Art 99), which allows the CoJ to return cases with a reasoned order where a question is identical to a question on which the CoJ has already ruled, where the answer to such a question may be clearly deduced from existing case law, or where the answer to the question is not open to reasonable doubt. It sends a clear signal to the national courts that they, too, could have reached the same conclusion, thus strengthening further the evolution of the Art 267 TFEU procedure. Whilst part of this evolution, the *acte clair* development has, however, caused some concern, especially when it is abused by member state courts, which results in injustice to individuals who are denied their EU law rights, although the *Köbler* and *Traghetti* cases discussed earlier appear to narrow the scope for the application of the doctrine to courts, other than last-instance courts where it began.

6.5.10 **Reforms and Future**

In the context of the growing numbers of references, many reforms have been considered and changes suggested. Those most recently made (including the case law changes noted earlier) include the expansion of the General Court (formerly the Court of First Instance) jurisdiction to include Art 267 TFEU references (under Art 256 TFEU), and the ability to set up specialized courts (formerly judicial panels) under Art 257 TFEU. Furthermore, two procedural changes have been made in order to expedite specific types of case in which delay might lead to injustice: an accelerated procedure, set out in Art 104a of the CoJ's Rules of Procedure, whereby the national court may request the reference to be considered as a matter of urgency and which, if accepted, subjects the stages of the case to reduced time limits; and the urgent procedure relating to persons in custody, now incorporated into the body of Art 267 TFEU by the Lisbon Treaty, which requires the CoJ to act with the minimum of delay, and allows for both the written procedure and the opinion of the AG to be omitted. It is also to be found in the Rules of Procedure, Art 104b.

---

[50] See, among others: S. Douglas-Scott, *Constitutional Law of the European Union*, Longman, Harlow, 2002, pp 249–52, and the articles cited in Further Reading.

[51] See P. Craig and G. de Búrca, *EU Law: Text, Cases, and Materials*, 5th edn, Oxford University Press, Oxford, 2011, p 477.

Further suggestions for reform include:

(a) limiting the national courts able to make a reference by removing the right of first-instance courts to refer

(b) only allowing novel or complex cases, that is, those involving new questions of law

(c) permitting national courts to make suggestions regarding the answer

(d) permitting national courts to decide themselves, subject to an appeal to the Court of Justice

(e) setting up regional Community courts, again with an appeal to the Court of Justice.

These last two suggestions represent a much more radical shake-up of the system and seem very unlikely in the short to medium term.

6.5.11 **Interim Measures within an Art 267 TFEU Reference**

Interim measures may also be highly relevant to EU law questions that are the subject of a reference to the Court of Justice, particularly because a reference may take an average of 16 months (at the time of writing). In that time, the lack of relief may lead to great damage and, in many cases, insolvency of the companies involved. The clearest leading case on this is Case C-213/89 *Factortame*, in which the CoJ held that, regardless of national rules on whether interim relief should be granted, if rights under Community law were at stake pending a ruling on a reference on the substantive question, interim relief should be granted. Cases C-143/88 and 92/89 *Zuckerfabrik Süderdithmarschen AG* involved the possibility of granting interim relief in a preliminary ruling on the validity of a Community law provision. The CoJ took the opportunity to provide guidelines for the national courts along the lines of those developed already by the CoJ under its Art 243 EC (now Art 279 TFEU) jurisdiction in direct actions.[52] It held that relief should only be granted provided that there was sufficient evidence before the CoJ that serious doubts existed about the validity of the Community law in question, the case was urgent, and relief was necessary to avoid serious and irreparable damage. The grant of interim relief was extended to positive, rather than only suspensory, measures in Case C-465/93 *Atlanta Fruchthandelsgesellschaft*, which concerned whether a licence to import bananas be granted whilst awaiting the ruling on whether a Community act regulating the banana market was valid. The CoJ held that national courts could do this, provided that they did so in light of existing Community case law, the Community interest in the matter, the consequences for the Community regime, and the effect on all interested parties. Hence, a common rule has been established that is nevertheless subject to national legal procedure, but only to the extent that the EU law right is not endangered, which topic is considered in further detail in the section following.

6.6 National Procedural Law and the System of Remedies

It has already been mentioned that the development of individual remedies, as established and developed by the Court of Justice, has added a second system of vigilance to

---

[52] Which will be dealt with in Chapter 7, under Art 258 TFEU actions.

the existing direct enforcement of EU law by the Union institutions and member states. Inevitably, though, because direct and indirect effects, incidental effect, and state liability are individual remedies that are pursued before the national courts, their overall effectiveness is dependent on national rules of procedural law that are per se outside the jurisdiction and direct influence of the EU law and the Court of Justice. These rules can affect and interfere with the realization of EU law rights at the national level and, in comparison between member states, this situation can be complicated by different rules on standing, or time limits, or burden of proof, or because certain remedies are simply not recognized in some member states.

However, because procedural rules were not within the scope or competence of any of the treaties, they were originally considered to be within the reserved and exclusive competences of the member states. This idea is wrapped up within the term 'national procedural autonomy'. To counter this, new principles of EU law have been developed to protect individual rights, which can be referred to generally as 'principles of effective legal protection' of EU law rights.

6.6.1 The Principle of National Procedural Autonomy

In the absence of harmonized rules on procedure, rights conferred by EU law must be exercised before national courts in accordance with the traditions laid down by national procedural rules that, in strict terms, are autonomous from the EU legal system. To what extent, though, should they be respected where they interfere with EU law rights? There are general arguments for and against, including that the rule of law and legal certainty would be undermined if not entirely respected, or that differences in remedies would arise between member states that may distort the uniformity of EU law and the realization of the internal market. On the other hand, it is arguably better to leave the provision of remedies to those who know their own systems best.

The position of the Court of Justice up to the 1980s was one that essentially respected national procedural rules, subject to certain guidelines as developed through its case law. In Case 33/76 *Rewe-Zentralfinanz*, the CoJ held that national courts were entitled to apply national procedural limits provided that national rules are no less favourable for Community law rights as for domestic situations and do not make the Community right impossible to realize. In Case 45/76 *Comet*, the CoJ held that it was up to each member state to determine the procedural conditions governing those actions, but that such conditions cannot be less favourable than those relating to similar actions of a domestic nature and should ensure the protection of the rights that citizens have from the direct effect of EU law. Thus, where an EU law right is involved, national procedural law must not deprive a litigant of their rights under EU law, so that the general principle of Art 18 TFEU (ex Art 12 EC) that there be no discrimination on the grounds of nationality is not breached.

From the first cases and other early case law, stem the principles of practical impossibility and equivalence; the latter holds that EU law rights should be treated in the same way as national rights. It was already seen in relation to cases in respect of supremacy, such as Case 6/64 *Costa v ENEL*, that the CoJ will not allow national rules to stand in the way of a reference to the CoJ or the supremacy of EU law. As was also seen in the *Simmenthal* and *Factortame (No 2)* cases, it is not only national substantive laws that must give way to EU law, but also any national rules of procedure, including constitutional rules that might get in the way of the effective application of an EU law right, regardless of the origin of these rules. However, it was clearly stated by the CoJ in Case 158/80 *Rewe v Hauptzollamt Kiel* that no new remedies were intended to be created in the national courts to ensure the observance of Community law over and above that already existing in national law, but it became clear that, in some cases, further intervention was necessary. The alternative, which would require the agreement of the member states to harmonize national procedural rules or to replace them with common Union rules, is neither politically acceptable, because member states do not wish to hand over control of their legal systems, nor practically possible, due to the very different and nationally idiosyncratic legal systems in existence.

6.6.2 Further Intervention by the Court of Justice

Whilst the principle of equivalence would ensure the non-discriminatory application of national rules, this does not go far enough to remedy the situation in all cases. National remedies must also provide an effective remedy. Any rule that actually prevents individuals from relying on an EU law right, such as the Spanish domestic procedural rule considered by the Court of Justice in Case C-118/08 *Transportes Urbanos y Servicios Generales*,[53] discussed later in this section, would be incompatible with the principle of effective legal protection.

In Case 14/83 *Von Colson*, discussed earlier in relation to indirect effects, the compensation offered by the national court for the discrimination suffered was the payment of the rail fare home. This was held not to be a dissuasive and adequate remedy. The remedy, according to the Court of Justice, must guarantee real and effective judicial protection, and must have a real deterrent effect. Case C-213/89 *Factortame* highlighted just how radical the solution had to be to ensure the protection of EU law rights in the national courts, including in that case the right to interim relief against the UK Crown, something that was not constitutionally possible previously. Case C-208/90 *Emmott* concerned a national three-month time limit in which to bring benefits claims and the time ran from the date on which the claim arose, under the relevant legislation, in this case, the entry into force date of a Community directive. However, it was not clear, due to the faulty transposition of a Community directive, that the applicant's claim was valid and the claim was rejected in any event as being out of time. The CoJ held that whilst reasonable time limits are acceptable in respect of a claim based originally in Community law, time can only run from the date on which the directive is implemented properly and the applicant's rights are clear. In Case C-271/91 *Marshall II*, the award of compensation to Ms Marshall for discrimination was set at a statutory ceiling that was much lower than the real loss of earnings suffered. The Court of Justice held that unlawful dismissal based on a Community right should be subject to full compensation, including interest, despite the interpretation of the Court of Appeal that, under national law, damages could not include interest.

In a much more interventionist mode, EC law has also required national courts to provide specific and new forms of remedy, most notably in Case C-6/90 *Francovich*, and the establishment of the right to damages from the state where liable, as discussed fully in Section 6.4.

Thus, national rules are respected to the extent that they do not clash with an EU law right, but where they prevent an EU law right from being realized or applied in some way, then the national procedural law must give way. This period of judicial activism

---

[53] [2010] ECR I-635.

and creativeness on the part of the Court of Justice, particularly the *Emmott* case, which took things surprisingly far, gave way to a less intrusive period, because generally the CoJ was reacting to being criticized for its overtly judicial activism. Cases though do appear still before the CoJ, which considered in Case C-118/08 *Transportes Urbanos y Servicios Generales* a Spanish domestic procedural rule which required the exhaustion of domestic remedies before an applicant would be allowed to bring an action for damages against the Spanish state for a breach of EU law. This was not, however, a requirement when taking an action for a breach of national constitutional law. It was held by the CoJ to be a breach of the EU principle of equivalence.

6.6.3 **A More Balanced Approach**

A more balanced approach was shown by the Court of Justice in Case C-339/91 *Steenhorst-Neerings* involving the retroactive limitation of a claim to benefits to one year under Dutch law, which was held to be acceptable to the CoJ. This apparent step back from *Emmott* means that reasonable time limits are acceptable, even though these can vary from state to state. However, *Steenhorst-Neerings* was distinguished from the rule in *Emmott*, which applied after the three-month deadline expired to prevent bringing an action at all, because in *Emmott* the state itself had contributed to the failure of the applicant to comply with the strict time limit by advising a wait-and-see attitude to another case also questioning similar rights to equal treatment in payments. The rule in *Steenhorst-Neerings*, in contrast, permitted a claim, but limited the retrospective payments under it to one year. In Case C-188/95 *Fantask*, the CoJ gave general grounds for accepting time limits that could result in differences between the member states. It held that national time limits would continue to apply even in situations in which a directive had not been properly implemented into national law for reasons of legal certainty, and to protect the taxpayer and authorities. The case itself concerned a national five-year limitation period for the recovery of debts, held to be acceptable. Thus, no Community (EU) rule for the recovery of tax payments was established. Two further cases, both from Spain, concerned a bar on presenting claims too late and after the initial proceedings had closed. The first, Case C-168/05 *Claro v Milenium SL*, concerned an annulment action against an arbitration decision before which a claim should have been made that the arbitration clause was unfair, but had not been. Spanish law prohibited it being raised in the subsequent proceedings which would have meant there could be no contesting the alleged unfair clause. On reference to the CoJ, it effectively held that the national rule preventing the annulment action also deprived the consumer of the right to challenge an unfair clause, contrary to Directive 93/13 and that the national court is required to consider that plea even though not within national rules. Case C-40/08 *Asturcom v Rodriguez Noguiera* involved a similar attempt to challenge an arbitration decision but this time outside of the time limits of the domestic court. The CoJ this time accepted the final closure of the case in the interests of ensuring the sound administration of justice.[54]

Two similar cases concerned more closely with procedure within the action rather than time limits, were, however, decided differently. Both concerned a variation of a national procedural rule that states that it is up to the parties to introduce legal arguments and not the court. However, if EU law, which may be relevant, is not introduced, then a party may suffer as a result. In these circumstances, it was argued the national court must either introduce the EU law itself or at least make a reference to the Court of Justice, whether or

---

[54] [20016] ECR I-10421 and [2009] ECR I-9579.

not this infringed the national rule. Questions were referred as to whether, indeed, the national procedural law must give way. In Case C-312/93 *Peterbroeck van Campenhout*, the CoJ held that national procedural laws should not prevent references being made, but this was seemingly contradicted by Cases C-430–1/93 *Van Schijndel*, in which a similar procedural rule that prevented a reference taking place was upheld as acceptable because the rule applied also in similar domestic circumstances, and was there to ensure legal certainty and clarity. Somewhat unhelpfully in *Van Schijndel*, the CoJ held that each rule of procedural law, and thus each case, has to be judged on its merits, taking into account the rights of defence, legal certainty, and the role of the national procedure, before determining whether it renders the application of Community law impossible or excessively difficult. This would seem only to provoke further references to the Court of Justice each time a slightly new procedural law is brought into question.

In Case C-326/96 *Levez v Jennings*, the CoJ considered a UK procedural law that limited the period of claim for damages in sex discrimination cases to a period not exceeding two years running backward from the date of commencement of proceedings. The CoJ acknowledged that, in the absence of a Community regime on the matter, it was for member states to determine procedural rules governing Community law rights, provided that they are equivalent to similar domestic actions and were effective. A limit of two years was not criticized. However, Ms Levez had been misinformed or deliberately misled by the employer as to the higher earnings of a male predecessor, and had only learned the truth on leaving her job. Under such circumstances, the CoJ held that, if applied, the rule would serve to deprive an employee from effective enforcement of Community law because it would be almost impossible to obtain arrears of remuneration and would allow employers to avoid paying damages through deceitful means. In such circumstances, the rule would be manifestly incompatible with principles of EU law. Whilst following the *Emmott* case, each case requires a clear demonstration that the particular facts applicable to it will lead to a particular unjust result. This is not, though, consequentially very useful in helping to determine further cases.

The cases considered earlier under *Francovich* state liability are also relevant to this discussion, in that they also demonstrate the impact on the national legal systems of remedies developed by the Court of Justice, and the extension of those remedies against both other individuals under EU law and the courts of the member states. These EU remedies were simply not available previously, although some member states may have had national remedies that would have achieved the same result. The next case considers and summarizes the scope of the EU law remedy.

Case C-432/05 *Unibet* is a case referred to the Court of Justice by the Swedish Supreme Court about the compatibility of a Swedish law on lotteries with Community law. In order to determine this, the national court enquired specifically about the scope of the principle of effective judicial protection and whether Community law required a member state's legal order to provide a self-standing action for a declaration that a provision of its national law conflicted with Community law, and whether, in waiting for the determination, interim relief must be granted. The Court of Justice held that the principle of effective judicial protection is a general principle of Community law stemming from the constitutional traditions common to the member states, which is also enshrined in Arts 6 and 13 of the European Convention on Human Rights (ECHR) and which has also been affirmed by Art 47 of the Charter of Fundamental Rights of the European Union. It confirmed that Art 10 EC (now Art 4(3) TEU) required member states to ensure judicial protection of individuals' rights and refer to its earlier case law on this, including Cases 33/76 *Rewe*, 45/76 *Comet*, and C-312/93 *Peterbroeck*, noted earlier. The CoJ held, though, that, in the absence of a Community rule, the member states were left to decide according to their own procedural rules. Consequently, the principle of effective judicial protection does not require the national legal order of a member state to provide for a free-standing action for an examination of whether national provisions are compatible with Art 49 EC (now Art 56 TFEU), provided that other effective legal remedies, which are no less favourable than those governing similar domestic actions, make it possible for such a question of compatibility to be determined as a preliminary issue. Furthermore, the principle of effective judicial protection of an individual's rights under EU law must be interpreted as requiring it to be possible in the legal order of a member state for interim relief to be granted until the competent court has given a ruling on whether national provisions are compatible with EU law, where the grant of such relief is necessary to ensure the full effectiveness of the judgment to be given on the existence of such rights. This essentially confirms the position previously laid down in Case C-213/89 *Factortame*, which provides that this should be no more difficult to obtain than the application for interim relief in cases concerned with domestic law.

French constitutional procedural law was considered by the Court of Justice in Joined Cases C-188–9/10 *Melki and Abdeli*. The rule that national courts must refer first to the Conseil constitutionnel any questions of constitutionality including that of EU law, appeared to undermine the rights of parties to make preliminary ruling references to the Court of Justice under Art 267 TFEU. The CoJ held, though, that the rule did not offend EU law provided that national courts remained free nevertheless to refer to the Court of Justice and to disapply any national law they considered to be contrary to EU law.

The principle of effective judicial protection thus ensures that, regardless of the existence of national law remedies, EU law rights are subject to protection before the national courts.

6.6.4 Conclusions

National procedural autonomy is still protected under the EU legal order and is still the general rule, but the Court of Justice has intruded into the area by developing the demands for effectiveness and equivalence, or by providing new remedies in the member states, with the aim of ensuring a balance between the objectives to protect the national procedural autonomy and to protect the effectiveness of EU law. Until there is an agreement by all member states to try to harmonize procedural law, a very difficult task at best, the ad hoc case law development witnessed to date is not likely to change. Indeed, the only change in this respect introduced by the Constitutional Treaty and retained by the Lisbon Treaty is quite modest. New Art 19(1) TEU provides as a general statement that member states must provide remedies that are sufficient to ensure effective legal protection in the fields covered by Union law, which merely reflects (but in far simpler language) the *Unibet* case, considered earlier.

Further Reading

Books

BROBERG, M. and FENGER, N. *Preliminary References to the European Court of Justice*, Oxford University Press, Oxford, 2010.

PRECHAL, S. *Directives in EC Law*, 2nd edn, Oxford University Press, Oxford, 2005.

PRINSSEN, J.M. and SCHRAUWEN, A. (eds) *Direct Effect: Rethinking a Classic of EC Legal Doctrine*, 2nd edn, Europa Law Publishing, Groningen, 2004.

WARD, A. *Judicial Review and the Rights of Private Parties in EU Law*, 2nd edn, Oxford University Press, Oxford, 2007.

Articles

ANAGNOSTARAS, G. 'Preliminary Problems and Jurisdiction Uncertainties: The Admissibility of Questions Referred by Bodies Performing Quasi-judicial Functions' (2005) 30 EL Rev 878.

ANAGNOSTARAS, G. 'The Quest for an Effective Remedy and the Measure of Judicial Protection Afforded to Putative Community Law Rights' (2007) 32 EL Rev 727.

ARNULL, A. 'The Principle of Effective Judicial Protection in EU Law: An Unruly Horse?' (2011) 36 EL Rev 51.

BEBR, G. 'Casenote on *Francovich*' (1992) 29 CML Rev 557.

BEUTLER, B. 'State Liability for Breaches of Community Law by National Courts: Is the Requirement of a Manifest Infringement of the Applicable Law an Insurmountable Obstacle?' (2009) 46 CML Rev 773.

BRINKHORST, L. 'Case Note on the *Grad* and *SACE* Decisions' (1971) 8 CML Rev 380–92.

BROBERG, M. '*Acte Clair* Revisited: Adapting the *Acte Clair* Criteria to the Demands of the Times' (2008) 45 CML Rev 1383.

BROBERG, M. AND FENGER, N. 'Preliminary References as a Right—But for Whom? The Extent to which Preliminary Reference Decisions Can Be Subject to Appeal' (2011) 36 EL Rev 276.

BROBERG, M and FENGER, N. 'Variations in Member States' Preliminary References to the Court of Justice: Are Structural Factors (Part of) the Explanation? (2013) 19 ELJ 488.

CRAIG, P. 'The Legal Effects of Directives: Policy, Rules and Exceptions' (2009) 34 EL Rev 349.

DAVIS, R. 'Liability in Damages for Breach of Community Law: Some Reflections on the Question of Who to Sue and the Concept of "the State"' (2006) 31 EL Rev 69.

DICKSON, J. 'Directives in EU Legal Systems: Whose Norms Are They Anyway?' (2011) 17 ELJ 190.

DOUGAN, M. 'When Worlds Collide: Competing Visions of the Relationship Between Direct Effect and Supremacy' (2007) 44 CML Rev 931.

DRAKE, S. 'Scope of Courage and the Principle of "Individual Liability" for Damages: Further Development of the Principle of Effective Judicial Protection by the Court of Justice' (2006) 31 EL Rev 841.

EASSON, A. 'The Direct Effect of EEC Directives' (1979) 28 ICLQ 319–53.

EILSMANSBERGER, T. 'The Relationship between Rights and Remedies in EC Law: In Search of the Missing Link' (2004) 41 CML Rev 1199.

GRANGER, M.-P.F. 'National Applications of *Francovich* and the Construction of a European Administrative *Jus Commune*' (2007) 32 EL Rev 157.

GUTMAN, K. 'The Evolution of the Action for Damages against the European Union and its Place in the System of Judicial Protection' (2011) 48 CML Rev 695.

KOMAREK, J. 'In the Court(s) We Trust? On the Need for Hierarchy and Differentiation in the Preliminary Ruling Procedure' (2007) 32 EL Rev 467.

LEFEVRE, S. 'The Interpretation of Community Law by the ECJ in Areas of National Competence' (2004) 29 EL Rev 501.

LOCK, T. 'Is Private Enforcement of EU Law through State Liability a Myth?: An Assessment 20 Years after Francovich' (2012) 49 CML Rev 1675.

LOHSE, E. 'Fundamental Freedoms and Private Actors: Towards an "Indirect Horizontal Effect"' (2007) 13(1) EPL 159.

NASSIMPIAN, D. '. . . And We Keep on Meeting: (De)fragmenting State Liability' (2007) 32 EL Rev 819.

PRECHAL, S. 'Member State Liability and Direct Effect: What's the Difference After All?' (2006) 17 EBL Rev 299.

PRECHAL, S. and DE VRIES, S. 'Seamless Web of Judicial Protection in the Internal Market' (2009) 34(1) EL Rev 5.

TIMMERMANS, C. 'The European Union's Judicial System' (2004) 41 CML Rev 393–405.

TRIDIMAS, T. 'Knocking on Heaven's Door: Fragmentation and Defiance in the Preliminary Reference Procedure' (2003) 40 CML Rev 9.

VAJDA, C. 'Liability for Breach of Community Law: A Survey of the ECJ Cases Post-*Factortame*' (2006) 17 EBL Rev 257.

Special Report of the EU Commission of 15 July 2009 on the 'Case Law of the Court of Justice of the European Union Connected with Claims for Damages Relating to Breaches of EU Law by Member States': available at **http://eur-lex.europa.eu/LexUriServ/LexUriServ.do?uri=C OM:2010:0281:FIN:EN:PDF.**

7

The Direct Jurisdiction of the Court of Justice

7.1 Introduction

This chapter considers the actions that are commenced before the Court of Justice, the most important of which are the actions to enforce EU law against the member states and actions against the Union institutions. It includes actions by the Commission and other member states against a member state (Arts 258–60 TFEU), judicial review of acts of the institutions (Art 263 TFEU), the action against the institutions for a failure to act (Art 265 TFEU), and actions for damages (Arts 268 and 340 TFEU). Interim measures under Arts 278 and 279 TFEU will also be considered, but staff actions under Art 270 TFEU will not. Finally, actions arising from the Commission enforcement of EU competition law against individuals will also be considered briefly.

7.2 Actions against Member States

Direct actions against the member states to ensure compliance with EU law were the first part of the system of dual vigilance enforcement of EU law noted in Chapter 6. The treaty-based remedies were provided from the outset in the EC Treaty, and at first were not regarded as being particularly efficient, although improvements have been made. Breaches of member states' obligation to comply with EU law, which is now imposed generally by Art 4(3) TEU, are officially established by the Court of Justice following a procedural action against the state. Article 258 TFEU is the treaty basis for Commission action against member states for failures to fulfil obligations under the treaties. The Commission is acting under its duties to ensure the application of the treaties and to oversee the application of Union law under its duties outlined in Art 17 TEU. In addition, Art 259 TFEU provides for actions by one member state against another member state. Furthermore, in support of both these actions, Art 260 TFEU imposes an obligation on member states to comply with judgments of the Court of Justice. This was revised by the TEU and provides a system of penalties that can be imposed on member states. This will be considered towards the end of this section.

7.2.1 Enforcement Actions by the Commission

In contrast to other international organizations, the EU has a much more effective control mechanism under Art 258 TFEU to ensure compliance with its own laws by member states. The procedure, though, also serves the purposes of re-inforcing the establishing and efficacy of the policies of the EU and the clarification of EU law where its meaning and requirements are sometimes disputed.

Article 258 TFEU provides:

> If the Commission considers that a Member State has failed to fulfil an obligation under the Treaties, it shall deliver a reasoned opinion on the matter after giving the State concerned the opportunity to submit its observations. If the State concerned does not comply with the opinion within the period laid down by the Commission, the latter may bring the matter before the Court of Justice of the European Union.

In addition to the action under Art 258 TFEU, there are further actions that the Commission can take against the member state in respect of specific subject matters: Art 108(2) TFEU in respect of infringements of state aids provisions; Art 114(9) TFEU in respect of derogations from the internal market; and Arts 346–8 TFEU in respect of emergency security measures. The Commission is empowered under those Articles to take alleged infringements directly before the Court of Justice without having to go through the procedural requirements of Art 258 TFEU; however, none of those actions will be covered in any further detail in this volume.

7.2.1.1 The Breach

Article 258 TFEU is silent as to what constitutes a 'breach' of a duty. The Court of Justice has determined that a breach can be constituted not only by an act of a member state, but also by the *failure* to act by a member state. A failure to act is most often observed where a member state has failed to implement EU legislation, mainly directives, or has failed to remove national legislation that is now in conflict or inconsistent with EU legislation, or has implemented the directive incorrectly, either deliberately, inadvertently, or incompletely, or has considerably delayed its implementation or has failed to stop administrative practices which get in the way of the application of EU law. Failing to comply with a previous judgment of the Court of Justice also constitutes a breach, as will be considered later. Increasingly now, as there are general requirements to notify technical standards to the Commission and to notify the Commission of when and how directives have been implemented in national law, failure to do so may and probably will result in an infringement proceeding being commenced. Apart from the general good-faith clause (otherwise termed the 'solidarity clause') under Art 4(3) TEU and the Art 18 TFEU duty not to discriminate on the grounds of nationality, there are more specific duties under the various chapters of the treaties and the very detailed duties imposed by secondary legislation. Thus, breaches may arise from the treaties, secondary legislation, international agreements, Court of Justice decisions, and general principles.

There are numerous examples of breaches by a member state to be found in the chapters of this book.

Failure to remove inconsistent legislation constitutes a breach even if the authorities no longer apply the national legislation and apply the EU rules in preference. For example, in Case 167/73 *Commission v France*, provisions of the French Maritime Code restricted the numbers of foreign workers on French vessels, but the French pleaded that the national law was not being applied. The Court of Justice held that this law, even if it is not being applied, might influence the behaviour of people who rely on the law being applied and thus its non-repeal would create uncertainty. Also, in Case C-265/95 *Commission v France (Spanish Strawberries)* over a period of time the French enforcement agencies simply stood by and observed illegal action by French farmers in destroying Spanish goods as they came over the border. It was held by the Court that doing nothing or little to prevent other persons from restricting the movement of goods, when action could and should have been taken, will also constitute a breach of an obligation.

7.2.1.2 Identifying and Reporting Breaches

A possible breach can come to light by the Commission's own investigations or from the failure of the member states to notify how they have implemented EU law, because they are required to do so now under secondary legislation.[1] In those cases, the failures are most likely to be notified to the Commission by its own implementation monitoring software.[2] Breaches can be reported by other member states, the European Parliament and other institutions and agencies of the EU, or concerned or affected individual citizens or companies. Note that, with regard to these last, they are unable to force the Commission to do anything about a complaint that has been lodged (see Case 247/87 *Star Fruit Company v Commission*, also discussed in Section 7.2.2.1). The Art 258 TFEU action was not intended to be an individual remedy, so whilst complaints might have been welcomed by the Commission, that was as far as the complainant's interest in the matter formally extended. The Commission was thus neither under an obligation to act on the complaint nor even to inform the complaining individual of what, if anything, was being done. This was further confirmed in Case T-47/96 *SDDDA v Commission* in which the General Court held that there was no right for individuals to require the Commission to adopt a particular position.

Although the formal position of an individual in the matter has not changed, the Commission has demonstrated more sympathy with the position of individual complainants in its annual reports on the monitoring and application of EU law,[3] and also publicizes its progress much more widely than before by issuing notices in the Official Journal (OJ). The Commission has set up a number of systems now to assist it in monitoring the application of EU laws as well as infringement complaints and procedures. The *CHAP* system registers and monitors complaints from individuals but also keeps the complainants informed, the result of which is that many complaints are satisfied before further action might be necessary on the part of the Commission against the member states.[4] It also takes into account the impact of breaches on individuals and affected economic operators for the purposes of calculating the amount of penalty.[5]

7.2.1.3 Defendants in an Art 258 TFEU Action

A breach of EU law can arise from any part of a state and is not restricted to purely governmental action or inaction. For example, in Case 77/69 *Commission v Belgium (Belgium*

---

[1] See e.g. Art 33 of Directive 2006/54, which provides: 'Member States shall communicate to the Commission the text of the main provisions of national law which they adopt in the field covered by this Directive.' (Reproduced in N. Foster (ed), *EU Treaties and Legislation*, latest edn, Oxford University Press, Oxford.)

[2] The increases in the use of this can be found in the latest annual monitoring report, at the time of writing, for 2013: **http://ec.europa.eu/atwork/applying-eu-law/infringements-proceedings/annual-reports/index_en.htm#**.

[3] In this respect, see generally 31st Annual Report on the Monitoring and Application of Community Law, see n 2.

[4] See **http://ec.europa.eu/community_law/infringements/infringements_decisions_en.htm**. See also the details on the CHAP complaints handling system at **http://ec.europa.eu/atwork/applying-eu-law/docs/annual_report_31/com_2014_612_en.pdf**.

[5] This is not to compensate the individuals affected or redress the balance but to reflect the overall seriousness of the breach—that is, put crudely, to reflect how many individuals may be adversely affected from none to a whole industry or sector of the economy. See point 16.4 of SEC (2005) 1658 final.

Wood case), the government pleaded that it should not be held responsible for the negligence of the Belgian Parliament, which, being out of session, was not able to implement a Community directive in time. The Court of Justice held that 'Obligations arise whatever the agency of the state whose action or inaction is the cause of the failure to fulfil its obligation even in the case of a constitutionally independent institution'. Thus actions of the legislature, the executive, and local and regional authorities are included and even the failures of federal authorities (Cases C-227–30/85 *Commission v Belgium*). It could include and now has included breaches by the judiciary in a member state for rendering an incorrect decision. In Case C-129/00 *Commission v Italy*, the failure to repeal a law that was interpreted by the Italian courts in such a way as to make a Community law right excessively difficult to realize was held by the CoJ to be a breach on the part of the Italian state.[6] In Case C-154/08 *Commission v Spain*, the Spanish state was held in breach for the erroneous interpretation of the Sixth VAT Directive by the Spanish Supreme Court, which also did not make a preliminary ruling reference to the CoJ. The national ruling was subsequently followed by many other Spanish courts and led to the national tax administration causing considerable economic harm. The defence of the independence of the judiciary raised by Spain was rejected by the CoJ. This ground-breaking judgment, if followed in the future, allows the Commission to police the judgments of the national courts and, whilst correct in EU law, is not something one supposes the national supreme or constitutional courts or member state governments will be too happy about.

The unlawful actions of individuals in breach of EU law with whom the state is compliant or against whom the state takes no action will also render the state liable. In Case 249/81 *Commission v Ireland (Buy Irish)* a 'buy Irish' campaign was administered by the Irish Goods Council, a registered private company. However, because the Irish government largely sponsored the campaign to buy Irish products, appointed the management committee, and set the broad outlines of the campaign, it was held accountable for the breach of Article 28 (now 34 TFEU) which was held to be applicable.[7] In C-265/95 *Commission v France (Spanish Strawberries)*, the situation whereby individuals had disrupted fruit and vegetable imports, against which the French authorities effectively did nothing, rendered the state in breach of Community law for its omission to act.

7.2.2 Article 258 TFEU Procedure

Article 258 TFEU requires that certain informal and formal stages be completed before the matter can be brought to the Court of Justice.

7.2.2.1 The Informal and Administrative Stages

The first part of Art 258 TFEU states rather tersely and without any acknowledgement of the much more involved informal procedure, 'If the Commission considers that a Member State has failed to fulfil an obligation under the Treaties, it shall deliver a reasoned opinion on the matter after giving the State concerned the opportunity to submit its observations.'[8] This means that the Commission must have reached a conclusion that the member state is probably in breach of an obligation before it can commence

---

[6] In the parallel development of accepting that member states may be liable for damages caused by national courts' incorrect interpretation of EU law, so might member states in the future be found in breach in an Art 258 procedure for the same. See Case C-224/01 *Köbler* which is also considered in Chapter 6.

[7] This case is also considered in Chapter 8, Sections 8.8.1, 8.8.2, and 8.8.5.1.

[8] A very good overview of the procedure can be found at: **http://ec.europa.eu/atwork/applying-eu-law/ infringements-proceedings/index_en.htm**.

an action before the CoJ. However, a lot more goes on in the background now. Having formed a view during the pre-procedural investigations and discussions with member state officials, in what are described as the 'package meetings', that a state has breached its obligations, the Commission will inform the state of its view on a potential breach and give the state the opportunity to answer the allegation or to correct its action or inaction before the formal administrative procedure of Art 258 TFEU begins. Central to this now is the 'EU Pilot' scheme which transfers the complaints after initial investigation by the Commission to the member state for consideration and comment. Again this has led to many complaints being solved without further action being necessary. In view of the discretion that the Commission enjoys, there is no obligation on it to take action. Individuals who complain or who are concerned have been held by the Court of Justice not to be able to force the Commission to take action: see Case 48/65 *Lütticke v Commission* or Case 246/81 *Bethell v Commission*. In Case 247/87 *Star Fruit Company v Commission*, the CoJ held that the Commission was not bound to commence the proceedings, but has a discretion that excludes the right for individuals to require that institution to adopt a specific position. In view of that discretion, both the formal letter and reasoned opinion cannot be challenged in Art 263 TFEU actions, which are considered in Section 7.4.[9] Each year, the Commission prepares a report on the application of EU law that provides statistics for the number of cases being investigated and numbers for each of the stages of Art 258 TFEU actions.[10] The administrative part of the procedure consists of two distinct phases, as follows.

7.2.2.2 Letters of Formal Notice

Not every suspicion of infringement by the Commission will result in the initial formal letter of notice being sent to the member state. In a report by the European Parliament in 1982, it was estimated that only one in 1,000 cases suspected by the Commission resulted in a court action. Whilst, at this stage, the process is still administrative, it is nevertheless absolutely necessary as a prerequisite for the formal process should the member state fail to take action or correct the alleged breach.[11] The initial letter has been held also to be essential for the commencement of proceedings before the CoJ in Case 274/83 *Commission v Italy*. Case 293/85 *Commission v Belgium (Re University Fees)* held that the Commission must allow member states a period which is reasonable to reply to the letter of formal notice, which is generally 2 months.

In 1995, the Commission sent out 1,016 formal letters (1,552 in 2003 and 1,168 in 2010) stating its point of view. Generally, at least half of the investigations are settled before a formal notice is issued, although this figure varies from year to year and has been rising in recent years. Despite a rise to (at that time) 25 member states, in 2006, there was a reduction of formal letters sent out to 1,536. These letters simply seek a response from the member state and do not automatically lead to either of the next possible stages—the reasoned opinion or litigation stage. The Commission has a national infringement database (NIF) which monitors the cases being pursued formally by the Commission.

---

[9] The Commission has though responded informally to complaints about the exercise of its discretion in 'Communication from the Commission to the Council and the European Parliament: Updating the handling of relations with the complainant in respect of the application of Union law' COM (2012) 154 final OJ (2012) C171/10.

[10] The latest published report (for the year 2013) can be found at **http://ec.europa.eu/atwork/applying-eu-law/docs/annual_report_31/com_2014_612_en.pdf**. A newer version may be available after this textbook has been published.

[11] Case C-191/95 *Commission v Germany* or Case C-230/99 *Commission v France*.

7.2.2.3 **The Reasoned Opinion**

Following the reply from the member state to the formal notice, or after the time given by the Commission for an answer (which is usually two months), if no reply has been received, the Commission can then deliver a reasoned opinion that records the factual and legal reasons why the Commission considers there has been a failure on the part of the member state. This is delivered to the member state and also provides a further time limit within which the member state is required to bring the alleged infringement to an end. The reasoned opinion is confidential and cannot be obtained by third parties during the course of investigations or where the Commission exercises its discretion and decides not to proceed further against a member state (see, for example, Cases T-105/95 *WWF* and T-191/99 *Petrie*). Many of the original complaints are settled informally during this stage and the resulting number of reasoned opinions in 1995 was 192 (533 in 2003, 680 in 2006, and 288 in 2010). In Case 39/72 *Commission v Italy (Slaughtered Cows)*, the CoJ determined that, if the state should fail to comply with the reasoned opinion of the Commission within a reasonable time or as stipulated by the Commission (normally two months), the Commission then has the right, which is still discretionary, to bring the matter before the Court of Justice, further specifying its grounds for action.

In terms of the total number of cases each year, about 90 per cent will have been solved by the end of this stage and about 10 per cent only of the original cases will be referred to the CoJ. In 1995, 72 cases were brought, 215 in 2003, 189 in 2006, and 120 in 2010, which represent about 10 per cent of all procedures opened.[12] The administrative proceedings are subject to the judicial review of the CoJ during the judicial stage and the action can be declared void if, for example, the member state has not been given sufficient time in which to respond (Case 293/85 *Commission v Belgium (University Fees)*) or has substantially altered the complaint or submissions between the reasoned opinion and the application to the CoJ (Case 232/78 *Commission v France*). Furthermore, decisions by the Commission to pursue an action or to close the proceedings may be, and usually are, published in the OJ.

7.2.2.4 **The Judicial Stage**

The final stage of the procedure is action before the CoJ and its judgment, which at first is merely declaratory, which means that the CoJ essentially states at the time of judgment, whether the member state is in breach or not. Only about 5 per cent of cases reach final judgment, because a number are withdrawn beforehand, due mainly to member state compliance. After the judgment, the state is required to take the necessary measures to comply. Judgments rendered by the CoJ in 1995 were 72, 86 in 2003, and 90 in 2006.

The Court of Justice can proceed to judgment even if the member state has complied with the Commission's reasoned opinion, but did so outside the time limit set (Case C-147/00 *Commission v France*). In Case C-240/86 *Commission v Greece*, the CoJ held that the Commission action remained admissible despite compliance before the deadline or judgment and that the CoJ was still entitled to establish the breach, or where the member state has persistently failed to comply with EU law on a particular issue as in Case C-147/03 *Commission v Austria*, concerned with qualifications required by EU citizens for entry to Austrian educational establishments. This can be important for the

---

[12] The percentages given in the 2011 monitoring report are 77% settled by formal letter, 89% by reasoned opinion, 96% settled by referral, leaving just 4% of cases going on to the final stage. See **http://ec.europa.eu/ eu_law/docs/docs_infringements/annual_report_27/com_2010_538_en.pdf**. For more up-to-date statistics refer to the later reports up to 2013, cited in the earlier footnotes in this chapter.

Commission in establishing exactly what the law is or for setting a precedent to control other member state behaviour or, as in Case 22/87 *Commission v Italy*, the breach that was declared by the CoJ was the basis for determining liability on the part of the Italian state in the later Cases C-6 and 9/90 *Francovich* which established the principle of state liability. The matter of referral remains, however, a matter of discretion on the part of the Commission.

At the moment, there is about a 17-month delay in the CoJ hearing enforcement actions, but if the matter is very important, the CoJ is able to speed up the case.[13] Where a delay would also cause severe difficulties, it is possible for the Commission to request, and the CoJ to order, interim measures (considered in Section 7.2.2.6).

7.2.2.5 Defences Raised by the Member States

The member states have raised various defences, often acceptable in international law, but without success in the EU legal order, to justify their non-compliance with obligations. *Force majeure* or overriding necessity was relied on in Case 77/69 *Commission v Belgium (Belgium Wood* case), in which the Belgian government pleaded that the dissolution of Parliament and the separation of powers had forced the failure to implement an EC directive. It was used again in Case 101/84 *Commission v Italy*, in which a data-processing centre had been bombed, which might have actually allowed the defence to be used if it were not for the fact that the delay in implementing was four-and-a-half years, far too long for the CoJ. Furthermore, arguments have been raised that EU measures were the cause of political or economic difficulties such as by the UK in Case 128/78 *Commission v UK (Tachographs)*, in which the UK pleaded that the cost and interruption to industry of fitting tachographs in lorry cabs would cause extreme difficulties. A similar argument was used by Italy in Case 7/61 *Commission v Italy*, in which Italy claimed that it could take action in the case of an emergency, but this could only be done if expressly sanctioned by the Commission which, in this case, it was not. A further defence is that of reciprocity, by which the member state claimed in Cases 90–1/63 *Commission v Belgium and Luxembourg* that because the Council has failed to act or, as in Case 232/78 *Commission v France*, that other member states have not complied with their obligations, the member state challenged was justified in not complying. This was similarly rejected by the CoJ. Likewise, arguments that a conflicting national law is not, in fact, applied or that the administrative practice is in compliance, as in Case 167/73 *Commission v France (Re Merchant Seaman)*, also fail. In Case 29/84 *Commission v Germany*, Germany had even attempted to claim there was no need to implement an EU law because individuals were already able to enforce the EC law via direct effect in the national courts. Not unsurprisingly, this was held by the Court not to be a defence against infringement proceedings for Germany.

A threat to public order pleaded by France in Case C-265/95 *Commission v France (Spanish Strawberries)* was also rejected. The Court of Justice found that 'the French Government has manifestly and persistently abstained from adopting appropriate and adequate measures to put an end to the acts of vandalism which jeopardize the free movement on its territory of certain agricultural products originating in other Member States and to prevent the recurrence of such acts'. However, the CoJ did suggest that under the appropriate circumstances, a defence of public order might be upheld, but has so far not given a judgment supporting that view.

---

[13] See Art 23a of the Protocol on the Statute of the Court of Justice, reproduced in N. Foster (ed), *EU Treaties and Legislation*, latest edn, Oxford University Press, Oxford.

About the only defence that will work, given the robust dismissal by the Court of Justice of virtually all other defences raised, is that the Commission got it wrong on the facts or law; in other words, that there was no breach. The Commission success rate measured over a ten-year period was between 90 and 99 per cent.

7.2.2.6 Suspensory Orders and Interim Measures

One of the criticisms of the Art 258 TFEU procedure was, and remains, the length of time that it takes to get to a final judgment. This is now about 17 months in terms of the formal judicial stage of proceedings, but that does not take account of the informal stage, which can extend the whole process by years. During this time, a member state's breach can cause considerable economic hardship and damage to individuals affected by it. In order to overcome these, the Court of Justice may order a contested act to be suspended under Art 278 TFEU or, in any case before it, the CoJ may proscribe necessary interim measures under Art 279 TFEU, both of which have been ordered occasionally in Art 258 TFEU actions. A case for the requested measure must specifically be made. Interim measures must be requested prior to final judgment and applied only in urgent circumstances. Interim measures are not in any strict sense a direct sanction, but they can nevertheless have the effect of rectifying the alleged breach until it has been determined by the CoJ whether the conflicting national legislation should be removed or not applied. In Case 53/77 *Commission v UK (Pig Producers)*, the UK was ordered to halt subsidies to pig producers until the CoJ could decide whether the scheme was compatible with the rules of the common market. In Case 293/85 *Commission v Belgium (University Fees)*, the CoJ ordered Belgium, under Art 243, to allow access on equal terms to other non-Belgian Community nationals to vocational training in Belgian universities when non-Belgians were asked to pay enrolment fees but nationals were not. It also made an interim order in Case 61/77 R *Commission v Ireland (Irish Fisheries)* for Ireland to cease certain fishing measures that the Commission claimed were contrary to Community fishing rules. In all three cases, the member states complied immediately. In Case C-195/90 *Commission v Germany*, the CoJ ordered that a special road tax for lorries be suspended pending the outcome of the Commission Art 258 TFEU (ex Art 226 EC) action against Germany. In response, Germany had requested a security undertaking from the Commission, in case the Commission's application was not upheld, but this was judged not to be required by the CoJ. In the *Factortame* litigation, Case 246/89 R *Commission v UK*, the Commission requested, and was granted, the suspension of the alleged incompatible UK laws that were causing, and would have caused further, considerable economic damage to the Spanish fishermen in the UK, although the UK did not initially comply with the order for an extended period. As a consequence, the UK was required in a later case in the same saga of litigation to pay considerable compensation to the Spanish fishermen who had been damaged by the UK breach.

Note that interim measures are also available in other actions and not just in enforcement actions under art 258 TFEU.[14]

7.2.2.7 The Application and Effect of Judgments

Other international tribunals are unable to enforce their judgments against miscreant member states: for example, the International Court of Justice (ICJ) at The Hague, or the European Court of Human Rights (ECtHR) in Strasbourg. The best that can really be

---

[14] E.g. in Case 113/77R *NTN v Council* [1977] ECR 1721 in which an application for a suspension order was successful whilst awaiting the outcome of the substantive issue.

achieved is the issue and discussion of a report on the failure or breach, whilst waiting for political pressure to bear on the state concerned. In the EU legal order, whilst the initial judgment of the Court of Justice is only declaratory and carries no specific sanctions, it does however establish the necessary basis for a follow-up procedure under Art 260 TFEU, considered at 7.2.2.8. The initial position stands in contrast with its greater powers of suspension at the interim stage, noted earlier, but the member states are then placed under a further obligation under Art 260 TFEU to comply with the judgment by taking the necessary measures. If they do not do this, a further action may lie against them by the Commission under Art 258 TFEU for a further breach, but this time of Art 260 TFEU. This has taken place a number of times.[15] An early instance of this is Case 48/71 *Commission v Italy (Second Art Treasures* case*)*. The Commission discerned that because Italy had not complied with the CoJ's judgment in Case 7/68 (the *First Art Treasures* case), judgment should be given that Italy had also failed in its obligation under Art 228 EC (now Art 260 TFEU), despite the fact that Italy complied with the original decision prior to judgment. This unsatisfactory situation, without ultimate sanction to encourage compliance, allowed matters to drag on, as in cases against France for the same infringement that spanned 20 years.[16] These and other cases prompted the member states to reform the Art 226 EC (now Art 258 TFEU) procedure and Art 228 EC (now Art 260 TFEU) in particular.

7.2.2.8 Article 260 TFEU

The TEU amended Art 228 EC (now Art 260 TFEU) to enable the Court of Justice to fine member states for breaches of EU law. Furthermore, under the changes introduced by the Lisbon Treaty, the Commission is no longer required to give a further reasoned opinion in this second procedure on the continued failure but simply issue a formal notice and state a time limit for compliance. If it is not satisfied with the member state reply, or if the member state fails to meet the time limit, the Commission may then refer the case directly to the Court of Justice, which will allow the CoJ to levy the fine (Art 260(2) TFEU). This is estimated to speed up those secondary proceedings by 8 to 18 months.[17] Article 261 TFEU provides that the penalties will be determined by regulations to be adopted by the Council and a penalty calculation system was established by the Commission[18] whereby it will state what penalty, if any, it considers appropriate. The basic penalty is fixed at €650 per day, but will rise soon to €660 per day for the periodic penalty and €220 per day for the lump sum penalty,[19] multiplied by factors reflecting the gravity and duration of non-compliance, the financial situation of the member state, and the number of votes in Council. The amount of the fines may also take into account the impact of breaches on individuals and affected economic operators. This is not to compensate the individuals

---

[15] Over the decade 1997–2006, there were 22 Art 228 EC (now Art 258 TFEU) actions for a failure to comply with a judgment under (now) Art 260 TFEU. Three countries account for over 50% of all cases: France for seven; Germany for four; and Luxembourg for three.

[16] See Case 163/73 *Commission v France* and Case C-334/94 *Commission v France*.

[17] See now SEC (2010) 1371 final for details. In 2011, 77 actions under Art 260(2) TFEU had been commenced.

[18] See Commission Communications: SEC (2005) 1658, SEC (2010) 923, SEC (2010) 1371, and SEC (2012) 6106. Updated notices are noted in n 20.

[19] From fn 7 of SEC (2012) 6106: 'The lump sum will result from multiplying a daily (lump sum) amount (resulting from multiplying the flat-rate for lump sum payments by the coefficient for seriousness and the result of this calculation being multiplied by the special factor "n") by the number of days the infringement persists between the date of the first judgment and the date that the infringement comes to an end or the date of delivery of the judgment under Article 260(2) TFEU.' Updated notices are noted in n 20 below.

affected or redress the balance but to reflect the overall seriousness of the breach—that is, put crudely, to reflect how many individuals may be adversely affected from none to a whole industry or sector of the economy.[20]

The penalty can be levied in the form of a lump sum or periodic payment or, as is usually the case now following the judgment in Case C-304/02 *Commission v France*, both. The penalty will apply from the date of the first judgment in the action and not from the date of original non-compliance, hence member states have the chance to minimize the penalty. A number of cases have resulted in fines being imposed: the first two were Case C-387/97 *Commission v Greece* and Case C-278/01 *Commission v Spain*, in which the CoJ held that the form of the Commission penalty request does not bind the CoJ, which can decide the appropriate type and amount of penalty according to the circumstances. The case against Spain involved the quality of bathing water, which was assessed only annually, and therefore the CoJ considered a daily penalty not appropriate and instead imposed an annual penalty based on the percentage of beaches not meeting the directive's standards. In Case C-304/02 *Commission v France*, both a lump sum and periodic fine were imposed. The Court of Justice also held in Case C-304/02 that, contrary to initial interpretations, the duration of the infringement and, thus, penalty is to be calculated from the date of the first judgment.[21] The Commission now is likely to request both.

The Lisbon Treaty also changed the procedure under Art 260 TFEU and removed the need for the entire second procedure under Art 260 TFEU when seeking a penalty fine under the circumstances in which a member state has failed to notify measures transposing a directive, presumably on the basis that the failure to comply is self-evident. Instead, the Commission simply proceeds under Art 258 TFEU and requests a fine at the same time, the level of which cannot be raised by the Court of Justice.[22] The considerable saving of time that this would achieve should further encourage compliance on the part of the member states. According to the 2008 monitoring report, these cases accounted for around 50 per cent of all enforcement actions and, by the end of 2012, 11 cases had been brought under this expedited Art 260 TFEU procedure.[23]

7.2.3 Actions Brought by One Member State against Another

Article 259 TFEU is the basis for an action by one member state against another, when one member state considers another to have breached an obligation under EU law. Article 344 TFEU obliges the member states not to pursue methods of dispute resolution other than those provided by the treaty, therefore member states are obliged to use Art 259 TFEU to resolve differences under EU law, although this is not always observed to the letter of the law. It must be noted, though, that the previous use of

---

[20] See now the updated communication in the calculation of fines: C (2013) 8181 final 21.11.13, **http:// ec.europa.eu/atwork/applying-eu-law/docs/c_2013_8101_en.pdf** and update C (2014) 6767 final 17.9.14, **http://ec.europa.eu/atwork/applying-eu-law/docs/c_2014_6767_en.pdf**.

[21] As was also done in Case C-77/07 *Commission v France*. The fifth case is Case C-212/99 *Commission v Italy*, but the fine requested by the Commission was denied by the Court of Justice on the basis that Italy had corrected the breach in a timely manner and the CoJ was thus of the opinion that the fine would serve no useful purpose.

[22] By the end of 2011, nine cases against five states had been brought under this expedited Art 260 TFEU procedure. For further details and information on this revision, see SEC (2010) 1371 final. The latest report on such actions is from 2013: **http://ec.europa.eu/atwork/applying-eu-law/docs/annual_report_31/ com_2014_612_en.pdf**.

[23] There were 14 cases in 2013 according to p 6 of the 2014 annual monitoring report: **http://ec.europa. eu/atwork/applying-eu-law/docs/annual_report_31/com_2014_612_en.pdf**.

Art 227 EC (now Art 259 TFEU) by the member states has been minimal. The preference is almost exclusively to request the Commission to take action under Art 258 TFEU. The member states have full *locus standi* in relation to Art 259 TFEU, which procedure is set out later.

7.2.3.1 Complaining State Refers the Matter to the Commission

Before an action can take place, the member state must bring the matter before the Commission.

7.2.3.2 The Commission Issues a Reasoned Opinion

The Commission will ask both states to submit their observations and will then deliver a reasoned opinion on the matter. The Commission seeks to bring about a solution before Court action is necessary and may even intervene to take over the action, as it did in Case 232/78 *Commission v France*, which commenced as an action by Ireland against France, or in Case 1/00 *Commission v France*, which was commenced by the UK, concerning the French measures that continued after the Commission UK beef export ban had been lifted.

7.2.3.3 Complaining State May then Refer the Matter to the Court of Justice

If a settlement or solution is not reached at this stage and three months have elapsed, or if the Commission fails to submit an opinion within three months of being informed of the matter, the member state can take the matter before the CoJ. Judgment has been reached, up to the date of writing, in only a handful of Art 227 EC (now Art 259 TFEU) actions:[24] for example, in Case 141/78 *France v UK*, in which France successfully challenged the UK's unilateral fishery conservation measures. Another case brought to judgment under Art 227 was Case C-388/95 *Belgium v Spain*, in which Belgium failed in its action to challenge the denial of the use of the 'Rioja' designation for bulk-transported wine,[25] as an impediment to the free movement of goods.

These rare cases aside, member states usually prefer to ask the Commission to bring actions under Art 258 TFEU as an alternative, because this is a less politically obvious and contentious manner in which to secure compliance of EU law in the interests of the member states concerned. However, an example of an Art 227 EC (now Art 259 TFEU) action ignoring political sensitivities is Case C-145/04 *Spain v UK*, in which Spain had challenged what it claimed to be the excessive extension of UK voting rights for the residents of Gibraltar to the European Parliament. This extension had, in fact, followed an ECtHR judgment against the UK for not providing EU citizens voting rights in that territory. Spain lost the case. Spain has an outstanding territorial claim to Gibraltar. There is a further very political case between Hungary and Slovakia (Case C-364/10) involving the challenge by Hungary that, in failing to invite the Hungarian president to an official ceremony, Slovakia had breached citizenship and free movement rules. The date of the ceremony coincided with the anniversary of the Soviet invasion of Czechoslovakia in 1968 (Hungarian troops had been amongst the Soviet pact troops entering and occupying Czechoslovakia). The action was dismissed by the ECJ as only involving the president in his diplomatic status and not individually as a citizen and was thus to be governed by national and international law and not by EU law. Furthermore, under Art 273 TFEU,

---

[24] Three against the UK (one France and two Spain), *Belgium v Spain*, and *Ireland v France*.

[25] As opposed to cellar-bottled wine which could use the denomination 'Rioja'. This case is also considered under Free Movement of Goods, Chapter 8, Section 8.8.5.4.

member states may agree to refer any dispute relating to the subject matter of the treaty to the Court of Justice for adjudication, which appears never to have been employed.

7.3 Alternative Actions to Secure Member States' Compliance

Whilst actions to secure member states' compliance have been considered in the previous chapter, it is appropriate to mention such actions again here, because they are equally, if not a lot more, effective in ensuring compliance with EU obligations by member states. They include actions in which individuals point to the breach of a Union obligation or duty by a member state as a defence against prosecution by that member state, or in which they seek to challenge national rules that operate against their interest. The doctrine of direct effects thus additionally placed the policing of EU law in the hands of private individuals, who often have more reason, and thus more incentive, to bring actions than the Commission officials. Individuals may benefit by their actions, as well as help to bring about the compliance by member states parallel to Art 258 TFEU actions, as exampled by Case 152/78 *Commission v France (Advertising of Alcoholic Beverages)*. It was held in that case that a French ban on advertising foreign spirits was discriminatory and contrary to Community law. France failed to remove its legislation and prosecuted an importer for advertising. Waterkeyn, which was the advertiser, referred to the previous judgment as a defence. In the follow-up Cases 314–16/81 *Procureur de la Republique v Waterkeyn*, it was held that individuals could rely on such past judgments as a defence to protect their rights. In addition, there is the possibility for individuals to sue a state for loss caused by a breach of EU law, under the state liability principle established first in the case of *Francovich*, which was considered in Chapter 6. This will also play a strong part in encouraging member states to comply with EU law obligations if they find themselves having to pay out significant damages in an increasing number of cases.

The next procedures considered in this chapter are those taken directly against the institutions of the Union, and commence with the action to annul acts of the institutions under Art 263 TFEU.

7.4 Actions to Annul EU Acts

Article 263 TFEU is the action to annul acts of the Union, its institutions, and other bodies, the acts of which are intended to produce legal effects in relation to third parties.[26] It was held in Case 294/83 *Parti Ecologiste Les Verts v European Parliament* that the EC is a Community based on the rule of law, in as much as neither its member states nor its institutions can avoid a review of the question whether the measures adopted by them are in conformity with the basic constitutional charter, the treaty. To this end, Art 263 TFEU provides for actions to be brought before the Court of Justice to allow it to review the validity of acts of the Union. If it finds them to be invalid, the CoJ has the sole right to declare those acts void. This action helps to ensure that the Union institutions and bodies comply with all requirements of EU law when they take action.

---

[26] Please see the schematic for this in the Online Resource Centre: **www.oxfordtextbooks.co.uk/orc/foster5e/.**

There are two main aspects of this action: admissibility and the merits or substance of the action. After these technical elements have been covered, we will also consider the suggestions for the reform of Art 263 TFEU, raised largely due to its apparent strictness and alternatives to it. First, though, the complex question of admissibility will be addressed.

7.4.1 **Admissibility**

The issue of the admissibility of Art 263 TFEU actions includes the questions of which institutions are subject to review, which acts can be reviewed, the time limit for challenging acts, and the applicants who are able to bring an action. All of these will be considered in turn, but the last aspect presents the greatest barrier to applicants in practice and understandably demands most emphasis in case law, and thus also textbooks. One of the problems previously in getting to grips with this topic is the wide choice of relevant cases, many of which appeared to discourage applications by individuals challenging general legislation. The Lisbon Treaty, though, has made some reforms to this Article, which may help to clarify the requirements of the Article and which will be considered in turn later.

7.4.1.1 **The Institutions whose Acts Are Reviewable**

Article 173 EEC (now Art 263 TFEU), as originally constituted, stated that the acts of the Commission and Council are subject to review, but case law extended this to acts of the European Parliament. Over a series of cases, the Court of Justice justified this on the basis that, as the European Parliament's powers grew, it should be responsible for acts that create legally binding effects in respect of third parties and these should therefore be open to review: see Case 230/81 *Luxembourg v European Parliament* in respect of the choice of the European Parliament's seat, Case 294/83 *Parti Ecologiste Les Verts v European Parliament* in respect of a challenge to the apportionment of election campaign funds, and Case 34/86 *Council v European Parliament (Budgetary Procedure)* with regard to a budgetary decision of the President of the European Parliament. The development is thus very much allied to the democratic deficit debate and as the European Parliament's role increased in making law (that is, its rights and duties), so correspondingly have its duties; thus, there should be a right to challenge decisions of the European Parliament. This is reflected in the further amendments extending the range of institutions expressly, which were included in the new Art 263 TFEU by the Lisbon Treaty, which now provides:

> The Court of Justice of the European Union shall review the legality of legislative acts, of acts of the Council, of the Commission, of the European Central Bank, other than recommendations and opinions, and of acts of the European Parliament and of the European Council intended to produce legal effects vis-à-vis third parties.

The Court of Justice has held that to be subject to a challenge, an institution must be empowered under the treaty to enact binding measures; therefore this does not include, for example, the Committee of Permanent Representatives (COREPER) (see Case C-24/94 *Commission v Council*).

The Lisbon Treaty thus makes it clear that all Union institutions, bodies, or agencies, or combinations of them, which enact legislative acts per se and institutions the acts of which produce legal effects for third parties are bodies that can be subject to challenge under Art 263 TFEU. The new inclusion of the European Council is significant, because this subjects for the first time the political-policy driving force of the EU to legal judicial control and, as such, bolsters the claim of the EU that it too respects the rule of law.

7.4.1.2 **Reviewable Acts**

Prior to the Lisbon Treaty reforms, the jurisdiction of the CoJ under old Art 230 EC (now Art 263 TFEU) applied to the legally binding acts of the institutions, which were given in Art 249 EC (now Art 288 TFEU) as regulations, directives, and decisions, and did not therefore include recommendations or opinions, or indeed anything else. However, the term 'act', and the definition of what constitutes an act or a decision, had already been given a very wide interpretation by the Court of Justice so as to bring many other forms of act within the review of Art 230 EC (now Art 263 TFEU) that would not, on the face of it, be admissible. The reason for such an extension is that these create binding legal effects or affect the legal status of third parties, and therefore they should be subject to review. Article 263 TFEU has been amended to reflect the previous case law by expressly including not only legislative acts, but also all acts intended to produce legal effects for third parties, noted earlier. For example, it was held in Cases 8–11/66 *Noordwijks Cement Accord* that other acts may be subject to review and that the test to apply to a particular act is whether it has binding legal effects or changes the legal position of the applicant. The case involved a letter that changed the immunity from prosecution of certain companies. Further, in Case 22/70 *Commission v Council (ERTA)*, it was held that Art 249 EC (now Art 288 TFEU) is not exhaustive and that special acts such as the minuted discussions of the Council, for the European Road Transport Agreement (ERTA), could also be challenged. The reasoning for this was that despite being negotiated by the member states as an international agreement, this was a Community competence and was thus within the review jurisdiction of the CoJ. As already mentioned, Case 294/83 *Parti Ecologiste Les Verts v European Parliament* and the TEU extended the list of reviewable acts to those of the European Parliament where they give rise to legally binding effects on the position of third parties. However, there remain exceptions to this, in that some acts that nevertheless produce legal effects are still not subject to challenge. For example, in Case 7/61 *Commission v Italy*, it was held that the reasoned opinion given by the Commission under the Art 226 EC (now Art 258 TFEU) proceedings did not constitute an act that can be subject of review under Art 230 EC (now Art 263 TFEU). Similarly, in Case 48/65 *Lütticke v Commission*, the applicants had requested that the Commission take action against the German Federal Republic regarding a breach of Community law, but the Commission refused. Lütticke applied under old Art 230 EC to annul the decision not to act, but it was held that the refusal to act was not a legally binding act and therefore not reviewable. Equally the reasoned opinion of the Commission with regard to the possible member state breach was held not to be reviewable.

The Lisbon Treaty has confirmed the position previously made clear by the Court of Justice in cases in which challenges are not restricted to the binding legal forms outlined in Art 288 TFEU. The textbooks abound with examples of which only three are offered here. In Case C-57/95 *French Republic v Commission*, the CoJ ruled on a French action to annul a Commission 'communication' that it was argued imposed new obligations on the member states. It held that the communication in question, which was published in the OJ 'C' series and was not a legislative act envisaged by old Art 249 EC, was a measure that could be the subject of an annulment action. The content of the communication was considered, and the CoJ thought that it had 'imperative wording' and that the content was the same subject matter as a withdrawn draft directive. Hence, it held that the communication constituted an act intended to have legal effects on its own, distinct from the treaty provisions, and an action to annul it could be upheld.

In Case C-106/96 *UK v Commission*, the Council had decided not to support 'Poverty 4', a programme to combat poverty and social exclusion, but the Commission decided nevertheless to fund a number of projects amounting to an expenditure of 6 million European currency units (ecus) and issued a press release to advertise this. The CoJ held that the Commission lacked the competence to commit the expenditure and the decision was annulled. However, in view of the fact that much of the expenditure had already taken place, the CoJ decided in the interests of legal certainty to exercise the discretion given to it under Art 231 EC (now Art 264 TFEU) and rule in favour of the payments made or promised.

Finally, a more recent case appears to have helped to define an 'act' for the purposes of admissibility. In Case C-131/03 P *Reynolds Tobacco Holdings and ors*, the Commission took the decision to commence legal proceedings against the US company, which it suspected of smuggling cigarettes into the EU. Reynolds challenged that decision, but the Court of First Instance (CFI, now the General Court) and Court of Justice held that the decision to take legal action was not a reviewable act. The decision had legal effects, but not ones that satisfied the test for Art 230 EC, because the decisions did not per se determine definitively the obligations of the parties to the case. That determination can result only from the judgment of the court. The Court of Justice confirmed that only acts that were binding on, and capable of affecting the interests of, the applicant by bringing about a distinct change in his legal position could be challenged. In this case, the decision to take legal action—that is, the decision to prosecute or commence proceedings that might lead to a fine—would not affect the outcome of the legal position, but the judgment on the case would, against which would lie an appeal.

Hence, a wide array of measures can be subject to review dependent on the legal effects that they produce or their nature and not only the three formal acts listed in Art 288 TFEU.

7.4.1.3 Time Limits

Article 263(6) TFEU provides that the applicant has two months from the date of publication of the measure or from the date of notification, or in the absence of publication or notification, from the date on which it came to the notice of the applicant, regardless of the status of the applicant. The time limit for challenging a regulation has been determined to run from the end of the fourteenth day following publication: see Art 50 of the CoJ's Rules of Procedure. This was introduced in the days before the electronic publication and dispatch of the OJ to take account of postal delivery time to the furthest regions of the EU—certainly this is arguably less necessary now with electronic dispatch of legislation and now that the online edition of the *Official Journal of the European Union* is the only one deemed authentic.[27] The allowance of 14 days remains though.[28]

The very short time limits have been held by the CFI (now the General Court) not to apply where there are such serious defects in the measure that it is to be regarded as non-existent (see Case T-79/89 *BASF v Commission*).

7.4.1.4 Who May Apply: *Locus Standi*

The question of who may apply relates to what is known as the *locus standi* of applicants. *Locus standi* means, literally, 'the place of standing'. It relates to the recognition of a legal

---

[27] See Council Regulation 216/2013 (OJ 2013 L69/1).

[28] Art 51 of the Rules of Procedure in fact still provides an additional ten days to be added to the time limit on account of distance, although this is not defined and hardly seems necessary now that the paper version is not official.

interest in a matter, which is expressed in the treaty but defined and interpreted by the Court of Justice, that produces the right to mount a legal challenge against a legal provision. 'No standing' means no right to challenge, hence this is absolutely crucial to an applicant's chances.

There are three categories of applicants:

privileged

semi-privileged

non-privileged.

Privileged Applicants The privileged applicants are named by Art 263 TFEU as the member states, the Council, and the Commission, and, following the Treaty of Nice, the European Parliament, which have the right to challenge any act. Notably absent now, though, despite its elevation to a full institution by the Lisbon Treaty in Art 13 TEU, is the European Council.

Semi-Privileged Applicants The semi-privileged applicant is a category first established in case law for the European Parliament by the Court of Justice, but extended to the European Central Bank (ECB) and, following its elevation to a full institution, the Court of Auditors. They have the right to challenge acts of the institutions, but only for the purpose of protecting their prerogatives. The term 'protection of prerogatives' is one that was essentially developed in case law and means 'where their interests are clearly affected'. See, for example, Case 138/79 *Maizena (Roquette Frères) v Council*, as confirmed in Case C-70/88 *European Parliament v Council (Chernobyl)*, and the successful challenge in Case C-295/90 *European Parliament v Council (Students Residence Directive)* to the legal base used by the Council, which undermined the right of the European Parliament to participate. This limited right of challenge is now confirmed in Art 263 TFEU. The new *locus standi* requirements reflect the increase in the law-making and participatory roles of the European Parliament in the EU. The Lisbon Treaty has added the Committee of the Regions (CoR) to the category of semi-privileged applicants due arguably to its greater democratic credentials in comparison to the European Economic and Social Committee (EESC) which was not added. The European Council was also not added and is thus excluded from any privileged applicant status. The member states individually, though, still possess full privilege.

All other persons are non-privileged applicants, which must satisfy certain conditions before their right of access to the General Court or Court of Justice will be recognized.

7.4.2 *Locus Standi* for Non-privileged Applicants

Article 263(4) TFEU provides three situations in which non-privileged applicants can bring actions for judicial review. It provides:

Any natural or legal person may, under the conditions laid down in the first and second paragraphs, institute proceedings against

[i]   an act addressed to that person

[ii] or which is of direct and individual concern to them,

[iii] and against a regulatory act which is of direct concern to them and does not entail implementing measures.

The first thing to note is that all three conditions have been changed in some way by the Lisbon Treaty, which previously provided that proceedings could be instituted against a decision addressed to that person or against a decision that, although in the form of a regulation or a decision addressed to another person, is of direct and individual concern to the former. The import of this change will be explained in the sections following.

7.4.2.1 An Act Addressed to the Applicant

This first situation has been revised in a rather subtle way. 'Decision' in Art 230 EC has been replaced by 'act' in Art 263 TFEU, which is not defined and thus suggests that, provided that something is addressed to the applicant, whatever its form, it may be subject to review. Hence, where the applicant is directly addressed, the applicant will have automatic standing and this is most likely to occur in specific circumstances in which, for example, the applicant has been the subject of a formal decision of the Commission under the competition rules of Arts 101–2 TFEU and Regulation 1/2003. For the purposes of the addressee mounting a challenge, there is no barrier to admissibility provided that the time limit has been observed. In Case T-138/89 *BBV v Commission*, it was held by the CFI (now General Court) that it was not possible to challenge a potential decision (in other words, a decision that might be made, but which had not actually been made at the time of the challenge) to the claim that the potential decision would affect the applicant's interest. 'Natural or legal person' has been interpreted to include non-member states in Case C-298/89 *Gibraltar v Council*.

The next two situations or categories have reformulated significantly the circumstances under which individuals may challenge acts of EU institutions and bodies that have not been addressed to them.

7.4.2.2 The Challenge to Acts not Addressed to Applicants

Condition (ii) requiring direct and individual concern reflects previous case law, which will thus be referred to, that demonstrating 'individual' was and is the most important aspect of the application and thus admissibility.

Condition (iii) which refers to regulatory acts not entailing implementing measures is new and refers to non-legislative acts. This will be considered in Section 7.4.5.

7.4.2.3 An Act (not Addressed to Them, but) of Direct and Individual Concern

The second circumstance concerns acts addressed to another person. 'Another person' was held in Case 25/62 *Plaumann v Commission* to include decisions addressed to the member states and not just to other individuals (natural or legal).

Article 263 TFEU no longer specifically mentions 'decision' or 'regulations', but instead refers more generally to 'acts', which is not then defined but presumably was intended to apply to all legal acts affecting the legal status of the applicant providing they are of direct and individual concern. The focus of attention therefore remains on the phrase 'direct and individual concern', but more importantly 'individual'. This was precisely the subject of the focus developed by the CoJ in previous case law in establishing the circumstances in which individuals could challenge regulations, which, by their nature, are not addressed to individuals because they are acts of general application; that is, to everyone.

Very often, 'individual' was considered first, as it was in the leading Case 25/62 *Plaumann*, because if that requirement is satisfied, the type of act becomes irrelevant. Therefore the reform of Art 263 TFEU made good sense by simply requiring an investigation of 'direct and individual' and not first whether the act challenged was a regulation or some other form of EU law.

7.4.3 **Direct and Individual Concern**

Acts addressed to other people are only challengeable if they concern the applicant directly and individually.

7.4.3.1 **Direct Concern**

With 'direct concern', the general rule is that if a member state is granted discretion to act under the provision, then the provision cannot, by its nature, give rise to direct concern. The 'act must affect directly the legal situation of the individual and leave no discretion to its addressees, who are entrusted with the task of implementing it' (Cases 41–4/70 *International Fruit v Commission*). A good example is Case 62/70 *Bock v Commission (Chinese Mushrooms)* which involved the authorization for a member state to restrict imports; that is, it had the discretion. An application was made by Bock to import Chinese mushrooms, but had been refused by Germany on 11 September and only authorized by the Commission on 15 September. Hence the decision was a retroactive measure in direct response to the application from Bock, which was therefore held to be directly concerned. The discretion to act was already waived. This trend was continued in Case 11/82 *Piraiki-Patraiki v Commission*, in which the French authorities applied for and were authorized to impose quotas on yarn imports from Greece. In considering an application to review this decision, the CoJ held that where interested parties could be identified with certainty or a high degree of probability, direct concern would be satisfied, despite the theoretical discretion on the part of the member state. In other words, the country applied for permission to restrict imports and the Commission had granted it, so whilst in theory the country had the discretion to restrict imports or not, in reality it had already exercised and thus extinguished that discretion.

7.4.3.2 **Individual Concern**

'Individual concern' has been traditionally very hard to demonstrate. The case law which established that position will be considered. An applicant must show some factors that distinguish themself uniquely. This was the position taken in the leading and still very much valid judgment of Case 25/62 *Plaumann v Commission* in which a decision was addressed to the German government refusing permission to reduce duties on clementines, which was challenged by Plaumann. The test decided for individual concern was whether the decision affects the applicant by virtue of the fact that he is a member of the abstractly defined class addressed by the rule: for example, because he is an importer of clementines, or because of attributes peculiar to him that differentiate him from all other persons. Plaumann was held to be one of a class of importers and not therefore individually concerned; the reasoning is that anyone could become an importer. It was held in *Plaumann* that persons other than those to whom a decision is addressed may claim to be individually concerned only if that decision 'affects them by reason of certain attributes that are peculiar to them or by reason of circumstances in which they are differentiated from all other persons and by virtue of these factors distinguishes them individually', just as in the case of the person addressed. In *Plaumann*, the CoJ went on to state that 'the applicant is affected by the disputed decision as an importer of clementines, that is to say, by reason of a commercial activity which may at any time be practised by any person and is not therefore such as to distinguish the applicant in relation to the contested decision as in the case of the addressee'. Effectively Plaumann would have to have been addressed personally by the decision.

A much more vivid version of this, Case 231/82 *Spijker Kwasten BV v Commission*, involved an import ban requested by the Dutch and approved by the Commission in a decision which was imposed on Chinese brushes. Spijker Kwasten was the only importer in the Netherlands and although it had previously requested a licence, it was held that the company could not be individually concerned. The reasoning and distinguishing factor was that, because the decision restricting imports was valid not for the previous application but for the forward period of the next six months, it remained possible that others could apply for licences in that period, even though this was very unlikely. Hence there was no individual concern, as it was theoretically possible that others could seek to import and thus also challenge, and drive a coach and horses through, any attempt by the government to restrict imports.

In Case 62/70 *Bock v Commission*, the company was individually concerned because applications made by Bock to import Chinese mushrooms were refused by Germany on 11 September, but the required authorization by the Commission was only passed on 15 September. Hence, the decision was a retroactive measure in direct response to the application from Bock, which was held to have a vested legal interest and therefore was individually concerned.

In Cases 41–4/70 *International Fruit Company v Commission*, a group of fruit import-ers were held entitled to challenge a regulation where the identity of the legal persons affected was already known, and thus fixed and identifiable. Apple importers had applied in advance for import licences and the decision to issue a limited quantity of licences was made on the basis of applications previously received, therefore finite and known at the time the act entered into force. The regulation was a response to the individuals; no new persons could be added at the time of challenge or thereafter to the list of applicants. The case though does not sit well with *Spijker Kwasten*. See also Case C-152/88 *Sofrimport v Commission* concerning a regulation restricting the import of Chilean apples, which was adopted whilst some apples were in transit and of which the Commission was specifically notified to take into account when the ban was enacted. Sofrimport was thus part of a closed group of companies with goods in transit when the regulation was adopted and which could not be added to. It was thus individually concerned and the application was held to be admissible.

Alternatively, where the applicant is named in the regulation or where the applicant has played a part in the issue of legislation, individual concern will be much easier to estab-lish. In Cases 138–9/80 *Roquette Frères v Council and Maizena v Council*, the CoJ held that, despite being a measure of general application, certain individuals may challenge regulations as if they were decisions, especially when one of the Articles of the regulation specifically referred to the applicant companies.

A number of cases are concerned with alleged breaches of competition law by other companies or the dumping of goods on the EU market. The applicants are those that have made a complaint to the Commission about the activities of another company that appear to breach competition or anti-dumping rules. As a result of an investigation of individual importers, the Commission may take action by issuing a decision seeking to correct the situation or a general regulation is issued to catch all imports; thus the complaint has led to the enactment of a regulation, as in the following examples. In Case 264/82 *Timex v Commission*, the Timex company had complained about the dumping of watches on the European market, which led to an anti-dumping regulation being imposed by the Commission. However, Timex was not satisfied as it thought the duty imposed on the Russian-dumped import watches was not high enough. Timex therefore challenged the regulation and was held to have direct and individual concern. Likewise, the application for review in Case C-26/76 *Metro-SB-Grossmarkte v Commission* was held to be admissi-ble because Metro had a legitimate interest in the decision aimed at another person. Metro had made a complaint, which was expressly provided for by Art 3 under the Competition

Law Regulation 17, in respect of the exclusion from a distribution network by another company (SABA). They had thus shown a legitimate interest as well as having played a part that led directly to the Commission decision.

See also Case C-358/89 *Extramet Industrie v Council*, concerning an anti-dumping regulation which imposed a 22 per cent import duty on goods imported by Extramet and which it challenged. The CoJ accepted the special economic circumstances, which were that in the EU the company was the largest importer and end-user of calcium from China and the Soviet Union, and the only other producer and supplier of calcium was a competitor, which had refused to supply Extramet. The company was also involved in the Commission investigations. The high import duty on calcium import would have affected it severely in view of the limited suppliers and manufacturers of the product. The CoJ held that the applicant had established the existence of a set of factors constituting such a situation which was peculiar to the applicant and which differentiated it, as regards the measure in question, from all other traders. The Extramet case does not serve though as a very good precedent or example case for how future cases may be decided because of the exceptional factual circumstances which make it unique. If it was similar to a number of other cases with the same or similar facts, by definition they would not be unique, therefore not demonstrate individual concern and would not succeed. It does though highlight that, if there are truly unique circumstances, 'individual' will be established to the satisfaction of the CoJ and not by precedent or the future application of the *Extramet* case.

It would not include those who have merely written to the Commission to complain without direct involvement in the particular situation complained of.

Other successful cases include Case C-389/89 *Codorniu v Council (Spanish Wine Producers)* involving a regulation limiting the use of the term 'Cremant'. Despite the CoJ confirming that the regulation was a legislative measure applying to traders in general, it could still be of individual concern to one of them. Codorniu had distinguished itself by the ownership of a trademark for the term 'Cremant' from the year 1924, which the Community had tried to reserve for French and Luxembourg producers. Codorniu was able to challenge a regulation that prevented its use of a registered trademark 'Gran Cremant di Codorniu', because this fact isolated it from other wine producers who had not registered this term or a similar term including the word 'Cremant' and were similarly restricted from using the name. Hence, it was a regulation for all others but it was a decision for Cordoniu because of its individual concern.

The judicial position on 'individual concern' has been maintained in the post-Lisbon Treaty case law. In Case T-49/07, *Sofiane Fahas v Council of the European Union*, the General Court defined 'individual' in virtually the same words as used in *Plaumann*. Furthermore in Case T-18/10 *Inuit*, and on appeal in Case C-583/11 P *Inuit v EP & Council*, both the General Court and the Court of Justice made clear that whilst Art 263 TFEU must be interpreted in the light of the fundamental right to effective judicial protection, such an interpretation could not go beyond the conditions expressed in Art 263 TFEU. In other words *Plaumann* continues to be good law.

7.4.4 Interest Groups and Party Actions

By their very nature, non-individual applications might expect not to have standing because it would be expected that, by definition, the application cannot be of individual concern. However, a trade association's application has been recognized in Cases T-447–9/93 *AITEC v Commission*, in which it represented the individual interests of some or all of its members.[29]

---

[29] And confirmed in the later Case T-122/96 *Federolio v Commission* in which the General Court further qualified the conditions as requiring the association to have expressly had grants granted and also be itself affected by the act.

However, in Case T-585/93 *Greenpeace v Commission*, the plea that all individuals with an environmental interest and not only an economic interest in the consequences of a decision should be collectively able to be represented by a group failed. The CFI (now the General Court) rejected this view, which was confirmed on appeal in Case C-321/95 P by the Court of Justice, which held that the decision had affected individuals only in an abstract and general fashion, and that the applicants representing them were thus similarly affected and similarly without standing.

7.4.5 **The Challenge to Regulatory Acts**

This third condition or circumstance is new to Art 263 TFEU, introduced with the Lisbon Treaty reforms as a response to the calls to make it easier for non-privileged applicants to challenge, and provides individual applicants with a right to make an application against a regulatory act that is of direct concern to them and does not entail implementing measures. It is to be stressed that the applicant need show direct concern only, but there was no definition provided in the treaties for what is meant by a 'regulatory act', so it was unclear from the start whether the changes made would in fact, makes things easier. If the second circumstance does refer to a legislative act, then it is to be assumed that this refers to non-legislative acts—hence, the easier condition without the need to show individual concern for *locus standi*. Whilst legislative acts are described in Arts 288–9 TFEU, regulatory acts are not. Regulatory acts are, according now to the General Court and CoJ, the non-legislative acts described in new Arts 290–1 which are the delegated and implementing administrative acts taken by the Commission and which may include acts labelled as regulations, directives, or decisions. In Case T-18/10 *Inuit*, the General Court held that 'the meaning of "regulatory act" for the purposes of the fourth paragraph of Article 263 TFEU must be understood as covering all acts of general application apart from legislative acts'. This position was confirmed on appeal by the Court of Justice in Case C-583/11 P *Inuit v EP & Council*, which also held that the 'Direct' requirement was to be understood in the same way as for a category [ii] application. In the case itself, a legislative act, a regulation, was involved and the applicants were denied standing.

This means we have first to know what legislative acts are to be able to exclude them from a consideration under category [iii]. To determine whether an act is legislative, the General Court in *Inuit* considered the decision-making process which was used.

In Case T-262/10 *Microban*, the General Court considered the legal basis under which the directive was adopted. If the challenged act was expressly adopted under Art 289 TFEU or any Article which refers to Art 289 or the ordinary or general legislative process and also all of those enacted under any of the special legislative processes (Art 289 (2) TFEU), it is a legislative act and thus not a category [iii] act. That leaves us with the conclusion that regulatory acts are indeed the general delegated and implementing acts of Arts 290–1 TFEU. Furthermore, the regulatory act challenged must be direct and not entail any implementing measures but again there is no definition of 'implementing measures' in the TFEU. In Case T-262/10 *Microban*, the General Court confirmed the generally understood view that implementing measures related to any action of intervention by either the Commission or member states in the application of a general non-legislative act of the Commission. Any intervention would thus remove/exclude a right to challenge. For these challenges the applicant need only show direct concern, noted earlier, which was addressed in *Microban* with the Court holding that the test for 'direct' be no stricter than in the challenge to legislative acts under condition [ii]. In the case, the three requirements of non-legislative act, direct, and not involving implementing measures were satisfied and Microban was granted standing and was ultimately successful in challenging a decision which had banned a substance it used in manufacturing products. Following the *Microban* case, Case T-380/11 *Souliotis v Commission* addressed the issue whether direct concern and not involving implementing measures amounted to the same thing or the same test. It held that direct concern, essentially relating to discretion on the part of the addressee, was different from an implementing measure, which was held by the CoJ in Case C-274/12 P *Telefónica v Commission* to mean any measure at all taken or needed to be taken by the addressee of the act.[30] If there was any measure taken by the addressee, who would in normal circumstances most likely be a member state, then the route to challenge would be via the national courts and an Art 267 reference. The problem that leaves is demonstrating that there was neither a discretion nor a need for an implementing measure; in other words, the act had to be in force without anything else happening, something arguably only applicable with any certainty to non-legislative regulations, which enter into force as they are without any implementation.

It would seem, therefore, that it is still unclear whether it is an easier condition for *locus standi*. To reach firmer conclusions will require yet further guidance by the Court of Justice.

7.4.6 Merits or Grounds for Annulment

Once admissibility has been established, the grounds or substantive merits must be proved. These are laid down in Art 263(2) TFEU and can often overlap in individual cases.

7.4.6.1 Lack of Competence or Authority

The lack of competence on the part of an institution to adopt a particular measure is really the equivalent of ultra vires ('beyond the power to act') and concerns the requirement that all measures must have the appropriate legal authority. Article 13(2) TFEU requires each institution to act within the limits of power conferred on it (and also Art 5(2) TEU). Case 9/56 *Meroni v High Authority* concerned the successful challenge to decisions taken by the High Authority, to which at the time no delegated decision-making powers had been granted.

There is a fair degree of overlap with the fourth category—misuse of power. Further examples of this ground include Case C-327/91 *France v Commission*, whereby the Commission exceeded its competence when it concluded an international agreement with the USA, because Art 300 EC (now Art 218 TFEU) required it to be concluded by the Council. Case C-57/95 *French Republic v Commission* involves a French action to annul a Commission 'communication'. The CoJ held that the Commission had no such power to adopt an act imposing new obligations on the member states that was not inherent in the treaty, thus the Commission lacked competence and the act was annulled.

The most important and clearest of these cases now is probably Case C-376/98 *Germany v European Parliament and Council (Tobacco Advertising)*, in which a directive banning tobacco advertising was introduced under a treaty Article concerned with the completion of the internal market and which was held not to authorize the enactment of legislation concerned primarily with public health. The directive was annulled.

---

[30] Case T-380/11 *Souliotis*, judgment of 12 September 2013 (OJ 2013 C313/23) and Case C-274/12P *Telefónica v Commission*, judgment of 19 December 2013, nyr.

7.4.6.2 **Infringement of an Essential Procedural Requirement**

Specific requirements are laid down by Art 296 TFEU that all EU secondary law must give reasons, and refer to any proposals and opinions made in respect of the provisions. The Court of Justice has held that insufficient or vague or inconsistent reasoning would constitute a breach of this ground. It was held in Case 24/62 *Germany v Commission (Wine Tariff Quotas)* that reasons must contain sufficient details of the facts and figures on which they are based. In Case 139/79 *Roquette and Maizena v Council*, the Council failed to consult the European Parliament, as required under old Art 43(2) EC. It had asked for an opinion, but did not wait long enough for the answer before going ahead with the regulation, which was subsequently annulled. In Case C-325/91 *France v Commission* it was held that there was a requirement to state the treaty base, the failure to observe this leading to the annulment of the measure. And, finally, in Case 17/74 *Transocean Marine Paint Association v Commission*, a measure that is not notified will deprive an applicant of the right to protest and to have their views made known or represented to the relevant institution, and is thus susceptible to annulment under Art 230 EC (now Art 263 TFEU).

7.4.6.3 **Infringement of the Treaty or any Rule Relating to Its Application**

This is the most frequently argued ground because it is capable of embracing all errors of EU law, including breaches of general principles or human rights including the EU Charter of Fundamental Rights, such as non-discrimination, proportionality, legitimate expectation, and right to a fair hearing. In the following cases, the CoJ recognized the general principles pleaded: Case 101/76 *KSH v Intervention Board* considered the principle of equality; Case 17/74 *Transocean* was concerned with the right to be heard; legitimate expectation was pleaded in a case challenging the milk quota Regulation in Cases C-104/89 and 37/90 *Mulder*; non-retroactivity was raised in Case 63/83 *R v Kirk*; and Case 112/77 *Töpfer* concerned legitimate expectation and legal certainty.

Case C-325/91 *France v Commission* would also be applicable here for infringing a treaty requirement, which was the requirement to state the treaty base.

7.4.6.4 **Misuse of Powers**

The basis of this ground concerns the use of power for the wrong purpose, as in the very early Case 8/55 *Fédération Charbonniere v High Authority*, which held, in respect of Art 33 of the European Coal and Steel Community (ECSC) Treaty, that the substance of the power must be related to the end result, and Case 105/75 *Giuffrida v Council* concerning the appointment of a Community official. This category comes very close to the first one, in that the use of power as the basis of unauthorized action is the equivalent of having no lawful basis for the action undertaken or acting beyond power.[31]

7.4.7 **The Effect of a Successful Action and Annulment**

Article 264 TFEU provides that if the action is well founded, the CoJ shall declare the act concerned to be void.[32] Article 264(2) TFEU provides that the CoJ shall, if it considers this necessary, state which of the parts of an act can be considered as definitive and can sever parts where possible. This means that the CoJ can specify those parts of the measure that will be annulled and those that may remain in force.

---

[31] More recently: Case C-442/04 *Commission v Spain* [2008] ECR I-3517.

[32] A schematic for the entire Art 263 action can be found in the Online Resource Centre (**www.oxfordtextbooks.co.uk/orc/foster5e/**).

In Case C-106/96 *UK v Commission (Poverty 4)*, considered in Section 7.4.1.2, the CoJ held that the Commission lacked the competence to commit the expenditure and the decision in the guise of an advertisement was annulled. However, in view of the fact that much of the expenditure had already taken place, the CoJ decided in the interests of legal certainty to exercise the discretion given to it under Art 231 EC (now Art 264 TFEU) and rule in favour of the payments made or promised.

Article 266 TFEU provides that where an act has been declared void, the institutions are obliged to take the necessary measures to comply with the judgment of the CoJ. The Court can also delay the date on which the annulled act becomes inoperative in order to give the institutions concerned the chance to enact a replacement where this is necessary as in the case of Case C-295/90 *EP v Council* on the free movement of students Directive 90/366. The CoJ may only annul the act referred to it or dismiss the action, but cannot order an institution to pay a sum of money; that is, it cannot fine the institution. The institution may, though, be liable to compensate under Art 340 concerned with the non-contractual liability of the institutions, considered in Section 9.3. The requirement to take action, however, does not go beyond the scope of the challenge leading to the annulment or apply, for example, to parties who have not challenged the decision imposing fines in competition proceedings. In Case C-310/97 P *Assidomän Kraft*, the company and others who had not challenged a competition decision fine attempted to require the Commission to refund fines on the basis of a Court ruling in respect of other companies who had successfully challenged the decision. The Court of Justice rejected that claim.

7.4.8 **A Restrictive Approach?**

The reasons for the difficulties in demonstrating *locus standi* have been subject to much debate and policy factors feature large in this discussion. For example, is there a floodgate policy whereby *locus standi* requirements have been interpreted particularly restrictively by the Court of Justice to reduce the number of cases coming before the Court of Justice and the General Court? Litigants face a lengthy wait to take their case to Luxembourg and so keeping the number of cases down will help to reduce delay. Another argument is the suggestion that there is a desire to promote the Court of Justice more as a supreme court of the member states and not as one directly accessible as a first-instance court for individuals, as was considered in Chapter 6. In this suggestion, it is argued that the national courts are best placed to defend individuals' interests and that, if required, cases for annulment should be referred by the national courts under Art 267 TFEU. To some extent, both these arguments were answered by the establishment of the CFI (now General Court) primarily to handle the rise in cases, elevating the Court of Justice to the role of an appeal court in relation to these categories of case.

Other arguments revolve around discussions about balancing the interests of the Union and individuals. The decision-making procedure in the EU is a much more complex procedure and is often the result of compromise, which makes legislation more difficult to enact. The inevitable economic choices of the Union are bound to affect individuals and sometimes in an adverse way, but they must be allowed to be made, otherwise the ability of the Union and Commission to operate would be undermined. Individuals' actions should not hinder the institutions' ability to operate. Comparisons with the member states may be made; such challenges nationally are also subject to equally tight *locus standi* requirements under the constitutional traditions of the member states, which often restrict or prevent individual challenges to general legislative measures or primary laws.

In those areas, by contrast, in which individuals find it easier to achieve standing, such as competition law, state aids, and anti-dumping measures, it may be argued that the very often closer involvement of particular individuals makes the difference. The applicants are likely to be the ones involved in the process by informing the Commission of certain situations or can be seen clearly to be affected by the measures complained about. This then sets them apart from the many other challengers, arising most frequently against legislative decisions made under the CAP. Furthermore, there are those cases that arise from the application of retroactive legislation in which the applicants are seen clearly as belonging to a fixed and identifiable group, and which would suffer an injustice if not allowed standing. In other words, the system works well when it needs to do so.

However, arguments for a more liberalized test were made by Advocate General Jacobs in Case C-50/00 *Union des Pequeños Agricultores (UPA) v Council*, influenced by the Charter of Fundamental Rights which provides that individuals are entitled to expect an effective judicial remedy. It was argued that the Art 230 EC (now Art 263 TFEU) restrictive *locus standi* test led to a possible denial of justice, because the law for individuals is complex and unpredictable. Introducing a less strict test would fit in with a general tendency to extend the scope of judicial protection in response to the growth of powers of the Union. Hence, the suggestion that applicants should be regarded as individually concerned where, by reason of their particular circumstances, the measure has, or is liable to have, a substantial adverse effect on their interests.

Whilst initially approved by the CFI in Case T-177/01 *Jégo-Quéré v Commission*, it was rejected by the CoJ in Case 50/00 *UPA*, making clear that the test established in Case 25/62 *Plaumann* remains valid and applicable. Furthermore, it stated in the appeal Case C-263/02 P *Commission v Jégo-Quéré* that any revision to the standing rules was not for the CoJ, but for the member states in the context of a treaty amendment, for which there have been a number of opportunities not taken up. Thus, it overturned the CFI decision, which it held had erred in law.

In Case C-167/02 *Willi Rothley and ors v European Parliament*, a plea for standing based on the right to judicial protection was dismissed by the Court of Justice, which stated that protection is still available through an Art 234 EC (now 267 TFEU) reference raising a question of the validity of Community law. However, as was noted in Chapter 6 and will be noted further later, there is no guarantee that such a reference will be made by the national court or accepted by the CoJ. The overall picture remains that of a continuing restrictive *locus standi* for applicants under Art 267 TFEU, although indirect alternatives are available to individuals, albeit with mixed success, which are considered next.

It may be argued that the inclusion of new Art 19(1) TEU, which requires that 'member states shall provide remedies sufficient to ensure effective legal protection in the fields covered by Union law', reinforces the argument that the Court of Justice should not be a court of direct access, but that matters be filtered first by the national courts or alternatively that the General Court or Court of Justice may now interpret more liberally the rights of individuals to challenge Union acts, but as yet that has not been the case.

7.4.9 Alternatives to Art 263 TFEU

7.4.9.1 A Reference under Art 267 TFEU

The first alternative, as noted earlier, is a reference from a national court to the Court of Justice for a preliminary ruling on the validity of acts of the institutions, which is a question that must be referred (see Case 314/85 *Firma Foto-Frost v Hauptzollamt Lübeck-Ost*). In general terms, actions under Art 267 TFEU avoid the strict time limits of Art 263 TFEU and are instead subject to the national time limits. For example, the challenge to the Commission regulations in Case 101/76 *KSH* had failed when raised directly before the CoJ, but was successful when made within an Art 234 EC (now Art 267 TFEU) reference in Cases 103 and 145/77 before the UK courts. See also Case 133/85 *Walter Rau v BALM* involving a challenge to a Community decision in a national court that was questioned by the national court because of the possibility that Art 230 EC (now Art 263 TFEU) could have been used. The CoJ held that if the outcome of the case depended on the validity of the decision, then a reference under Art 234 EC (now Art 267 TFEU) was permissible without having to decide if Art 230 could have been used. Hence, the possibility of an Art 263 TFEU action does not preclude an attempt to challenge an EU decision before the national courts.

However, Art 267 TFEU cannot be used simply to get round the time limits of Art 263 TFEU and, in Case C-188/92 *Textilwerke Deggendorf GmbH v Germany*, the CoJ held that the time limits in Art 230 (263 TFEU) apply equally to national court proceedings, and Art 234 (267 TFEU) rulings on invalidity and references will be barred if the applicant would undoubtedly have had standing under Art 230, but failed to take advantage of it within the time limit. The CoJ is more sympathetic to the Art 267 TFEU route where it can be shown that there was uncertainty as to whether the applicant would have had standing under Art 263 TFEU, or where a directive was involved that would clearly exclude individual challenge (Cases C-241/95 *Accrington Beef* and C-408/95 *Eurotunnel*).

There are further difficulties or requirements facing individuals wishing to raise a question of validity via Art 267 TFEU: there needs to be an element of national law to be able to raise a matter before the national courts. An Art 267 TFEU reference also increases the time involved in getting an answer by about two years and may lead to contrived cases being concocted in the national courts in order to challenge EU legislation. Finally, the national court retains the discretion whether to refer or not, and may not consider a reference necessary. Hence, Art 267 TFEU as an alternative is a very uncertain and unpredictable one.

7.4.9.2 The Plea of Illegality: Art 277 TFEU

If there are other proceedings taking place before the CoJ, a party can raise an issue of illegality of an EU regulation, but only indirectly or incidentally, and not as an independent cause of action. Thus, Art 277 TFEU is not simply a second chance to get around the strict time or *locus standi* limits of Art 263 TFEU; rather, it is designed to overcome the strict *locus standi* requirements for private parties in cases that would otherwise be unjust.

In reflecting previous Court of Justice case law, the new Art 277 TFEU has been amended from the old Art 241 EC to apply not only narrowly to regulations, but also all acts of general application. The Court of Justice already had held, in Case 92/78 *Simmenthal v Commission*, that the action would also cover acts that produce similar effects, but were not in the form of a regulation, on the grounds that individuals should be given the chance to have reviewed implementing decisions that are of direct and individual concern, thus echoing the *locus standi* requirements under old Art 230 EC (now Art 263 TFEU).

The grounds in the action are the same as in Art 263 TFEU. The effects are a declaration of inapplicability of the general act contested and an annulment of the individual decision due to illegality. They are considered in further detail later.

7.4.9.3 Action for Damages under Arts 263 and 340(2)

The action under Art 263 TFEU only annuls the act and does not provide compensation for a damaged but successful applicant; therefore damages must be pursued under Art 340 TFEU as a parallel or follow-on action. However, the Art 340 TFEU action is a separate and autonomous action, and not dependent on an earlier Art 263 TFEU or Art 267 TFEU action: see Case 4/69 *Lütticke v Commission*. Therefore it could be commenced without pursuing an Art 263 TFEU action first. Article 340 TFEU will be also considered in detail later.

7.5 Action for Failure to Act: Art 265 TFEU

Article 265 TFEU concerns actions against the European Parliament, the European Council, the Council, the Commission, the ECB, or other bodies, offices, or agencies of the Union for a failure to act, and constitutes an attempt to compel the institution or institutions concerned to take action. The unlawfulness of the institution is the failure to act in violation of a treaty duty, which clearly presupposes that there was a duty imposed on the institution to act in the first place. It complements an Art 263 TFEU action and can be pleaded at the same time. In Case 15/70 *Chevalley v Commission*, the Court of Justice held that it was not necessary to state that action was the subject of the application.

There are a number of similar features between the two Articles, but they were designed to cover different situations: Art 263 TFEU, illegal action; and Art 265 TFEU, illegal inaction. Both provisions, however, have as their objective the ending of a situation of illegality. Actions are heard at first instance by the General Court, with an appeal to the Court of Justice.

7.5.1 Admissibility and *Locus Standi*

7.5.1.1 Privileged Applicants

The EU institutions and member states have, under Art 265(1) TFEU, a privileged right of action that is not subject to restrictions on admissibility and, although not express, it was implicit that the European Parliament was a privileged applicant, as confirmed by Case 13/83 *European Parliament v Council (Transport Policy)*, in which it was established that the privileged applicants can request actions requiring general legislative acts, as well as decisions, without having to show any special interest. The ECB was given the right to take action by the TEU amendment to Art 265 TFEU in areas falling within its field of competence and now, according to Art 265 TFEU, all the institutions of the Union have the right to commence an action. These are now defined in Art 13 TEU, and include the European Council and the Court of Auditors.

7.5.1.2 Non-privileged Applicants

Individuals, on the other hand, have a restricted right of *locus standi* under Art 265(3) TFEU because there is no equivalent within the Article itself of directly and individually concerned, but they have instead to be potential addressees:

> Any natural or legal person may, under the conditions laid down in the preceding paragraphs, complain to the Court of Justice that an institution, body, office or agency of the Union has failed to address to that person any act other than a recommendation or an opinion.

It was established by case law that to challenge under Art 232 EC (now Art 265 TFEU), an individual must have been legally entitled to make a claim for action as a potential addressee: see Case 246/81 *Lord Bethell v EC Commission*, involving a complaint of a failure to act on price-fixing by the airlines. In the case, though, any potential act was to be addressed to the airlines and not Lord Bethell.

This strict view on the *locus standi* requirements has been tempered by the Court of Justice in subsequent cases, and now the requirements are analogous to the direct and individual concern of Art 263 TFEU (see Case C-68/95 *T Port v Bundesanstalt für Landwirtschaft und Ernährung*) in that a potential act would have concerned an individual in the same way.

7.5.2 Acts Subject to an Art 265 TFEU Action

In many cases, the CoJ has rejected applications by individuals for measures of general legislative content: see Case 15/70 *Chevalley v Commission* and Case 42/71 *Nordgetreide v Commission*, in which it was held that applications are restricted to decisions. Regulations cannot be requested because, by their nature, they are not capable of being addressed to specific individuals only. Directives are addressed to the member states thus it is only decisions on the face of it that are capable of being addressed to individuals. There must be an obligation under the treaty to adopt a reviewable act that is enforceable on the part of the institution. A demand for an opinion is not admissible (Case 15/70 *Chevalley v Commission*). Case 13/83 *European Parliament v Council (Transport Policy)* holds, though, that the acts requested need not be spelt out in detail, but must be sufficiently identified. Following the reforms to Art 263 TFEU, it is surprising that the same changes were not made to Art 265, although it is always possible that this might be done by judicial interpretation.

7.5.3 Procedural Requirements

7.5.3.1 The Invitation to Act

There is a preliminary procedural step that must be taken before Court action can ensue. Article 265(2) TFEU provides:

> If, within two months of being so called upon, the institution, body, office or agency concerned has not defined its position, the action may be brought within a further period of two months. The action shall be admissible only if the institution concerned has first been called upon to act.

The applicant must request the institution to take a specific action as legally required and advise that failure to do so will result in a Court action under Art 265 TFEU. The invitation to act need not follow any precise form to qualify for the purposes of Art 265 TFEU. Only if the institution fails to define its position within the two-month period can the matter be brought before the CoJ.

The application to the CoJ must be made within a further two-month period from the end of the initial two-month period. If the institution complies with the request to act, as in Case 302/87 *European Parliament v Council (Comitology)*, the CoJ will not allow the action to proceed.

7.5.3.2 Definition of Position

This requirement has been seen to defeat most actions, because where the institution has explained its refusal to act already—that is, defined its position—the action is inadmissible. In Case 48/65 *Lütticke v Commission*, the applicants had requested that the Commission take action against the German Federal Republic regarding a breach of Community law. The Commission was of the opinion that there had been no breach, so therefore refused to take action, but also notified the applicant of this. The CoJ declared the application inadmissible on the grounds that the notification of the refusal was a definition of position.

In Case 8/71 *Deutscher Komponistenverband (German Composers Group) v Commission*, a complaint that a decision taken by the Commission was wrong did not allow an applicant to proceed under Art 232 EC (now Art 265 TFEU) on the basis that the right decision was not taken by Commission; that is, it had failed to act in the right way.

In Case 125/78 *Gema v Commission*, a competition law complaint was made to the Commission under Regulation 17 (now replaced by Regulation 2003/1) about Radio Luxembourg. When the Commission failed to take any action, GEMA attempted an Art 232 EC (now Art 265 TFEU) action against the Commission. It was held that the letter from the Commission to GEMA stating its decision not to take action was a sufficient definition of position to defeat GEMA's action. Until Case 13/83 *European Parliament v Council (Transport Policy)*, a declaration by an institution of its unwillingness to act was regarded by some as constituting a sufficient definition of position for the purposes of the CoJ. However, the CoJ in the *Transport Policy* case stated that:

> In the absence of taking a formal act, the institution called upon to define its position must do more than reply stating its current position which in effect neither denies or admits the alleged failure nor reveals the attitude of the defendant institution to the demanded measures.

7.5.3.3 The Substantive Action

In the *Transport Policy* case (in the previous section), the European Parliament had complained that the Council had failed in its treaty obligations under Arts 3, 61, 74, 75, and 84 EEC to introduce a common policy for transport, lay down a framework for this policy, and act on 16 specific proposals of the Commission. The CoJ held, with regard to the first claim, that because the treaty requirements were so vague, there could not be said to exist sufficiently specific obligations as to amount to a failure to act, although, even so, the obligations should have been long since completed. The CoJ held that the obligation of Art 61 EEC could be identified with sufficient precision as to constitute a failure on the part of the Council to lay down a framework.

The second claim of failure to act on 16 proposals of the Commission was only successful regarding the proposals in respect of the freedom to provide services. The other measures were within the greater margin of discretion left to the Council by the treaty.

7.5.3.4 Results of a Declaration of a Failure to Act

The institution is required under Art 266(1) TFEU to take the necessary measures to comply with the judgment of the CoJ within a reasonable time. A continued failure to act would, of course, be actionable under Art 265 TFEU. Article 266 TFEU states that it is without prejudice to any action for damages under Art 340 TFEU, the action that is considered next.

7.6 Non-contractual Liability of the EU

While the TFEU specifically refers EU contractual liability disputes to the jurisdiction of national courts, Art 268 TFEU confers jurisdiction over disputes relating to claims for non-contractual liability damages under Art 340 TFEU to the Court of Justice. The General Court hears at first instance actions by individuals and the Court of Justice actions by the member states, although in the case of the latter, there have been none.

Article 340(2) TFEU requires the Union to make good damage caused by the institutions or servants in the performance of their duties in accordance with the general principles common to the laws of the member states. The term 'non-contractual' is employed to take account of the different legal traditions and to ensure that the Union is responsible for all its actions outside of contractual liability. Non-contractual liability thus covers the civil wrongs caused by the legislative and administrative activities of the Union, whether created by the institutions or the servants.[33]

7.6.1 Admissibility

As with Art 263 TFEU actions, there are four elements of admissibility to consider: the defendant institution; an act or inaction; a time limit; and *locus standi*. Unlike Art 263 TFEU actions, the latter aspect of standing is much more easily satisfied and will be considered first this time.

7.6.1.1 *Locus Standi*

In contrast to Arts 263 and 265 TFEU, there is not a restrictive *locus standi* imposed on applicants by either Art 268 or 340(2) TFEU. Applicants still need to show that some act of an institution was the source of the damage, and then show that the applicant has been affected and damaged in some tangible and provable way. They must be able to demonstrate some degree of loss without necessarily calculating the exact amount, but this can be quantified later if the action is found to be admissible and the claim upheld. For example, in Case T-376/04 *Polyelectrolyte Producers Group v Council and Commission*, the application was rejected as inadmissible by the CFI (now the General Court), because the allegations of loss made were unsupported by any evidence of loss.

7.6.1.2 The Defendant Institution and Act/Action

In an action against the Union, the appropriate institution—the legislative or administrative act, or the action or inaction, of which caused the damage—should be named as defendant. This can be the Commission or the Council, or both, which jointly legislate in many areas of EU law, as confirmed by the Court of Justice in Cases 63–9/72 *Werhahn v Commission*. Indeed now, in view of its greater powers, this can include the European Parliament either alone or in connection with the Council of Ministers. The ECB is also named in Art 340 TFEU as an institution that can be sued. Member states would only be sued where they are responsible for the implementation of Union measures and have exceeded the discretion that they were given. If there is no discretion on their part, the Commission would be the proper defendant (Case 175/84 *Krohn v Commission*). The action under Art 340 (2) TFEU does not extend to the treaties or accession acts which cause damage as these are the acts of the member states and not the institutions (see Case 169/73 *CCT v Commission* and Case C-95/98 *Dubois v Council & Commission*).

7.6.1.3 Time Limit

There is a five-year limitation period on actions, which commences from the occurrence of the event causing the damage (Case 5/71 *Schöppenstedt v Council*) or, if not discovered until later, from when the event causing the damage is discovered (Case 145/83 *Adams v Commission*).

---

[33] It does not however, include damages caused as a result of treaty requirements, specifically the creation and completion of the internal market which led to a claim by a customs agent that, understandably, his business had collapsed. In Case T-113/96 *Dubois v Commission* the agent sought damages for the loss suffered but his claim was dismissed by the General Court as being un-actionable against the agreements (as contained within the treaties) between the member states.

7.6.2 **An Autonomous or Independent Action**

The action for damages has been held by the CoJ to be an autonomous form of action having its own particular purpose to fulfil within the treaty system of remedies, and subject to conditions on its use dictated by its specific nature. In Case 4/69 *Lütticke*, damage had been suffered as a result of the Commission failing to act against Germany. The Commission argued that the action under Art 288 EC (now Art 340 TFEU) was an attempt to circumvent the *locus standi* requirements of a previous unsuccessful Art 230 EC (now Art 263 TFEU) action. The CoJ rejected this argument and declared that:

> the action for damages provided by Arts 235 and 288(2) [now Arts 268 and 340 TFEU] was established by the Treaty as an independent form of action and whose object was to compensate a party for damage sustained and not to secure the annulment of an illegal measure.

Further, in Case 5/71 *Zuckerfabrik Schöppenstedt v Council*, in an action for damages arising from a regulation, the Council had argued that the action should be ruled inadmissible because to allow it would frustrate the system of judicial remedies provided by the treaty by allowing a challenge to a regulation not allowable under Art 230 EC (now Art 263 TFEU), namely those applications ruled out as a result of a lack of *locus standi* or outside the short time limit. This was firmly rejected by the CoJ. However, in Case T-86/03 *Holcim (France) v Commission*, the General Court held that an action will be inadmissible if it was intended to have the same effect as an annulment action in respect of an individual administrative decision only. In such a case it is regarded as an abuse of process as an attempt to get round the much stricter time limits of Art 263 TFEU.

Therefore little difficulty faces applicants in respect of admissibility; the problem lies in proving an act of the Union caused damage and was a sufficiently serious breach.

7.6.3 **The Requirements of Liability**

Under Art 340 (2) TFEU, the liability of the Union is to be determined in accordance with the general principles common to the laws of the member states. When the Court of Justice looks to national laws for guidance and general principles, as in other instances of this practice, it is not required to accept the lowest common denominator, but makes a comparative review and selects principles of law appropriate to the situation. Therefore, a body of EU law is being built up in this area. From the case law, requirements have been identified to establish liability for the purpose of Art 340(2) TFEU that the Union is liable for either:

(a) damage caused by one of its institutions; or

(b) damage caused by its servants in the performance of its duties.

There must be a wrongful act or omission on the part of the Union that has breached a duty, the applicant must have suffered damage, and there must be a causal link between the act or omission and the damage.

7.6.4 **The Standard of Liability and Fault**

Liability can be imposed not only for administrative acts or omissions, but also for legislative acts, such as regulations, directives, or decisions. Liability can thus be incurred as a result of failures of administration, the negligence of employees of the institutions in the performance of their duties (but not extending to personal faults of employees), and the adoption of invalid legal acts. The act or omission of the Union must be shown to be wrongful; however, the degree of wrongfulness or fault varies depending on whether the wrong committed was the result of an administrative act, an act of one of the employees, or resulted from a legislative act.

Note now, however, that since Case C-352/98 P *Bergaderm* the CoJ has provided the view that a single test should apply to both administrative and legislative acts.

This section will, however, chart the development of the law in this area in respect of both types of act as previously developed and return to the new test later.

7.6.4.1 Administrative Acts

While a requirement of fault is not express from the treaty, case law indicates that it is necessary for the establishment of liability for damage caused by administrative acts. In Case 14/60 *Meroni*, the CoJ ruled that the liability is based on fault in that there must be negligence in the administration or construction of a scheme of regulation for ferrous scrap before there can be liability when the scheme malfunctions. The CoJ held that the mere existence of errors in the administration of the scheme is not in itself evidence of a wrongful act or omission, since they might be caused by the fact that the problems tackled by the scheme are difficult to resolve. In Cases 19, 20, 25, and 30/69 *Richez Parise*, the Commission had supplied wrong information to its staff about pension rights. This information was based on an incorrect interpretation of the rules concerning rights that they could claim on the termination of their service. The CoJ held that only in exceptional circumstances would an incorrect interpretation constitute a wrongful act. However, in this case, the Commission was at fault by failing promptly to remedy the error of interpretation as soon as it became obvious that its interpretation was erroneous. Therefore its failure to issue a correction within a reasonable time was of such nature as to render the Commission liable.

There is a notorious case in EU law concerning the liability of the Union institutions in respect of acts of its servants.[34] Case 145/83 *Stanley Adams v Commission* concerned the liability of the Community for a breach of the duty of care owed to its informants in the sphere of competition law. Adams claimed a breach of confidence of information by releasing documents by which Hoffmann-La Roche could identify Adams as the person blowing the whistle when it was investigated and fined under competition law. Article 287 EC (now Art 339 TFEU) imposes a duty on members of staff of institutions not to disclose information covered by professional secrecy. It was held that the Commission remained under a duty not to reveal its source even when Adams left his employment. Hoffmann-La Roche discovered his identity and the Swiss public prosecutor was informed. Adams was tried in his absence and convicted of industrial espionage, which is a criminal offence in Switzerland. The Commission was aware of the risk that Adams would be identified by handing over documents and failed to tell Adams of the threats to prosecute the informant. On return to Switzerland, Adams was arrested and jailed. His wife, who was suffering from depression, committed suicide when informed about a possible 20-year jail sentence for her husband. The Commission was held liable to make good the damage resulting from the discovery of the applicant's identity, but Adams was held to have been contributorily negligent by not informing the Commission that he could be identified from documents and failing to ask the Commission to keep him informed of progress.

---

[34] There has even been a film on this: *A Song For Europe/A Crime of Honour* (1985), directed by John Goldschmidt (see **http://www.imdb.com/title/tt0088964/** for more information).

The *Adams* case is an illustration of the rules relating to duty, vicarious liability, causation, and contributory negligence.

7.6.4.2 Liability for Employees

The possibility of vicarious liability for employees was raised in Case 9/69 *Sayag v Leduc*, in which Mr Sayag was employed by the European Atomic Energy Community (EURATOM) and, whilst showing guests of the Community round in his own car, was involved in an accident in which his passengers were injured. They sued Sayag who claimed the Commission should be held responsible. It was held that the Commission was not liable because it was not an official act of the Community: 'the Community is only liable for those acts of its servants which, by virtue of an internal and direct relationship, are the necessary extension of the tasks entrusted to the institutions of the Community'. There was also the possible policy reason that the person's own insurance should cover the damage. The scope of liability was thus limited to activities of institutions or the performance of institutional tasks.

7.6.4.3 Liability for Legislative Acts

The principle that there can be liability on the part of the institutions for damage resulting from the adoption of legislative acts, which is the most important one in terms of the potential damage that can be caused by wide-reaching legislative acts, was confirmed in Case 5/71 *Schöppenstedt v Council*. However, the CoJ has laid down a strict test, which became the standard required to establish liability. In the case, the plaintiffs claimed that a regulation breached the principle of non-discrimination in Art 34(2) TFEU. The Court of Justice held that 'The Community does not incur liability on account of a legislative measure which involves choices of economic policy unless a sufficiently flagrant violation of a superior rule of law for the protection of the individual has occurred'. In *Schöppenstedt*, it was held that discrimination was a superior rule of law, but that it had not been breached.

The reasoning for the strict test is very similar to the strict requirements for *locus standi* for Art 263 TFEU in that the high degree of discretion that the institutions need to carry out the economic tasks for which they are responsible necessarily affects many persons, hence the imposition of a higher burden when choices of economic policy are involved. The point is that the act concerned is not just an administrative decision of the Commission, but a legislative act that has been brought about as the result of reaching the agreement of, if not all 28 member states in the Council, at least a significant majority of them when voting by QMV. Therefore it is not only unlawful conduct that will attract liability, but it is also the degree of unlawful conduct required under the formula developed by the CoJ. All types of legislative act can be subject to an action under Art 340(2) TFEU.

The *Schöppenstedt* formula can be divided into two parts, although in some treatments it is divided into three parts, as follows:

(a) a violation or breach of superior rule of law (which can be linked with the next part)

(b) the rule must exist for the protection of natural or legal persons

(c) the violation must have been sufficiently serious.

Case C-352/98 P *Bergaderm v Commission* appears to have modified the test laid down in *Schöppenstedt* in that the CoJ now requires there to be a sufficiently serious breach of a rule of law intended to confer rights on individuals, which is the same for member state liability as developed from the *Francovich* case (see Chapter 6 for details).

Whilst this has been followed up in some CFI (now General Court) and ECJ cases,[35] there is not as yet a completely definitive line of authority to be sure that the more complex approach in *Schöppenstedt* has been abandoned for ever.

7.6.4.3.1 The Rules of Law Covered

The rules of law include specific legal rules contained in legislation, fundamental rights, and general principles. The principles of proportionality, legal certainty, equality/discrimination, and legitimate expectation seem most often to be raised.[36]

The treaty Article in *Schöppenstedt* was regarded as a superior rule of law. Article 40(2) TFEU (ex Art 34(2) EC) provides that the CAP and measures taken under it 'shall exclude any discrimination between producers or consumers within the Union'. In Case 64/76 *Dumortier Frères v Commission (Gritz and Quellmehl)*, the ending of a subsidy was held to be a breach because it was retained on starch that was in direct competition. (See also Case 83/76 *HNL* and Cases 103 and 145/77 *KSH v Council and Commission (Royal Scholten Holdings)*, which are also often cited in respect of the same rule of law.) The rule that there should not be unjustified enrichment was recognized in Case T-166/98 *Cantina* and confirmed in Case C-47/07 P *Masdar (UK) v Commission*.

7.6.4.3.2 The Protection of the Individual

The protection of the individual, which includes either natural and legal persons, has been interpreted to include the protection of classes of persons also, as with the importers in Cases 5, 7, 13, and 24/66 *Kampfmeyer*, in which a regulation aimed generally at the agricultural markets was held to include individuals within those markets. In Case 74/74 *CNTA v Commission*, involving the general principle of legitimate expectation, the Commission was held liable to pay compensation for losses incurred as a result of a regulation that abolished with immediate effect and without warning the application of compensatory amounts. It was considered a serious breach of the principle of legitimate expectation, which was designed to provide individual protections. See also Case T-69/00 *Fiamm*, in which individuals were held to be affected indirectly by Community acts, but which action was held to be admissible, although it was not successful ultimately on a damages issue.

7.6.4.3.3 The Breach Must Be Sufficiently Serious

This is required because it is a challenge to an economic policy choice of the Union involving exercise of wide discretion. So, whilst a breach of an important rule of law that is hierarchically superior to more general rules of law is required, a mere breach is not sufficient to trigger liability; a sufficiently flagrant or serious breach is required. In Case 83/76 *HNL v Commission*, a regulation requiring cattle food manufacturers to use more expensive skimmed milk than cheaper soya in their foods (to use up the 'milk lake') was held to be invalid, and declared null and void, because it offended the principles of proportionality and discrimination (Art 34(2) EC, now Art 40(2) TFEU). However, whilst in the Art 288 EC (now Art 340 TFEU) action, the breach was acknowledged, it was held not to be a sufficiently serious or flagrant breach. Almost inevitably in the regulation of the CAP and particular food products, a legislative decision by the Commission to allow or restrict the production will affect, often adversely, the economic position of individual farmers. To

---

[35] See e.g. Case T-16/04 *Arcelor*, which also focused on the degree of discretion rather than the seriousness or arbitrariness of the breach. See also Case C-282/05 P which did, though, apply *Bergaderm*.

[36] All of these are discussed in Chapter 3.

permit them to succeed in actions for damages each time would completely undermine any attempt to control the market. The Commission and Union would be rendered useless. In *HNL*, the CoJ held:

> The legislative authority . . . cannot always be hindered in making its decisions by the prospect of applications for damages whenever it has occasion to adopt legislative measures in the public interest which may adversely affect the interests of individuals.

Thus, liability is incurred only where there has been a manifest and grave disregard of the limits on the exercise of their powers. This was itself later interpreted in Cases 103 and 145/77 *KSH v Council and Commission* as conduct verging on the arbitrary.

Preliminary rulings in Cases 117/76 and 16/77 *Rucksdeschel*, and Cases 124/76 and 20/77 *Moulins de Pont à Mousson (Maize, Gritz, and Quellmehl Cases)*, had held that regulations providing higher production refunds for maize starch than maize gritz were incompatible with Art 34(2) EC (now Art 40(2) TFEU) and thus invalid. New lower refunds had been set for maize gritz and the companies claimed damages. The question was: had the Council of Ministers manifestly and gravely disregarded the limits of power? In the cases known collectively as the *Maize, Gritz, and Quellmehl* cases,[37] the CoJ held that the Council had manifestly and gravely disregarded the limits of power for the following reasons:

1. Article 34(2) (ex Art 40(2)) was important protection of individuals.
2. Only a small defined and closed group of commercial applicants were affected.
3. The damage must be over and above economic risks normal in business.
4. The equality of treatment ended without sufficient justification.
5. The Council ignored a Commission proposal.

The *Quellmehl* cases had the same result with regard to a discriminatory treatment by the Commission of maize starch and quellmehl, both products used in the baking industry. In both cases, damages plus interest were awarded.

Another product-specific series of cases dealt with the production of isoglucose, an artificial sweetener that competed with sugar. It was heavily penalized by a regulation, which was later annulled, but the consequence was that the producers had already suffered massive losses, including some producers going out of business. Their claims for losses failed, because the breaches were not 'verging on the arbitrary'. This is typified in the *Isoglucose* cases (Cases 116, 124, and 143/77 *Amylum and Tunnel Refineries*).

Factors that influence the CoJ in its determination of whether the breach is sufficiently serious include the clarity of the rule breach, the effect of the breach, and the manner or nature of the breach. The effect of a measure relates to its scope, the number of people affected, and the damage caused and if that damage was unusual. The manner of the breach relates to whether it was intentional or accidental or whether it was excusable such as the difficulty in reaching decisions in complex situations or difficulties in interpreting the legislation. Other important factors are whether there is a higher Union public interest involved and the numbers involved. Previously, it was considered that only a small defined and closed group of applicants could successfully pursue a claim (see Case 152/88 *Sofrimport*), and that if large numbers were involved, this would defeat a claim, but in

---

[37] The *Maize Gritz and Quellmehl* cases (which also include Cases 64 and 113/76, 239/78, 25, 27, and 28/79 *Dumortier Frères v Council*; Cases 241, 242, and 245–50/78 *DGV v Commission and Council* [1979] ECR 3017; Case 238/78 *Ireks Arkady v Commission and Council* [1979] ECR 2955; and Cases 261 and 262/78 *Interquell v Commission and Council* [1979] ECR 3045).

Cases C-104/89 and 37/90 *Mulder v Council*, the CoJ suggested that a large group of applicants need not be fatal to a claim. They were ones who had previously been compensated for not producing milk, in one of the attempts to reduce or prevent over-production of milk, a scheme that was abandoned following understandable widespread criticism. The new regime allowed all farmers to produce a certain percentage of previous years' production only. These farmers' cows had produced none, of course, so the farmers were therefore disadvantaged. Hence the CoJ held that the presence of a large group of claimants did not defeat a claim, although a serious breach still had to be demonstrated and that there was no higher public interest of the Union involved. The application in the case itself though was not successful because the Commission had not exceeded its discretion, therefore the breach was not sufficiently serious.

7.6.5 A New Single Test for Liability?

According to the AG in the *Factortame* case up to 1995, only eight awards had been made against the Community institutions,[38] which seemed to indicate that the *Schöppenstedt* formula, as it had been applied, had been far too strict and needed to be modified. As previously discussed in Chapter 6, the CoJ applied the standard established for Art 340 TFEU in the *Schöppenstedt* case to the member states when it came to assessing whether damage caused by them to individuals because of a breach of EU law should be compensated. There had been discussion, however, about whether the standard in fact had been maintained in the same way for both the institutions and the member states. Thus, in Case C-352/98 P *Bergaderm v Commission*, the Court of Justice took the opportunity to modify or simplify the test laid down in *Schöppenstedt*. The CoJ considered the parallel developments in the cases on state liability, including, in particular, Cases C-46 and 48/93 *Brasserie du Pêcheur* and *Factortame*, and adapted the test for liability from those cases. The modification requires there to be a sufficiently serious breach of a rule of law intended to confer rights on individuals, and whether there had been a disregard of the limits of discretion by the institution involved.

The slight change in emphasis from superior rules of law for the protection of individuals to those rules conferring rights and the emphasis on discretion brings into line the test for liability under state liability and Art 340 TFEU actions. It suggested that where the institutions and member states had manifestly and gravely disregarded the limits of their discretion, then the breach would be sufficiently serious to incur liability. It also extended the test for all acts, rather than only for legislative acts—a point that was considered in Chapter 6. Hence, then, as with member states, where there is no discretion, a mere infringement will suffice but, where there is discretion, it will be a matter of the degree by which the institution exceeded that discretion. The matters, taken from the *Factortame* case, that the Court in *Bergaderm* considered affected this degree, in addition to the discretion already noted, included the clarity and precision of the law, whether intentional or not, and whether excusable or not.

Whilst the new formulation has been followed up in some General Court cases and on appeal to the Court of Justice, there is not as yet clear authority to be sure that the more complex approach in *Schöppenstedt* has been abandoned entirely.

See, for example, Case T-212/03 *My Travel Group plc v Commission*, in which there were grave and manifest faults in the Commission's consideration of a proposed merger which led to the blocking of the merger and loss to My Travel Group. It was held that as a

---

[38] [1996] ECR 1029, 1101.

consequence of the complexity of the merger and market combined with the difficulties in applying the relevant EU law within tight time constraints and the margin of discretion enjoyed by the Commission, it was not to be liable. Also Case T-16/04 *Arcelor* focused on the degree of discretion enjoyed by the Commission and less on the seriousness or arbitrariness of the breach.

However, in Case C-282/05 P *Holcim* which did, though, apply *Bergaderm*, the sheer difficulty encountered by the Commission in investigating an extremely complex competition market was again the most important factor in holding the Commission not to be liable and thus the result was the same as if the more complete *Schöppenstedt* formula had been applied.

It therefore remains very difficult to assess whether the *Bergaderm* case is actually changing how cases are analysed by the General Court or Court of Justice in the determination of liability and still further case law is required.

7.6.6 Individual (Non-legislative) Acts

The *Schöppenstedt* test was developed specifically to apply to general legislative acts, and because the subsequent *Bergaderm* case was a modification of this, it might have been expected that it would not be appropriate for acts applying to or affecting an individual only. However, in *Bergaderm*, the CoJ also addressed this point and held that it was not material whether the act alleged to have caused damage was legislative or administrative, but rather, as noted earlier, whether the institution exceeded the limits of its discretion. This was confirmed in the later Case C-282/05 P *Holcim v Commission*, in which the CoJ held that the requirement to show a sufficiently serious breach should also apply to individual acts.

It would be helpful to see further cases from the CoJ supporting this development.

7.6.7 Liability for Lawful Acts

In a further development, the possibility that the Union may be liable, in certain circumstances, for damage caused by lawful acts has been explored. In the earlier Case C-237/98 P *Dorsch Consult v Council*, which concerned the banning of trade in Iraq under an EC regulation complying with a United Nations (UN) Resolution and resultant losses, the CoJ held that, in order to be held liable, such losses would have to be unusual and special. Case T-69/00 *FIAMM & FIAMM Technologies et al v Council and Commission*, and now the appeal case C-120/06 P, concern regulations enacted under the infamous EU banana regime, which were incompatible or alleged to be incompatible with the World Trade Organization (WTO) agreements. As a result, the USA took retaliatory measures by increasing customs duties on other products, causing loss to the applicants for damages as a result of the impact on their imports to the USA. Whilst the disputed regulations were lawful in the EU regime, internationally they were not. The CFI (now General Court) held that although the conduct was not unlawful, an action for damages could be admissible where the economic operators had borne a disproportionate burden as a result of the countermeasures to the EU regulation of the banana market contrary to WTO rules. The applicants still need to show actual damage, a causal link between the conduct of the EU institution and the damage, and the unusual and special nature of the damage.

Whilst the case was not successful, it has widened the category of potential acts that can incur liability. On appeal, the Court of Justice confirmed the judgment on the facts of the CFI that no liability accrued in this case, and disapproved the principle that lawful acts could, given the appropriate facts, give rise to liability. Further case law is thus required on this point.

7.6.8 The Damage

Having established the existence of an act or omission attributable to the Union, damage to the applicant must be proved. Damage can be purely economic, as in Cases 5, 7, 13, and 24/66 *Kampfmeyer* involving a cancellation fee and loss of profits, but this must be specified and not speculative, or damage can take the form of moral damage (Case 110/63 *Willame v Commission*). In Case 74/74 *CNTA*, compensation for the losses caused by a sudden change to export refunds contrary to the legitimate expectations of the company was upheld, although in the case itself currency fluctuations meant that no actual loss was recorded.

It has been held that the damage must be over and above the risk of damage normal in business (see Case 64/76 *Dumortier Frères v Council*). In Case C-152/88 *Sofrimport v EC Commission*, concerned with Chilean apples in transit, import licences were suspended whilst the cargo was on the high seas. The applicants in *Sofrimport* were successful in obtaining damages because of the complete failure of the Commission to take into account the interests of the applicants when they were required to do so, which therefore amounted to a sufficiently serious breach of legitimate expectation. The damage went beyond the limits of economic risk inherent in business.

As noted earlier, Case T-69/00 *FIAMM & FIAMM Technologies et al v Council and Commission*, and now the appeal Case C-120/06 P, concern regulations enacted under the infamous EU banana regime. The CFI (now General Court) held that although the conduct disputed was not unlawful, an action for damages could be admissible, but that the applicants still need to show actual damage, a causal link between the conduct of the EU institution and the damage, and the unusual and special nature of the damage. In this case, it was held that the conduct of the defendant institutions had led to retaliatory measures being adopted that were the cause of the damage sustained. However, the CFI considered that the extent of damage suffered was neither unusual nor beyond the economic risks that might be expected in their economic sector, and the actions failed.

A claim for compensation for damage caused has also been held to include a claim for an injunction to prevent further future damage as held by the General Court in Case T-279/03 *Galileo*. Part of the Court's reasoning was that this should be available as it is in national legal orders dealing with tortious or delictual claims.

7.6.9 The Causal Connection

Lastly, it must be proved by the applicant that the act of the Union caused the damage with a sufficiently direct connection between the act and the injury. The damages must be ascertainable (Cases 5, 7, 13, and 24/66 *Kampffmeyer*). In Cases 64 and 113/76 *Dumortier Frères v Council (Gritz and Quellmehl)*, it was held that there was no need to make good every harmful consequence, especially where remote. Damage must be a sufficiently direct consequence of the unlawful conduct of the institution concerned. In Case 169/73 *Compagnie Continentale Française*, it was held that the causal link was only established if the misleading information given would have caused an error in the mind of a reasonable person. In Case 132/77 *Sugar Export*, it was held that the chain of causation may be broken by an independent act of a third party.

In summary, the damage must be certain, specific, proven, and quantifiable, and it may cover imminent foreseeable damage and lost profits (Cases 5, 7 and 13–24/66 *Kampffmeyer*).

7.6.10 **Concurrent Liability/Choice of Court**

For the most part, the application of EU legislative measures, especially in the agricultural sector, are actually administered by and thus dependent on the national intervention agencies that make payments and receive payments. However, if a claim is based on a Union act that was wrongful, the question arises of whether the appropriate forum is a national court or the Court of Justice. Where the claim involves return of sums unlawfully paid to national authorities, compensation must be sought from the national authorities before the national courts, followed if necessary by a reference under the Art 267 TFEU procedure (Cases 5, 7, 13, and 24/66 *Kampffmeyer*) especially where joint liability of the member state and the EU can be proved. It is only really the conduct of the institutions or servants that would require application to the CoJ or where the claims are for unliquidated damages; that is, those involving loss of profits suffered as a result of illegal Union action (Case 74/74 *CNTA*; see also Case 175/84 *Krohn v Commission*).

7.7 **The Plea of Illegality**

This action under Art 277 TFEU provides a right to plead the illegality of an EU regulation in different circumstances from the direct challenge of Art 263 TFEU.

Article 277 TFEU reads:

> Notwithstanding the expiry of the period laid down in the fifth paragraph of Article 263, any party may, in proceedings where an act of general application adopted by an institution, body, office or agency of the Union is at issue, plead the grounds specified in Article 263, second paragraph, in order to invoke before the Court of Justice of the European Union the inapplicability of that act.

Article 277 TFEU is not an independent or direct cause of action to the CoJ, as confirmed in Case 33/80 *Renato Albini v Council and Commission* and Cases 31 and 33/62 *Wöhrmann v Commission*. The Court of Justice held that Art 241 (now Art 277 TFEU) was only available in proceedings already brought before the CoJ under some other action, and only as an incidental or indirect action. For example, it may be that, during the course of an Art 263 TFEU challenge to a decision, it comes to light that another EU act, such as a regulation, which was the legal base for the decision, was for some reason unlawful, but was beyond challenge itself due to the time limit or a lack of *locus standi* under Art 263 TFEU, as considered earlier. This would provide the grounds under which Art 277 TFEU might apply. It cannot be used in Art 340 TFEU actions, considered earlier, nor in Art 258 TFEU actions against member states.[39]

7.7.1 *Locus Standi*

The Art 277 TFEU action is available to any party including, it is argued, but without clear authority from the CoJ, the member states. However, it is more likely to benefit individuals who, for good reason, are unable to comply with the *locus standi* and time-limit

---

[39] See Case 70/72 *Commission v Federal Republic of Germany*.

requirements of Art 263 TFEU. However, it is not designed or intended to provide a back-door for those who have simply failed to meet the requirements of Art 263 TFEU. The conditions for *locus standi* under this action are exactly the same as Art 263 TFEU. This means when challenging legislative acts, direct and individual concern must be demonstrated and when challenging non-legislative acts (the delegated regulations), only direct concern need be shown but as with Art 263 TFEU, the act must not entail implementing measures.

In Case 156/77 *Commission v Belgium*, a Community decision was challenged directly before the CoJ; however, the CoJ refused the application because Belgium had allowed its right under Art 230 EC (now Art 263 TFEU) to expire.

Article 277 TFEU is designed more for those who either have no rights under Art 263 TFEU or were unable to meet the *locus standi* requirements, but who nevertheless are affected by the illegality of a Union act, usually a decision. For example, in Case 216/82 *University of Hamburg v Hauptzollamt Hamburg*, the university was able to challenge a decision addressed to the German government indirectly before the national court because it was directly and individually concerned by it but, because the decision was not published, it was unable to challenge it under Art 230 EC (now Art 263 TFEU).

7.7.2 Acts that Can Be Reviewed

Article 277 TFEU refers to acts of general application only, which can be challenged only if they form the legal basis of the subject matter of the direct action, as in Case 9/56 *Meroni v High Authority*. Article 277 TFEU does not envisage the challenge of decisions or other forms of binding act. However, in Case 92/78 *Simmenthal v Commission*, a decision was challenged that was based generally on prior regulations and notices. The regulations could not be challenged directly under Art 173 EEC (now Art 263 TFEU) because of the restrictive *locus standi* requirements, but could be challenged indirectly via Art 184 EEC (now Art 277 TFEU). The CoJ held that it was not the form of the act that is important, but the substance. Therefore, other acts that were normative in effect should be regarded as a regulation for the purposes of Art 277 TFEU and can be challenged under Art 277 TFEU, thus applying to notices and decisions that, in substance, have the effect of general or normative acts.

Addressees of an individual act such as a decision cannot challenge it indirectly in the Court of Justice because they should have done so directly under Art 263 TFEU within the time limits. To allow otherwise would render the time limit meaningless, as confirmed in Case 156/77 *Commission v Belgium*.

7.7.3 Grounds of Review

The substantive grounds of the action are those listed for Art 263 TFEU. Case 92/78 *Simmenthal* succeeded on its merits that the general measure had been used for purposes other than that for which it was intended; that is, its proper purpose.

7.7.4 Effect of a Successful Challenge

The result of such an action is that the regulation is declared inapplicable in that case and not generally void (see Case 9/56 *Meroni v High Authority*). Any acts based on this voidable regulation will, however, be void and withdrawn. Also, in practice, the regulation will not be applied in subsequent cases, as is the consequence in Art 267 TFEU (ex Art 234 EC) references; for example, refer to Case 66/80 *ICC*.

7.8 Actions against Natural or Legal Persons

This category represents the third set of direct actions, this time against legal and natural individuals, but is only relevant in certain limited circumstances. The TFEU permits action by the Commission against legal and natural persons to ensure that they comply with Union law. Mainly under the competition rules, the Commission is provided with the possibility of taking a decision that companies have breached the competition rules and is empowered to fine them, against which there is an appeal to the General Court, with the possibility of a further appeal to the Court of Justice.

Article 261 TFEU provides the Court of Justice with unlimited jurisdiction to review such penalties as may be imposed by the Commission under EU law provisions. The power of the Commission to impose fines is provided by Regulation 1/2003 and under the Merger Regulation 139/2004.

Note the growing potential size of the fines. In Case T-51/89 *Tetra Pak Rausing SA v Commission*, the company was fined 75 million European currency units (ecus), which was upheld by the Court of Justice in Case C-333/94 P *Tetra Pak Rausing SA v Commission*; and in Commission Decision 98/273, Volkswagen was fined 102 million ecus, which was about £67 million, but which was reduced before the CFI to 90 million ecus in Case T-62/98. In Case T-201/04, the fine imposed on Microsoft by the Commission of €497 million was upheld by the CFI.[40]

Further Reading

Books

GORDON, R. *EC Law in Judicial Review*, Oxford University Press, Oxford, 2007.

HARTLEY, T. *The Foundations of European Community Law*, 6th edn, Clarendon Press, Oxford, 2007 (especially chs 10–13 and 15–17).

LENAERTS, K., ARTS, D., and MASELIS, M. *Procedural Law of the European Union*, 2nd edn, Thompson, London, 2006.

WARD, A. *Judicial Review and the Rights of Private Parties in EU Law*, 2nd edn, Oxford University Press, Oxford, 2007.

Articles

ALBORS-LLORENS, A. 'The Standing of Private Parties to Challenge Community Measures: Has the European Court Missed the Boat?' (2003) 62 Cambridge LJ 72.

ALBORS-LLORENS, A. 'Remedies against the EU Institutions after Lisbon: An Era of Opportunity?' (2012) 71 Cambridge LJ 507.

---

[40] Most recently, the Commission handed out a fine of €1.38 billion to four glass-making firms that had acted as a cartel in fixing prices and customers, with the largest fine of €896 million going to Saint-Gobain of France (Cases T-56/09 and T-73/09 [2014] ECR nyr) but which was reduced for that company; and in the *Intel* case IP/09/745, Intel was fined €1.06 billion for its infringements of EU competition law (Case C-413/14 P *Intel v Commission* [2014] ECR I-547 and appeal pending).

ARNULL, A. 'The Principle of Effective Judicial Protection in EU Law: An Unruly Horse?' (2011) 36 EL Rev 51.

BALTHASAR, S. 'Locus Standi for Challenges to Regulatory Acts by Private Applicants: The New Article 263(4) TFEU' (2010) 35 EL Rev 542.

CORTES MARTIN, J.M. 'Ubi ius, ibi remedium? Locus Standi of Private Applicants under Article 230(4) EC at a European Constitutional Crossroads' (2004) 11 Maastricht Journal of European and Comparative Law 233–61.

ENCHELMEIER, S. 'No One Slips Through the Net? Latest Developments, and Non-developments, in the European Court of Justice's Jurisprudence on Art 230(4) EC' (2005) 24 YEL 173.

GUTMAN, K. 'The Evolution of the Action for Damages against the European Union and its Place in the System of Judicial Protection' (2011) 48 CML Rev 695.

HARLOW, C. and RAWLINGS, R. 'Accountability and Law Enforcement: The Centralised EU Infringement Procedure' (2006) 31 EL Rev 447.

HILSON, C. 'The Role of Discretion in EC Law on Non-contractual Liability' (2005) 42 CML Rev 677–95.

KILBEY, I. 'Financial Penalties under Art 228(2) EC: Excessive Complexity?' (2007) 44 CML Rev 743.

KILBEY, I. 'The Interpretation of Article 260 TFEU (ex Art 228 EC)' (2010) 35 EL Rev 370.

PEERS, S. and COSTA, M. 'Judicial Review of EU Acts after the Treaty of Lisbon' (2012) 8 ECLR 82.

PRETE, L. and SMULDERS, B. 'The Coming of Age of Infringement Proceedings' (2010) 47 CML Rev 9.

USHER, J. 'Direct and Individual Concern: An Effective Remedy or a Conventional Solution' (2003) 28 EL Rev 575.

VOGT, M. 'Indirect Judicial Protection in EC Law: The Case of the Plea of Illegality' (2006) 31 EL Rev 364.

WARD, A. 'Locus Standi under Article 230(4) of the EC Treaty: Crafting a Coherent Test for a "Wobbly Polity"' (2003) 22 YEL 45–77.

WENNERAS, P. 'A New Dawn for Commission Enforcement under Arts 226 and 228: General and Persistent (GAP) Infringements, Lump Sums and Penalty Payment' (2006) 43 CML Rev 31.

WENNERAS, P. 'Sanctions against Member States under Article 260 TFEU: Alive but not Kicking?' (2012) 49 CML Rev 145.

Web-based Materials

http://ec.europa.eu/community_law/index_en.htm
Website concerned with monitoring the application of Community law in the member states, which includes access to the Annual Reports.

PART II

Introduction to the Substantive Law of the European Union

As was indicated in the introduction to Part I, this second part of the book is concerned with the substantive law of the EU and assumes that the reader has already acquired an understanding of the topics covered within Part I. Although it would not be impossible to study the substantive law without such understanding, doing so would be more difficult. The subjects chosen for Part II are those most commonly found in EU law courses, covering probably about 90–95 per cent of all such courses. Substantive law topic choice is no longer dictated by the Law Society and Bar Council because they appear no longer to have a specific requirement; therefore in theory this offers a free choice of topics to include. While previously the Law Society and the Bar Council required that only an introduction to the internal market and free movement of goods was to be studied, most courses understandably included that topic in full; in addition, most university courses also consider the free movement of persons, including citizenship. EU competition law is often included in general EU law courses, but mainly in introductory form, leaving more detailed coverage to specialist courses at either undergraduate or postgraduate level. Further, many courses also include equality/non-discrimination law, although often restricted to discrimination on the ground of sex. As a consequence, the subjects included in this volume are: the internal market and the free movement of goods; the free movement of persons including citizenship; competition law and sex discrimination law. These substantive law topics have been covered in four chapters only, which, while not common practice, allows all of the relevant material to be gathered in one place, thus avoiding as far as possible the division and repetition of material.

In turning to the content of the chapters themselves, the 'freedoms' are clearly part of the wider aims of the Union, as expressed in the preambles to the treaties and Art 2 TFEU. By freeing the basic factors of production, it was intended that economic development and expansion would be encouraged and promoted throughout the Union. The four fundamental factors are the freedom of movement of goods, persons, services, and capital—the last not being covered in this text.

Competition law concentrates on the leading topics of agreements and concerted practices, abuse of dominant positions, merger control, and a brief consideration of state aid. Social policy, in particular sex discrimination, falls outside the four freedoms, but is nonetheless discussed.

There is often an overlap of areas of substantive law that is both inevitable and necessary in the context of the internal market. The prohibition of discrimination also imposes itself in the other areas of substantive law where appropriate: for example, within the free movement of persons and free movement of goods. As was also indicated in Chapter 4, the European Court of Justice has, for a long time, referred to the support that must be given to the four freedoms of the Union that it regards as fundamental elements or cornerstones of the Union and will do its best to uphold them. It will interpret the EU rules of law generously—that is, wherever possible, it will try to uphold the EU rules in the face of national legislation. The exceptions or derogations allowed to the member states in some of the provisions are interpreted narrowly against the member states. The aim is to give the greatest possible effect to EU rights and less scope to member state derogations that, if allowed free rein, would undermine the aims of the Union.

Whether EU law is studied in two or more courses or all in one course, it can be observed that many of the cases that appear in Part I are those that have arisen in an action in one of the substantive law topics. *Van Gend en Loos*, for example, which first established direct effects, is a case concerned with customs duties in the common market; *Von Colson*, establishing indirect effects, arises from a sex discrimination case; and *Factortame*, concerned with nationality discrimination, supremacy, and national procedural rules, is a case based essentially on the right of establishment without nationality discrimination within the free movement of persons. EU law and this book abound with many more examples. Studying the institutional, procedural, and substantive parts together very often reinforces the study and understanding of each.

8

The Free Movement of Goods

8.1 Introduction

The free movement of goods is, following the European Coal and Steel Community (ECSC), the foundation and very core of the European Union today. It is very much concerned with the economic ideals of the Union to create a single trading bloc in which all factors of production—and particularly goods—flow freely. The free movement of goods is essential to the creating and running of the customs union and the common market, and provides the infrastructure for the rest of the Union. Amongst the prime reasons for establishing the European Economic Community (EEC) and the very concept of a common European market was to create a stable trading and producing bloc capable of competing with the USA and the then strongly emerging Japanese economy, and as a bulwark against the then rising threat of communism in the era of the Cold War. Today, we would add the BRICS[1] economies to the list of principal economic competitors. In particular, these countries benefit from their own huge internal markets even before considering their export markets and potential. They help to emphasize the benefits of achieving economic integration and having a large internal market to allow companies to realize growth and to specialize which, in turn, allows them to compete on the world economic stage. This, it is argued, creates a dynamic, competitive market for the benefit of producers, consumers, and the member states. The broader underlying advantages are, though, more than merely the creation of an economic Community and, indeed, as was dealt with in Chapter 1, one of the original main aims of integration was to make the member states interconnected and interdependent, and thus less likely to go to war with each other. However, creating and maintaining the common market has proved to be much more difficult than first envisaged in view of the member states' attempts to protect their own national producers and industries.

At this early stage, the significance of a complementary competition law policy should be stressed, because it is vital to the successful running of the internal market. The establishment or foundation of the EU is premised on the desire to promote integration and to create a single unified market. A competition policy within the overall treaty regime prevents companies from setting up their own rules and obstacles to trade to replace the national rules and obstacles that the Union is trying to abolish. The two go hand in hand: without either, the aims of creating a single unified market would be defeated. To have prevented the member states, on the one hand, from restricting the movement of goods only to allow private companies to do it by means of agreements and practices

---

[1] BRICS = Brazil, Russia, India, China and South Africa. There are now additional acronyms for rising/emerging economies: MINT, PIGS, MIST, and CIVETS but these are overlapping and none have yet established themselves clearly. See, of the very many articles you can find on this topic, from the *Wall Street Journal* 2014: **http://www.wsj.com/articles/SB10001424052702304250204579431392126736568**.

would defeat the objectives of the first policy; to prevent companies from artificially dividing the markets, but to allow the member states to do so would undermine a competition policy. Hence, there is a need for both. However, since those beginnings, the expansion of the Communities and Union into many more policy areas, including regional and social policies, has significantly rebalanced the focus of the Union into one that is no longer driven primarily by the internal market or purely economic policies, although these still figure prominently.

8.2 Legislative Provisions

8.2.1 Treaty Articles

The preamble to the former EC Treaty has proved instrumental in the Court of Justice rulings on cases involving the free movement of goods, as have Arts 2 and 3, 10 (the fidelity clause), and 12 EC (the prohibition of discrimination on the grounds of nationality). The relevant treaty Articles today are: Arts 3 and 4 TEU and Arts 3, 4, and 18 TFEU.

There are four main groups of provisions in the TFEU connected with the internal market, which are set out initially in Arts 26 and 27 TFEU:

(a) customs duties and charges having equivalent effect (Arts 28–30 TFEU)

(b) the Common Customs Tariff (CCT) (Arts 31 and 32 TFEU)

(c) the prevention of national taxation systems from discriminating against goods imported from other member states (Art 110 TFEU)

(d) quantitative restrictions or measures having an equivalent effect on imports and exports (Arts 34–6 TFEU).

In this chapter in particular, it is worth taking a careful note about the Treaty of Amsterdam and Treaty of Lisbon Article number changes which have made life difficult in this area of law, because old Art 30 EEC, which provides one of the basic prohibitions in this area, became Art 28 EC and then Art 34 TFEU, while the old Art 36 EEC concerned with derogations became Art 30 EC (the old Article number for the prohibition) and is now returned to Art 36 TFEU under the Lisbon Treaty. More frequently than for other chapters, both numbers will be provided where confusion might otherwise arise.

As one of the cornerstones and one of the fundamental freedoms of the Union, the free movement of goods has been stoutly defended by the Court of Justice, as will be seen in the case law considered later in the chapter. The free movement of goods objectives have been set out in a revised, briefer form in Art 3 TFEU than was the case previously under Arts 2–4 EC:

(3) The Union shall establish an internal market.

(4) The Union shall establish an economic and monetary union whose currency is the euro.

The internal market is then defined in Art 26 TFEU as 'an area without internal frontiers where the free movement of goods, persons, services and capital is ensured in accordance with the provisions of the treaties'.

Therefore, the aim is to achieve the circulation of goods without customs, duties, charges, or other financial or other restrictions, and to promote unlimited trade and to remove from the member states the control over export and import matters. The Union is exclusively responsible for import and export duties and tariffs by the grant of exclusive competence in this area under Art 3 TFEU.

Articles 114 and 115 TFEU are important treaty Articles designed to help to achieve and maintain the single internal market. Article 114 TFEU specifically provides additional competences for the achievement of the internal market by the use of qualified majority voting (QMV) and the co-decision procedure. Article 115 TFEU provides the Council, acting unanimously, with powers to enact directives to approximate member states' laws that directly affect the establishment or functioning of the common market.[2]

8.2.2 Secondary Legislation

There is very little secondary legislation of direct importance in this area of EU law, but Directive 70/50 will be considered, as will Regulation 764/2008 and Directive 98/34. There is, however, a large amount of case law to consider.

8.3 Progress Towards the Treaty Goals

Whilst the goals of integration have been outlined, progression towards them is not, of course, an overnight thing and has to be achieved over a series of moves. Various stages in economic integration have been generally recognized which, in crude terms, are as follows.

8.3.1 A Free Trade Area

The free trade area involves the removal of customs duties between member states, but the members of a free trade area decide themselves their external policies and any duties payable by third-party countries wishing to export goods to the free trade area countries. It is this latter aspect that is regarded as of little use, because third countries may target the country with the lowest external duties. Any goods entering will compete with internal goods of the Union and thus certification of origin is often required, which is difficult and expensive to administer.

8.3.2 A Customs Union

The next stage is a customs union, which builds on the stage outlined in the previous section by creating a common external tariff, presenting a common position to the outside world. The same duties are imposed on goods entering the customs union regardless of from where they are imported or which entry port to the customs union is used. Once imported, the goods circulate freely as union goods throughout the union.[3]

8.3.3 A Common Market

A common market, which may also be called the 'internal' or 'single' market, is the next stage, which adds to the defined customs union in the previous section the free movement

---

[2] The use and abuse of these Articles has been considered in the context of the competences discussion in Chapter 3, and will be considered further briefly later in this chapter in relation to harmonization.

[3] In the EU, this is established and governed by Arts 28(1), 31, and 207 TFEU.

of the factors of production (goods, persons, and capital) and a competition policy. Its definition was emphasized by the CoJ in Case 15/81 *Schul* as the 'elimination of all obstacles to intra-Community trade in order to merge the national markets into a single market bringing about conditions as close as possible to those of a genuine internal market'.[4]

8.3.4 An Economic Union

Almost finally, an economic union would be all of the previous stages plus the harmonization or unification of economic, monetary, and at a very advanced stage fiscal policies, but including primarily the creation of a common currency controlled by a central authority. The final step would then be full political union in a confederation or federal state with one overall or umbrella governing body exercising a number of common policies.

8.3.5 Which Stage Has the EU Reached?

Whilst its goals are clear, as outlined previously, just how far has the EU progressed? Articles 26 and 28–32 TFEU make it clear that a customs union should be established, which includes a common—or single, or internal—market. The EU certainly has a customs union with a CCT that is exclusively regulated by the Commission. The degree to which a true common market has been achieved is more doubtful, given the considerable case law still arising that is evidence of the sheer number of obstacles still in the way of the unified market. However, 18 countries,[5] which now represent more than half the member states, have gone further and established an economic and monetary union, with a European Central Bank (ECB) and a single currency.

8.3.5.1 Internal Market Developments to Date

The initial means by which the goals of the Union were to be achieved commenced with an attempt at total harmonization. In line with the original views, outlined in Chapter 1, that success or harmonization in one area would lead to 'spillover' to related areas (workers' rights, for example), it was considered that progress would be steady; however, for various reasons, legislative stagnation set in relatively swiftly. Amongst those reasons, the French boycott and subsequent Luxembourg Accords, the late 1960s economic downturn, the 1970s oil crises and world economic recession, and the increase in the number of member states all possessing a veto over legislation not in their national interest all featured to slow progress. Consider, as a classic example, the Architects Harmonization Directive, which took 18 years to enact. To a large and necessary extent, this was countered by judicial innovation in, for example, Case 26/62 *Van Gend en Loos*, the creation of the doctrine of direct effects, and other leading cases that demonstrated that the Court of Justice was to interpret the treaty in a purposive approach and not the actual words used. (A further example, Case 2/74 *Reyners*, is considered in Chapter 9.) However, the member states remained reluctant to carry the common market project forward themselves.

From the late 1970s, these problems were acknowledged and when new Commission President Delors took office there was sufficient support from commerce and industry and the member states for the single market project. This led to the Commission White

---

[4] [1982] ECR 1409.

[5] Latvia became the 18th member state to join the single currency on 1 January 2014 and Lithuania became the 19th member on 1 January 2015: see http://www.eurozone.europa.eu/euro-area/euro-area-member-states/.

Paper *Completing the Internal Market*,[6] which was endorsed by the European Council in 1985. It set out 300 legislative measures needed to complete the single market and 1992 was set as the target date by which those measures should have been enacted. '1992' then became the recognized term for that goal. This also marked a shift in approach in that whilst national rules would be harmonized where needed, other means of achieving the goals were emerging, including a shift to new, broadly construed, technical harmonization and moves towards mutual recognition, spurred on by the Court of Justice decision in Case 120/78 *Cassis de Dijon*. The Single European Act (SEA) provided the needed institutional and legal reforms to facilitate the meeting of the targets set by the '1992' project (for example, by the introduction of Art 95 EC, now Art 114 TFEU, to allow for harmonization measures and QMV in Council to ease the passage of legislation). In addition, other policies started to be put into place that were regarded as necessary to support the single market as a result of the realization that the single market could not be achieved in isolation—so an environmental policy was introduced, along with, for example, an economic and social cohesion policy.

The single market was given a particular boost by the Treaty of Maastricht (TEU), which established economic and monetary union (EMU), although not for all of the then 15 member states. This nevertheless led to the expansion of other EU competences in order to complement the internal market, the latter being regarded as incorporating more than economic concerns and more of an ongoing and dynamic project, rather than as one with a definable end. It might be argued that this demonstrates a return to functional integration or creeping federalism, noted in Chapter 1, in that the desire to move to economic and monetary union led to the establishment at the EU level of other policies that were regarded as vital to support and, indeed, sustain economic and monetary union.

Following the entry into force of the Lisbon Treaty, new Art 4(2) TFEU provides that the internal market is a shared competence of the Union and the member states.

8.4 Integration Methods

Integration of what were a number of separate national markets was, and is, to be achieved by two main integration strategies: namely, positive and negative integration. *Negative integration* is the removal of existing impediments to free movement, such as striking down national rules and practices that obstruct or prevent achievement of the internal market, and *positive integration* is achieved by the modification of existing national laws and institutions, either by harmonization of the divergent national laws or the creation of new common European laws.

8.4.1 Negative Integration

Negative integration involves the outlawing of national rules and practices that obstruct the fundamental free movement regimes. In the EU legal order, this form of integration is found in the statutory attempt to ensure the free movement of goods under Arts 28–37 TFEU, workers under Arts 45–8 TFEU, the provision of services and establishment under Arts 49–62 TFEU, and capital under Arts 63–6 TFEU. In the area of goods, Art 34 TFEU provides that 'Quantitative restriction on imports and all measures having equivalent effect shall be prohibited between member states'. However, there are statutory

---

[6] OJ 1985 COM (85) 310 final.

exceptions to the total prohibition for specific agreed reasons under Art 36 TFEU, which provides that Art 34 TFEU shall not preclude prohibitions or restrictions that are justified on certain grounds contained within an exhaustive list in the Article, which will be considered later in this chapter.

Negative integration represents a deregulatory approach—that is, an attempt to reduce regulation rather than to increase regulation in order to remove obstructive laws and practices so that free movement can be achieved. Negative integration has been vastly assisted by the judicial development of direct effects and the other forms of individual enforcement that help to police the member states, and highlight member states' laws and actions that do not conform with the free movement provisions. The leading Case 26/62 *Van Gend en Loos* cannot be beaten as an example. In addition, the provision of Art 18 TFEU (ex Art 12 EC), the general rule prohibiting discrimination, is also vitally important in this area because, prior to the establishment of the common market, free movement of goods could be restricted solely on the basis of the country from which the goods came.

8.4.1.1 The Prohibition of Discrimination

Article 18 TFEU provides: 'Within the scope of application of the Treaties, and without prejudice to any special provisions contained therein, any discrimination on the grounds of nationality shall be prohibited.' Thus, the nationality of goods or persons within this internal market should not play a role again. In the history of Europe, this is an incredible concept, which is perhaps not appreciated today by most of the readers of this book. Previously (and this applies still to those outside the EU), discrimination of different persons—namely, all those outside a single state—solely on the basis of nationality was perfectly lawful—and, worse still, perfectly acceptable! Now, for many, it seems astonishing that a state, or we ourselves, would treat people and goods differently simply on the basis of where they come from. But if either comes from outside the EU, this is still acceptable. Consider an example very close to home: in the UK, the state and other universities charge non-EU and EU students different tuition fees, although the education and the provision is the same, purely on the basis of where those students come from. Within the EU, though, the new internal market regime means that this is no longer possible or acceptable between the 28 member states.

Discrimination can appear in the form of direct discrimination, which is usually clear and easy to spot in a difference in treatment of, or different rules being applied to, imports from that of domestic products. It is not restricted to intentional discrimination, but also unintentional discrimination, if the effect of a rule is nevertheless to discriminate against imports. The prohibition of discrimination in the EU legal order, though, also includes indirect discrimination and thus catches restrictions that, on the face of it, do not apply nationality criteria, although the effects are as if that were the case.

Indirect discrimination has now been given statutory definition in the EU legal order.

> Indirect discrimination: Where an apparently neutral provision, criterion or practice would put persons of one class at a particular disadvantage compared with persons of the other class, unless that provision, criterion, or practice is objectively justified by a legitimate aim, and the means of achieving that aim are appropriate and necessary.[7]

Indirect discrimination, however, can be justified objectively. The best case to demonstrate this in the area of goods is Case 120/78 *Cassis de Dijon*, which will be considered

---

[7] See Directives 2000/43 (OJ 2000 L180/22), 2000/78 (OJ 2000 L303/16), and 2006/54 (OJ 2006 L204/23).

later in detail, but the criteria that must be met by the objective justification are equally clearly set out in a case from the free movement of persons. In Case C-55/94 *Gebhard*, the Court of Justice held that restrictions albeit applying to both nationals and non-nationals:

- must be applied in a non-discriminatory manner
- must be justified by imperative requirements in the general interest
- must be suitable for securing the attainment of the objective that they pursue
- must not go beyond what is necessary in order to attain it.

More recent developments in case law have gone beyond the need to show discrimination and it has been held that any measures that do not discriminate against, but nevertheless make life more difficult for, exporters or importers may also be caught by the free movement of goods prohibitions. These will be considered in further detail towards the end of this chapter.

8.4.2 **Positive Integration**

Positive integration involves the introduction of new laws or, viewed in another light, marks a return to regulation as a means of ensuring that there is a level playing field for imported and domestically produced goods by the introduction of new EU-wide laws, or by the setting up of new institutions to provide EU-wide regulation and control: for example, the ECB and the single currency.[8] It also includes the harmonization or approximation of national legislation by replacing multiple and divergent national rules or, where relevant, the absence of national law, with a single EU rule that advances free trade. However, in seeking to establish common rules, the EU has been anxious to avoid agreeing on the lowest common denominator, but instead is keen to achieve a common rule that protects other important interests (essentially social interests) and which thus avoids, in the EU jargon, the 'race to the bottom' like the US Delaware Corporation legislation.[9]

In the EU, harmonization is achieved by legislative intervention empowered by specific treaty bases, such as for the free movement of workers (Arts 45 and 46 TFEU) and also by the provision of the general legal bases, Arts 114, 115, and 352 TFEU, which we have already seen in Chapter 3 in the section on competences. There are, however, limits to the scope and, thus, use of the general legal bases, and therefore to harmonization itself. This was seen in Case C-376/98 *Germany v European Parliament and Council (Tobacco Advertising Ban Directive)*, whereby the measure was annulled for being based on the internal market Art 95 EC (now Art 114 TFEU), which could not support the motive for the tobacco advertising ban, which was essentially motivated by the concern for public health. In the second *Tobacco Advertising* case, Case C-380/03 *Germany v European Parliament and Council*, it appears, however, that the Court of Justice has erred more in favour of harmonization, due to the potential obstacles to the market as a result of the differing national regimes on the advertising of tobacco products. Complete harmonization—that is, the same rule, which amounted to a complete ban in certain circumstances—was then

---

[8] '[T]he modification of existing instruments and institutions, and more importantly, to the creation of new ones so as to enable the market of the integrated area to function properly and effectively and also to promote other broader policy aims of the [integration] schemes': El-Agraa, *The EU: Economics and Policies*, Cambridge University Press, Cambridge 2001, p 3.

[9] The US state with the most lax company registration and regulation laws, which attracts many companies to register in that state and thus get away with lower standards for workers and minority shareholders, amongst others.

argued and accepted as an internal market measure to stop market fragmentations. It was thus justified and could be based on Art 95 EC. In particular, in the second Tobacco Advertising Directive (2003/33) were provisions excepting advertising in tobacco trade journals as a part of the exception from the ban on free movement of products complying with the directive. Harmonization, therefore, is not without its problems and the extent to which harmonization methods can be used has also been questioned.

In Case C-66/04 *UK v Council and European Parliament (Smoked Flavourings)*, the UK challenged the use of Art 95 EC (now Art 114 TFEU) to set up a regulatory body, which, in turn, issued opinions on food safety that were the basis for Commission regulations restricting the marketing of products on health and safety grounds, in this case the use of certain smoked flavourings. The CoJ held that, in order to achieve harmonization in certain markets that require scientific analysis, it may be necessary to set up appropriate bodies or procedures to undertake this and report to the Commission, which must then take the final decision. Hence, the establishment of new levels of regulatory bodies can be regarded as part of the process of harmonization under Art 114 TFEU, provided that they are closely defined and controlled by the Union institutions, and are in pursuit of harmonization for the improvement and better functioning of the internal market.[10] This area, then, may see a considerable expansion of the use of Art 114 TFEU, which, whilst contributing to the internal market, is of concern to the member states as yet another example of competence creep.[11]

8.4.3 Methods of Harmonization

There are different forms of harmonization that can be undertaken, as follows.

8.4.3.1 Total or Complete Harmonization

Total, or complete, harmonization—also known as 'exhaustive' harmonization—involves one rule being enacted for the whole Union, which precludes the member states from legislating in the same area. This means that each member state is prevented from raising an additional standard that would serve to exclude imports. For example, see Directives 70/156 and 76/756 on car headlights, which were considered in Case 60/86 *Commission v UK (Dim-dip Headlights)*. The directives covered all car lighting, but did not address the dim-dip facility that the UK had previously required for both imports and domestically produced cars. Following the enactment of the directives, the UK could not impose this on cars made in other EU countries that did not provide this facility.

This form of harmonization requires that the standards, and thus products, must be exactly the same, with no regional variations. It is criticized largely because of the images it produces of the 'Euro-sausage' or the 'Euro-banana' and the idea that Brussels wants to harmonize everything in the EU—hence, the view that it is best used in cases in which there is compelling evidence, for safety reasons, that a single common rule is needed.[12]

---

[10] See also the later Case C-217/04 *UK v Council and European Parliament (Network and Information Security Agency)*, again involving a challenge to an agency set up under Art 95, but again condoned by the Court of Justice providing that the agency contributed to harmonization by advising on how measures to be adopted in the area of ICT might be affected by, and might impact on, security issues.

[11] The concern about the division of competences is considered in Chapter 3, but was something that was addressed specifically by both the Constitutional Treaty and Lisbon Treaty, although rejected respectively by the French, Dutch, and Irish electorates when they voted against those treaties.

[12] Thankfully, there has been a step back from this kind of thinking recently, in that regulations banning non-standard-shape vegetable and fruit produce have been repealed. See Commission Press Release IP/08/1694, 'The return of the curvy cucumber: Commission to allow sale of "wonky" fruit and vegetables', available at **http://europa.eu/rapid/pressReleasesAction.do?reference=IP/08/1694**.

8.4.3.2 **Optional Harmonization**

Optional harmonization incorporates the idea that producers need only follow the provisions of a directive where they intend to trade the goods across an EU member state frontier. If they do not intend to export, they can still choose to follow the directive, but it is not regarded as very satisfactory and can lead to two differing standards in each member state. It does not take account of the fact that those products may subsequently be imported and traded in other member states, and would not then meet the appropriate standard. Also, in the home state, there would be products on the market meeting both home and EU standards, thus leading to possible confusion amongst consumers. Thus, it is no surprise that it has not been resorted to very often.

8.4.3.3 **Minimum Harmonization**

As it suggests, minimum harmonization involves the establishment of a minimum standard, but does not mean that the member states cannot go further and insist on higher domestic standards. The latter would not apply, though, to imported goods. For example, Directive 89/622, now replaced, concerning tar and nicotine labelling was considered in Case C-11/92 *R v Secretary of State for Health, ex p Gallaher Ltd and ors*, in which the CoJ held that the member states can retain or adopt much higher standards than the minimum standards provided in the Community legislation. In Case C-84/94 *UK v Council (Working Time)*, the CoJ advised that 'minimum standards' does not mean *minimal* standards, as in necessarily adopting the lowest common denominator; the Union minimum may be set at a fairly high level and member states remain free in any case then to set higher standards domestically, although any such national standards must still conform to the general free movement of goods rules and not prevent imports.

8.4.3.4 **The New Approach Legislation**

The New Approach Directives (Directives 83/189 and 98/24, Regulations 764 and 765/08, and Decision 768/2008, for example) are those so-called following a change of approach to harmonization by the Commission by which directives were aimed very broadly at a whole industry and which provided general principles rather than detailed rules. They rely very much on the technical standards being set by private bodies; that is, those industrial bodies, especially research and standards institutes, that are in the know and are more appropriate in devising the appropriate technical standards, especially for consumer products and safety standards, considered further under Section 8.10.3.

8.4.4 **Alternatives to Legislative Harmonization**

Rather than harmonize, which can be a very long-winded process, an alternative led by a judicial development is that of the 'mutual recognition' of standards. This principle was one of two leading principles affecting the free movement of goods established by the CoJ and made prominent in the landmark case of *Cassis de Dijon* (Case 120/78 *Rewe-Zentrale AG v Bundesmonopolverwaltung für Branntwein*), which will be considered in full in Section 8.10.1. This decision essentially holds that if a product is lawfully produced in one state meeting the safety and health standards of that state, then states into which the product is imported should accept those standards, and thus the products, as the equivalent of domestic standards and products. They should not then ban the import for not complying with different domestic standards.

Following this case, the Commission picked up the ruling as a crucial tool in completing the internal market by insisting, for example, on 'mutual recognition clauses' in national product regulations, whereby a state would be required, in setting its own standard for a product, to include a mutual recognition clause that it would accept other national standards.[13] In Case C-184/96 *Commission v France (Foie Gras)*, the CoJ held France at fault for not including such a clause, which has now become a standard requirement as a result.

8.5 The Establishment of the Internal Market

8.5.1 The Common Commercial Policy and the Common Customs Tariff

The common market, which is a customs union, provides not only for the elimination of duties regarding goods originating in other member states, but also regarding goods originating in third countries that are in free circulation in the common market and on which customs duties have been paid. The external duties are fixed by the Union for goods imported from outside the Union and a single set of common tariffs is adopted in trade relations with the outside world (Art 31 TFEU). The Common Commercial Policy (CCP, Arts 206–7 TFEU) is the overall policy basis for the establishment and maintenance of the CCT. The CCT is also referred to as the 'common external tariff', and imposes a single tariff for all imports, and it is exclusively established and regulated by the Commission. Once a product has been imported into the EU, it is then in free circulation and further tariffs cannot be imposed on the product (Art 29 TFEU). This aspect is now within the entire competence of the Union and is ever more tied up with world developments on customs duties—most notably, the World Trade Organization (WTO).[14]

8.5.2 The Prohibition of Customs Duties

These sections concern not only customs duties in the strict sense, which are a hindrance to free trade, but also any financial barriers that have an equivalent effect, however named. Necessarily, we must also consider aspects of member states' tax regimes, because these may be a disguised way of imposing additional financial burdens on imported products, thus making them less competitive or even uncompetitive. Therefore the treaty also includes provisions (Art 110 TFEU) to deal with these, but the treaty Articles concerned with customs duties will be considered first. (Note that the provisions on goods and tax are mutually exclusive sets of provisions, even though often dealing with the same factual situation—an aspect that will be considered more fully later.)

Articles 28 and 30 TFEU are aimed at the abolition of customs duties and charges having equivalent effect, and at prohibiting the introduction of any such measures.

---

[13] This also prompted the Commission to issue its 'Communication from the Commission concerning the consequences of the judgment given by the Court of Justice on 20 February 1979 in Case 120/78 ("*Cassis de Dijon*")', OJ 1980 C256/2. Reproduced in N. Foster (ed), *EU Treaties and Legislation*, latest edn, Oxford University Press, Oxford.

[14] The general aspects of external relations are considered briefly in Chapter 1. See also C. Barnard, *The Substantive Law of the EU: The Four Freedoms*, 4th edn, Oxford University Press, Oxford, 2013, pp 29–34, and ch 7. In the early days of the EU, the CCP and CCT were given extensive treatment in textbooks, but this is no longer regarded as warranted with the extensive developments elsewhere in the EU and EU law, hence its lack of detailed consideration in this volume.

Article 28 TFEU states that the Union shall be based on a customs union, with a CCT, involving the prohibition of all customs duties on imports and charges having equivalent effect.

8.5.2.1 Definition of Goods

This provision covers 'all trade in goods', with goods being defined by the Court of Justice in Case 7/68 *Commission v Italy (Art Treasures)* in which Italy claimed an export tax on art treasures was to protect the artistic heritage of Italy. The Court held goods to be 'products which can be valued in money and which are capable, as such, of forming the subject of commercial transactions'. The definition of goods was extended in Case 45/87 *Commission v Ireland (Dundalk Water Supply)* to include the provision of goods within a contract for the provision of services and further in Case C-2/90 *Commission v Belgium (Waste)* to include even those goods of no commercial value. In the case this involved non-recyclable waste. Electricity has also been classified or defined as coming within the concept of goods.[15]

Article 30 TFEU prohibits customs duties or charges having equivalent effect, and applies both to imports and exports. It also specifically mentions that it applies to customs duties of a fiscal nature. It was held to be directly effective, under the previous numeration of Art 12 EEC, in the leading Case 26/62 *Van Gend en Loos*. Whilst it is relatively easy to recognize a customs duty, which is usually designated as such and is a clear duty applied at the border, it is less easy to identify 'a charge having an equivalent effect'; thus a considerable body of case law has arisen trying to define this, although there has been relatively little case law for a few years now, which is arguably a sign that the law in this area is not only settled, but adhered to by the member states. The total prohibition of customs duties per se means that cases of such an obvious breach rarely arise, hence the concentration on charges having equivalent effect (CHEE).

8.5.3 A Charge Having Equivalent Effect (CHEE)

In Cases 2 and 3/62 *Commission v Belgium & Luxembourg (Gingerbread* case), involving a tax on imported gingerbread to compensate for a domestic tax on wheat used to make gingerbread internally, the Court of Justice held that:

> a duty, whatever it is called, and whatever its mode of application, may be considered a charge having equivalent effect to a customs duty, provided that it meets the following three criteria: (a) it must be imposed unilaterally at the time of importation or subsequently; (b) it must be imposed specifically upon a product imported from a member state to the exclusion of a similar national product; and (c) it must result in an alteration of price and thus have the same effect as a customs duty on the free movement of products.

In certain circumstances, a charge may be acceptable if it is a service rendered for the benefit of the importer, if it is specifically required by EU law, or if it is part of a system of internal taxation. These criteria are all subject to further refinement by the Court of Justice.

In Case 24/68 *Commission v Italy (Statistical Levy* case), a small (10 lira) levy, which was imposed on imports and exports for the purpose of financing statistical surveys, was held to breach Community law. Whilst there was no discrimination between imports and exports, the CoJ stressed that the purpose of using the concepts of customs duties and

---

[15] Case C-393/92 *Almelo* [1994] ECR I-1477.

CHEEs was to avoid the imposition of any pecuniary charge on goods circulating within the Community by virtue of the fact that they cross a frontier. The CoJ stressed that any charge must be considered in the context of the achievement of one of the fundamental objectives of the EC Treaty, and in modification of its stance in *Commission v Belgium & Luxembourg*, the CoJ offered the following definition of a CHEE to include 'any pecuniary charge, however small and whatever its designation and mode of application, that is imposed unilaterally on domestic or foreign goods by virtue of the fact that they cross a frontier'.

Such a charge is a CHEE:

- even if it is not imposed for the benefit of the member state concerned
- even if it is not discriminatory or protective in effect
- even if the product on which it is imposed is not in competition with any domestic product.

In this case (Case 24/68), the levy was found to hamper the interpenetration of goods that the EEC Treaty aimed to secure and thus had an effect equivalent to a customs duty. It was further held that the levy could not be regarded as the consideration for a specific benefit actually conferred on the importer, because the advantages of the survey were so general and difficult to assess. This aspect will be considered further in Section 8.5.3.1 following.

In Cases 2 and 3/69 *Sociaal Fonds voor de Diamantarbeiders*, a levy on the import of uncut diamonds was used to go towards a social fund for workers in the diamond industry. It was not used in any protective way over national products but was held nevertheless to be a charge regardless of the purpose or motive. It was thus irrelevant that Belgium does not produce diamonds. The effect of the charge is to create an obstacle to free movement.

The concept of border also includes internal borders where charges are levied on the movement of goods.[16]

Claims by member states concerning charges for services rendered, such as for health inspections and warehousing fees during clearance of customs formalities, have been carefully considered by the Court of Justice, and are considered next.

8.5.3.1 The Validity of Charges for Services Rendered

The CoJ has developed its rules over a number of cases regarding when it is lawful to charge for services rendered. In Case 132/82 *Commission v Belgium (Customs Warehouses)*, the CoJ considered the questions of whether a charge having equivalent effect may be permitted as a consideration for services rendered. The Belgian authorities allowed customs formalities for goods originating in, or in free circulation in, another member state to be completed either at the frontier or within the country. When the goods were presented for customs clearance at special stores of public warehouses, a fee fixed and levied by the municipal authorities was payable. This fee was payable in consideration of the use by the importers of the premises made available to them to store their goods pending clearance through customs. The state did not receive the money. The only role played by the state was to fix the maximum fee payable. The CoJ held that when payment of storage charges is demanded solely in connection with the completion of customs formalities, it cannot be regarded as consideration for services actually rendered to the importer.

In Case 340/87 *Commission v Italian Republic (Customs Posts)*, Italian legislation required importers that presented themselves at Italian customs outside normal Italian

---

[16] See Case C-363/93 *Lancry* [1994] ECR I-3957 and Case C-72/03 *Carbonati Apuani* [2004] ECR I-8027.

opening hours (six hours a day) to pay a fee. Article 5 of Directive 83/643 required customs offices at frontier posts to open for normal business hours of at least ten hours a day, Monday to Friday. Therefore, in order to comply with the directive, Italian customs officials would have to work four hours' overtime and Italian law sought to impose a charge during that four-hour period. The Italian government maintained that this was a charge for a service rendered that was commensurate to the value of the service. The CoJ said that it had already held on several occasions that a charge imposed on goods by reason of the fact that they cross a frontier might not be a charge having equivalent effect to a customs duty, provided that it constituted a benefit specifically or individually conferred on the economic operator concerned, of an amount proportional to that service. In this case, the CoJ held that the charge constituted a breach of the treaty.[17]

In Case 170/88 *Ford of Spain v Spanish State*, a claim that a charge levied by the Spanish customs for granting customs clearance at the Ford factory was a charge for services rendered and not a charge having equivalent effect to a customs duty was rejected. The charge was calculated at a rate of 0.165 per cent of the declared value of the goods. The CoJ held that even if the contested charge were, in fact, remuneration for a service rendered to the importer, the amount charged could not be regarded as proportionate to the service. The Spanish government's argument that, in some cases, the charge would be less than the cost of carrying out the inspections only served to confirm this argument. A charge calculated on the basis of the value of the goods could not correspond to the costs incurred by the customs authorities.

8.5.3.2 **Justified Charges for a Genuine Service**

There are circumstances in which charges may be justified but distinct criteria must be met in order to satisfy the EU free movement regime. In Case 87/75 *Bresciani*, the CoJ held that veterinary checks performed as a service and the charges for them are acceptable, but, on the facts of that particular case, they were not because the inspections were in the public interest at large and not in the interest of each importer, hence the argument is that as such it should be paid by the member state from public funds. In Case 46/76 *Bauhuis v The Netherlands*, the Court of Justice held that a fee for health inspections would be acceptable if required by a Community regulation and covering the actual cost incurred only. This was followed up in Case 18/87 *Commission v Germany (Animal Inspection Fees)*, in which the CoJ held that it is possible under certain circumstances that an inspection charge may escape classification as a CHEE. In this case, fees for inspections carried out under the requirements of Council Directive 81/389 were held to be acceptable. According to the CoJ, they satisfied the criteria that:

(a) the fees constituted a payment for a service, not exceeding the cost of the actual inspections in respect of which they are charged

(b) the inspections in question were mandatory and uniform for all of the products in question in the Community

---

[17] Such is the success now of the internal market and the Schengen Agreement area that it has led not just to the complete removal of the formalities of importation but also to the actual customs posts between a number of member states being a thing of the past and to their removal—many quite literally torn down. There is simply no need to stop when leaving one country to enter another in the Schengen area; one simply drives straight through. Hence, there is no opportunity or need for charges to be levied. It may be then in the future that this too will be an area receiving less treatment in textbooks or, indeed, none at all. However, particularly in view of the potential impact of internal charges or taxes being applied to imports, which does not take place on the border, and which can have the same detrimental impact on imports, the area still remains important.

(c) the inspections were provided for by Community law in the interests of the Community

(d) the inspections promoted the free movement of goods in particular, by neutralizing the obstacles that may result from unilateral inspection measures adopted under Art 30 of the EC Treaty (now Art 36 TFEU).

The fees in the case were charged by some of the German *Länder* on the importation of live animals from other member states and their purpose was to cover the cost of health inspections carried out under Council Directive 81/389. The charges in this case satisfied the conditions and were justified.

Case C-111/89 *Netherlands v Bakker Hillegom* extended the criteria to include the requirements of international conventions.

8.5.3.3 Where the Charge Is in Fact a Tax

If the charge does relate to a system of internal dues applied systematically and in accordance with the same criteria to domestic products and imported products alike, and is therefore a genuine, non-discriminatory tax, it falls to be classified under Art 110 TFEU and not under Art 30 TFEU. In Case 90/79 *Commission v France (Reprographic Machines)*, a levy was charged on all copy machines in order to compensate authors for the breaches of copyright that often occur by the use of such machines. Whilst very few copy machines were manufactured in France and the tax looked like disguised discrimination, it was held to be a genuine non-discriminatory tax and thus justifiable. This situation is sometimes referred to as the 'exotic import rules', whereby a product is available by import only and not manufactured in the importing state, although this case does not exactly fit that rule. However, in order to justify an import tax on such a product, there must be a genuine reason, as in Case 184/85 *Commission v Italy* and a tax on dried bananas which were held not to compete with fresh table fruits. Thus, an exotic or unique product tax was held not to be contrary to Art 110(2) TFEU.

These cases highlight the often subtle difference between what is a charge and what is a genuine tax—a distinction that will be considered next.

8.5.4 The Distinction between Internal Taxation and CHEEs

If a charge imposed by a member state on imported goods is a measure of internal taxation that is non-discriminatory, then it cannot be a CHEE and cannot be caught by Arts 30–2 TFEU. It is governed by Art 110 TFEU instead of the rules on free movement and member states have not been slow to realize the potential of Art 110 TFEU as a way of justifying a financial charge on imported goods. Whilst the customs duties and CHEEs mentioned in Arts 30–2 TFEU must be abolished, tax measures are allowed because, as a general principle, Art 110 TFEU allows each member state to establish the system of taxation that it considers most suitable. However, Art 110 TFEU prohibits tax from discriminating against imports in the organization or application of an internal system of taxation, and was regarded as crucial to complement the free movement provisions where taxation policy was being employed by a state to circumvent the customs rules by the imposition of discriminatory internal taxes. Article 110 TFEU thus represents an early intervention into the member states' tax regimes, which is likely to be more intrusive in future. Article 30 TFEU also specifically prohibits customs charges of a fiscal nature.

The difference between a charge and a tax is crucial. A financial imposition regardless of how it is designated, which is defined by the Court of Justice as an internal tax to which Art 110 TFEU applies, cannot be at the same time a charge having equivalent effect to a customs duty and therefore be subject to Arts 30–2 TFEU. In Case 78/96 *Steinlike und Weinlig v Germany*, the CoJ held that 'Financial charges within a general system of internal taxation applying systematically to domestic and imported products according to the same criteria are not to be considered charges having equivalent effect'. It may be one thing or the other, but cannot be both; they are mutually exclusive categories. There is now a considerable body of Court of Justice case law on the distinction between an internal tax (to which Art 110 TFEU might apply) and a CHEE (which might be prohibited by Arts 30–2 TFEU). In Case 20/76 *Schöttle & Söhne v Finanzamt Freuenstadt*, the CoJ held that the purpose of Art 90 (now Art 110 TFEU) is to remove disguised restrictions on the free movement of goods that may result from the tax provisions of a member state. It was held that a German tax on transportation of goods for more than a certain distance levied, in this case, on a lorry load of gravel was an indirect tax on the gravel itself. It would discriminate against lorries travelling from greater distances—that is, mainly affecting those from other countries. However, it might in the future, if not now, be justified on environmental grounds, as in Case C-132/88 *Commission v Greece*, considered later.

Case 132/78 *Denkavit v French State* also concerned this distinction. It arose out of a charge on the importation of meat products that was the equivalent to a similar charge imposed on the slaughter of meat in French slaughterhouses.[18] The CoJ noted that a charge could escape classification as a CHEE only if it related to a general system of internal dues applied systematically, and in accordance with the same criteria for domestic products and imported products alike. At [8] of its judgment, the CoJ further emphasized that, in order to relate to a system of internal taxation:

(a) the charge to which an imported product is subject must be imposed at the same rate on the same product;

(b) the charge to which an imported product is subject must be imposed at the same marketing stage; and

(c) the chargeable event giving rise to the duty must be the same for both products.

It is therefore not sufficient that the objective of the charge imposed on imports is to compensate for similar charges imposed on domestic products at a production or marketing stage prior to that at which the imported products are taxed.

The CoJ held that it was bound to regard the charge in this case as a CHEE for the following reasons:

(a) It was charged on imported goods by virtue of the fact that they had crossed a frontier.

(b) The tax was imposed at a different stage of production and on the basis of a different 'chargeable event'.

(c) No account was taken of fiscal charges that had been imposed on the products in the member state of origin.

(d) To find otherwise would render the prohibition on CHEEs empty and meaningless.

Finally, in Case 77/76 *Fratelli Cucchi*, the CoJ confirmed the mutually exclusive nature of the charges and internal taxation regimes, but stressed that, because it is often difficult to

---

[18] This is the language used by the CoJ (or the translation thereof)—which was, that the meat is slaughtered—but you might spot the inaccuracy: it is not meat, but animals, which are slaughtered; one cannot slaughter meat! See para [4] of the judgment.

tell the difference, both Arts 25 and 90 EC (now Arts 30 and 110 TFEU) should be invoked together before the CoJ, and the CoJ should be asked to determine which should apply.

8.6 The Prohibition of Discriminatory Taxation

Article 110(1) TFEU provides that no member state shall impose directly or indirectly on the products of other member states any internal taxation of any kind in excess of that imposed directly or indirectly on similar domestic products. This prohibits discrimination in favour of the domestic products.

Article 110(2) TFEU further provides that no member state shall impose on the products of other member states any internal taxation of such a nature as to afford indirect protection to other products. Article 90 EC (now Art 110 TFEU) was held to be directly effective and an indispensable foundation of the common market in Case 57/65 *Lütticke v Hauptzollamt Saarlouis*.

Taxation was defined in Case 90/79 *Commission v France (Reprographic Machines)* as a general system of internal dues applied systematically to categories of product in accordance with objective criteria irrespective of the origin of the products. However, internal taxes can never be imposed solely by virtue of the fact that the goods cross a frontier. The reason for their imposition must be that domestic products are subject to taxation and that, for competition reasons, imported goods should be subject to the same tax. That Art 110 TFEU should also apply to exports, despite not being mentioned in the article itself, was confirmed by the Court of Justice in Case C-234/99 *Nygard*.

8.6.1 Direct and Indirect Taxation

Article 110 TFEU seeks to outlaw both directly discriminatory taxation and indirect discrimination in tax regimes. Direct discrimination arises when imports and domestic products are deliberately treated differently, and is thus automatically unlawful and cannot be justified, whereas indirect discrimination, on the face of it, imposes the same rule on both domestic and imported products, but the result is that the import is, in fact, disadvantaged.

Indirect discrimination may be objectively justified, as in Case 196/95 *Commission v France*, in which a regional subsidy was granted for the production of sweet wines in poor growing areas. On the face of it this favoured domestic growers, but was held to be acceptable particularly as the subsidy was also open to importers who could prove similar conditions. In Case 28/76 *Molkerei-Zentrale Westfalen v Haupzollamt Paderborn*, the Court of Justice ruled that the words 'directly or indirectly' were to be construed broadly, and embraced all taxation that was actually and specifically imposed on the domestic product at earlier stages of the manufacturing and marketing process. This means that member states cannot escape the conclusion, in line with the earlier considered *Denkavit* case, by arguing that a tax at an earlier stage on a domestic product is a lawful equivalent on a tax on imports. If it does not conform to the *Denkavit* criteria, it is unlawful.

It is also capable of including taxes on raw materials and to the assessment of the tax. In Case 20/76 *Schöttle & Söhne v Finanzamt Freuenstadt*, it was held that a German tax on transportation of goods for more than 50 km, levied in this case on a lorry load of gravel, was an indirect tax on the gravel itself. In Case 127/75 *Bobie v HZA Aachen-Nord*, beer production in Germany was taxed at a level according to the quantity produced, with small producers being favoured with a lower tax. All beer imports were taxed on a mid-range rate not connected with the amount of production. Whilst this would be favourable to imports from large producers, it was held to be indirectly discriminatory against a small Belgian producer. In Case C-302/00 *Commission v France (Cigarettes)*,[19] light and dark tobacco cigarettes were held to be similar but were subject to different tax rates with dark tobacco, mainly produced in France, enjoying a more favourable tax regime and light tobacco, mainly imported, a higher rate. There was no discrimination in terms of origin but the tax regime was held to breach Art 110 TFEU.

8.6.2 'Similar' or 'Other Products'

The criteria for determining whether there is discrimination differs according to whether the case is brought under Art 110(1) TFEU, concerned with 'similar products' or Art 110(2) TFEU, 'other products'. The last of these serves to cover imported products that may be different, but are nevertheless in competition with the domestic products. To avoid discrimination taking place in breach of Art 110(1) TFEU, not only must the rates of tax on the imported product and the domestic product be the same (prima facie non-discrimination), but also the basis of imposition of the taxes must not be such that differences between imported and domestic goods may result from it. The rates of tax, the basis of assessment, and the rules for levying and collecting it must all be non-discriminatory. In the case of Art 110(2) TFEU, to be caught by the prohibition on discrimination, it has to be proved that the taxation has a protectionist effect. At the root of this difference is the fact that direct comparisons are possible under Art 110(1) TFEU, whereas under Art 110(2) TFEU they are not. So, even where the level of taxation is the same, a delay in the collection in favour of domestic goods was held to be discriminatory and a breach of Art 90 (now Art 110 TFEU). In Case 55/79 *Commission v Ireland (Excise Payments)* under Irish law, domestic producers of beer, wine, and spirits enjoyed an extension of four to six weeks of the period for payment of excise duties, whereas taxes on imported beers wines and spirits had to be paid immediately on importation or on delivery from the bonded warehouse. The delay in favour of domestic goods was held to be discriminatory and in breach of Art 90 EC.

In Case 112/84 *Michel Humblot v Directeur des Services Fiscaux*, the French authorities imposed a higher tax on cars with a higher horsepower rating, none of which were manufactured in France, meaning that the tax applied in practice only to imported cars. The Court of Justice recognizes that a tax that appears to discriminate against a category of imported goods, because no goods in that category are produced domestically, will not necessarily always be in breach of Art 90 EC (now Art 110 TFEU). However, it held that because many of the imported cars thus taxed would still be in competition with cars produced in France taxed at the lower rate, the indirect tax was nevertheless in breach of Art 90 EC (now Art 110 TFEU). In contrast is Case C-132/88 *Commission v Greece (Taxation of Motor Cars)*, in which a Greek tax on both new and second-hand cars, whether produced in Greece or imported from outside, rose steeply in respect of cars above 1800cc cylinder capacity. The cars affected were all imported, because no cars above 1600cc were produced in Greece. The CoJ held that this measure would only be indirectly discriminatory if it were shown that the taxation had the effect of discouraging Greeks from purchasing foreign cars. On the face of it, the tax was motivated by other considerations and there was no protective effect.

Even where there may even be benefits for the imported goods, a difference in the way in which a tax is levied may be held to breach Art 110 TFEU. In Case C-213/96 *Outokumpu*

---

[19] [2002] ECR I-2055.

Oy, a flat-rate tax on imported electricity from Sweden was held to infringe Art 90 EC (now Art 110 TFEU) because the tax rate on domestic electricity was calculated according to the product that was used for its manufacture for environmental reasons. The fact that only in limited circumstances would the rate of tax on imported electricity be higher was immaterial to the CoJ. The ease of administration in setting up a general system and the fact that it was extremely difficult to determine precisely the method of production of imported electricity were not accepted as grounds justifying the system adopted.

8.6.2.1 Similar Products

Article 110(1) TFEU requires that if there is a difference in the way in which similar products are taxed, the levels of tax have to be equalized. First of all, in determining what constitutes 'similar products', whilst obviously including same products, the Commission and Court need to take into account the composition, physical characteristics, and method of production of the product, as well as to consider whether they both meet the same consumer needs or are in competition with each other and therefore substitutable. For example, in Case 243/84 *John Walker Ltd v Ministeriet for Skatter og Afgifter*, the question of 'whether whisky was similar to fruit wine' was posed. Whilst it was clear that both were alcoholic drinks, the CoJ held that the two drinks were not similar, since they exhibited manifestly different characteristics. The wine was fruit-based and relied on natural fermentation, whereas the Scotch whisky was a cereal-based drink produced by distillation. There were also significant differences in the alcohol volume.

In Case 184/85 *Commission v Italy (Italian Fruit)*, the similarity between bananas, on the one hand, and peaches and pears, on the other, was considered and, according to the CoJ, they were not similar. The CoJ referred to the organoleptic[20] characteristics and the water content, which were different and which meant that they were suited for different markets. In Case 106/84 *Commission v Denmark*, the Court of Justice held that wine made from grapes and wine made from other fruits which had very similar alcohol content and were produced in the same way and substitutable were therefore similar products.

8.6.2.2 Other Products

As far as Art 110(2) TFEU is concerned, for a tax to be caught by the prohibition on discrimination, it has to be proved that the taxation has a protectionist effect to the detriment of imported goods that may be in competition with the other domestic goods. The main question focuses on whether the products can be substituted by each other. Probably the most important case on Art 90(2) EC (now Art 110(2) TFEU) is Case 170/78 *Commission v UK (Wine Excise Duties No 2)*, in which the Court of Justice held that the fact that the UK imposed a higher duty on table wines than it did on beer was held to give indirect protection to beer (a domestic product) over light table wines (a predominantly imported product) and contravened Art 90(2) EC (now Art 110(2) TFEU). The UK government had argued that wine and beer could not be regarded as competing beverages, since beer was widely consumed in public houses and wine was generally only drunk on special occasions, and pointed out the difference in the alcoholic volume. The CoJ took the view that it was necessary not only to examine the present state of the market, but also

---

[20] Essentially meaning 'sensory', organoleptic refers to any sensory properties of a product, involving taste, colour, odour, and feel. Organoleptic testing involves inspection through visual examination, feeling, and smelling of products.

whether the two products were potentially in competition.[21] The CoJ decided that such a relationship existed on the basis of volume, price, and alcoholic strength and mentioned the thirst-quenching qualities of both products, even though UK beer was then about 3 per cent alcohol and the lightest wines 8–9 per cent. [22]

After such a finding, the member state may abolish discrimination either by lowering the tax on imported goods or by raising the tax on domestic products, or may use a combination of both to remove the discrimination or protection.

8.7 Summary on Tariff Barriers

In fact, it is hoped that it is apparent that the main aspects considered in the cases were not, in fact, customs duties or tariffs, which are now extremely rare, but that instead the emphasis is more on CHEEs, although these too are much rarer today than they were in the past. The main focus of attention in the future is therefore likely to be on taxation aspects of this topic, because taxation is still, for the most part, within the competences of the member states, unless it is unfairly levied on imports in a discriminatory manner. In that case, the policy or tax provision can be reviewed by the CoJ to see if it conforms to the free movement of goods and tax provisions of the treaty. Such taxation can, though, be justified if a genuine reason and taxation for environmental reasons is a likely ground for taxation in the future. It must not, though, discriminate against imports.

8.8 Quantitative Restrictions and Measures Having Equivalent Effect

This section considers the non-financial barriers to the free movement of goods contained within the phrase 'quantitative restrictions and measures having equivalent effect'. Restrictions or obstacles to free movement are caused mainly now by divergent national laws regulating products and trade or technical standards, rather than the very crude or obvious, and clearly prohibited, import or export bans. As was discussed earlier, harmonization of all products was neither practical nor desirable, and therefore the creators of the internal market adopted a means of negative integration to tackle the obstacles to free movement caused by these divergent national laws, which were often very different in each member state. So this becomes the focus of attention in this area of free movement. Quantitative restrictions are straightforward: either a ban or quota. It is the extent to which member states can insist that imported products comply with national standards in the face of the attempt to create a genuinely unified single market that causes the real difficulties.

The development of the rules on the free movement of goods reflects the general approach to the fundamental freedoms in that the Court of Justice has interpreted the principle of free movement as liberally as it can to promote free movement, and the

---

[21] Given that the case was over 30 years ago, that was a pretty shrewd judgment, because they are probably far more in competition with each other now than then.

[22] A more recent beer and wine case C-167/05 *Commission v Sweden* [2008] ECR I-2127 did not hold though that the Swedish tax rates on wine, mainly imported, being much higher than strong beers, mainly domestic, were in breach of Art 110. The differential was not as great as in the UK, prior to the ruling but nevertheless notable at twice the rate for wine.

derogations allowed the member states as restrictively or narrowly as possible. (See Case 8/74 *Dassonville* as a good example of this approach.)

8.8.1 **The General Scope of the Treaty Prohibition**

Article 34 TFEU lays down a general prohibition on quantitative restrictions and measures having equivalent effect, and Art 35 TFEU extends that prohibition to exports. Article 36 TFEU, which details exceptions to the general rule, provides:

> The provisions of Articles 34 and 35 shall not preclude prohibitions or restrictions on imports, exports or goods in transit justified on the grounds of:
>
>> public morality, public policy or public security;
>>
>> the protection of health and life of humans, animals or plants;
>>
>> the protection of national treasures possessing artistic, historic or archaeological value;
>>
>> or the protection of industrial and commercial property.

The application of these exceptions is subject to the limitation in the second sentence of Art 36 TFEU, that they may not be used as a means of arbitrary discrimination or a disguised restriction on trade between member states.

Both Arts 28 and 29 EC (now Arts 34 and 35 TFEU) have been found to be directly effective, vertically against measures taken by the state: see, respectively, Cases 74/76 *Ianelli and Volpi SpA v Meroni* and 83/78 *Pigs Marketing Board v Redmond*. However, 'state measures' has been interpreted fairly liberally to include public, semi-public, and even private bodies in certain circumstances in which there has been a fair degree of state involvement or financing that then taints an otherwise private body with aspects of statehood to include actions taken by those bodies. For example, in Cases 266–7/87 *R v Pharmaceutical Society of Great Britain, ex p Association of Pharmaceutical Importers*, the activities of the association, which regulates the conduct of and sets standards for chemists and pharmacists who were required to be members and follow the rules set and were subject to disciplinary sanction, was included. Also, in Case 249/81 *Commission v Ireland (Buy Irish)*, a 'buy Irish' campaign was administered by the Irish Goods Council, a registered private company. However, because the Irish government largely sponsored the campaign to buy Irish products, appointed the management committee, and set the broad outlines of the campaign, Art 28 EC (now Art 34 TFEU) was held to apply. In Case 222/82 *Apple and Pear Development Council v Lewis*, a government-sponsored development council was under a duty not to run an advertising campaign to encourage the purchase of domestic fruit at the expense of imported products. Its other activities involving research and dissemination of information were held to be acceptable. In this way, it may be argued that the scope of Art 34 TFEU (ex Art 28 EC) has been extended to the activities of non-governmental organizations.

In Case C-171/11 *Fra.bo SpA v DVGW*, an independent-of-state, private body, DVGW, which was responsible for certifying plumbing fittings, refused to certify copper fittings made by Fra.bo in Italy for use in Germany. There was no direct state involvement in DVGW but it regulated those goods in place of the state which by national legislation accepted and approved DVGW's certification. When the refusal was challenged, the Court of Justice held that Article 28 EC (now Art 34 TFEU) applied to the standardization and certification activities of a private-law body, where accepted and approved by national legislation. The body then effectively restricted the marketing of products which were not certified and was thus caught by Art 34 TFEU.

The Court though did not specifically address whether Art 34 TFEU was being applied vertically (with DVGW representing some form of extension of the state) or horizontally (with DVGW as a private party). So even with these cases, there remains thus some scope for doubt that Art 34 TFEU does apply horizontally without any involvement of the state at all.

8.8.2 What Are 'Measures' for the Purposes of Art 34 TFEU?

The concept of 'measures' includes not only legally binding acts, but also practices 'capable of influencing the conduct of traders and consumers' (see Case 249/81 *Commission v Ireland (Buy Irish)*) and may include state inaction in the face of private individuals' actions that obstruct the free movement of goods: for example, Case 265/95 *Commission v France (French Farmers/Spanish Strawberries)*, in which the state did not take effective action to stop the protests that destroyed or prevented Spanish produce entering France. This case is to be contrasted with Case C-112/00 *Schmidberger*, in which the protest that blocked the Brenner motorway pass was in fact authorized by the Austrian state and thus held to be acceptable and not a breach by the Austrian state for not preventing it. The cases were distinguished on length of protest because, in *Schmidberger*, it was a single one-off event that was not repeated and was a lawful protest (a fundamental right) which was notified to and acknowledged by the Austrian State, unlike the repeated illegal sabotages of imported goods that took place in *Commission v France (Spanish Strawberries)*. The term 'measures' has also been interpreted to include administrative practices, if they have a certain degree of consistency and generality, as was held by the Court of Justice in Case 21/84 *Commission v France (Franking Machines)*. Whilst in that case, an import banning law in breach of Art 34 was removed, the administration had failed over a period of time to issue an approval for the import of machines from the UK. The preamble to Directive 70/50[23] supports this generous view of measures or rules by including non-legally binding administrative practices.

The following issues will be considered in turn: the meaning of 'quantitative restrictions' and 'equivalent measures'; the derogations of Art 36 TFEU; and the particular problems of measures that apply both to imports and domestic goods.

8.8.3 The Meaning of 'Quantitative Restrictions'

A quantitative restriction is a measure restricting the import or export of a given product by amount or by value. In Case 2/73 *Geddo v Ente Nationale Risi*, the CoJ held that a prohibition on quantitative restrictions covers measures that amount to a total or partial restraint of imports, exports, or goods in transit. The court also referred to any 'encumbrances' as having a similar effect. The most obvious examples of quantitative restrictions on imports and exports are complete bans on imports, or subjecting imports to quotas restricting the import or export by either quantity or value. These are clearly in contravention of Art 34 TFEU and thus prohibited. It was held by the CoJ in Case 34/79 *R v Henn and Darby* to cover measures capable of limiting imports to a finite quantity, including zero, and import bans. Case 231/78 *Commission v UK (Import of Potatoes)* and Case 232/78 *Commission v France (Import of Lamb)* are straightforward examples of total bans, which are prohibited.

---

[23] Administrative Practices. Any standard regularly followed procedure of a public authority, compared with recommendations, which are instruments issuing from a public authority that, while not legally binding on the addressees thereof, cause them to pursue a certain conduct. OJ Special Edn 1970 I L13/29.

A quantitative restriction also includes subjecting the import of goods to the condition of obtaining an import licence. In Case 124/81 *Commission v UK (Imports of UHT Milk)*, the failure to obtain an import licence meant that milk could not be imported even though the requirement was a formality and licences were issued on demand. The CoJ held that import licences or other similar procedures, even if a pure formality, are precluded by Art 28 EC (now Art 34 TFEU).

8.8.4 Measures Having Equivalent Effect (MHEE)

The concept of measures having equivalent effect[24] has been defined by secondary legislation (Directive 70/50) and by the Court of Justice jurisprudence. The directive, which was introduced to provide guidelines at the time when the common market was being established, continues to provide guidance as to what measures may be considered a breach of the prohibition under Art 34 TFEU. Whilst it appears not to have been formally repealed and thus still in force, and indeed is to be found under the 'legislation in force' section of EUR-Lex (the EU legislation site),[25] its treaty base was removed by the Treaty of Amsterdam amendments. However, it defines 'measures having equivalent effect on imports' as including distinctly applicable measures—that is, those that apply to imports, but not domestically produced goods, and which 'make imports, or the disposal at any marketing stage of imported products, subject to a condition, other than a formality, that is required in respect of imported products only' (Art 2). They also include any measures that subject imported products or their disposal to a condition that differs from that required for domestic products and which is more difficult to satisfy.

Equally, it covers, in particular, measures that favour domestic products or grant them a preference, other than an aid, to which conditions may or may not be attached. Basically, therefore, any measure that makes import or export unnecessarily difficult and thus discriminates between the two would clearly fall within the definition.

It also covers, under Art 3, national marketing rules that, on their face, are non-discriminatory or 'indistinctly applicable'; deal in particular with size, shape, weight, composition, presentation, identification, or putting up; and are equally applicable to domestic and imported products, where the restrictive effect of such measures on the free movement of goods exceeds the effects intrinsic to trade rules. We will return to this aspect later.

Further help in understanding this concept comes from the Court of Justice and the starting point is Case 8/74 *Procureur du Roi v Dassonville*, in which the term 'measures having equivalent effect' was held to include 'all trading rules enacted by a Member State which are capable of hindering, directly or indirectly, actually or potentially, intra-community trade'. The case concerned criminal proceedings in Belgium against a trader who imported Scotch whisky, in free circulation in France, into Belgium without being in possession of a certificate of origin from the British customs authorities,[26] thus infringing Belgian customs rules. The CoJ held that:

> the requirement by a Member State of a certificate of authority that is less easily obtainable by importers of an authentic product, put into free circulation in a regular manner in

---

[24] Which may be abbreviated to either MHEE or MEQR, depending on which text you consult, although both mean the same thing.

[25] At **http://eur-lex.europa.eu/LexUriServ/LexUriServ.do?uri=CELEX:31970L0050:EN:NOT**.

[26] Before the UK became a member of the European Communities.

another Member State, than by importers of the same product coming directly from the country of origin, constitutes a measure having equivalent effect.

The CoJ added that, in the absence of a Community system to guarantee a product's origin, a member state may take reasonable measures for the protection of consumers in the area of designation of origin of products without necessarily infringing Art 28 EC (now Art 34 TFEU). However, this is subject to the further qualification that whether or not such measures were authorized by the terms of Art 36 TFEU (ex Art 30 EC), they could not constitute an arbitrary discrimination or a disguised restriction on trade between member states.

The scope of the prohibition thus defined is extremely wide and means that virtually any measure that hinders or even potentially hinders imports or exports in any way, whether intended or not, could be caught. A good example is the *Foie gras* case, C-184/96 *Commission v France*, which involved the imposition of production standards on foie gras. The argument that hardly any foie gras was produced outside France and that imports complied in any case was dismissed by the CoJ which stressed that whilst at the time the French standards imposed no restriction, there remained the potential to do so in the future. Thus the *Dassonville* criteria were satisfied without having to conduct any further investigation.

The *Dassonville* case also paved the way for a considerable development of EU law on free movement in the *Cassis de Dijon* case, which we shall consider in detail in Section 8.10.1.

8.8.5 **The Scope of the Prohibition**

8.8.5.1 **National Promotional Campaigns**

Measures that do not have clear visible direct effect on imports may still be caught by the prohibition in Art 34 TFEU. In Case 249/81 *Commission v Ireland (Buy Irish)*, the CoJ held that the activities of a company, which was government controlled and financed, which carried out a government policy of promoting the sale of national products by means of an advertising campaign, and which promoted the use of a 'home-produced' symbol, constituted a measure having equivalent effect. It was held not necessary for the government to have taken any compulsory measures and simply encouraging the purchase of domestic products through a campaigning body was sufficient to count as a measure having equivalent effect. The emphasis is therefore on those rules that are capable of having an effect rather than those rules actually having an effect. In Case 222/82 *Apple and Pear Development Council v Lewis*, the ruling in *Buy Irish* was qualified to hold that a member state could establish a development council for fruit production that was composed of members appointed by the minister responsible and financed only by the growers themselves, as long as the activities consisted of compiling statistics, promotion and undertaking of research, and giving technical advice, rather than trying to get consumers to purchase only home-produced fruit and not imports.

8.8.5.2 **Discriminatory National Marketing Rules**

National marketing rules often impose restrictions on the production, packaging, movement or distribution of goods that, as a consequence, infringe Art 34 TFEU. Import licences, which by their nature apply to imports only, were held to be a breach of the treaty early on in Cases 51–4/71 *International Fruit Co* and later in Case 124/81 *Commission v UK (UHT Milk)*. This remains the case even if they are issued as a matter of formality, because they still represent some form of hindrance. In Case 113/80 *Commission v Ireland (Metal*

Objects/Origin), the requirement to stamp the origin of goods as either Irish or foreign was held to breach the rule. In Case 261/81 *Rau v De Smedt*, the Belgian national rule that required margarine to be packed in cubes and in no other form, such as tubs or rectangular blocks, was held to be in breach of Art 28 EC (now Art 34 TFEU), because of the economic disadvantage that it imposed on exporters to Belgium. Price restrictions involving minimum and maximum pricing and maximum profit margins have all been found to breach Art 34 TFEU (see Cases 82/77 *Openbaar Ministerie v Van Tiggele*, 65/75 *Riccardo Tasca*, and 78/82 *Commission v Italy*). In Cases 266–7/87 *R v Pharmaceutical Society of Great Britain*, the rule of the Pharmaceutical Society prohibiting dispensing pharmacists from substituting for the product named on a doctor's prescription any other with identical therapeutic effect except under certain exceptional conditions was capable of coming within the operation of Art 28 EC (now Art 34 TFEU). However, in this case, it was held to be capable of being justified on the grounds of the protection of public health.

8.8.5.3 Product Classification

Cases C-387/99 *Commission* v *Germany* and C-150/00 *Commission* v *Austria* concerned the classification of food supplement products as medicines, which resulted in the restriction of imports where the daily doses of particular vitamins were exceeded. This practice was held to breach Article 28 EC (now 34 TFEU) and could not be justified by Article 30 EC (now 36 TFEU) because of the systematic nature of regulation rather than a case-by-case investigation. Classification by a private regulator is also now subject to Art 34 TFEU where the results of the classification are effectively condoned by national legislation as held in Case C-171/11 *Fra.bo SpA v DVGW*, noted in Section 8.8.1.

8.8.5.4 Exports

In Case C-47/90 *Delhaize v Promalvin*, a ban on the export of wine in bulk was held to breach Art 29 EC (now Art 35 TFEU), which states that quantitative restriction on exports, and all measures having equivalent effect, shall be prohibited between member states. There was no evidence to support the contention that bottling was necessary at the source of production, especially where the wine was transported in bulk internally. In another bulk wine export case, C-388/95 *Belgium v Spain*, a rule which provided that the designation 'Rioja' could only be used if it was bottled in that region prior to export and not when exported in bulk, was held to be a MHEE.[27] The CoJ held that Art 35 TFEU applies to measures which have the effect of specifically restricting patterns of exports and which establish a difference of treatment between trade within a member state and its export trade. It was a rule though which could be objectively justified.

8.9 The Derogations of Art 36 TFEU

Article 36 TFEU provides exceptions to the general prohibition of Art 34 TFEU. It states that Arts 34 and 35 TFEU shall not apply to prohibitions on imports, exports, or goods in transit that are justified on any of the following four sets of grounds:

   (a) public morality, public policy, or public security
   (b) the protection of health and life of humans, animals, or plants

---

[27] [2000] ECR I-3123; this case is also considered in Chapter 7, Section 7.2.3.3.

(c) the protection of national treasures possessing artistic, historic, or archaeological value

(d) the protection of industrial and commercial property.

The application of these exceptions is subject to the limitation, set out in the second sentence of Art 36 TFEU, that they may not be used as a means of arbitrary discrimination or a disguised restriction on trade between member states.

8.9.1 General Purpose and Scope

Article 36 TFEU provides the member states with a set and exhaustive list—that is, a list that cannot be added to—that allows the member states to restrict the free movement of goods for certain specific reasons only. The member state must prove that the national measure is both necessary and proportionate, not to fall foul of the second sentence of the Article. In Case 72/83 *Campus Oil v Ministry for Industry and Energy*, the CoJ held that the purpose of Art 36 EEC (now Art 36 TFEU) was not to reserve certain matters to the exclusive jurisdiction of the member states, but instead to allow national legislation to derogate from the principle of the free movement of goods to the extent to which this is, and remains, justified in order to achieve the objectives set out in the Article. In Case 113/80 *Commission v Ireland (Metal Objects)*, it was held that because the derogations were exceptions to a fundamental principle, namely, the free movement of goods, they were to be construed narrowly and could not, for example, be used for economic reasons, as was done by Italy in Case 7/61 *Commission v Italian Republic (Pig-meat Imports)* in order to protect its own pig industry, which was suffering economic difficulties.

8.9.2 Public Morality

Case 34/79 *R v Henn and Darby* concerned a ban on the importation of pornographic magazines, despite the fact that similar but less graphic magazines were lawfully available for purchase in the UK, although none similar to the imports were produced in the UK. It was therefore accepted that there was no lawful trade of the type of magazines which were the subject of the import ban. The CoJ ruled that a prohibition, which might be stricter than the laws applicable internally, was not designed to discriminate in favour of the domestic product and so was acceptable under the public morality clause of Art 30 EC (now Art 36 TFEU). It was up to member states to determine the requirements of public morality in their own state and they have, therefore, a margin of discretion in this area in view of the varying levels of pornography available. This was qualified, however, in Case 121/85 *Conegate v HM Customs and Excise*, the infamous case concerned with the importation of 'blow-up dolls'. It was held that member states did not have complete freedom to exclude such material when similar products could be manufactured, distributed, and marketed lawfully in the UK. The CoJ held that a member state might not rely on the ground of public morality to prohibit the importation of goods from other member states when its legislation contained no prohibition on the manufacture or marketing of such goods in its own territory. The prohibition was therefore a disguised restriction on trade and a means of arbitrary discrimination, and as such contrary to the second sentence of Art 30 EC (now Art 36 TFEU).

8.9.3 **Public Policy**

The leading case in the category of public policy is Case 7/78 *R v Thompson et al*, which concerned the ban on the unlawful importation into the UK of krugerrands and a ban on the export of coins, some of which were no longer legal tender and some of which were. The English coins that were no longer legal tender were held to be goods within the meaning of Art 28 EC (now Art 34 TFEU). However, it was held that the right to mint coinage was a fundamental interest of the state and therefore a state that prohibits the destruction of coinage, even when they are no longer legal tender and imposes an export ban to prevent their destruction abroad, will be justified under Art 30 EC (now Art 36 TFEU) on the grounds of public policy.

Other attempts by member states to invoke this exception have failed. See, for example, those cases dealing with lack of effective action by states to curb illegal protests in which the states have claimed that the threat to public order prevented them from intervening to ensure the free movement of goods. The CoJ has not accepted the invocation of Art 30 EC (now Art 36 TFEU) to justify the lack of action.[28]

8.9.4 **Public Security**

The leading case to deal with security is Case 238/82 *Campus Oil* concerning Irish rules requiring importers of petroleum products to purchase a certain proportion of their requirements from an Irish state-owned refinery at prices fixed by the minister. Although the claim to rely on the public policy exception failed, the Court of Justice held that the maintenance of essential oil supplies was covered by the public security exception and was accepted; however, any measures taken are subject to the principle of proportionality, considered later.

A further attempt by France to invoke Art 30 EC (now Art 36 TFEU) was also rejected in Case 231/83 *Cullet v Centre Leclerc Toulouse*, concerned with a law imposing a minimum retail price for fuel. Lower-cost imports could not realize their competitive advantage by being able to be sold at a lower and more competitive rate under this law. France argued that, in the absence of the pricing rules, there would be civil disturbances, blockades, and violence. The CoJ rejected this claim.

8.9.5 **The Protection of the Health or Life of Humans or Animals**

The protection of the health or life of humans or animals is a frequently argued ground for import restrictions and virtually every sort of good, especially foodstuffs, has been subjected to restrictions on health grounds, most of which have been held by the CoJ not to conform with Art 36 TFEU. In Case 322/01 *Deutscher Apothekerverband*, the CoJ held that 'the health and life of humans rank foremost among the assets or interests' protected by Art 36 EEC (now Art 36 TFEU), and the CoJ has been extremely vigilant in exposing the disguised restrictions of member states.[29] For example, in Case 124/81 *Commission v UK (UHT Milk)*, the systematic checking and re-packaging of sealed UHT cartons of milk for health checks, which dramatically increased the cost to the importer, amounted

---

[28] When the French authorities did not step in to prevent illegal action during a protest by French farmers, including the destruction of property: see Case C-265/95 *Commission v France (Spanish Strawberries)* considered in Chapter 7, Art 258 TFEU.

[29] See also Case C-170/04 *Rosengren and ors v Riksåklagaren*, in which the Court of Justice expressed the same sentiments.

to import restrictions. The CoJ held that the health of consumers would be adequately protected by the necessary controls being carried out in the country of production to meet all of the reasonable requirements of the country of import. Similarly, in Case 42/82 *Commission v France (Italian Table Wines)*, systematic checks on three-quarters of consignments of Italian wine, which were held up at the French border for long periods—sometimes months—was held not to be justified by Art 36 EEC (and TFEU). Whilst the Court of Justice acknowledged the right of the member states to carry out checks, it noted that the frequency of analysis of Italian wine was considerably higher than the occasional checks carried out on French wine transported within France. The CoJ held that the French authorities had no right to carry out systematic checks and that, in the absence of any reasonable suspicion on the basis of specific evidence in a given case, they ought to have confined themselves to random checks.

A series of cases has now been considered by the CoJ concerned with import bans on the grounds of protecting public health as a result of the content of food products and mainly concerning food additives. The CoJ has held in these cases that, in the absence of any EU regulation of the manufacture and marketing of products, the member states are free to regulate this matter as long as they do not infringe the EU provisions on the free movement of goods. In those cases, which are concerned with an import ban raised on the grounds of protecting the health of the population from harmful additives, the view of the CoJ is based on whether the additives were either permitted in another product or were allowed in another member state, or with regard to the results of international scientific research—in particular, the work of the World Health Organization (WHO)—and to eating habits in the country of importation. If the additive does not constitute a danger to public health, a ban would be a breach of Art 34 TFEU and not justified under Art 36 TFEU. Additionally, bans would be contrary to the principle of proportionality if there were no accessible procedure by which traders were able to request that the use of specific additives be permitted. Cases include: the ban on the import of beer in Case 178/84 *Commission v Germany (Beer Purity)*; a ban on the import of sausages containing certain non-meat ingredients in Case 274/87 *Commission v Germany (Sausage Purity Law)*; and a ban on the import of low-fat cheese in Case 210/89 *Commission v Italy*. However, a ban would not infringe Art 34 TFEU if additives were also not permitted in domestic products and if there were a system to allow the assessment and addition of additives to the list of permitted additives: see Cases 95 and 293/89 *Commission v Italy and Greece*. States must make out, on the basis of latest scientific data, that a real risk to health exists. However, the CoJ recognizes 'that such an assessment of the risk could reveal that scientific uncertainty persists as regards the existence or extent of real risks to human health'. In such circumstances, it must be accepted that a member state may, in accordance with the precautionary principle,[30] take protective measures without having to wait until the existence and gravity of those risks are fully demonstrated, as stated by the CoJ in Case C-192/01 *Commission v Denmark* and a number of similar cases. Finally, in this category, is Case C-358/95 *Tommaso Morellato v Unita Sanitaria Locale*, which concerned the import of frozen bread that contravened national statutory limits by having a moisture content exceeding 34 per cent, an ash content of less than 1.40 per cent,[31] and bran

---

[30] The precautionary principle has statutory form in the EU legal order in Art 191 TFEU on the environment and permits provisional measures to be taken where a clear risk to health is identified but cannot immediately be proved beyond doubt.

[31] You may wonder why the authorities might insist on there being a minimum ash content, which does not seem a very healthy ingredient. Frozen bread will be mass produced and part baked in industrial ovens heated by gas or electricity. Traditional ovens would be coal- or coke-fired and some ash would get into the bread. Insisting on ash is just a way of banning mass-produced bread. Non-ash-containing bread may well be less carcinogenic and thus actually healthier.

content, contrary to national standards. France was unable to demonstrate a threat to public health, and so it was easy for the CoJ to reach the conclusion that the national law constituted a quantitative restriction contrary to Art 28 EC (now Art 34 TFEU) and was not saved by Art 30 EC (now Art 36 TFEU).

An area in which the public health proviso in Art 36 TFEU is of great importance is that of the importation of pharmaceutical products, in which cases there are often vast price differences between the retail prices of drugs in different member states. Case 215/87 *Schumacher v Hauptzollamt Frankfurt* concerned the ban on the import of medicinal products purchased in France for personal use. The medicines in question were available in Germany without prescription, but at four times the price charged in France. The CoJ held that national rules or practices that have, or are likely to have, a restrictive effect on importation of pharmaceutical products are compatible with the treaty only insofar as they are necessary for the protection of health and human life. In this case, the purchase of the goods in a pharmacy of another member state in effect gives a guarantee equivalent to that resulting from the sale of the product in a pharmacy in the member state into which it is imported. The CoJ ruled that the rule prohibiting the importation of the goods in this case contravened Art 28 EC (now Art 34 TFEU) and was not protected by Art 30 EC (now Art 36 TFEU).

8.9.6 **Artistic, Historic, or Archaeological Heritage**

It was held in Case 7/68 *Commission v Italy (Art Treasures)* that the ground of artistic heritage does not justify a tax being levied on the export of art treasures, which was held to breach Art 25 EC (now Art 30 TFEU).

8.9.7 **The Protection of Industrial or Commercial Property**

Intellectual property (IP) rights, such as patents, trade-marks, and copyright, can nevertheless be protected even though they are on the face of it and actually designed to restrict the complete freedom of how goods covered by them are traded and if not excepted would breach Art 34 TFEU. They can though be justified under the Art 36 TFEU but the derogation must be read alongside Art 345 TFEU, which provides that the treaty shall in no way prejudice the rules in member states governing the system of property ownership. This justification has been held by the CoJ not to extend to prevent parallel imports of products lawfully marketed in another member state.[32] The leading case of Case 78/70 *Deutsche Grammophon v Metro* distinguished between the existence of the rights, guaranteed by Art 345 TFEU and the exercise of those rights which often impact on the free movement of goods and Art 34 TFEU. The case also made it clear that copyright and allied rights were also covered by Art 36 TFEU.

Only the specific subject matter can be protected by Art 36 TFEU when the rights have not already been exhausted by being put into circulation in the EU. Case 15/74 *Centrafarm v Sterling* dealt with the concept of the exhaustion of rights. In the case, drugs patented by Sterling and marketed in the UK and the Netherlands were bought by Centrafarm in the UK and resold in the Netherlands. Sterling attempted to uphold its patent to prevent the drugs from being marketed there. The Court of Justice held that the derogation in Art 36

---

[32] Whilst most of the cases on IP are dealt with under competition law and often beyond general courses on EU law, the leading cases showing the relationship with the free movement of goods will be nevertheless be considered here.

TFEU served only to protect the specific subject matter which was the exclusive right to put into circulation for the first time the products protected by the patent. However, once the goods protected have been lawfully put onto the market in more than one member state, those rights are said to be exhausted. This means that the holder cannot rely on the patent to prevent further lawful sales in another member state and importation back (known as parallel imports) into the first state of sale or manufacture. Case 16/74 *Centrafarm v Winthrop* extended the same reasoning and conclusions to trade-marks. The Court of Justice thus ensured that the exercise of patents and trade-marks was not such as to prevent the lawful free movement of goods between member states. It held that such a restriction of the free movement of goods would defeat the aims of the treaty and could not be justified under Art 30 EC (now Art 36 TFEU). This derogation was also considered in Case 388/95 *Belgium v Spain* in the context of the Spanish ban on using the protected designation 'Rioja' when exporting Rioja wine in bulk in order to protect the quality and thus name of the product. The ban was held to be a breach of Art 29 EC (now Art 35 TFEU), but which was justified to maintain its high quality and reputation under the Art 30 EC (now Art 36 TFEU) derogation for the protection of commercial property.

Because most undergraduate courses on EU law do not go into any further detail on this topic as a part of free movement of goods, neither shall this book.

8.9.8 Article 36 TFEU Second Sentence

The second sentence of Art 36 TFEU provides that such prohibitions or restrictions shall not, however, constitute a means of arbitrary discrimination or a disguised restriction on trade between member states, and that any measure must in any case be proportionate. In Case 42/82 *Commission v France (Italian Table Wines)*, the systematic checking of every consignment and subjecting inspections to very long delays of weeks, and even months, was held to be disproportionate. Similarly, in Case 124/81 *Commission v UK (UHT Milk)*, the requirement of an import licence was held to be a disguised restriction despite being issued automatically.

Case C-170/04 *Rosengren* involved a Swedish government measure prohibiting the private import of alcohol, unless sanctioned by the authorities and subject to additional import charges. The restriction was held to be contrary to Art 28 EC (now Art 34 TFEU), but was claimed by Sweden to be justified under the Art 30 EC (now Art 36 TFEU) health ground—in particular, to protect young persons. The Court of Justice dismissed this because the measure, contained in Ch 4(2)(1) of the Swedish Law on Alcohol, was unsuitable for attaining the objective of limiting alcohol consumption generally and not proportionate for attaining the objective of protecting young persons against the harmful effects of such consumption. The state monopoly was not a means of restricting alcohol imports or strength of drinks, but more of preserving state monopoly to import. The CoJ held, therefore, that it cannot be regarded as being justified under Art 30 EC (now Art 36 TFEU) on grounds of protection of the health and life of humans.[33] So whilst the CoJ is acutely aware of the health issues in alcohol abuse and consumption by young people, any measures ostensibly to address those issues must really be designed to do that. The Swedish measures were inadequate in that respect and only operated to ensure the state near-monopoly on alcohol sales. If health was the overriding concern and the product restricted a clear and proven risk to health, then a complete ban would probably be justified.

---

[33] See [58] of the judgment.

8.9.9 Decision 3052/95 and Regulation 764/2008

In an attempt to better regulate the introduction by member states of measures that dero-gate from the free movement of goods, Decision 3052/95[34] (now replaced by Regulation 764/2008) was adopted, which requires the member states to inform the Commission about any measures that ban the import of goods, or refuse goods to be admitted to the market, or require modification of goods for the market, or withdraw goods from the mar-ket. The Commission then informs the other member states and may decide to seek further details or take action if it concludes that the measures actually breach Art 34 TFEU.

The replacement Regulation 764/2008 is also intended to assist the free movement of goods by providing procedures to assess the impact of proposed technical rules by mem-ber states, which must advise the Commission when they propose to enact any such meas-ures. So far, it has not been very successful and further details will not be provided here.

8.10 Equally Applicable Measures (Indistinctly Applicable Measures)

Measures that apply only to imports or exports are called 'distinctly applicable meas-ures', but it is to be noted that Art 34 TFEU not only prohibits national rules that overtly discriminate against imported products, subject to the possibility of justifi-cation under Art 36 TFEU, but may also be used to challenge national rules that, on their face, make no distinction between domestic and imported goods but which actu-ally discriminate in fact, i.e. the end result. Article 3 of Directive 70/50 provides that measures that are equally applicable to domestic and imported goods will breach Art 34 TFEU only where the restrictive effect on the free movement of goods exceeds the effects necessary for the trade rules—that is, the measures are disproportionate to the aim and thus tend to protect domestic products at the expense of the imports:

> This Directive also covers measures governing the marketing of products which deal, in particular, with shape, size, weight, composition, presentation, identification or putting up and which are equally applicable to domestic and imported products, where the restric-tive effect of such measures on the free movement of goods exceeds the effects intrinsic to trade rules.
> This is the case, in particular, where:
> – the restrictive effects on the free movement of goods are out of proportion to their purpose;
> – the same objective can be attained by other means which are less of a hindrance to trade.

Those measures that apply to both imports and domestic goods are termed equally or indistinctly applicable.

The wide definition of this in *Dassonville* made no allowance for some measures intro-duced by member states that applied to both imports and domestic products, and might be justified on particular grounds such as the environment, but the judgment was actu-ally qualified by the statement that:

> in the absence of a community system guaranteeing for consumers the authenticity of a product's designation of origin, if a Member State takes reasonable measures to prevent

---

[34] Decision 3052/95 on exchange of information about national measures derogating from the principle of free movement of goods (OJ 1995 L321/1); Regulation 764/2008 (OJ 2008 L218/21).

unfair practices in this connection, Article 28 EC [now Art 34 TFEU] may not be contravened. It is, however subject to the condition that the means of proof required should not act as a hindrance to trade between member states and should, in consequence, be accessible to all Community nationals.[35]

Thus, the *Dassonville* case hints at the possibility that the member states could restrict imports for a good reason and marks the foundation of the so-called rule of reason. This was developed further in a landmark decision in EU law that seemed to address the difficulties with indistinctly applicable measures introduced by member states for arguably sound reasons: Case 120/78 *Rewe-Zentral AG v Bundesmonopolverwaltung fur Branntwein*, better known as *Cassis de Dijon*.

8.10.1 **The *Cassis de Dijon* Case**

The *Cassis de Dijon* case concerns a prohibition on the marketing in the Federal Republic of Germany of spirits with less than a 25 per cent alcohol content, which included Crème de Cassis de Dijon (a blackcurrant alcoholic liqueur), containing 15–20 per cent alcohol. The ban applied to all low-alcohol liqueurs regardless of origin, and did not distinguish between national and foreign drinks. The arguments made by Germany for the ban were that lower-alcohol liqueurs would lead to alcohol tolerance, thus leading to health problems in the future, and that the lower alcohol also provided a price advantage for the imported products, which was unfair and would force down alcohol rates of drinks and thus quality contrary to usual manufacture. However, the actual result was the effective ban, albeit indirect, of French imports. The Court of Justice made a number of statements of importance in its judgment. It held that there was no valid reason why, provided that they have been lawfully produced and marketed in one of the member states, alcoholic beverages should not be introduced without restriction into any other member state. As was seen in an earlier case—notably, *Commission v UK (UHT Milk)*—this is a restatement of the principle of equivalence.

The CoJ also held that obstacles to the free movement of goods resulting from disparities in the national laws on the marketing of products must be accepted as far as these provisions are necessary to satisfy certain mandatory requirements, considered further later. The judgment was a way of getting around too strict an application of the rule developed in the earlier *Dassonville* case. Therefore, equally applicable measures that hinder trade may be acceptable if they are in pursuit of a reasonable special interest that the member state has the right to protect. However, they must still be subject to the principle of proportionality and must neither be an arbitrary discrimination, nor a disguised restriction on trade. The latter two terms repeat those provided in Art 36 TFEU. The judgment in *Cassis de Dijon* makes it clear that Art 34 TFEU also covers indirect discrimination by reference to the term 'obstacles to movement within the EU resulting from disparities between national laws relating to the marketing of the products in question'. In other words, where a national rule has a different effect, although on the face of it applying equally to both imported and domestic products, it may also be caught by Art 34 TFEU, as the rule in the *Cassis de Dijon* case itself. The case is regarded as a very important tool for the Commission in creating the internal market by the simple rule that goods lawfully manufactured and sold in one member state should be able to move freely throughout the EU—and, indeed, the Commission later issued a Practice Note based on its interpretation of what the *Cassis de Dijon* case meant.[36]

---

[35] Para 6 of the judgment in Case 8/74 *Dassonville*.

[36] Communication from the Commission concerning the consequences of the judgment given by the Court of Justice on 20 February 1979 in Case 120/78 ('*Cassis de Dijon*'), OJ 1980 C256/2: N. Foster (ed), *EU Treaties and Legislation*, latest edn, Oxford University Press, Oxford.

8.10.1.1 Examples of the Types of Mandatory Measure

The national rules that may be raised by the member states referred to by the Court of Justice in *Cassis de Dijon* were 'the effectiveness of fiscal supervision, the protection of public health, the fairness of consumer transactions and the defence of the consumer'. They are not exhaustive and have been added to by the CoJ in subsequent cases:

- In Case 302/86 *Commission v Denmark (Disposable Beer Cans)*, environmental grounds were raised.

- Cultural interests were raised in Cases 60–1/84 *Cinéthèque SA v Fédération Nationale des Cinémas Français*, concerning the sale of video recordings.

- Environmental protection and conservation of the resources of the sea were held to be interests worthy of protection in Cases 3, 4, and 6/76 *Minister of Justice v Kramer*.[37]

- Laws for the protection of workers were raised in *Union Departemental des Syndicats CGT de l'Aisne v Sidef Conforama*, judgment of 28 February 1991, and Case C-332/89 *Criminal Proceedings against Marchandise*.

- The maintenance of the diversity of the press was raised in Case C-368/95 *Vereinigte Familiapress*.

- The financial balance of the social security system was raised in Case C-120/95 *Decker*.

- The protection of young persons was raised in Case C-244/06 *Dynamic Medien*.

- The protection of the fundamental rights of the freedom of speech and the right to protest were raised in Case C-112/00 *Schmidberger*.

8.10.2 The Application of the Rule of Reason: The Requirements in Detail

Once it has been established that the interest comes within the rule of reason, the criteria of the rule of reason must be satisfied, as follows.

8.10.2.1 There Must Be No EU System Covering the Interest in Question

There must be no EU system covering the interest in question—that is, EU legislation must not have occupied the field and there must be no harmonizing legislation. In Case 16/83 *Criminal Proceedings against Karl Prantl*, a German law provided that only certain quality wines from Franken and Baden could be marketed in the bottle known as *Bocksbeutel*. Anyone marketing any other wine in the *Bocksbeutel* committed an offence. The defendant in the main action was charged with selling quantities of Italian red wine in bottles of this type. In fact, red wine produced in the Italian Tyrol had been produced in bottles of this type for at least a century, as had Portuguese wines.[38] There was in place, though, a partial system of Community rules governing the types of wine that might be marketed in specific types of bottle, but these had not yet been concluded to rule out national competences in respect of the bottle in question. Thus, it was held that until Community rules are implemented, the rules adopted by the member states could be

---

[37] [1976] ECR 1279, [1976] 2 CMLR 440.

[38] The Portuguese wine Mateus Rosé is probably the most well-known wine using this shape of bottle. See http://www.chalicewine.com/sitecw201301/wp-content/uploads/bocksbeutelsonaWall.jpg for a picture of red, white, and rosé bottles.

maintained as long as they did not contravene Arts 28–30 EC (now Arts 34–6 TFEU). The CoJ held that the rules in question did, in fact, contravene Art 28 EC (now Art 34 TFEU) and were not saved by Art 30 EC (now Art 36 TFEU).

8.10.2.2 The Measure Must Be Indistinctly Applicable

The measure or rule or standard must apply without difference on the face of it to both imports and domestic products, otherwise it cannot be considered under the rule of reason and must be considered narrowly under Arts 34 and 36 TFEU only. Case 113/80 *Commission v Ireland (Metal Objects)* confirms the strict view of Art 36 TFEU. Irish legislation required souvenirs of Ireland that were not domestically produced to bear the designation 'Foreign'. The Commission considered the restrictions to contravene Art 28 EC (now Art 34 TFEU) and Art 2(3)(f) of Directive 70/50, because they were measures that had the effect of lowering the value of an imported product or increasing its costs. The Irish government argued that the measures were justified on the grounds of consumer protection and therefore fell within the scope of the public policy derogation in Art 30 EC (now Art 36 TFEU). The Court of Justice held that since Art 30 EC (now Art 36 TFEU) constitutes a derogation from the basic rule that all obstacles to the free movement of goods between member states are to be eliminated, Art 30 EC (now Art 36 TFEU) must be construed narrowly. Since neither the protection of consumers nor the fairness of transactions were included amongst the exceptions set out in Art 30 EC (now Art 36 TFEU), it was held that they cannot be relied on in connection with that Article. The CoJ then considered whether the measures might be justified as necessary to meet mandatory requirements. However, the rules were not measures that applied to domestic and imported products without distinction; they applied only to imported products and were therefore discriminatory in nature, with the result that the measures were not covered by the decision in *Cassis de Dijon*, which applies only to provisions that regulate both imported products and domestic products. The rules were therefore in breach of Art 28 EC (now Art 34 TFEU).

8.10.2.3 The Measure Must Neither Be an Arbitrary Discrimination Nor a Disguised Restriction on Trade

The measure must neither be an arbitrary discrimination nor a disguised restriction on trade, as in Case 124/81 *Commission v UK (UHT Milk)*, in which the requirement of an import licence, a second heat treatment, and repackaging were held to be disguised restrictions despite the licences being issued automatically. The argument raised—that there was not a Community regime for UHT milk—was rejected on the grounds that the treatment of UHT milk was, in fact, very similar in the different member states and thus such a regime was not required.

8.10.2.4 The Measure Must Meet the Requirements of Proportionality

In addition to the *Cassis de Dijon* case itself, a number of others have addressed the requirement of proportionality. In Case 113/80 *Commission v Ireland (Irish Metal Objects)*, the CoJ took the view that the interests of consumers and fair trading would have been adequately protected if it were left to domestic manufacturers to take appropriate steps if they so wished, such as affixing their mark of origin to their own products or packaging. The Irish government requirement to stamp 'Foreign' was not reasonable.

In Case 261/81 *Walter Rau Lebensmittelwerke v De Smedt*, Belgian legislation prohibited the marketing of margarine that did not conform to a particular shape. This rule had a clear protective effect and was an obstacle to marketing for importers. The Belgian government argued that the measure was necessary for consumer protection.

The CoJ ruled that if a member state has a choice between various measures to attain the same objective, it should choose the measure that least restricts the free movement of goods. In this case, consumers might have been protected and informed that the product was margarine by other measures that would have constituted less of an interference with free movement of goods, such as labelling. Therefore, the rules contravened Art 28 EC (now Art 34 TFEU). In Case 16/83 *Prantl*, the wine bottle shape case, the CoJ held that the sale of a product may not be prohibited when a labelling requirement will adequately protect the consumer, so as not to confuse the particular wine in the wine bottle sold.

The various food additives and constituents considered in the cases noted earlier under the Art 36 TFEU derogations are also subject to this line of argument that adequate labelling will protect consumers rather than warrant a ban, which would be disproportionate: see Case 174/84 *Commission v Germany* concerning the Beer Purity Law, discussed earlier, which provided that only malted barley, hops, yeast, and water may be used in the manufacture of beer, and further that only drinks complying with those provisions could be marketed under the designation beer. A further law prohibited importation of beers containing additives unless the additives were specifically authorized. The CoJ held that whilst it was legitimate to seek to enable consumers, who attribute special qualities to beer manufactured from particular raw materials, to make their choice in an informed way, that could be achieved by labelling. The prohibition went beyond what was necessary for the protection of German consumers, since such protection could quite easily be ensured by the compulsory affixing of labels informing consumers about the nature of the product sold.

More recent cases have suggested that in determining whether a particular measure chosen by a member state is proportionate, the member state is not required to go to the extent of demonstrating beyond doubt that no other measure could have been adopted but that they must consider any suggestions made by the Commission (see Cases C-110/05 *Commission v Italy* and C-28/09 *Commission v Austria*, both considered in Section 8.11.2).

8.10.3 **Technical Standards and Legislative Interventions**

In order to try to regulate the free movement of goods more effectively and more comprehensively, and to avoid some of the difficulties of relying on piecemeal litigation to challenge measures introduced from time to time by the member states, the Commission introduced Directive 83/189, now updated and consolidated by Directive 98/34.[39] These required member states to notify technical standards of products before being adopted, so that the Commission could consider whether they created barriers to the free movement of goods. Whilst it was not intended to create rights for individuals, and merely to provide a channel of communication between the member states and the Commission, the directives have nevertheless been instrumental in some cases between individuals (see Section 6.3.4.4, on incidental horizontal direct effect). These cases have prompted significant use and notifications under the directives, and have probably helped to prevent some national measures that would have created barriers. While further discussion in a book of this nature is not warranted, it is nevertheless useful to know of their existence.

---

[39] OJ 1998 L204/37, reproduced in N. Foster (ed), *EU Treaties and Legislation*, latest edn, Oxford University Press, Oxford.

8.10.4 **Summary of *Cassis de Dijon***

We can take the view of the rule of reason in the *Cassis de Dijon* case that it either classifies measures as falling outside the scope of Art 34 TFEU in the first place, or that it justifies measures that would otherwise have breached Art 34 TFEU as a result of the fact that the mandatory requirements provide further derogations to Art 34 TFEU. The case of *Cassis de Dijon* certainly allowed member states to maintain some rules that protected an interest. Nevertheless, it was often unclear whether the national mandatory requirement fell outside, or would be in breach of, Art 34 TFEU except for the fact that it was an interest worthy of protection and thus justified (provided that all other criteria were satisfied). As a consequence, in some cases there has been a blurring of the difference between 'distinctly' and 'indistinctly' applicable measures. Normally, the route taken would be to decide if the measures are distinctly or indistinctly applicable, and to decide if they have breached Art 34 TFEU; then, if distinctly applicable, to decide whether any of the derogations of Art 36 TFEU apply or, if indistinctly applicable, whether any of the mandatory requirements from *Cassis* or an Art 36 TFEU derogation applies.

Occasionally, though, as in Case C-67/97 *Bluhme* or Case C-2/90 *Commission v Belgium (Walloon Waste)*, the Court of Justice has extended the mandatory requirements to a situation concerned essentially with a distinctly applicable rule permitting one local good only to the exclusion of all others. The first case concerns the ban on keeping certain species of bee in a particular small area of Denmark, which was held to fall within Art 34 TFEU. In the latter case, a Belgian region prohibited the transfer of waste from other countries or other parts of Belgium to Wallonia for storage, tipping, or dumping. This distinctly applicable restriction was effectively ignored by the CoJ in both of the mentioned cases in the interests of environmental protection. However, for the most part, a difference remains between indistinctly and distinctly applicable measures.

To this must be added a consideration of the difference between equal burden and dual burden rules that was provoked by the *Cassis de Dijon* development. The problem was that whilst dual burden rules could be isolated and easily regarded as being in breach of Art 34 TFEU, equal burden rules were often left to the national courts to decide whether the national interest (the mandatory requirement) was one that was worthy of protection and thus satisfied the requirements of the *Cassis de Dijon* case, often with different outcomes.

8.10.5 **Equal Burden/Dual Burden**

An indistinctly applicable rule is one that applies, at least on the face of it, to imported and domestic products alike; it is the same rule in play and therefore the face-value conclusion is that the rule imposes an equal burden on both products. However, this is not the conclusion if one takes into account the fact that the importer may have already satisfied a similar or, indeed, slightly different rule applied in the state of export and that the imported product may therefore have to comply with two sets of product requirements in order to be marketed lawfully in the state of import: those operated by the state of origin and those of the state of importation. In this situation, the imported product is placed under an additional dual burden. For example, in Case 261/81 *Walter Rau (Margarine)*, noted earlier, the Belgian authorities required margarine to be packed in cube-shaped containers only; therefore a separate production line would have to be set up for the Belgian market and more if other countries were to adopt similar requirements—maybe round for Luxembourg, and so on—which would not be economically viable for the manufacturer. Hence, the conclusion is that it is unfair that two sets of rules must be adhered to, with the consequence that the additional, or dual burden, rule is caught by Art 34 TFEU unless justified by either Art 36 TFEU or the rule-of-reason mandatory requirements.

Equal burden rules, in contrast, should not have been considered as even coming within Art 34 TFEU because, by definition, the burden of the rules in question in the state of import falls equally on home and domestic products; the imported product suffers no discrimination or disadvantage. Unfortunately, the CoJ appeared in some cases to extend the scope of Art 34 TFEU to cover the equal burden rules that applied fairly to both imported and domestic products by national measures, which were neither directly nor indirectly discriminatory. The same requirement applied to both without adding an additional burden on the imports. For example, Cases 60–1/84 *Cinéthèque* concerned the prohibition on hire or sale of videos of films within the first year of release in order to protect the film industry from production through to the cinemas. The rule applied equally to domestic and imported videos. The CoJ held nevertheless that the rule was a measure having equivalent effect because it did restrict the overall import of videos, as indeed it equally restricted sales of domestically produced videos, although these were fewer in number. However, it could be justified for a specific reason which, in this case, was the addition of 'the protection of artistic works' to the list of mandatory requirements of *Cassis*. Otherwise, it would have breached Art 34 TFEU. However, the extension of the scope of the Article 28 EC (now Art 34 TFEU) prohibition to equal burden rules had taken place. The *Cassis* case is beneficial to free movement of goods and supports national diversity by allowing regional variations under the mutual equivalence rule. Further, under the rule of reason and mandatory requirements rule, member state interests covered by national rules would be recognized. However, if those equal burden rules were also potentially in breach of Art 34 TFEU, then, as happened, all sorts of national rules would be seized upon by traders to attack virtually any nationally imposed restriction on trade practices or commercial freedom that restricted in any way the level of imports. Particularly, it was seized upon by traders who had been caught infringing the national rules, who claimed that their right to import goods and sell them had been infringed. Many of the national laws were concerned with sales and marketing rules, and actually had no impact on the access of imported goods to the national market. Increasingly, however, national laws were questioned, not on the basis that they hindered imports only, but on the basis that they affected the volume of trade regardless of origin, as in Case 61/84 *Cinéthèque*, noted earlier.

The Sunday trading case law, and in particular Cases 145/88 *Torfaen Borough Council* v *B&Q plc* and *B&Q Ltd* v *Shrewsbury Borough Council*, serve as good examples of the confusion that can arise, because it was assumed that the national laws did affect Community (EU) trade and were in breach of Art 28 EC (now Art 34 TFEU), unless justified. However, as was demonstrated in these cases, the interest worth protecting could vary. The previous ban that used to exist in the UK prohibited the trading of very many goods on a Sunday and was not discriminatory, but applied to imported and domestic goods alike. However, traders claimed that it breached Art 28 EC (now Art 34 TFEU) because, by reducing the volume of sales, it reduced the volume of imports and thus it was a measure having equivalent effect. The grounds stated by the member state to justify the law were not contained in Art 36 TFEU, but arguably fell within the mandatory requirements of *Cassis*. The case law from the UK in respect of this question has not been particularly helpful—partly as a result of the Court of Justice deciding that national courts must determine for themselves whether the reason for a rule was justified under the rule of reason. However, the ban on Sunday trading concerned both the idea of 'keeping Sunday special' and the protection of workers, and as a result led to contradictory decisions depending on whether the UK courts took into account the protection of workers, which would appear to justify a ban on Sunday trading, and the attempt to keep Sunday special, which appears not to justify a ban (see Case 145/88 *Torfaen BC v B&Q plc* and *B&Q Ltd v Shrewsbury BC*[40]).

Before a further UK case reached the Court of Justice, two decisions had been reached by the CoJ in Case C-312/89 *Conforama* and Case C-332/89 *Criminal Proceedings against Marchandise*, which were more instructive from the EU law point of view. In a request for preliminary rulings from French and Belgian courts, the CoJ held that national restrictions on the opening of shops on Sundays (the French *Code de Travail* provides for a mandatory day's rest on Sundays, whilst the Belgian *Loi sur le Travail* prohibits the employing of retail shop workers after noon on a Sunday) were not in breach of Community law. It was considered that this area was a matter for the regulation of each individual member state and thus the measures were held not designed to control patterns of trade between member states, nor were they applied so as to discriminate against goods from other member states. So, when another reference on Sunday trading was referred from the UK, the CoJ held in Case C-169/91 *Stoke City Council v B&Q plc* that the UK's restrictions on Sunday trading do not conflict with Community law. It held that such rules reflected 'choices relating to particular national or regional socio-cultural characteristics'; the member states have the discretion to make such choices.

This series of cases did, however, raise the question of whether the Court of Justice had gone too far in upholding the sanctity of free movement over national rules by finding that all obstacles to free movement, and not merely those concerned with discrimination and protectionism, were in breach of Art 28 EC (now Art 34 TFEU) unless justified—hence, the next development.

8.11 *Keck and Mithouard*: Certain Selling Arrangements

Faced with many similar arguments by traders against national rules, when presented with a suitable occasion, the CoJ was able to redefine its position. Cases C-267–8/91 *Keck and Mithouard* concerned the French prohibition of the sale of unaltered goods at a loss. Although this was applicable to both imported and domestic products, it was argued by the company to be a restriction of sales contrary to Art 28 EC (now Art 34 TFEU) as a defence when the company was prosecuted by the French authorities. France counter-claimed that the rule was nevertheless justified under the *Cassis De Dijon* mandatory rules exception. The CoJ stated that:

> In view of the increasing tendency of traders to invoke Article 30 [now Art 34 TFEU] of the Treaty as a means of challenging any rules whose effect is to limit their commercial freedom even where such rules are not aimed at products from other member states, the Court considers it necessary to re-examine and clarify its case law on this matter.

The CoJ considered that traders had been using EU law to try to challenge laws that were not aimed at restricting imports, but restricted the sales of all goods, domestic and imported. The CoJ then stated that it considered that selling or marketing arrangements did not come within the concept outlined in *Dassonville* or Art 30 EEC (now Art 34 TFEU). The CoJ held that:

> Contrary to what has previously been decided, the application to products from other member states of national provisions restricting or prohibiting certain selling arrangements is

---

[40] [1990] 3 CMLR 535.

not such as to hinder directly or indirectly, actually or potentially, trade between member states within the meaning of the *Dassonville* judgment provided that those provisions apply to all affected traders operating within the national territory and provided that they affect in the same manner, in law and in fact, the marketing of domestic products and of those from other member states.

Looked at in another way, an impediment to trade is acceptable where the rule in question is merely a selling arrangement that applies to both the trade in domestic and imported products equally. It was an attempt to remove many national rules that were introduced for genuine reasons and not introduced with the intention to be a restriction on imports. So, provided that national rules do not impede access to markets, but merely regulate them without any form of discrimination either in law or in fact, they will be acceptable and will not fall within Art 34 TFEU. For example, many of the Sunday trading restrictions in the UK were enacted in Victorian times—well before the EU and Art 34 TFEU ever came into existence and so clearly were not enacted with the intention to restrict EU imports. So, that should have been the end of it; such rules would not then be considered either under Art 36 or *Cassis de Dijon*. However, there were problems with the *Keck* judgment because it did not provide an instant clarification of the law—most notably the question 'what are "selling arrangements"?' The scope of this expression was explored in subsequent cases.

8.11.1 Post-*Keck* Case Law

'Selling arrangements' are broadly defined as rules relating to the market circumstances in which the goods are sold. Selling arrangements are usually equal burden rules, which now fall outside the scope of application of Art 34 TFEU. In contrast to the rules relating to the product itself or its characteristics, such as those concerned with the shape, size, weight, composition, presentation, identification, packaging, or putting up (preparing for sale),[41] selling arrangements are measures dealing with where, when, how, and by whom goods may be sold. For example, Cases C-401–2/92 *Tankstation 't Heukske* involved Dutch laws about the opening times of shops at petrol outlets; Case C-292/92 *Hunermund* involved product advertising rules; Belgian laws prohibiting offering products for sale at a loss of profit were considered in the *Keck* case itself and in Case C-63/94 *Belgapom*; and Case C-391/92 *Commission v Greece* related to the prohibited sale of any processed milk for babies other than in pharmacies. In all these cases, the Court of Justice found that the rules were acceptable under Art 28 EC (now Art 34 TFEU), as it did a rule that required a licence to open a new shop in Case C-140/94 *DIP* in view of the public interest and concern for planned commercial development. The rule did not concern itself with the origin of goods traded.

It would have seemed that, post-*Keck*, provided that a rule was classified as a selling arrangement, it fell outside Art 34 TFEU. However, if the rule were shown to create a requirement physically to alter the imported product, it would breach Art 34 TFEU unless justified. For example, in Case C-470/93 *Mars*, a national law was challenged that prohibited the selling of Mars Bars, which had been labelled as providing an extra 10 per cent. The CoJ held that the law concerned product presentation in the form of labelling or packaging and was thus a physical requirement. Therefore, if the law were upheld, it would have meant that it imposed a dual burden. It was therefore held to be a breach of Art 28 EC (now Art 34 TFEU). It could though be justified, either under Art 36

---

[41] Termed 'product requirements' or sometimes 'product bound measures'.

TFEU or under the *Cassis de Dijon* rule of reason. See also Case C-368/95 *Vereinigte Familiapress Zeitungsverlags v Bauer Verlag*, which considered the difference between a selling arrangement and physical requirement. An Austrian law prohibiting the offering of free gifts linked to the sale of goods was the basis for an Austrian publisher's action against a German magazine containing a prize crossword puzzle. The CoJ repeated its position established since *Keck* that certain national rules would not breach Art 28 EC (now Art 34 TFEU) unless imposing additional requirements and that the Austrian rules would constitute a hindrance to free movement if the content of the magazine were to have to be altered for the Austrian market. However, it could be justified because maintaining the diversity of the press (as coming within *Cassis de Dijon* and not an Art 36 TFEU exception) was the legitimate public interest objective given by the authorities and accepted by the CoJ.

Unfortunately, the next twist in the case law was the recognition that some selling arrangements, although equal burden and not relating to physical characteristics, nevertheless had an effect that disadvantaged imports by hindering market access or which seemed to favour domestic products—in particular those in respect of advertising and sales promotion rules. This is then compounded by a few cases that, on the face of it, concern rules relating to the product, such as packaging, but which, on closer examination by the CoJ, are really selling arrangements and thus to be considered as falling outside Art 34 TFEU; hence, the search for a new test to be able to classify these developments and to provide some form of predictability for the future.

8.11.2 Market Access or Discrimination, or Both?

In the post-*Keck* case law, cases have considered whether Art 34 TFEU has been breached because market access has been hindered in some way or because of a selling arrangement that, although equal burden, is nevertheless discriminatory in some way or has a differential impact. See Case C-412/93 *Leclerc Siplec*, concerning certain goods that could not be advertised on television, but only in the press and in particular the local press, in order to maintain a certain level of advertising revenue for local papers and thus ensure the survival of local and independent press. Advocate General Jacobs argued that the test should be to consider if there were an impediment to market access, and that Art 28 EC (now Art 34 TFEU) should catch measures that directly and substantially impede access to the market. This was seen previously in the free movement of persons area of law in Case C-415/93 *Union Royale Belge des Sociétés de Football Association v Bosman*, in which it was held that non-discriminatory rules that prevented football player transfers and that prevented market access should be outlawed.

This was taken up in Cases C-34–6/95 *Konsumentombudsmannen v De Agostini*, in which television advertising directed at children under the age of 12 was prohibited. The measure was considered to be a selling arrangement that applied without discrimination and which was thus equal burden. However, it was held that would seem to have a greater impact on products from other member states, because of the difficulties faced in trying to get access to the market, advertising being the only effective form of promotion. If the national court found that the impact of the prohibition resulted in different treatment of or impact on imported goods, it would therefore breach Art 28 EC (now Art 34 TFEU) unless justified by Art 30 EC (now Art 36 TFEU) or the mandatory requirements under *Cassis*.

In the subsequent Case C-405/98 *Gourmet International*, a ban on alcohol advertising was challenged under the same argument that it had a greater impact on imported products trying to gain access to the Swedish market because, without advertising, consumers would only be familiar with domestic products. Thus, it was held that the measure would be caught by Art 28 EC (now Art 34 TFEU) if it were to prevent access to the market by products from another state, or impede access any more than they impede access of domestic products.

In Case C-254/98 *Heimdienst*, a non-discriminatory Austrian law that applied to all operators trading in the national territory (Austrian and other EU states) required goods sold on the doorstep to come from locally established premises. It was held to be a selling arrangement, but one that impeded access to the market of the member state of importation for products from other member states more than it impeded access for domestic products—that is, there was a difference in the way in which it affects domestic and other member state products. Thus, selling arrangements that either in law or in fact discriminate against non-national providers and thus impede or hinder market access, will not escape Art 34 TFEU, but might still be justified.

Case C-416/00 *Morellato* involved packaging and the requirement that partly baked bread be packaged by the retailer completing the baking. Thus, it appeared to be the same as the *Mars* case noted earlier and thus product alteration, but it was, however, held to be a selling arrangement, because the rule applied only at the final stage of marketing, not physically altering the product prior to distribution.

In a further 'bake-off' bread case, a requirement that, under normal circumstances, would be regarded as a selling-arrangement case was, in fact, used in a way that did restrict market access. This concerned the requirement to have a full baker's licence and all of the practical needs of a full bakery in order to sell bake-off bread, which is merely thawed and reheated at the sales outlet after otherwise full preparation elsewhere, including transportation whilst frozen from other member states. In Cases C-158–9/04 *Alfa Vita Vassilopoulos*, that requirement, which resembled a selling arrangement in terms of who is permitted to sell a product, nevertheless represented a barrier to imports and was not a selling arrangement due to its discriminatory impact on imports. The differential treatment in the *Alfa Vita* case was not justified under public health grounds.

Selling arrangements that either in law or in fact discriminate against non-national providers and thus impede or hinder market access will not escape Article 34 TFEU. They might, however, still be justified under either Art 36 TFEU or the rule in *Cassis de Dijon*. Thus, this test of differential impact—that is, a measure or requirement that affects imports more than domestic products—focuses both on market access and the fact that the effective result is discriminatory. For example, in Case C-28/09 *Commission v Austria*, to tackle pollution, a prohibition of the use of a section of the Inn motorway in the Tirol by lorries over 7.5 tons, which of course applies to both the transport of national and imported goods, was held to be a MHEE because of its impact on long-distance freight carrying goods across Europe. It hindered access to markets. The justifications of the protection of human health and the environment, which on the face of it certainly appear plausible, were not accepted by the Court of Justice because the measure itself was disproportionate. The retort for Austria was that other less disruptive measures to tackle the pollution had not been considered.

8.11.3 Restriction on Use Rules

Finally, or finally thus far in the post-*Keck* case law, are cases of a further development dealing with so-called 'residual rules' which concern restrictions on the use of products. These have added yet another gloss on the free movement rules.

Case C-110/05 *Commission v Italy (Trailers)* concerned not a ban on the product but a ban on mopeds towing trailers. It was held to have a significant impact on the marketing and thus import of such trailers and was therefore in breach of Art 34 TFEU. However, in this case it was considered an argument based on road safety could justify the measure especially as there were no EU common rules on this activity. Case C-265/06 *Commission v Portugal* involved Portugal's ban on the fixing of tinted film on vehicle windows. It applied to both imports and domestic products so was indistinctly applicable. It is to be noted though that vehicles manufactured with tinted windows were acceptable. The Court of Justice considered the market access approach as well as returning to the *Dassonville* formula and found that the impact of the ban on potential purchasers would probably reduce imports. The products would have a smaller and less attractive market. It was therefore considered a MHEE and thus in breach of Art 34. The justifications of crime prevention and road safety were not accepted by the Court. In Case C-142/05 *Aklagaren v Mickelsson and Roos*, the Swedish ban on the use of jet-skis on navigable waterways was not considered to be a selling arrangement because it concerned how a product was to be used. It was though held to be a MHEE but justified on the grounds of the protection of health and life and environmental protection. However, as the ban was a general one and not confined to waterways where jet-ski use constituted a threat to humans, it was held to be disproportionate.

These residual rules cases thus far appear to be with the market access group of cases and not selling arrangements. The Court did though categorize types of MHEEs in the *Italian Trailers* case as follows:

- those rules whose object or effect is to treat imports less favourably and are distinctly applicable measures
- secondly, the indistinctly applicable product requirements rules
- any other measures which either hinder access to the market via a differential (discriminatory) impact or those residual rules not being classified as selling arrangements but which nevertheless impacted on market access without discrimination.

It is because of the complexity of the types of rules and regulations which are applied to goods in the member states that finding one or more catch-all tests to tackle all of the rules employed by the member states has proved to be extremely difficult, to say the least. *Dassonville* and *Cassis de Dijon* went too far and *Keck* was not distinguishing enough. Hence the development of the market access test and differential impact, but which did not cover situations where there was no discrimination, therefore the need to tackle these residual rules via a return to something closer to the *Dassonville* formula.

This area of law is still in need of clarification and if possible, simplification.

8.12 Overall Summary

Non-tariff barriers have proved to be more difficult to eradicate than the tariff barriers, because of the huge variety of national rules that can apply and the fact that not all national rules regulating trade law should be considered as coming within Art 34 TFEU. Hence, the difficulty has been determining where to draw the line, and deciding which rules offend Art 34 TFEU and which do not. We start with a perfectly sound rule (Art 34 TFEU), which seeks to ensure that there are no restrictions on the free movement of goods. To this, we add a further statutory rule (Art 36 TFEU), which provides exceptions to the first rule because it is recognized that there are genuine circumstances in which restrictions and different treatment are justified—so far, so good. Then there are statutory guidelines (Directive 70/50) and case law, which help to determine how the

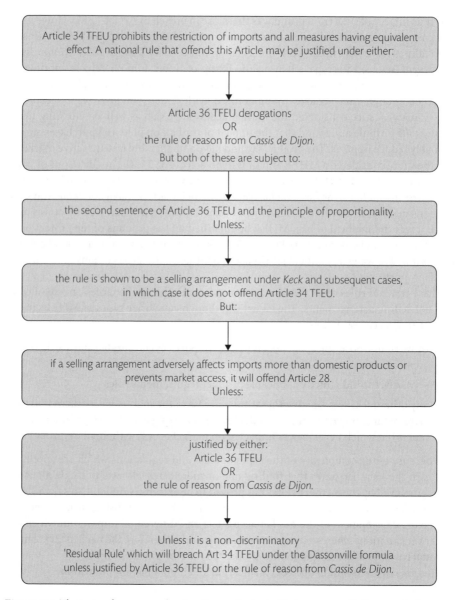

Article 34 TFEU prohibits the restriction of imports and all measures having equivalent effect. A national rule that offends this Article may be justified under either:

Article 36 TFEU derogations
OR
the rule of reason from *Cassis de Dijon*.
But both of these are subject to:

the second sentence of Article 36 TFEU and the principle of proportionality.
Unless:

the rule is shown to be a selling arrangement under *Keck* and subsequent cases, in which case it does not offend Article 34 TFEU.
But:

if a selling arrangement adversely affects imports more than domestic products or prevents market access, it will offend Article 28.
Unless:

justified by either:
Article 36 TFEU
OR
the rule of reason from *Cassis de Dijon*.

Unless it is a non-discriminatory
'Residual Rule' which will breach Art 34 TFEU under the Dassonville formula unless justified by Article 36 TFEU or the rule of reason from *Cassis de Dijon*.

Figure 8.1 The tests of a measure having the equivalent effect as a quantitative restriction

rule applies and the circumstances that breach the rule or come within the exceptions. Additionally, there is a focus on the concepts of distinctly applicable measures, which can only be justified by Art 36 TFEU, which are easy to see, and indistinctly applicable measures, which start to become complex and require us to be aware of the very important case of *Cassis de Dijon*. The indistinctly applicable measures are presumed to come within, and thus breach, Art 34 TFEU unless justified by Art 36 TFEU or a further set of justifications introduced by *Cassis* and subsequent cases (the mandatory requirements). It is worth noting that Art 36 TFEU applies to both direct and indirect discrimination, but has an exhaustive—that is, a limited—list of exceptions, whereas *Cassis de Dijon* applies to indirect discrimination only, but potentially includes a much wider range of exceptions. Thus, certain national rules or laws could escape the prohibition of Art 34 TFEU because they meet either one of the Art 36 TFEU derogations or the mandatory requirements of *Cassis de Dijon*. However, strict criteria were laid down so that member states would not be able to exploit this possibility of avoiding the prohibition of Art 34 TFEU. These were contained within the second-sentence requirement of Art 36 TFEU and in the application of the principle of proportionality which apply both to Art 36 TFEU derogations and *Cassis de Dijon* exceptions.

Then, because all sorts of national rules that applied to goods started to be considered to come within the ambit of the *Cassis de Dijon* case, there is another important case (*Keck*). This seeks to lay down another rule, or gloss, on the original rules to say that certain types of law applicable to the marketing of goods (selling arrangements) should not even be considered as coming within the original rule (Art 34 TFEU)—*and* there is further case law now to provide clarification of what was meant in *Keck*. Indistinctly applicable selling arrangements are thus presumed to be outside Art 34 TFEU unless they introduce discrimination or prevent market access by adversely affecting imports more than domestic products (see *Heimdienst*), but these can be justified by Art 36 TFEU or *Cassis* (*Familiapress*).

On top of all of those now, are a set of rules which have somehow escaped classification previously and which relate to the use of products and are known as 'residual rules'. These are rules which are indistinctly applicable, are not product requirements or selling arrangements, but which do appear to hinder access to markets but not in a discriminatory way. They nevertheless, potentially if not actually, hinder imports. They will therefore breach Art 34 TFEU unless justified either by Art 36 TFEU or the rule of reason from *Cassis de Dijon*. With these levels of complexity, it may actually be helpful, when the occasion arises, for the member states to make statutory changes to try to regulate these continuing developments or, failing that, for the Commission to issue another practice note.[42] Whether they do or not, the CoJ is sure to be involved further. Figure 8.1 illustrates these principles.

Further Reading

Books

BARNARD, C. *The Substantive Law of the EU: The Four Freedoms*, 4th edn, Oxford University Press, Oxford, 2013.

OLIVER, P. et al *Oliver on Free Movement of Goods in the European Union*, 5th edn, Hart Publishing, Oxford, 2010.

Articles

CONNOR, T. 'Accentuating the Positive: The "Selling Arrangement", the First Decade, and Beyond' (2005) 54 ICLQ 127.

DAVIES, G. 'Can Selling Arrangements be Harmonised?' (2005) 30 EL Rev 371–85.

DAWES, A. 'A Freedom Reborn? The New Yet Unclear Scope of Article 29 EC' (2009) 34 EL Rev 639.

ENCHELMAIER, S. '*Moped Trailers, Mickelson & Roos, Gysbrechts*: The ECJ's Case Law on Goods Keeps Moving' (2010) 29 YEL 190.

---

[42] The last rethink was 2008; see the single market webpages generally at **http://ec.europa.eu/enterprise/ policies/single-market-goods/index_en.htm**.

MÖSTL, M. 'Preconditions and Limits of Mutual Recognition' (2010) 47 CML Rev 405.

OLIVER, P. and ENCHELMAIER, S. 'Free Movement of Goods: Recent Developments in the Case Law' (2007) 44 CML Rev 649.

OLIVER, P. and ROTH, W.-H. 'The Internal Market and the Four Freedoms' (2004) 41 CML Rev 407.

PAPADOPOULOUS, T. Criticising the Horizontal Direct Effect of the EU General Principle of Equality' (2011) EHRLR 437.

SNELL, J. 'Non-discriminatory Tax Obstacles in Community Law' (2007) 56 ICLQ 339.

SNELL, J. 'The Notion of Market Access: A Concept or Slogan?' (2010) 47 CML Rev 437.

VAN HARTEN, H. and NAUTA, T. 'Towards Horizontal Direct Effect for the Free Movement of Goods?' (2013) 38 EL Rev 677.

WEATHERILL, S. 'Harmonisation: How Much, How Little' (2005) 55 ICLQ 457.

WEATHERILL, S. 'Recent Developments in the Law Governing the Free Movement of Goods in the EC's Internal Market' (2006) 2 ECRL 90.

WENNERAS, P. and MOEN, K.B. 'Selling Arrangements: Keeping *Keck*' (2010) 35 EL Rev 387.

WILSHER, D. 'Does *Keck* Discrimination Make any Sense? An Assessment of the Non-discrimination Principle within the European Single Market' (2008) 33 EL Rev 3.

Web-based Materials

http://europa.eu/legislation_summaries/internal_market/
internal_market_general_framework/l21001b_en.htm

On mutual recognition

9

The Free Movement of Persons

9.1 Introduction

Before European citizenship was introduced as an EU law concept and was provided with teeth, EU law was concerned with the free movement of economically active persons only. However, it was not long in the life of the Communities that the Court of Justice started to expand our understanding of the range of persons who could take advantage of the treaty provisions and the first phase of secondary legislation provided rights for non-economically active members of a worker's family. Originally, free movement of persons concerned the direct freedom of movement for workers and self-employed persons only, the latter establishing themselves or providing services in a host member state. In this book, all aspects of the free movement of persons including workers, establishment, services, and citizenship will be dealt with together in one chapter. The reasons for this are that, increasingly, case law, and, in particular, the new case law, concerned with citizenship applies without distinction across all these categories and new secondary law has also brought many of the statutory rules for all categories of person in line. See, for example, the Services Directive (2006/123) which covers both services and establishment, discussed later. It therefore seems of less merit to try to maintain increasingly irrelevant distinctions.

Whilst the original treaty Articles on free movement of persons have altered little since 1957, their scope and our understanding of them have developed considerably since then. It is not only the original personal scope of the legislation that has been expanded by both additional statutory law and judicial interpretation, but also the consequences for the Union and national legal regimes, which are much greater than those that may have been anticipated by the member states. Free movement of persons is now a much wider concept, and has become inextricably linked with the concept of European citizenship and other wider issues of free movement, including third-country nationals (TCNs). As ever, in considering a legal regime, we need to start with the basics for each of these categories, and these are the treaty provisions, followed by any pertinent secondary legislation and the now extensive case law of the Court of Justice. A particular feature of this area of law is the extensive rights that apply to the family members of EU citizens who take advantage of rights of free movement, by virtue of the so-called 'derived rights'. Finally, integrated into these aspects are the more recent provisions of secondary legislation[1] that have both consolidated the existing secondary legislation, and introduced amended and new rules

---

[1] In particular, Directive 2004/38 of the European Parliament and of the Council of 29 April 2004 on the right of citizens of the Union and their family members to move and reside freely within the territory of the member states (OJ 2004 L158/77), which entered into force on 30 April 2006, and the Internal Market Services Directive 2006/123, which is actually a bit of a misnomer because it is concerned with both services and establishment. The directive came into force on 28 December 2009.

relating to those taking advantage of free movement rights, and have further organized the provision of services and establishment in the EU. These will be considered where appropriate in the text.

However, before looking at any of these particular provisions, it is useful to outline and discuss the original reasons and intentions behind the free movement of persons. Was free movement, as originally conceived, only a necessary appendage to the free movement of goods and capital in order to complete the freedom of the factors of production for economic or capitalist development? In other words, would the development of economic activities and the balanced expansion and accelerated raising of the standard of living referred to in the preamble to the old EC Treaty not have been realizable unless capital could also take advantage of freely moveable labour without border restrictions? Hence, the argument that the rights were provided merely or deliberately to help to create the 'common market' in the same way as the free movement of goods. By ensuring the free movement of workers across the member countries of the common market, capital (namely, employers operating productive facilities) can easily import labour when required, which in turn ensures that economic conditions in all member states of the market are broadly similar, and thus competition is not distorted by labour shortages and higher labour costs in some parts of the market.

What is clear is that the free movement of persons section is firmly anchored in the economic part of the treaty, concerned with a basic definition of the internal market and outlined in Art 26 TFEU, and not within the social policy section much further on in the treaty. Whilst there have always been claims that the rights were also imbued with a social quality and concern for individual rights, it is really only since the extensive development of the rights by both statutory supplement and generous interpretation by the Court of Justice that this argument takes on credibility. A review of both the literature of the time and more recent articles and books will reveal that there has been, and remains, support for both points of view. The truth probably lies somewhere in between, in that whilst it was originally restricted to the pursuit of those engaged in an economic activity in another member state, and the rights were perceived as a form of support for the common market and economic progress in the Community, a view also acknowledged by the Commission in its early documentation,[2] the rights as developed have undoubtedly become a clear part of the social policy of the EU. This is evidenced by the growing tendency in textbooks to treat the subject as a part of social policy. This transition of treatment may also have been encouraged by the way in which the free movement provisions were actually used in society. By this is meant that the evidence of migration in Europe does not show large-scale movement by West Europeans of the original six member states (with the exception of Italians moving to Germany).[3] Whilst large numbers of workers were imported into some countries, notably West Germany, France, and the UK, to feed growing industrial capacity in the 1950s and 1960s, this was mainly from non-European countries. For the most part, movement within Europe was small-scale, not large-scale movement from employment black spots in Europe to other parts of the EU.

Furthermore, it is now clear that the movement of large numbers of persons is no longer an economically efficient or sensible option for capital. It is far more effective and cheaper

[2] 'Even if initially the free movement of persons was mainly an economic matter, concerning only workers, the concept has gradually expanded to allow any citizen of the Union to move and stay freely within the member states': available at **http://ec.europa.eu/justice_home/fsj/freetravel/fsj_freetravel_intro_en.htm**.

[3] Most employment migration was from outside the EC member states. See, inter alia, K. Foster, 'The Free Movement of Workers' in B.A. Wortley (ed) *The Law of the Common Market*, Manchester University Press/Oceana Publications, Manchester/New York, 1974, pp 170, 179–80.

to set up new factories where labour is cheaper than it is for labour to move to capital. The examples of China and India could not be clearer. This view was actually formed rather quickly by both capital and the European Commission and, regardless of the original intentions, free movement rights were not being used as originally intended as an instrument of encouraging economic progress, but were really being used as individual social rights by member-state nationals.[4] By the time that the first legislative expansion of the rights had been carried out, the view was clearly that such rights were dual in purpose and effect. Another reason for the fact that the original provisions did little to facilitate free movement of persons is not that the rights themselves were toothless, but more that, until 1961, member states could maintain a priority for national workers. Then, up to 1965, member states needed only to accept other member-state workers if no nationals had applied for the vacancy within three weeks and, after 1965, member states could insist that potential host workers first notify employment authorities. Finally, member states could rely on escape clauses in Regulation 15/61[5] and Regulation 38/64,[6] up to the end of the transition period (1968), which allowed them to suspend the treaty provisions in favour of nationals where national or local interests required it.

Putting into effect the right of free movement for the self-employed also proved to be slow and much more difficult than the simple treaty expression of the rights would suggest. The attempts by the Commission to harmonize the various professions proved to be very arduous and time-consuming, and it was not until the intervention of the Court of Justice in leading cases that much more rapid and expansive progress took place, as considered later.

So, instead of becoming a tool for economic development, the use of the free movement provisions by individuals has established it more as a social right. In support of the view that social concerns predominate, the CoJ has adopted a very liberal approach for the interpretation of the free movement of workers provisions, both the treaty principles and the further extensions of these principles in the secondary legislation, such as the widely construed concept of 'worker'. In contrast, the exceptions to the rights granted to the member states are interpreted strictly; for example, see the case law on Art 45(4) TFEU, the public service proviso, in Section 9.6.3.

Whilst the view now might be generally that the rights are as much (if not more) social, there are some cases along the way that cause us to question this. For example, in Case C-159/90 *Grogan*, the economic rights to move to receive services abroad took priority over the legislative provisions of the member state, which were the product of deep ethical and moral considerations of the sanctity of life. In the *Grogan* case, it was the right to travel to receive abortion services that took priority despite the fact that the national Constitution prohibited abortion, although that free movement facilitated other personal social rights.

---

[4] In a Recommendation and Opinion of July 1962, 1962 JO (2118), the Commission argued that this freedom was not concerned with traditional notions of emigration and immigration. These notions assumed that individuals migrated because they were unable to secure satisfactory living standards in their own countries. The Community, however, sought to ensure uniformly high living standards throughout its territory. The problems of depressed areas of high unemployment should be remedied through investments in those areas rather than through emigration. In effect capital should be moved to the unemployed rather than vice versa. Consequently, in the context of the Community the traditional motive for migration would cease to exist. Therefore, the freedom of movement in Community law represented a considerable expansion of personal freedom.

(A. Evans, 'European Citizenship' (1982) 45 MLR 497, 499)

[5] JO 1961, 1073.   [6] JO 1964, 965.

9.2 The Legal Framework: Primary and Secondary Legislation

9.2.1 Treaty Provisions

Article 3(2) TEU provides:

> The Union shall offer its citizens an area of freedom, security and justice without internal frontiers where the free movement of persons is ensured...

Article 18 TFEU generally prohibits discrimination on the grounds of nationality, as is considered in Section 9.2.2.

Articles 19–24 TFEU are concerned with citizenship of the Union and the rights thereunder and will be considered in Section 9.9.3.

Article 20(2) TFEU, which is concerned with citizenship and will be considered further in Section 9.9.3, further provides:

> Citizens of the Union . . . shall have, inter alia:
>
> (a) the right to move and reside freely within the territory of the Member States[.]

Article 26 TFEU provides, in paragraph 2, that:

> The internal market shall comprise an area without internal frontiers where the free movement of goods, persons, services and capital is ensured in accordance with the provisions of this Treaty.

The following treaty Articles outline the basic requirements to facilitate the free movement of the economically active: Arts 45–8 TFEU for workers; Arts 49–55 TFEU for those wishing to establish; and Arts 56–62 TFEU for those wishing to provide services.

For workers, Art 45(1) TFEU provides that freedom of movement for workers shall be secured within the Union and, in the second paragraph, that such freedom of movement shall entail the abolition of any discrimination based on nationality between workers of the member states as regards employment, remuneration, and other conditions of work and employment.

Article 39 (now Art 45 TFEU) was held to be vertically directly effective in Case 167/73 *Commission v France Re French Merchant Seamen* and, later, horizontal direct effects were implied in Case 36/74 *Walrave and Koch*, concerned with a private body, but established under public law. The horizontal direct effects of Art 39 EC (now Art 45 TFEU) were definitively established in Case C-281/98 *Angonese v Cassa di Risparmio di Bolzano SpA* involving an action between an individual and a private bank.

Article 45(3) TFEU describes in broad outline the rights of workers, but subjects those rights to the limitations on grounds of public policy, public security, or public health, amplified now in the new Directive 2004/38, considered later. The rights as listed are:

(a) to accept offers of employment actually made

(b) to move freely within the territory of member states for this purpose

(c) to stay in the member state for the purpose of employment in accordance with the provisions governing the employment of nationals of that state laid down by law, regulation, or administrative action

(d) to remain in the territory of a member state after having been employed in that state and governed by Regulation 1251/70.

Article 45(4) TFEU provides that 'The provisions of this Article shall not apply to employment in the public service'.

For establishment, Art 49 TFEU provides that the freedom of establishment shall include the right to take up and pursue activities as self-employed persons, and to set up and manage undertakings, in particular companies or firms.

And, finally, for the provision of services, Art 56 TFEU provides that 'restrictions on freedom to provide services within the Union shall be prohibited in respect of nationals of member states who are established in a Member State other than that of the person for whom the services are intended'.

9.2.2 Secondary Legislation

With regard to secondary legislation, Directive 2004/38 and the consolidating Regulation 492/2011, which has repealed and replaced Regulation 1612/68, comprehensively cater for the rights of workers and their families in the EU.

9.2.3 The Basic Right of No Discrimination

The most basic or fundamental right in free movement is that there shall be no discrimination on the grounds of nationality. Article 18 TFEU, which prohibits discrimination on the grounds of nationality, has also been highly influential in the development of this area of law by allowing the Court of Justice to outlaw various discriminatory rules and practices by member states and organizations, which were not a clear and direct breach of the provisions on workers, establishment, or services, but which nevertheless discriminated against non-nationals. It has been applied, inter alia, for workers in Case 59/85 *Netherlands v Reed*, for services in Case 2/74 *Reyners v Belgium*, and for establishment in Case 246/89 *Commission v UK (Nationality of Fishermen)*, all of which are considered later.

The CoJ has often stressed that the concept of discrimination not only covers direct discrimination, in which different rules apply to nationals and non-nationals, but also covers covert or indirect discrimination, which leads to the prejudicial treatment of non-nationals by rules that seem to apply fairly to both, but which have an indirect discriminatory effect on non-nationals. The measure may, however, be objectively justified on other grounds. Furthermore, the prohibition of national rules has also been expanded to catch not only those involving discrimination, but all those rules that hinder market access. Parallel developments have also taken place in the other very significant free movement of goods area considered in Chapter 8.

Indirect discrimination was demonstrated in Case 33/88 *Alluè and Coonan v University of Venice*. The applicants, after five years of employment as foreign-language lecturers, were informed that they could not be retained under a 1980 Italian Decree that limited the duration of employment of foreign-language lecturers. Not all the foreign-language lecturers were non-national. Some 25 per cent were nationals; therefore, there was no dissimilar treatment; that is, no overt discrimination. Although the rule applied regardless of nationality, it nevertheless mainly affected the nationals of other member states, who made up 75 per cent of such language teachers. It was held by the CoJ to be discriminatory where such limitations do not exist in respect of other workers. The rules may also be objectively justified if there is a legitimate aim compatible with the treaty, the measure is justified by pressing reasons of public interest, and the measure is proportionate.[7]

---

[7] For a more detailed discussion of objective justification, refer to the text following the *Cassis de Dijon* case in Chapter 8 (free movement of goods).

There are now statutory definitions of indirect discrimination in EU secondary legislation dealing with other forms of discrimination. Directives 2000/43, 2000/78, and 2006/54 all have a similar Art 2, which provides that indirect discrimination arises if an apparently neutral provision, criterion, or practice would put persons of one sex, age, nationality, etc. at a particular disadvantage compared with persons of the other sex, etc., unless that provision, criterion, or practice is objectively justified by a legitimate aim, and the means of achieving that aim are appropriate and necessary.

In the same way as will be seen for services and establishment in Section 9.3.1.3, there has been an attack on national rules that, although applying to both home professionals and those establishing in the host country, are regarded as inappropriate for host professionals because they hinder access to movement. Case 415/93 *Bosman* concerns football transfer fee rules that certainly restricted transfers, but applied to both national and cross-border transfers, hence there was no discrimination and nationality was not a factor. The CoJ held that they were nevertheless an obstacle to movement. The *Bosman* ruling was applied to a similarly restrictive German handball rule in Case C-438/00 *Kolpak*, which limited the number of foreign players to two in each squad, which was found to be discriminatory by the CoJ and not justified on sporting grounds. It clearly limited the chances of non-Germans entering the market. Thus, for persons, the prohibition of harmful rules goes beyond discrimination to cover rules that impede market access.

9.3 The Scope of the Basic Rights

This section determines who may benefit or claim from the rules provided and considers two elements: the personal and material scope. The personal scope is both determined by nationality and comes within the definition of those persons granted the right to move freely by legislation. The material scope of the rights has been determined largely by secondary legislation and concerns the actual rights provided, considered in Section 9.4.

9.3.1 Personal Scope

Two basic definitions have to be established: 'nationality'; and whether the person concerned is a 'worker' or 'self-employed' by establishing or providing services, or otherwise entitled to remain in the member state as an EU citizen, for example, which is a category of growing importance. This definition essentially determines which persons can take up the rights provided by the legislation. The categories of the economically active persons will be considered first and the free movement of citizens in Section 9.9.4.

9.3.1.1 Nationality

For workers and the self-employed, the right to move freely and obtain other benefits, especially those rights that can be taken up by members of the worker's family, is initially dependent on being defined as a national of one of the member states.

The actual determination of member state nationality is a matter for each of the member states, as was expressly stated in Declaration No 2 on Nationality attached to the Treaty on European Union (TEU) before its removal by the Lisbon Treaty. It provided that nationality shall be settled solely by reference to the national law of the member state concerned. This position was upheld in Case C-192/99 *Manjit Kaur*, in which the CoJ held that it is for each member state to lay down the conditions for the acquisition and loss of nationality. This was confirmed in Case C-135/08 *Rottmann*[8] in which Rottmann lost German citizenship and became stateless. His claim not to lose EU citizenship failed as the Court of Justice held that it was up to the member states themselves to decide matters of nationality and statehood, but the Court emphasized that because he would lose his entitlements as an EU citizen as a consequence, this was something the member state concerned had to be sure was proportionate.

It is not, however, necessary for the members of a worker's family to be member-state nationals to obtain benefits, as will be seen in the secondary legislation and case law considered later.

9.3.1.2 Union Status as a Worker or Self-employed

The second part of the personal scope of the law is that, in order for a person to benefit personally, or for their family to benefit from rights arising under Arts 45–62 TFEU and law made thereunder, the person needs to be classified as a worker or self-employed person or now enjoys another status recognized by the CoJ as coming within the scope of the concept. Article 45 TFEU secures freedom for workers of the member states. Establishment under Art 49 TFEU and services under Art 56 TFEU refer to the right of nationals of the member states either to establish or to provide services in the other member states. Establishment also includes legal persons, predominantly in the form of companies, registered in one of the member states which are also included within the personal scope of the rights. The definition of these concepts, as indicated in the heading, is a matter for Union law and not for each of the national legal systems to determine. For example, the persons who may rely on free movement of workers rights under Art 45 TFEU also include an employer (Case C-350/96 *Clean Car Autoservice*) and a recruitment agency (Case C-208/05 *ITC*).

9.3.1.2.1 Worker

Turning first to the term 'worker', there was no definition of the term in the EEC Treaty, but the Court of Justice has held that the term must have a Union meaning, and cannot be the subject of differing interpretations by the courts of the member states. In Case 75/63 *Hoekstra v BBDA*, the CoJ declared the reason for this view:

> If the definition of this term were a matter for the competence of the national courts, it would be possible for every member state to modify the term 'worker' and so to eliminate at will the protection afforded by the EEC Treaty to certain categories of person.

In the case itself, the CoJ gave this limited definition: 'A worker is any employed person, irrespective of whether he is wage earning or salaried, blue collar or white collar, an executive or unskilled labourer.' But it has, in subsequent cases, gone on to expand the definition in a series of cases to include part-time workers, work seekers, and, under certain circumstances, those undertaking a period or course of study.

9.3.1.2.2 Part-time Work

Case 53/81 *Levin v Minister of Justice* concerned the value of work that a person needs to do before he or she can be classed as a worker. The woman plaintiff was a British citizen working in the Netherlands as a chambermaid for 20 hours a week and whose earnings

---

[8] [2010] ECR I-1499.

were below the subsistence level in the Netherlands. The Dutch government argued that because she was a part-time worker earning below the government-set subsistence level, she was not a 'favoured [European Economic Community] EEC citizen' and could not benefit from the provisions of EEC law guaranteeing freedom of movement of workers. The Court of Justice held that these considerations were irrelevant to her status as a worker and declared that, whether she was a full- or part-time worker, she was entitled to the status of worker, provided that the work was genuine and effective, and not so infinitesimal as to be disregarded. The CoJ ruled that work will only be disregarded if it is so minimal that it does not constitute economic activity at all. The essential defining characteristic of work is therefore that it is activity of an economic nature.

In Case 139/85 *Kempf v Minister of Justice*, a German national worked as a part-time flute teacher for 12 lessons a week only. His limited income was topped up to the Dutch minimum income level with supplementary benefit under national legislation. He, too, was refused a residence permit on the grounds that he was not a 'favoured EEC citizen'. The CoJ ruled that if a person is in effective and genuine part-time employment, he or she may not be excluded from the sphere of application of the rules on freedom of movement of workers merely because the remuneration that he or she derives from it is below the minimum level of subsistence set by national law. In this regard, it is irrelevant whether the supplementary means of subsistence are derived from property, from the income of another member of his or her family (as in *Levin*), or from the public funds of the member state of residence (as in *Kempf*). The Dutch court had found that the work was genuine and effective.

Although not expressly stated to be the situation, Case C-313/02 *Wippel v Peek & Cloppenburg* dealt with the common phenomenon of 'zero hours' contracts where no fixed hours are arranged and employees work only when asked to do so by the employer. The case itself concerned an equal treatment claim, and is considered in Chapter 11, but also considered Directive 97/81 on part-time workers—hence the conclusion that even if it was not already obvious, zero-hours employees are considered to be workers under EU law.

The Court of Justice has held in Case C-357/89 *Raulin v Netherlands Ministry of Education and Science* that, in considering whether work is genuine and effective, the national court should take account of all the occupational activities of the person in the host state only and the duration of the activities. This appears to be a decision that hands back the discretion to the member states to define who is a worker at the very margins of those possibly coming within the term. The case concerned a French national who worked for 60 hours in total as a waitress in the Netherlands but who, whilst doing so, was granted the status of worker.[9]

In Case 66/85 *Lawrie-Blum v Land Baden-Württemberg*, the CoJ considered the compatibility of German rules restricting access to a preparatory service stage that was necessary to become a teacher. It laid down three essential characteristics to establish an employment relationship:

- the provision of some sort of service
- being directed by another person (that is, *not* self-employed)
- working in return for remuneration.

---

[9] See also the similar Case C-413/01 *Ninni-Orasche* involving two-and-a-half months' work in three years, which would qualify according to the Court of Justice, but again it was up to the national authorities to decide, as in *Raulin*.

This was applied in Case 196/87 *Steymann v Staatssecretaris van Justitie*, whereby remuneration for work in Bagwhan Religious Community's commercial activities was paid in the form of pocket money and the meeting of material needs. Some limits to the definition appear to have been found in Case 344/87 *Bettray v Staatssecretaris Van Justitie*. The CoJ held that a national of a member state employed in another member state under a social employment scheme involving therapeutic work as part of drug rehabilitation merely as a means of retraining or reintegration cannot be regarded as a worker for the purposes of Community law. The activities could not be carried out as real and genuine economic activities. Here, the position was artificially created with government money and not therefore genuine. Although carried out under supervision and remunerated, the CoJ (in contrast to its position in *Levin*) looked at purpose and found that Bettray was not a worker. However, this *Bettray* decision might not be so secure in view of the decision in Case C-456/02 *Trojani*. Trojani had secured accommodation in a Salvation Army hostel, where, in return for board and lodging and some pocket money, he undertook various jobs for about 30 hours a week as part of a personal socio-occupational reintegration programme, thus straddling both previous cases in terms of fact. He applied for social assistance, which was refused. The CoJ held that he had a direct right of residence under Art 18 EC (now Art 21 TFEU), and that where such EU citizens are in possession of a residence permit, they are thus entitled, according to Art 12 EC (now Art 18 TFEU), to social assistance on the same basis as nationals. So, no real decision was taken on his actual status, which was left to the national court to decide and which will be discussed later, although it can be argued that, under citizenship rights, status is of lesser importance now.

9.3.1.2.3 Frontier Workers

Frontier workers had the potential to create novel legal problems because they are workers who continue to reside in their home state, but work across a frontier in another state or, in less frequent circumstances, continue to work in their home state, but move to another state to live. The argument that presented itself to member states in some of the cases was that where a national continued to live in the home state, he or she had not moved as such and should therefore be treated the same as another national, because the matter was an internal one for the home state and not a matter for EU law.[10] However, the Court of Justice, in a series of cases, has ensured that workers who nevertheless take advantage of the opportunities either to work in another member state, but to reside in the host state, or to work in the home state, but to reside across a frontier, are able to take advantage of EU law rights and not be discriminated against in either the home or host state.

For example, in Case 419/92 *Scholz*, it was held that a frontier worker who continues to live in his or her home state and is only employed in another state, but who crosses the border to work, triggers Community rights that can be claimed within the home state. In Case C-385/00 *De Groot*, the CoJ confirmed that Art 39 EC (now Art 45 TFEU) applies also to frontier workers and thus so does Regulation 1612/68,[11] Art 7(2), which provides that there should be no discrimination in tax matters. Thus, any discrimination such that personal and family circumstances are taken into account, where this results in less favourable treatment of the frontier worker, amounts to an obstacle to the free movement guaranteed by Art 45 TFEU. This judgment is despite, but in full recognition of, the fact that, ostensibly, member states are still in possession of full competence to decide their own tax regimes, but which must be non-discriminatory.

---

[10] This 'wholly internal' situation will be explored in greater detail in Section 9.7.

[11] Now repealed and replaced by Regulation 492/2011.

Case C-212/05 *Hartmann* concerns a German national who moved to Austria but retained his job in Germany. His wife applied for a child benefit from Germany, but was refused. It was argued by member states that Mr Hartmann was not a migrant worker, but the Court of Justice, in line with the earlier cases, dismissed this and held that Art 39 EC (now Art 45 TFEU) applied to the situation of Mr Hartmann. The CoJ also held that, as a consequence, such workers could rely on the freedom from discrimination in social advantages under Art 7(2) of Regulation 1612/68, including child benefit claimed by a spouse. The further argument that, by living in another country, the applicants were not in residence and thus did not have a real link with Germany was also dismissed by the CoJ, in that Mr Hartmann continued to work in Germany and contribute to the German labour market and society. Finally in this selection of frontier workers' cases is Case C-213/05 *Geven*, in which a Dutch national, Ms Geven, had worked in Germany part-time for about a year, but continued to reside in the Netherlands and claimed child benefit from Germany. The status as worker under Art 39 EC was confirmed by the CoJ and thus also the rights under secondary legislation, as in the *Hartmann* case noted earlier. However, in this case it was acknowledged that the contribution to the labour market was less substantial and thus a difference in treatment may be objectively justified as not constituting a real link.[12] In view of the fact that the social-benefit regimes remain within the competences of the member states, the CoJ concluded that it was up to the national courts to decide, but would be legitimate if they were to conclude that the level and length of previous work were not sufficient to establish the close connection required. This latter case also demonstrates how EU law developments are further blurring the distinctions between the previous clear categories of economically and non-economically active EU citizens, which will be discussed later.

The term 'worker' is, however, wider than referring only to those in employment and, in certain circumstances, also applies to those who are seeking work and those who, having lost one job involuntarily, are capable of taking another.

9.3.1.2.4 Work Seekers

Having established in the *Hoekstra* case that certain rights were retained by the worker losing a job, including the status of worker,[13] the proposal for Directive 68/360[14] was discussed in Council, which promoted a myth that the period to look for work sanctioned by the minutes of the directive was three months. This was the period during which EC nationals made unemployed could claim unemployment benefit whilst seeking work under Regulation 1408/71, Art 69. It was then argued before the Court of Justice to be the time after which a member state could lawfully deport a person who had not found work. Two cases follow that have considered these matters.

In Case 316/85 *Marie-Christine Lebon*, the CoJ held that those in search of work are not entitled to receive workers' benefits (in this case, a social security support payment). Miss Lebon no longer lived with her parents, who were ex-workers; therefore, she did not qualify for benefits as a dependent of a worker. She then asked if she qualified for workers' benefits if she was looking, or intended to look, for work. The CoJ held that the benefits provided by legislation on free movement were only for those in actual employment, and not for those who migrate in search of work and have not found it. She could temporarily be classified as a worker, but not for the purposes of benefits—although the later Case

---

[12] This is something that will also be taken up in the citizenship cases in Section 9.9.4.

[13] And confirmed in the later Case C-43/99 *Leclere and Deaconescu*.

[14] Now repealed and replaced by Directive 2004/38.

C-138/02 *Collins*, noted briefly in the next section, has cast doubt on that part of the judgment. Case C-292/89 *Antonissen* clarifies how long the temporary status entitles a person to remain to look for work. The UK wished to deport Antonissen, who had been convicted of possession of cocaine with intent to supply, and asked the CoJ whether it could do so. UK legislation gave EC citizens six months in which to find employment. Antonissen was in the country for over three years without work before his imprisonment. The Court of Justice held that statements recorded in minutes regarding the acceptable time for the pursuit of work before deportation would not be allowable, have no legal significance, and cannot be used to interpret the relevant legislative provisions. A member state may deport an EU migrant worker subject to an appeal if he or she has not found employment after a period of six months, which is to be taken as a guideline only, unless there is evidence that indicates that he or she is continuing to seek employment and that there are genuine chances of being engaged—language that is repeated in Directive 2004/38, Art 14.[15] Therefore, after the expiry of a reasonable period, depending on the circumstances, persons may no longer be afforded the status and benefits of worker under EU law, and may lawfully be deported by the member state. The CoJ based this right on the treaty itself and not Directive 68/360.

Article 7 of Directive 2004/38 makes it clear that workers and the self-employed may retain their status and right to remain if made temporarily unfit for work or involuntarily unemployed,[16] and Art 14 of the same directive provides that residence may be retained provided that the persons concerned do not become an unreasonable burden on the host state. But EU citizens not possessing a sufficiently close link to the host state will be ineligible for benefits according to the CoJ in Case C-138/02 *Collins*, considered further later and in Section 9.7 on citizenship.

9.3.1.2.5 Worker Training, Education, and Benefits

A further extension to the scope of the concept of worker took place in favour of those no longer in employment, but who were employed previously and now engaged in some form of study. This category was rather limited, but its boundaries may now have been considerably extended by the respect shown by the CoJ to the concept of citizenship, considered in Section 9.7.

The leading case is Case 39/86 *Lair v Universität Hannover*, in which a French national employed in Germany was refused a grant by the university for a maintenance award and training fees because she had not worked in the country continually for at least five years, and therefore, whilst at university, was not considered a worker. It was stated in this case

---

[15] The *Collins* case (C-138/02) considered later and in Section 9.7 essentially repeats the guidance time of six months in *Antonissen* as the period which should be granted jobseekers before either expelling them or determining whether they have genuine chances of being employed. It they are not looking, they are hardly going to get a job.

[16] Directive 2004/38, Art 7(3), makes it clear that workers and also the self-employed may retain their status and right to remain in the following circumstances:

(a) he or she is temporarily unable to work as the result of an illness or accident

(b) he or she is in duly recorded involuntary unemployment after having been employed for more than one year and has registered as a jobseeker with the relevant employment office

(c) he or she is in duly recorded involuntary unemployment after completing a fixed-term employment contract of less than a year or after having become involuntarily unemployed during the first 12 months and has registered as a jobseeker with the relevant employment office (in which case, the status of worker shall be retained for no less than six months)

(d) he or she embarks on vocational training (but unless he or she is involuntarily unemployed, the retention of the status of worker shall require the training to be related to the previous employment).

that the period at university would lead to a vocational qualification and that the time at university represented a break in employment only. The Court of Justice held that since there was no fixed legislative definition of 'worker', there was nothing to say that the definition must always depend on a continuing employment relationship. Certain rights have been guaranteed to workers after employment has finished, such as the right to stay and social security rights. This could also apply to university training, provided that there was a link or continuity between the previous work and university. Therefore the university support could be considered one of the social rights coming within Regulation 1612/68 (now 492/2011). The status of worker would therefore be retained if a link were to exist between the previous occupation and the studies in question.

In contrast, in Case 197/86 *Brown v Secretary of State for Scotland*, the Scottish education department refused Brown a grant for university. He had worked for eight months in the UK prior to, and as a precursor to, university and gained the status of worker. The CoJ held that, whilst university training is to be regarded as mainly vocational, it was only covered by Art 12 EC (now Art 18 TFEU) generally outlawing discrimination. This covers tuition fees, but not the maintenance grant; therefore, a person who enters employment for eight months, and who did so as a precursor or requisite to attend university, did not retain the status of worker for the purposes of claiming a grant. Whether this would be decided in the same way again if presented now bears close inspection in light of the *Grzelczyk* and subsequent cases discussed later.

Returning to Case C-357/89 *Raulin*, the Court of Justice held that the 60 hours' work had enabled Raulin to claim the protection of Art 39 EC (now Art 45 TFEU), despite its very temporary nature. However, a migrant worker who then left that employment to begin a course of full-time study unconnected with the previous occupational activities did not retain the status of worker—a finding upheld by the Dutch court. Raulin, however, did have a right of residence in the host state for the duration of the course of study, regardless of whether or not the host state had issued a residence permit.

Thus, definitions of what constitutes vocational training and the link to work are crucial for the determination of the status of a worker, and the consequent benefits and rights, as is the number of weeks or hours worked. This case law is essentially confirmed in the consolidating Directive 2004/38 which, under Art 7(3)(d), provides that the status of worker is retained if the EU citizen concerned embarks on vocational training that is related to the previous employment. However, in Case C-184/99 *Grzelczyk*, a French national who studied and worked on a part-time basis to help to support himself for three years in Belgium applied at the beginning of his fourth and final year of study to the CPAS (a government social assistance agency) for payment of the *minimex*, a non-contributory minimum subsistence allowance. The CPAS granted Mr Grzelczyk the *minimex*, but then later denied this on the basis that he was not Belgian, hence, clear discrimination on the grounds of nationality. This case did not consider whether Grzelczyk enjoyed the status as a worker. The Court of Justice emphasized that the new citizenship provisions and new competences in education, albeit limited, allowed it to hold that Arts 12 and 17 EC (now Arts 18 and 21 TFEU) preclude discrimination as regards the grant of a non-contributory social benefit to Union citizens where they are lawfully resident. Hence, it would seem that, under these or similar circumstances, a link to previous work is no longer required.

In Case C-138/02 *Collins*, the CoJ held that, once citizenship had been established, then even work seekers could claim certain benefits, in contrast to *Lebon* discussed earlier, but some benefits could be denied on objective grounds, in this case the habitual residence requirement for a jobseeker's allowance which, according to the CoJ, can be made dependent on the existence of a genuine link between the work seeker and the state. A further case now appears to confirm *Collins*, but to step back slightly from the previous generous interpretation of individual's rights. Case C-158/07 *Förster v IB-Groep* concerns Ms Förster, a German national in the Netherlands who, from 2000, worked from time to time there and qualified for a study maintenance grant, which was withdrawn when the responsible authority (IB-Groep) discovered in 2003 that she was no longer working. Her challenge to the decision failed because she was not sufficiently integrated in the Netherlands and she had not satisfied the requirement of five years' residence there. On reference to the Court of Justice, the CoJ upheld its previous decision in Case C-209/03 *Bidar* that member states were entitled to require a certain degree of integration; in this case, a five-year period was justified and proportionate. The work–study relationship did not play a role in the CoJ's decision.

Case C-256/01 *Allonby* concerned the re-employment of former college lecturers in the same establishment, but under a self-employed scheme paid by a private independent company. Effectively, the definition of the term 'worker' was also extended to cover self-employed persons. In considering the new relationship, the CoJ held: 'The formal classification of a self-employed person under national law does not change the fact that a person must be classified as a worker within the meaning of that Article if his independence is merely notional.'

9.3.1.3 Freedom of Establishment and the Provision of Services

The self-employed are granted rights under the treaty to move to another member state to establish either permanently or on a long-term basis (Arts 49–55 TFEU) or to provide services temporarily (Arts 56–62 TFEU). The definitions for the personal scope of establishment and for the provision of services are much more straightforward than for workers, because the primary treaty Articles have laid down the basic concepts, which have not then been subject to an expansive interpretation by the Court of Justice. Article 49 TFEU deals with rights of freedom of establishment as the right to enter another member state and stay on a long-term or permanent basis, to take up and pursue activities as a self-employed person, and to set up and manage undertakings. This includes legal, as well as natural, persons. A basic definition has been given in Case C-221/89 *Factortame*: 'the actual pursuit of an economic activity through a fixed establishment in another member state for an indefinite period'. In Case C-268/99 *Jany*, the CoJ characterized self-employment as a relationship outside a relationship of subordination, as would be the case with workers, and in which the remuneration earned was paid directly and in full to the self-employed person.

'Services' under Art 56 TFEU envisages a temporary state of affairs and appearance, if at all, in the host state would only be for a limited period to provide specific services. There would be no permanent personal or professional presence in the host state or a necessity to reside. The concept of services is defined by Art 57 TFEU as those 'provided for remuneration, in so far as they are not governed by provisions relating to freedom of movement of goods, capital and persons'; in particular, Art 57(d) TFEU specifically includes activities of industrial and commercial characters, and those of craftsmen and the professions. The provision of services is potentially a much wider category, and can be associated with the areas of banking, finance, insurance, and legal services, and now, with modern technology, telephone, broadcasting, and internet services will become big services areas—notably without the need to move from the home state to provide services in other member states (see, for example, Case C-384/93 *Alpine Investments*, concerned with cross-frontier telephone-sales calling). The scope of the term 'services' has been held by the CoJ to include the recipients of services, considered later, and even to include prostitution in Case C-268/99 *Jany et al.*

Originally, the concepts of 'services' and 'establishment' were regarded as, if not absolutely distinguishable, certainly clearly distinct concepts with no overlap. At times, however, the distinction between them can be difficult to ascertain.

In Case 205/84 *Commission v Germany (Insurance Services)*, the provision of insurance included the setting up of offices on a long-term basis staffed by nationals of the host state, which was considered by the Court of Justice as establishment even though the legal entity (the owner or principal) remained in the home state. This ruling is very important, because the application of home rules may be stricter for establishment since it appears to be based on achieving complete equality of treatment. The provision of services under Art 57 TFEU, on the other hand, whilst allowing for the same conditions to be imposed by the host state, has developed on the basis that not all home rules have been found by the CoJ to be suitable or acceptable to those providing services. The distinction, therefore, between establishment and services is important. The CoJ has now advised that the provision of services may even justify the setting up of infrastructure in the host state. In Case C-55/94 *Gebhard v Milan Bar Council*, the CoJ characterized 'establishment' as the right of a Community national to participate on a stable and continuous basis in the economic life of a member state other than his or her own, and 'services' by the temporary, precarious, and discontinuous nature of the services. The CoJ held:

> The temporary nature of the activities in question has to be determined in the light, not only of the duration of the provision of the service, but also of its regularity, periodicity or continuity. The fact that the provision of services is temporary does not mean that the provider of services within the meaning of the Treaty may not equip himself with some form of infrastructure in the host member state (including an office, chambers or consulting rooms) in so far as such infrastructure is necessary for the purposes of performing the services in question.

In this case, the setting up of chambers in Italy by a German lawyer on a long-term basis, although still practising in Stuttgart, was held to be establishment.[17]

In Case C-386/04 *Stauffer*, the Court of Justice stated that establishment required the permanent presence in the host state and that merely renting property from an agent to carry out activities of an Italian organization in Germany was not establishment. In Case C-215/01 *Schnitzer*, a long-term (three-year) contract for plastering services by a Portuguese company in Germany was held by the CoJ to be exactly that, the provision of services and not establishment, which was argued to be the case by the German skilled trades register. There was no intention to remain beyond the contractual period; hence the actual classification very much depends on the view taken on the facts of the case.

9.3.1.4 Establishment of Companies

Whilst the study of company law is not usually an intense study in EU law courses, a brief note should be included on the leading cases in this area that have had general implications for establishment.

Article 49 TFEU specifically refers to the right to 'manage undertakings, in particular companies or firms within the meaning of the second paragraph of Article 54'. Article 54

---

[17] The Services Directive, a considerable intervention in this area, is considered in Section 9.5.2.2.

TFEU, in turn, provides that those coming within the scope of Art 49 TFEU are those formed in accordance with the law of a member state and which have their registered office, central administration, or principal place of business within the Union, which includes companies or firms constituted under civil or commercial law.

In Case C-212/97 *Centros Ltd*, two Danish directors registered a company in the UK and requested registration of a branch office in Denmark, which was refused on the grounds that it was an attempt to circumvent the Danish company capital requirements, particularly because there was an intention to trade only in Denmark and not in the UK. Denmark required a much higher minimum paid-up capital than the UK. Upon reference to the Court of Justice, the CoJ held that the case came within the scope of Art 43 EC (now Art 49 TFEU), and that any concerns that creditors would be at risk had already been catered for in national and Community law. Article 43 EC (now Art 49 TFEU) conveyed the right to set up companies in one member state and trade via a branch in another member state, subject to the regulation in the host state provided that any such regulation satisfies the following requirements, observed elsewhere in free movement law, namely that it be non-discriminatory, justified by imperative requirement in the general interest, and proportionate. The CoJ held that the complete ban by Denmark did not fulfil those conditions.

Members states of original establishment, may though, impose conditions or restrictions on companies wishing to transfer, move or split their registered office to another state. In Case C-81/87 *Daily Mail*, the newspaper company attempted to move its central management to the Netherlands for tax advantages but nevertheless remain a UK company. It was not permitted to exit the UK by the UK Treasury. In a challenge to that by the Daily Mail, under Art 49 TFEU, the CoJ held that the right of establishment was not unconditional and could be restricted lawfully by member states, particularly as company law is not harmonized and is still within the competence of the member states. In the similar case C-210/06 *Cartesio*, a Hungarian company wanted to move its head office to Italy but continue to operate under Hungarian law. Hungary refused to sanction this unless it ceased to operate entirely as a Hungarian company and the CoJ held this was acceptable under EU law.

In Case C-208/00 *Überseering*, a Dutch-registered company was transferred to Germany, but was denied legal capacity in Germany by a German court. This was argued to breach the freedom of establishment in Art 43 EC (now Art 49 TFEU). The Court of Justice agreed with this view. Both *Centros* and *Überseering* have been criticized for allowing companies to be registered in the state with the least restrictive requirements and thus for introducing a lowest common denominator into EU company law, resembling the Delaware clause from the USA (Delaware being the state with the most lax regulation). The judgments are, thus, a strong support for the free choice of company registration and free movement. Case C-167/01 *Inspire Art* did, though, allow for the possibility that the host state could impose restrictions or conditions on an establishing company in order to protect creditors and investors, provided that the restrictions or conditions were objectively justified. In this case, the requirement that the company register itself additionally as a 'former foreign company' and use that in business, which was already quite clear, and an additional requirement of minimum capital, not imposed on national companies, were not. The rights obtained under establishment operate not only against the host state but also against the home state. Case C-446/03 *M&S*, concerning UK tax rules which did not allow losses from subsidiaries located in other member states to be deducted, challenged this rule as being an obstruction to free movement. The Court of Justice agreed even though M&S, at that time, was merely contemplating setting up branches out of the UK.

9.4 **The Material Scope of the Rights**

Apart from the basic rights being provided by the central Arts 45, 49, and 56 TFEU, the material rights of free movement have largely been provided in secondary law.

9.4.1 **Secondary Legislation: Introduction**

Each of the free movement sections has its own treaty base to empower the enactment of secondary legislation in pursuit of the treaty objectives. Consequently for workers under Art 40 EC (now Art 46 TFEU) and the self-employed under Arts 53 (now repealed), 47, and 52 EC (now Arts 53 and 59 TFEU), the Commission was empowered to issue directives to obtain the general objectives set out in the treaty. Most of the earlier secondary legislation enacted over the course of a number of years has now been comprehensively replaced and updated by consolidating legislation and therefore the focus of attention will now be on the new provisions.

Three measures, Directive 64/221, Regulation 1612/68, and Directive 68/360,[18] were enacted both to facilitate the original rights provided and to provide genuinely new rights, particularly when it came to members of the member state national's family.

Regulation 1612/68, repealed and replaced by Regulation 492/2011, provided for equality of access to employment for all community nationals, equality of treatment in employment rights and housing rights, the right of a worker to be joined by his or her family, and the right for his or her children to be educated on the same terms as the children of nationals of the member state concerned. For the self-employed, Directives 73/148 and 75/34 were the equivalents of Directives 68/360 and 1251/70, and they too have been repealed and replaced by Directive 2004/38.

Directive 2004/38 is now the main and most important provision of secondary legislation for the free movement of Union citizens, and, as noted, has replaced most of the previous secondary legislation. It covers both workers and the self-employed, and both generally revises the law and encapsulates much of the case law of the Court of Justice, which has often advanced legal rights prior to statutory change. The directive clarifies who should be regarded as a member of the family or person otherwise provided with rights derived from an economically active EU citizen. It also establishes permanent rights of residence for citizens after a certain period and restricts the member states' right to refuse entry on the grounds of public policy. Whilst the right of permanent residence appears new, in reality it merely reflects the existing situation for many Union citizens and families who have chosen to live in another member state. Its provisions will be considered where appropriate in the sections of text following, along with, when considered useful, reference to the previous provisions applicable.

9.4.2 **Rights of Entry, Residence, and Exit**

The rights to enter, move freely, seek, and take up employment are governed by a combination of Art 45(3) TFEU; Regulation 492/2011, Arts 1–5; and Directive 2004/38, Arts 4–14, although much of the case law is based on previous legislation.[19]

---

[18] All of these earlier directives have been repealed and replaced by Directive 2004/38, but are mentioned here in brief because they may arise in literature and case law; however, in the text, the new directive and Article numbers have been inserted.

[19] Hence in older cases you will see reference to Regulation 1612/68 and Directive 68/360.

Regulation 492/2011, Arts 1 and 2, provide the right to take up employment in the host state under the same conditions as nationals without discrimination.

Regulation 492/2011, Art 3(1), permits imposition on non-nationals of conditions relating to linguistic ability required by the nature of the post to be filled. This is illustrated and interpreted by the Case 379/87 *Groener v Minister for Education*, in which the Court of Justice upheld an Irish requirement that teachers in Ireland should be proficient in Irish as part of a public policy to maintain and promote the Irish language and culture. Any requirement, though, must be proportionate.

Directive 2004/38 provides the rules to regulate the conditions by which workers can leave one member state and enter the territory of another. It prescribes the entry formalities that it is permissible for member states to impose; in particular, the rules regarding the issue and withdrawal of residence permits. Cases arising under the previous directive sought to remove the unnecessary restrictions on free movement.

Article 4 provides that exit states are obliged to allow nationals and their family with a valid passport to leave with an exit visa or other formality. The exit state is obliged to issue a passport or identity (ID) card.

Article 5 provides that entrance states cannot demand an entry visa or equivalent documents from EC nationals. They can, however, require a passport or valid ID card and visas from non-Union members of the family, or in the absence of the correct documents, unequivocal proof of the right to enter and reside (see Case C-215/03 *Salah Oulane*).

In Case C-68/89 *Commission v Netherlands (Entry Requirements)*, the Court of Justice held generally in respect of Directive 68/360 that the requirements for documentation do not give the member state the right to further questioning regarding the purpose and duration of stay once the correct papers have been shown. Whilst this is reasonable in theory, in practice it is not so likely in today's more security-conscious climate.[20] In Case C-344/95 *Commission v Belgium*, a delay in issuing documents, the limited duration of residence permits, and payments demanded in excess of that comparable for national ID cards were all measures held by the CoJ to breach Directive 68/360.

Article 6 provides that the right to enter, travel, and reside in a host member state for a period of up to three months by an EU citizen and his or her family is not restricted to the economically active, but to any EU citizen without any other conditions other than the requirement to hold valid ID and/or visa documentation, the latter covered by Arts 5 and 6. The financial self-sufficiency requirements that were contained in the repealed general free movement directives are not imposed for the initial period of residence up to three months; however, Art 24 of the directive makes it clear that there is no right of social assistance in that three-month period.[21] The right to reside for a period of more than three months is made conditional, under Art 7, on being engaged in a gainful activity, being self-employed, being a recipient of services, being self-sufficient with comprehensive sickness insurance cover, attending a recognized educational establishment, or being a family member of a lawfully resident EU citizen. After that period EU citizens may lose

---

[20] It is now quite common to be asked questions on leaving or entering countries which still maintain border controls about the purpose and duration of a visit. This is justified on the ground of security but whether this would stand up to the scrutiny of the Court of Justice is not known as recent case law on this aspect is not available.

[21] See Art 24(2) of Directive 2004/38: '2. By way of derogation from paragraph 1, the host Member State shall not be obliged to confer entitlement to social assistance during the first three months of residence or, where appropriate, the longer period provided for in Article 14(4)(b).' The latter reference refers to where EU citizens are looking for work and have genuine prospects of obtaining it, essentially the statutory rendering of the ruling in *Antonissen*.

their right to remain if they become an unreasonable burden on the host state. Article 8(4) further provides that in determining the right to stay and financial self-sufficiency, the member states may not fix a minimum amount but must assess each case on its merits, but must not be above the threshold for national eligibility for pure safety net social assistance.

As well as residence permits for family members, a registration certificate can be demanded, which must be granted to any worker who produces a passport and certificate of proof of employment. Members of the worker's family must also be afforded a registration certificate on production of a passport and proof of relationship or proof of dependence. In Case C-459/99 *MRAX*, the Court of Justice considered that it was disproportionate and therefore prohibited to send back a third-country national (TCN) married to a national of a member state not in possession of a valid visa where he or she is able to prove his or her identity and conjugal ties, and there is no evidence to establish that he or she represents a risk to the requirements of public policy, public security, or public health. Directive 2004/38, Art 8, reflects the previous case law by providing that the failure to comply with the registration requirement may render the person concerned liable to proportionate and non-discriminatory administrative sanctions only. For example, in Case 159/79 *R v Pieck*, Mr Pieck, a Dutch national, re-entered the UK after his original six-month entry permit had expired and he had failed to renew it. The authorities sought to deport him. The CoJ held that a failure to obtain a permit could only result in penalties for minor offences. In Case 118/75 *Watson v Belman*, Miss Watson, a UK national, was acting as an 'au pair' whilst staying in Italy with Mr Belman. Both had failed to report this to the national authorities as required, and faced imprisonment and fines under national law. In addition, Miss Watson was to be deported. The Italian magistrate asked the CoJ if the punishments were compatible with EC law. The CoJ held that the use of internal rules—in this case, the requirement to report—was acceptable, but that the penalty must be in proportion to the offence or damage caused (that is, a small fine). Therefore, any decision to deport would be contrary to the treaty. In line with previous case law, Directive 2004/38, Art 25 provides that the registration certificate and residence permit are not preconditions for residence, but merely evidence of the entitlement to enter and reside, in other words not the right itself but merely the proof of it. Administrative rules requiring registration are acceptable, as is an appropriate sanction for their breach, but not deportation, which would be regarded as disproportionate.

Previously, Art 6 of Directive 68/360 provided that the permits must be valid for the whole territory of the member state and valid for at least five years with automatic renewal. These requirements are reproduced in Arts 22 and 11 of the Directive 2004/38. However, Art 22 does provide that member states may impose territorial restrictions on the rights of permanent residence only where the same restrictions may be applied to their own nationals. It was confirmed in Case 36/75 *Rutili v Minister of Interior* that an administrative prohibition restricting movement to parts of France, where justified, could only be for the entire territory of the member state. Although, as held in Case C-100/01 *Olazbal*, when it comes to criminal measures being taken to restrict movement, this would be acceptable provided that the action was justified, the seriousness of the crime would otherwise lead to a complete banishment, and nationals would be subject to similar punitive measures. Article 15 of the directive states that the expiry of the documentation does not constitute a ground for expulsion.

Temporary involuntary unemployment does not remove the employed or self-employed status (Art 14). Whilst the period is not specified, previous case law (Case C-292/89 *Antonissen*) suggests that six months would be the limit, after which the favoured status would then be lost. Whether then the host member state would be entitled to deport the citizen concerned is doubtful in view of the case law considered later in this chapter, unless there were serious grounds for deportation other than involuntary unemployment or that the person concerned had become a burden on the state.[22]

9.4.3 **The Rights Provided by Regulation 492/2011 and Directive 2004/38**

Of all the earlier legislation, Regulation 1612/68 (now replaced by Regulation 492/2011) certainly proved to be the most supportive of free movement, in particular, Art 7. The regulation details access to employment and rights for workers and introduced the rights of free movement for members of the workers' family. Whilst economically active persons received confirmation that their rights extended to matters such as tax and social advantages, vocational training, trade union membership, and housing rights and benefits under Arts 7–9 of Regulation 492/2011, the most significant provisions introduced by the first expansion of the rights were to the members of the family of the EU worker or the self-employed person moving. These additional rights to take up employment, education, or vocational training applied also to non-EU member-state family members.

These rights of equality of treatment are further emphasized by Art 24 of Directive 2004/38, which provides that 'all Union citizens residing on the basis of this Directive in the territory of the host Member State shall enjoy equal treatment with the nationals of that Member State within the scope of the Treaty'.

Article 5 of Regulation 492/2011 obliges member states to give the same assistance to other EU nationals as their own nationals when seeking employment; that is, by the various national employment agencies.

Regulation 492/2011, Art 7(1), prohibits discrimination against workers on grounds of nationality, and specifically mentions terms and conditions of employment, dismissal, and, where relevant, reinstatement.

It has been decided that when a worker commences a job in another country, the same as that previously undertaken in the home state, this previous service may count for advantages in the host state. The Court of Justice held that to ignore this is to discriminate contrary to Art 7(1). In Case C-187/96 *Commission v Greece*, the CoJ held that a Greek administrative regulation and practice that did not take into account periods of employment in the public service of another member state when determining seniority increments and salary grading breached Art 39 EC (now Art 45 TFEU) and Art 7(1) of Regulation 1612/68 (now of 492/2011)—in other words, service elsewhere counts.

Article 7(2) of Regulation 492/2011 has proved to be a provision with extremely wide scope. It refers specifically to equality in social and tax advantages, which also apply to the family of workers. 'Family' is open to wide interpretation, as are the benefits under Art 7(2).

In Case 32/75 *Fiorini aka Christini v SNCF*, a reduced fare entitlement was claimed by the widow of an Italian SNCF worker. Widows of French workers were allowed such a family entitlement, but it was denied to the Italian. The SNCF claimed that, since it was not express in the contract of employment, it was not available to foreign workers. The CoJ was asked if this was the kind of social advantage envisaged by Art 7 and it held that Art 7

---

[22] A UK Employment Appeal Tribunal held, though, in *Giangregorio v Secretary of State for the Home Department* [1983] 3 CMLR 472, that voluntary unemployment would remove the continued right to a residence permit and thus arguably permit deportation, but it is unclear whether the Court of Justice would agree with this view.

applies to all advantages, not only those limited to a contract of employment. It therefore applies to the family of an EU worker in the same way as those of nationals.

In Case 94/84 *ONE v Deak*, an unemployed Hungarian national living with his mother, an Italian national working in Belgium, was refused special unemployment benefits for non-nationals on the basis that no agreement for such benefits existed between Belgium and Hungary. The Court of Justice held that special unemployment benefits were a social advantage within the meaning of Art 7 and that Deak, regardless of nationality, could derive rights as the descendant of a worker, otherwise a worker might be hindered from moving if the descendants were discriminated against, thus causing financial difficulty.

In Case 137/84 *Mutsch*, a Luxembourg national living in a German-speaking commune in Belgium was denied the use of German before a court, a right granted to the Belgian German minority. The Court of Justice held that the right was a social advantage under Art 7(2) despite there being no link to a contract of employment. Article 7(2) has even been interpreted to include a grant to cover funeral expenses in Case C-237/94 *O'Flynn*, although some limit to Art 7(2) appears to have been found in Case C-43/99 *Leclere*, which involved a Belgian national who was working in Luxembourg, but was injured in an accident. He was granted an invalidity allowance by the Luxembourg authorities, but was later refused child allowance, because he was no longer a worker. Whilst the invalidity benefit was regarded as linked to former work, the child allowance was not held to be connected and therefore could lawfully be refused.

In Case C-385/00 *De Groot*, Art 7(2) applies to provide that there should be no discrimination in tax matters, and that any discrimination in the way in which personal and family circumstances are taken into account that results in less favourable treatment of the frontier worker amounts to an obstacle to the free movement guaranteed by Art 39 EC (now Art 45 TFEU). This judgment is despite, but in full recognition of, the fact that member states are still able to decide their own tax regimes.

The rights under Regulation 492/2011, Art 7 (2) were summed up by the Court of Justice in Case 207/78 *Even* as 'all those which, whether or not linked to a contract of employment, are generally granted to national workers primarily because of their objective status as workers, or by virtue of the mere fact of their residence' in the host member state. The CoJ stressed that these were the rights which helped facilitate their mobility within the EU. In the case though a further right to an increased pension due to war service claimed by a French national in Belgium was not to be included in the understanding of social advantage as this was for a service rendered to a country and not generated by reason of the status of an EU worker. As noted already, the ECJ held in Case 316/85 *Lebon* that equal treatment with regard to social and tax advantages laid down by Article 7(2) of Regulation 1612/68 operates only for the benefit of workers and does not apply to nationals of member states who move in search of employment.

Article 7(3) of Regulation 492/2011 provides for the same rights and access to vocational training (see, for example, the *Lair* case considered previously). Article 7(3) appears, however, to be less expansive, so that Art 7(2) equally applies to education as a social advantage—see, for example, Case C-3/90 *Bernini*.

Article 9 of Regulation 492/2011 provides that workers shall enjoy all of the rights and benefits accorded to national workers in matters of housing, including ownership and access to local authority housing lists.

9.4.3.1 Family Members

Directive 2004/38 provides that the rights enjoyed by the Union national under the directive also apply to family members, who are defined more generously now in Art 2 as spouses, registered partners, descendants, and ascendants. Article 2 has provided that the status of partners will be equated with that of spouses in those member states that recognize such a registered or attestable stable relationship, and thus brings statute law in line with the case law of the Court of Justice in the *Reed* and *Diatta* cases considered later. Article 2(c) considerably widens the definition of 'the family' in providing that members of the family include the direct descendants and ascendants of the spouse and partner also. Article 3 also provides rights of entry and residence for any other family members not within the definitions in Art 2 who, in the country from which they have come, are dependents or members of the household of the Union citizen having the primary right of residence, or where there are serious health or humanitarian grounds for doing so.

Members of the family can be any nationality, and include those under the age of 21 and adult children over the age of 21 where they are dependent on the worker. 'Dependency' was defined in Case 316/85 *Lebon* as a factual situation of support provided by the worker. By way of example, in Case 261/83 *Castelli v ONPTS*, the Italian mother of a retired Italian worker in Belgium claimed an old-age pension. Mrs Castelli had never worked herself in Belgium, therefore her claim was based on her status as a member of her son's family. The Belgian authorities refused to pay on the grounds that she was not Belgian and they did not have a reciprocal agreement with Italy. The Court of Justice held that Mrs Castelli was entitled to install herself with her son under Art 10 of Regulation 1612/68. She was also entitled to remain after her son's retirement and had a right to the pension under Art 7.

In a judgment concerned with both Arts 7 and 10 of Regulation 1612/68, but which has now been partly overtaken by Directive 2004/38, the CoJ was required to consider whether the term 'spouse' included cohabitees in Case 59/85 *Netherlands v Reed*. Miss Reed applied for a residence permit in the Netherlands, claiming that her right to remain was based on her cohabitation with a UK national working in the Netherlands. The Dutch government refused to recognize this. The Court of Justice was aware that provisions of national laws regarding cohabitees' legal rights could be quite varied. It was unable to overcome the clear intention of Art 10, which referred to a relationship based on marriage. The CoJ referred instead to the social advantages guaranteed under Art 7 of the Regulation as being capable of including the companionship of a cohabitee, which could contribute to integration in the host country. The CoJ held that where such relationships amongst nationals are accorded legal advantages under national law, these could not be denied to nationals of other member states without being discriminatory, and thus breaching Arts 7 and 48 EC (now Arts 18 and 45 TFEU). This is a somewhat convoluted decision, but it does provide justice to free movement in the case. The cohabitee does not have rights in his or her own right, but the companionship of a cohabitee is merely regarded as one of the advantages to which workers are entitled. Hence, the case merely supports the well-established right in EU law not to be discriminated against on the grounds of nationality. Of course, in some countries cohabitees are not afforded the same rights as married couples. The reasoning of the CoJ has been carried over into Art 2 of the new directive in respect of same-sex partner rights. Where national law supports this, EU law will demand that other Union nationals are equally treated, and where national law does not support such rights, EU law cannot impose them on member states. The UK does, of course, now formally recognize same-sex partnerships. The *Reed* case remains important for its wide interpretation of Art 7(2) of Regulation 492/2011.

The rights of a spouse have been held not to be dependent on residence with the entitled worker. In Case 267/83 *Diatta v Land Berlin*, Mrs Diatta, a Senegalese citizen, was married to a Frenchman living and working in Berlin. She obtained work in Berlin, shortly after which the couple separated to live apart. Upon application to extend her residence permit, the German authorities refused on the ground that she was no longer a member of the family for the purposes of Regulation 1612/68. The Court of Justice ruled that the rights under the regulation were not dependent on the requirements as to how or where members of the family lived. Therefore, a permanent common family dwelling cannot be implied as a condition of the rights granted thereunder. In Case C-413/99 *Baumbast*, the CoJ had confirmed that divorce will bring to an end the spousal relationship for the purposes of free movement rights and, thus, the right to remain in the host state unless saved by any other reason, as it was in the case. However, under Art 13 of Directive 2004/38, in certain circumstances this will not affect the right to remain in the host state; that is, where the spouse is a national of another member state or, if not, where the marriage or relationship has lasted at least three years, including one year in the host state or, reflecting the *Baumbast* case, where the person is a carer of the Union citizen's children.

In reviewing a case that has the appearance of a marriage of convenience, the CoJ has held, in Case C-109/01 *Akrich*, that Art 10 of Regulation 1612/68 and now by analogy Directive 2004/38, applies to TCNs only if they are lawfully resident in a member state before they can move to another one and is not applicable where a marriage of convenience has been arranged to circumvent a member state's immigration laws. There have been cases subsequent to the *Akrich* case on related family issues, the first of which, Case C-01/05 *Jia*, held that Community law does not require member states to make the grant of a residence permit to TCNs who are members of the family of a Community national subject to the condition that those family members have previously been residing lawfully in another member state. The second of these, Case C-127/08 *Metock et al*, confirms *Jia*, but this time was based on Directive 2004/38 and expressly reverses part of the judgment in *Akrich* by making clear that the directive is not conditional on a requirement that a TCN must have been lawfully resident in another member state to stay in a member state as a spouse or member of the family of an EU citizen. *Metock* considered numerous Articles of Directive 2004/38 and involved four TCNs who had been refused asylum in Ireland and had then married EU citizens lawfully resident there. The facts of the case stated that these were not marriages of convenience.

Article 23 of Directive 2004/38 (previously Art 11 of Regulation 1612/68) entitles the family members of an entitled Union citizen to take up any activity as an employed person, to include any activity or profession provided that the appropriate qualifications and formalities are observed. For example, in Case 131/85 *Emir Gül v Regierungspräsident Düsseldorf*, the Court of Justice held that this right includes the right of such concerned persons to access to employment also under the same conditions as nationals of the host state. This was also affirmed in the case of *Diatta v Land Berlin* in favour of Mrs Diatta.

9.4.4 **Education and Carer Rights**

Article 10 of Regulation 492/2011 provides that the children of a national of a member state shall be admitted to the general educational, apprenticeship, and vocational training courses under the same conditions as nationals. Case 9/74 *Casagrande* had already extended the right (then Art 12 (1612/68)) to include not only access to educational facilities, but also equality of measures intended to facilitate educational attendance. In Case C-7/94 *Gaal*, the CoJ extended the right to an independent and over-21-year-old child of a migrant worker who had been employed in another member state. Gaal was the Belgian son of an EC worker in Germany who had since died. Gaal was attending university and applied for a grant to undertake an eight-month period of study in the UK. This was refused on the grounds that he was over the age of 21 and not a dependent. Thus, he was considered ineligible and denied his rights as a descendant of an EC worker. The Court of Justice held that he still fell within the personal scope of Art 12 (1612/68), because the definition of 'child' was not subject to the same definition as in Arts 10 and 11 (1612/68).

Article 12 (1612/68) extends to all forms of education, including university education, and must include older children no longer dependent on their parents. The case was, however, decided on the basis that the child must have lived at some time with a parent who was an EU worker and thus derived his rights in this manner.

Two cases heard together have extended the CoJ's view of the effect of Art 12 (1612/68, now Art 10 of Regulation 492/2011) to provide rights for carers of Union-citizen children who are receiving education. In Case C-413/99 *Baumbast and R v Home Secretary*, the non-EU national mothers in the case would have been deported had the CoJ not held that their children had the right to be cared for, in circumstances in which the original basis of their right to stay in the UK had disappeared (one as a result of divorce and the other because there was no longer an EU national working in the UK or, indeed, any member state). It is probable that such a convoluted decision is no longer necessary under new rights provided by Directive 2004/38, considered later.

The protection of carers was taken even further in Case C-200/02 *Chen*, in which the child in question was born in Northern Ireland to two Chinese nationals who had not even moved from one member state to another. The baby daughter was granted Irish nationality under the then Irish law granting Irish nationality to anyone born on the island of Ireland and thus became an EU national under Art 17 EC (now Art 20 TFEU). In view of the fact that the baby was an EU national with a right to remain, but was below school age and thus unable to care for herself, the Chinese nationals gained a right to remain in the UK to care for her.[23] This case will also be considered in further detail in Sections 9.8 and 9.9.

9.4.5 Right to Remain

Article 45(3)(d) TFEU provides the right to remain after retirement or incapacity applies also to members of the family even if workers die, and to whom Art 7(2) of Regulation 492/2011 continues to apply. The right to remain has been expanded by Directive 2004/38 to include permanent residence rights. Article 12 of Directive 2004/38 provides that the Union citizen's death or departure from the host member state shall not affect the right of residence of his or her family members who are nationals of a member state, and also of non-member-state family members who were living with the Union citizen for at least one year before his or her death or departure. Any children also retain the right to attend educational establishments. Article 13 (2004/38) provides that divorce, annulment of marriage, or termination of the partnership or relationship shall not affect the right of residence of a Union citizen's family members who are nationals of a member state and also those who are not nationals of a member state. The latter category is subject to the requirement that the marriage or partnership has lasted at least three years, one of these in the host state, or where the spouse or partner has custody of family children, or where it is warranted by particularly difficult circumstances. The rights to remain under Arts 12 and 13 are further dependent on the persons being considered not to be a burden on the host state (Art 14 of 2004/38).

---

[23] Following this decision, Ireland made a constitutional amendment (the 27th Amendment), so that not everyone born in Ireland still has a right of Irish, and thus EU, nationality. A person born in Ireland who does not have, at the time of his or her birth, at least one parent who is an Irish citizen or who is entitled to be an Irish citizen is no longer entitled to Irish citizenship or nationality, thus ensuring that there will not be similar cases in future.

Article 16 of Directive 2004/38 provides that Union citizens who have resided legally for a continuous period of five years in the host member state shall have the right of permanent residence there, and that continuity of residence shall not be affected by temporary absences not exceeding a total of six months a year, or by longer absences not exceeding 12 months at a time for important reasons such as compulsory military service, serious illness, pregnancy and childbirth, study or vocational training, or a work assignment in another member state or a third country. Paragraph 1 shall apply also to family members who are not nationals of a member state and have resided with the Union citizen in the host member state for five years. Furthermore, Art 17 provides that this period may be reduced in cases of the death of or injury to the Union national. In respect of family members who are not nationals of a member state, Art 18 provides that they shall acquire the right of permanent residence after residing legally for a continuous period of five years in the host member state. This right to remain under EU law is only gained if the conditions of Directive 2004/38 are satisfied, in particular not being a burden and may not be the same as an expired right of lawful residence previously granted by the member state. In Cases C-424–5/10 *Ziolkowski and Szeja*, two polish nationals who had been dependent on German economic support and thus lawfully resident there until their status had changed, were unable to rely on EU to prevent deportation from Germany.

9.5 Free Movement Rights of the Self-employed

The basic treaty rights providing for free movement of the self-employed are subject to national rules including rules, regulations, and conditions of the various professional organizations and bodies (Arts 49 and 57 TFEU). These, in fact, were very often the biggest impediments to free movement and it was first considered by the Commission that these could be removed by harmonization only. Furthermore, both main treaty Articles (Arts 43 and 49 EC, now Arts 49 and 56 TFEU) envisaged that the basic freedoms provided would be fleshed out by the enactment of secondary legislation issued under Arts 44 and 52 EC (now Arts 50 and 59 TFEU).

The initial approach of the Commission, therefore, was the harmonization of rules by the adoption of a general programme of directives to abolish the restrictions on free movement, and the mutual recognition of qualifications in all sorts of trades and professions on an occupation-by-occupation basis. This, however, was only achieved painfully slowly by the enactment of around 40 sectoral directives, and this attempt to harmonize the conditions of the various professions proved extremely difficult and time-consuming. As an example, it took 18 years for the Architects Directive[24] alone to be agreed upon and finally enacted. This approach also encouraged the view throughout the EU that the only way in which these rights could be promoted and relied on was if directives were enacted to establish them, and not directly from the treaty. Thus, little progress was made and, even prior to the issue of some directives considered essential in the process, case law had developed the law considerably.

9.5.1 The Intervention of the Court of Justice

Whilst the Commission was attempting to realize the free movement of establishment and services by negotiation with all the interested national bodies, and the harmonization of

---

[24] Directive 85/384 (OJ 1985 L223/15).

the various nationals rules governing the professions, legal disputes were starting to reach the Court of Justice that were concerned with self-employed persons who were facing severe restrictions in trying to practise their professions in another country. Two leading cases, in particular, had a considerable impact on the thinking and approach of the Commission in trying to achieve free movement in these areas. They had highlighted the slow progress and denial of the most basic rights of free movement. The cases, in which Arts 52 and 59 (now Arts 49 and 56 TFEU) were held to create direct effects by the CoJ, were decided in favour of the applicants, in the absence of the assumed completing secondary legislation, largely on the basis of the general prohibition of discrimination (Art 12 EC (now Art 18 TFEU)).

Concerned with establishment, Case 2/74 *Reyners v Belgian State* involved the attempt by a suitably qualified Dutchman to get access to the Belgian Bar, but who was refused on the grounds of nationality. The Dutch government argued that Art 52 EEC (then) was not directly effective because it was incomplete without the issue of directives required by that Article. The Court of Justice held that the prohibition of discrimination under Art 52 EEC (now Art 49 TFEU) was directly effective and declared that nationality could be no barrier to appropriately qualified lawyers entering a country to practise. The directives were simply to facilitate free movement and not to establish it, which had already been done by the treaty by the end of the initial transition period of the Communities (1969).

In Case 33/74 *Van Binsbergen*, it was not nationality that was the problem, but a residence requirement. The case concerned a professionally qualified Dutchman, resident in Belgium, who was refused audience rights before the Dutch courts. The Court of Justice held that Art 59 (now Art 56 TFEU) was directly effective and was not conditional on the issue of a subsequent directive in respect of the specific professions, nor on a residence requirement in the Netherlands.

These decisions meant that the CoJ had opened the way so the basic treaty rights to establish and provide services in a host state could be realized without discrimination or the imposition of unnecessary requirements. This was on the basis of the direct effects of the treaty Articles themselves, and without having to wait for the enactment of directives for each and every profession. Other cases soon followed that fleshed out even further the rights available under the treaty. As with workers, free movement cases tackled the various ways in which national or professional rules restricted free movement, either by direct or indirect discrimination, and rules that were non-discriminatory, but nevertheless prevented access.

Case 71/76 *Thieffry v Paris Bar Council* backs up the *Reyners* and *Van Binsbergen* cases. In *Thieffry*, the applicant was refused access to the Paris Bar despite having obtained a Belgian diploma in law, recognized by the University of Paris as the equivalent of a French diploma, and having sat and passed the French Certificate for the Profession of Advocate. The Court of Justice held that the relevant national authorities should apply any laws or practices that allow for the securing of freedom of establishment in accordance with the EEC policy, although no directives may have been enacted in that particular area. Therefore, where the competent authorities have recognized a foreign diploma as equivalent to a domestic qualification, recognition of that diploma may not be refused in an individual case solely because it is not a diploma of the host state.

Moving beyond clear-cut discrimination, in Case 205/84 *Commission v Germany (Insurance Services)*, Germany had required the providers of insurance to be resident on German soil. The Court of Justice held that member states were under a duty not only to eliminate all discrimination based on nationality, but also all restrictions based on the free provision of services on the grounds that the provider is established in another member state. It also emphasized that all of those national rules that apply to the providers of services permanently established in a member state will not necessarily automatically apply to those 'activities of a temporary character which are carried out by enterprises established in other member states'. It was held that the residence requirement was not justified.

The CoJ has moved further in the development of a rule that prevents the restriction of services from other member states, but may still persist to limit activities of the home providers of services. The next cases parallel developments in the free movement of goods in that they move further from prohibiting not only discriminatory rules but also any that restrict or hinder the movement of the self-employed, unless objectively justified by the host state. In Case C-76/90 *Säger v Dennemeyer*, Dennemeyer wished to provide patent services in Germany, something requiring a licence, the issue of which was restricted. His right to obtain a licence was challenged by a German patent agent. Dennemeyer claimed breach of Art 59 EEC (now Art 56 TFEU). The rule was non-discriminatory in that it applied to all patent agents regardless of residence. The CoJ held that not only discriminatory rules are prohibited, but also any rules that are liable to prohibit or otherwise impede persons providing a service that they already lawfully carry out in the state of their establishment. Laws applying to the temporary provision must comply with all of the following:

(a) They must be justified by imperative reason relating to the public interest.

(b) The public interest must not already be protected by the rules of the state of establishment.

(c) The same result must not be achievable by less restrictive means.

In view of the limited activities undertaken by the patent agents, the Court of Justice was of the view that the national measures went too far.

In Case C-55/94 *Gebhard*, a German lawyer had set up a second chamber in Milan and was prevented from using the title *Avvocato*. No secondary law was held to apply to the situation. The issue was whether the Italian rules could be imposed on him. In principle and according to the general treaty provision Art 43 (now Art 49 TFEU), he was required to comply with national rules, but the Court of Justice held that national measures that hinder or make less attractive the exercise of fundamental freedoms must fulfil four conditions. They must be:

(a) non-discriminatory in application

(b) justified by imperative reason relating to the public interest

(c) suitable to secure the objective sought

(d) proportional.

In Case 340/89 *Vlassopoulou*, a Greek lawyer who had worked in Germany, and gained some partial qualifications and experience in German law, had her request for admission to the German Bar rejected on the grounds that she did not have the necessary German qualifications. On reference to the Court of Justice, it was held that national authorities must take into account qualifications and experience that fall short of full qualification, and undertake a comparison of the qualifications to see if they are the equivalent of the national requirements; they should not dismiss them out of hand.[25]

---

[25] See also Case C-313/01 *Morganbesser*, in which it was held that training does not constitute a regulated profession for the purposes of mutual recognition; however, member states are required to take account of all qualifications of the migrant to assess objectively what was needed to make up the shortfall.

It is left to the national courts to determine whether qualifications are equivalent, and here the danger is that some will and some will not. The consequence of these decisions is that establishment is now very close to services. Perhaps this is a fair result to achieve; that is, it does not matter where or how a person practises, either on a temporary or permanent basis, provided that qualifications are roughly equivalent. Rules that seek to prevent this must satisfy the criteria or be struck out, at least as far as non-national EU citizens are concerned. Eventually, this might also lead to internal pressure in member states and thus the rules could be abolished in respect of nationals also, who then appear to be placed in a worse and discriminatory position in comparison with EU nationals who take advantage of the free movement rights. Hence, as with goods and as with workers, the prohibited rules applying to the self-employed also include indirect discrimination and thus market access, but similarly such rules may be objectively justified.

In Case C-384/93 *Alpine Investments*, a Dutch law that prevented financial services providers from making cold-calling telephone calls either within or outside the Netherlands was challenged as breaching Art 59 EEC (now Art 56 TFEU). The Court of Justice held that the rule was not to be equated with the selling arrangements rule established in the case of *Keck and Mithouard* for goods, and thus outside the scope of EC law, but held instead that because the rule affects access to other markets and thus is capable of hindering intra-Community trade in services, it will breach the treaty. Even still, such measures can be objectively justified by imperative reasons of public interest that are necessary and proportionate. In the case itself, it was decided that the Dutch government's arguments of consumer protection and safeguarding the reputation of Dutch financial markets satisfied those criteria, therefore the prohibition did not offend Art 59 (now Art 56 TFEU).

In Case C-438/05 *ITWF & FSU v Viking*, the right to establish was balanced with the rights of workers to strike. The Viking Line wanted to re-register a Finnish ship under the Estonian flag to employ lower-paid Estonians, to reduce costs, and increase competitiveness with other lines plying the same route, but was prevented from doing so by the threat of strike action and a general boycott of Viking Line ships by the unions ITWF and FSU. Viking's claim that this was a breach of Art 43 EC (now Art 49 TFEU) was recognized by the Court of Justice between the two private parties, but the right to strike was a fundamental right and a public interest right that could be a justified breach of Art 43 EC (now Art 49 TFEU) provided that action was necessary to safeguard jobs and that any action was proportionate. It is for the national courts to undertake the final balancing of those rights according to the facts.

In a similar case, Case C-341/05 *Laval*, concerned with the provision of cross-border services, a Swedish union and workers attempted to force a Latvian company undertaking work in Sweden, but employing lower-paid temporary workers, to observe the Swedish collective bargaining terms and conditions. The CoJ held that provided that the conditions observed by the company were lawful, which they were, the attempt to force higher standards represented a breach of Art 49 EC (now Art 56 TFEU).

In Case C-17/00 *De Coster*, a tax on satellite dishes which amounted to a tax on receiving satellite services, with no equivalent on cable services was held to breach Art 56 and the argument that this was on environmental grounds to prevent the proliferation of dishes was not accepted. The tax would apply disproportionately to services broadcast from outside the country, whereas cable services would be provided mainly by national service providers.

9.5.2 **Legislative Developments**

Even as a result of the early case law, the Commission realized that the harmonization approach was not the best solution with which to realize free movement and commenced work on a new approach to achieving free movement that was applicable to many professions across the board.

9.5.2.1 **Mutual Recognition**

With regards to establishment and the provision of services, a change of tactic was undertaken by the Commission to overcome the problems of tackling one profession at a time, which involved the enactment of the Mutual Recognition Directives to apply to many professions. Three reasons prompted the new approach. First, the progress on specific professions was painfully slow; for example, as mentioned previously, the Architects Directive took 18 years. Also, following the case law, especially *Reyners* and *Van Binsbergen*, the Commission decided that it was not necessary to issue directives for each individual trade and profession, especially in the case of establishment, and it was observed that the progress by the Court of Justice with regard to lawyers' rights and others not subject to specific directives was minimal and uncertain.

All three of the general mutual recognition directives, along with 12 medical and health sector directives, have now been consolidated and replaced by Directive 2005/36, which came into force on 20 October 2007.[26] Mutual recognition of professional qualifications remains the underlying basis of the this directive (Arts 1 and 2), and it covers both the provision of services on a temporary basis and establishment of regulated professions, as well as employment of qualified professionals, with the exception of lawyers, whose specific directives (Directives 77/249 and 98/5) remain in force. Along the lines of the previous directives, the new one is designed for persons who are qualified to practise a profession in one member state and wish to have their qualifications recognized in another, so that they can practise the same profession in the host state, where that state requires a qualification to practise that profession.[27] The directive is intended to make it much easier than the previous regimes by providing for more automatic recognition of qualifications (Art 21) and increased flexibility in the procedures for updating the directive by the use of common platforms to compensate where there are substantial differences in training (Art 15).

9.5.2.2 **The Provision of Services Directive**

Finally, in this area, the enactment, after some considerable delay and debate, of the Provision of Services Directive 2006/123 needs to be noted.[28] This was designed to consolidate further the freedoms to provide services and to establish in the new, much-liberalized markets of the member states, but seems rather to have maintained and possibly increased the distinction between them. Unfortunately, this new directive is riddled with exceptions and will overlap with existing directives; thus, its entry into force from December 2009 was predicted to give rise to many difficulties, both in application by the member states and in its interpretation, especially in light of the potential clash with existing legislative regimes. In view of its comprehensiveness and complexity, it is

---

[26] OJ 2005 L255/22. The author suspects, though, given the detail of this directive and the next to be considered, Directive 2006/123, that there will be little, if any, coverage in general EU courses in universities.

[27] A guide to mutual recognition can be found at **http://ec.europa.eu/internal_market/qualifications/docs/guide/guide_en.pdf**.

[28] OJ 2006 L376/36.

unlikely to be covered in any detail in general and introductory courses on EU law, and is likely to feature in detail only in postgraduate courses, which is reason to introduce only the main elements of it here.[29]

The directive is complex in its application despite the simple statement of coverage in Art 2(1) that it applies to services supplied by providers established in a member state. Apart from certain sectors, which are excluded from its application in Art 2(2a-l) and (3),[30] any services already covered by existing sectoral directives are also excluded (Art 3(1)), hence there are immediately considerable gaps in its coverage. Furthermore, where there is only limited or no EU law coverage, the directive takes second place to the main Arts 49 and 56 TFEU, which cover a large number of other areas.[31] As much as anything, the directive aims to simplify the national administrative procedures for allowing providers of services and those wishing to establish to do so in the host state. Articles 9–15 apply to establishment, Arts 16–18 to exceptions, Arts 19–21 to the receipt of services, and Arts 22–7 to the provision of services.

9.5.3 **The Free Movement of Lawyers**

Whilst not dealing with any other professions, as an exception in a book on EU law, it is appropriate to consider briefly the legislative provisions applicable to the legal professions.

9.5.3.1 **The Provision of Services by Lawyers**

It was considered against the trend of moving away from sectoral directives to issue a directive to realize the freedom to provide services for lawyers. Directive 77/249[32] is limited to the recognition of practising lawyers from member states, who must be accepted on the basis that the training of lawyers in other member states is as strict as that of those in the host state. Article 4(1) dispenses with residence and registration requirements for 'the representation of a client in legal proceedings'. Article 4(2) provides that lawyers providing services in judicial proceedings are required to observe those sets of rules of professional conduct of both the home and the host states. Article 4(4) states that, where justifiable, the same rules apply to those providing services as nationals. Article 5 provides that:

> for the pursuit of activities relating to the representation of a client in legal proceedings, a member state may require lawyers . . . to work in conjunction with a lawyer who practises before the judicial authority in question and who would, where necessary, be answerable to that authority.

The requirements of Directive 77/249 have been specifically considered in Case 427/85 *Commission v Germany (Lawyers' Services)*. The Court of Justice held that local rules were acceptable, but could not go beyond the strict requirements of Community law as to

---

[29] The preamble and recitals alone contain 118 lengthy paragraphs on its purpose, scope, and application. It is simply beyond both general EU law courses and any book trying to do justice to such course coverage. A 64-page handbook on the directive can be found at **http://ec.europa.eu/internal_market/ services/docs/services-dir/guides/handbook_en.pdf**. Updates on the Services Directive are available from European Movement at **http://www.euromove.org.uk/index.php?id=11780** and the European Free Trade Association (EFTA) at **http://www.eftasurv.int/media/internal-market/Report_on_the_ implementation_of_the_Service_Directive.pdf**. See also reading on the directive in Further Reading at the end of the chapter.

[30] Financial services, private security services, social services, and transport, amongst others.

[31] See Art 1(2) and (3).   [32] OJ 1977 L78/17.

become a hindrance to free movement. The requirement to have local lawyers alongside at all times and also before courts, where there was no compulsory representation, and the requirement to live locally, when only providing services, was far too restrictive and therefore a breach of the treaty. The rule that lawyers could operate only in strictly defined areas was not justified by Art 5 of the directive and could not be applied to activities of a temporary nature carried out by lawyers established in another member state, although they may still apply to national lawyers. This case is an example of reverse discrimination, whereby the rule cannot be applied to Community lawyers from other member states, but can still be applied to national lawyers. Germany has now repealed that rule.

9.5.3.2 Establishment by Lawyers (Practice under Home Title)

After a considerable period of discussion not only about the content, but also about whether such an establishment for a lawyers' directive was required, the Lawyers' Home Title Directive[33] was enacted, which essentially provides under Art 2 that any lawyer shall be entitled to practise on a permanent basis, in any other member state, under his or her home country professional title as an independent or salaried lawyer. To practise, lawyers need only register with the competent authority in the host state on the basis of their registration in the home member state (Art 3).

Article 5 provides that the host lawyer may give advice on the law of his or her home member state, on Community (now EU) law, on international law, and on the law of the host member state. He or she must comply with the rules of procedure applicable in the national courts.

Article 5(3) provides that activities relating to the representation or defence of a client in legal proceedings may be reserved to lawyers practising under the professional title of that state, where the host state law provides for this. The state may require lawyers practising under their home country professional titles to work in conjunction with a lawyer who practises before the judicial authority in question and who would, where necessary, be answerable to that authority. In addition, access to supreme courts may be reserved to specialist lawyers.

Article 6 provides that, in addition to the professional rules of the home state, a lawyer practising under his or her home country professional title shall be subject to the same rules of professional conduct as lawyers practising under the relevant professional title of the host member state in respect of all of the activities that he or she pursues in its territory.

Article 10 provides that a lawyer practising under his or her home country professional title, who has effectively and regularly pursued for a period of at least three years an activity in the host member state in the law of that state, including EU law, shall, with a view to gaining admission to the profession of lawyer in the host member state, be exempted from the conditions set out in Art 4(1)(b) of Directive 89/48/EEC. There are detailed rules on providing the necessary proof of practice, training, and qualifications.

This so-called 'third approach' provides an easier way of acquiring the professional title of the host member state and, in effect, circumvents the necessity under Directive 89/48 of undertaking the aptitude test to establish in another member state. The reason given for providing this is that it was primarily directed at experienced professionals, for whom an aptitude test would constitute an obstacle on account of the time that has elapsed since they obtained their qualifications, but it is hard to see how it would not be used by lawyers of any length of service.

---

[33] 98/5, OJ 1998 L77/36.

In Case C-313/01 *Morgenbesser*, the Court of Justice ruled that the refusal to enrol paid trainee lawyers because their prior academic legal qualifications were obtained in other member states was unjustified. Hence, the CoJ held that national authorities are obliged to compare the applicant's professional knowledge, as certified by his or her qualifications or acquired through professional experience either in the member state of origin or in the host member state, with the professional knowledge required by national law. If the comparison reveals that these correspond only partially, the host member state is entitled to require the person concerned to show that he or she has acquired the knowledge that was lacking. When Luxembourg required non-national lawyers to take linguistic tests, not to act on behalf of companies, and to show annual proof of professional registration with their home state, Luxembourg was taken before the CoJ by the Commission (Case C-193/05 *Commission v Luxembourg*). The CoJ found Luxembourg to have breached EU law for all of those requirements.

9.6 Derogations from the Free Movement Regimes

Before considering the substantive grounds that member states may invoke in order either to refuse entry in the first place or to justify deportation, which are considered later, it makes sense first to consider any procedural rights that persons may have who are faced with such decisions. If immediate deportation can be prevented, then there is more time to consider the substantive grounds given.

9.6.1 Procedural Safeguards

Articles 30 and 31 of Directive 2004/38 further support free movement by providing for non-discriminatory rights of appeal, rights to remain to hear the appeal result, rights to be given reasons for deportation, and rights to the judicial review of decisions.

There is a right to remain in the member state pending a decision either to grant or refuse a residence permit, save in emergency situations. Article 30 provides that the grounds for deportation must be precisely and comprehensively stated. The concerned person has a right to be informed of the grounds of refusal or deportation unless security is at stake.

These rights were first developed in case law, for example in Cases 115 and 116/81 *Adoui and Cornuaille v Belgian State*, in which two French ladies, euphemistically described by the Court of Justice as 'waitresses', had their residence permits withdrawn by the Belgian authorities on the grounds that their personal conduct justified the invocation of the public policy proviso. The conduct was described by the CoJ as 'Displaying themselves in windows in scant dress and being able to be alone with clients'. Basically, Belgium was trying to clamp down on the number of French prostitutes settling in Belgium. A reference was made to the Court of Justice, which held that the public policy proviso does not allow expulsion where similar conduct by nationals does not incur penalty or repressive measures. However, it does not require illegality to be invoked. It was noted that Belgian prostitutes were tolerated and not prosecuted. The CoJ held that the reasons must be sufficiently detailed to allow a migrant to defend his or her interests, and drafted in such a way and in such language as to enable the person to comprehend the content or effect.

Article 30(3) provides the right to be notified of any decision to expel or the refusal of a permit. The decision should also state the minimum period given to leave the country, which cannot be less than one month in any circumstance.[34] Article 31 provides that there should

---

[34] Try to avoid February!

also be a system for appeal against decisions on their merits, as well as legality. Previously, Case C-175/94 *Gallagher* considered the body hearing the appeal. Gallagher, who had been convicted of the possession of rifles for unlawful purposes in Ireland, had been deported from the UK. In questioning this decision, he was interviewed in Ireland before the case was heard by the Home Secretary. He challenged these bodies as not being independent. The Court of Justice held, however, that it was a matter for the national courts to decide whether the body hearing an appeal was independent, but that the directive did not specify how it should be appointed. It should, however, be genuinely independent.

In Case 98/79 *Pecastaing v Belgium*, a French prostitute was asked by the Belgian authorities to leave on grounds of personal conduct. She claimed under Directive 64/221, Arts 8 and 9, that she should be able to stay in the country whilst the decision was being reviewed, which could be up to three years during the course of an Art 234 EC (now Art 267 TFEU) reference. The Court of Justice held that, even under Art 234 EC (now Art 267 TFEU), the right of appeal is not to be diluted and only in cases of emergency should automatic expulsion take place. However, the urgency could only finally be determined by the member states. Articles 8 and 9 of the repealed directive did not grant rights to remain in the host state pending hearing provided a fair hearing and full facilities were nevertheless possible even whilst out of the country (see now Art 31 of Directive 2004/38).

9.6.2 Restrictions on the Grounds of Public Policy, Security, and Health

Member states are able to restrict entry and deport EU nationals on the grounds set out in Art 45(3) TFEU, which are public policy, security, and health. Articles 52 and 62 TFEU subject establishment and provision of services to the same derogations as workers, which is now confirmed by Directive 2004/38 Arts 27 et seq. These grounds were held to be exhaustive by the Court of Justice in Case 352/85 *Bond van Adverteerders et al v The Netherlands*, in which economic grounds were pleaded, but rejected by the CoJ.

Directive 2004/38, Art 27 requires that measures taken on grounds of public policy or public security shall comply with the principle of proportionality, and shall be based exclusively on the personal conduct of the individual concerned. It also provides that previous criminal convictions shall not in themselves constitute grounds for taking such measures. It further provides that the personal conduct of the individual concerned must represent a genuine, present, and sufficiently serious threat affecting one of the fundamental interests of society. Justifications that are isolated from the particulars of the case or that rely on considerations of general prevention shall not be accepted. Personal conduct may not be considered a sufficiently serious threat unless the member state concerned takes serious enforcement measures against the same conduct on the part of its own nationals. Furthermore, in Art 28, the member states are now required to take a number of factors into consideration, including how long the individuals concerned have resided within its territory; their age, state of health, family, economic situation, and social and cultural integration into the host member state; and the extent of the links with their country of origin, before taking the decision to remove an EU citizen or a member of his or her family. Removal decisions cannot be taken against Union citizens or family members, irrespective of nationality, who have the right of permanent residence within its territory, or against family members who are minors (Art 28(2)). Article 28(3) increases the seriousness of the grounds needed for deportation for EU citizens who have resided for more than ten years in the host state and for minors. In these cases, the decision to deport must be based on 'imperative' grounds of public security. Furthermore, any deportation orders that are made must be subject to review for possible lifting under Directive 2004/38, Art 32, at least three years after being made.[35]

Personal conduct was defined in Case 67/74 *Bonsignore v Köln*, in which an Italian national faced deportation as a general preventative nature, after conviction for fatally shooting his brother in a firearms accident. The Court of Justice held that:

> measures adopted on grounds of public policy and for the maintenance of public security against the nationals of member states of the Community cannot be justified on grounds extraneous to the individual case, and that only the personal conduct of those affected by the measures is to be regarded as determinative. As departures from the rules concerning the free movement of persons constitute exceptions which must be strictly construed, the concept of 'personal conduct' expresses the requirement that a deportation order may only be made for breaches of the peace and public security which might be committed by the individual affected.

In Cases 115 and 116/81 *Adoui and Cornuaille*, French prostitutes facing expulsion from Belgium on public policy grounds could not be denied residence on the basis of their personal conduct when similar conduct on the part of nationals did not attract similar repressive measures to combat such behaviour, hence Belgium was denied the use of the proviso.

In a somewhat less liberal judgment in Case 41/74 *Van Duyn v The Home Office*, the CoJ held that restrictions on the grounds of public policy must be interpreted very strictly and be subject to judicial review. In this case, a Dutch woman obtained a position as secretary with the Church of Scientology in the UK, but was refused entry by the Home Office on the grounds that public policy declared the Church to be socially harmful. The Court of Justice held that to rely on public policy, the member state must have defined it position with regard to the organization and have taken administrative but not necessarily legislative measures against it, which the UK had in fact done. The UK could therefore rely on the public policy exception. Additionally in the case, Miss Van Duyn claimed that the refusal was not made on the basis of personal conduct, but on the conduct of the group. The Court of Justice held that personal conduct must be an act, or omission to act, on the part of the person concerned and must be voluntary. It need not, however, be illegal or criminal to offend public policy. The CoJ further held present association reflecting participation in the activities and identification with the aims of a group may be considered a voluntary act, and could therefore come within the definition of conduct, which hands back some of the discretion to the member states to determine whether an individual's association in a group constitutes personal conduct. This latter part of the judgment must now be somewhat suspect in view of both later case law and Directive 2004/38.

Article 27 provides that previous criminal convictions should not be taken into account. Case 30/77 *R v Bouchereau* involved a Frenchman who had been convicted in the UK on a number of occasions for drugs possession. The UK magistrate asked the Court of Justice whether he could be deported to stop him committing acts in the future. The CoJ held that it was not possible to look at his past record to decide future conduct unless it constituted a present threat. Public policy measures could only be relied on where conduct and criminal convictions were a genuine and sufficiently serious threat affecting one of the fundamental interests of society. (See also *Antonissen*, considered earlier, whereby the lack of employment and the lack of any serious chance of obtaining one would justify expulsion.)

---

[35] Most of the case law, thus far, relates to the previous legislation.

In Case C-348/96 *Donatella Calfa*, involving the provision of services, a Greek rule of automatic life expulsion from Greek territory was applied following conviction and imprisonment for certain offences including prohibited drugs. As an exemption, the CoJ held that it must be interpreted restrictively, and where a person has been convicted, expulsion could only be based on personal conduct outside of the conviction itself, but, in any event, a life ban was disproportionate and would now not conform with the requirement in Directive 2004/38 for a review of the expulsion after a minimum of three years (Art 32).

The public security proviso was specifically considered in Case C-100/01 *Otieza Olazabal*, which involved the French imprisonment and ban on residence for activities undertaking for ETA, the Basque separatist movement. This was challenged, but upheld, by the CoJ as coming within the public security proviso.

Articles 27 and 28 have now been considered by the Court of Justice.

Case C-33/07 *Jipa* concerned a national decision to expel a non-national, in which it was held that, in deciding on the matter, member states could not simply rely on a previous expulsion or information from the home state. Both could be considered but only in the context of the overall decision and provided that the conclusion was that personal conduct was judged to be a threat to society. In Case C-145/09 *Land Baden-Württemberg v Tsakouridis*, Art 28(3) was considered. The case involved the criminal activity of an organized gang dealing in narcotics. The Court of Justice held that, as a deliberate raising of strictness, the measures taken under Art 28(3) had to be exceptional. Whilst the CoJ concluded that organized drug trafficking could be such an exceptional circumstance, the member states nevertheless still had to consider the personal conduct of the individual, as still required by Art 27(2) of Directive 2004/38, and that any decision must be proportionate having regard to the time spent and degree of integration in the host state, especially where the person had spent most, even all, of his childhood in the host state. The national court must also consider the sentence passed on conviction and take account of fundamental rights in both the EU Charter of Fundamental Rights and the European Convention on Human Rights and Fundamental Freedoms (ECHR). The Court of Justice though defined public security as 'A threat to the functioning of the institutions and essential public services and the survival of the population, as well as the risk of a serious disturbance to foreign relations or to the peaceful co-existence of nations, or a risk to military interests', thus emphasizing its internal and external aspects.

A national court thus has quite a balancing act to come to a decision on whether authorities can lawfully, under EU law, deport an EU citizen of more than ten years' residence in a host state.

Public health measures are given further definition in Art 29 of Directive 2004/38 and, rather than listing particular diseases as was the previous practice, the directive now provides that:

> The only diseases justifying measures restricting freedom of movement shall be the diseases with epidemic potential as defined by the relevant instruments of the World Health Organization and other infectious diseases or contagious parasitic diseases if they are the subject of protection provisions applying to nationals of the host member state.

9.6.3 **The Public Service Proviso**

Article 45(4) TFEU exempts employment in the public service from the provisions of Art 45 TFEU. The initial difficulty was that there is no treaty definition of 'public service', which can vary considerably from state to state, and thus its understanding in different member states could vary considerably and could be claimed by the member states to apply to a vast range of workers employed by the state. Hence, the Court of Justice has constantly stressed the need for a strict interpretation of this Article. It has been held to apply to entry and not to conditions of employment.

In Case 152/73 *Sotgui v Deutsche Bundespost*, Mr Sotgui, an Italian national, was employed by the German Post Office, but was not paid the same travel allowance as German nationals on the basis of the public service proviso. This was held to be discrimination contrary to Art 39(1) EC (now 45 TFEU) and not excused by Art 39(4). In Case 149/79 *Commission v Belgium (Public Employees)*, the CoJ held that the public service derogation only applies to typical public service posts that exercise powers conferred by public law and which are there to safeguard the interests of state, regardless of the actual status in each of the member states. Belgium had reserved all manner of jobs across the public sector to Belgium nationals. This case, which was actually two cases, required Belgium to discuss and negotiate with the Commission, the scope of those jobs which fell within and without the exception and thus helped develop the Commission guidelines, noted next.

The CoJ has, on this basis, excluded from the scope of Art 39(4):

- nurses (Case 307/84 *Commission v French Republic*)
- trainee secondary school teachers (Case 66/85 *Lawrie-Blum v Land Baden-Württemberg*)
- secondary school teachers (Case C-4/91 *Bleis v Ministry of Education*)
- secondary school teachers and foreign language lecturers (Case 33/88 *Alluè and Coonan v Università degli Studi di Venezia*).

In order to try to clarify the posts that the member states claim to come within Art 39(4), the Commission has issued a notice[36] of those sectors in which it thinks positions would rarely be covered by the public service proviso. These include public health care, teaching in state educational establishments, non-military public research, and public administration of commercial activities. Occasionally, restrictions are accepted by the CoJ, as in Case C-47/02 *Anker et al*, in which restricting the appointment of ships' masters of private vessels also to German nationals was held to be acceptable in view of the public duties that had to be undertaken by the masters of ships. However, the CoJ advised that such duties should not be only a minor part of the activity of a master.[37]

There is the equivalent of the public service exception for establishment in Art 51 TFEU, but only on the more tightly defined ground of 'positions concerned with the exercise of official authority'. The CoJ held, in the case of *Reyners*, that the derogation was more concerned with the exercise of the prerogative power of the state rather than with the preventing of particular occupations from exercising rights under Community law. In Case C-438/08 *Commission v Portugal*, for example, vehicle testing inspectors acting under public law but working for private companies were held not to be connected with the exercise of public power. Equally the office of notary in six countries could not be reserved for nationals under the public service exception, as was argued to be the case (Cases C-47, 50, 52–4, and 61/08 *Commission v (Belgium, France, Portugal, Luxembourg, Austria & Germany)*).

---

[36] OJ 1988 C72/2, confirmed in the 2002 Commission Communication COM (2002) 694 final, p 17, available at **http://eur-lex.europa.eu/LexUriServ/site/en/com/2002/com2002_0694en01.pdf**.

[37] In the case, Anker did not satisfy this requirement.

9.7 **The Extension of Free Movement Rights**

Freedom of movement now exists for persons other than workers and the self-employed, because this concept has been widened to include those receiving services as well as those providing services and because rights to free movement are no longer solely anchored to an economic activity. This was initially facilitated by three general directives, then by the introduction of a citizenship section into the EC Treaty. It is further supported now by Directive 2004/38, which has replaced the three general rights of movement directives. In the following two subsections, those receiving services and those having a right to move not based on an economic activity are considered.

9.7.1 **Receiving Services**

The concept of 'services' has been expanded to those who, rather than actively pursuing an economic activity, instead passively receive services of an economic activity. Whilst there is nothing to confirm this category within the treaty, it was expressly mentioned in Art 1 of Directive 64/221, now repealed, but not in Directive 2004/38. Services can be received either by movement to another member state or by receiving services from another state in the home state. Initially, cases that first confirmed this arose from the areas of educational provision and tourist travel.

In Case 286/82 *Luisi and Carbone v Ministero del Tesoro*, two Italian nationals were prosecuted under Italian currency regulations for taking money out to pay for tourist and medical provisions abroad. These were held by the Court of Justice to be payments for services and thus to come under the provisions of the EEC Treaty, payments also being a fundamental freedom of the Community, and the case was covered by Arts 59, 60, and 7 EEC (now Arts 56, 57, and 18 TFEU).

In Case 293/83 *Gravier v City of Liège*, a decision to charge foreign students a fee for vocational training courses, but not nationals, was claimed to be contrary to Community law (Arts 6, 59, and 128 EEC, now Arts 18, 56, and 166 TFEU). This was upheld in the case and in two cases following, Case 24/86 *Blaizot v University of Liège* and Case 263/86 *Belgium v Humbel*, which confirmed that university study was, for the most part, vocational training in EU law terms, and that Union nationals have a right to equal access to receive that under equal conditions to those of nationals even where fees were financed by the host state. Note, though, that the judgments did not extend to establishing a right to scholarships and grants, although the *Grzelczyk* case, considered later, may have altered the view on this.

Case 186/87 *Cowan* confirms that tourists travelling and receiving services bring themselves within the protection of EU law not to be discriminated against even in areas, as in the case itself, such as participation in the French criminal injuries compensation scheme.

Case C-109/92 *Wirth* involved a question from a German court of whether courses available in an institute of higher education had to be classified as services under Art 50 EC (now Art 57 TFEU). A German national was attempting to get a grant from German authorities to study in the Netherlands. The Court of Justice held that courses given in a university or institute of higher education that is financed essentially out of public funds do not constitute services within the meaning of Art 50 EC. However, it noted that many courses were financed by the students themselves paying fees, with the aim that the course would be able to generate profit and could, in these circumstances, be regarded as coming within the concept of services. The conclusions from this case are therefore that member states remain able to determine their own system of grants and so discriminate against non-nationals, but that access to institutions and tuition fees are subject to EU law. However, the citizenship cases, and in particular *Grzelczyk*, may cause us to alter our conclusions on grants.

Fees, though, are now another matter: in many countries, university fees have become the norm. In Case C-147/93 *Commission v Austria*, Austria was held to account for imposing more demanding conditions for university entry on other EU nationals than those imposed on Austrian students, which served to restrict access. The CoJ stressed the EU desire to promote the mobility of students and their right to receive education. The measure was not justified by the argument that, by not imposing stricter requirements, it would lead to a flood of non-Austrian students, swamping the universities and resources, because Austria had offered no evidence on this. The CoJ held that access to education under the same conditions was the very essence of the free movement of students.

The conclusions from this case law are that access to institutions and tuition fees are subject to EU law. The earlier judgments did not extend to establishing a right to grants or other social assistance whilst studying. However, more recent case law, including the citizenship cases, and, in particular, *Grzelczyk* and *Bidar*, seems to indicate that this is no longer the case.

In Case C-209/03 *Bidar*, a French person residing in the UK decided to undertake study and applied for a student loan, which was refused on the grounds that Bidar was not 'settled' in the UK for the purposes of obtaining a student loan. The CoJ held that, despite the previous case law, including the *Brown* and *Lair* cases, which excluded student maintenance grants from the scope of the treaty, as a result of the introduction of the citizenship Article and a chapter on education and training, student assistance can now be counted as falling within the scope of the treaty. As such, then, as in the previous cases, Arts 12 and 18 EC (now Arts 18 and 21 TFEU) in combination provided Bidar with the right to equal treatment in loans. However, in building on the *Collins* case considered later, a member state could require a certain amount of integration before awarding a loan, but national laws that completely excluded the possibility of students from other member states obtaining the status of a settled person would be incompatible with Art 12 EC (now Art 18 TFEU).

In Case C-73/08 *Bressol*,[38] the mass migration to Belgium to take up courses in medicine by Austrian students, who had difficulty in gaining a place in Austria, was restricted in Belgium on the grounds that they were not resident in Belgium at the time of registration. Whilst the Court of Justice held the rule to be discriminatory and a breach of EU law, it also held that it was up to the Belgium authorities to see if the rule could objectively be justified on the grounds that Belgium was entitled to reserve a certain minimum of finite places for Belgium nationals to ensure the provision of medical services in certain parts of Belgium.

This is an argument that could be expanded into other areas of the economy, no doubt with some relief on the part of national authorities.

Finally in this section, the receipt of services without physical cross-movement needs to be considered, because it is an increasing means by which services are obtained. The receipt of services can be incorporeal, such as receiving services over the telephone,

---

[38] [2010] ECR I-2735.

or—more probably these days, over the internet. If the simple receipt of services, irrespective of the manner of delivery of these services, triggers the application of EU law, then it could be argued that potentially any receipt of services will do, regardless of how minimal, such as telephoning another country to get advice or other services, or downloading advice packages from a computer server in another member state. The *De Coster* and *Mobistar* cases, considered in Section 9.8, lend some support to this view that receiving incorporeal services will trigger EU law rights.

In view of the ease by which EU law rights may be triggered for persons otherwise not entitled to those more extensive rights, the AGs in the *Carpenter, Angonese,* and *Collins* cases have suggested a new test to determine whether EU law is triggered, which relates specifically to the connection to the state of the person concerned; that is, an economically determined level of activity could be set, below which EU rights would not be triggered for the reason that the services received were marginal. The Court of Justice adopted this test in the *Collins* case.

The receipt of services will be additionally governed by the Services Directive 2006/123, noted previously in Section 9.5.2.2.

9.7.2 **The General Free Movement Directives**

There were three general free movement directives (Directives 90/364, 90/365, and 93/96),[39] but these have now been replaced by Directive 2004/38, considered earlier, and are only mentioned here in respect of the case law generated by them. Indeed, shortly after initial enactment, the directives were soon overtaken by the introduction of the citizenship rights and other developments in EU law, which are considered elsewhere in this chapter. The directives allowed for free movement not linked to an economic activity in the same way now provided by the Directive 2004/38. In place of an economic activity, proof of self-sufficiency is instead required (Art 7(1)(b) of Directive 2004/38). The Court of Justice has confirmed that member states may ask for evidence of self-sufficiency, but cannot dictate of what that evidence should consist (Case C-424/98 *Commission v Italy*) and the CoJ held in Case C-184/99 *Grzelczyk* that it may be possible to make a claim on the social funds of a member state, provided that the burden on the state is not unreasonable. 'Unreasonable burden' were the qualifying words used in the preamble to the directives rather than simply 'burden', which appeared in the Article itself. In other words, a reasonable burden on the state, particularly if temporary in nature, would be acceptable, which is a quite different matter and category. The decision leaves open the question of who should define reasonableness in similar circumstances: is it a matter for the CoJ or for the member states? Presumably, in line with the CoJ's comments in *Grzelczyk*, this would be within the member states courts' discretion. The CoJ has also considered Directive 90/364 in Case C-413/99 *Baumbast* and held, in view of the facts that Baumbast and family were not a burden on UK social security, and had German insurance cover, albeit not for emergency treatment, that the requirement for all-risks insurance did not have to include emergency insurance, which the CoJ noted was provided as a matter of course in the UK. The new directive does not use 'unreasonable' in Art 7(1)b, but, as did the previous directives, includes it in the preamble and in Art 14 in respect of retaining an existing right of residence; thus, the same Court of Justice qualification should apply.

---

[39] OJ 1990 L180/26, OJ 1990 L180/28, and OJ 1993 L317/59.

9.7.3 **European Citizenship**

The TEU, signed at Maastricht, introduced a small section on European citizenship to the EC Treaty, now contained in Arts 20 et seq TFEU.

Article 20 TFEU provides that 'Citizenship of the Union is hereby established. Every person holding the nationality of a member state shall be a citizen of the Union. Citizenship of the Union shall complement and not replace national citizenship.' Furthermore, Art 21 TFEU provides that every citizen of the Union shall have the right to move and reside freely within the territory of the member states, subject to the limitations and conditions laid down in the treaty and by the measures adopted to give it effect.

The rights provided by the treaty under citizenship remove the economic activity requirement of the previous free movement of persons regime. However, its true scope was not immediately obvious and this has only become clearer as a result of Court of Justice judgments. It must also be noted that the right of residence under Art 21 TFEU is still subject to the limitations and conditions laid down in the treaty, and by the measures adopted to give it effect; that is, limitations already in existence and those that might be contained in future implementing measures.

The first matter to be considered is a definition of EU 'citizenship', which Art 21 TFEU bases on the nationality of the member states, considered in Section 9.3.1.1. Thus, there can be no Union definition of 'European citizenship' and the concept can only be determined as the collective definitions of national citizenship from all of the member states.[40] Thus, if a person is a national or citizen of a member state, then Arts 20 and 21 TFEU apply. Building on the *Micheletti* and *Manjit Kaur* cases considered in Section 9.3.1.1, Case C-135/08 *Rottmann* v *Bayern* considered whether the false/illegal acquisition of nationality nevertheless brought the person within the material scope of EU citizenship. Mr Rottmann, an Austrian, had failed to reveal pending criminal proceedings when he applied for and was granted German citizenship (which necessitated the loss of his Austrian citizenship). The revocation of the German citizenship would however lead to him being stateless. The Court of Justice, not following the opinion of the AG, held that EU law did apply to him. The Court considered it had not interfered with the right of the member states to decide nationality themselves, but the consequence of withdrawing nationality by a state had the result that a once-enjoyed right, EU citizenship, was also lost. The Court rather fudged the decision, though, by concluding that, ultimately, it was up to the national court to decide whether the decision to withdraw citizenship was proportionate in view of both national law and the loss of EU citizenship, even if the German citizenship was acquired by a lack of disclosure. It should also take into account whether his original nationality could be recovered and the gravity of the wrong committed by Rottmann, especially in view of the effect on his family.

The scope and restrictions of citizenship rights need then to be determined. Article 21 TFEU is subject to restrictions, but it does not expressly state that restrictions apply to it. It is, however, reasonably clear that the restriction on the grounds of public policy, security, and health provisos, which are stated in Art 45 TFEU and now clarified in Directive 2004/38, Arts 27–9, will apply to the rights. These matters have already been subjected to the consideration of the Court of Justice in a number of cases coming before it.

---

[40] Declaration 2 which was attached to the Maastricht Treaty reserved to the member states the definition of nationality for their own states. This declaration, though, was not carried forward to the Lisbon Treaty.

The Lisbon Treaty has reorganized the provisions on citizenship slightly by providing new overriding general Articles in new Art 9 TEU and Art 20 TFEU, consolidating the rights previously in Arts 19–21 EC, and then expanding those rights in new Arts 21–4 TFEU. Article 25 TFEU provides that the Council, acting under the special legislative procedure and with the consent of the European Parliament, can adopt acts that add to or strengthen the rights provided in Art 20(2) TFEU. In addition, the Maastricht Treaty added a number of so-called political citizenship rights including in Art 22 TFEU, the right to vote and stand as a candidate at municipal and EP elections in their host country. Article 23 TFEU provides that EU citizens have the right to diplomatic protection and assistance by the consular offices of other member states in third countries and now governed by Decision 95/533. Article 24 TFEU provides that EU citizens have a right of initiative granted by Art 11 TEU and which was considered in Chapter 2. Article 24 TFEU also provides for a right to petition the EP in accordance with Art 227 TFEU and to apply to the European Ombudsman as governed by Art 228 TFEU. Finally Art 24 TFEU provides that EU citizens can write to and be answered by any of the institutions, bodies, offices, or agencies in any of the official languages.

9.7.4 Case Law on the Citizenship Articles

For the first time in Case C-274/96 *Criminal Proceedings v Bickel and Franz*, the self-standing status of Art 18 EC (now Art 21 TFEU) was acknowledged by the CoJ, although not as an overriding EU law right, but one that could be pleaded in support of other rights. In this case, it was to support the view that the refusal to allow Germans the use of the German language in the Italian South Tirol courts would be contrary to Art 12 EC (now Art 18 TFEU), where Italian citizens of Austrian extract in South Tirol were allowed to use German. In Case C-85/96 *María Martínez Sala v Freistaat Bayern*, Sala, a Spanish national who had worked in Germany for many years, lost her job but had remained in Germany and had received social assistance from 1989. Her residence permit had expired, but the German authorities supplied her with certificates stating that she had applied for an extension to her permit. The authorities refused her child allowance because she did not have a valid residence permit, which she claimed was contrary to Art 12 EC (now Art 18 TFEU) because German nationals were not subject to the same condition. Although in this case her actual status as a worker was not determined, the CoJ held in any event that she was lawfully resident in Germany. Sala thus came within the personal scope of treaty citizenship and Art 8(2) EC (now Art 21 TFEU) acted to attach other rights, including the right to be protected against discrimination under Art 12 EC (now Art 18 TFEU); this, in turn, applied to a right within the material scope of the treaty, such as the child allowance claimed in the case on an equal basis with nationals.

In Case C-184/99 *Grzelczyk*, noted in Section 9.3.1.2.4, the Court of Justice emphasized that the new citizenship provisions and new competences in education, albeit limited, allowed it to hold that Arts 12 and 17 EC (now Arts 18 and 21 TFEU) preclude discrimination as regards the grant of a non-contributory social benefit to Union citizens where they are lawfully resident, even though not economically active.

In Case C-224/98 *D'Hoop*, a Belgian national had studied in France. She was refused a tide-over allowance between study and work granted to nationals by the Belgian authorities on the ground that she had studied in another member state. The Court of Justice had held that the tide-over allowance was a social advantage under Art 7(2) of Regulation 1612/68, but that to take advantage of it, the person must either have participated in the employment market or obtained a derived right in some way. She was not a worker and her parents had remained in Belgium; therefore she had neither rights in her own right nor derived rights from the parents. The CoJ referred to the new contribution to education by the EC in encouraging mobility of students and teachers (Arts 3(1)(q) and 149(2) EC, now Arts 6 and 165 TFEU) and, citing *Grzelczyk* at [31] of the judgment, held that it would be incompatible with the right of freedom of movement if a citizen who had taken advantage of free movement were then to suffer discrimination as a consequence.

Such inequality of treatment is contrary to the principles that underpin the status of citizen of the Union; that is, the guarantee of the same treatment in law in the exercise of the citizen's freedom to move. The condition at issue could be justified only if it were based on objective considerations independent of the nationality of the persons concerned and if it were proportionate to the legitimate aim of the national provisions.[41] The Belgian authorities offered none, hence the limiting of places of education that qualify for the tide-over allowance, according to the CoJ, went beyond what is necessary to attain the objective pursued.

In Case C-413/99 *Baumbast*, Mr Baumbast was self-employed in the UK, where he resided with his Colombian wife and two children, who were being educated in the UK. He was subsequently employed by a German company and worked outside the EU. His family remained in the UK. Their residence permits were not renewed, however, and Mrs Baumbast and the children faced deportation. The case was referred to the Court of Justice, which emphasized the right of children of EU nationals under Regulation 1612/68 to continue their education even if the worker, from whom their rights derived, was no longer working in the EU. The CoJ further held that the text of the treaty does not permit the conclusion that citizens of the Union who have lawfully established themselves in another member state as an employed person are deprived, where that activity comes to an end, of the rights that are conferred on them by virtue of that citizenship. In the most important statement of the judgment, the CoJ held that his or her right to stay under Art 18(1) EC (now Art 21 TFEU) is conferred directly on every citizen of the Union by a clear and precise provision of the EC Treaty. Purely as a national of a member state, and consequently a citizen of the Union, Mr Baumbast therefore had the right to rely on Art 18(1) EC (now Art 21 TFEU). It held:

> The answer to the first part of the third question must therefore be that a citizen of the European Union who no longer enjoys a right of residence as a migrant worker in the host member state can, as a citizen of the Union, enjoy there a right of residence by direct application of Article 18 (1) EC [now Art 21 TFEU].[42]

In summary, the citizenship law, as developed through the Court of Justice cases, would appear to be as follows. Article 21(1) TFEU has been declared to be directly effective and it can be activated in favour of EU citizens in a variety of ways, such as: by exhausted free movement rights, that is, those once enjoyed by a member state national and which gained him or her lawful entrance and residence in the host state when exercised, but who no longer is or can be relied upon because of changed circumstances (as in the *Baumbast* case); and by the movement to another member state to receive services (as in *D'Hoop*), which movement then serves as the economic activity to trigger the general rights of citizenship.

The right of residence under Art 21 TFEU continues, according to the Court of Justice, to be subject to the requirement that it is lawful. However, a clear definition of what constitutes 'lawful residence' is thus far missing in EU law, with only the Court of Justice judgments to suggest that, provided that an EU citizen had a lawful right to enter the

---

[41] At [35]–[36] of *Grzelczyk*.   [42] At [94] of the judgment.

host state in the first place and has not done anything to endanger his or her residence subsequently, the right to remain continues. In *Grzelczyk*, the CoJ held that its judgment does not, however, prevent a member state from taking the view that a student who has recourse to social assistance no longer fulfils the conditions of his or her right of residence or from taking measures, within the limits imposed by EU law, either to withdraw his or her residence permit or not to renew it. Nevertheless, in no case may such measures have the automatic consequence that a student who is a national of another member state requiring recourse to the host member state's social assistance system is required to leave as a matter of fact.

This would seem to suggest that if a member state does decide to withdraw the status of lawful residence, the member state would be entitled to deport the individual. Such a decision is subject to proportionality and the review of the Court of Justice. See, for this review of the right of member states to determine whether EU citizens can or cannot remain in the UK, Case 159/79 *R v Pieck* and Case C–292/89 *Antonissen* in which, respectively, the CoJ held that deportation of Pieck would be disproportionate and thus contrary to EU law, whereas Antonissen could be deported. Hence, it would seem that previous case law provides a workable model of how to decide lawful residence: a deportation that could be condoned by the CoJ would remove lawful residence.

9.7.5 Citizenship and Welfare Rights

If an EU citizen is lawfully resident in a host state, this will trigger EU citizenship and the rights that conveys. The most important of these are not the political rights contained in Art 22 TFEU, but the general right to be treated without discrimination compared to nationals. Court of Justice judgments that have arisen under the citizenship provisions are not only concerned with the scope and meaning of the term 'citizenship', but also evidence an assertive approach by which the CoJ has upheld welfare, not only through its interpretation of EU law, but also by reference to the ECHR. A number of the decisions appear to go further than intended by the general free movement directives by extending the welfare benefits rights of EU citizens who were not supposed to be a burden on the host member state. These developments appear to show that the Union is more concerned with the welfare rights of EU citizens and the sanctity of their family than it is with any national concerns about the possible drain on national resources by the welfare claims of other-member-state EU citizens or the claim to a right of residence by TCNs, although there are also cases which appear to clarify the scope of such rights, as will be considered following.

In *Sala*, the individual's right to rely on treaty citizenship triggered other rights, including most importantly Art 12 EC (now Art 18 TFEU), the right not to be discriminated against according to nationality. This, in consequence, included the right to receive, on equal terms, social welfare benefits including the non-contributory child allowance, the subject matter of the case. Similarly, in *Grzelczyk*, a French national, who studied and worked on a part-time basis to help support himself for three years in Belgium, applied at the beginning of his fourth and final year of study to the *Centre Public d'Action Sociale* [the Public Social Welfare Centre] (CPAS), for payment of the *minimex*, a non-contributory minimum subsistence allowance. The CPAS granted Mr Grzelczyk the *minimex*, but then later denied this on the basis that he was not Belgian; hence clear discrimination on the grounds of nationality. The CoJ held that the new citizenship provisions and new competences in education, albeit limited, allowed it to hold that Arts 12 and 17 EC (now Arts 18 and 20 TFEU) preclude discrimination as regards the grant of a non-contributory social benefit to Union citizens where they are lawfully resident, even though not economically active. In *D'Hoop*, a Belgian national had studied in France. She was refused a tide-over allowance between study and work granted to nationals by the Belgian authorities because she had studied in another member state. The Court of Justice had held that the tide-over allowance was a social advantage under Article 7(2) of Regulation 1612/68, but to take advantage of it the person must either have participated in the employment market or obtained a derived right in some way. She was not a worker and her parents had remained in Belgium; therefore she had no rights in her own right nor derived rights from the parents. The Court of Justice referred to the new contribution to education by the EC in encouraging mobility of students and teachers (Articles 3(1)(q) and 149(2) EC (now 6 and 165 TFEU)) and, citing *Grzelczyk* at [31], held that it would be incompatible with the right of freedom of movement if a citizen who had taken advantage of free movement were then to suffer discrimination with regard to a social benefit right as a consequence. It held:

> Such inequality of treatment is contrary to the principles which underpin the status of citizen of the Union, that is, the guarantee of the same treatment in law in the exercise of the citizen's freedom to move. The condition at issue could be justified only if it were based on objective considerations independent of the nationality of the persons concerned and were proportionate to the legitimate aim of the national provisions.[43]

The Belgian authorities offered none; hence the limiting of places of education that qualify for the tide-over allowance, according to the Court of Justice, went beyond what is necessary to attain the objective pursued.

In the next case, a distinct test has been imposed on those EU citizens who seek to claim benefits in a host state that certainly starts to answer the concerns of member states about benefit or welfare tourism. In Case C-138/02 *Collins v Secretary of State for Work and Pensions*, Collins entered the UK in 1998 on an Irish passport to seek work. He claimed an income-based jobseeker's allowance on the strength of ten months' part-time work that he had undertaken as a US citizen from 1980 to 1981. The UK authorities refused the benefit on the grounds that he was not habitually resident in the UK. Collins claimed that this was discrimination, because nationals were advantaged by automatically satisfying the time period required, whereas other EU nationals would have to fulfil this extra requirement. The Court of Justice held that it was permissible for member states first to require that there be a genuine link between the work seeker and the state for the purposes of claiming a jobseeker's allowance. There was indirect discrimination, in that nationals could far more easily establish this link but, for the reasons given by the UK, it was objectively justified, because the jobseeker's allowance was designed to reduce national unemployment for those living long-term in the UK.

The link requirement was confirmed in the next case, but which also confirms that, where appropriate, welfare rights can nevertheless be claimed by EU citizens.

In Case C-256/04 *Ioannidis*, a Greek national spent three years in Belgium obtaining a graduate diploma followed by a training course in France. On his return to Belgium to look for work, he claimed a tide-over allowance (as in *D'Hoop* earlier). This was refused on the grounds that he had not completed secondary education in Belgium nor pursued education of the same level in another member state; nor was he the dependent of a migrant worker residing in Belgium. The Court of Justice held that Ioannidis fell within the scope of Art 39 EC (now Art 45 TFEU) whilst seeking work and that, according to the citizenship provisions of the treaty, under certain conditions, financial assistance cannot be denied Union citizens. In line with the *Collins* case, the CoJ acknowledged that a link with

---

[43] Paras 35–6 of the judgment.

the employment market could be required, but the fact that Ioannidis had completed a diploma in Belgium had already provided such a link.

In Case C-406/04 *De Cuyper*, a Belgian national claimed unemployment benefit but moved to France whilst continuing to claim. Once that information was revealed to the authorities, his claim was denied on the grounds that he was not in residence. The CoJ held that the requirement to reside in Belgium whilst claiming was contrary to Art 18 EC (now Art 21 TFEU), but that Art 18 EC (now Art 21 TFEU) breaches can be objectively justified. In this case, the public interest in being able to verify and monitor the right to benefit, which would be very difficult or impossible if the claimant were not in the country, was held to be proportionate.

In Cases C-11–12/06 *Morgan and Bucher*, two students moved to study abroad, but claimed the benefits to do so from their home state, which demanded that they study in the home state for at least one year. This would add a considerable disincentive by adding a year to, or at best complicating, their studies, but was insisted on by the home state to establish a clear link to the state for the purposes of receiving the benefit. The Court of Justice approved a need to demonstrate a sufficient level of integration with the home state in line with its previous case law. However, it held that, in the cases before it, that need was satisfied, because both persons were raised and schooled in the home state. Consequently, the home state could not demand that they study there first for one year.

A further case now appears not only to confirm *Collins*, but also steps back slightly from the previous generous interpretation of individuals' rights. Case C-158/07 *Förster v IB-Groep* concerns Ms Förster, a German national in the Netherlands who, from 2000, worked from time to time there and qualified for a study maintenance grant, which was withdrawn when the responsible authority (IB-Groep) discovered in 2003 that she was no longer working. Her challenge to the decision failed because she was not sufficiently integrated in the Netherlands and she had not satisfied the requirement of five years' residence. On reference to the Court of Justice, the CoJ upheld its previous decision in Case C-209/03 *Bidar* that member states were entitled to require a certain degree of integration and that, in this case, a five-year period was justified and proportionate. The student status in this case may have distinguished it from the following case.

In Cases C-22–3/08 *Vatsouras and Koupatantze v ARGE Nürnberg*, the Court of Justice was asked to consider the rights to social welfare under Arts 18 and 21 TFEU and the ability of member states under Art 24 of Directive 2004/38 to deny social welfare to EU migrant jobseekers and their families. The CoJ held, in view of the treaty Articles and previous case law, that, provided that the EU citizens can establish a genuine link with the host state, such as previous employment, then a jobseeker's allowance, which is designed to facilitate access to the labour market, should be available. It was not to be regarded as a safety net social assistance, which could still be excluded under EU law, but a clear link must nevertheless be established.

Thus, as far as welfare rights entitlement is concerned, it would seem now that the economic status of the person—that is, whether worker or self-employed—is no longer an important factor. Provided that there is movement in some way, even back to the home state or lawful residence in the host state, EU citizens will be entitled to be treated without discrimination compared to nationals. This is the situation now in cases concerning a variety of claims, the only limitation appearing to be the requirement in some cases, according to circumstances, of a close link between the person seeking benefit and the host states or a period of residence requirement, as in the *Collins, Ioannidis, Morgan and Bucher* and *Förster* cases.

The next cases are concerned, for the most part, with family members, who are very often non-EU citizens. There is a degree of overlap with the cases considered in the section above on welfare rights and the following section concerned with TCNs, because members of the family are often also those claiming additional rights.

9.8 Citizenship and Family Rights (including TCN Family Members)

These cases, in which a greater respect for family life has emerged, are also a product of the move from regarding free movement rights in the EU legal order as wholly dependent on the pursuit of an economic activity to recognizing them as rights that are equally based on citizenship and fundamental freedoms.[44]

In the *Carpenter* case, the CoJ was more concerned with family rights than with arguments regarding the basis for lawful residence of TCN members of the family. The CoJ referred to Art 49 EC (now Art 56 TFEU) and Regulation 1612/68, which, read strictly, does not apply to the provision of services. These provisions, according to the CoJ, provide rules protecting the family life of nationals of the member states in order to eliminate obstacles to the exercise of the fundamental freedoms guaranteed by the treaty. It held:

> It is clear that the separation of Mr. and Mrs. Carpenter would be detrimental to their family life and, therefore, to the conditions under which Mr. Carpenter exercises a fundamental freedom. That freedom could not be fully effective if Mr. Carpenter were to be deterred from exercising it by obstacles raised in his country of origin to the entry and residence of his spouse.[45]

The CoJ considered that the rights of residence could be subjected to objective restrictions, but which must comply with fundamental rights, and that:

> The decision to deport Mrs. Carpenter constitutes an interference with the exercise by Mr Carpenter of his right to respect for his family life within the meaning of Article 8 of the Convention for the Protection of Human Rights and Fundamental Freedoms and does not strike a fair balance between the competing interests, that is, on the one hand, the right of Mr. Carpenter to respect for his family life, and, on the other hand, the maintenance of public order and public safety.[46]

The CoJ noted that the marriage appeared genuine, that there were no official complaints against Mrs Carpenter, and that she looked after the children while Mr Carpenter was providing services. Read in light of the fundamental right to respect for family life, the CoJ's judgment is that Art 49 EC (now Art 56 TFEU) should be interpreted as ensuring that the spouse of a provider of services established in the provider's member state of origin (where those services are provided to recipients established in other member states) cannot be denied the right to reside in the provider's member state of origin, even if the spouse is a TCN. *Baumbast* also highlights the support of the Court of Justice for family rights. It is settled law according to the CoJ in Cases 389–90/87 *Echternach and Moritz*, that rights enjoyed by members of an EU worker's family under Regulation 1612/68 can, in certain circumstances, continue to exist even after the employment relationship has

---

[44] I have decided that because there is so much overlap of family rights in general and those concerned with the rights of third-country nationals as family members, to merge these two sections thus cutting out a lot of repetition and cross referencing. EU legislative moves to regulate completely independent TCNs are however dealt with in Section 9.10

[45] At [39] of the judgment.   [46] At [42]–[43].

ended. Case C-413/99 *Baumbast* actually covers, under the same name, two sets of fac-tual circumstances and concerns derived rights for TCNs. The case also involves 'R', an American woman who, on the face of it, had neither personal nor derived rights to remain in the EU and whom the UK authorities wanted to deport. R moved to the UK with her then French husband who had obtained work in the UK. Later, they were divorced and, in line with the jurisprudence of the *Diatta* and *Reed* cases, R lost her own legal right to remain in the host state under Regulation 1612/68, Art 10 but her children, who remained the children of an EU national, but one who was no longer working in the UK, were enti-tled to and granted indefinite leave to remain. R was not. The Court of Justice though held that R had a right of residence under Community law enabling her to resist an attempt to deport her. This was because the children had a right to remain and to pursue their education, under the best possible conditions, in the host member state and therefore the CoJ reasoned that this necessarily implies that those children have the right to be accompanied by the person who is their primary carer and, accordingly, that the carer be able to reside with them in that member state during their studies. To refuse to grant permission to remain to a parent who is the primary carer of the child exercising his or her right to pursue his or her studies in the host member state infringes that right. The CoJ held that Regulation 1612/68, interpreted in light of Art 8 ECHR, entitled the parent who is the primary carer of those children, irrespective of nationality, to reside with them in order to facilitate the exercise of that right, notwithstanding the fact that the parents have meanwhile divorced. The facts that only one parent is a citizen of the Union, that the parent has ceased to be a migrant worker in the host member state, and that the children are not themselves citizens of the Union are irrelevant in this regard.

Hence, then, there is an implied right within Art 12 of the Regulation that the child of a migrant worker can pursue his or her education in the host member state and that the child has the right to be accompanied by the person who is his or her primary carer. Furthermore, that person is able to reside with him or her in that member state during his or her studies. According to the CoJ, to refuse to grant permission to remain to a par-ent who is the primary carer of the child exercising a right to pursue studies in the host member state infringes that right (at [73] of the judgment). Obviously, in that particular case, there was still a connection with the host state that provided the right to remain, but nevertheless it represents another slight widening of the scope of EU free movement. This derived right stems this time not directly from the worker, but from the children of the worker, who are themselves recipients of derived rights. This could be termed 'indirect derived rights'.

A further case that provides express support for family life is Case C-459/99 *MRAX*, which involves the challenge by an interest group to the Belgian authorities' applica-tion of Community law in respect of the visa requirements for TCN family members. Certainly, according to Art 3 of Directive 68/360, member states are entitled to demand a visa from the TCN family members. The CoJ reasoned that it is apparent, in particu-lar from the Council regulations and directives on freedom of movement for employed and self-employed persons within the Community, that the Community legislature has recognized the importance of ensuring protection for the family life of nationals of the member states in order to eliminate obstacles to the exercise of the fundamental free-doms guaranteed by the treaty.[47] In this light, the CoJ considered that it is, in any event, disproportionate and therefore prohibited to send back a TCN married to a national of a member state not in possession of a valid visa where he or she is able to prove his or her

---

[47] At [53] of the judgment.

identity and conjugal ties, and where there is no evidence to establish that he or she represents a risk to the requirements of public policy, public security, or public health within the meaning of Art 10 of Directive 68/360 and Art 8 of Directive 73/148.[48] Hence, the right to a family life protected by Art 8 ECHR has been instrumental in achieving far-reaching judgments on the rights of family members of EU citizens and clearly beyond any strict interpretation of EU law rights.

In Case C-109/01 *Akrich*, the position of a non-lawfully resident TCN who was married to a UK national was considered. Although Akrich entered the UK unlawfully and the CoJ held that Regulation 1612/68 did not apply to the situation to provide rights before the move to Ireland on a temporary basis, after that move Akrich should be accorded a right to stay unless the member state took the view that the marriage was not genuine. *Akrich* also concerns Art 8 ECHR which, if the marriage in this case was determined to be genuine, should be taken into account when considering the importance of the unlawful residence of the TCN seeking to stay in the UK, although the CoJ attached no actual weight to the consideration that must be given.

In Case C-1/05 *Jia*, also noted in Section 9.4.3.1, the Court of Justice held that neither the *Akrich* judgment nor Community law in general permitted member states to restrict the entry of a TCN relative of the spouse of a Community citizen to allow him or her to do so only if the TCN relative had first been resident in another EU country. In other words, the TCN could move directly to join her relative in the EU direct from the third country. The case also held, though, that the proof of dependency for such moves, required previously under Directive 73/148, but now catered for by Directive 2004/38, required real proof of factual dependency from any appropriate means, and not only an undertaking from a member of the family.

Case C-127/08 *Metock et al*, also noted in Section 9.4.3.1, considered numerous Articles of Directive 2004/38, in which four TCNs who had been refused asylum in Ireland then married EU citizens lawfully resident in Ireland. The CoJ held that rights provided for spouses to accompany EU citizens apply irrespective of where the marriage took place and how the TCN entered the host member state. The facts of the case stated that these were not marriages of convenience, although under Art 35 of the directive, member states can take action to penalize those who do abuse rights or engage in fraud. The member states are somewhat concerned as to the further consequences of this judgment.

Where TCNs are members of the family of a Union citizen who has exercised his or her rights under EU law, then Directive 2004/38 certainly provides the most secure rights, with, after five years, the right of permanent residence, even in the event of the death of, or divorce from, the Union citizen. Whilst Case C-200/02 *Chen*, considered in more detail in Sections 9.4.4 and 9.10, showed the strong support of the CoJ for both the strength of the right of EU citizenship, and family and carer rights, its unique factual base and the fact that the Irish Constitution has since been amended means that similar cases will not arise in the future. In Case C-34/09 *Zambrano v ONEM*, Zambrano and his wife, Colombian nationals seeking asylum in Belgium, had two children in Belgium who acquired Belgian nationality; their own applications for Belgian residence had, though, been rejected. In the national court reviewing that decision, they asked whether Arts 12, 17, and 18 EC (now Arts 18, 20, and 21 TFEU) confer rights of residence in the state in which the EU citizen was born. Despite interventions by member states that the situation was wholly internal and thus beyond the scope of EU law, the Court of Justice held that Art 20 TFEU did, indeed, prevent a member state from denying residence to the parents (and carers)

---

[48] At [61].

of an EU citizen by reason of the fact that the EU-citizen dependent would otherwise be denied full exercise of his or her rights, including most importantly the right to reside in the EU and thus to exercise all of his or her rights under EU law.

Thus, the CoJ (and the AG before it) upheld the sanctity of EU citizenship once acquired, in the face of member state objections.

More palatable to the member states would be the ruling in Case C-434/09 *McCarthy*, which followed shortly after the *Zambrano* ruling. An EU citizen born and living exclusively in the UK with British and Irish nationality was denied residence based on EU law. She had hoped to obtain that residence so that her Jamaican husband could also obtain residence under the treaty and Directive 2004/38. The Court this time rejected those claims as not being based on the exercise of any movement by a national of the state in which the rights were claimed. The CoJ did distinguish the case from *Zambrano* on the ground that there was no fear that she would have to leave the state or residence.

Case C-256/11 *Dereci and others* may though add a further gloss. It involved the refusal of residence permits by Austria for five non-EU nationals living with Austrian nationals but each in different circumstances. They sought to rely on the *Zambrano* case to obtain the right to stay but this was distinguished by the Court of Justice in that in *Zambrano* the derived EU rights gained by the non-EU nationals would be completely lost if forced to return to Columbia whereas, in the five situations in *Dereci*, the option of moving to another EU country and thus obtaining those rights for family members existed and thus those EU rights could be realized.

Thus EU law does not require member states to admit non-EU spouses or family members where no such right in national law exists and the possibility of moving to another EU state exists.

Finally, for the moment, is another case involving both family member and TCN elements. Joined Cases C-356–7/11 *O, S & L* asked the question of the Court of Justice whether a TCN step-father of an EU child born to a TCN mother in a previous marriage with an EU national could derive residence rights from that child. The Court answered no, provided the substance of the rights of the EU citizen concerned (the EU child of the previous marriage) would not be denied by such a decision. Further any decision on an application for a residence permit must under the circumstances be considered by the national court under both the Family Reunification Directive 2003/86 and Arts 7 and 24 of the EU Charter of Fundamental Rights.

The cases, *Zambrano* in particular, appear to reduce even further the concept of 'wholly internal', considered next.

9.9 The Wholly Internal Rule

A number of cases have highlighted how EU law has benefited persons and families who have taken advantage of the right to move to another member state, but when compared to nationals of a member state who have not moved, those nationals appear to be disadvantaged and thus to be suffering a form of reverse discrimination. This is because, without the movement of EU citizens, there is nothing actually to trigger EU law rights and the situation is thus described as wholly internal. This means domestic national law is the law that applies to those nationals. Hence EU law will not apply when a factual situation is regarded as being within the wholly internal legal competence of a member state and there is no personal fulfilment of the EU law rights to trigger any material rights under EU law. For example, strict professional rules continue to apply to nationals established and providing services, but are held by the Court of Justice not to be suitable or appropriate to apply to EU lawyers providing services temporarily in the host state: see the restriction on areas of practice for lawyers in Germany in Case 427/85 *Commission v Germany (Lawyers)*. The consequence of this judgment was that the German lawyers could still be restricted in the geographical areas in which they could practise, because this was an entirely internal matter of the application of national rules to nationals. EU law in such a circumstance was not invoked in any way, and the CoJ could not and would not interfere in a wholly internal matter. Note, though, that the internal German rules on this have now been changed.

In Case 175/78 *R v Saunders*, a criminal sanction imposing a mobility restriction on Saunders was applicable within the UK only. This was claimed by Saunders to be contrary to Art 48 EEC (now Art 45 TFEU). The CoJ held that there was no factor connecting the situation with EU law, because there was no movement to or from another member state. Hence, the provisions on free movement of workers cannot be applied to situations that are wholly internal to a member state.

The *Saunders* case can be compared with another to demonstrate the difference when EU law applies. In Case 36/75 *Rutili v France*, a restriction by France on the Italian national Rutili entering certain departments of France was regarded as contrary to both the treaty and EU secondary legislation. The Court of Justice held that Art 48(3) EEC (now Art 45 TFEU) derogations may be imposed only in respect of the whole of the national territory.

However, Case C–299/95 *Kremzow v Austria*, concerning a national imprisoned in his own state, suggests that non-interference with wholly internal situations is still the position taken by the CoJ. It ruled that whilst the deprivation of liberty might prevent the person from exercising the EU right to freedom of movement, the purely hypothetical possibility did not involve a sufficient connection with EU law. Further, in Case C-100/01 *Olazbal*, dealing with the restriction of movement of a Spanish national who had connections with the Basque ETA organization to specific regions in France, the CoJ held that when criminal measures are taken to restrict movement, they are acceptable if the action was justified due to the seriousness of the crime, which would otherwise lead to a complete banishment. Furthermore, in similar circumstances, nationals would also be subject to similar punitive measures. This is now supported by Art 22 of Directive 2004/38, which provides that member states may impose territorial restrictions on the rights of permanent residence in situations in which the same restrictions may be applied to their own nationals.

Two further cases illustrate how the wholly internal rule appears to give rise to unfair and arbitrary results, and thus discrimination, because nationals or those lawfully resident in the member state in question are denied rights on which EU nationals from other member states and family members from outside the EU are able to rely.

In Cases 35–6/82 *Morson and Jhanjan*, the applicants, both Surinamese nationals, claimed the right to stay in the Netherlands with their Dutch-national son and daughter, who were working there. It was held by the CoJ that there was no application of Community law to the wholly internal situation in which national workers had not worked in any other member state. There was no movement from one member state to another and therefore Community law did not apply and movement from a third country does not qualify. This was confirmed in Cases 64–5/96 *Land Nordrhein-Westfalen v Uecker and Jacquet* concerning two TCNs trying to rely on Community law as spouses of German nationals living in Germany. The case was deemed to be wholly internal and thus not within the scope of application of EU law. If, in both cases, there were, for example, Spanish nationals moving to either the Netherlands or Germany, they would be allowed to take TCN spouses or relatives with them. Of late, however, there appears to be some softening of the wholly internal rule. Some cases look wholly internal, but because some prior movement is involved, EU law rights can be triggered against the home state. The amount of movement or degree of economic activity deemed necessary to take a situation out of being wholly internal to one to which EU law applies appears to be decreasing.

In Case C-370/90 *Surinder Singh*, an Indian spouse of a British national was able to use EU law to derive a right of residence in the UK on the basis that the spouse had previously exercised the right of free movement by providing services in another member state, but who then re-established herself in the UK. In Case 419/92 *Scholz*, it was held that a frontier worker who continues to live in his or her home state and is only employed in another state, but who crosses the border to work, triggers EU rights that can be claimed within the home state.[49]

In Case C-60/00 *Carpenter*,[50] a Philippine national claimed a right of residence in the UK with her British spouse on the grounds that he provided services from time to time in other member states. The case is similar to *Singh* in relation to the fact that services had been provided in another member state before returning to the UK, but Mrs Carpenter had not left UK soil whilst services were being provided by her husband both from the UK and travelling to other member states. The argument put forward by the applicants was that, if Mrs Carpenter were also to have gone to another member state, both would have rights of residence and the right to work in the other host EU states. However, she chose to remain in the UK to look after the children and thus to assist her husband in providing services in other member states. The Commission regarded the case as a wholly internal matter for the member state and thus subject to its law alone. The Court of Justice referred to Regulation 1612/68, which strictly does not apply to the provision of services, but provides rules protecting the family life of nationals of the member states in order to eliminate obstacles to the exercise of the fundamental freedoms guaranteed by the treaty:

> It is clear that the separation of Mr. and Mrs. Carpenter would be detrimental to their family life and, therefore, to the conditions under which Mr. Carpenter exercises a fundamental freedom. That freedom could not be fully effective if Mr. Carpenter were to be deterred from exercising it by obstacles raised in his country of origin to the entry and residence of his spouse.[51]

The CoJ held that Art 49 EEC (now Art 45 TFEU) is to be interpreted as preventing a member state from refusing the TCN spouse of an EU national established in that member state, but providing services to recipients established in other member states, a right to reside in its territory.

In Case C-281/98 *Angonese*, an Italian citizen applied for a job in Italy, but was refused entry to the selection process because he did not have the appropriate local authority certificate of bilingualism, despite being accepted by the local court as perfectly bilingual and possessing certificates of language study from the University of Vienna at which he had studied. The Italian government and defendant bank argued that the matter was wholly internal, and had no connection with Community law. Whilst there was movement in this case, in that Mr Angonese had studied in Austria, the only economic activity was the receiving of educational services. The Court of Justice held that the previous movement for the purposes of study had triggered Community law rights.

A further case in this category is Case C-403/03 *Schempp*. Divorce maintenance was being paid in another member state, which meant that the German tax regime that would normally apply was denied in this case and a tax exemption on the payments was lost.

---

[49] Other frontier workers cases were considered in Section 9.3.1.2.2.
[50] Also considered in Section 9.9.   [51] At [39] of the judgment.

It was argued by Germany and other governments that this was a wholly internal situation that had involved no movement on the part of Mr Schempp. The Court of Justice held, however, that the exercise of the right of free movement by the former spouse of Mr Schempp had an effect on his right to deduct tax in Germany and was therefore not a wholly internal situation with no connection to Community law. The difference in treatment offended Art 12 EC (now Art 18 TFEU), although the CoJ stressed that, in view of the difference in tax regimes, Community law does not guarantee neutrality of treatment if a person takes advantage of the free movement rights under Art 18 EC (now Art 21 TFEU).

Case C-109/01 *Akrich* raised some important questions in respect of the scope of the *Singh* judgment, in particular, whether a situation that would otherwise be wholly internal can be deliberately engineered to become one with an EU context. The case involves a Moroccan who, after both lawful and unlawful attempts to enter and remain in the UK, married a UK national and moved to Ireland for a short period expressly in order to take advantage of EU law rights and, in particular, the judgment in *Singh* to return to the UK. The Secretary of State considered that Mr and Mrs Akrich's move to Ireland was no more than a temporary absence deliberately designed to manufacture a right of residence for Mr Akrich on his return to the UK, and thereby to evade the provisions of UK legislation, and that Mrs Akrich had not been genuinely exercising rights under the EC Treaty as a worker in another member state. The Court of Justice was asked, amongst other questions, whether a situation engineered to evade national immigration laws was an abuse of Community law rights and, if so, whether the UK authorities could lawfully refuse entry. The CoJ held that the motive for going to Ireland is not relevant to the status of a worker, nor the decision to return to the home state, but it did acknowledge that there would be an abuse if the facilities afforded by Community law in favour of migrant workers and their spouses were invoked in the context of marriages of convenience entered into in order to circumvent the provisions relating to entry and residence of nationals of non-member states. If, however, genuinely married, Art 8 ECHR should be taken into regard in considering the unlawful residence status of the TCN. The CoJ held that Art 10 of Regulation 1612/68 applies to TCNs only if they are lawfully resident in a member state before they can move to another one to take advantage of the rights provided by the Regulation. It is not applicable where a marriage of convenience has been arranged to circumvent a member state's laws and to engineer the application of EU law instead. So, if the marriage is genuine, despite a lack of lawful residence, member states should pay regard to Art 8 ECHR. The question that is left to the member state is whether the marriage was genuine or not.

Case C-148/02 *Garcia Avello* looks very much wholly internal, with no movement taking place directly connected with the facts of the case. It involved dual nationality children of a Spanish father living in Belgium, who wished to register the children's names according to Spanish custom and practice, and not Belgian. The CoJ, relying on Arts 17 and 12 EC (now Arts 20 and 18 TFEU), held that the children's future rights to move back to Spain might be prejudiced by Belgium, therefore contrary to the treaty, and that by denying them the right to follow the Spanish tradition Belgium discriminated against them on grounds of nationality. Another name case is Case C-208/09, *Ilonka Sayn-Wittgenstein v Landeshauptmann von Wien*, in which the CoJ held it was acceptable for a member state (Germany) to refuse to recognize titles of nobility from another country (Austria) if justified by a general aim and principle which was upheld evenly and uniformly. In the case, this judgment was support for the concept of the equality of all citizens.

Case C-17/00 *De Coster* was concerned in strict terms with only the domestic tax regime but was held by the CoJ to be considered under EU law. The taxation was applicable to the installation of satellite dishes that could receive television broadcasts from other member states only, and not applied to the installation of receiving equipment capable of receiving purely domestic broadcasts. However, television signals could also easily be received broadcast from another member state, thus confirming the cross-border element.

In similar vein, Case C-544/03 *Mobistar*, concerned with mobile phone masts, also triggered the application and consideration of EU law because, equally, mobile phone signals satisfy the cross-border service element.

Finally, in this context, is C-200/02 *Chen*, considered in Section 9.9.4, which involved no movement from one member state to another but, because of the particular legal rules in Ireland, nevertheless triggered the application of EU law.

So, bearing in mind the developments so far, a factual circumstance that, on the face of it, appears to be wholly internal may nevertheless be subject to EU law, provided that there has been some previous movement into another member state or that services have been received in another member state. It is further arguable that the movement can also be incorporeal, such as receiving services over the telephone or, more probable these days, over the internet. If the simple receipt of services, irrespective of the manner of delivery of these services, triggers the application of EU law, then it could be argued that potentially any receipt of services, albeit clearly on the face of it wholly internal, will qualify regardless of how minimal, such as telephoning another country to get advice or other services, or downloading advice packages from a computer server in another member state.

9.10 Third-country Nationals—Legislative Moves

TCNs lawfully or unlawfully resident in a member state were not subject to EU law unless specifically catered for in some way, such as family members of EU persons taking advantage of the free movement rules, which were considered earlier in this chapter. Here, we are concerned only with independent TCNs who obtain no rights under EU law to reside in the EU or to move from country to country. Their rights were originally entirely a matter for national law regulation. TCNs, according to European Commission estimates, comprised about 4 per cent of the population of the 15 member states in 2000, which translates to roughly 13 million TCNs lawfully or unlawfully resident in the EU. This figure has risen now that the EU has increased to 28 member states and now stands at around 20 million.[52]

Whilst it might have been the case in the past that the treatment of TCNs was regarded as being below the standards of treatment to be expected from the EU, more recently, the Court of Justice has been addressing the rights of TCNs in the latest case law and there now has been legislative intervention on the part of member states in Council. A lot of attention has been directed to the immigration policies, and the Schengen Agreement regarding the entry and visa regulation of TCNs, whereas less attention has been paid to the free movement rights of those already in the EU—although of late those aspects, too, have been receiving attention, considered later. Previously, the CoJ has held, for example, in Case 238/83 *Mr and Mrs Richard Meade*, that the treaty Articles on free movement of workers apply solely to EU nationals and not therefore to TCNs.

The first of the exceptions to this position is where TCNs have been provided with rights under the various association and cooperation agreements with countries such as

---

[52] Commission Communication COM (2007) 0780 final, 'Towards a Common Immigration Policy', provided the figure of 18.5 million. For a full report of EU demography see **http://epp.eurostat.ec.europa.eu/cache/ITY_OFFPUB/KE-ET-10-001/EN/KE-ET-10-001-EN.PDF.**

Turkey, Algeria, and Morocco. The second arises when TCNs form part of the workforce of a company established in the EU that sends workers abroad to complete a contract in another member state. In Case C-43/93 *Van der Elst*, the CoJ confirmed that TCNs also have the right of free movement within the context of the right of free movement of companies that are established within the EU, provided that the non-EU nationals are part of the legal labour force of the company established in the home member state and where the employer provides services in another member state.

There has also now been legislative intervention in this area and further proposals have also been made. Regulation 1091/2001[53] was enacted, which provides limited rights of free movement for those TCNs in the EU on a long-stay visa. TCNs may also be helped by Directive 2000/43,[54] which prohibits discrimination based on race; however, Art 3(2) states that it is without prejudice to the provisions and conditions relating to the entry and residence of TCNs, and to any treatment that arises from the legal status of TCNs. So whilst it may prevent unequal treatment in the country of residence, it is unlikely to provide a right of free movement.

Specifically addressing the situation of divided families with TCN family members, the institutions have enacted Directive 2003/86,[55] which provides that lawfully resident TCNs in member states may apply to have their family join them from a third country, provided that they are self-sufficient and have been in the member state for a year or more. Furthermore, Art 3 requires that they must have a reasonable prospect of remaining longer. The definition of 'family' has been restrictively drawn and member states retain much discretion in deciding whether to grant an application. The directive does not apply to the UK, Ireland, and Denmark, all of which have opted out of this section of the treaty.[56]

A directive has been enacted concerning the status of TCNs who are long-term residents in a member state.[57] Directive 2003/109 provides TCNs who have been lawfully resident in the EU for a minimum of five years with the right to apply for, and acquire, a certain status that entitles them to long-term residence in the host state and limited rights of movement within the EU. These rights are subject to the public policy and security derogations, self-sufficiency, sickness insurance requirements, and quotas and restrictions on movements imposed by the other secondary states. The directive extends to core family members, as defined by the Reunification Directive, but these may not be admitted by a second EU state. Indeed, whilst the directive does provide new rights for TCNs, it does so only without prejudice to all of the other legislative provisions already providing rights and is subject to interpretation by the member states, which may dilute some of its provisions. It came into force on 23 January 2006 and is nevertheless a welcome if, in the end, somewhat modest improvement.

Finally, there are two further directives to take note of. Council Directive 2004/114[58] provides details on the conditions of admission of TCNs for the purposes of studies, pupil exchange, unremunerated training, or voluntary service, which entered into force in 2007. Directive 2009/50,[59] which is known as the 'Blue Card' Directive because it provides for the entry and residence of highly qualified TCNs who would otherwise have no rights to enter the EU. Persons wishing to benefit from the directive must, however, also satisfy the national regulations of the particular state they wish to enter or are being recruited to.

---

[53] OJ 2001 L150/4.   [54] OJ 2000 L180/22.   [55] OJ 2003 L251/12.
[56] See Arts 77–80 TFEU and the protocols attached to the TEU and the TFEU.
[57] Directive 2003/109 (OJ 2004 L16/44).   [58] OJ 2004 L375/12.   [59] OJ 2009 L155/17.

Article 59 EEC (now Art 56 TFEU) was amended by the SEA, and now provides that the European Parliament and the Council, acting in accordance with the ordinary legislative procedure, may extend the provisions of the chapter to TCNs who provide services and who are established within the Union. After many years of lying dormant, a proposal was made under this Article, but there has been no further action on this since 8 May 2000, when an amended proposal was sent to the European Parliament. A further proposal has been made that concerns common conditions of entry and residence for TCNs who seek paid employment, or self-employment, within the EU, but it was never adopted.[60] Things may be moving for TCNs in the future, but only very slowly.

The Lisbon Treaty has provided a better basis for the rights of TCNs and, under Art 67(2) TFEU, aims to frame a common policy on asylum, immigration, and external border controls that is fair towards TCNs. The provisions from both the TEU and EC Treaty have been regrouped in Arts 67–74 TFEU. In order to achieve the broad objectives of Art 67, Art 75 provides for the ordinary legislative procedure to be used, which involves the co-decision procedure—a very positive move away from intergovernmentalism to supranationalism in this more controversial area of Union activity. The individual areas of border controls, asylum, and immigration are then set out respectively in Arts 77–9 TFEU, the further details of which go beyond the necessary remit of this book.

9.11 Concluding Remarks

The EU law provision for the free movement of persons has changed considerably from its inception. Whilst the treaty Articles themselves have hardly changed since 1957, the scope of the rights available now to individuals has expanded considerably. This is due to both secondary legislation and judicial interpretation, and recently most widely to the introduction of a section on European citizenship and the consideration of a number of cases considering wholly internal situations, the position of TCNs, and family rights.

Thus far, we can tentatively say that if one is an EU citizen lawfully resident in another member state, one does not have to be economically active to be entitled to equal treatment. This includes, for example, equal treatment in non-contributory welfare benefits on the same basis as nationals. One may be a burden on the state, albeit a reasonable one only. However, the *Carpenter, Angonese*, and *Collins* cases have suggested a new test to determine whether EU law is triggered, which relates specifically to the connection to the state of the person concerned; that is, an economically determined level of activity, below which EU rights would not be triggered for the reason that the services received were marginal.

The expansion of the receipt of services also opens up the possibility of the expansion of EU rights to situations hitherto coming within the wholly internal rule. So if a national returns to his or her home EU member state after receiving services in another EU member state, he or she and members of his or her spouse's or partner's family, who are or who are not EU citizens, will be entitled to reside with him or her and also obtain benefits on the same basis as nationals. Given that the Court of Justice has already held that services

---

[60] COM (2001) 386 final. The latest developments can be found at **http://ec.europa.eu/justice_home/fsj/ immigration/fsj_immigration_intro_en.htm**.

include the provision of telephone services (Case C-384/93 *Alpine Investments*), it could easily therefore include provision of services over the internet, and possibly the receipt of services over the internet, as being a sufficiently strong cross-border element to trigger EU law rights in the areas of family and welfare law. For example, would the receipt of advice from a professional in another member state over the internet be sufficient to help a TCN family member to assert residence rights in any of the member states?

Hence, the limit of the range of rights to which EU law now applies is far from clear. Whether it should apply to rule out all discrimination against host EU citizens in comparison with nationals in all areas of law is the burning question left by the present development of the law. Does, for example, an unemployed tourist on holiday receive services? If so, do these activate Art 21 TFEU citizenship rights? Again, if so, does this then trigger the general right of equal treatment, such as access to needed benefits on the same basis as nationals, if, for the sake of argument, he or she runs short of money whilst on holiday? These dangers of an over-expansive interpretation of EU law may now mean that EU citizens who have established lawful residence in a host state will have equal rights to the full spectrum of contributory and non-contributory social benefits. If so, the spectre of 'benefit tourism' has effectively been raised, whereby EU nationals and their TCN family members can roam the member states in search of the 'good life'.

It would seem that EU citizens who do not move at any time to another member state to receive or provide services are the only ones unable to obtain these welfare and family rights, unless provided for under national law.

When we turn to TCNs we see that they may derive rights from their EU family members, including children, even where the children are non-EU nationals, but who nevertheless have rights of their own to stay in the host state, as in the case of R in *Baumbast*. EU nationals and TCN family members can derive rights in situations previously regarded as wholly internal, or in which the degree of movement or activity appears to be minimal, or even, arguably according to the case of *Akrich*, in which the movement is deliberately engineered. The statutory and case law developments represent some slight improvement in the position of lawfully resident TCNs in the EU. The EU legislature and the Court of Justice are having to be very careful in trying to provide rules for TCNs who have a good claim to reside and exercise rights of free movement, without opening the door too widely, so that unlawful residents gain a right to remain and obtain state benefits, matters that are highly politically charged in the present day. Another way of regulating TCNs and simultaneously prompting further recognition of their rights in the EU is by the policies pursued by the Schengen Agreement, which is not considered in this text.[61]

It is clear that the legal regime regulating the free movement of persons has come a long way from the near-empty and little-used original treaty provision for it. It is ironic, then, at the present stage of the evolution of free movement rights, that the concern is whether those rights have now actually gone too far and encroached too much on areas of the member states' own national laws and more than is universally acceptable.

However, as is often the case with the very dynamic system of law that is EU law, the burning questions with which we are left will be answered only by either the Court of Justice in future cases or by the intervention of the member states by treaty or secondary legislative amendment.

---

[61] See http://ec.europa.eu/justice_home/fsj/freetravel/fsj_freetravel_intro_en.htm.

Further Reading

Books

BARNARD, C. *The Substantive Law of the EU: The Four Freedoms*, 4th edn, Oxford University Press, Oxford, 2013.

SHAW, J. *The Transformation of Citizenship in the European Union*, Cambridge University Press, Cambridge, 2007.

WHITE, R. *Workers, Establishment and Services in the European Union*, Oxford University Press, Oxford, 2005.

Articles

ACIERNO, S. 'The *Carpenter* Judgment: Fundamental Rights and the Limits of the Community Legal Order' (2003) 28 EL Rev 398.

BARNARD, C. 'Unravelling the Services Directive' (2008) 41 CML Rev 323.

BARRETT, G. 'Family Matters: European Community Law and Third-country Family Members' (2003) 40 CML Rev 369.

CARRERA, S. 'What Does Free Movement Mean in an Enlarged EU?' (2005) 11 ELJ 699.

COSTELLO, C. '*Metock*: Free Movement and "Normal Family Life" in the Union' (2009) 46 CML Rev 587.

COUSINS, M. 'Citizenship, Residence and Social Security' (2007) 32 EL Rev 386.

CYGAN, A. 'Citizenship of the European Union' (2013) 62 ICLQ 492.

DAVIES, G. 'The High Water Point of Free Movement of Persons: Ending Benefit Tourism and Rescuing Welfare' (2004) 26 Journal of Social Welfare & Family Law 211–22.

DOUGAN, M. 'The Constitutional Dimension to the Case Law on Union Citizenship' (2006) 1 EL Rev 613.

FOSTER, N. 'Family and Welfare Rights in Europe: The Impact of Recent European Court of Justice Decisions in the Area of the Free Movement of Persons' (2003) 25 Journal of Social Welfare & Family Law 291–303.

HATZOPOULOS, V. and Do, T. 'The Case Law of the ECJ Concerning the Free Provision of Services 2000–2005' (2006) 43 CML Rev 923.

HOFSTOETTER, B. 'A Cascade of Rights, or Who Shall Care for Little Catherine? Some Reflections on the *Chen* Case' (2005) 30 EL Rev 548.

JACOBS, F. 'Citizenship of the European Union: A Legal Analysis' (2007) 13 ELJ 1591.

KOCHAROV, A. 'What Intra-Community Mobility for Third-country Workers?' (2008) 33(6) EL Rev 913–26.

KOCHENOV, D. 'The Right to Have What Rights? EU Citizenship in Need of Clarification' (2013) 19 ELJ 502.

KOCHENOV, D. and PLENDER, R. 'EU Citizenship: From an Incipient Form to an Incipient Substance? The Discovery of the Treaty Text' (2012) 37 EL Rev 369.

KOSTAKOPOULOU, D. 'European Union Citizenship: Writing the Future' (2007) 13(5) ELJ 623.

KUNOY, B. 'A Union of National Citizens: The Origins of the Court's Lack of Avantgardisme in the *Chen* Case' (2006) 43(1) CML Rev 179–90.

LEE, R. 'Liberalisation of Legal Services in Europe: Progress and Prospects' (2010) 30 Legal Studies 186.

NEWDICK, C. 'Citizenship, Free Movement and Health Care: Cementing Individual Rights by Corroding Social Solidarity' (2006) 43 CML Rev 1645.

NIC SHUIBHNE, N. 'Free Movement of Persons and the Wholly Internal Rule: Time to Move On?' (2003) 39 CML Rev 731.

NIC SHUIBHNE, N. 'The Resilience of EU Market Citizenship' (2010) 47 CML Rev 1597.

PEERS, S. 'Implementing Equality? The Directive on Long-term Resident Third-country Nationals' (2004) 29 EL Rev 437–60.

REICH, N. and HARBACEVICA, S. 'Citizenship and Family on Trial: A Fairly Optimistic Overview of Recent Court Practice with Regard to Free Movement of Persons' (2003) 40 CML Rev 615.

RITTER, R. 'Purely Internal Situations, Reverse Discrimination, *Guimont, Dzodzi* and Article 234' (2006) 31 EL Rev 690.

SPAVENTA, E. 'From *Gebhard* to *Carpenter*: Towards a (Non-)economic European Constitution' (2004) 41 CML Rev 743.

TRYFONIDOU, A. 'In Search of the Aim of the EC Free Movement of Persons Provisions: Has the Court of Justice Missed the Point? (2009) 46 CML Rev 1591.

TRYFONIDOU, A. 'Redefining the Outer Boundaries of EU Law: The *Zambrano, McCarthy* and *Dereci* Trilogy' (2012) 18 EPL 493.

WEATHERILL, S. 'Fair Play Please! Recent Developments in the Application of EC Law to Sport' (2003) 40(1) CML Rev 51.

WHITE, R. 'The Citizen's Right to Free Movement' (2005) 16 EBLR 547.

10

An Introduction to EU Competition Policy and Law

10.1 Introduction

Competition law applies to regulate the activities of mainly commercial undertakings to curb the excesses of the free market or to remedy situations which in an unregulated free market would be harmful to some parties or the system of competition itself. Cast more widely though it is also concerned with state aid which can also distort the market. The idea of competition lies at the heart of the capitalist system and at the heart of EU economic law. It conjures up images of the free market in a free market economy with minimal state intervention. It suggests the efficiency of the actors in the marketplace determining what should be made where and for what price and, more to the point, free from state planning or state production. 'If, as the metaphor goes, a market economy is governed by an invisible hand, competition is surely the brass knuckles by which it enforces its decisions.'[1]

It is often commented that competition is desirable for many reasons. Competition is supposed to ensure efficiency by giving the greatest awards to the keenest in the marketplace. This efficiency is meant to provide a benefit to all in that it improves living standards, it creates employment, and allows the consumer to benefit from a competitive market. Competition is therefore seen as a healthy and desirable state of affairs by economists particularly of the right wing who would point to the obvious failure of the planned uncompetitive economies of the communist world which were unable to provide the gains in the standard of living achieved in the West. Thus, if competition is good, then more competition is surely better. It is therefore desirable to increase the scale over which competition can be achieved; that is, create a larger and freer market. The internal market of the EU must therefore be a good thing for the industry and economy of the member states. European-wide competition should stimulate the entire economy of the EU for both the domestic and world markets.

However, unfettered competition does not maintain the status quo, left unregulated it is ultimately self-destructive. The most efficient undertakings will finally drive other competition out of business leaving a monopoly which can then exploit the market to the detriment of consumers and the economy generally. So, in order to retain fair competition, some form of intervention on the part of a state is required. To continue to reap the benefits of competition, given that perfect competition is well-nigh impossible, a state between perfect competition and oligopoly or monopoly must be maintained. For this, certain criteria must be fulfilled. There must be no discrimination between buyers and

---

[1] *US v Syufy*, Case No 89-15475 United States Court of Appeals for the Ninth Circuit. Case reproduced at **http://notabug.com/kozinski/syufy**.

sellers and producers. This is actually a requirement of the Common Agricultural Policy (CAP), see Art 40(2) TFEU. There should be a supply of homogeneous commodities; that is, the same or at least very similar products must be available and, thus, in competition with each other. There should be a large number of buyers and sellers. Where there are a limited number (known as an 'oligopoly') or only one or two ('monopoly' or 'duopoly') the market can be severely affected or influenced by these companies. There should be close and free contact between buyers and sellers in all parts of the market; that is, no artificial obstacles to trade, by tariffs or geography, etc. Without these, the market distorts or becomes imperfect with the upper hand being achieved by one side or the other; today this is usually the producer or seller rather than the consumer or buyer, although the massive supermarket chains are able to exploit their power over producers.

10.2 Competition Law Relevance to the EU

Competition law regulation was regarded as a necessary and essential element in the building and functioning of the Community and Union. A view confirmed by the Court of Justice in paragraph 36 of Case C-126/97 *Eco Swiss China Time Ltd*. Apart from the previously noted general reasons, the EU needed an integrated competition policy to complement and to ensure the maintenance of the internal market—the whole establishment or foundation of the EU is premised on the desire to promote integration and create a single unified market. One of the wider aims of the internal market is to establish and maintain European-wide competition to stimulate the entire economy of the EU for both the domestic and world markets. A competition policy within the overall treaty regime prevents companies from setting up their own rules and obstacles to trade to replace the national rules and obstacles the EU is trying to abolish. The two go hand in hand: you cannot have one without ensuring you have the other. To have prevented the member states on the one hand from restricting the movement of goods just to allow private companies to carve up the EU into national territories or dictate terms and conditions in those divided territories by their agreements and practices would defeat the objectives of the first policy and, vice versa, to prevent companies from artificially dividing the markets but to allow the member states to do so would undermine a competition policy. It is worth noting that some multinational companies are in a better position to divide the market than states. They have the same or greater turnover than the gross or national domestic product of some states. Without regulation, it would be the companies and not the member states which took the decisions on trade flows. In order to retain fair competition in the EU, some form of intervention on the part of the EU is therefore required.

10.2.1 Basic Outline of EU Competition Policy

The broad policy objective remains to maintain and encourage competition for the benefit of the EU and its citizens, to achieve an open and unified market and the integration of the EU, to encourage economic activity amongst small and medium-sized enterprises, and to maximize efficiency by allowing the free flow of goods and resources. Competition law is there also to enhance consumer welfare and to ensure an efficient allocation of resources.

Much of the basis of EU competition policy has been borrowed from the American experience of the concentration in too few hands of power over the marketplace and also to some extent post-war's German concern with the large firms and cartels which had obtained not only too much economic power but also consequently undemocratic political power particularly in the Weimar Republic and in Hitler's Germany.

Thus, in the period following World War II, German attitudes to competition were adopted in Europe. Attitudes were also influenced by the desire to protect emerging and expanding industries and companies and to encourage the rebirth of European industry after the devastation of World War II.

The EU is distinctly interventionist and increasingly so in order to outlaw abuses of industry to the detriment of consumers and the market. However, too much intervention hinders growth and results in inefficient small-scale production which cannot benefit from the economies of scale. Therefore, the EU must tread a middle path. One of the fundamental positions of the competition law to be established was that there should be no barriers against the entry to the market of new companies and industries so that there would be fairness and equality amongst businesses. It was also considered vital to promote European business to compete with American and Japanese capital and business ventures and now the BRICS[2] economies, which benefit from having a huge internal market on their doorsteps. So, the competition policy and rules chosen should also promote the integration of European business, especially small and medium-sized business but at the same time it must be ensured that companies do not become too competitive or over-concentrate and are then able to eliminate competition, thereby starting to dominate a market, or to cooperate in such a way as to act as one unit in the EU to the detriment of consumers and smaller firms. In the EU, regulatory action has been focused more on the larger players in the market rather than the small and medium business enterprises.

One of the problems with EU competition policy is in respect of the multiple objectives which exist. If they are complementary then there is no conflict but if they are in fact different—objectives which require different approaches to achieve them—some difficulties, not least at the legal level, will be experienced.

The overall policy is underpinned by conflicting ideologies of why or even of how it is to be achieved. On the one hand, a market-oriented approach defines the problems of competition as barriers to free trade which must be removed. This approach presupposes there is formal equality of all of individuals (undertakings) in the market and the Commission is merely interested in the regulation of the market per se and not on the part of any particular interest. This leads to difficulties in satisfying all objectives, especially in the area of merger policy. On the other hand, the 'structural approach' concerns changes to the market structure because the inequality of the actors has been recognized. Therefore, the Commission is entitled to regulate and structure the market in order to achieve the goals set by the inclusion of competition policy in the EU, which can lead to difficulties in rationalizing all the decisions. Thus, it is argued, you can easily achieve single objectives such as a competition policy which has the simple aim of preventing distortion in the market. The actual prevention of this may not be simple but the goal is unambiguous and not confused or subject to conflicting priorities. Or, you can have an industry policy to encourage small and medium-sized EU firms, or a customs policy to discourage external imports or rules to ensure the free movement of goods. However, when all these various policies are pursued within one supposed clear objective called competition policy, it will lead to difficulties because there is a need to regulate all of them with an eye on the others. In some quarters, this is seen as one of the steps on the way to political unity; that is, functionalism or the interrelatedness of everything. Furthermore, the particular aims pursued can change from time to time. Sometimes, the structural approach has

---

[2] Brazilian, Russian, Indian, Chinese, and South African.

the upper hand and is criticized because it is regarded as applying more overtly political rather than economic motives, in that it gives too much encouragement to the small and medium-sized business and is too heavy on the large-scale industry which is the only one capable of competing on the world markets with the American, Chinese, Indian, South Korean, Japanese and other rising country industries. Then, at other times, there seems to be more concentration on larger companies or on consumer protection. Thus, the Commission may be interpreting the competition rules to meet changing objectives as politically required, for example to make the rules lighter to promote certain industries so that they can compete worldwide, or tighter to discourage entry by others, or to take account of state-imposed distortions as with the French tobacco industry, or to protect certain agricultural products vital for the CAP. Worker protection and environmental considerations may also play their part. The point of all of this is that if you are not aware that this is happening and only seek to learn the rules, you will have difficulty in rationalizing rules between cases when rationality does not exist or has been undermined by conflicting policy objectives. Hence, the approach here is not to present all the rules in competition policy but just to outline the most important in the context of the leading cases.[3]

10.2.2 **Legislative Outline**

EU competition rules are generally designed to intervene to prevent agreements which fix prices or conditions or the supply of products, to prohibit agreements which carve up territories, and to prevent abuses of market power which have the effect of removing real competition and controlling mergers which would also remove competition. There are also rules to determine lawful and unlawful state aid. As with the free movement of goods, the rules cover all items capable of forming the subject of commercial transactions. The aims are set out in the preamble to the TFEU and Art 3 of TEU and TFEU.

The preamble to the TFEU states that the 'removal of existing obstacles calls for concerted action in order to guarantee steady expansion, balanced trade and fair competition'. Article 3 TEU refers to a 'highly competitive social market' and Art 3(1)(b) TFEU lists among the exclusive competences of the EU 'the establishing of competition rules necessary for the functioning of the internal market'. The previous formulation found in Art 2 EC, containing the requirement that there should be 'a system ensuring that competition in the internal market is not distorted', has been relegated to Protocol 27 attached to the treaties.[4] Given that protocols enjoy the same status as the treaties under Art 51 TEU, it would seem to make no difference to the overall regime and approach to competition law regulation in the EU.

The member state fidelity clause (Art 4(3) TEU) has in the past been pleaded with Arts 3(1)(b) and 101 TFEU as a general principle of law supporting the argument that competition law also applies in respect of the member states and not just undertakings so that they

---

[3] The overall and latest means to reach objectives can be found in the EU Commission competition law website: **http://ec.europa.eu/competition/** and in particular **http://ec.europa.eu/competition/consumers/ why_en.html**.

[4] Protocol (No 27) on the Internal Market and Competition: 'THE HIGH CONTRACTING PARTIES, CONSIDERING that the internal market as set out in Article 3 of the Treaty on European Union includes a system ensuring that competition is not distorted, HAVE AGREED that: To this end, the Union shall, if necessary, take action under the provisions of the Treaties, including under Article 352 of the Treaty on the Functioning of the European Union.'

are prohibited from encouraging or requiring acts or conduct by companies which may distort competition in the EU.

The broad aims are then expanded in three sets of rules: one relating to the activities of legal persons—that is, the business undertakings—which now includes rules on concentrations and mergers; one relating to anti-dumping measures; and, finally, one relating to the activities of the member states, principally, state aid. The rules concerned with private undertakings are further subdivided into: Art 101 TFEU for agreements between cartels involving more than one entity; Art 102 TFEU, concerned with dominant positions, dealing predominantly with one entity but also applicable to one or more undertakings; and the rules applicable to concentrations and mergers. The rules are designed to prevent a number of abuses, which will be considered in detail later. Article 103 TFEU supports Arts 101 and 102 by empowering the Council under a special legislative procedure to adopt regulations and directives to give effect to the principles of competition law in those articles. Article 107 TFEU seeks to prohibit any aid granted by member states which distorts or threatens to distort competition by favouring certain undertakings or the production of certain goods. There are a number of exceptions permitted which will be considered in Section 10.8.

This chapter will commence with the main competition rules of Arts 101 and 102 TFEU applicable, for the most part, to private companies and individuals and the relationship between these two Articles. It will also be concerned with the mergers policy of the EU and briefly with state aid and the procedural law of competition and merger law.

10.2.3 **Application and Interpretation**

The Commission is given the task under Art 105 TFEU and Regulation 1/2003 to ensure that competition in the EU is not distorted. The establishment of competition rules is an exclusive competence of the EU (Art 3(1)(b) TFEU). The application of the rules by the Commission and the interpretation of the rules of the Court of Justice has not been done in isolation by looking at the provision alone, but has been applied in light of the objectives of competition policy and the rules are also applied in light of the general objective of the treaty. In Cases 6–7/73 *Commercial Solvents v Commission*, the Court of Justice held:

> The prohibitions of Articles 85 and 86 EEC [now Arts 101 and 102 TFEU] must be interpreted and applied in the light of Article 3(f) [now Art 3(1)(b) TFEU] of the [EC] Treaty, which provides that the activities of the Community shall include the institution of a system ensuring that competition . . . is not distorted, and Article 2 of the [EC] Treaty which gives the Community the task of promoting 'throughout the Community harmonious development of economic activities'.[5]

Case 26/76 *Metro v Saba (No 1)* is also a good example, whereby the Commission, in pursuit of a goal, also relied on Art 2 EEC to justify particular decisions reached. The agreements in the case were deemed to satisfy competition rules because they helped to maintain employment. This latter case serves as an example of where the Commission, in carrying out its tasks in relation to competition law, is also required to balance this policy with other policies, such as regional development or concern for unemployment, and which may cause it to modify its position on the behaviour of companies. The general economic climate also influences the Commission, particularly in respect of merger policy,

---

[5] Presumably if the Court of Justice feels the need to resort to the general principles to justify a particular ruling it would now simply refer to Protocol 27, noted at n 4.

in that in times of poor economic growth, the Commission may treat mergers as being more acceptable because of the efficiency gains to be achieved and the greater ability the emerging company will have in the world market.

10.3 Article 101 TFEU (Anti-competitive Behaviour)

Article 101 TFEU is designed to tackle the agreements and collusion between companies which result in restrictive practices and anti-competitive behaviour. It sets out the prohibitions and details of the consequences of the failure to observe the prohibitions. Finally, it provides a framework by which exemptions from the prohibitions can be obtained. Article 101(1) TFEU prohibits agreements between undertakings, decisions by associations of undertakings, and concerted practices which may affect trade between the member states, and which have as their object or effect the prevention, restriction, or distortion of competition within the internal market. Article 101(2) TFEU provides that any agreements or decisions prohibited pursuant to Art 101 TFEU shall be automatically void. Article 101(3) TFEU concerns the exemptions to the basic rules but lays down criteria for them which must be met. The agreements must also not be too small such that, under the *de minimis* rule, it is not considered (looked at in Section 10.3.5.4). Article 101 TFEU has been subject to some considerable definition in the jurisprudence of the CoJ and was held to be capable of producing direct effects in Case 127/73 *BRT v SABAM*.

This section will consider in turn the basic definitions; in particular it will consider what is meant by three key terms: 'undertakings', the 'object or effect', and 'effect on trade'.

10.3.1 Article 101(1) Definitions

10.3.1.1 'Undertakings'

The term 'undertakings' has been interpreted to include both natural and legal persons as independent or complementary economic actors. According to the Commission in *Polypropylene Cartel Community v ICI*,[6] this includes any entity engaged in economic or commercial activities and regardless of how it is financed (Case C-41/90 *Höfner and Elser*). Any form of business undertaking is included: artists, as in *Unitel* an opera singer;[7] *AOIP v Beyrard*, an inventor;[8] and groups of companies in *Re Kodak*.[9] If, however, the activity is more in support of public or social services, then they are likely to be held not to be an undertaking carrying out an economic activity caught by Art 101 (or, indeed, Art 102) TFEU, especially where non-profit-making (see Cases C-364/92 *SAT v Eurocontol*, C-264/01 *AOK Bundesverband*, and C-205/03 P *FENIN*).

Groups of companies have caused problems, not least in deciding whether Art 101 or 102 TFEU should apply. As far as Art 101 TFEU is concerned, the Court of Justice addressed this in Case C-73/95 P *Viho Europe BV v Commission* (also known as the *Parker Pen* case). The problem is that if a group of companies, consisting of a parent and a number of wholly owned subsidiaries, are deemed to be one entity, then by definition Art 101 TFEU does not apply. Article 102 may have to be applied but requires the fulfilment of the criteria for such application (considered in Section 10.6). In the *Viho* case, Viho in the Netherlands was refused supply of Parkers Pens by the German Parker company and was referred to the Dutch Parker company. The Court held the Parker Group to be a single

---

[6] Commission Decision [1988] 4 CMLR 347.   [7] Decision 78/516.
[8] [1976] 1 CMLR D14.   [9] [1970] CMLR D9.

entity and that the subsidiaries did not enjoy any real autonomy from the controlling parent company and, whilst their refusal to supply did effectively divide the market, Art 81 EC (now Art 101 TFEU) did not apply to a single entity. The CoJ, though, acknowledged that it might breach Art 82 EC (Art 102 TFEU). However, a group-controlling or group-owning parent company may nevertheless be held liable for the anti-competitive activities of 100 per cent-owned subsidiaries which breach Art 101 TFEU. The Court assumed in Case C-97/08 *AKZO Nobel v Commission* that the parent company exercises a decisive influence over the conduct of the subsidiary unless proved otherwise and could then be lawfully fined by the Commission. The rebuttable presumption is that the higher the percentage holding the parent company has the more likely it is to exert control[10] and even down to a 51 per cent holding.[11] This applies also if the parent company is based outside the EU, as was held in Cases 48–9 and 51–7/69 *ICI v Commission (Aniline Dyes)*, considered also in Section 10.3.1.4.[12]

10.3.1.2 'Agreements'

The term 'agreements' is not limited to written and legally enforceable agreements only, and it is not the form of the agreement that is important from the Commission's point of view but its effect on competition. Therefore, a broad interpretation is given to the term agreement, whether it is termed a decision or a concerted practice. It includes non-binding agreements, as in, for example, the *Polypropylene Decision*, noted earlier.

The terms apply to both horizontal (where the parties are at the same level of the economic process) and vertical (where the parties are at different levels of the economic process) agreements, as is illustrated by the rulings of the Court of Justice in Cases 56 and 58/64 *Consten & Grundig v Commission* and Case 56/65 *Société Technique Minière v Maschinenbau Ulm* (the *STM* case). Gentlemen's agreements consisting of an oral or tacit agreement with nothing committed to writing are, thus, included in this definition: see Case 28/77 *Tepea v Commission*. The Ford Motor Company's refusal to supply right-hand drive cars to German dealers, to stop them being imported into the UK at lower cost, was held to be an agreement or concerted practice with its contractual partners, the dealers (Cases C-25–6/84 *Ford v Commission*). The Court of Justice judgment in the appeal Case C-199/92 P *Hüls AG v Commission* held that to be a concerted practice, there is no need to demonstrate either conduct in the market or that it is restricted competition, merely to demonstrate that there was participation, which is similar to showing the intent to do something. So if no clear agreement, the approach then is to see whether there has been collusion and if that is not obvious or apparent, to see whether the behaviour in the market is such that indicates or points to a breach of Art 101 TFEU. The terms are then, according to the case law, capable of being interpreted very widely.

So-called 'unilateral action', though, on the part of a supplier in dictating terms to distributors would not normally breach Art 101 unless it can be shown there was some sort of agreement with the policy or action of the supplier. In Case C-2–3/01 P *Commission v Bayer*, an agreement was not found to exist by the CoJ that the distributors in France and Spain of the drug Adalat, manufactured by Bayer, stopped exporting to the UK. Supplies to those distributors had been reduced by Bayer. Where a supplier's policy is followed

---

[10] See inter alia Case T-299/08 *Elf Aquitaine v Commission* [2011] ECR II-2149, Case C-97/08 P *Akzo Nobel v Commission* [2009] ECR I-8237.

[11] Cases 6–7/73 *Commercial Solvents v Commission* [1974] ECR 223.

[12] Also confirmed in Cases 89, 104, 114, 116–17, and 125–9/85 *Ahlstrom* and known as the *Woodpulp* cases.

voluntarily, as in Case C-74/04 P *Commission v Volkswagen*, this also does not amount to an agreement for the purposes of Art 101 TFEU.

10.3.1.3 'Decisions by Associations of Undertakings'

Decisions by associations of undertakings includes the coordinating activities of a trade association which has been held liable for behaviour by its members in *AROW v BNIC*,[13] whereby the Bureau National Interprofessionel de Cognac was fined because it had fixed a minimum distribution price for cognac, arguing that this was necessary to guarantee quality. The Commission decided that, given all the other quality-control measures which existed in the cognac industry, this argument could not be sustained.

Non-binding recommendations made by trade associations may also amount to decisions as held in Case 8/72 *Vereeniging van Cementhandelaren v Commission* (the *Cement Association* case) and Case 96/82 *IAZ International Belgium NV v Commission*. In the latter, an association of water supply undertakings recommended its members not to connect dishwasher machines to the mains system unless they had a label supplied by the Belgian association of dishwasher manufacturers indicating that they complied with relevant Belgian standards. The Court of Justice upheld the Commission's view that this recommendation, despite the fact that it was not binding, could restrict competition since its effect was to discriminate against appliances produced in other member states.

Professional bodies which regulate the activities of their members in a particular way may also come within the definition of associations as was made clear by the Commission in Case C-309/99 *Wouters*, in which the Dutch Bar Association sought to prohibit multi-disciplinary practices This was a breach of Art 85 EC (now Art 101 TFEU).[14]

10.3.1.4 'Concerted Practices'

The term 'concerted practice' is potentially very broad and includes many forms of informal collusion between undertakings. An important example of a 'concerted practice' is found in Cases 48–9, and 51–7/69 *ICI v Commission (Aniline Dyes)*. ICI was the first among a number of undertakings, accounting for 85 per cent of the market, to raise prices. The companies all said that the price coordination was simply a reflection of parallel behaviour in an oligopolistic market, where each producer followed the price leader, very often seen, for example, with petrol prices. The Court of Justice held that this was a concerted practice arising out of coordination which becomes apparent from the behaviour of the participants, and which was designed to replace the risk of competition and the hazards of competitors' spontaneous reactions by cooperation constituting a concerted practice. This case is also a precedent for the extraterritorial application of the competition rules, with the head office of ICI being in the UK, at the time of the facts of the case outside the EEC; nevertheless, it was fined for activities which affected trade within the then EEC.

In Cases 40–8, 50, 54–56, 111, and 113–14/73 *Suiker Unie (Sugar Union) v Commission*, the Community's main sugar producers had made deliveries in the Netherlands only, with the assent of the producers in that country, so as to weaken considerably the competitive pressure which unrestricted sugar imports would have engendered. They said that they had not agreed to any plan to that effect, and hence there was no concerted practice.

[13] OJ 1982 L379/1, [1983] 2 CMLR 240.

[14] See also the Commission Communication on Competition in Professional Services (COM (2004) 83 final (09.02.2004) and two follow-up reports: Professional Service—scope for more reform (COM (2005) 405 final (05.09.2005)) and Report on Progress made by Member States (SEC (2005) 1064 (05.09.2005)). See http://eur-lex.europa.eu/LexUriServ/LexUriServ.do?uri=CELEX:52005DC0405:EN:NOT and http://ec.europa.eu/competition/sectors/professional_services/reports/annex.pdf.

The Court of Justice held that there was no need for an actual plan and a concerted practice included 'any direct or indirect contact between such operators, the object or effect of which is either to influence the conduct on the market of an actual or potential competitor or to disclose to such a competitor the course of conduct which they themselves have decided to adopt or contemplate adopting on the market'.

A concerted practice is present when it enables the firms concerned to set positions which they have secured to the detriment of free movement of goods in the internal market and the freedom of consumers to choose their suppliers. Each trader must independently decide on the policy it proposes to follow on the internal market. This requirement does not deny traders the right to adapt their conduct to the way their competitors are behaving or are likely to behave but it does rule out any direct or indirect contact where the object or effect is to influence the conduct of an existing or potential market competitor or to reveal to it market policy decisions or intentions. However, in Cases C-89, 104, 114, 116–17/85, and 125–9/85 *Ahlström Oy et al v Commission* (the *Woodpulp Cartel* cases), the Court of Justice held that the burden be placed on the Commission to prove a concerted practice by establishing a 'firm, precise and consistent body of evidence' that a concerted practice existed. Parallel price increases would not satisfy this unless there was no other plausible explanation for them. Agreements which were taken by the parties within their trade association to fix recommended prices was not upheld as restricting competition contrary to Art 81(1) EC (now Art 101 TFEU). Here, the price increases could be explained by the fact that there was an oligopolistic market in which prices set by the limited number of producers in the market would tend to follow each other closely, without there being any understanding or agreement.

Even the supply of information such as future pricing strategies by one party, especially if a leading party in the market, at a meeting can amount to being an agreement of concerted practice as, in the view of the Court, the other parties could not fail to take account of the information. It would thus breach Art 101 TFEU.[15]

Article 101 TFEU applies to both horizontal and vertical agreements and concerted practices; an example of the latter can be seen in the following case. Even unilateral conduct on the part of a manufacturer has been deemed by the Court of Justice to be capable of amounting to an agreement or a concerted practice. In Cases 25–6/84 *Ford v Commission*, until May 1982, Ford of Germany supplied to its German dealers a quantity of right-hand drive cars for sale in the Federal Republic. Since spring 1981, there had been a great increase in demand for right-hand drive cars because German prices were considerably lower than those in Britain. Ford of Germany became concerned about the effects of this on the position of Ford Britain and notified the German dealers that, as from 1 May 1982, it would no longer accept their orders for right-hand drive cars, and all such cars would have to be purchased in Britain. The Commission decided that the dealer agreement and the termination of deliveries contravened Art 81(1) EC (now Art 101 TFEU). Ford argued that the cessation of deliveries was a unilateral act not caught by Art 81(1) EC. The CoJ rejected this argument (para [21]) stating that 'such a decision forms part of the contractual relations between the undertaking and its dealers. Indeed, admission to the Ford dealer network implies acceptance by the contracting parties of the policy pursued by Ford with regard to the models to be delivered to the German market.' The instruction

---

[15] The Commission has now issued a guideline note on how the exchange of information may be judged in 'Guidelines on the applicability of Article 101 of the Treaty on the Functioning of the European Union to horizontal co-operation agreements' (OJ 2007 C11/1), p 13: General Principles on Competitive Assessment of Information Exchange.

was held to form part of the contractual relations between the undertaking and its dealers and, hence, the restriction was held to be a breach of Art 81 EC (Art 101 TFEU).

10.3.2 **The Object or Effect of Restricting or Distorting Competition**

An agreement or practice is prohibited if it has either the object or effect of preventing, restricting, or distorting competition. Separated by 'or', in practice both object *and* effect must be considered but this is not a cumulative test; either will suffice but whilst one may be satisfied, the other element may not be so serious as to restrict or distort competition sufficiently to be held in breach of the treaty.

10.3.2.1 **Object or Effect**

Even if, as a result of a consideration of the terms of the agreement, it is clear that the object is to restrict competition, on the face of it, it will be contrary to Art 101 TFEU. However, it may still be necessary to consider the economic effects of the agreement to determine whether it is caught by Art 101 TFEU, as it may fall within the *de minimis* doctrine, considered later, or it may have no effect on trade between the member states. In Case C-8/08 *T-Mobile*, the Court of Justice held that when an agreement will inevitably result in an injury to normal competition, it will be regarded as having an anti-competitive object regardless or not of whether it actually restricts competition, e.g. price fixing agreements. If the object though is not to distort competition, then it must be seen if its effect is restrictive. See also Case 56/65 *STM* in which the Court held that 'It must be possible to foresee with a sufficient degree of probability on the basis of a set of objective factors of law or fact that the agreement in question may have an influence, direct or indirect, actual or potential, on the pattern of trade between member states'. The Court also held that:

> Where, however, an analysis . . . does not reveal the effect on competition to be sufficiently deleterious, the consequences of the agreement should then be considered and for it to be caught by the prohibition it is then necessary to find that those factors are present which show that competition has in fact been prevented or restricted or distorted to an appreciable extent.

If it is not established that the object of the agreement or practice is to restrict or distort competition, it is necessary for the Commission to undertake an examination of the effect of the agreement on the market.

In Case 23/67 *Brasserie de Haecht v Wilkin*, the Court of Justice said that the agreement, decision, or concerted practice had to be examined in the context of the market in which it operated and in the context of the effects surrounding its implementation. This entails scrutiny of the relevant product market and the relevant geographical market, the impact of national laws upon competition, the existence of intellectual property rights, and the level of competition on the rest of the market and the behaviour of other competitors. If the effect is insignificant, it is likely to be held not to distort the market enough to breach Art 101 TFEU. See now the Commission clarification of this *de minimis* doctrine.[16] The Commission therefore has to pay close attention to the definition of the market for the purposes of competition law. As a result of the case law of the Court of Justice, the

---

[16] Commission Notice on Agreements of Minor Importance which Do Not Appreciably Restrict Competition under Art 81(1) of the Treaty Establishing the European Community (now 101 TFEU) (OJ 2001 C368/1). See Section 10.3.5.4.

Commission presented its methodology in a Notice on the Definition of the Relevant Market.[17]

10.3.3 **Types of Prohibited Agreements**

Article 101(1) TFEU lists particular examples of such agreements, which have as their object the restriction of competition. The non-exhaustive list includes:

(a) directly or indirectly fix purchase or selling prices or any other unfair trading conditions (These are most often seen in the form of minimum price-fixing arrangements; see, for example, Case 8/72 *Cement Association* or the Decision in *Hennessy/Henkel*,[18] in which minimum and maximum prices were laid down, which breached Art 81 EC (now Art 101 TFEU). 'Other trading conditions' includes things like requiring distributors or retailers to provide suitable premises, or displays or training or minimum stocks or holding certain promotions. In return, the retailer may be guaranteed a specific protected area. In Case 26/76 *Metro*, it was held that such systems would not breach Art 81 EC provided that selection of dealers was done objectively. In Case 161/84 *Pronuptia v Schillgalis*, even a requirement that 80 per cent of wedding dresses were purchased from Pronuptia was held to be acceptable in order to protect the know-how and reputation of the franchisor.)

(b) limit or control production, markets, technical development, or investment; most often seen in market-sharing agreements (see, for example, market partitioning in Cases 56 and 58/64 *Consten and Grundig* and *Quinine Cartel*)

(c) share markets or sources of supply (see also *Consten and Grundig*)

(d) apply dissimilar conditions to equivalent transactions with other trading parties, thereby placing them at a competitive disadvantage (see, for example, Case 26/76 *Metro v Commission* where a difference in prices could be justified by objective factors such as volume of purchases or transport costs)

(e) make the conclusion of contracts subject to the acceptance by the other parties of supplementary obligations which, by their nature or according to commercial usage, have no connection with the subject of such contracts. An example of the last of the conditions listed would be the imposition by a producer on a distributor of an export ban (see the *Henessy/Henkel* Decision in which a clause prohibiting the sale of competing products was held to be acceptable but not a clause prohibiting the sale of any other product).

10.3.4 **Which May Affect Trade between Member States**

To be caught by the provisions of Art 101 TFEU, the practice complained of must be capable of affecting EU trade. Trade is given a wide definition and encompasses the production and distribution of goods, trade in agricultural produce, the services sector (including banking insurance and professional services), and even opera singers have been held to be involved in trade.

In Cases 56 and 58/64 *Consten and Grundig*, the Court of Justice stated that this phrase is intended to set the boundary between the areas covered by Community law and the law of the member states. It held that the question to be asked is whether it is probable

---

[17] OJ 1997 C372/5.   [18] [1981] 1 CMLR 601.

in law or fact that the agreement in question may have an influence, direct or indirect, actual or potential, on the pattern of trade between member states to hinder the attainment of a single market. The case was concerned with exclusive territorial sales licences which served to encourage the volume of trade. Consten and Grundig had granted a distributor a sole representation agreement for the whole of France, Saar, and Corsica. The distributor undertook not to sell similar articles liable to compete with the goods of the contract and not to deliver, either directly or indirectly, for or to other countries from the contract territory. An analogous prohibition was imposed on concessionaires from other territories. The result was to grant absolute territorial protection, and to insulate the French market against parallel imports. The result in this case was that it actually promoted trade. The Court of Justice held that the fact that an agreement encourages an increase, even a large one, in the volume of trade between states is not sufficient to exclude the possibility that the agreement may affect trade between member states. Although this may seem strange, the requirement that the agreement must affect inter-state trade goes to the jurisdiction of EU law. The contract between Grundig and Consten, on the one hand by preventing undertakings other than Consten from importing Grundig products into France, and on the other by prohibiting Consten from re-exporting those products to other countries of the common market, indisputably adversely affected the flow of trade between the member states. These limitations on the freedom of trade were enough to satisfy the requirement in question.

In Case 56/65, the *STM* case, in similar terms to that seen in the *Dassonville* case in the free movement of goods in Chapter 8, the Court of Justice provided the basic test that if the agreement may have an influence, direct or indirect, actual or potential, it would satisfy this requirement.

In Case 23/67 *Brasserie de Haecht SA v Wilkin and Wilkin*, network or series agreements were considered. In the case, the brewery had entered into a contract whereby it had furnished the Wilkins' cafe and had granted several loans. The agreement stipulated that the Wilkins were obliged to obtain all their supplies of liquor, beer, and soft drinks for the cafe and for their own personal use exclusively from the de Haecht brewery. They had purchased supplies of liquor from other undertakings and the brewery had sought to rescind the contract and claim repayment of the loans, return of the furniture, and damages. The Tribunal de Commerce asked the Court of Justice whether to judge the agreement on its own or in light of all such agreements. The CoJ ruled that indeed the 'economic and legal context' had to be taken into account, such as in this case the fact that the arrangement tying the cafe proprietors to receiving their beer and other drink supplies from one brewery was one which was extensively used, and the extensive use of such contracts would adversely affect competition in the Community at large. The CoJ further ruled that in order to satisfy the 'capable of affecting trade between member states' requirement:

> it must be possible for the agreement, decision or practice, viewed objectively to appear to be capable of having some influence, direct or indirect on trade between member states, partition the market, and hampering the economic interpenetration sought by the Treaty. When this point is considered the agreement, decision or practice cannot therefore be isolated from the others of which it is one.

Therefore, if it forms a series of agreements, a single contract should not just be considered on its own.

In Case 8/72 *Vereniging van Cementhandelaren v Commission*, the members of a Dutch cement dealers association argued that since the cartel was purely national in its activities, limited to the territory of the Netherlands, it could not be caught by Art 81(1) EC (now

Art 101 TFEU). The Court of Justice upheld the Commission decision declaring that an agreement extending over the whole of the territory of a member state, by its very nature, has the effect of reinforcing the compartmentalization of markets on a national basis.[19] Therefore, one country on its own can be used to establish an effect on trade between member states. The ability to affect trade between members can be direct or indirect, actual or potential.[20]

10.3.5 Exemptions from Art 101(1) TFEU

Apart from the justification considered later under Art 101(3) TFEU, certain agreements have been deemed by the Court of Justice and Commission not to fall within the category of a 'restriction of competition'. These judicial exemptions from the application of Art 101 are also referred to as coming within a type of 'rule of reason' in competition law, in that the Court (the General Court which hears these cases at first instance) will balance the effects of an agreement to see whether the alleged benefits outweigh the anti-competitive effects. However, the Court of First Instance (CFI, now General Court) appeared clearly to rule out the existence of a rule of reason in EU competition law in Case T-112/99 *Metropole Television v Commission* whilst confirming, nevertheless, that the Court's approach is to take account of the actual conditions and economic context in which the agreement operates. Hence some public policy considerations may apply even though they may be categorized as coming within an overall 'rule of reason', for example, where on balance social policy or agricultural policy considerations take priority over a possible breach of competition law.[21]

Prior case law on Art 101(3) TFEU has discussed a number of circumstances which may, though, be taken into account in assessing whether a particular agreement which may have the effect of restricting competition, does not breach Art 101 TFEU.

10.3.5.1 Objective Necessity

There are cases where the restrictions are objectively necessary for the performance of a particular type of contract, as in franchising agreements. See Case 161/84 *Pronuptia de Paris v Schillgalis*, in which the Court of Justice held that the compatibility of distribution franchise agreements with Art 81(1) EC (now Art 101 TFEU) depended on the clauses contained in the agreements and on the economic context in which they are included.

Clauses which were indispensable to prevent the know-how and assistance provided by the franchisor from benefiting competitors and clauses which implemented the control necessary for the preservation of the identity and reputation of the organization represented in the trademark, did not constitute restrictions on competition within the meaning of Art 81(1) EC. The fact that the franchisor communicated suggested prices to the franchisee did not constitute a restriction on competition, on condition that there has not been a concerted practice between the franchises with a view to effective application of those prices. However, clauses which fixed prices or which affected a partitioning of markets between franchisor and franchisee or between franchises and were capable of affecting trade between member states, constituted restrictions on competition contrary to

---

[19] See also the Decisions in *Re Vacuum Interrupters* [1977] 1 CMLR D67 and *Re Italian Flat Glass* [1982] 3 CMLR 366 supporting Case 8/72.

[20] Case C-238/05 *Asnef-Equifax* [2006] ECR I-11125.

[21] For social policy see Case C-67/96 *Albany International* [1999] ECR I-5751 concerning employment collective agreements and Art 42 TFEU and Regulation 1184/2006 (OJ 2006 L214/7) exempting some food production agreements from the application of Art 101 TFEU.

Art 81(1) EC. Very many of these franchise agreements, including Pronuptia's, were granted individual exemption under Art 81(3) EC (now Art 101 TFEU) before the modernization in 2004 of this area of competition law.

10.3.5.2 High Commercial Risks

The Court of Justice has held that where the commercial risk undertaken by a distributor, licensee, or franchise is so great, some exclusivity must be conferred on him to induce him into the market. Case 56/65 *STM v Maschinenbau* is an example of this. In this case the French company La Société Technique Minière purchased 37 earth-levelling machines, and were given exclusive sales rights for the territory of France. The agreement with the producers, Maschinenbau Ulm, stipulated that they could only sell other goods to compete with these levelling machines with the consent of Maschinenbau Ulm. The agreement left STM entitled to export the machines. The Court of Justice held that in order to assess the effect of the agreement on competition, examination should take place of the severity of the clause granting the exclusive right; the nature and quantity of the products which are the subject matter of the agreement; the position of the grantor and the concessionaire on the market for the products in question; the number of parties to the agreements; and the possibilities left for other commercial currents upon the same products by means of re-exports and parallel imports. The Court of Justice held that due to the high cost of the product and its specialized nature, the agreements would not offend Art 81 EC (now Art 101 TFEU).

10.3.5.3 Quality Control

Cases involving selective distribution systems, such as in Case 26/76 *Metro v Commission*, to ensure the quality of sales and service, to benefit the consumer in terms of safety of electrical goods, and to maintain employment in an important industry would not breach Art 81 EC (now Art 101 TFEU) even though that might mean supplies to other low-price distributors might be restricted and higher prices maintained. Price competition was recognized as not the only form of competition in the market. The restrictions could promote other forms of competition such as service and after-sales commitment, particularly as the consumer still had sufficient choice of supplier.

10.3.5.4 The *De Minimis* Doctrine

The doctrine of *de minimis* means some agreements which affect competition may nevertheless not be caught by Art 101 TFEU because they do not have an appreciable effect on intra-Community trade. It was first formulated in Case 5/69 *Volk v Vervaecke*, where Volk granted an exclusive dealership to Vervaecke for washing machines in the Belgian and Luxembourg market. Vervaecke undertook to place a monthly order for 80 appliances, and Volk undertook to protect Vervaecke's sales territory against parallel imports. There was a dispute as to the nature of the agreement and the Court of Justice held that an agreement falls outside the scope of Art 81(1) EC (now Art 101 TFEU) when it has only an insignificant effect on the market, taking into account the weak position which the parties concerned have on the market of the product in question. Consequently, an exclusive dealing agreement, even with absolute territorial protection, may, having regard to the weak position of the persons concerned in the market in question and in the area covered by the absolute protection, escape the prohibition; that is, it represented too small an effect significantly to affect competition and, thus, did not fall within Art 101(1) TFEU. From a strict reading of the article, this does not support it; that is, other motives underpin the policy of the Commission and the judgment of the Court, for example not to suppress small and medium-sized businesses from expanding or only restricting small business when predatory.

In 2001, the Commission provided an updated Notice on Agreements of Minor Importance which Do Not Appreciably Restrict Competition[22] setting out the criteria which will be used in determining whether a practice may affect trade between member states. The basic criterion is that the undertakings have less than a 10 per cent market share in the EU as a whole. In line with a general concern which has arisen and has been responded to by the Commission about vertical agreements, the threshold for vertical agreements has been raised to 15 per cent of market share. It is 10 per cent for horizontal agreements. Market share below this removes agreements from the scope of Art 101 TFEU, unless they are serious or intended breaches of the competition rules or they fix prices. Even above these thresholds, small and medium-sized enterprise agreements will be considered leniently by the Commission. Although such notices are not binding in law and certainly cannot amend the treaty provisions, they are a clear indication that, providing an agreement falls within the exception allowed, the Commission will not take action under the competition rules. There is general concern about the rigidity of the present application of the rules to vertical agreements (see *Consten and Grundig*). There is flexibility in applying the Commission notice and that even where the threshold has been exceeded, at least marginally, the Commission and Court are able still to review generally the economic effect of an agreement.[23]

The same pressures also led to the enactment of the block exemptions, which are discussed in Section 10.5.3.

Finally, in respect of a number of the issues noted earlier, Case C-234/89 *Delimitis v Henniger Bräu* should be considered. In this case a tied-in contract between *Delimitis* and a brewery, which on its own would certainly fall within the *de minimis* doctrine, was argued to be part of a network of similar agreements and thus subject to Art 81 EC (now Art 101 TFEU). The CoJ observed the benefits to both parties of tied agreements and concluded that the object was not to restrict competition but that the cumulative effect, when all such agreements were taken into account, might be to restrict competition and make market entry difficult if not impossible unless within a tied relationship.[24] Hence, regardless of whether there is a rule of reason or not, all the consequences of an agreement, whether restrictive or not, will form part of the analysis of whether the agreement breaches Art 101.

10.4 Article 101(2) TFEU and the Consequence of a Breach

Article 101(2) TFEU provides that 'Any agreements or decisions prohibited pursuant to this Article shall be automatically void'. In Case 56/65 *STM v Maschinenbau Ulm*, the Court of Justice held that this provision only applies to those parts of the agreement

---

[22] OJ 2001 C368/13 which replaces the previous 1997 Notice (OJ 1997 C372/13) but is itself now under review: **http://ec.europa.eu/competition/consultations/2013_de_minimis_notice/de_minimis_notice_en.pdf**.

[23] See Cases T-374–5/94 *European Night Services* [1998] ECR II-3141.

[24] In those circumstances, the 2001 minor importance reduces the market share to 5% to reflect such reasoning. See point 8, reproduced in N. Foster (ed), *Blackstone's EU Treaties & Legislation*, latest edition, Oxford University Press, Oxford.

affected by the prohibition in Art 81(1) EC (now Art 101 TFEU) or to the agreement as a whole if those parts are not severable from the agreement itself.

10.5 Article 101(3) TFEU Exemptions

In advance of the Court of Justice-developed grounds, whereby certain agreements have been held not to constitute a restriction of competition, and which were considered under Section 10.3.5, the treaty had provided in Art 101(3) certain circumstances where Art 101(1) will not apply to an agreement or concerted practice. Article 101(3) circumstances where Art 101(1) will not apply to an agreement or concerted practice:

> which contributes to improving the production or distribution of goods or to promoting technical or economic progress, while allowing consumers a fair share of the resulting benefit, and which does not:

(a) impose on the undertakings concerned restrictions which are not indispensable to the attainment of these objectives;

(b) afford such undertakings the possibility of eliminating competition in respect of a substantial part of the products in question.

They are most likely to apply to individual agreements but can also apply to all types of agreement in the same way as block exemptions as they both outline the criteria by which agreements may be judged to comply with or to be contrary to the competition law provisions. If the particular agreement envisaged falls within a block exemption, considered in Section 10.5.3, it will save an individual trying to determine whether it might fall within Art 101(3) and thus breach Art 101 or not.[25]

10.5.1 Individual Notification

Previously, and for most of the life of the Communities it was the first and main way to obtain an exemption, parties to an agreement must have made an individual notification to the Commission. Failure to notify meant that the agreement would have been void and the parties would have been liable to fines. Once notified, the Commission considered whether the agreement could have been exempted and issued an official decision which could be challenged under Art 230 EC (now Art 263 TFEU) before the CFI (now the General Court). However, because the Commission simply could not investigate and come to a decision on all the applications made, it dealt with them very often by the so-called comfort letter which provided an immunity from fines, considered in the following section. This led, though, to the revision of this procedure which was contained in a new enforcement of competition law regulation (Regulation 1/2003[26]) which came into force on 1 May 2004 and abolished the individual notification. This was done to remove the drain on resources that this procedure was for the Commission and coincided with ten new member states joining in 2004, which would have imposed even greater demands on the Commission. The decision-making was handed over to the national competition law authorities and facilitated this by expressly making Art 81(3) EC (now Art 101 TFEU) directly effective so that any disputes can be adjudicated in the national courts. Essentially,

---

[25] The Commission has published guidelines for the application of Art 101(3): **http://ec.europa.eu/competition/antitrust/legislation/art101_3_en.html** (OJ 2004 C101/97).

[26] OJ 2003 L1/1.

the private parties will decide if their agreement falls within the legal exceptions (rather than the previous exemptions) in Art 101 TFEU, which decision can then be challenged and defended in the national courts. To assist parties in this, the Commission has issued guidelines on the application of Art 81(3) EC (now Art 101 TFEU).[27] Novel and uncertain cases may still find their way to the Commission for a decision in a procedure under Art 10 of Regulation 1/2003.[28] A further policy initiative that was undertaken to deal with the quantity of applications was the issuing of block exemptions, which if undertakings ensured that their agreement was in compliance, would exempt the application of Art 101 TFEU to those agreements. These are considered later.

10.5.2 **Negative Clearance and Comfort Letters**

Although this no longer applies, it is very useful to know. The previous notification regime put strain on the time and resources of the Commission, so as an alternative to taking every individual application for exemption through to a decision, the Commission frequently settled cases informally by way of a so-called comfort letter. A comfort letter was simply a notification to the parties that, in the Commission's opinion, the agreement does not infringe Art 101(1) TFEU or that it qualifies for exemption. The Commission then closes the file after sending the comfort letter. These comfort letters do not bind the national courts or produce legal effects in national law or EU law. This was made clear in a series of cases involving perfume manufacturers, Cases 253/78 and 1–3/79 *Guerlain SA, Rochas SA, Lanvin SA and Nina Ricci SA*. Obviously, a statement of this nature from the Commission would be of persuasive authority, but a national court would not necessarily be bound by it. In an action by French shops which were unable to get supplies from Lancôme and Guerlain, the Court of Justice rejected the view that the comfort letters provided a defence to such actions against the refusal to supply. This, too, has now been replaced by the system of assuming that the agreement constitutes a legal exception by the parties, subject to a possible challenge in the national courts and reference to the General Court where relevant, thus comfort letters will no longer be needed or issued.

Whilst to some extent of historical interest only, there remain a lot of previous agreements still subject to comfort letters or provisional validity. This was considered in Case C-39/96 *Koninklijke Vereeniging ter Bevordering van de Belangen des Boekhandels v Free Record Shop BV*, and concerns competition agreements which were concluded prior to Regulation 17 and notified to the Commission prior to the deadline of 1 November 1962. Normally such agreements would carry provisional validity until the Commission had either given positive clearance or had taken a negative decision holding them to be contrary to EC law. Many agreements similar to this one about the retail price maintenance for books have continued in this legal limbo ever since. The Commission is simply unable to investigate all of them and many are left without interference. The agreement in question, however, had been challenged as contrary to Art 81 EC (now Art 101 TFEU) by a shop selling below the imposed retail price. Having lain dormant for so long, questions about the continued validity were raised by the national court. The Court of Justice held that until the Commission decides one way or the other the agreement remains provisionally valid even if it has been amended but only insofar as the amendments render the agreement less restrictive. More restrictive amendments would end the validity unless

---

[27] OJ 2004 C101/97.
[28] There are guidelines: Notice on Informal Guidance Relating to Novel Questions Concerning Arts 81 and 82 of the EC Treaty that Arise in Individual Cases (Guidance Letters) (OJ 2004 C101/78).

these were severable from the original agreement. It is to be noted that Art 8 of the otherwise repealed Regulation 17, which permits the Commission to amend or revoke previous decisions, remains in force.[29]

From May 2004, individual companies must decide whether an agreement complies with the four conditions specified in Art 101(3) TFEU and if they conclude that they do, there is no need to take any further action or to notify the Commission or national competition authorities. However, in case of doubt a new procedure, not too dissimilar to the negative clearance and comfort letter of old, noted earlier, has been introduced by which guidance on grey area agreements can be sought from the Commission. The Commission may issue this guidance in a 'guidance letter' but only if the situation is genuinely novel and not coming within any previous case law on decisions dealing with block exemptions, considered next.

10.5.3 **Block Exemptions**

In order to avoid unnecessary work for all involved, companies and the Commission, it was decided that certain categories of common or typical types of commercial agreement, which were considered not to infringe free and fair competition could be exempted from the prohibition in Art 81(2) EC (now Art 101 TFEU) by virtue of a block exemption, sometimes within certain industries or areas. In such cases, there was no need to apply for individual notification. In particular, vertical agreements were considered as more beneficial than harmful to competition in that they often increase investment in the specialization and knowledge of certain products which is of benefit to the ultimate consumers of the products. The block exemptions set out types of restriction or provision which do not infringe Art 101(1) TFEU or would be exempted. The following are now the main block exemptions and guidelines following the revision and reissue in 2010–11:

Regulation 330/2010[30] on vertical agreements and concerted practices

Regulation 1217/2010[31] on research and development agreements

Regulation 1218/2010[32] on specialization agreements

Regulation 461/2010[33] on distribution agreements in respect of motor vehicles

Regulation 772/2004 (OJ 2004 L123/18) on technology transfer agreements.

There are a number of guides now published by the Commission which help to clarify the block exemptions.[34]

The pattern of these block exemptions is to provide examples of agreements and clauses that are permitted, those which are expressly forbidden, and those which, depending on the actual details contained within, may or may not offend competition law. The first category means that there is no need to take any action or inform the Commission. Agreements of clauses coming within the second category render the entire agreement in breach of Art 101 TFEU and liable to a fine, and the third type under the previous regime required notification and clearance from the Commission and are those which would

---

[29] See N. Foster (ed), *EU Treaties and Legislation*, latest edn, Oxford University Press, Oxford.
[30] OJ 2010 L102/1.   [31] OJ 2010 L335/36.   [32] OJ 2010 L335/43.   [33] OJ 2010 L129/52.
[34] See, for examples, in addition to the general guideline on horizontal agreements in n 11, the 2010 Guidelines on Vertical Restraints (OJ 2010 C83/88) and Guidelines on the Application of Art 81 of the EC Treaty to Technology Transfer Agreements (OJ 2004 C101/2). Further details in the Commission website: **http://ec.europa.eu/competition/antitrust/legislation/legislation.html**.

now probably fall to be considered as to whether they come within the new concept of the legal exception.

Most of the regulations listed are replacements for previous regulations which were revised in light of practical application and in response to criticisms made by the various industries and companies affected. The new regulations now focus more on market share and market power in relation to the particular agreements rather than the agreements themselves. For example, for companies with less than a 30 per cent market share, Regulation 330/2010 removes the need to make an assessment as to whether their agreements fall within the competition law rules, thus further reducing the bureaucratic workload on the part of companies and the Commission. Without going into unnecessary detail in this introduction, the Vertical Agreements Regulation provides in:

- Art 1—definitions of what is meant by vertical agreements covered by the block exemption
- Art 2—that vertical agreements meeting this are exempt from Art 101
- Art 3—the 30 per cent market share threshold
- Art 4—the hard-core restrictions which do not receive exemption
- Art 5—that certain clauses of long-term (over five years) or indefinite duration which restrict competition are prohibited.

Any restrictions which fall within Art 4 render the agreement void and unenforceable, whereas those which offend Art 5 can be severed or amended. In what is now, with the various exemptions in place, a rare case, *JCB* was found to infringe Art 81 EC (now Art 101 TFEU) by its restrictive distribution agreement and not to be exempted by Regulation 2790/1999 (now 330/2010) because its market share was between 40 and 45 per cent; see Case T-67/01 *JCB v Commission*.

10.6 Article 102 TFEU and the Abuse of a Dominant Position

Article 102 TFEU applies where individual organizations have a near monopoly position or share an oligopolistic market with a small number of other companies and take unfair advantage of this position to the detriment of the market, other companies, and the end-consumers. Companies with a large market share, about 40 per cent, do not infringe Art 102 TFEU by that alone but are at the position where their behaviour needs to be closely monitored in case their practices stray into abuse. Such large and larger market shares bring with them a responsibility under competition law to act only in ways which do not distort or restrict the competitive market in which their large share or dominance exists.

Article 102 TFEU proscribes 'Any abuse by one or more undertakings of a dominant position within the internal market or in a substantial part of it shall be prohibited as incompatible with the internal market in so far as it may affect trade between member states'. Article 102 TFEU then goes on to give specific examples of such abuse, considered later.

10.6.1 Article 102 TFEU Requirements

For Art 102 TFEU to be applicable, there must be domination of the internal market or a substantial part of it by one or more undertakings. This requires a definition of the relevant market by reference to both the product and the geographical area and to a lesser extent the temporal market. The necessary requirements are finding that a dominant position exists within a relevant market, and that there has been abuse of the dominant market which has affected trade between member states. The leading and best case for many of the points and issues arising from Art 102 TFEU is Case 27/76 *United Brands v Commission* which will be referred to frequently in the following sections.

Hence Art 102 TFEU requires these essential elements to be considered: an undertaking (or undertakings) which is (or are) in a dominant position within the relevant markets; the 'abuse' of that dominant position; which then affects or has the potential to affect trade between Member States.

10.6.2 **Definition of Undertakings**

The understanding of the term 'undertaking' rather than just concerning an individual company has been extended. The CFI (now the General Court) confirmed in Cases T-68 and 77–8/89 *Re: Italian Flat Glass* that Art 82 EC (now Art 102 TFEU) could apply to activities of more than one undertaking where the companies together could constitute a dominant position. Furthermore, oligopolies (a small number of competing companies in a particular market) may also find their activities being considered under the Merger Regulation, considered in the text later.

10.6.2.1 **A Dominant Position**

The *United Brands* case arose out of a complaint by a number of banana importers about the activities of United Brands Company (UBC). Some of the facts of this case are as follows (they might put you off bananas!). Bananas are picked and transported whilst green and only begin to ripen after they have been gassed, which usually takes place when they reach the country in which they are to be sold. UBC grew, shipped, and distributed bananas requiring its distributors/ripeners not to sell on bananas whilst still green (the green-banana clause). It charged distributors in different member states different prices, sometimes by as much as 138 per cent without objective justification. UBC had also refused to supply a Danish company with Chiquita bananas because they had advertised another brand. As a result of these activities (and others), the Commission considered United Brands to have infringed Art 82 EC (now Art 102 TFEU) and imposed a fine of 1 million units of account (the forerunner of the ecu and euro). UBC sought the annulment of the decision and fine before the Court of Justice.

The issues for the Court of Justice were: the proof of dominance in the market and the abuse of this which affected trade. It defined a dominant position as:

> a position of economic strength enjoyed by an undertaking which enables it to hinder the maintenance of effective competition on the relevant market by allowing it to behave to an appreciable extent independently of its competitors and customers and ultimately of consumers.

This takes us immediately on to the next points of determining the relevant markets, by defining the product market and the geographical market area. Sometimes, the temporal market must be defined, in which dominance has to exist over a period of time (Cases 6–7/73 *Commercial Solvents*). This is more relevant in markets which change over time, which most markets do not. These are important questions as the definition is very often crucial to determining whether dominance exists. More recently, in line with general reforms to competition law, other factors than just the raw market share are taken into account, such as the position of competitors, if any, the ease or difficulty there is for new companies to enter the market, and the overall market structure.

10.6.2.2 **The Relevant Product Market**

The test for the relevant product market concerns itself with the interchangeability of the products or product substitution. A number of factors can influence this. For example:

(a) Cross-elasticity; that is, if the price of one product rises, will consumers change to another, for example lager for beer, frozen vegetables for fresh vegetables, margarine for butter, artificial sweeteners for sugar? This can change over time according to fashion.

(b) Physical characteristics which are similar. These are factors which may mean a product is not unique and is capable of being replaced by something else.

The Commission has published a Notice on the Definition of the Relevant Market[35] which provides a summary of the case law and Commission methodology for determining the relevant markets.

What was the product market in the *United Brands* case? UBC said the product market was fruit. The Commission said bananas, clearly a difference. UBC controlled 40–45 per cent of the banana market, but argued that bananas were only a small part of a larger market in fresh fruit, and that although they might occupy a dominant position in the banana market, they did not occupy a dominant position in the fruit market. Which market was pertinent?

The Commission argued, and the CoJ considered, the special characteristics of the banana (sounds like a joke) and stated that the relevant product market turned on whether the banana could be 'singled out by such special features distinguishing it from other fruits that it is only to a limited extent interchangeable with them and is only exposed to their competition in a way that is hardly perceptible'.

It then identified a number of characteristics of the banana which would help to determine whether the banana had a market of its own:

(a) its physical appearance, chemical composition, taste, shape, softness, vitamin content

(b) the fact that it is functional easy, hygienic, convenient, has high nutritional value, and is easily digestible

(c) the fact that it is economic, in that the constant level of production maintained throughout the year lends itself to advance planning of sales.

All that in a banana!

The Commission and Court actually went further and identified a special sub-market of the old, young, and infirm who rely on bananas. You might ask why and you might also come to the conclusion that the common characteristic might be the absence of teeth! The Court of Justice held 'a very large number of consumers being in constant need for bananas are not noticeably or even appreciably enticed away from the consumption of this product by the arrival of other fruit on the market'. Therefore, other fruits were not substitutable and the relevant product market for the CoJ was the banana market.

It is easier to demonstrate dominance the more narrowly the relevant product market is defined. Hence companies will seek to widen that definition as much as possible

---

[35] OJ 1997 C372/3.

so that there are more potential competing products and consequently dominance will be much more difficult to establish. The next case focuses on the supply substitutability issue, which refers to the ease by which other suppliers or producers can enter the market and compete with the product under investigation.

In Case 6/72 *Europemballage and Continental Can v Commission*, the Court of Justice stressed the crucial importance of defining the relevant product market and, because the Commission had failed to define the product market properly, the decision was quashed. The Commission had said that the companies had a dominant position in the market for cans for meat, cans for fish, and metal tops. It did not explain why these markets were separate from each other, or from the general market in cans and containers. The Court of Justice held it necessary to identify the 'characteristics of the products in question by virtue of which they are particularly apt to satisfy an inelastic need and are only to a limited extent interchangeable with other products'.

In Cases 6 and 7/73 *ICI Commercial Solvents v Commission*, ICI were found to have a dominant market in one possible product raw material used for the manufacture of drugs. Although others were available, the CoJ held the difficulty of substitution was a deciding factor in determining a dominance. The concept of non-interchangeability is an important test which is applied by the Commission in identifying the relevant product market; see, for example, Case 85/76 *Hoffmann-La Roche*. The same product may, in fact, be classified into different markets; for example, in Case 322/81 *Michelin v Commission*, replacement tyres were held by the Court of Justice to constitute a different market from the same tyres supplied to the car production factories.

The key feature in determining product demand substitution and one incorporated into the Commission Notice on the relevant market is the 'small but significant nontransitory increase in price' test (SSNIP) whereby if a product price was raised permanently by 5–10 per cent and as a result a significant number of customers bought another similar competing product. This would show that those products are in the same market and interchangeable such that even a dominant company would be unlikely to raise prices much or undertake other forms of abuse in fear of losing customers. This does not always work though, especially with products with a very strong customer brand loyalty such as Coke and Pepsi.[36]

10.6.2.3 The Relevant Geographical Market

In *United Brands* the Court of Justice held that this required consideration of the opportunities for competition 'with reference to a clearly defined geographical area in which the product is marketed and where the conditions are sufficiently homogeneous for the effect of the economic power of the undertaking concerned to be able to be evaluated'—in other words, it should be plain to see how the competition is affected.

The whole or at least a substantial part of the EU is required but whatever market is demonstrated, it must be drawn to show market dominance. In a narrowly drawn geographical market, a firm which operates on a comparatively localized basis might possess

---

[36] An *American Journal* paper (M.A. Lemley and M.P. Mckenna, 'Is Pepsi Really a Substitute for Coke? Market Definition in Antitrust and IP') looked at this very question and, on the basis of the SSNIP test alone, it would seem that Coke and Pepsi are not in the same product market and not substitutable, certainly for a significant number of their loyal customers. Strange but true! See also the discussion on what is known as the 'Cellophane Fallacy' whereby a product argued by the manufacturer to be in competition, thus not abusive of a monopoly position, is in fact already priced at an abusive monopoly price because there is no competition as such at anywhere near the price sold. See Jones and Sufrin, *EU Competition Law*, 4th edn, Oxford University Press, Oxford, 2010, pp 72–4.

adequate market power to occupy a dominant position, but if the market is too narrowly drawn, it will not be sufficiently large to be a substantial part of the internal market. This latter problem should be seen in the context of the decision in case *Suiker Unie* whereby the Court of Justice held that dominance of the sugar market in Belgium and Luxembourg, then only about 10–15 per cent of the Community, was dominance of a substantial part of the common market. In Case T-83/91 *Tetra Pak v Commission*, the geographic market was defined as the whole Community.

In *United Brands*, the area was agreed to be six (from the then nine states) hence a substantial part in which trading conditions were similar. The market and supply conditions in the three countries (France, Italy, and the UK) were held to be sufficiently different to be excluded.[37]

The temporal market is rarely investigated but was considered in the *United Brands* case as UBC argued that banana sales were subject to seasonal changes particularly when summer fruits competed with them, thus trying to show a seasonal variation widened the market. This was not accepted as banana sales remained steady throughout the year.

10.6.2.4 Market Share and Dominance

After determining what the relative markets are for both product and territory, the market share must be considered. Whilst this is an important consideration for determining dominance, it is not definitive. In Case 85/76 *Hoffmann-La Roche* had market shares of 70–80 per cent in some drugs; in Case 6/72 *Continental Can* had 70–80 per cent share of the can market in Germany; in Cases 6–7/73 *ICI* had a virtual monopoly of the raw material; and in *Suiker Unie v Commission*, the Sugar Union had 85 per cent of the Belgium production. A market share of 50 per cent or over will, though, raise a presumption of dominance on the part of the Court of Justice (Case 62/86 *AKZO*), which was easily observed in the *Microsoft* case (Case T-201/04) in which a market share of over 90 per cent was identified. If not clearly dominant, the actual share must then be considered in the light of the overall market structure.

United Brands had only 40–45 per cent share of the banana market but the share of the nearest competition becomes relevant. In this case, the next company had only about 16 per cent of the market. Other factors were also critical in the *United Brands* case, such as their control of production, shipping, and dock facilities of bananas which made market entry for any new companies very costly and thus difficult. It also ensured the ability of UBC to act independently of other banana producers and distributors. In *United Brands* dominance was therefore satisfied.

The Commission suggested in its Tenth Report on Competition Policy that in the case of a highly fragmented market, a share of 20–40 per cent might constitute dominance and in Case T-219/99 *Virgin/British Airways* the CFI (now General Court) upheld the Commission's finding that the 39.7 per cent share that British Airways have of total airline sales in the UK, was sufficient to establish dominance. The Commission has subsequently published Guidance on the Commission's Enforcement Priorities in Applying Article 82 (now Art 102 TFEU) of the EC Treaty to Abusive Exclusionary Conduct by Dominant Undertakings[38] which reveals that 40 per cent is the rule-of-thumb bar on the likelihood of dominance, below which it is unlikely but not impossible. At 50 per cent it is very likely

---

[37] The Commission Notice of 1997 is also helpful in determining this in paras 44–6, similar prices being one of the most important but also taking account of exchange rate movements (not the case now in the eurozone of 18 countries), taxation, language, culture, and lifestyle.

[38] OJ 2009 C45/7, **http://eur-lex.europa.eu/legal-content/EN/ALL/?uri=CELEX:52009XC0224(01)**.

that dominance exists unless there are other overriding contradictions and between 70 and 80 per cent, there is a very strong presumption of dominance but still not conclusive on its own.

In the *British Airways* case, a very important factor was the share of the nearest rival, Virgin, which was just 5.5 per cent. The position of potential competitors or the ability of other competitors to enter the market is one of the other considerations taken into account by the Commission in determining dominance. Various entry barriers may be present which hinder or prevent market entry, such as the length of time a company has been dominant. This was considered in the *United Brands, Continental Can*, and *Tetra Pak* cases amongst others. In Case 85/76 *Hoffmann-La Roche*, the ability of competitors to enter the vitamins market to compete was all but non-existent, such was the very high cost of investment and Hoffmann's existing dominance. Market entry is very relevant with leading firms in areas such as IT technologies, where they possess or indeed own significant financial resources, technical know-how, access to markets, and access to raw materials. There are also often considerable legal barriers including various intellectual property rights such as patents and trademarks. Hence, there may well be temptations to exploit those advantages of a dominant position, for example in the *Intel* and *Microsoft* cases.[39]

Dominance, or in this case near-total domination (also called super-dominance) in one market, in the particular example for drinks containers, may be enough to lead to abuse in an associated market for containers, even though dominance in that associated market has not been demonstrated or exists, where the products, manufacturers, and consumers were largely the same in both markets: see Case 333/94 P *Tetra Pak International v Commission (No 2)*. In *Continental Can*, the Court of Justice held that the acquisition of a position of dominance through takeover or merger might amount to an abuse of a dominant market position.

10.6.2.4.1 Joint Dominance

Collective or joint dominance has also now been established where two or more companies act sufficiently closely as to present themselves on a particular market as a collective entity, although legally independent, as held in Cases C-395–6/96 P *Compagnie Maritime Belge SA v Commission*. Article 102 TFEU does allow for joint dominance in the phrase 'one or more undertakings'. For Art 102 TFEU, rather than the companies reaching an agreement that would breach Art 101 TFEU, it is the fact that the combined market share of the companies involved established dominance. In Case T-342/99 *Airtours plc v Commission* the Court identified three conditions required to establish joint dominance which included, mutual awareness of trading and operating policy, the tacit agreement that they maintain the status quo, and no other effective competition.[40]

10.6.2.5 The Abuse of the Dominant Position

Dominance on its own is not a problem; it must be abused to breach Art 102 TFEU. Article 102 TFEU provides four categories of example abuses, dealing essentially with unfairness, prejudice, discrimination, and unnecessary conditions. These categories, though, are not exhaustive and other forms of abuse can be found. The four categories,

---

[39] Cases T-201/04 *Microsoft* [2007] ECR II-3601 and T-286/09 and Case C-413/14P *Intel* (OJ 2009 C220/41) [2014] ECR I-547 and appeal pending.

[40] Joint dominance is also considered under merger control in Section 10.10.

along with cases which fit within those categories, follow with a more detailed look at two cases thereafter:

(a) directly or indirectly imposing unfair purchase or selling prices or unfair trading conditions: for example, unfair low prices, loss leaders, or unfair high prices as in *United Brands, Hoffmann-La Roche,* or *Tetra Pak*[41]

(b) limiting production, markets, or technical development to the prejudice of consumers: for example, restrictions on exports in the *Sugar* cases; restrictions on resale in *United Brands*; refusal to supply which might eliminate competitors in *Commercial Solvents*

(c) applying dissimilar conditions to equivalent transactions with other trading parties, thereby placing them at a competitive disadvantage, as in *United Brands*

(d) making the conclusion of contracts subject to acceptance by the other parties of supplementary obligations which, by their nature, or according to commercial usage, have no connection with the subject of such contracts, for example the green-banana clause in the *United Brands* case or tying-in clauses in *Hoffmann-La Roche*. A more recent case in this category is that of Microsoft in Case T-201/04 *Microsoft v Commission* and its bundling of Windows Media Player with the Windows operating system, which was found to be an abuse of its super-dominant position.

Abuse was defined in Case 85/76 *Hoffmann-La Roch*e as:

relating to the behaviour of an undertaking in a dominant position which is such as to influence the structure of the market where, as a result of the very presence of the undertaking in question, the degree of competition is weakened and which, through recourse to methods different from those which condition normal competition in products or services on the basis of transactions of commercial operators, has the effect of hindering the maintenance of the degree of competition still existing in the market…

In the *United Brands* case, the company had been found to have infringed Art 82 EC (now Art 102 TFEU) in that it had required its distributors not to sell bananas whilst still green (the green-banana clause) and had charged distributors in different member states different prices, sometimes by as much as 138 per cent without objective justification. UBC had also refused to supply a Danish company with Chiquita bananas because they had advertised another brand. In the *Continental Can* case, the Court of Justice held: 'Abuse may therefore occur if an undertaking in a dominant position strengthens such a position . . . that the degree of dominance reached subsequently fetters competition.'

Case C-7/97 *Oscar Bronner GmbH & Co KG v Mediaprint Zeitungs- und Zeitschriftenverlag GmbH & Co* helps to define, perhaps in a more positive way, the boundaries of what may be regarded as the abuse of a dominant position, in that this was not found to be the legal position from the facts. A media undertaking holding a clear dominant position (46.8 per cent circulation) in one market was not obliged to allow access to a home delivery scheme, the only one in the market, to a smaller rival newspaper which could not economically set up its own scheme. There was, in other words, no breach of Art 82 EC (now Art 102 TFEU) although there was a dominant position in the market. The case stresses that the exploitation of the advantages achieved by reaching a dominant position does not necessarily amount to unlawful abuse.

---

[41] See also Case C-62/86 *AKZO V Commission*, [1991] ECR I-3356, in which the predatory pricing regime of AKZO was held to be an abuse of its (50%) dominant position in the market for organic peroxides.

The Commission approach and priorities in respect of Art 102 TFEU enforcement have been set out in a guidance document along with a comprehensive volume on antitrust enforcement.[42]

10.6.2.6 **May Affect Trade between Member States**

The effect on trade is virtually taken as read under Art 102 TFEU if abuse has been found.

The principles developed in Art 101 TFEU cases also apply here. In Cases 6–7/73 *Commercial Solvents*, ICI claimed that the company to which they had refused to supply raw materials sold 90 per cent of its production of a tuberculosis drug made from those materials outside the EC and, in particular, in the developing countries. The applicants therefore argued that the abuse of the dominant position would not come within the ambit of the prohibition in Art 82 EC (now Art 102 TFEU), because it did not have an effect on trade between member states. The CoJ held that the expression could not be interpreted so as to limit the sphere of application of the prohibition to industrial and commercial activities supplying the member states.

By prohibiting the abuse of a dominant position within the market insofar as it may affect trade between member states, Art 102 TFEU therefore covers abuse which may directly prejudice consumers as well as abuse which indirectly prejudices them by impairing the effective competitive structure. The Commission must consider all the consequences of the conduct complained of without distinguishing between production intended for sale within the market and that intended for export. When an undertaking in a dominant position within the internal market abuses its position so that a competitor within the internal market is likely to be eliminated, the area of trade is unimportant, once it has been established that this will have repercussions on the competitive structure within the internal market. In *United Brands*, the higher prices and the various restrictions were the equivalent of a prohibition on exports and held to have an appreciable effect on trade between member states. This element is also covered in the 2009 Commission guidance on enforcement priorities relating to Art 102 TFEU; see footnote 42.

10.6.2.7 **The Consequences of Breaching Art 102 TFEU**

Unlike Art 101 TFEU which pronounces agreements in breach of that Article as being void, Art 102 TFEU is silent as to the consequences, although subsequent enforcement legislation provides for fines which can be very substantial. See, for example, the fine of €1.06 billion imposed on Intel for abusing its dominant market position! This was upheld by the General Court but is on appeal to the Court of Justice.[43]

10.7 The Relationship between Arts 101 and 102 TFEU

Articles 101 and 102 TFEU are not mutually exclusive categories and both may be considered as applicable to the same set of facts where, for example, dominant companies then

---

[42] Guidance on the Commission's Enforcement Priorities in Applying Article 82 of the EC Treaty to Abusive Exclusionary Conduct by Dominant Undertakings (OJ C45/7, 24.2.2009) at **http://ec.europa.eu/competition/antitrust/art82/index.html** and its comprehensive volume from 1 December 2011, EU Competition Law Rules Applicable to Antitrust Enforcement, Vol 1: General rules, which may be found at **http://ec.europa.eu/competition/antitrust/legislation/handbook_vol_1_en.pdf**.

[43] See **http://europa.eu/rapid/pressReleasesAction.do?reference=IP/09/745**, Case T-286/09 and Case C-413/14P *Intel v Commission* [2014] ECR I-547 and appeal pending.

abuse their strength by forcing unfair and restrictive agreements on their customers: see Case 85/76 *Hoffmann-La Roche*. Case 6/72 *Europemballage Corp and Continental Can* concerned an attempt by the Commission to use Art 86 EEC (now Art 102 TFEU) to tackle a merger which, in its view, resulted in anti-competitive behaviour; however, the Commission had failed to establish the relevant markets in a case in which a merger had created dominance, and because of that failure the Commission had failed to establish an abuse of a dominant position. The CoJ's views in the case were, however, instructive in respect of the relationship of Arts 101 and 102 TFEU and the restrictive approach to the problem adopted by the Commission, that by refusing to consider the use of Art 81 EC (now Art 101 TFEU) as well for mergers it had handicapped itself. The Court of Justice held that Arts 85 and 86 EEC (now Arts 101 and 102 TFEU) seek to achieve the same aim on different levels, viz the maintenance of effective competition within the common market. The restraint of competition which is prohibited if it is the result of behaviour falling under Art 85 EEC (now Art 101 TFEU) cannot be permissible by the fact that such behaviour succeeds under the influence of a dominant undertaking and results in the merger of the undertakings concerned. In the absence of explicit provisions, one cannot assume that the treaty, which prohibits in Art 85 EEC (now Art 101 TFEU) certain decisions of ordinary associations of undertakings restricting competition without eliminating it, permits in Art 86 EEC (now Art 102 TFEU) that undertakings after merging into an organic unit, should reach such a dominant position that any serious chance of competition is practically rendered impossible. Such diverse legal treatment would make a breach in the entire competition law which could jeopardize the proper functioning of the common market.

In other words, merger cannot alleviate the application of Art 101 or 102 TFEU to concerted actions of companies. The CoJ further held that Arts 85 and 86 EEC (now Arts 101 and 102 TFEU) cannot be interpreted in such a way that they contradict each other, because they serve to achieve the same aim.

This was the first attempt to use the treaty provision to tackle the assault on competition resulting from mergers. The Commission then realized that a new approach was required to tackle the problems of concentrations and, after some delay, a Mergers Regulation (4064/89) was enacted, considered in Section 10.11.1.

The difficulties in dealing with the realities of complex commercial cross-holding were highlighted by Cases 142 and 156/84 *BAT and Reynolds v Commission*. In this case the CoJ had to determine whether the Commission decision that the acquisition of a minority holding in a competing company was not an infringement of Arts 81 and 82 EC (now Arts 101 and 102 TFEU) was correct. Two applicant competitive companies objected to this decision. The original companies remained independent after the agreement and therefore Art 81 EC, which the Court of Justice considered could apply to mergers, was considered first. The Court of Justice upheld the Commission decision that no anti-competitive object or effect had been established and there was no control, thus there was no case under Art 82 EC either. However, although an acquisition itself might not restrict competition, it may influence conduct to restrict or distort competition. The case is an example of the need to consider both in such complex situations.

The Court of Justice has, though, held that an agreement within the meaning of Art 101(1) TFEU between legally separate undertakings may nevertheless result in undertakings being so linked that they become and act as a collective entity as far as their competitors and customers are concerned. As such, then, it can lead to a position of collective dominance which is then capable of being abused. See Cases C-395–6/96 P *Compagnie Maritime Belge Transports*. However, in a later case the Court of Justice considered that the Mergers Regulation is more suitable to situations of collective dominance than Art 82

EC (now Art 102 TFEU). See Cases C-68/94 *France v Commission* and C-30/95 *Société Commerciale des Potasses et de l'Azote (SCPA) v Commission* and comments in Section 10.11 on mergers.

Therefore, some circumstances need to be considered in light of both Arts 101 and 102 TFEU and the Mergers Regulation.

10.8 State Aid

In this short section, the rudiments of the principal legislative provisions[44] and leading cases concerning state aid will be outlined. In order to assist the creation and mainten-ance of a single market and fair competition, rules were introduced to prevent member states from supporting companies in a way which gave them an unfair economic advan-tage over competitors and indeed countries and which would distort fair competition. The treaty therefore prohibits state aid unless it can be justified in a permitted way for eco-nomic development. As with the other competition law provisions, the rules are enforced by both the European Commission and national authorities and courts. There are more specific exemptions which along with its own *de minimis* doctrine and block exemption, will be considered subsequently. Articles 107–9 TFEU govern state aid, the concept and understanding of which will be defined next.

10.8.1 Defining State Aid

Article 107 TFEU provides that 'any aid granted by a Member State or through State resources in any form whatsoever which distorts or threatens to distort competition by favouring certain undertakings or the production of certain goods shall, in so far as it affects trade between Member States, be incompatible with the internal market'. So state aid means selectively conferring an advantage of some kind on undertakings by the national public authorities. Legislation, supportive notices and guidelines, and case law have further defined what state aid is.[45] To be classified, for the purposes of EU law as state aid, the following elements are required:

1. aid or an advantage in some form, granted by the state or through state resources or measures

2. which is given to a specific undertaking or sector or region on a selective basis

3. which distorts or has the potential to distort competition

4. which is likely to affect trade between member states.

State aid will only be held to be present if all four conditions are met.

State aid can come in many forms including, as examples and by no means a comprehen-sive list: subsidies, exemptions from tax or social security payments, reduced cost land, real estate or loans, writing-off debts, and any help or assistance not coming within the excep-tions or approved by the Commission. The concept of aid was defined early in the life of the EU as 'wider than that of a subsidy because it embraces not only positive benefits, such as

---

[44] A complete compilation of state aid legislation and other provisions put together by the EU Commission can be found at: **http://ec.europa.eu/competition/state_aid/legislation/compilation/index_en.html**.

[45] In this brief outline, I shall not go into detail on these developments. For a comprehensive guideline see Community Guidelines for State Aid (OJ 2006 C319/01).

subsidies themselves, but also interventions, which…mitigate the charges which are normally included in the budget of an undertaking'.[46] The CoJ though has required that there be a clear connection to the public accounts of a state for such assistance to be considered state aid (Case C-189/91 *Kirsammer-Hack*). Government public statements of support including the making available of a €9 billion credit line, but which was not taken, was held not to constitute state aid by the General Court in Cases T-425, 444, 450, and 456/04 *France v Commission*, because, inter alia, it involved no transfer of state resources.

The effect on inter-state trade is easily satisfied in that in comparison with other undertakings not receiving aid, a company receiving aid will be financially strengthened and in a better position to conduct trade. The Commission need only show a potential effect on trade and not an actual effect.[47]

10.8.2 **Exceptions**

When the general prohibition of Art 107 TFEU was established it was recognized that there would be circumstances which would require government intervention to assist in difficult circumstances or to compensate for market failure which would otherwise lead to economic and social hardship.

In particular, Art 107(2) TFEU lists aids which are automatically compatible. It provides:

The following shall be compatible with the internal market:

(a) aid having a social character, granted to individual consumers, provided that such aid is granted without discrimination related to the origin of the products concerned;

(b) aid to make good the damage caused by natural disasters or exceptional occurrences[.]

Article 107(3) TFEU provides that certain other policy objectives may be supported by state aid and thus compatible with the internal market, as considered next.

10.8.2.1 **Article 107(3) Exceptions**

In order to provide aid under the following exceptions, the proposed assistance must first be notified to the Commission, which may comment on it, require amendment or even block it (Art 108(2)–(3) TFEU). Article 107(3) provides:

The following may be considered to be compatible with the internal market:

(a) aid to promote the economic development of areas where the standard of living is abnormally low or where there is serious underemployment, and of the regions referred to in Article 349, in view of their structural, economic and social situation; [48]

(b) aid to promote the execution of an important project of common European interest or to remedy a serious disturbance in the economy of a Member State; [49]

---

[46] Case 30/59 *Steenkolenmijnen v HA* [1961] ECR 1. See also e.g. Case 323/82 *Intermills v Commission* [1984] ECR 3809.

[47] See Case 730/79 *Philip Morris v Commission* [1980] ECR 2671.

[48] Essentially constituting a form of regional aid, assistance was provided by Holland to a tobacco company but was held not to comply with the general prohibition of Art 107. Any such consideration of Art 107(3)(a) must be made in view of EU standards of living and not just the particular state. Case 730/79 *Philip Morris v Commission* [1980] ECR 2671. See generally Guidelines on Regional State Aid for 2014–2020 (OJ 2014 C209/1).

[49] This heading assumes some form of cross-border project as in Case 62/87 *Glaverbel v Commission* [1988] ECR 1573, in which aid to the glass industry by Belgium was held to lack the transnational element and was therefore not compatible with Art 107 TFEU.

(c) aid to facilitate the development of certain economic activities or of certain economic areas, where such aid does not adversely affect trading conditions to an extent
contrary to the common interest; [50]

(d) aid to promote culture and heritage conservation where such aid does not affect
trading conditions and competition in the Union to an extent that is contrary to the
common interest;

(e) such other categories of aid as may be specified by decision of the Council on a proposal from the Commission. [51]

10.8.2.2 The State Aid Block Exemption

A new block exemption regulation for state aid was recently enacted and entered into
force in July 2014. [52] It and its predecessors essentially increase the forms of state aid which
are acceptable providing the aid leads to new activities being developed and promotes
economic development without distorting competition excessively. Member states are
not required to notify the Commission for approval if their state aid measures fall within
the provisions of the block exemption.

10.8.2.3 State Aid *De Minimis*

The *de minimis* rule has now been enacted as a *De Minimis* Regulation which in the brief-
est of summaries, provides that aid can be granted provided it does not exceed €200,000
over any period of three fiscal years. [53]

10.8.3 Procedures under Articles 108 and 109 TFEU

The Commission is primarily responsible for enforcing the EU state aid rules, largely by
the Directorate-General (DG) for Competition. [54] Procedures for considering the compatibility of state aid can be triggered either by notification by the state, considered next,
or by third parties with an interest, considered in Section 10.8.3.2. The procedures are
primarily governed by Council Regulation 659/1999 as amended. [55]

10.8.3.1 Notification Procedure

The system is essentially based on a mandatory prior notification procedure which
requires the member states to notify contemplated aid clearly not coming within Art
107(2), or the block exemption or *de minimis* regulations, considered earlier. Article
108(3) TFEU states the notification must be made in sufficient time to enable the

---

[50] This overlaps with (a) in that it envisages regional aid in some form but judged instead by national
criteria and comparison as well as with other EU states and regions. See generally Guidelines on Regional
State Aid for 2014–2020 (OJ 2014 C209/1).

[51] A catch-all not covered by the other heads which allows directives to be made for specific sectors, e.g.
shipbuilding has been provided with significant aid over the decades.

[52] Commission Regulation 651/2014 declaring certain categories of aid compatible with the internal
market in application of Arts 107 and 108 of the treaty (OJ 2014 L187/1).

[53] Commission Regulation 1407/2013 on the application of Arts 107 and 108 of the Treaty on the
Functioning of the European Union to *de minimis* aid (OJ 2013 L352/1), **http://ec.europa.eu/competition/
state_aid/legislation/de_minimis_regulation_en.pdf.**

[54] Competition DG is supported in their respective fields by DG Agriculture and Rural Development
and DG Maritime Affairs and Fisheries to deal with the agricultural and fisheries sectors.

[55] Full procedural rules can be found at: **http://ec.europa.eu/competition/state_aid/legislation/rules.
html.**

Commission to submit its comments. From notification, the Commission has two months to decide whether:

1. there is no aid within the meaning of the EU rules, therefore the measure may be implemented
2. the aid is compatible because on balance it has been decided that the positive effects outweigh any possible distortions of competition, and may therefore go ahead
3. there are serious doubts as to the compatibility of the notified measure with state aid rules.

In the event of the latter, the Commission will open an in-depth investigation, during which time the measure may not be transferred until the investigation is concluded. This is known as the suspension obligation which has been held to have direct effect, which in turn means if breached, it can be upheld in the national courts to recover payments already made. It can also be used to support an action for damages by competitors or others who may have suffered as a result of the breach of the obligation.

10.8.3.2 Investigation

An in-depth investigation under Article 108(2) TFEU by the Commission can be triggered by state notification or a third-party complaint, in which case the Commission will notify the state. The Commission may then request further information from the member state. The Commission will open a formal investigation if it has serious doubts about compatibility with state aid rules, or where there are procedural difficulties in obtaining the necessary information. The decision, when taken, is published in the Official Journal and member states and interested third parties have one month from the date of publication to submit comments. The member state concerned is in turn invited to comment on observations submitted by interested parties. The Commission adopts a final decision at the end of the formal investigation.

There are essentially three possible outcomes:

1. positive decision: where the measure is held not to be aid or the aid is considered to be compatible with the internal market
2. conditional decision: where the measure is found compatible but its implementation is made subject to conditions stated in the decision
3. negative decision: where the measure is incompatible and cannot be implemented, in which case the Commission would normally order the member state to recover any aid that has already been paid out, from the beneficiaries.

10.8.3.3 Recovery of Incompatible/Unlawful Aid

Aid granted without prior Commission authorization can be ordered to be repaid by the Commission, which may use injunctions to obtain information from member states and suspend the granting of further aid and impose a provisional recovery obligation on the member state. If the Commission has taken a negative decision in the context of aid that has already been paid out, the Commission can require the member state to recover the aid with interest from the beneficiary. The Commission may open a 'recovery case' to enforce the implementation of its decision. If the member state does not comply with the decision in due time, the Commission may refer it to the CoJ. The aim of recovery is to remove the unfair advantage granted to an undertaking and to restore the market to the state before the aid was granted. There is a limitation period of ten years for recovery. In Case C-24/95 *Land Rheinland-Pfalz v Alcan*, recovery was possible even in the face of national-rule time limits which would have prevented recovery and, in Case C-5/89 *Commission v Germany*, recovery could also be undertaken by the Commission in the face of an argument of legitimate expectation on the part of the recipient.

10.8.3.4 Judicial Review and National Court Proceedings

All decisions and the procedural conduct of the Commission are subject to review by the General Court and on appeal by the CoJ under Art 263 TFEU. Applications can be made by the states concerned, the beneficiaries or intended beneficiaries, and competitors. See the details on Art 263 TFEU actions in Chapter 7, Section 7.4.

Challenges are also possible in the national courts either by way of national judicial review proceedings or actions for damages. Whilst the Commission has the exclusive right to determine the compatibility of the aid with the internal market, the national court can determine questions of liability where unlawful aid has been granted and has the power to order the recovery of allegedly unlawful state aid, grant injunctive relief, award damages, or adopt any other necessary measures to remedy the unlawfulness of the aid. The judgment in Case C-284/12 *Deutsche Lufthansa and Frankfurt-Hahn Airport*[56] has now given national courts the ability to order repayment of the alleged unlawful state aid before the Commission has reached a final conclusion to an investigation.[57]

10.9 The Enforcement of EU Competition Law

Under Art 103 TFEU the Council was provided with the power to adopt any appropriate measures to give effect to and ensure the effectiveness of Arts 101 and 102 TFEU. Additionally, the Commission was given extensive independent enforcement powers quite early in the life of the Communities under Art 105 TFEU and originally under Council Regulation 17 which was the first regulation to be enacted implementing Arts 85 and 86 EEC (now Arts 101 and 102 TFEU). As was outlined in Section 10.5.2, the system of enforcement of competition law was changed from a centralized to a devolved system relying far more on the member states. As a result the supportive legislation had to be extensively amended and Regulation 17 has been replaced, with the exception of Art 8 which is still in force, with Regulation 1/2003 which now provides the system of enforcement. Enforcement is essentially undertaken by both the Commission and national competition authorities and by private parties pursuing actions where they consider they have suffered damage as a result of the anti-competitive behaviour of other parties.

10.9.1 Council Regulation 1/2003

Regulation 1/2003 empowers the Commission to carry out its function of ensuring that the provisions of the TFEU are applied; to address undertakings, decisions, and recommendations for the purpose of bringing to an end infringements of Arts 101 and 102 TFEU; and to enforce these by way of fines and periodic payments. It sets out the powers and duties of the Commission in the conduct of investigations of competition law abuses, which can be prompted by individuals and companies, the member states, or on the Commission's own initiative. The ethos of the new system of enforcement of competition law introduced and

---

[56] [2013] ECR I-755, http://curia.europa.eu/juris/liste.jsf?language=en&num=C-284/12.
[57] For further details and a summary of case developments, see the Commission Notice: Commission Notice on the Enforcement of State Aid Law by National Courts (OJ 2009 C85/1).

enabled by this regulation is that of cooperation between the Commission and national competition authorities and the respective courts. The regulation allows national authorities and courts to apply Arts 101 and 102 TFEU directly themselves and levy fines.[58]

The main details of the regulation follow, but since this new regulation replaced Regulation 17, much of the case law arising from the previous Regulation 17 remains relevant. In particular, the rights of parties to be heard and present their view of matters still need to be considered here as analogous authorities for the new Articles in Regulation 1/2003. The existence of Regulation 773/2004 should be noted as it provides details on how Art 101 and 102 TFEU enforcement proceedings should be conducted; however, no details will be provided here.

Regulation 1/2003, Arts 1–16 are mainly concerned with the respective powers of the Commission and national authorities, interim measures, cooperation between the Commission and national authorities, and with the procedure of the declarations by the Commission that the agreement either infringes the treaty Articles or is exempt from the treaty provisions.

Articles 17–21 concern the powers of the Commission in conducting investigations; Arts 23–8 concern sanctions available to the Commission in the case of infringements which have been established by it and the rights of the parties under investigation; and Arts 17–18 concern requests for information. It generally empowers the Commission to request information to assist its investigations from both the authorities of the member states and from the undertakings. The owners of undertakings or their representatives are obliged to supply the information requested. If this is not forthcoming, the Commission can adopt a formal decision requiring the information to be supplied (Art 18(3)). Penalties may then be imposed for non-compliance with the terms of the decision.

10.9.1.1 Investigations

Article 20 empowers the Commission to undertake all necessary investigations including the right of its officials to examine books, take copies of records and books, ask for oral explanations, and enter the premises of undertakings, including now extended powers under Art 21 to search the homes of directors, managers, and other members of staff where there is a reasonable suspicion that records relevant to the investigation are stored there. This can be undertaken without the consent of the undertaking involved providing it is specifically authorized in advance by the Commission: see Case 136/79 *National Panasonic*. Alternatively, a formal decision may be adopted for a mandatory investigation. There is no need to approach the company in advance and the Commission should not be subjected to a delay before the investigation can take place. The investigations authorized under this provision include the infamous 'dawn raids' on the premises of companies under investigation. In Decision 80/334 *Fabbrica Pisana*, it was established that a duty of the company existed to assist the Commission to find documents. In Cases 46/87 and 227/88 *Hoechst*, the authority to raid was challenged on the ground that it lacked precision but the Court of Justice held that it was acceptable providing the Commission indicated clearly its suspicions rather than have to supply full information; however, force cannot be used by Commission officials to gain entry and examine documents, but assistance to

---

[58] This is assisted and facilitated by the establishment of the European Competition Network to exchange information and try to ensure the consistent application of EU competition law: **http://ec.europa. eu/competition/ecn/index_en.html**.

gain entry must be obtained via the national authorities: Case 85/87 *Dow v Commission* and Case 374/87 *Orkem v Commission*. In the latter case, it was held by the Court of Justice that the power to compel the production of information does not extend to requiring the company to admit breaches of the competition rules and, thus, incriminate itself. In effect, a company can be obstructive but may suffer the penalty of fines being imposed on it under Art 23. This can be up to 1 per cent of the previous year's turnover, where a company has misled the Commission: see Cases 40–8/73 *Sugar Union*. Article 23(1) covers a number of situations of not supplying information or supplying false, misleading, or incomplete information, books, or records.

10.9.1.2 Conduct of Hearings and Professional Secrecy

Previously largely established by case law but now contained within the regulation, Arts 27 and 28, contain details concerning the conduct of hearings, the rights of individuals and companies in those hearings and rights of confidentiality, and professional secrecy.[59] The types of documents which are subject to legal privilege and professional secrecy have been the subject of case law. Legal privilege is recognized and covers correspondence between the company and an independent lawyer; see Case 155/79 *AM & S*. In-house lawyers do not enjoy such privilege, so it depends on the nature of the correspondence. Case T-30/89 *Hilti* decided that the privilege extends to in-house lawyers' reports of the independent lawyers' findings but not the stand-alone work of the in-house lawyer. In Case C-36/92 P *Samenwerkende*, a refusal to hand over documents considered to be confidential was held to be unjustified in light of the existing protections in Community law under which the Commission is required to notify undertakings of the documents that it intends to release to the national authorities and thus give the undertakings the chance to seek judicial review to protect these documents. As such, the refusal to supply would be unjustified. In the end, the General Court and Court of Justice must be the arbiters of what is privileged.

The principle of professional secrecy does not apply to allow a company to protect documents from the Commission but to ensure that information received by the Commission in an investigation is not disclosed to competitors: refer to Arts 27 and 28 and Cases 209–15 and 218/78 *Dow Benelux & Van Landewyck* and Case 53/85 *AKZO*.

Case C-550/07 P *AKZO* was appealed on various points to the ECJ, which confirmed the earlier case of Case 155/79 *AM & S v Commission*, to the extent that the Court of Justice confirmed that the principle of legal privilege does not extend to in-house lawyers. It held that it made no difference even if the in-house lawyer was a member of the relevant national Bar or Law Society and was subject to the same rules of professional conduct and discipline as an independent lawyer.

10.9.1.3 Fining

For a substantive breach of Arts 101 or 102 TFEU, Art 23 provides the Commission with the right to fine an undertaking not exceeding 10 per cent of the total turnover of the

---

[59] As with many aspects of competition law, guidelines and notices provide additional information. In this area see the Notice on Best Practices in Proceedings Concerning Articles 101 and 102 TFEU (OJ 2011 C308/6) and Decision 2011/695 on the Terms of Reference of the Hearing Officer (OJ 2011 L275/29).

preceding business year, which, given the huge turnover of some multinational companies, means that fines can be substantial. The Commission takes into account the duration of the infringement and how serious it was.[60] In Case T-51/89 *Tetra Pak Rausing SA v Commission*, the company was fined 75 million ecu, which was upheld by the Court of Justice in Case C-333/94 P *Tetra Pak Rausing SA v Commission* and in *Volkswagen*, Commission Decision 98/273, Volkswagen were fined 102 million ecu which was about £67 million but which was reduced before the CFI (now General Court) to 90 million ecu in Case T-62/98. This was topped in 2003 when the Commission fined a number of companies who had been operating a vitamin cartel a total of €855.22 million in Decision 2003/2, with Hoffmann-La Roche in that case fined €462 million. The latest records are those set in March 2004 when Microsoft was fined €497 million and in 2009 when Intel were fined €1.06 billion. Latest fine is €1.8 billion.[61]

As noted in Section 10.9.1.1, fines can also be imposed during the course of investigations where companies fail to supply requested information or mislead.

10.9.2 **Leniency Notice and Settlements**

To encourage informant companies, a policy of leniency in fining was partly formalized in a system of so-called leniency notices, whereby companies which volunteered information and cooperated with the Commission in cartel investigations could have their fines drastically reduced, up to 100 per cent if they are the first company in a cartel to provide information to either launch an investigation into a previously undetected cartel or information to secure a prosecution in an ongoing investigation which lacked evidence. There is now a revised leniency notice covering this area.[62]

In addition, a system of settlement has been established which complements the voluntary participation above, by allowing companies under investigation to acknowledge a breach and thus effectively plead guilty, to bring the matter to a swift conclusion. This too would be rewarded by a reduction in the fine.[63]

10.9.3 **Judicial Review of Enforcement**

All decisions taken by the Commission under Regulation 1/2003 are subject to review by the General Court under Art 263 TFEU with the possibility of an appeal on points of law only to the Court of Justice. Article 261 TFEU provides the Court of Justice with unlimited jurisdiction to review such penalties as may be imposed by the Commission under EU law provisions. Fines can be increased or reduced by the GC and CoJ or if there are errors by the Commission in fact of law, the decision can be quashed entirely.[64]

---

[60] For details see Guidelines on the Method of Setting Fines Imposed Pursuant to Article 23(2)(a) of Regulation No 1/2003 (OJ 2006 C210/2).

[61] Case COMP/C–3/37.792 *Microsoft* and Case T-286/09 and Case C-413/14 P *Intel v Commission* [2014] ECR I-547 and appeal pending. The fine of €1.38 billion was levied against glass manufacturers in Cases T-56/09 and T-73/09 [2014] ECR, not yet reported.

[62] Commission notice on immunity from fines and reduction of fines in cartel cases, as updated to 2006 (OJ 2006 C298/17).

[63] See Commission Regulation 622/2008 (amending Regulation 773/2004) as regards the conduct of settlement procedures in cartel cases (OJ 2008 L171/3) and a notice: Commission Notice on the Conduct of Settlement Procedures in View of the Adoption of Decisions Pursuant to Article 7 and Article 23 of Council Regulation No 1/2003 in Cartel Cases (OJ 2008 C167/01).

[64] See n 45 for reference to further details on the conduct of competition law hearings.

10.9.4 **Private Enforcement**

As with other areas of EU law, enforcement of the EU rules can also take place by individuals before the national courts via the vehicle of direct effects. This is particularly important now that, as was noted earlier, the new Regulation 1/2003 has made Art 101(3) TFEU, concerned with exemptions, directly effective, which was previously not the case. If the other areas of EU law are anything to go by, this will greatly complement the Commission's power to enforce competition law, which because of its stretched resources is rather limited. It enables the vigilance of thousands of individuals who may be affected by anti-competitive practices to pursue actions and claims against offending companies. The Commission has also noted in paragraph 16 of its Notice on the Handling of Complaints by the Commission (OJ 2004 C101/05) that actions before the national courts are possible and may be advantageous to aggrieved parties.

A leading case has started to explore this development. Case C-453/99 *Courage v Crehan* concerns a pub tenant party to an agreement which tied him into buying beer from a particular brewery, Courage plc. He claimed this was in breach of Art 81 EC (now Art 101 TFEU) and claimed damages. As a party thus also tainted by the agreement, the UK court was minded to dismiss the claim but nevertheless made a reference to the Court of Justice under Art 234 EC (now Art 267 TFEU). The Court of Justice, in looking back at the importance in securing enforcement rights for individuals and the effectiveness of Community law (*Van Gend en Loos* and *Francovich*),[65] held that the competition law rules were fundamental rules in the EC, and if the agreement was in breach of Art 81 EC (now Art 101 TFEU) and not able to be exempted, it was void and could not be relied on by anyone, including a party to the agreement. Then, also in line with case developments in other areas, the CoJ held that in order to ensure the effectiveness of Community law, the procedural rules of the member states should not deprive individuals of rights in the absence of a Community regime. That matter was ultimately up to the member states' courts, but there should be no absolute bar to an action where the contract was held to breach Art 101 TFEU. Hence, *Courage v Crehan* can rely on a breach of Art 101 TFEU and should not be barred from seeking damages for any loss incurred as a result, but national law can exclude a claim where the party him or herself is also responsible for the agreement in breach. The party in this case did win damages and there is no doubt that this case and many others will assist Commission enforcement of competition law significantly.

In support of the ability of private parties to pursue claims in the national courts, the Commission proposal for a directive on anti-trust damages actions to iron out some of the differences and difficulties in the member states has been approved by the Council and EP.[66]

10.10 **Conflict of EU and National Law**

In theory, the division should be easy; one or more companies' activities will only come within EU competition law jurisdiction if they also affect trade between member states, otherwise it will be up to the member states' competition authorities to prosecute the

---

[65] See the details in Chapter 5.

[66] Directive 2014/104 (OJ 2014 L349/1), **http://eur-lex.europa.eu/legal-content/EN/TXT/?uri=uriserv: OJ.L_.2014.349.01.0001.01.ENG**, and the Commission had previously set up a European Competition Network to exchange information and facilitate the consistent application of EU competition law: **http:// ec.europa.eu/competition/ecn/index_en.html**.

breach. However, the question of the resolution of potential conflicts between EU and national competition law and the problem of double jeopardy was initially addressed in Case 14/68 *Walt Wilhelm v Bundeskartellamt*. The Federal Cartel Authority in Germany and the Commission had instituted proceedings against Walt Wilhelm for breach of competition rules. Walt Wilhelm submitted that the Bundeskartellamt could not maintain proceedings for an offence which was at the same time the object of investigation by the Commission. The Court of Justice ruled that conflicts between Community law and national law in the matter of cartels must be resolved by applying the principle that Community law takes precedence. This was subsequently confirmed in Case 13/77 *GB-INNO-BM*, which considered a clash between Belgian law and EC competition law in which the Court of Justice held that the member states had a duty not to adopt or retain any national measures which might deprive, in the case, Art 82 EC (now 102 TFEU) of its effectiveness. In order to clarify the procedure and assist national courts in considering cases which involve issues of EU competition law, the Commission had issued a Notice to National Courts on the Application of Articles 81 and 82 EC (now 101 and 102 TFEU)[67] setting out the procedure which should be followed. The notice also indicates that national courts should take notice of 'comfort letters' although they remain non-binding. However, Regulation 1/2003 has now taken over the field in this area to govern the relationship between the national courts and the Commission. It provides under Art 16 that if a decision has been reached by the Commission on a competition law matter, the national authorities and courts can no longer reach their own conclusion which conflicts with that decided by the Commission or even that in the process of being decided by the Commission. This means, in practice, that they must wait for the Commission conclusion before taking any action. Article 15 allows for a cross-flow of information between the Commission and national competition authorities to assist both in investigations.

Regulation 1/2003, though, has made other changes which affect the relationship. By scrapping, at least on the face of it, the individual notifications procedure and by making Art 101 TFEU directly effective, the legal exceptions to Art 101 TFEU can be the subject matter of national court adjudication. However, the bottom line is that any decision reached on them cannot run contrary to established or pending EU law and Commission decisions dealing with the same matter. The national courts must apply EU law where relevant.

10.11 EU Merger Control

It is in the area of mergers and acquisitions—or, as termed in the EU, concentrations—that the relationship of Arts 81 and 82 EC (now Arts 101 and 102 TFEU) with each other previously came under closest scrutiny. Originally, the Commission was of the view that Art 81 EC would not apply to concentrations. Thus, if competition was restricted or distorted by a concentration of companies, Art 82 EC was the appropriate measure with which to tackle it. This policy was pursued by the Commission in Case 6/72 *Continental Can* whereby the Commission tried to remedy an abuse of a dominant position which had been achieved by takeovers and substantial holdings in European companies by an American company. It was the first attempt at merger control by the Commission. It was not successful, mainly because the Commission failed to establish the relevant markets, rather than it being a failure to show abuses by the concentration. The Court of Justice's

---

[67] OJ 1993 C39/5.

views in the case were, however, instructive in respect of the relationship of Arts 81 and
82 EC and the restrictive approach to the problem adopted by the Commission, that by
refusing to consider the use of Art 81 EC as well for mergers it had handicapped itself.
(See Section 8.7, Case 6/72 *Europemballage Corp and Continental Can*, and the Court of
Justice's view on the aims of Arts 81 and 82 EC.)

The CoJ further held that Arts 81 and 82 cannot be interpreted in such a way that they
contradict each other, because they serve to achieve the same aim.

In Case T-51/89 *Tetra Pak v Commission*, Tetra Pak were found to be in breach of Art 82
EC (now Art 102 TFEU) following the acquisition of another company which held an
exclusive licence to manufacture sterilized milk cartons. Whilst the acquisition itself did
not offend Art 82 EC, the consequent dominant position which was immediately abused
did do so.

The difficulties in dealing with the realities of complex commercial cross-holding were
highlighted by Cases 142 and 156/84 *BAT and Reynolds v Commission*. The Court of
Justice had to determine whether the Commission decision was correct that the acquisition of a minority holding in a competing company was not an infringement of Arts 81
and 82 EC. Two applicants, competitive companies, objected to this. The original companies remained independent after the agreement; therefore Art 81 EC, which the Court
of Justice considered could apply to mergers, was considered first. The Court of Justice
upheld the Commission decision that no anti-competitive object or effect had been established and there was no control, thus there was no case under Art 82 EC either. However,
although an acquisition itself might not restrict competition, it may influence conduct to
restrict or distort competition. The case is an example of the need to consider both in such
complex situations.

10.11.1 The Mergers Regulations (4064/89 and 139/04)

It was following the *Continental Can* case that the Commission realized that a new
approach was required to tackle the problems of mergers, otherwise known as 'concentrations'. The Commission put forward a proposal for a regulation on merger control, but it was 16 years later, on 21 December 1989, that the Council adopted Council
Regulation 4064/89 on the control of concentrations between undertakings. Under it,
the Commission jurisdiction under Arts 81 and 82 EC (now Arts 101 and 102 TFEU) and
Regulation 17 was repealed in respect of concentrations. The first mergers regulation has
now been replaced by Mergers Regulation 139/04 which provides the legal foundation of
EU policy control of mergers and acquisitions. Mergers Regulation 139/04 establishes a
division between large mergers with a European dimension, over which the Commission
will exercise supervision, and smaller mergers which will fall under the jurisdiction of
national authorities. The concept of a concentration was set out in a Commission notice.[68]

Article 1 states that the regulation applies to mergers and takeovers with an EU dimen-
sion, where there is a worldwide turnover of more than €5,000 million, and an aggregate
EU wide turnover of each of at least two of the undertakings of more than €250 million.
An EU dimension may nevertheless pertain, if:

(a) the combined aggregate worldwide turnover of all the undertakings is more than
€2,500 million

(b) in each of at least three member states, the combined aggregate turnover of all the
undertakings is more than €100 million

[68] OJ 1998 C66/2.

(c) in each of at least three member states, the aggregate turnover of each of at least two of the undertakings concerned is more than €25 million

(d) the aggregate EU-wide turnover of each of at least two of the undertakings concerned is more than €100 million.

However, if each of the undertakings concerned achieves more than two-thirds of its aggregate EU-wide turnover within one and the same member state, a concentration will fall outside the scope of the regulation, and the merger will be subject to national rather than EU control.

Article 2 provides the power of review to determine whether mergers are compatible with the common market. The creation or strengthening of such a position will be declared incompatible with the common market where it would significantly impede effective competition in the common market as a whole or in a substantial part of it. In making this appraisal, the Commission is required to take into account the following matters: the need to preserve and develop effective competition within the common market; the structure of all the markets concerned (product and geographic markets); the actual or potential competition from undertakings located within or without the EU, and which includes the market position and economic and financial power of the undertakings concerned; suppliers' and users' access to supplies or markets; legal barriers to entry into the market; supply and demand trends for the relevant goods and services; the interests of intermediate and ultimate consumers; and the development of technical and economic progress provided that it is to consumers' advantage and does not form an obstacle to competition.

The last requirements are similar to the exemptions under Art 101(3) TFEU.

Where a merger is found by the Commission not to impede effective competition, it will be declared compatible with the common market (Art 2(2)). The member states, however, retain the right in such circumstances to veto mergers in particularly sensitive areas of their economies, providing this is compatible with the general requirements of EU law. Article 2(3) then declares that where a merger is found by the Commission to impede effective competition, it will be declared in a decision incompatible with the common market.

Article 3 defines a concentration to include mergers, acquisitions of direct or indirect control of undertakings by persons already controlling at least one undertaking, partial mergers, and merger-like joint ventures. However, it excludes from the scope of the regulation coordination of market behaviour of firms which remain independent of each other. Such coordination, if adverse to competition in the common market, would fall within the scope of either Art 101 or Art 102 TFEU as in Cases 142 and 156/84 *BAT and Reynolds v Commission*. However, more recent cases would seem to contradict this view. In Joined Cases C-68/94 *France v Commission* and C-30/95 *Société Commerciale des Potasses et de l'Azote (SCPA) v Commission*, the Court of Justice determined that the Merger Regulation may apply also to collective dominance. The case concerned a proposal that potash companies in Germany be concentrated, thus creating a de facto monopoly in the German market and a dominant position with the French company SCPA in the Community market. To obtain Commission approval, the parties agreed to certain conditions relating to cooperation between the dominant firms and the distribution of products in the markets identified. France objected to the Commission decision before the Court of Justice and SCPA, before the CFI (now the General Court). As they both concerned the same decision, the CFI declined jurisdiction and the whole matter was referred to the Court of Justice. The decision is important because it is the first time the CoJ has clearly stated the Merger Regulation to be applicable to collective dominance, despite the lack of express words to that effect in the regulation and the doubts of the member states when the regulation was enacted that it would apply to oligopolies. The Court of Justice, on the other hand, thought that there was nothing in the regulation to exclude its application. That collective dominance was not sufficiently established by the Commission in the case itself does nothing to upset this. See also Case T-102/96 *Gencor v Commission* which confirms this position.

The effect of the regulation is described as one-stop shopping, in that only one authority, Commission, or national authority need take action depending on the area of dominance. It provides for the operation of a so-called principle of exclusivity whereby all decisions on EU-wide mergers are taken by the Commission, member states having undertaken not to apply their national competition rules to such cases (Art 21(1) and (2)), although there is provision for referral to national authorities in certain cases.

10.11.2 **Enforcement of Regulation 139/04**

Article 4(1) requires the notification of a concentration with a Union dimension within one week after the conclusion of the agreement, the announcement of the public bid, or the acquisition of a controlling interest, whichever of these shall occur first. Fines for a failure to notify can be imposed up to a maximum of €50,000 (Art 14(1)).

Article 7(1) provides that a concentration with a Union dimension shall not be put into effect before notification or in the three weeks following notification. The validity of transactions in securities on stock exchanges is not affected (Art 7(5)).

Under Art 10(1) the decision to open proceedings referred to in Art 6 must be taken within one month of the day following receipt of the notification. Article 6 provides that the Commission is under a duty to examine all notifications as soon as they are received, and to notify its decision to the undertakings concerned and the national authorities without delay. If the Commission considers that the proposed concentration falls outside the scope of the regulation, it must record that finding by way of a decision. Where it finds that the proposed concentration has a Union dimension, but does not raise serious doubts as to its compatibility with the common market, it must decide not to oppose it and must declare it compatible with the common market. Where the concentration both falls within the scope of the regulation and raises serious doubts as to its compatibility with the common market, the Commission must decide to issue proceedings.

Article 10(3) requires that a decision that a concentration is incompatible with the common market must be taken within four months of the decision to open proceedings. During this period, the parties to the proposed concentration will be free to propose changes to their merger in order to avoid a negative decision.

Where the Commission has found a proposed concentration to be incompatible with the common market, it may require the separation of the undertakings brought together, or the cessation of joint control, or any other action that may be appropriate to restore the conditions of effective competition (Art 8(5)). So far, the regulations have been sparsely used to prevent mergers, most of which have been cleared. An exception was the proposed merger of Aerospatiale, Alenia, and de Havilland (M053)[69] which was prohibited under the regulation for the reason that the merger would have had an unacceptable impact on customer choice and the balance of competition in the EU. Following this first blocking by the Commission, another seven mergers have been blocked.

---

[69] [1992] 4 CMLR M2.

A Commission decision which was made to block a merger was overturned by the CFI (now General Court) in Case T-342/99 *Airtours plc v Commission* when Airtours wished to take over First Choice in the UK. The reason given by the CFI was that the Commission had failed to establish clearly that a position of collective dominance would have been reached following the merger.

Article 13 confers the power to undertake 'all necessary investigations' on the Commission, including the power for officials to examine and take copies of or extracts from books and other business records; to ask for oral explanations on the spot; and to enter any premises, land, or means of transport of the undertakings concerned.

The regulation also allows for the imposition of fines and periodic payments for failure to notify, for supplying incorrect or misleading information, and for obstructing an investigation by Commission officials (Arts 14 and 15). Where the parties intentionally or negligently fail to comply with an order to suspend the concentration or disregard a decision to stop a merger or undo a merger, the Commission may impose a fine of up to 10 per cent of the aggregate annual turnover of the undertakings (Art 14(2)).[70]

10.12 Summary

Competition policy and law remain a central element of the EU internal market. As outlined in the introduction, this is an area very much influenced by the market and market forces. Presently, during the economic recession, merger activity has declined considerably and most competition law concerns now focus on state aid to ailing sectors of the economy. Generally though, competition law activity, whilst quieter and concentrating on larger abuses, remains as set out here. There are arguments to suggest it should be applied just as rigorously as companies seek to bolster falling profits by engaging in anti-competitive behaviour. Hence the general consensus that it should continue to be applied in the same way, albeit sympathetically where needed, for example, to protect employment.

Further Reading

Books

BELLAMY and CHILD, *European Union Competition Law*, ed. V. Rose and D. Bailey, 7th edn, Oxford University Press, Oxford, 2013.

CAHILL, D. *The Modernisation of EU Competition Law Enforcement in the European Union*, Cambridge University Press, Cambridge, 2004.

COLINO, S.M. *Competition Law of the EU and UK*, 7th edn, Oxford University Press, Oxford, 2011.

FURSE, M. *Competition Law of the EC and UK*, 5th edn, Oxford University Press, Oxford, 2006.

JONES, A. and SUFRIN, B. *EU Competition Law*, 5th edn, Oxford University Press, Oxford, 2014.

KORAH, V. *An Introductory Guide to EC Competition Law and Practice*, 9th edn, Hart Publishing, Oxford, 2006.

---

[70] Considerable further information, legislation, notices, and general guidelines on all aspects of merger control can be found at **http://ec.europa.eu/competition/mergers/procedures_en.html**.

Articles

BAILEY, D. 'Restrictions of Competition by Object under Article 101 TFEU' (2012) 49 CML Rev 559–99.

BAILEY, D. 'Single, Overall Agreement in EU Competition Law' (2010) 47 CML Rev 473.

BAXTER, S. and DETHMERS, F. 'Collective Dominance under EC Merger Control—After *Airtours* and the Introduction of Unilateral Effects Is there Still a Future for Collective Dominance?' (2006) 27 ECLR 148.

CAMILLERI, E. 'A Decade of EU Antitrust Private Enforcement: Chronicle of a Failure Foretold?' (2013) 14 ECLR 531.

GERBER, D. and CASSINIS, P. 'The Modernisation of European Community Competition Law: Achieving Consistency in Enforcement' (2006) 27 ECLR 10.

MEZZANOTE, F. 'Tacit Collusion as Economic Links in Article 82 EC Revisited' (2009) 30 ECLR 137.

NEBBIA, P. 'Damages Actions for the Infringement of EC Competition Law: Compensation or Deterrence?' (2008) 33 EL Rev 23.

REICH, N. 'The *Courage* Doctrine: Encouraging or Discouraging Compensation for Antitrust Injuries?' (2005) 42 CML Rev 35.

SLOT, P.J. 'A View from the Mountain: 40 Years of Developments in EC Competition Law' (2004) 41 CML Rev 443.

VENIT, J. 'Brave New World: The Modernization and Decentralization of Enforcement under Articles 81 and 82 of the EC Treaty' (2003) 40 CML Rev 545–80.

VICKERS, J. 'Merger Policy in Europe: Retrospect and Prospect' (2004) 25 ECLR 455–63.

VOGELAAR, F. 'European Competition Law Revisited: The "Great Overhaul" of 2004 Analysed' (2005) 32 Legal IEI 105–9.

WITT, A. 'From Airtours to Ryanair: Is the More Economic Approach to EU Merger Law Really about More Economics' (2012) 49 CML Rev 217–46.

Web-based Material

http://ec.europa.eu/competition/index_en.html
Commission Competition Policy website

11

Sex Discrimination Law

11.1 Introduction

This chapter is principally concerned with sex discrimination law, which is the classical or typical area of EU social law study dealing only with a single, albeit multifaceted, example of discrimination on the grounds of sex. Whilst it would be interesting to continue to expand coverage of this area of law into all areas of the rapidly expanding equality law of the EU, it would go beyond what is useful for a textbook intended to provide a comprehensive introduction to the more popular areas of EU law for undergraduate courses. Hence, then, this development of a general equality law will only be sketched out and sex discrimination law is the focus of the chapter.

11.2 A General Principle of Equality in EU Law?

Equality or non-discrimination has also been mentioned earlier in the book under general principles in Chapter 4. From the outset, it has to be stressed that whilst there is a debate as to whether the terms 'equal treatment', 'equality', and 'non-discrimination' are synonymous, they are taken as meaning the same thing, without spending time on the subtleties of the differences, if any.

There are a number of examples of express prohibitions of discrimination on different grounds within the treaty, but there is not, as such, an express general principle of non-discrimination or equality in the treaty, although new Art 10 TFEU is close. The specific prohibitions do, however, support the existence of a general principle in the EU legal order that is additionally confirmed by the judgments of the Court of Justice and academic commentary.

The treaty Articles that seek either to prohibit discrimination or promote equality are:

- Arts 2 and 3 TEU (equality between men and women)
- Art 8 TFEU (ex Art 3 EC Treaty)
- Art 10 TFEU (which sets out the policy goals to combat discrimination across a range of issues)
- Art 18 TFEU (ex Art 12 EC) (nationality)
- Art 19 TFEU (ex Art 13 EC) (general power to prohibit discrimination across a range of issues)
- Art 40(2) TFEU (ex Art 34(2) EC) (concerned with equality between producers and between consumers in the Common Agricultural Policy (CAP))
- Arts 45, 49, and 56 TFEU (ex Arts 39, 43, and 50 EC) (providing for equal treatment of workers and the self-employed)

- Art 106 TFEU (ex Art 86 EC) (public undertakings)
- Art 110 TFEU (ex Art 90 EC) (taxation)
- Art 153 TFEU (ex Art 137 EC) (equality of men and women in the work environment)
- Art 157 TFEU (ex Art 141 EC) (equal pay).

Without going into details, all of these Articles support the development of a general principle of equality by the establishment of a legal culture that does not tolerate the different treatment of like, or the same treatment of unequals, across a range of subject matters.

Added to these now, since the Lisbon Treaty, is the Charter on Fundamental Rights, which has provided a section (Arts 20–3) prohibiting discrimination on any ground and which will be considered at the end of this chapter.[1] Hence the existence and value of a general principle of equal treatment has been acknowledged and confirmed by the Court of Justice in a number of cases: for example, in Case C-149/10 *Chatzi*, in which the Court held that the principle of equal treatment is one of the general principles of EU law and is now affirmed by Art 20 of the EU Charter of Fundamental Rights (in that case, to support the right to parental leave on an equal basis).

11.2.1 **Article 18 TFEU**

Article 18 TFEU, the prohibition of discrimination on the grounds of nationality, clearly stands out as already being close to a general principle itself because it has become a fundamental basis for integration, harmonization, and the removal of inequalities in the EU legal order through its application in various policy areas of the Union, most notably, the free movement of persons and, more recently, citizenship, considered in Chapter 9. The reason for this is that the Court of Justice has relied on Art 18 TFEU in many subject areas, including those areas outside those covered by specific equality Articles noted earlier. As such, then, the CoJ has been able to fill any gaps in equality provision by resorting to Art 12 EC (now Art 18 TFEU).

Whilst the various prohibitions of discrimination on the grounds of nationality can be readily understood within the general framework of a Union and legal order that seeks to promote the integration of different countries, the prohibition of discrimination on the grounds of sex can be less readily understood. Therefore, before looking in depth at sex discrimination provisions, the reasons for its inclusion will be discussed.

11.3 The Reasons for the Original Inclusion of Sex Discrimination Provisions in the Treaty

The prohibitions of discrimination in other Articles of the treaty can be quite readily understood because they all relate, more or less, to nationality, and therefore go to the very foundation of the establishment of the Community and now Union; that is, the removal of national barriers to the establishment of the internal market. Nationality should not play a role in the free movement of goods, persons, or capital. Non-discrimination on the grounds of sex, though, is less readily understandable in this context. On the face of it, it would appear to be essentially a socially based discrimination and not economic. It was, however, originally framed in the EC Treaty as a form of workplace-based discrimination.

---

[1] It is also considered in Chapter 4, along with other general principles outlawing discrimination.

Therefore, as was considered in Chapter 9 on the free movement of persons, it is helpful and informative to go back to the drafting of the Treaty Establishing the European Economic Community (the EEC Treaty) to see why what has clearly become a social law right was included in the EEC in the first place. Additionally, and viewed in the context of the initial, more limited, aims of the Communities to eliminate discrimination based on nationality, there is an odd feature to sex discrimination law, in that it does not require a cross-state or community context; that is, there needs to be no movement between member states, unlike the fundamental freedoms of goods, persons, and capital, which do require such movement. EU sex discrimination law is applicable in entirely or wholly internal situations. This begs the question why sex equality rights were included.

Given the original, more economic, nature of the Community, the European Community (EC) would seem an unlikely source of women's equality rights. Fundamentally, it was first a vehicle to promote economic integration and development of the member states, rather than to provide equality between the sexes, which is, arguably, really an internal matter for the member states. However, it is now generally accepted that the immediate reason for including Art 119 in the EEC Treaty was not for reasons of social justice, but out of economic considerations; that is, the creation of level playing fields for industry in terms of the application of national social laws. The Article was alleged to have been included at the request of the French, whose law provided for equality of pay between male and female workers. It was feared that French industry would be at a disadvantage if equal pay were not enforced in the other member states. It is also rumoured that this was aimed as much at Germany because, although having the principle in law, in reality French industry at the time had very few women workers, whilst Germany in the post-war period relied on far more women workers to make up for the lack of male workers, because many men of working age had been killed during the war. Pay equality enforced on member states would help to curb the resurgent German economic primacy. Regardless of the exact underlying motive, its inclusion would appear to be based on economic arguments the aim of which was to ensure that similar economic conditions apply in all of the member states. There appears to be no social justification for its inclusion, but one thing we know is that things never stay still in EU law; the Court of Justice's view on the matter can be seen in Case 43/75 *Defrenne v Sabena (No 2)*. The CoJ declared that:

> Article 119 also forms part of the social objectives of the Community, which is not merely an economic union, but is at the same time intended, by common action, to ensure social progress and seek the constant improvement of the living and working conditions of their peoples, as is emphasized by the preamble to the Treaty . . . This double aim, which is at once economic and social, shows that the principle of equal pay forms part of the foundations of the community.

Hence, it was regarded in 1976 as one part of a joint economic and social aim, but was promoted in status in subsequent judgments to a prime aim. In Case 149/77 *Defrenne v Sabena (No 3)*, a couple of years later, the CoJ declared the elimination of discrimination based on sex as part of the fundamental rights within Community law. It was confirmed in Case C-234–5/96 *Deutsche Telekom v Vick* that the social aims of Art 119 (now Art 157 TFEU) prevail over those of the economic aims and subsequently confirmed in Case C-50/96 *Deutsche Telekom v Schröder*:

> it must be concluded that the economic aim pursued by Article 119 of the Treaty, namely the elimination of distortions of competition between undertakings established in different member states, is secondary to the social aim pursued by the same provision, which constitutes the expression of a fundamental human right.

Hence, then, a seemingly complete turnaround in a 30-year journey from an instrument of economic levelling or harmonization to a primary individual fundamental social right.

Sex equality law has developed much more slowly and much later than the central internal market areas of law, notably the free movement of goods and persons. This is argued to be because of the less extensive original provision for it in the treaty, and the delays by the member states in implementing the principle of equal pay and those caused by the Commission in not introducing secondary legislation until prompted to do so by the Council of Ministers. There now exists a considerable body of EU law on the subject, in the form of treaty additions, introduced notably by the Treaty of Amsterdam, a growing body of EU directives, and the very many progressive decisions of the Court of Justice. As a result this has become a relatively developed area of EU law, which is notable from its limited beginnings. I make this comment because I observe that new cases concerning novel points arise less frequently now than in the past, which can be interpreted as this being an area of law which is settled and that the ground-breaking rulings are those in the past, for the most part. To some extent, but for different reasons, this can be equated with the area of the free movement of goods and tariff barriers. Not very much new now happens in that area of law, as the removal of tariff barriers and charges having equivalent effect has largely been achieved. That's not to suggest the same is the case with discrimination on the grounds of sex; the most obvious and direct discriminations have been addressed, but many indirect discriminations continue. Perhaps when the present economic recession has passed, we can turn again to social and not just economic justice.

11.4 The Legislative Framework

11.4.1 Treaty Articles

Article 157 TFEU (previously Art 119 EEC and Art 141 EC) (equal pay for equal work) originally provided the only specific mention of equal treatment in the treaty, but it has formed the basis upon which the principle of non-discriminatory treatment has been expanded into areas beyond equal pay. Now, following amendments by the Treaty of Amsterdam, treaty references to the promotion of equality are more extensive. In addition to the main treaty Article, which is now Art 157 TFEU, the Treaty of Amsterdam introduced as one of the goals now outlined in Art 2 TEU 'equality between men and women' and Art 3 TEU, which states the aim to promote equality 'between men and women'. This aspiration is also repeated in Art 8 TFEU: 'In all its activities, the Union shall aim to eliminate inequalities, and to promote equality, between men and women.'

Equality between men and women in the working environment was also included in the 1989 Community Social Charter, which was incorporated into Art 151 TFEU. Article 153 TFEU provides that, inter alia, the Union shall complement and support the activities of the member states in the field of equality between men and women with regard to labour market opportunities and treatment at work.

Article 157 TFEU has been expanded beyond its simple original provision to ensure that men and women should get equal pay for equal work. The Treaty of Amsterdam amended and added two sentences to locate within the treaty base the principles of equal pay for work of equal value and action to promote equality, but which falls short of out-and-out positive discrimination. These rights were previously contained in directives only, which meant that they could not give rise to direct effects against other individuals. The Lisbon Treaty amended the Art 157(4) TFEU 'positive discrimination' aspect by removing that actual term and rewording it, as considered under Section 11.6.6.

Finally, as far as the treaty is concerned, an enabling power has been provided in Art 19 TFEU that provides that the Council, acting unanimously in accordance with a special legislative procedure and after obtaining the consent of the European Parliament, may take appropriate action to combat discrimination based on sex or sexual orientation.

Added to the primary law now must be included the section in the EU Charter of Fundamental Rights, Arts 20–3, which prohibits discrimination on any grounds in Art 21. It is starting to be referred to by the Court of Justice and will no doubt feature much more in case law in the future.

11.4.2 **Secondary Legislation**

It was only after the completion of the transition period for the common market in 1968 that the member states and Commission started to turn towards developing a social policy for the Union. The European Summit meetings of 1972/73, and in particular the Paris Summit of 1972, requested the Commission to produce proposals for a Social Action Programme (SAP), as the first of what transpired to be a number of action programmes. The first report was published in 1974.[2] Amongst a number of measures dealing with redundancy and transfer of undertakings, three directives concerned with equality between men and women were adopted, which will be considered as appropriate later: the Equal Pay Directive 75/117, the Equal Treatment Directive 76/207, and the Social Security Directive 79/7.[3]

A second SAP was commenced in 1982,[4] which led, as far as equality legislation is concerned, to the enactment of Directive 86/378 on equal treatment in occupational pensions, and Directive 86/613 on equal treatment of the self-employed and protection of self-employed women during pregnancy and motherhood.[5]

After the long period of stagnation of the Communities, the political will to complete the single market and at last to allow for institutional reform of the Community brought in its wake a strengthening of social policies in the EC Treaty by the amendment by the Single European Act (SEA) in 1986. This helped to create the environment that led to the adoption of the Charter of Fundamental Social Rights of Workers (known as the 'Social Charter') in 1989 by 11 of the then 12 member states (not the UK). It provided, amongst other measures, under (g), the equal treatment of men and women. This, in turn, led to another SAP in 1989,[6] which resulted in the enactment of the Pregnancy and Maternity Directive 92/85.[7]

The next step on this seemingly tortuous path to provide a comprehensive set of enactments covering equal treatment was the EC Treaty amendment by the Maastricht Treaty (TEU), which attached an Agreement and Protocol on Social Policy (known as the 'Social Chapter') to the treaty, to which 14 of the then 15 member states signed up (the UK having secured another opt-out from social legislation). This led to the enactment of further directives, including the Parental Leave Directive 96/34, repealed and replaced now by Directive 2010/18, the Burden of Proof in Sex Discrimination Cases Directive 97/80 now absorbed into Directive 2006/54, and the Part-time Workers Directive 97/81.[8]

---

[2] OJ 1974 L14/10.

[3] OJ 1975 L45/19, OJ 1976 L39/40, and OJ 1979 L6/24. The first two were repealed and replaced by Directive 2006/54 (OJ 2006 L204/23) on 15 August 2009, which will be considered where appropriate.

[4] OJ 1982 C186/3.

[5] OJ 1986 L225/40 and OJ 1986 L359/86, the first of which was repealed and replaced by Directive 2006/54 (OJ 2006 L204/23) on 15 August 2009, and will be considered where appropriate.

[6] COM (1989) 568.   [7] OJ 1992 L348/1.

[8] OJ 1996 L145/9, OJ 1998 L14/6, and OJ 1998 L14/9, the second of which was repealed and replaced by Directive 2006/54 (OJ 2006 L204/23) on 15 August 2009, and will be considered where appropriate.

While this last directive is not directly aimed at addressing sex discrimination, it has this effect, because it aims to reduce the inequality between full-time workers and part-time workers—the majority of the latter being women and thus likely to be indirectly discriminated against (a matter considered later in this chapter).

The more recent secondary legislation includes Directive 2004/113[9] on equality in the access to and the supply of goods and services, Directive 2010/41[10] on equal treatment between self-employed men and women, and Directive 2010/18[11] on parental leave.

Article 157 TFEU and the early legislation in particular have been subject to very liberal interpretation by the Court of Justice, far beyond a literal reading of the provisions and due, no doubt in large part, to the fact that, for the first 20 years of the Community's life, there was only Art 119 (now Art 157 TFEU) to provide for equal treatment—and that was confined to equal pay. During the subsequent ten years, this was supplemented by only the first three directives dealing with equal treatment. The CoJ had to be inventive in order to make any progress. Whilst greater effort is being shown now by the Union institutions and the member states by the setting up of various fora in which to promote equality, in the beginning, action was more likely to be taken by individuals, sometimes with the support of the national equality agencies, such as the Equal Opportunities Commission (EOC) in the UK, rather than the Commission in enforcement actions. (See, for example, the *Defrenne, Garland*, and *Marshall* cases, considered later.)

This chapter will concentrate on the core aspects of sex equality law in the EU, notably, Art 157 TFEU, and the old and now repealed Directives 75/117 and 76/207 (the Equal Treatment Directive), both of which have been replaced by the consolidating Directive 2006/54 on equal treatment between men and women, which came into force on 15 August 2008. The old directives will still be referred to in this chapter, with either the new or old directive Article numbers in brackets. At the end of the chapter, other less prominent secondary legislation will also be considered.

The consolidating directive carries the extended concept of discrimination under Art 2, which provides that discrimination includes:

(a) harassment and sexual harassment, as well as any less favourable treatment based on a person's rejection of or submission to such conduct

(b) instruction to discriminate against persons on grounds of sex

(c) any less favourable treatment of a woman related to pregnancy or maternity leave within the meaning of Directive 92/85/EEC.

11.5 Article 157 TFEU and the Scope of the Principle of Equal Pay

Article 157 TFEU originally provided that 'member states shall ensure the application of the principle that men and women should receive equal pay for equal work'. Article 157 TFEU was amended along the way by the Treaty of Amsterdam to refer to 'equal pay for work of equal value', a concept that was first introduced by Directive 75/117. Article 157(1) TFEU now states first that 'Each member state shall ensure that the principle of equal pay for male and female workers for equal work or work of equal value is applied', and then attempts to define what 'equal pay' actually means. Article 157(2) TFEU narrowly

---

[9] OJ 2004 L373/37.   [10] OJ 2010 L180/1.   [11] OJ 2010 L68/13.

defines pay as 'the ordinary basic or minimum wage or salary or any other consideration, whether in cash or in kind, that the worker receives either directly or indirectly in respect of his employment from his employer'. Article 157(2) TFEU defines 'equal pay without discrimination' to mean:

(a) that pay for the same work at piece rates shall be calculated on the basis of the same unit of measurement

(b) that pay for the same work at time rates shall be the same for the same job.

Payment by piece rates is not so common now and basically means that a person is paid per unit of a product that is made; it was previously found in factory work or in home working, such as the assembly of biro parts. The more assembled or made, the more is paid.

It took a long time, however, until the principle of equal pay was realized. Much of the delay was due to a deliberate postponing of the application of the principle by the member states, and it was only court action by individuals that allowed the Court of Justice to step in and at last provide for the application of the principle, and simultaneously to condemn the member states' efforts not to provide for equal pay. The first significant case under Art 119 EEC (now Art 157 TFEU) concerned an applicant who was previously unsuccessful in challenging a discriminatory pension system based on national legislation and, thus, held to be outside Community law competence. However, she commenced a second action to challenge unequal pay. In Case 43/75 *Defrenne v Sabena (No 2)*, a claim for compensation was made for the damage suffered from February 1963 until February 1966, because Gabrielle Defrenne was paid at a substantially lower rate than her male colleagues for the same work. The case was sympathetically received by the CoJ and Gabrielle Defrenne was successful. The CoJ held that the principle of equal pay was sufficiently clear and precise as to have direct effects both vertically and horizontally. However, in response to the fears expressed by employers and the interventions of some member states about the costs to industry if the judgment were applied back to 1957 (namely, all of the back pay that would have to be paid), the CoJ declared the ruling to be prospective only from the date on which the original litigation by Defrenne commenced and any cases in the pipeline. This prospective-only ruling is a type of ruling that is rare, but repeated again in equality law in the *Barber* case, considered later. With *Defrenne* having opened the gate, many more cases were referred to the CoJ, which was then able to refine the definition of 'pay' and thus the scope of Art 119 EEC (now Art 157 TFEU).

11.5.1 The Meaning of 'Pay'

Although previously, Case 80/70 *Defrenne v Belgium (No 1)* seemed to rule out a wider definition of 'pay' to exclude, as considered in the case, 'pension benefits in retirement', the term 'pay' has been progressively defined. In Case 12/81 *Garland v British Rail Engineering*, Art 119 EEC (now Art 157 TFEU) was held to include concessionary rail-travel facilities for the family of an ex-employee. The Court of Justice held that the travel facilities in question were granted in kind by the employer to the retired male employee or his dependants directly or indirectly in relation to his employment, and could be regarded as an extension of travel facilities granted during employment. Pay, as interpreted by the CoJ, also includes:

- rules by which seniority or loyalty payments are achieved in favour of full-time employees in Case C-184/89 *Nimz v Hamburg*
- sick pay, even though part of a statutory scheme in Case 171/88 *Ingrid Rinner-Kuhn v FWW Spezial-Gebäudereiningung*

- a severance grant in Case C-33/89 *Kowalska v Hamburg*
- compensation for lost wages for attendance on a training course for works council members in Case C-360/90 *Arbeiterwohlfahrt der Stadt Berlin v Monika Botel*.

Unfair dismissal compensation and redundancy pay have also been confirmed to come within Art 141 EC (now Art 157 TFEU) in Case C-167/97 *Seymour-Smith & Perez*. Hence, 'pay' is given a very wide meaning, and any payments and benefits that arise from the employment relationship may be held to be pay under Art 157 TFEU.

One particular problem was the status of pensions because of the link that exists with retirement, and the fact that EU secondary legislation appeared to retain this whole area within the competence of the member states and not the Union.

11.5.1.1 The Concept of Pay and Its Relationship to Pensions

This topic has particular complications not only because the concept of pay is being stretched, but also because it straddles the very grey area of the boundary between the jurisdiction of the member states and that of the Union and Court of Justice. Directive 79/7, Art 7, stipulates that member states have the right to exclude from equal treatment the determination of pensionable age for the purposes of granting old-age and retirement pensions, and the possible consequences for other benefits. It was the meaning of the last part of the Article, 'the possible consequences for other benefits', that caused the uncertainty due to its vagueness.

Case 152/84 *Marshall* had determined that the retirement age itself was not to be linked to the pension age, and had to be equal for men and women. We had already learned, though, in the first *Defrenne* case that contributions into a statutory pensions or social security scheme were not to be considered as coming within the concept of pay under Art 157 TFEU. It was widely assumed that this ruling was good for all forms of pension scheme.

The reasons for the allowance in Union law for a difference in pension ages are probably becoming lost in time. It was previously the case, and still is under transitional arrangements in many states, that men and women retired and gained pensions at different ages: women usually five years earlier than men. This might seem odd, given that the life expectancy of women is on average greater than that of men and women might be expected to have to work longer in order to pay for this. However, historically, it was precisely because of the greater life expectancy that women should gain their pension earlier, for the following reasons. Pension ages and retirement ages in the eighteenth and nineteenth centuries were the same, but in those centuries, there was an average of three years' age difference between men and women at marriage, men being the older. However, men tended to die first and if they died at any time up to the age of 65 (which was the expected life expectancy of the working classes, and many died before they got the chance to retire or soon thereafter), their state pension entitlement died with them (which it did, because it was personal and not transferable to the wife). Therefore, if pension ages were the same (which they were), the wife, aged on average between 60 and 63, would be without any means of support until she reached the age of 65. So, to protect women from being evicted from their homes and being thrown into the poor houses, the law was changed to enable them to get their state pension earlier. Being able to get their pension earlier, it soon followed that they would retire earlier—not a legal requirement, but why carry on working when you could stop and get a pension? It then became the contractual standard for women to retire at the age of 60, and thus it was generally considered that pensionable age also meant retirement age, which in turn became lawfully enforceable because it became part of a standard contract of employment for women, hence the reason for the Directive 79/7, Art 7 exception. Also, it is the case that, in the past, almost all pensions were state pensions, with a few exceptions for high earners in private employment. However, pension schemes have developed in both sophistication and complexity from the 1970s onwards, and often involve a wholly or partly private or contractual element. Furthermore, there has been an increasing privatization of pensions without any state involvement that only serves to further complicate this area—so how are these now regarded by the Court of Justice?

In Case 69/80 *Worringham & Humphries v Lloyds Bank*, the bank operated an arrangement whereby male workers under the age of 25 were paid 5 per cent more than their female counterparts to enhance a pension. The reason for this was that part of the social and historical thinking up to that stage, and indeed factually correct according to the calculations of the actuaries, was that males were more likely to be breadwinners and more likely to die before their usually younger female spouses, so therefore it was regarded as not a bad idea to enhance the pension pay-ins of males at an early stage and thus increase the level of pension pay-outs later to the benefit of those surviving, namely the female spouses and offspring. The total enhanced payment package, however, formed the basis of calculation of other social advantages and welfare benefits. The defendant bank argued that the enhancement was linked to pensions; therefore, it could lawfully discriminate. The CoJ ruled that such a contribution, which determined other benefits linked to salary paid by the employer, is pay within the meaning of Art 119 (now Art 157 TFEU), even if they were deducted at source and paid on behalf of the employee; that is, the employee never sees them directly. This could include anything supplied by the employer to, or on behalf of, the employee on a pro-rata basis, such as annual bonuses. Thus, as a result of this case, whilst it was not the pension itself that was considered to be pay, not all linked consequences were to be automatically excluded under Art 7a of Directive 79/7.

Case 170/84 *Bilka Kaufhaus v Karin Weber Van Hartz* concerned different access rules to a pensions scheme for full-time and part-time workers, the part-timers being mainly female. It was held that where supplements were made by the employer to the basic state pension under a contractual agreement and where the amount was linked to pay (that is, as a proportion or percentage), it was pay for the purposes of Art 119 EEC (now Art 157 TFEU). Furthermore, if access to this scheme was discriminatory, as it was proved to be in the case, it also breached Art 119 EC (now Art 157 TFEU).

The next case was, like the second *Defrenne* case, highly significant in the Community legal order because of the impact it had on employers. In Case C-262/88 *Barber v Guardian Royal Exchange Assurance Group*, Barber was made redundant by GRE at the age of 52. There was an agreed contracted-out (that is, private) pension scheme. His redundancy package included a statutory redundancy payment, and an ex gratia payment (a top-up), but entitlement to his occupational pension was deferred until the agreed pension age under the scheme age of 62 for men and 57 for women. There was an agreement in the redundancy package that if redundancy were to take place within ten years of the state pension ages, the pension could be obtained earlier. A redundant woman aged 52 would be entitled to immediate access to her pension, because she was within ten years of the statutory pension age, whereas Barber and other male employees were not (being ten or more years adrift), which was the basis for the claim of unlawful discrimination. The defence claimed that there was a link to the pension age and the case therefore fell under the Directive 79/7 exemption, in which case it would be lawful discrimination. The UK government, intervening, claimed that the scheme, which replaced the state scheme, should be regarded as coming within the realm of social security provision and not Art 119 EEC (now Art 157 TFEU). The Court of Justice concluded that the statutory redundancy pay and the benefits from the contracted-out occupational pension scheme—that is, the pension itself—were 'pay' within Art 119 EEC (now Art 157 TFEU). The deciding factor is whether the rules, and thus payment of the specific scheme, are a part of the employment contract or are a voluntary inclusion of the employer. Only if entirely to do with the compulsory state pension, does a case fall outside Art 157 TFEU. The CoJ emphasized the importance of the fact that the occupational pension scheme was funded without any contribution being made by the public authorities.[12]

The *Barber* decision gave rise to severe concern. It was not expected that pensions should be pay; indeed, the first *Defrenne* case suggested that they were not. It would mean that there would be unlawful discrimination not previously thought to be the case, for which huge amounts of compensation, not previously contemplated, would be payable. This would not have been taken account of in the actuarial calculations and the pension schemes would have had severe difficulties in making payments not previously foreseen. Hence, the CoJ declared Art 119 EEC (now Art 157 TFEU) to be directly effective for pensions from the date of judgment only—namely, 17 May 1990—and for any cases in the pipeline. In other words, like the second *Defrenne* judgment on the direct effects of Art 119 EEC (now Art 157 TFEU) before it, the judgment was prospective only, applying from the date of judgment onwards and not validating any backdated claims for equal treatment, which would cost the industry severely. Indeed, the member states were so concerned about the judgment and possible future interpretations of it that they attached a specific protocol (Protocol No 2) to the TEU, which has now been replaced by Protocol No 33 attached to the treaties by the Lisbon Treaty. It states that the benefits arising from social security schemes shall not be considered as remuneration in respect of periods of employment prior to 17 May 1990, with the exception of those who had instigated proceedings prior to that date; that is, only for benefits payable for service after 1990. This, like the *Defrenne* judgment, was to overcome the economic effect on employers in the case of a retroactive application of the ruling. Thus, the period of earnings before the *Barber* judgment do not give rise to a claim.

The protocol clarified the judgment and was expressly accepted by the CoJ in Case C-109/91 *Ten Oever*, which also extended the *Barber* ruling to pension benefits payable to the pension holder's survivors and further confirmed by the CoJ as coming within Art 141 EC (now Art 157 TFEU) in Case C-117/01 *KB v NHS Pensions*.

The *Barber* case, however, sparked off many more cases seeking to establish its exact meaning and consequences, only one or two of which are considered here. It also led to the extensive amendment of Directive 86/378 on occupational social security schemes.

In Case C-152/91 *Neath v Hugh Steeper*, it was held that inequality in employees' contributions arising from actuarial factors such as life expectancy, which differed according to sex, would not be caught by Art 141 EC (now Art 157 TFEU). The case involved a conversion of a periodic payment to a lump-sum pay-out. Whilst benefits and pay-outs must be regarded as pay, this is not the case for the contributions that determine the size of the fund, because other factors other than a simple difference in sex are involved. The funding system to provide the amount of pension to be available does not come under Art 141 EC (now Art 157 TFEU). The amount needed for a pension is determined by actuaries, who base their figures on the fact that women live longer after retirement and have a right to a pension at an earlier age, thus they need more capital available to supply this. If they work for the same time, they must pay more. This becomes quite clear when converted to a lump sum: women will get more. In this case, the male applicant got less and claimed that

---

[12] At [25] of the judgment.

this was unlawful discrimination. However, according to the Court of Justice the difference in treatment was objectively justified as a result of the actuarial factors.

It has subsequently been established that the time limit in *Barber* and Protocol No 33 do not apply to discrimination in relation to the right to join—that is, access to an occupational pension scheme—which remains governed by the judgment in *Bilka Kaufhaus*. (See, as confirmation, Case C-57/93 *Vroege v NCIV Instituut*.)

There are still very many cases arising from this very complex relationship between pay and pensions. It is complicated because there remains a lawful discrimination on the part of member states as to when females and males receive state pensions. Any difference that relates to the amount paid in or out to achieve a pension is, in law, entirely acceptable, unless, according to *Barber*, it has become part of the contractual relationship by the intervention of an agreement between the employer and employee. It is then pay and comes within Art 141 EC (now Art 157 TFEU), meaning that the employer cannot lawfully discriminate.

11.5.2 The Original Equal Pay Directive 75/117

The Equal Pay Directive added little to the legal interpretations of Art 119 EEC (now Art 157 TFEU), but did extend the principle of equal pay to 'work to which equal value is attributed' and extends to 'all aspects and conditions of remuneration' (Art 1).[13] This is now contained in the amended Art 157 TFEU and makes the situation much easier for claimants who work for a private employer—that is, the vast majority of workers.

It was with these concerns in mind that many of the cases that were originally raised in respect of Directive 75/117 alone, or in combination with Art 141 EC (now Art 157 TFEU), were decided upon by the Court of Justice with reference to Art 141 EC only. If the CoJ were not able to bring the case circumstances within the scope of Art 141 EC, there would have been severe difficulties for many of the applicants, because of the absence of horizontal direct effects in directives. A more concise equal pay principle is now to be found in Directive 2006/54, Art 4, although, of course, the case law still relates to the previous directive and treaty Article. The definition of 'pay' found in Art 157 TFEU is also contained in Art 2(1) of Directive 2006/54.

11.5.3 The Basis of Comparison

In most situations in which there is direct discrimination, it is usually clear and obvious that there is discrimination. For example, it is easy to compare a man and woman who are doing the same job in the same workplace for the same employer, but who are paid differently. There are, however, many complications that could be added to this, whereby the comparison is not so obvious: the times of work differ, or the job differs slightly or the workplace differs. It then becomes important that there is a valid comparator. In Case 129/79 *Macarthys Ltd v Wendy Smith*, Smith was employed from March 1976 at a salary of £50 per week and complained of discrimination because her predecessor, a man, had received a salary of £60 per week. The CoJ held that although the work actually performed by employees of different sex must be within the same establishment, the employees need not be employed at the same time. However, the CoJ was careful to point out that: 'It

---

[13] Although replaced by Directive 2006/54, it is still useful to see the development of the law in this earlier directive.

cannot be ruled out that the difference in pay between two workers occupying the same post but at different periods in time may be explained by the operation of factors which are unconnected with any discrimination on grounds of sex'. This is a question of fact for the national courts to decide. In this case, the CoJ therefore expressly left open the possibility of a genuine material factor defence. Hence, the scope of the concept of equal pay for equal work (the same work) could not be restricted by a requirement by member states that the person whose work was being compared be contemporaneously employed.

Comparison can also be made with members of the other sex who do work of a lesser value to ensure that women doing work of higher value cannot be paid less than the male comparator, as was held in Case 157/86 *Mary Murphy v An Bord Telecom Eireann*.

The Court of Justice had also expressed the view in the *Macarthys* case that it would not entertain a hypothetical comparator. Equally it held in Case C-313/02 *Wippel v Peek & Cloppenburg* that a woman who was working only when required (a form of zero hours contract) who claimed unfair treatment because her working hours had not been specified could not be compared with a male working full time. The reason given was that no worker working full time had a contract the same or similar to Wippel; in other words, whilst EU legislative provisions on equal treatment Directive 76/207 and part time workers Directive 97/81 would apply, the case was distinguished on the facts.

However, in light of the new statutory definitions of direct discrimination in the new Equality Directives (Directives 2000/43 and 2000/78), and now Directive 2006/54, it is quite possible that the CoJ could also now provide a more generous interpretation. Directive 2006/54 defines direct discrimination as 'where one person is treated less favourably on grounds of sex than another is, has been or would be treated in a comparable situation'. It is thus arguable that 'would be' opens the door for even a hypothetical comparator to be sufficient. It may also encourage the CoJ to adopt a hypothetical comparator test in view of the disturbing consequences arising from some recent cases considering comparators.

11.5.4 Comparison Revisited

Comparison, or the lack of it, has become a crucial factor in two cases that have arisen from the contracting out of jobs to outside private companies under the compulsory competitive tendering schemes that were imposed on local authorities in the UK. In these schemes, some members of staff (predominantly women) have been removed from direct employment by the local authority and then re-employed by an independent employer. They are then returned to the same job, but on less money than their (mainly) male counterparts doing the same job or work previously evaluated to be of equal value. In Case C-320/00 *Lawrence v Regent Office Care Ltd*, dinner ladies, who were previously employed directly by the local authority, had their contracts taken over by a private company. They continued to work in the same job, but were paid less than they had been and less in comparison with male colleagues who were retained by the local authority, but who had been rated to be doing work of equal value. The CoJ held that whilst Art 141 EC (now Art 157 TFEU) was not restricted to employees working for the same employer, it could not apply where there was not a single overall authority responsible for deciding pay. Similarly, in Case C-256/01 *Allonby*, teachers who were mainly female had been made redundant by a college, but taken on by an agency in a self-employed capacity and returned to work in the same college, but were paid less than an alleged male comparator employed by the college. The CoJ held that because there was not a single source that led to the unequal pay, the work and the pay of those workers could not therefore be compared on the basis of Art 141 EC (now Art 157 TFEU).

With the Court of Justice having held twice now that a comparison is not possible, the conclusion is that there can be no factual, let alone illegal, discrimination, because there is no single-body employer responsible to make the pay adjustment if inequality were found to be unlawful. These cases would appear to open up a very big loophole, which allows the rolling back of the gains that have been made over the decades to ensure equal pay for women, by condoning the hiving-off of employment contracts according to sex in order to be able to pay unequally, thus either directly or indirectly discriminating against women under the ostensible reason given of delivering local authority services more economically and more efficiently. Although the compulsory competitive tendering scheme itself has now been abandoned, it is possible that there will be more cases following this particular development, as other forms of outside contracting, agency contracting, and various public–private initiatives[14] have been developed.

These cases have also involved an issue that occurs a lot in discrimination law, that of indirect discrimination rather than direct, and this will be considered next.

In the UK, there is a Scottish case, which was not referred to the Court of Justice, but which was decided by the Scottish court itself, that allowed a comparison across local authorities and from which the Court of Justice might take a leaf: *South Ayrshire Council v Morton*.[15]

11.5.5 Part-time Work and Indirect Discrimination

It is in the area of part-time work that the concept of indirect discrimination was most thoroughly explored by the Court of Justice. Whilst direct discrimination on the grounds of sex can arguably never be justified—either it is discriminatory and thus contrary to EU law, or it is not—indirect discrimination can be justified. Article 157 TFEU and Directive 2006/54, Art 2(1)(a) clearly outlaw direct discrimination where a distinction is drawn between the rights of men and women overtly on the basis of sex. It is still factually possible to show that the discrimination was not based on sex, but on some other factor. Indirect discrimination, which has already been encountered in relation to the free movement of persons, is more difficult to determine. In this area, it covers cases in which a class of persons is mainly or entirely constituted of one sex (usually women), and a difference is drawn between that class and another class, which can consist of members of both sexes. In either class, no direct discrimination takes place—that is, both genders are treated the same—but, in comparison with the other class, a rule or measure operates in a discriminatory manner against the predominant sex, which can be either women or men. Whether the discrimination is actually unlawful is often dependent on the motives behind it and whether it can be justified objectively by those motives.

There is a statutory definition of indirect discrimination, now contained in Directive 2006/54, Art 2(1)(b), as follows:

'indirect discrimination': where an apparently neutral provision, criterion or practice would put persons of one sex at a particular disadvantage compared with persons of the

---

[14] See **http://webarchive.nationalarchives.gov.uk/20130129110402/http://www.hm-treasury.gov.uk/ppp_index.htm**.

[15] [2002] IRLR 256. Legislative intervention to correct this has not happened and despite the fact that recital 10 of Directive 2006/54 states that 'The European Court of Justice has established that, in certain circumstances, the principle of equal pay is not limited to situations where men and women work for the same employer', there was nothing to that end introduced into the body of the directive. Thus, it appears that this will have to wait for suitable cases to come along for the Court of Justice to make its own correction—perhaps encouraged by recital 10.

other sex, unless that provision, criterion or practice is objectively justified by a legitimate aim, and the means of achieving that aim are appropriate and necessary.

Even with the statutory definition, it is nevertheless still instructive to see how this was developed by the Court of Justice, which has considered indirect discrimination in a number of cases concerning pay differences between full-time and part-time workers. These are also usually combined with objective justifications as elements of the cases.

In Case 96/80 *Jenkins v Kingsgate*, the employers paid full-time workers 10 per cent more per hour than part-time workers, in order, it was claimed, to discourage absenteeism and to achieve a more efficient use of their machinery. All but one of the part-time workers were women. The CoJ held:

A difference in rates of remuneration between full and part-time employees did not offend against Article 119 EEC [now Art 157 TFEU] provided that the difference was attributable to factors which were objectively justified and did not relate directly or indirectly to discrimination based on sex.

It also held that:

If it is established that a considerably smaller percentage of women than men perform the number of hours necessary to be a full-timer, the inequality will contravene Article 119 EEC [now Art 157 TFEU] where, regard being had to the difficulties encountered by women in arranging to work the minimum number of hours per week, the pay policy of the undertaking cannot be explained by factors other than the discrimination based on sex.

In other words, it is more likely that women find it harder to work full time and that they seek part-time work because of commitments to family and home, but this does not make it lawful to discriminate against them.

11.5.5.1 Objective Justifications

The existence of an objective justification becomes crucial but in EU law we do not, for the most part, see this because it is usually a matter of factual consideration for the national court. For example, the justification given by an employer may be that the company needs to encourage the recruitment of full-time employees, in which case the national court might require evidence that demonstrates the relative number of full-time and part-time vacancies, and applications for those posts, to see whether the facts bear out the claim made by the company. Where there is no plausible explanation to account for the difference in pay, it is likely to be discrimination contrary to Art 157 TFEU.

In Case 170/84 *Bilka-Kaufhaus v Karin Weber Van Hartz*, a store gave all full-time employees a non-contributory pension on retirement, whereas part-timers only qualified if they had been employed permanently for at least 15 years. The undertaking claimed that it needed to pay full-timers more to attract them in sufficient numbers. The Court of Justice ruled that Art 119 EEC (now Art 157 TFEU) is infringed where a company excludes part-time workers from its occupational pension scheme and where that exclusion affects a far greater number of women than men, unless the undertaking shows that the exclusion is based on objectively justified factors unconnected with discrimination based on sex. The CoJ went on to consider the question of whether the undertaking could justify that disadvantage on the ground that its objective is to employ as few part-time workers as possible, even though, in the department-store sector, there are no reasons of commercial expediency that call for the pursuit of such a policy.

In order to show that the discrimination was objectively justified, the employer must show that the measures giving rise to the difference in treatment:

(a) correspond to a genuine need of the enterprise

(b) are suitable for attaining the objective pursued by the enterprise

(c) are strictly necessary for that purpose—that is, they are proportional.

The further requirement laid down by the CoJ, that it was for the company to show that the discrimination was not based on sex rather than the complainant having to prove discrimination, was part of a move by the CoJ to shift the burden of proof to the company over a number of cases. In the particular case, the German court applying the ruling held that the difference was not objectively justified. In Case 171/88 *Rinner-Kuhn*, the Court of Justice suggested that an objective factor that was based on a social policy might be acceptable, but not the reason for a difference in pay in the case, based on the assumption that part-time workers were not integrated into the business in the same way as full-time workers, even where based on national law.

In Case C-167/97 *Seymour-Smith and Perez*, for example, the CoJ held that national courts should look at the numbers of both men and women who can and cannot satisfy a particular requirement (full-time work, for example) to determine whether there is a disproportionate effect on one sex, in which case discrimination will be assumed unless justified.

Part-time work and overtime were considered in two cases in which indirect discrimination was claimed, both involving a predominance of women in the part-time group of workers. In Case C-399/92 *Helmig*, part-time workers were not paid overtime rates for work in excess of their part-time hours but only, as with full-time workers, when they worked more hours than full-time workers. In Case C-300/06 *Vob*, the part-time workers were paid less for overtime than full-time workers regardless of the overall number of hours worked. The Court of Justice was satisfied that in *Helmig*, there was no discrimination as pay calculations were the same, but in *Vob*, pay rates were reduced for part-time overtime but it was left open whether they could be objectively justified within the national court.

The case law on part-time work has essentially been put into statutory form by Directive 97/81.[16]

The next section considers equal value claims, but is also instructive in terms of the investigation that the national court should undertake to assess the grounds for the indirect discrimination.

11.5.6 Work of Equal Value

'Work of equal value' claims cause further difficulties because it is not often clear that two jobs are of the same value and an appraisal has to be done, either by the national court or using a formal job evaluation scheme. Case C-127/92 *Enderby v Frenchay Health Authority* involved an equal value claim and the comparison of lower-paid, mainly

---

[16] OJ 1998 L14/9.

women, speech therapists with higher-paid, mainly men, pharmacists and clinical psychologists. The Court of Justice held that it was for the national court to determine, if necessary, by applying the principle of proportionality, whether and to what extent the shortage of candidates for a job and the need to attract them by paying higher pay constituted an objectively justified ground for the difference in pay between jobs of equal value. The CoJ held that it was up to the national court to decide whether the available statistics are representative enough to provide sufficiently significant evidence to decide the justifications given. The difficulty with indirect discrimination is that the higher demand for lower-paid, but flexible, jobs especially where this demand is from women, can be argued by the employer to constitute evidence that it needs to pay less flexible and thus less attractive jobs, occupied mainly by men, at a premium or, in the alternative, to pay the more flexible and more sought-after jobs at a lower rate.

In Case 157/86 *Mary Murphy v An Bord Telecom Eireann*, an employee claimed equal pay for her work, which was considered to be of even higher value than her comparator. The CoJ held that Art 119 EEC (now Art 157 TFEU) must be interpreted as covering the case in which a worker who relies on that provision to obtain equal pay is engaged in work of higher value than that of the person with whom a comparison is to be made. The conclusion that has to be drawn from the case was that Art 119 EEC could also be applied to equal value claims, although not expressly stated in the Article at the time. Under the amended Art 157 TFEU, it is expressly covered. The CoJ reasoned that whilst it was true that Art 119 EEC applies only in the case of equal work, nevertheless, if that principle forbids workers of one sex engaged in work of equal value to be paid a lower wage than the other sex, it prohibits much more strongly such a difference in pay where the lower-paid category of workers is engaged in work of higher value. Interestingly, in this case the defendant was a public body, and if the CoJ had so wished, it could have resolved the case under Directive 75/117, because it would involve vertical direct effects, but it chose instead to widen the scope of Art 119 EEC which, in the long run, would assist more potential litigants than would the directive.

11.5.6.1 Job Evaluation Schemes and the Burden of Proof

In order to back up the principle of equal pay for work of equal value, old Directive 75/117 provided, under the second sentence of Art 1, that where a job classification scheme is used for determining pay, it must be drawn up so as to exclude discrimination based on sex. That is now reproduced in the second sentence of Art 4 of Directive 2006/54.

The UK was brought to task in Case 61/81 *Commission v UK (Equal Pay for Equal Work)* for failing to put in place a job classification system in this case in which employers refused to make an assessment. This was then corrected by the national Equal Pay (Equal Value Amendment) Regulations 1983. In a number of cases, the Court of Justice has ruled that any job evaluation schemes used must not be based on criteria that valued one sex only and must be transparent, so that a claimant can see how particular wages were achieved. For example, in Case 237/85 *Rummler v Dato-Druck*, a job evaluation scheme that was based on muscular effort, fatigue, and physical hardship was held by the CoJ not to be in breach of Art 1 of Directive 75/117 as long as certain conditions were met. First, it must, insofar as the nature of the tasks carried out in the undertaking permits, take into account criteria for which workers of each sex show particular aptitude. The CoJ said that criteria based exclusively on the values of one sex contain a 'risk of discrimination'.

Secondly, as was noted in the *Bilka* and *Enderby* cases, the CoJ has reversed the burden of proof so that the employer has to prove that there was no discrimination, direct or indirect, rather than the employee having to show that there was discrimination—something that would be much harder for the employee, particularly in such cases as Case 109/88

Handels-og Kontorfunktionaerernes Forbund i Danmark v Dansk Arbejdsgiverforening (Danfoss). This case involved a pay structure so complex that it was impossible for a woman to identify the reasons that led to a difference in pay between her and a man doing the same job. The results of this case law were consolidated into Directive 97/80,[17] which itself has now been replaced by Directive 2006/54, Art 19.

The *Danfoss* case also made it clear that a length-of-service criterion for higher pay was acceptable with special justification. This has now been clearly confirmed in Case C-17/05 *Cadman*, in which a significant difference in pay between men and women existed based on length of service. It would be only in the case of doubt that the burden would fall on the employer to justify the difference, but quite what would constitute justiciable 'doubt' is unclear.

11.5.7 Enforcement and Remedies

The remedies and enforcement procedures have been consolidated in the new Directive 2006/54 for all of the directives that it has replaced.[18] Member states are required under Arts 17 and 18 of Directive 2006/54 to ensure that judicial or conciliation procedures are available, with adequate compensation measures. Article 17(1) of Directive 2006/54 requires member states to provide the legal means by which all employees who consider themselves discriminated against are able to pursue a claim. Member states shall ensure that, after possible recourse to other competent authorities, including, where they deem it appropriate, conciliation procedures, judicial procedures for the enforcement of obligations under this directive are available to all persons who consider themselves wronged by failure to apply the principle of equal treatment to them, even after the relationship in which the discrimination is alleged to have occurred has ended. Article 23 of Directive 2006/54 requires member states to take the necessary measures to ensure that any provisions in collective agreements, wage agreements, or in individual contracts that breach the principles of the directive are to be null and void or to be removed. Article 24 of Directive 2006/54 requires the member states to take measures to protect employees against dismissal as a result of a complaint of discrimination made by them to an employer, or where the employee takes legal proceedings aimed to enforce the principles provided by the directive. The member states were required under Art 6 of Directive 75/117 to take the necessary measures to ensure that the principle of equal pay is applied and see that effective means are available to take care that the principle is observed. This requirement has not been carried over verbatim, and appears to have been consolidated with the overall requirement to ensure equal treatment in Arts 1 and 4 of the new Directive 2006/54.

11.6 Equal Treatment

The original Equal Treatment Directive (76/207) went well beyond the original scope of Art 119 EC (now Art 157 TFEU), which was concerned only with pay; therefore, the directive had to be enacted under the general legislative power of Art 235 EEC (now Art 352 TFEU). It extended the prohibition of discrimination on the grounds of sex into many facets of the employment relationship including, inter alia, access, appointment, dismissal,

---

[17] OJ 1998 L14/6.

[18] The enforcement provisions in the original directives have been consolidated into an overall enforcement and remedies section of the chapter: see Section 11.5.7.

retirement, training, and working conditions. It has now been repealed and replaced by Directive 2006/54, which was enacted under the amended Art 141(3) EC (now Art 157(3) TFEU) now allowing for direct intervention under a dedicated treaty legal base.

Article 14(1) of Directive 2006/54 (previously Art 1 of Directive 76/207) refers to equal treatment for men and women, which is required to be applied to working conditions, access to employment (including promotion), and vocational training. Social security matters, covered by later directives, were expressly excluded from the ambit of this directive. A previous Art 1a of Directive 76/207, which set out what is known as 'gender mainstreaming', is now to be found in Art 23 of Directive 2006/54. It requires member states actively to take into account the objective of equality between men and women when formulating and implementing laws, regulations, administrative provisions, policies, and activities in the areas referred to in all of the new directives.

11.6.1 **The Concept of Equal Treatment/No Discrimination on the Grounds of Sex**

The concept of 'equal treatment', which was defined in Directive 76/207 as no discrimination on the grounds of sex directly or indirectly by reference in particular to marital or family status, has not been carried over into Directive 2006/54, which has adopted the extended definition of discrimination noted in Section 11.4.2. The now single exception to the principle of equal treatment is that relating to particular occupational activities previously contained in Art 2(6) and now to be found in Art 14(2) of Directive 2006/54, which will be considered after the cases that previously helped to determine the extent of discrimination covered by the earlier directive.

As was discussed earlier, whilst the concepts of 'equal treatment' and 'no discrimination' are treated as being synonymous, in the context of equal treatment (rather than only equal pay), the distinction took on greater significance because of the much greater subject-matter coverage of the earlier directive. Does equal treatment mean *more* than no discrimination? Case law has considered the scope of the protection provided for by these provisions insofar as what is meant by the right to equality within the framework agreed by the member states and interpreted by the Court of Justice. For example, in Case C-13/94 *P v S and Cornwall County Council*, a male-to-female transsexual was dismissed from employment in an educational establishment after informing his employers that he was going to undergo gender reassignment. The CoJ, in moving away from a simple interpretation of no discrimination on the grounds of sex simply to mean by a comparison of how each gender is treated, held that the dismissal was unlawful discrimination on the grounds of sex because it was 'based essentially if not exclusively on the sex of the person concerned'. One of the difficulties in sex discrimination law is that the need to find a comparator is not always convenient or helpful in determining whether discrimination has been suffered, especially in relation to the pregnancy cases, considered later. In this case, if this is discrimination based on sex, as the CoJ held, with whom can a comparison be made? There is no direct comparator as such, for example, a female-to-male transsexual. The CoJ held that, where a person is dismissed on the ground that he or she intends to undergo, or has undergone, gender reassignment, he or she is treated unfavourably by comparison with persons of the sex to which he or she was deemed to belong before undergoing gender reassignment.

P engendered some debate that the directive appeared not to be limited to discrimination on the grounds of sex (namely, not only the difference between genders), but also any discrimination where sex is a deciding or decisive factor. The question that was raised after this case was whether the concept of no discrimination on the grounds of sex had been transformed into 'no discrimination on the grounds of sexuality' or even, 'no sexual orientation discrimination'. The answer was soon forthcoming in a same-sex female cohabitees case. In Case C-249/96 *Grant v South West Trains*, South West Trains' regulations specifically excluded benefits from same-sex partnerships. Whereas opposite-sex partners were included even where they were not married, but provided that a stable relationship was established, same-sex partners were not. The Court of Justice held that this was not discrimination based on sex, because the rule would apply also using a direct comparison to male same-sex relationships. This was discrimination based on sexual orientation. The CoJ discussed a number of points in connection with this and found that, in some member states, such a relationship would, but only for a limited range of rights, be treated the same as an opposite-sex relationship and that, in some states, such relationships were not recognized in any particular way. The CoJ referred to the then new Art 13 EC (now Art 19 TFEU) by which the member states in Council were empowered to take action to outlaw sexual orientation discrimination, but stated that the (at that time) present state of law in the EC did not equate same-sex relationships with opposite-sex ones. Therefore, the discrimination in respect of sexual orientation, although present, was not contrary to Art 141 EC (now Art 157 TFEU) or the directive. The CoJ confirmed this stance in Case 125/99 P *D and Sweden v Council*. In both cases, the CoJ decided to leave the response to this form of discrimination to the legislative intervention of the member states, which have now responded with Directive 2000/78, providing a framework for combating discrimination on grounds of sexual orientation, considered later.

However, Case C-117/01 *KB v NHS Pensions*, which although decided on the basis of Art 141 EC (now Art 157 TFEU) and not the directive, is worthy of a brief note here because of the much more sympathetic judgment given by the Court of Justice in a case involving transsexual rights under the then-existing Community legislation. The case concerned the inability to nominate as a pension beneficiary a transsexual partner, because national legislation required the partner to be an opposite-sex spouse. National legislation would not allow the original sex of the partner to be altered to enable him or her to marry and thus satisfy the pension law requirement. The CoJ held that national legislation must be regarded as being, in principle, incompatible with the requirements of Art 141 EC on the grounds that it had already been found to be in breach of the European Convention on Human Rights (ECHR), and had prevented a couple such as KB and R from fulfilling the marriage requirement necessary for one of them to be able to benefit from part of the pay of the other. However, the CoJ was not specific as to how exactly Art 141 EC might be offended, apart from the fact that Art 141 EC would regard the benefit as pay. The CoJ acknowledged, though, that it was up to the member state to determine the conditions under which legal recognition is given to the change of gender of a person in R's situation and that it would be up to the national court to decide whether KB can rely on Art 141 EC (now Art 157 TFEU). Equal treatment in this case, then, has been given a very wide scope to include the right to have a change in sex officially testified. Quite where a comparison fits in is difficult to see. Now that same-sex civil partnerships have been given statutory recognition in the UK, this would no longer be a problem.

Finally, in Case C-423/04 *Richards*, it was held that the correct comparator for a male-to-female transgendered person when determining pensionable ages was a female who had not undergone gender reassignment. Directive 79/7, Art 4(1), was held not to permit a distinction in national law as to how a pension was determined.

The new Directive 2006/54 adds a little light to this area in that it states, in recital 3, that:

> The Court of Justice has held that the scope of the principle of equal treatment for men and women cannot be confined to the prohibition of discrimination based on the fact that a person is of one or other sex. In view of its purpose and the nature of the rights which it seeks to safeguard, it also applies to discrimination arising from the gender reassignment of a person.

This is not, however, addressed in the body of the directive.

11.6.2 The Scope of Equal Treatment

The scope of the prohibition of discrimination within the new directive is spelt out in detail in Art 14(1) of Directive 2006/54 (previously the amended Art 3 of Directive 76/207, which had consolidated much of the previous case law). It provides that the application of the principle of equal treatment means that there shall be no direct or indirect discrimination in the public or private sectors, including public bodies, in relation to:

(a) conditions for access to employment, to self-employment, or to occupation, including selection criteria and recruitment conditions, whatever the branch of activity and at all levels of the professional hierarchy, including promotion

(b) access to all types and to all levels of vocational guidance, vocational training, advanced vocational training, and retraining, including practical work experience

(c) employment and working conditions, including dismissals, as well as pay as provided for in Art 157 TFEU

(d) membership of, and involvement in, an organization of workers or employers, or any organization whose members carry on a particular profession, including the benefits provided for by such organizations.

Now, as provided in Art 23 of Directive 2006/54, member states are required to take the necessary measures to ensure that:

(a) any laws, regulations, and administrative provisions contrary to the principle of equal treatment are abolished

(b) provisions contrary to the principle of equal treatment in individual or collective contracts or agreements, internal rules of undertakings, or rules governing the independent occupations and professions and workers' and employers' organizations or any other arrangements shall be, or may be, declared null and void or are amended.

The scope of application can be avoided for specific reasons given in the directive only.

11.6.3 Equality with Regard to Employment Access, Working Conditions, Dismissal, and Retirement Ages

Article 14 of the new Directive 2006/54, noted earlier, provides that there shall be no direct or indirect discrimination relating to all aspects of employment, and notably access to jobs and conditions of employment. Cases that were until then considered under the previous directive, notably Art 5, which required equality of treatment in working conditions and conditions governing dismissal, are now covered by Directive 2006/54.

Most of the case law arising from the principle of equal treatment appears to have concerned retirement and pensions.

There are one or two exceptions, as in the first case following. In Case C-177/88 *Dekker v VJM Centram*, VJM (a social training centre) refused to employ Mrs Dekker because she was pregnant and this would mean that insurance law, which did not recognize pregnancy as a reason for paying insurance money, would not reimburse the employer during her maternity leave. As a social institution, it argued that it could not afford to hire a replacement for her. The Court of Justice held that the employer was in direct contravention of Arts 2(1) and 3(1) of Directive 76/207 by its refusal to employ even though national rules economically forced this situation. Furthermore, it was pointed out by the Court of Justice that direct discrimination removed the need to compare the treatment with that of a man.

In Case C-312/86 *Commission v France (Protection of Women)*, French legislation allowed certain privileges for women, including extended maternity leave, a reduction in working hours of women aged 59, bringing forward retirement age, time off for sick children, an extra day's holiday each year per child, a day off on the first day of a school term, and others. The CoJ considered that these special provisions only for women discriminated against men contrary to the directive. They were not justified by Art 2(3) (now Art 14 of Directive 2006/54), which protects women during pregnancy and maternity, because the reasons given for the protection applied equally to male and female workers.

Turning to dismissal and retirement, we know from the earlier section on equal pay that member states can, under Art 7 of Directive 7/79, exclude the determination of pensionable age for the purposes of granting old-age and retirement pensions, and the possible consequences thereof for other benefits. It was thought and argued that this meant that any difference to do with either pensions entitlements or pensionable ages was excluded, and thus, retirement and dismissal ages were also excluded. In Case 151/84 *Roberts v Tate and Lyle*, Mrs Roberts was aged 53, and a redundancy scheme allowed access to a redundancy for both men and women at the age of 55. Roberts claimed unlawful discrimination because men could gain access ten years before their pensionable age, but women only five. The CoJ held that access to a redundancy scheme was concerned with dismissal and therefore covered by Art 5, and not excluded by Art 7 of Directive 79/7. Access was not linked to the state security system. The CoJ held that Art 5(1) of Directive 76/207 must be interpreted as meaning that a contractual provision that lays down a single age (55) for the dismissal of men and women under a mass redundancy involving the grant of an early retirement pension (although the normal retirement age is different for men and women) does not constitute discrimination on grounds of sex contrary to Community law.

In the leading case concerned with retirement, Case 152/84 *Marshall*, the compulsory earlier retirement of women was considered. National legislation allowed employers to retire women earlier than men. The Court of Justice, though, held that retirement also came within the scope of working conditions, including dismissal, and was thus covered by the directive. When the CoJ came to consider whether the retirement age was linked to pensions, it decided relatively easily that the enforced earlier retirement for women than for men did not fall within the justification of Art 7 of Directive 79/7 and was therefore direct discrimination. Directive 76/207 was held by the CoJ to be directly effective, but only vertically. Other means of enforcement must be pursued if a private employer is involved.

Case C-136/95 *Thibault* is notable for the clear statement from the CoJ about how Community law on equal treatment should be regarded and thus applied. Pay rises and promotion were assessed on the basis of the previous six months' work presence, which was argued to discriminate clearly against women on maternity absence, who lost the chance to be assessed for pay increases or promotion. The CoJ held that this amounted to unlawful discrimination contrary to Arts 2(3) and 5(1) (as they were then) of Directive 76/207. These provisions, in the view of the CoJ, required substantive, and not only formal, equality; namely real rights, not only those on paper.

Finally, in this section, Case C-116/94 *Meyers* is worth noting because it extended the scope of the directive to the social security benefit, family credit, something that quite reasonably might be considered to come under the Social Security Directive 79/7 and not 76/207. The credit was designed to supplement low-paid workers in an attempt to persuade them to remain in work, thus satisfying the Court of Justice that it could be construed under the terms 'access to employment' and 'working conditions', covered by Arts 3 and 5 (then of Directive 76/207), because it would both encourage employees to take up job offers and also be considered to be a condition of work. 'Working conditions' thus applies to all aspects of the working relationship and not only those contained within the contract of employment.

Having regarded the widening scope of the principle of equal treatment, we now need to consider the derogations or exemptions that are provided under the directive to exclude certain circumstances or situations from being subject to the principle of equal treatment. The first provision seeks to take out of the application of the principle of equal treatment circumstances in which factors other than sex allow discriminatory treatment; the second seeks to take account of the unique circumstance of pregnancy; and the third seeks to allow for the possibility of promoting further equality for women.

11.6.4 **Member States' Ability to Exempt Certain Occupations**

Article 14(2) of Directive 2006/54 provides member states with the ability to exempt certain occupations from the application of the equal treatment principle where a characteristic not related to sex itself is a factor. The characteristic must constitute a genuine and determining occupational requirement in order not to constitute unlawful discrimination on the grounds of sex. Previously, cases showed that the member states were perhaps permitted a greater degree of discretion than under more recent cases. For example, in Case 165/82 *Commission v UK (Equal Treatment for Men and Women)*, the restriction of access of males to midwifery was held to be acceptable but, in such cases, member states are required to assess the restrictions periodically in order to decide, in light of social developments, whether there is justification for maintaining the exclusions concerned. They must notify the Commission of the results of this assessment under Art 9(2) of Directive 76/207. Indeed, it is now the case that male midwives are accepted in the UK and other countries. In the same case, a blanket exemption from the provisions of the directive that applied to all companies with fewer than six workers was held by the CoJ not to be sanctioned by the exemption and thus contrary to the directive.

In Case 222/84 *Johnston v Chief Constable of the RUC*, the Royal Ulster Constabulary did not renew the contracts of a number of female police officers and justified this under Art 2(2) of Directive 76/207, because of a policy decision that women could not carry firearms. The Court of Justice held that the exception might apply to certain activities carried out by police officers, but not to police activities in general. The member states might therefore restrict such specific activities and the training for that activity to men, provided that the situation was reviewed regularly to ensure that the restrictions remained justified and that the restrictions complied with the principle of proportionality. The CoJ suggested that the women could be assigned other duties not involving use of firearms, rather than suffer outright dismissal.

More recent case law concerning employment in the armed forces, however, questions the restrictions permitted in *Johnston*. In Case C-273/97 *Angela Sirdar v The Army Board*, the CoJ said that although EC law can also apply to employment in the army, in the present case, the exclusion of a woman as a cook in the Royal Marines was acceptable because of the Marines' requirements of interoperability and front-line duties (namely, the unit's cook was expected to undertake all duties and also be involved in front-line duties, and therefore sex was a determining factor and the UK could rely on the exemption). Sirdar, who was previously a cook for a commando regiment not having these same requirements, could not be a cook for the Marines.

In Case C-285/98 *Kreil v Germany*, a case that resembles *Johnston*, but which deals with the army rather than the police force, the CoJ did not accept a general exclusion from military posts that meant that all armed units could remain exclusively male. The CoJ held that the national authorities contravened the principle of proportionality in taking the general position that the composition of all armed units in the *Bundeswehr* had to remain exclusively male. By rejecting out of hand the application by Ms Kreil to the weapons electronics maintenance service of the Federal German army, the German authorities had unlawfully discriminated against her. The armed forces are thus categorically included, but with a discretion preserved for the member states to discriminate for particular circumstances as in *Sirdar*.

Finally in the trio of army cases, in Case C-186/01 *Dory*, the compulsory military service for males only in Germany was challenged. The CoJ held 'that the Equal Treatment Directive applies to equality in the access to posts, it does not govern the member states' choices of military organization for the defence of their territory or of their essential interests'. Germany's choice of compulsory male-only military service, enshrined in its Constitution, was immune from Community law scrutiny. The CoJ was, however, certainly showing an unusually high degree of respect for the German Constitution. The negative consequences for males as a result of their time spent in military service, such as a delay in comparisons to females in getting to the job market, can therefore only be remedied by the national authorities and courts—but see, however, *Schnorbus* in Section 11.6.6.

11.6.5 The Protection of Women Regarding Childbirth and Maternity

Article 28(1) of Directive 2006/54 provides: 'This Directive shall be without prejudice to provisions concerning the protection of women, particularly as regards pregnancy and maternity.' This is another derogation from the principle of equal treatment and a different legal regime can apply here, but this time specifically to protect women. However, these provisions should not be used to disguise discrimination. Directive 2006/54, Art 15, continues to state that a woman on maternity leave shall be entitled, after the end of her period of maternity leave, to return to her job or to an equivalent post on terms and conditions that are no less favourable to her, and to benefit from any improvement in working conditions to which she would be entitled during her absence. Directive 2006/54, Art 2(2)(c), now repeats that 'less favourable treatment of a woman related to pregnancy or maternity leave within the meaning of Directive 92/85/EEC' shall constitute discrimination within the meaning of Directive 2006/54.

Directive 92/85 concerns the protection of pregnant and breastfeeding workers. Its title comes across as somewhat inelegant, but it also helps to determine the rights to which women are entitled when pregnant and on maternity leave. Article 10, in combination with Art 8, designates the period of special protection as from the beginning of pregnancy to the end of maternity leave (which must be a 14-week minimum continuous period of leave), during which women are protected from dismissal for any reasons connected to pregnancy. After the period has expired, the special protection is lost. Note that even during the period of special protection, they can be dismissed in the normal course of events where the reason for dismissal is not connected to pregnancy; for example, for theft. In this particular area of law, the need to make a comparison is rejected in favour of allowing action that removes the substantive inequality suffered by reason of the pregnancy, which cannot be compared. Case law had, however, already expanded and clarified existing EU law ahead of Directive 92/85 coming into force.

In a case that predates the Parental Leave Directive, Case 184/83 *Hoffman v Barmer Ersatzkasse*, a father claimed that the refusal to grant six months' paternity leave following the birth of his child, while the mother went back to work, was discrimination contrary to Arts 1, 2, and 5(1) of the Equal Treatment Directive 76/207. The Court of Justice held that the directive was not designed to settle questions concerned with the organization of the family, or to alter the division of responsibility between parents, and that parental leave may therefore be reserved to the mother by the member states by virtue of Art 2(3). The case makes it clear that Art 2(3) was an exception to the general principle of equal treatment established by the directive exclusively in favour of women. Note, now, that the protection against dismissal during a period of parental leave is extended to workers of both sexes by the Parental Leave Directive 96/34, but because this is not usually the subject of study in most EU courses, it is not considered further here.[19]

11.6.5.1 Dismissal During or After Pregnancy

A series of cases has now allowed us to see just how protective the EU legal regime for pregnant women is. The first case deals with a national law designed to protect pregnant women, albeit by excluding them from a certain type of work.

In C-421/92 *Habermann-Beltermann v Arbeiterwohlfahrt*, HB was employed on a permanent nights' contract and was dismissed when discovered to be pregnant on the basis of a national law prohibiting the night-time work of pregnant women. The employer argued that the prohibition of night work was allowed by the directive and, to that extent, the Court of Justice agreed with the employer, but not so as to justify dismissal. The CoJ held that neither national legislation nor employment contract rules could render void an employment contract by reason of the fact that the female worker was found to be pregnant. Dismissal was clearly disproportionate and the employer should, for example, find other work for her.

In Case C-32/93 *Webb v EMO Air Cargo (UK) Ltd*, a woman who was employed on an indefinite contract to replace her predecessor, who was on pregnancy and maternity leave, was dismissed when it was discovered that, as a replacement, she was also pregnant. The CoJ held this to be direct discrimination contrary to Arts 2(1) and 5(1) of Directive 76/207. This case arose before Directive 92/85 came into force and could not therefore be applied in the case, which was then decided exclusively on Directive 76/207. The clear and forthright position taken by the CoJ in the case was confirmed in Case C-207/98 *Mahlberg*

---

[19] It is to be noted that the requirement of equal treatment has been extended to time off for breastfeeding for men and women, because in the view of the Court the time off has in fact been detached from the physical aspect of breastfeeding into time being spent feeding and caring for the child, time which can be carried out and enjoyed by both the father and mother. Hence, then, a national measure which reserved this time off exclusively for women was held to breach both Art 157(4) and Directive 76/207. See Case C-104/09 *Roca Alvaraz*. The time taken for maternity leave cannot be discounted when calculating seniority as was held in Case C-294/04 *Herrero*.

in respect of the appointment of full-time permanent employees. Dismissal because a woman is pregnant is a clear and direct breach of EU law.

The next form of employment relationship that was considered by the CoJ to determine if they, too, are included with the scope of the directive, was the temporary employment contract.

In Case C-438/99 *Melgar*, a woman was employed on a series of back-to-back fixed-term contracts. Her fourth one expired, allegedly, according to the employee, without being renewed or extended as in the past. Prior to that occurring, her employer learned of her pregnancy. However, the employers had offered a fifth contract, but Melgar refused to sign it on the basis that her last contract had not expired and she had been dismissed unfairly. The national court did not determine as a matter of fact whether the case concerned a dismissal from an indefinite employment contract or a failure to employ on a new contract. The Court of Justice held that the failure to renew a fixed-term contract was not strictly a case of dismissal discrimination contrary to Art 10 of Directive 92/85. However, it considered that the non-renewal could be regarded as a refusal to employ based on pregnancy and, thus, directly discriminatory and contrary to Directive 76/207, Arts 2(1) and 3(1). The facts in the case, however, do not seem to support the view that there was a refusal to appoint, with the employer having offered a contract.[20]

In a clearer fixed-term contract case, Case C-109/00 *Tele Danmark*, the following set of facts arose. A post was advertised as a six-months-only temporary contract. Training for the post, however, required two months before the person appointed could undertake full duties usefully. Ms Brandt-Nielsen was appointed as from 1 July 1995 but, in mid-August, she informed her employer that she was pregnant and due to give birth in early November. Under Danish law, she was entitled to paid maternity leave as from 11 September 1995—that is, after two weeks' work. She had not previously informed the employer that she was pregnant and was dismissed with effect from 30 September 1995. She claimed unlawful dismissal. The CoJ held that it was direct discrimination contrary to both Art 5(1) of Directive 76/207 and Art 10 of Directive 92/85, and that the fact that employment was fixed-term was irrelevant because the inability to work was due to pregnancy. The duration of employment was also not a factor that would influence the result. The CoJ held that: 'Had the Community legislature wished to exclude fixed-term contracts, which represent a substantial proportion of the employment relationships, from the scope of those directives, it would have done so expressly'.

Not much later was Case C-320/01 *Busch*, in which a woman, who was on parental leave after the birth of her first child, became pregnant a second time and sought, whilst pregnant, to return early to work and before the full amount of paid parental leave for the first pregnancy had expired. Her employer had a vacancy and she was permitted to return to work. She was seven months pregnant when she did so. She had not mentioned her pregnancy to her employer, nor had her employer asked whether this was so. On 9 April 2001 she started work, and on 10 April 2001 she informed her employer that she was seven months pregnant and was entitled to paid maternity commencing 23 May 2001 (that is, after just six weeks of work). The employer rescinded the permission to return to work (not actually dismissal) on grounds of misrepresentation and mistake as to an essential characteristic. The reason given subsequently for returning to work early by Ms Busch

---

[20] Both these provisions also featured in Case C-400/95 with the same result, the only noticeable difference being that the dismissed woman was a director of a company rather than a worker. The Court of Justice was not dissuaded by that difference that the dismissal was direct discrimination and contrary to both provisions.

was that the maternity leave allowance was higher than the parental leave allowance. The Court of Justice held that an employee is not under an obligation to inform her employer in seeking to return to work that, because of certain legislative prohibitions, she is not able to carry out all of her duties. Furthermore, the CoJ held that an employer is not entitled to withdraw consent given to return to work because it was in error as to the employee being pregnant.

These last two cases may seem to be acting increasingly harshly on the employers, but there is not much doubt about the clear-cut support of the CoJ for the law as it presents itself. It is helping to provide substantive support for women in achieving equal treatment in circumstances in which it is impossible to compare how a man might have been treated and in which the Union has provided a special protective legal regime because of this. These laws may not have universal support from employers, but the point is that, as a society, we have decided to correct an iniquitous situation, namely, that pregnancy is an acceptable ground for dismissal or non-appointment.

To counter the cynical preparation of a notice of dismissal prepared to be delivered after the period of protection expired, the Court of Justice held this to be included in the prohibition under Art 10 of Directive 92/85 in Case C-460/06 *Paquay*. Dismissal and pregnancy by *in vitro* fertilization (IVF) treatment has also come under the judicial spotlight in Case C-506/06 *Mayr*, in which there had been a dismissal of a woman who was undergoing IVF treatment. Whilst her ova had been fertilized, they had not been re-implanted and the national court asked whether this was to be regarded within the protected period of pregnancy under Directive 92/85. The Court of Justice held that, at this stage of the treatment, it was not. However, if the woman were to have been dismissed as a consequence of undergoing the treatment, this would amount to direct discrimination contrary to Directive 76/207. It was left to the national court in this case to determine the exact reasons for the dismissal.

11.6.5.2 Pregnancy and Illness

Cases that involve illness resulting from pregnancy are particularly difficult ones to resolve and have caused the Court of Justice to reach hard decisions on both sides of the line. In Case C-179/88 *Hertz v Aldi*, Mrs Hertz was dismissed because of repeated absence due to illness, which originated from her prior pregnancy. The CoJ held that although pregnancy-related discrimination was a form of direct discrimination, the directive did not apply to dismissals due to illness absence that took place outside the maternity leave time granted. In such circumstances, it was necessary to look at national legislation to consider whether there was any direct or indirect discrimination in the grounds of dismissal. In this case, when the period of special protection has expired, it becomes possible again to make a comparison with men to see how they are treated if absent through illness over a long time.

The approach taken in *Hertz* was confirmed even after the entry into force of Directive 92/85 in Case C-400/95 *Larsson v Dansk Handel & Service*. The directives thus do not prevent dismissals for absences due to illness attributable to pregnancy even where the illness arose during pregnancy, and continued during and after the period of maternity leave. Dismissal is prohibited and thus unlawful during the period of protected maternity leave only. The dismissal after the leave period is not specifically catered for by EU law and the situation to determine unlawful discrimination reverts to comparing dismissal due to illness on a direct basis with the dismissal of a man for illness. With these cases, the CoJ recognizes that certain disorders are specific to one sex or another. For example, if a man were ill with prostate trouble or testicular cancer and took a lot of time off, but was sympathetically treated by his boss and not dismissed, the comparison would have to be with a woman who was ill for any reason. Similarly, a woman dismissed for taking too much time off due to illness arising from pregnancy could be compared with a man suffering from any illness. So, although pregnancy might play a role as the source of an illness, outside the protected period, it is the normal comparison that determines the legal position—something that is argued represents formal equality only and not the substantive equality supposedly upheld by the Court of Justice. This is pretty much the decision as confirmed by the CoJ in Case C-191/03 *McKenna*, in which it held that pregnancy-originated illness outside the protected period and absence by men under ordinary sick pay schemes were rightfully to be regarded as comparable.

Case C-394/96 *Brown v Rentokil* also concerned a dismissal that resulted from time taken off due to an illness originating during pregnancy, but before maternity leave had commenced. The CoJ made it clear that the period of protection incorporated the entire pregnancy and the maternity leave. The results in the *Hertz* and *Larsson* cases were corrected by the CoJ to the extent that any time taken off during pregnancy and maternity leave cannot now be taken into account in calculating the entire time taken off for the purpose of dismissal. In other words, time can only start to accrue for this purpose after the period of protection has ended. A woman would therefore be best advised to take her maternity leave as late as possible, if possible, to maximize the period of protection.

11.6.6 The Promotion of Equal Opportunity by Removing Existing Inequalities Affecting Opportunities

The statutory attempt to promote equal opportunity is often described in the term 'positive discrimination', although this is not an accurate description for what is allowed under the Union legal regime, as will be observed from the judgments of the Court of Justice. Both the treaty and Directive 2006/54 contain provision for some sort of action by the member states to try to promote equality. Directive 76/207, which was first on the scene, originally provided in Art 2(4) that the directive shall be without prejudice to measures to promote equal opportunity for men and women, in particular by removing existing inequalities that affect women's opportunities in the areas covered by the directive. The CoJ, in Case C-319/03 *Briheche*, concluded that Art 141(4) EC (now Art 157 TFEU) and Directive 76/207, Art 2(4), needed to be looked at separately, suggesting that their scope differed. Article 3 of Directive 2006/54 has replaced old Art 2(4) and provides that 'member states may maintain or adopt measures within the meaning of Article 141(4) of the treaty with a view to ensuring full equality in practice between men and women in working life'. Article 157(4) TFEU provides:

> With a view to ensuring full equality in practice between men and women in working life, the principle of equal treatment shall not prevent any member state from maintaining or adopting measures providing for specific advantages in order to make it easier for the under-represented sex to pursue a vocational activity or to prevent or compensate for disadvantages in professional careers.

Whilst the measures concerned mostly contemplate women, this is not exclusively the position, as can be observed in the case law. The extent to which the authorities of the member states can provide legislation or, indeed, the extent to which private employers are able to discriminate positively in favour of women by, for example, shortlisting or interviewing only female candidates or if dismissals are required, dismissing males only, is a difficult question. Article 3 of Directive 2006/54 would seem to allow more positive action than was previously the case by the use of the term 'equality in practice'—that is, not only on paper—but, as yet, no cases have arisen from the Article. There are, however, a number that have arisen under the old directive Article and the treaty amendment.

In Case 312/86 *Commission v France (Protection of Women)*, considered earlier, it can be seen that not all measures adopted by a member state to assist women will be considered to be fair by the Court of Justice. In contrast, in Case C-218/98 *Abdoulaye v Renault*, additional or guaranteed payments for females on maternity leave over and above those paid to males on paternity leave were recognized by the CoJ as acceptable due to the occupational disadvantages suffered by women during absence, and were held not to be discriminatory.

There is a series of cases concerned with appointment procedures that have been adapted to introduce an element of rebalancing in favour of the under-represented sex. In Case C-450/93 *Kalanke*, the CoJ ruled that a national rule which provided that, where equally qualified, men and women were candidates for a position with fewer women, women are automatically to be given priority, constituted direct discrimination on the grounds of sex contrary to the directive. According to the CoJ, the rule had gone beyond promotion and had overstepped the exception provided for in Art 2(4) of Directive 76/207. This decision was not taken to kindly in some quarters, because it seemed to undermine any possibility of providing affirmative action to improve the equality position of women; however, there was soon a refinement of the position, both in terms of the subtlety of approach by the member state authorities and the interpretation by the CoJ. Case C-409/95 *Marschall* involved an application for a teaching post by a qualified man being rejected by the local authority according to a law that provided that women should be given priority in the event of equal suitability. However, in contrast to *Kalanke*, a 'saving clause' provided that if a particular male candidate had grounds that tilted the balance in his favour, women were not to be given priority. Thus, the CoJ was able to conclude that the provision was one that could fall within the scope of Art 2(4) of Directive 76/207 and did not offend the prohibition of discrimination. There were, however, two safety mechanisms, which could otherwise be regarded as complications to the process, which should be set up: the first to avoid discrimination against men, and the second to stop the pendulum from swinging back against women. The CoJ considered such priority clauses to be acceptable provided that the candidates are objectively assessed to determine whether there are any factors tilting the balance in favour of a male candidate, but that such criteria employed do not themselves discriminate against women. This is a somewhat convoluted judgment, but probably gets to the result intended. Case C-158/97 *Badeck* confirms *Marschall* that such laws are not in breach of EU law, provided that the priority for women was not automatic and unconditional.

Article 157(4) TFEU now backs up the ability of the Court of Justice to pursue the more liberal approach adopted in *Marschall*. However, the first case reaching it under the amended treaty Article did not give the CoJ an opportunity to be expansive. In Case C-407/98 *Abrahamsson*, a woman was appointed to a university chair in preference to a man on the basis of a positive discrimination regulation and despite a clear 3–5 vote in favour of the man, based on his qualifications and the overall higher ranking of the male even after the positive discrimination factor had been taken into account. The university contended that the difference was not so great as to breach the objectivity requirement imposed by Community law in light of the recent case law of the Court of Justice. The CoJ held that EC law, primary or secondary, does not support appointments based on automatic preference for the under-represented sex irrespective of whether the qualifications are better or worse and where no objective assessment of each candidate has taken place. It seems that only where women have equivalent or perceptibly near qualifications will EU law permit any affirmative action to be exercised.

A case involving female only access to childcare facilities, save in emergency, was considered under Art 2(4) of Directive 76/207. In Case C-476/99 *Lommers*, a government ministry restricted access to subsidized childcare to women to address the lack of affordable facilities that caused many women to give up their jobs. Whilst this was held by the CoJ to be acceptable under Art 2(4), it could only be so provided that the emergency rule that permitted single fathers to seek places was applied on the same conditions as for female workers. It seems that there must always be a saving clause in the background to prevent positive discrimination from being too positive and thus unlawfully discriminatory.

Finally, in this area, is Case C-79/99 *Julia Schnorbus v Land Hessen*, a decision that addresses an imbalance disadvantaging men, the result of which is one way of addressing the army case conclusions reached by the CoJ in *Dory* earlier. In Germany, military or civilian service is compulsory, but for males only. According to which service is performed, this can take between 9 and 18 months, and means that men wishing to go to university enter later and that all men enter the job market later. The *Land Hessen* provided rules in respect of entry to the second stage of German legal training that gave priority to men by deferring acceptance of applications by females by up to 12 months in comparison with males who applied at the same time. It argued, when challenged by a female applicant, that the rule was designed to counterbalance the disadvantage suffered by men. It was accepted by the CoJ under Art 141 EC (now Art 157 TFEU) as being a proportionate response to the situation.

The measures found to be acceptable by the CoJ represent only modest steps in providing substantive, and not only formal, equality for men and women. However, as with all areas of EU law, it is an area that will certainly not stand still for long, and therefore it is always wise in EU law to be looking out for new cases and the impact that they have on the development of EU law.

11.6.7 **Judicial Enforcement and Remedies**

Judicial enforcement and the possibility of a remedy for those damaged by breaches of the provisions are now consolidated in Directive 2006/54.

Article 23 of Directive 2006/54 requires member states to take the necessary measures to ensure that any provisions in collective agreements, wage agreements, or in individual contracts that breach the principles of the directive are to be null and void, or to be removed.

Member states are required under Arts 17 and 18 of Directive 2006/54 to ensure judicial or conciliation procedures are available, with adequate compensation measures, even after the employment relationship has ended, but also that individuals can pursue claims for real and effective compensation without a fixed upper limit. Previous case law has helped to develop these principles. Case 14/83 *Von Colson and Kamann* concerned the reimbursement of the employees' travel expenses as damages for discrimination. The Court of Justice ruled that full implementation of the directive entails that sanctions must be such as to guarantee real and effective judicial protection, and must therefore have a real deterrent effect on the employer. Where a member state chooses to penalize the breach of the prohibition of discrimination by the award of compensation, it must be adequate in relation to the damage sustained and amount to more than purely nominal compensation. At the time, it held that Art 6 is not, however, itself directly effective, hence the development of the principle of indirect effect from this case. In Case C-271/91 *Marshall II*, it was held that 'damages' means full compensation not restrictively limited by national statutory rules. Despite the directive at the time providing that there be no limit to the damages, as the amended version also does, the CoJ confirmed that the directive gave a right to full compensation from date of breach.

Other notable cases include Case C-180/95 *Draehmpaehl v Urania*. A job was advertised to females only, contrary to both Community and German law. In the consequent claim, damages were limited to a maximum of three months' salary, but dependent on proving fault on the part of the employer. If more than one plaintiff sued, the aggregate compensation payable was limited to six months' salary. The CoJ held that liability to compensate cannot be made dependent on fault; compensation itself must guarantee real and effective judicial protection, have a real deterrent effect on the employer, and be adequate in relation to the damage suffered. Limits, such as three months' salary, are acceptable where the employer can prove that, notwithstanding the discrimination, a better qualified person was appointed and the complainant would not have been appointed in any event. However, an aggregate award ceiling regardless of the number discriminated against is not acceptable under Directive 76/207, because it might have the effect of dissuading applicants so harmed from asserting their rights.

These decisions are now reflected statutorily, as is Case C-185/97 *Coote v Granada* in which Ms Coote settled a sex discrimination claim with Granada outside court and the employment relationship was terminated by mutual consent. She found it difficult to obtain another job due to Granada's refusal to supply an employment agency with a reference. It was claimed that this was contrary to Art 6 of Directive 76/207 (the Equal Treatment Directive), under which member states should take measures to achieve the aims of the directive and must ensure that the rights can be enforced by individuals before the national courts. The Court of Justice held that this right of recourse to the courts is a general principle of Community law reflected in the member states' constitutions and Art 6 ECHR. The CoJ held that Art 6 of the directive also covers measures that an employer might take as a reaction against legal proceedings of a former employee outside dismissal, because if employees were to find it difficult to get other jobs, it might deter them from taking action where they considered they had been discriminated against on the grounds of sex. This extends the scope of EU protection beyond the protection against dismissal.

Article 23 of Directive 2006/54 requires member states to take the necessary measures to protect employees against dismissal by the employer as a reaction to a complaint within the undertaking, or to any legal proceedings aimed at enforcing compliance with the principle of equal treatment. This had been extended by Directive 2002/73 to protect employees' representatives who act in cases involving complaints against the employer.

Article 30 of 2006/54 requires the member states to ensure that provisions of implementing laws are brought to the attention of employees by all appropriate means; Arts 20–2 of Directive 2006/54 were introduced for member states to set up bodies to promote equality, and to engage in research and discussion to bring forward proposals for agreements and action to achieve equality.

11.7 Social Security Directive 79/7

As the third instalment of the first wave of secondary legislative additions to Art 119 EC (now Art 157 TFEU), Directive 79/7 was enacted to apply the principle of equal treatment to the field of social security and other elements of social protection. The scope of the directive is limited to statutory schemes, whereas private schemes and the increasing number of contracted-out schemes were catered for later by Directive 86/378, now replaced by Directive 2006/54 (but note that Directive 79/7 has not been replaced by that directive). Because most courses do not deal with this in any further detail than already dealt with here in respect of Article 7 and pensions, no further treatment will be given.

11.8 Directive 92/85

The Pregnant and Breastfeeding Workers Directive was enacted as a measure for the protection of workers under Art 118a EC (now Art 154 TFEU) rather than a measure of equal treatment under Art 141 EC (now Art 157 TFEU), which now allows general measures of equal treatment to be adopted rather than only pay, as was the case prior to amendment.[21] Directive 92/85 is essentially, then, a health and safety measure to protect pregnant and breastfeeding workers in the workplace, including part-time workers. We have already considered Art 10 earlier in relation to the special period of protection and dismissal for pregnant women from the beginning of pregnancy to the end of maternity leave. Dismissals, therefore, should now be considered under Directive 92/85. However, what constitutes a 'dismissal' and what constitutes a 'refusal to take on an employee' is not necessarily a clear-cut point, as was observed in Case C-438/99 *Melgar*, because of the practice of employment on back-to-back or fixed-term contracts that is commonplace in industry and commerce. So, whilst strictly concerning health and safety issues, the directive is nevertheless important in providing a level of protection for women in a situation that is not comparable with that of men, and which, without such protection, might otherwise result in further inequality for women. For example, if paid time off to attend antenatal clinics were not required by Art 9, not only might the time off not be paid, but also the time taken off might be counted towards the amount of time absent from work for the purposes of dismissal.

Directive 92/85 has not featured in case law to any significant extent, so whilst it was originally assumed following its enactment that all cases concerned with dismissal during pregnancy or maternity would come under its provisions, the *Melgar* case shows that we still need to have an eye on Directive 2006/54, which replaces Directive 76/207, hence no further treatment will be given to it in this volume.

11.9 Related Secondary Legislation

11.9.1 Occupational Pensions

The Occupational Pensions Directive 86/378, which has also been replaced by Directive 2006/54 and was repealed on 15 August 2009, extended the equal treatment principle to occupational, as opposed to statutory, pension schemes and applies similar rules to those of Directive 79/7. The wide definition given to pay in the *Barber* judgment meant that much of this directive was no longer relevant, because some of the schemes concerned by it have been judged to constitute deferred pay and thus to be covered by Art 157 TFEU. Further analysis of this directive would go beyond the depth of most undergraduate courses on EU law and for that reason is not undertaken here.

---

[21] A proposal for the amendment for this directive, COM (2008) 637 final, appears to have been lost along the way somewhere, last seen heading towards the Council in 2012 after consideration by the EP in 2010 (although not published in the OJ until 2012 (OJ 2012 C70/162)). It may have been the victim of the recession as its main element was the increase in paid maternity leave from 14 to 18 weeks.

11.9.2 **Self-employed Equal Treatment**

A new Self-employed Equal Treatment Directive (2010/41) was enacted in 2010 and provides for the application of the equal treatment principle to the self-employed, especially in respect of self-employed women during pregnancy and motherhood. It complements Directive 76/207 to the extent that the matter is not already covered by Directive 2006/54 and Directive 79/7. As with Directive 86/378, further analysis here is beyond the scope of most undergraduate courses.

11.9.3 **The Part-time Workers Directive 97/81**

The Part-time Workers Directive 97/81[22] was also adopted under the Social Policy Agreement and was later extended to the UK by Directive 98/23.[23] Whilst not primarily aimed at addressing discrimination against women, the purpose of the directive, which is to remove the discrimination against part-time workers, had the potential of helping more women than men simply because historically more women are in part-time work than men, although the current economic crisis has resulted in far more part-time jobs for both sexes.[24] The directive also seeks to improve the quality of part-time work and to develop part-time work opportunities in a manner that takes account of both employers' and workers' needs (clause 1). Clause 4 provides that part-time workers should not be treated less favourably than full-timers unless objectively justified. It allows the principle of pro-rata application of time-qualifying rules to part-time workers with the clear exception of pay, which has been explored in detail earlier. For example, where a full-time worker would take three months to obtain a particular benefit, a part-timer working half the number of hours would be expected to take six months. Such rules would, however, have to satisfy the requirements of proportionality and not constitute indirect discrimination. The directive would seem to make it easier for claimants, in that any different treatment of part-timers from full-timers appears to be regarded as discriminatory unless justified by the employer.

11.9.4 **Summary of Secondary Legislation**

The EU is tackling a number of inequitable situations with the array of secondary EU legislation noted earlier and to a greater degree than many of the member states. Some of these laws were enacted under the specific treaty Article concerned with discrimination on the grounds of sex (Art 157 TFEU), whilst others were enacted either under the general and vestigial law-making power under Art 308 EC (now Art 352 TFEU), because of the lack of a clear EU competence for them, or under the Social Policy Agreement for similar reasons, or under worker protection, for example the Pregnancy Directive. Article 157 TFEU was amended, though, and now is considered an adequate legal base for secondary legislation in this area, as is evidenced by the enactment of the recast Directive 2006/54 on equal treatment. However, a further treaty amendment was made by the Treaty of Amsterdam that should remove any difficulties with finding an appropriate treaty base to tackle even wider issues of inequality. This is briefly considered next.

---

[22] OJ 1998 L14/9.   [23] OJ 1998 L131/10.
[24] This is not just a UK phenomenon but reflected across the EU: see **http://epp.eurostat.ec.europa.eu/statistics_explained/index.php/Employment_statistics**.

11.10 Article 19 TFEU: The Expansion of EU Equality Law

The introduction of Art 13 by the Treaty of Amsterdam provided the EC Treaty (now Art 19 TFEU) with a new legal base for the enactment of legislation to tackle discrimination across a range of issues. Take note that the Article does not actually prohibit anything in its own right, but rather empowers the Council to take action to combat discrimination based on sex, racial or ethnic origin, religion or belief, disability, age, or sexual orientation. This also has to be tempered with the fact that the Article restricts the EU to acting within the scope of its competences and cannot therefore encroach on member state competences, which means, bearing in mind the still economic basis of the EU and the type of legislation conceived, that any legislation enacted will always be close to the borderline between the EU and the member state competences. Directives were issued with little delay under this treaty Article and before a further ten member states came on board, which would have made it even more difficult to reach the unanimity required for measures under the Article. It can be said, though, in contrast with the debate about the reasons for the inclusion of the original Art 119 EEC in the first place, that there is no suggestion that Art 13 EC was included on economic grounds, but instead is a clear representation of the social concerns of the EU and is to be welcomed for this reason. Legislation to combat discrimination has now been enacted under Art 13 EC (now Art 19 TFEU).

11.10.1 Secondary Legislation Enacted under Art 19 TFEU

Two directives were enacted in 2000, which, between them and the new 2006 recast Equal Treatment Directive, encompass all of the matters identified in Art 19 TFEU for which action was deemed necessary to combat discrimination. It may be concluded that they were enacted remarkably quickly following the treaty addition of Art 19 TFEU; however, the types of discrimination covered by them have been of increasing concern within the member states and the EU for many years, with many reports and suggestions for action having been produced over the years. Perhaps what is more remarkable is that they were passed relatively quickly by the Council under the consultation procedure, whereby Council unanimity is required. As a consequence of the compromise required to enact them, there are differences between the directives in how equal treatment is to be achieved, and the implementation periods and exceptions permitted to the member states in their application.[25] In view of the concentration in this chapter on discrimination on the ground of sex, no further coverage will be provided here.

11.10.2 Directive 2004/113

In 2004, a directive (Directive 2004/113[26]) was enacted under Art 13 EC (now Art 19 TFEU) to implement the principle of equality between men and women in the access to, and supply of, goods and services. It applies to the provision of all public and private

---

[25] See T. Jones, 'The Race Directive: Redefining Protection from Discrimination in EU Law' (2003) 5 EHRLR 515–26.

[26] OJ 2004 L373/37.

sector supply of goods and services outside the sphere of private and family life transactions and, apart from a notable derogation in the directive dealing with insurance leading to case law and in particular a 2011 judgment,[27] it has not provoked much attention in academic and university studies of EU law.[28]

The insurance services case, Case C-236/09 *Test-Achats*,[29] concerned the application of Directive 2004/113 (equal treatment between men and women in access to and the supply of goods and services) and in particular Articles of the directive dealing with insurance contracts. The case was brought against a Belgian law that implemented the derogation permitted under Art 5(2) of the directive allowing for gender to be used as one of the criteria in the determination of insurance premiums. The directive, whilst clear about the fundamental nature of the equality between men and women as outlined in various Articles of the treaties and the directive, was conscious of the widespread use in insurance and financial services of gender as an actuarial factor to determine risk and thus premiums or pay-outs. Hence, the directive permitted an exception from the general requirement of unisex premiums and benefits, if supported by reliable and transparent data. The derogation could last up to five years after the transposition date—namely, 21 December 2007 plus five years—but after that the directive required a re-examination of the relevant data. The Court of Justice noted the wealth of general provisions aimed at the elimination of discrimination between men and women, but also noted that legislative attempts to achieve that end must be undertaken with regard for the economic and social conditions, and therefore allow, for limited transitional periods, derogations where appropriate—hence, the derogation in Art 5(2) of the directive. However, the directive failed to specify a date limit and thus there was a risk, in the view of the CoJ, that the derogation would be employed without limit by the member states contrary to the general rule requiring unisex premiums in Art 5(1). The result was a simple statement making it clear that the derogation expired on 21 December 2012.

In light of the high visibility of this ruling, which affected car insurance, pensions, and life insurance, it attracted much comment.[30]

In 2008, a new directive was proposed that aimed to combat discrimination based on religion or belief, disability, age, or sexual orientation, and to put into effect the principle of equal treatment, but outside the field of employment. Its scope is social protection, including social security and health care, social advantages, education, and access to and supply of goods and services that are available to the public, including housing, but only professional or commercial activities are covered. Following wide consultation, with reported opposition from some countries to the inclusion of sexual orientation, the proposal has been made but then amended and forwarded to the CoR for an opinion and awaits further progress; it faces the severe difficulty of obtaining unanimous approval by the Council.[31]

---

[27] Case C-236/09 considered in the following paragraph.

[28] Although specialist insurance law courses may well have taken note of it.

[29] Search at **http://curia.europa.eu/jcms/jcms/j_6/**.

[30] Start with **http://www.bbc.co.uk/news/business-12606610** and **http://www.guardian.co.uk/money/2011/mar/01/gender-insurance-ruling-premiums**, but note that not all articles report the ruling very accurately.

[31] And still awaiting as of January 2015. See COM (2008) 426 of 2 July 2008, available at **http://ec.europa.eu/prelex/detail_dossier_real.cfm?CL=en&DosId=197196**, **http://ec.europa.eu/social/main.jsp?langId=en&catId=423**, and **http://eur-lex.europa.eu/LexUriServ/LexUriServ.do?uri=CELEX:52008PC0426:EN:NOT**.

11.11 The Lisbon Treaty and Equality Rights

Gender equality and equality generally were issues that were discussed during the drafting of the Constitutional Treaty, which was abandoned and replaced by the Lisbon Treaty, but which dealt with these rights in a radically different way. It is worth noting that, with regard to their inclusion in the Constitutional Treaty, the burning question was not whether they should feature in the treaty at all, but where they should be placed. The Constitutional Treaty contained in its preamble the equality of persons as one of the European values, which was then repeated in Art I-2. The Lisbon Treaty attached the Union Charter to the treaties by way of a declaration, but with opt-outs for Poland and the UK applying internally in those two countries, and a political deal to do the same for the Czech Republic agreed prior to its ratification of the Lisbon Treaty (see Chapter 1).

The Union Charter includes a third title dealing with equality rights in Arts 20–3:

Article 20 Equality before the law
Everyone is equal before the law.

Article 21 Non-discrimination

1. Any discrimination based on any ground such as sex, race, colour, ethnic or social origin, genetic features, language, religion or belief, political or any other opinion, membership of a national minority, property, birth, disability, age or sexual orientation shall be prohibited.

2. Within the scope of application of the Constitution and without prejudice to any of its specific provisions, any discrimination on grounds of nationality shall be prohibited.

Article 22 Cultural, religious and linguistic diversity
The Union shall respect cultural, religious and linguistic diversity.

Article 23 Equality between men and women
Equality between men and women must be ensured in all areas, including employment, work and pay. The principle of equality shall not prevent the maintenance or adoption of measures providing for specific advantages in favour of the under-represented sex.

As set out, the rights provided would appear neither to disturb, nor indeed to add to, the existing provision of equality law in the Union, with the possible exception of Art 20, which could be argued to apply to third-country nationals, not presently covered by the EU equality regime and Art 21, which provides that any discrimination based on any ground shall be prohibited.

The Lisbon Treaty made a change to Art 19 TFEU requiring the consent of the European Parliament to legislation rather than only to consultation, but otherwise preserving unanimity voting in Council. No change was made to Art 157 TFEU, but the main principles of equality law are emphasized in Art 2 TEU, and Arts 8 and 10 TFEU. Article 51 of the Charter defines the scope of the application of the Charter as not extending to the member states when not implementing EU law and not extending the field of application of EU law nor modifying its powers and tasks, a proviso that is repeated in Declaration No 1 attached to the treaties. Time and case law will determine just exactly how it will be employed in the EU legal system.

11.12 **Concluding Comments**

From the original and quite limited Art 119 EEC (now Art 157 TFEU), which strictly concerned equal pay for equal work only, EU equality law appears to have developed genuine and comprehensive legal instruments for the combating of discrimination in a range of areas. A general principle of equality is emerging more and more visibly, thanks in large part to the judgments of the Court of Justice, which is now being confronted with cases arising under the new directives issued under Art 19 TFEU. The CoJ will thus have many more opportunities to expand on the general principle endorsed, for example, in Case C-144/04 *Mangold* and Case C-555/07 *Kükükdeveci*. Thus, a general principle of Union equality law is now a reality and no longer merely an aspiration without substance.

Further Reading

Books

ELLIS, E. and WATSON, P. *EU Anti-Discrimination Law*, 2nd edn, Oxford University Press, Oxford, 2012.

SOMEK, A. *Engineering Equality: An Essay on European Anti-Discrimination Law*, Oxford University Press, Oxford, 2011.

TRIDIMAS, T. 'The Principle of Equality' in *The General Principles of EC Law*, 2nd edn, Oxford University Press, Oxford, 2006, ch 2.

Articles

AHTELA, K. 'The Revised Provisions on Sex Discrimination in the European Law: A Critical Assessment' (2005) 11 ELJ 58–78.

ANAGNOSTARAS, G. 'Sex Equality and Compulsory Military Service: The Limits of National Sovereignty over Matters of Army Organisation' (2003) 28 EL Rev 713–22.

BELL, M. and WADDINGTON, L. 'Reflecting on Inequalities in European Equality Law' (2003) 28(3) EL Rev 349–69.

BESSON, S. 'Never Shall the Twain Meet? Gender Discrimination under EU and ECHR Law' (2008) 8 Human Rights L Rev 647.

BURROWS, N. and ROBINSON, M. 'An Assessment of the Recast of Community Equality Laws' (2006) 13 ELJ 18.

BURROWS, N. and ROBINSON, M. 'Positive Action for Women in Employment: Time to Align with Europe?' (2006) 33 J Law & Soc 24.

COSTELLO, C. and DAVIES, G. 'The Case Law of the Court of Justice in the Field of Sex Equality since 2000' (2006) 43 CML Rev 1567.

HOWARD, E. 'The European Year of Equal Opportunities for All 2007: Is the EU Moving Away from a Formal Ideal of Equality?' (2008) 14 ELJ 168.

JONES, T. 'The Race Directive: Redefining Protection from Discrimination in EU Law' (2003) 5 EHRLR 515–26.

KOLDINKSI, K. 'Case-law of the European Court of Justice on Sex Discrimination 2006–2011' (2011) 48 CML Rev 1599.

MASSELOT, A. 'The State of Gender Equality Law in the European Union' (2007) 13 ELJ 152.

PRECHAL, S. 'Equality of Treatment, Non-discrimination and Social Policy: Achievements in Three Themes' (2004) 41 CML Rev 533.

TRYBUS, M. 'Sisters in Arms: European Community Law and Sex Equality in the Armed Forces' (2003) 9 ELJ 631–58.

Index

Abuse of dominance (Art 102 TFEU)
abuse
effect on trade between
Member States 381
essential
requirement 379–81
applicability 374
consequences of breach 381
markets
geographical
markets 377–8
product markets 376–7
share and
dominance 378–9
problems with merger
control 392–3
relationship with Art
101 381–3
requirement for
dominance 374–5
undertakings 375
see also Merger control
Abuse of procedure 193–4
Acquis communautaire
body of EU law 97
defined 17
'*acte clair*' 198
Admissibility
annulment of
community acts
applicable
institutions 223
non-privileged
applicants 226–7
reviewable acts 223–6
standing 225–7
time limits 227
failure to act (Art 265
TFEU) 237–8
non-contractual
liability 239–40
preliminary rulings 191–5
**Annulment of community
acts**
admissibility
applicable
institutions 223
non-privileged
applicants 226–7
reviewable acts 223–6
standing 225–7
time limits 227
alternatives remedies 235–7
direct and individual concern
direct concern 228

individual
concern 228–30
regulatory acts 231–2
effect of successful
action 233–4
grounds
lack of competence 232
procedural
infringements 233
treaty infringements 233
interest groups and party
actions 230–1
introduction 222–3
restrictive approach 234–5
**Anti-competitive agreements
(Art 101 TFEU)**
consequences of breach
block exemptions 373–4
exemptions 370–1
individual notification to
Commission 371–2
negative clearance and
comfort letters 372–3
definitions
'agreements' 362–3
'concerted
practices' 363–5
'decisions by associations
of undertakings' 363
'undertakings' 361–2
effect on trade between
Member States 366–8
exemptions 368–70
objectives 361
problems with merger
control 392–3
relationship with Art
102 381–3
restriction or distortion of
competition 365–6
types of prohibited
agreement 366
Artistic protection 282

Belgium 155
Budgetary processes
Commission procedure 69
early UK participation 11
parliamentary functions 59

Carers 320–1
**Charges having equivalent
effect (CHEE)**
charges for services 265–8
internal taxation
distinguished 268–70

meaning 265
**Charter of Fundamental
Rights**
direct effects 173
sources of law 101–4
Citizenship
case law 338–40
Maastricht Treaty on
European Union (TEU)
1992 337–8
welfare and family
rights 340–6
Commercial Property *see*
Intellectual Property (IP)
Commission
application of competition
law 360–1
appointment and
removal 44–5
budgetary processes 69
composition and
organization 43–4
control by Parliament 57–9
delegation of powers 132–3
direct actions against
Member States 211–12
law-making
initial proposals 126–7
Ordinary Legislative
Procedure 127–30
Special Legislative
Procedure 130–1
origins 42–3
role 43
tasks and duties 46–7
**Committee of Permanent
Representatives
(COREPER)** 52
Committee of the Regions 68
**Common Agricultural
Policy**
establishment 6
progress towards
federalism 15
UK problems 10
**Common Commercial
Policy** 24, 264
**Common Foreign and Security
Policy (CFSP)**
establishment and
background 3
key features of Maastricht
Treaty 31–2
Competences
annulment of community
acts 232

Competences (*Cont.*)
　division of competences
　　exclusive and concurrent
　　　competences 79–81
　　extension of
　　　competences 81–2
　　implied powers 84–5
　　residual powers 82–4
　　role of subsidiarity and
　　　proportionality 78
　Lisbon Treaty 2007 90–1
　transfer of sovereign powers
　　to EU 71–2
　wholly internal rule 346–50
Competition law
　abuse of dominance
　　(Art 102 TFEU)
　　applicability 374
　　consequences of
　　　breach 381
　　markets 376–8
　　problems with merger
　　　control 392–3
　　relationship with Art
　　　101 381–3
　　requirement for
　　　abuse 379–81
　　requirement for
　　　dominance 374–5
　　undertakings 375
　anti-competitive agreements
　　(Art 101 TFEU)
　　consequences of
　　　breach 370–1
　　definitions 361–5
　　effect on trade between
　　　Member States 366–8
　　exemptions 368–70
　　objectives 361
　　problems with merger
　　　control 392–3
　　relationship with Art
　　　102 381–3
　　restriction or distortion of
　　　competition 365–6
　　types of prohibited
　　　agreement 366
　conflicts with national
　　law 391–2
　enforcement
　　judicial review of
　　　enforcement 390
　　leniency notices 390
　　powers and duties of
　　　Commission 387–90
　　private enforcement 391
　introduction 356–7
　legislative outline 359–60
　merger control
　　enforcement 395–6

problems with Arts 101
　and 102 392–3
relevant Regulations 393–5
policy objectives 357–9
relevance to EU 357
role of Commission and
　ECJ 360–1
Confidentiality 117–18
Consent procedure 131
Constitutional issues
　abandonment of
　　Constitutional Treaty 76–8
　division of competences
　　overview 74–5
　　role of subsidiarity and
　　　proportionality 78
　insistence of
　　constitutionality 76
　protocols and
　　declarations 75–6
　reception of EU law
　　Belgium 155
　　Czech Republic 162–3
　　Denmark 163–4
　　France 160–2
　　Germany 155–9
　　Hungary 164
　　Ireland 164–5
　　Italy 159–60
　　Poland 165
　　Spain 166
　　United Kingdom 146
　supremacy of EU law
　　ECJ approach 138–40
　　introduction 146
　　Member States 140–3
　treaty basis 74–5
Constitutional Treaty
　abandonment 76–8
　democratic deficit 90
Conventions 105–7
Council of the Union
　Committee of Permanent
　　Representatives
　　(COREPER) 52
　Council of Europe
　　distinguished 5
　functions and powers 47–8
　lack of transparency and
　　open governance 73–4
　law-making
　　consent procedure 131
　　Ordinary Legislative
　　　Procedure 127–30
　　Special Legislative
　　　Procedure 130–1
　legislative procedures 48–52
　name changes 47
　origins 42–3
　Presidency 48

see also European Council
Court of Auditors 67
Court of Justice
　approach to
　　supremacy 138–40
　composition and
　　organization 60–1
　direct actions against
　　Member States
　　actions by other Member
　　　States 220–2
　　enforcement actions by
　　　Commission 211–12
　　introduction 211
　　preliminary informal
　　　procedures 214–15
　direct actions against natural
　　or legal persons 251
　free movement of
　　self-employed
　　persons 322–9
　interpretation of competition
　　law 360–1
　intervention over national
　　rules 194–5
　judgments 62
　jurisdiction 62–3
　methodology
　　interpretation 64–5
　　precedent 65
　positive role towards
　　integration 28
　preliminary rulings
　　'*acte clair*' 198
　　applicability to courts and
　　　tribunals 189–91
　　courts of last instance 197
　　discretionary remedy 195
　　effect of ruling 200–1
　　evolution of
　　　references 201–2
　　interim measures 203
　　questions referred 191–2
　　reform proposals 202–3
　　time limits 196
　　procedure 61
　　reporting of cases 62
　　source of law 110–11
　specialized courts 66–7
　working style 94–5
Customs union
　defined 13
　progress towards treaty
　　goals 257
　see also Tariff and tax barriers
Czech Republic 162–3

Damages
　alternatives to
　　annulment 236–7

equal treatment
claims 426–7
non-contractual liability 241
Decisions
annulment of community
acts 227
direct effects 176
sources of law 109
Declarations 239
Delegation of powers 132–3
Democratic deficit
balance between Parliament
and Council 135–6
governance issues 134
key feature of TEU 32
lack of transparency and
open governance 73–4
law-making procedure 127
Lisbon Treaty 2007 90
Parliament 72–3
rationale for law-making
changes 131–2
role of Parliament 56–7
Denmark
reception of EU law 163–4
widening of Union 16
Derogations
free movement of
economically active
persons
health and safety 330–2
procedural
safeguards 329–30
public policy 332–3
public service
employees 332–3
security 330–2
free movement of goods
artistic protection 282
health and safety 280–2
Intellectual Property
(IP) 282–3
notification of
Commission 284
proportionality 283
public morality 279
public policy 280
purpose and scope 279
security 280
treaty provisions 278–9
Direct actions
actions against institutions
annulment of community
acts 222–37
competition
enforcement 390
failure to act (Art 265
TFEU) 237–9
illegality 249–50
introduction 222

non-contractual
liability 239–49
jurisdiction 63–4
against Member States
actions by other Member
States 220–2
enforcement actions by
Commission 211–12
introduction 222
preliminary informal
procedures 214–15
against natural or legal
persons 251
Direct applicability 170–1
Direct effects
Charter of Fundamental
Rights 173
competition law
enforcement 391
decisions 176
directives
extending 'State'
definition 177–8
general principles 180–2
incidental horizontal
direct effect 182–4
international
agreements 176–7
meaning 171–2
regulations 174
treaties 172–3
see also State liability
Directives
direct effects 174–6
extending 'State'
definition 177–8
general principles 180–2
incidental horizontal
direct effect 182–4
indirect effects 178–80
sources of law 108–9
Dualism
incorporation of EU
law 145–6
UK approach 146–7

**Economic and Financial
Committee** 68
**Economic and Social
Committee (EESC)** 42,
67–8, 124
Economic development
free movement of
economically active
persons
derogations 329–30
family members 318–20
introduction 299–301
legislative
provisions 302–4

material scope of
rights 314–22
scope of basic
rights 304–13
self-employed
persons 322–9
free movement of
goods: derogations 278–9
free movement of
goods: indistinctly
applicable measures
Cassis de Dijon case 285
effect of *Cassis de Dijon*
case 289
equal or dual burden
rules 289–91
introduction 284–5
legislative
interventions 288
rule of reason 286–8
free movement of
goods: non-tariff barriers
export bans 278
general scope of
treaty 274–5
introduction 273–4
marketing rules 277–8
meaning 275
promotion campaigns 277
free movement of
goods: tariff and tax
barriers
charges having equivalent
effect (CHEE) 265–8
overview 264
prohibition of customs
duties 264–5
prohibition of discrimin-
atory taxation 270–3
summary on tariff
barriers 273
measures having equivalent
effect (MHEE)
introduction 273–4
Education
family members 320–1
free movement
rights 309–11
Elections 55–6
Enlargement
assimilation of East
Germany 17
challenges from further
widening and
deepening 39–40
expansion after 1995 17–18
expansions in 2004 and
2007 18–19
first and second
expansions 17–18

Enlargement (*Cont.*)
future widening
accession
preconditions 22
six official
candidates 19–23
Entry rights 314–17
Equal pay
basis of comparison 408–10
equal value work 412–14
extension to work of equal
value 408
meaning of pay 404–8
overview 403–4
part-time workers 410–12
remedies 414
Equal treatment
employment terms 417–19
equal opportunities 424–6
exempt occupations 419–20
legislative provisions 414–15
maternity rights 420–4
remedies 426–7
scope 417
underlying concept 415–17
Establishment
intervention of ECJ 322–5
lawyers 327–9
legislative developments 326
Provision of Services
Directive 2006 327
EU Fundamental Rights
Charter *see* Charter of
Fundamental Rights
EU law
classification
institutional law 95–7
procedural law 96
substantive law 96–7
division of competences
exclusive and concurrent
competences 79–81
extension of
competences 81–2
implied powers 84–5
residual powers 82–4
role of subsidiarity and
proportionality 78
general principle of
equality 398–9
principle treaties 93–4
reception by Member States
Belgium 155
Czech Republic 162–3
Denmark 163–4
emerging trend 166–7
France 160–2
Germany 155–9
Hungary 164
Ireland 164–5

Italy 159–60
Poland 165
Spain 166
United Kingdom 146–54
sources
acquis communautaire 97
Charter of Fundamental
Rights 101–4
conventions 105–7
Court of Justice 110–11
decisions 109
declarations 101
directives 108–9
fundamental
rights 111–13
human rights 111–13
international
agreements 105–7
legally binding acts 109
natural justice 117–21
non-discrimination 116
opinions 110
other legislative acts 109
procedural
requirements 110
protocols 100–1
recommendations 110
regulations 108
secondary legislation 107
'soft law' 122–3
treaties 99–100, 105–7
supremacy
ECJ approach 138–40
introduction 138
Member States 140–3
theories of
incorporation 145–6
working style 94–5
see also Procedural law;
Substantive law
Euratom Treaties 8, 9, 15
European Central Bank
(ECB) 67
European citizenship
case law 338–40
Maastricht Treaty on
European Union (TEU)
1992 337–8
welfare and family
rights 340–6
European Coal and Steel
Community (ECSC)
establishment and
background 7–8
establishment of institutional
scene 42
progress towards federalism 15
European Communities (EC)
completion of internal
market 29

establishment and
background 5–6, 8–9
increasing degree of
integration
Luxembourg
Accords 25–6
positive role played
by ECJ 28
primary treaties and early
amendments 24
revival attempts 26–8
stagnation 26
relationship with UK
early period to 1970 9–10
membership and
acceptance 10–12
Single European Act 28–9
completion of internal
market 29
evaluation 30
institutional and policy
changes 29–30
need for further institu-
tional change 30–1
terminology 3
widening and deepening 16
European Council
Council of Europe
distinguished 5
High Representative for
Foreign Affairs and
Security Policy 54
history and development 53
legal basis for
legislation 123–6
Presidency 53–4
see also Council of the
Union
European Defence Community
(EDC) 7–8
European Economic and
Social Committee
(ECOSOC) 67–8
European Free Trade Area
(EFTA)
impact on, 1995
enlargement 18
progress towards treaty
goals 257
UK membership 9
European Investment Bank 68
European Political Community
(EPC) 7–8
European Regional
Development Fund 30
European Union (EU)
basic objectives 12–13
challenges from further
widening and
deepening 39–40

constitutional basis
  abandonment of
    Constitutional
    Treaty 76–8
  insistence of
    constitutionality 76
  protocols and
    declarations 75–6
  treaties 74–5
establishment and
  background
  defence proposals 7–8
  founding of EEC 5–6
  impact of Spaak
    Report 8
  motives for integration 4
  Schuman Plan 6–7
  Treaty of Rome and
    establishment of
    EURATOM 8
external relations
  commercial activities 24
  overview 23–4
forms of integration 13
key treaties
  Amsterdam
    Intergovernmental
    Conference and Treaty
    1996 33–4
  Constitutional Treaty 37
  Lisbon Treaty 2007 38–9
  Maastricht Treaty on
    European Union (TEU)
    1992 31–3
  Nice Intergovernmental
    Conference and Treaty
    2001 35–7
progress towards
  federalism 14–15
relevance of competition
  law 357
terminology 3
widening and deepening 16
see also Enlargement
'**Eurosclerosis**' 26
Exit rights 314–17

Failure to act (Art 265 TFEU)
  admissibility 237–8
  introduction 237
  procedural
    requirements 238–9
  relevant acts 238
Family rights
  free movement 317–20
  free movement of
    economically active
    persons 317–20
  maternity
    Directive, 92/85 428

legislative
  provisions 420–4
pregnancy and
  illness 423–4
unfair dismissal 421–3
pregnant and nursing
  mothers 428
widening concept of free
  movement 340–6
Federalism
  defined 14–15
  economic and monetary
    union 259
France 160–2
***Francovich* remedy**
  development by ECJ 185–7
  extensions of principle 187–8
  general principle 206–8
Free movement of goods
  derogations
    artistic protection 282
    health and safety 280–2
    Intellectual Property
      (IP) 282–3
    notification of
      Commission 284
    proportionality 283
    public morality 279
    public policy 280
    purpose and scope 279
    security 280
    treaty provisions 278–9
  establishment of internal
    market
    charges having equivalent
      effect (CHEE) 265–8
    overview 264
    prohibition of customs
      duties 264–5
    prohibition of discrimin-
      atory taxation 270–3
    summary on tariff
      barriers 273
  indistinctly applicable
    measures
    Cassis de Dijon case 285
    effect of *Cassis de Dijon*
      case 289
    equal or dual burden
      rules 289–91
    introduction 284–5
    legislative
      interventions 288
    rule of reason 286–8
  integration methods
    alternatives to
      harmonization 263–4
    harmonization 262–4
    negative integration 259–61
    positive integration 261–2

introduction 255–6
key features of Maastricht
  Treaty 32
legislative provisions
  secondary legislation 257
  treaty articles 256–7
measures having equivalent
  effect (MHEE)
  export bans 278
  general scope of
    treaty 274–5
  marketing rules 277–8
  meaning 275
  promotion campaigns 277
overall summary 295–7
particular selling
  arrangements
  leading case 291–2
  market access or
    discrimination 293–4
  post-*Keck* case law 292–3
progress towards treaty
  goals 257–9
quantitative restrictions
  general scope of
    treaty 274–5
  introduction 273–4
  meaning 275–6
Free movement of persons
  conclusions 352–3
  economically active persons
    derogations 329–30
    establishment of
      companies 312–13
    family members 317–20
    introduction 299–301
    legislative
      provisions 302–4
    material scope of
      rights 314–22
    scope of basic rights 304–13
    self-employed
      persons 322–9
  European citizenship 337–8
  general free-movement
    Directives 336
  key features of Maastricht
    Treaty 32
  services 334–6
  third-country
    nationals 350–2
  welfare and family
    rights 340–6
  wholly internal rule 346–50
Free trade 13
Frontier workers
  free movement rights 307–8
Fundamental rights
  establishment of European
    Union Agency 115–16

Fundamental rights (*Cont.*)
  non-contractual liability 244
  source of law 111–13
Fundamental Rights
  Charter *see* Charter of
    Fundamental Rights

Gender re-assignment
  concept of equal
    treatment 415–17
  general principle of
    equality 398–9
General Court 65–6
General powers 83–4
Germany
  assimilation of East
    Germany 17
  reception of EU law
    constitutional
      issues 155–6
    judicial recognition 156–9
Governance methods 134–5
Greece 16

Harmonization
  free movement of
    goods 262–4
  free movement rights 322
Health and safety
  free movement of
    economically active
    persons 306–8
  free movement of
    goods 280–2
High Representative for
  Foreign Affairs and Security
  Policy 54
Human rights
  establishment of ECHR 5
  source of law 105, 111–13
Hungary 164

Illegality
  alternatives to
    annulment 236
  effects of successful
    action 250–1
  grounds 250
  overview 249
  reviewable acts 250
  standing 249–50
Implied powers 84–5
Incorporation of EU law
  Belgium 155
  Czech Republic 162–3
  Denmark 163–4
  France 160–2
  Germany, constitutional
    issues 155–6
  Hungary 164

Ireland 164–5
Italy 159–60
Poland 165
Spain 166
theories 145–6
United Kingdom
  constitutional issues 146
  difficulties of
    acceptance 146
  dualist approach 146–7
  ECA 1972 147–9
  European Union Act
    2011 153–4
  judicial
    recognition 149–53
  parliamentary
    supremacy 147
Indirect actions 64
Indistinctly applicable
  measures
  Cassis de Dijon case 285
  effect of *Cassis de Dijon*
    case 289
  equal or dual burden
    rules 289–91
  introduction 284–5
  legislative interventions 288
  rule of reason 286–8
Industrial property *see*
  Intellectual Property (IP)
Institutions
  advisory bodies
    Committee of the
      Regions 68
    Economic and Financial
      Committee 68
    European Economic and
      Social Committee
      (ECOSOC) 67–8
    Political and Security
      Committee 68
  Commission
    appointment and
      removal 44–5
    composition and
      organization 43–4
    role 43
    tasks and duties 46–7
  Council of the Union
    Committee of Permanent
      Representatives
      (COREPER) 52
    functions and
      powers 47–8
    law-making powers 52
    legislative
      procedures 48–52
    name changes 47
    Presidency 48
  Court of Auditors 67

Court of Justice
  composition and
    organization 60–1
  General Court 65–6
  judgments 62
  jurisdiction 62–3
  methodology 64–5
  procedure 61
  reporting of cases 62
  specialized courts 66–7
direct actions against
  annulment of community
    acts 222–36
  competition
    enforcement 390
  failure to act (Art 265
    TFEU) 237–9
  illegality 249–50
  introduction 222
  non-contractual
    liability 239–49
European Central Bank
  (ECB) 67
European Council
  High Representative for
    Foreign Affairs and
    Security Policy 54
  history and
    development 53
  Presidency 53–4
European Investment
  Bank 68
governance issues 134–5
law classification 95–7
law-making
  initial proposals 126–7
  legal basis for
    legislation 123–6
  Ordinary Legislative
    Procedure 127–30
  Special Legislative
    Procedure 130–1
original framework 42–3
Parliament
  elections and political
    parties 55–6
  functions and
    powers 57–60
  location in Brussels and
    Strasbourg 54–5
  membership 55
  origins 54–5
Single European Act
  institutional and policy
    changes 29–30
  need for further
    change 30–1
Intellectual property (IP)
  derogation for protection
    of 282–3

Interest groups 230-1
Intergovernmentalism
  defined 14
  establishment of SEA 28
  key treaties establishing EU
    Amsterdam
      Intergovernmental
      Conference and Treaty
      1996 33-4
    Constitutional Treaty 37
    Lisbon Treaty 2007 38-9
    Maastricht Treaty on
      European Union (TEU)
      1992 31-3
    Nice Intergovernmental
      Conference and Treaty
      2001 35-7
  protocols and
    declarations 75-6
Interim measures
  direct actions against
    Member States 218
  preliminary rulings 203
Internal market
  completion under SEA 29
  defined 14
  division of competences 78
  free movement of goods
    charges having equivalent
      effect (CHEE) 265-8
    overview 264
    prohibition of customs
      duties 264-5
    prohibition of discrimin-
      atory taxation 270-3
    summary on tariff
      barriers 273
  key features of Maastricht 31
  progress towards treaty
    goals 257
  rationale 399-401
  relevance of competition
    law 357
  widening and deepening
    of EC 16
International agreements
  direct effects 176-7
  sources of law 105-7
International law
  Supremacy of EU law,
    and 143-4
International Monetary
  Fund (IMF)
  establishment 5
Interpretation
  jurisdiction 62-3
  methodology 64-5
Ireland
  reception of EU law 164-5
  widening of Union 16

Italy 159-60

Jobseekers
  free movement
    rights 308-9
Judgments
  Court of Justice 62
  enforcement against Member
    States 218-19
Judicial and Police
  Cooperation
  establishment and
    background 3
  key features of Amsterdam
    Treaty 31-2
  key features of Maastricht
    Treaty 31-2
Judicial review 390
Jurisdiction
  Court of Justice
    direct actions 63-4
    indirect actions 64
    interpretation 62-3
  General Court 65-6
    non-contractual
      liability 239-40

Laeken Summit 2001 22, 36, 73
Law reports 62
Law-making
  annulment of
    community acts
    effect of successful
      action 233-4
    introduction 222
    restrictive
      approach 234-5
  Council of the Union
    general powers 52
    voting 48-52
  delegation of powers 132-3
  division of competences
    exclusive and concurrent
      competences 79-81
    extension of
      competences 81-2
    implied powers 84-5
    residual powers 82-4
    role of subsidiarity and
      proportionality 78
  legal basis for
    legislation 123-6
  obtaining a democratic
    balance 135-6
  open method of coordination
    (OMC) 134-5
  principles and
    procedures 127
  procedure
    consent procedure 131

initial proposals 126-7
    Ordinary Legislative
      Procedure 127-30
    passerelle provisions 131
    Special Legislative
      Procedure 130-1
    rationale for changes 131-2
    role of Parliament 57
Lawyers 327-9
Legal certainty
  non-contractual liability 244
  source of law 118
Legal privilege 117-18
Legitimate expectations
  non-contractual liability 244
  source of law 119
Leniency notices 390

Marshall Plan 5
Maternity rights
  Directive 92/85 428
  legislative provisions 420-4
  pregnancy and illness 423-4
  pregnant and nursing
    mothers 428
  unfair dismissal 421-3
Measures having equivalent
  effect (MHEE)
  export bans 278
  general scope of treaty 274-5
  introduction 273-4
  marketing rules 277-8
  meaning 275
  promotion campaigns 277
Member States
  approach to
    supremacy 140-3
  direct actions against
    actions by other Member
      States 220-2
    enforcement actions by
      Commission 211-12
    introduction 211
    preliminary informal
      procedures 214-15
  occupations exempt from
    equal treatment 419-20
  reception of EU supremacy
    Belgium 155
    Czech Republic 162-3
    Denmark 163-4
    emerging trend 166-7
    France 160-2
    Germany 155-9
    Hungary 164
    Ireland 164-5
    Italy 159-60
    Poland 165
    Spain 166
    United Kingdom 146-54

Member States (*Cont.*)
  relevance to Ordinary
    Legislative Procedure 127
  State liability
    development by
      ECJ 185–7
    extensions of
      principle 187–8
    general principle 206–8
Membership
  Committee of Permanent
    Representatives
    (COREPER) 52
  Council of the Union 48
  Court of Justice 60
  European Council 53
  Parliament 55
Merger control
  enforcement 395–6
  problems with Arts 101 and
    102 392–3
  relevant Regulations 393–5
Monism
  French approach 160
  incorporation of
    EU law 145

National courts
  conflicts with EU
    competition law 391–2
  preliminary rulings
    '*acte clair*' 198
    applicability to courts and
      tribunals 189–91
    courts of last instance 197
    discretionary remedy 195
    effect of ruling 201
    evolution of
      references 201–2
    interim measures 203
    questions referred 191–2
    reform proposals 202–3
    time limits 196
  procedural remedies
    balanced approach 206–8
    conclusions 208
    intervention by
      ECJ 205–6
    introduction 203–4
    principle of
      autonomy 204–5
  reception of EU law
    Denmark 163–4
    France 160–2
    Germany 156–9
    Hungary 164
    Ireland 164–5
    Italy 159–60
    United Kingdom 149–53
  State liability 188

Nationality
  free movement of
    economically active
      persons 304–5
  non-discrimination
    general principle of
      equality 398–9
    rationale 399–401
  third-country
    nationals 350–2
  wholly internal rule 346–50
NATO 7
Natural justice
  confidentiality 117–18
  judicial review 117
  legal certainty 118
  legal privilege 117–18
  legitimate expectations 119
  non-retroactivity 118–19
  other new principles 120–1
  proportionality 119–20
  unjustified
    enrichment 120–1
Non-contractual liability
  admissibility 239–40
  autonomous action for
    damages 241
  causation 248–9
  concurrent liability 249
  EU liability for unlawful
    acts 247–8
  individual acts 247
  jurisdiction 239–40
  new single test for
    liability 246–7
  proof of damage 248
  requirements for
    liability 241
  standard of liability and
    fault 241–6
Non-discrimination
  development of
    comprehensive
    approach 432
  equal pay
    basis of
      comparison 408–10
    equal value work 412–14
    extension to work of equal
      value 408
    meaning of pay 404–8
    overview 403–4
    part-time workers 410–12
    remedies 414
  equal treatment
    employment terms 417–19
    equal
      opportunities 424–6
    exempt
      occupations 419–20

    legislative
      provisions 414–15
    maternity rights 420–4
    remedies 426–7
    scope 417
    underlying concept 417
  expansion of equality law
    new legal basis 430
    secondary
      legislation 430–1
  free movement of
    economically active
      persons 303–4
  free movement of goods
    integration methods 259
    particular selling
      arrangements 291–5
    prohibition of discrimin-
      atory taxation 270–3
  general principle of
    equality 398–9
  impact of Lisbon Treaty 432
  introduction 398
  legislative framework
    secondary
      legislation 402–3
    treaty provisions 401–2
  non-contractual liability 243
  pregnant and nursing
    mothers 428
  rationale 399–401
  secondary legislation
    occupational
      pensions 428
    part-time workers 429
    self-employed
      persons 429
    summary 429
  source of law 116
  treaty provisions 399
  welfare rights
    Social Security
      Directive 427–8
  see also Sex discrimination
Non-privileged applicants
  annulment of community
    acts 226–7
  failure to act (Art 265
    TFEU) 237–8
Non-retroactivity 118–19

Occupational pensions 428
Open method of coordination
  (OMC) 134
Opinions
  direct actions against
    Member States 214, 216
  source of law 110
Ordinary Legislative
  Procedure 127–30

Organisation for European
    Economic Co-operation
    (OEEC) 5
Organisation for European
    Economic Co-operation and
    Development (OECD) 5

Parliament
    democratic deficit 72–3
    elections and political
        parties 55–6
    functions and powers
        budgetary processes 59
        control of executive 57–9
        democratic
            legitimacy 56–7
        legislative powers 57
        litigation 59–60
    law-making
        consent procedure 131
        Ordinary Legislative
            Procedure 127–30
        Special Legislative
            Procedure 130–1
    legal basis for
        legislation 123–6
    location in Brussels and
        Strasbourg 54–5
    membership 55
    Ordinary Legislative
        Procedure 127–30
    origins 42–3, 54–5
Part-time workers
    equal pay 410–12
    free movement rights 305–7
    non-discrimination 429
Party actions 230–1
Passerelle provisions 131
Pensions 428
Poland 165
Political and Security
    Committee 68
Portugal 16
Precedent 65, 197–8
Pregnancy *see* Maternity rights
Preliminary rulings
    'acte clair' 198
    alternatives to
        annulment 235–7
    applicability to courts and
        tribunals 189–91
    courts of last instance 197
    discretionary remedy 195
    ECJ jurisdiction 64
    effect of ruling 200–1
    evolution of references 201–2
    interim measures 203
    overview 170
    purpose 188–9
    questions referred

abuse of procedure 193–4
lack of relevance or
    clarity 192–3
no genuine dispute 193–4
overview 194–5
references nevertheless
    accepted 194
relevance and
    admissibility 191–2
reform proposals 202–3
time limits 196
Privileged applicants
    annulment of community
        acts 226
    failure to act (Art 265
        TFEU) 237
Procedural law
    direct actions against
        institutions
        annulment of community
            acts 222–37
        competition
            enforcement 390
        failure to act (Art 265
            TFEU) 237–9
        illegality 249–50
        introduction 222
        non-contractual
            liability 239–49
    direct actions against
        Member States
        actions by other Member
            States 220–2
        enforcement actions by
            Commission 211–12
        introduction 211
        preliminary informal
            procedures 214–15
    direct actions against natural
        or legal persons 251
    direct applicability 170–1
    direct effects
        Charter of Fundamental
            Rights 173
        decisions 176
        directives 174–6, 178–80
        international
            agreements 176–7
        meaning 171–2
        regulations 174
        treaties 172–3
    grounds for
        annulment 232–3
    law classification 96
    national remedies
        balanced approach 206–8
        conclusions 208
        intervention by
            ECJ 205–6
        introduction 203–4

principle of
    autonomy 204–5
preliminary rulings
    'acte clair' 198
    alternatives to
        annulment 235–7
    applicability to courts and
        tribunals 189–91
    courts of last instance 197
    discretionary remedy 195
    effect of ruling 200–1
    evolution of
        references 201–2
    interim measures 203
    overview 170
    purpose 188–9
    questions referred 191–5
    reform proposals 202–3
    time limits 196
source of law 110
see also EU law;
    Substantive law
Proportionality
    division of competences 78
    free movement of goods 283
    meaning and effect 88–9
    non-contractual liability 244
    source of law 119–20
Protocols 100–1
Public morality 279
Public policy
    free movement of
        economically active
            persons 332–3
    free movement of goods 280
Public service
    employees 332–3

Qualified majority voting
    Council of the Union
        necessity 49–50
        workings 50–2
    key feature of Amsterdam
        Treaty 33–4
    Ordinary Legislative
        Procedure 127
    reintroduction under
        SEA 29–30
Quantitative restrictions
    export bans 278
    general scope of treaty 274–5
    introduction 273–4
    meaning 275–6

Recommendations 110
Regulations
    annulment of
        community acts
        direct and individual
            concern 228–30

Regulations (*Cont.*)
  annulment of community
    acts (*Cont.*)
      effect of successful
        action 233–4
      grounds 232–3
      non-privileged
        applicants 227
      restrictive
        approach 234–5
  direct effects 174
  source of law 108
Remain, right to 321–2
Remedies
  annulment of
    community acts
      admissibility 223–6
      alternatives
        remedies 235–7
      direct and individual
        concern 228–30
      effect of successful
        action 233–4
      grounds 232–3
      interest groups and party
        actions 230–1
      introduction 222
      restrictive approach 234–5
  direct actions against
    Member States
      actions by other Member
        States 220–2
      enforcement actions by
        Commission 211–12
      introduction 211
      preliminary informal
        procedures 214–15
  equal pay claims 414
  equal treatment
    claims 426–7
  failure to act (Art 265 TFEU)
    admissibility 237–8
    introduction 237
    procedural
      requirements 238–9
    relevant acts 238
  illegality
    alternatives to
      annulment 236
    effects of successful
      action 250–1
    grounds 250
    overview 249
    reviewable acts 250
    standing 249–50
  national law
    balanced approach 206–8
    conclusions 208
    intervention by
      ECJ 205–6

  introduction 203–4
  principle of
    autonomy 204–5
  State liability
    development by
      ECJ 185–7
    extensions of
      principle 187–8
    general principle 184–5
    see also Direct effects
Residence rights 314–17
Residual powers 82–4
Rule of reason
  Cassis de Dijon case 285
  detailed requirements 286–8

Schöppenstedt formula 243–4
Schuman Plan 6–7
Secondary legislation
  delegation of powers 132–3
  free movement of
    economically active
      persons 303, 314
  free movement of goods 257
  non-discrimination 402–3
    expansion of equality
      law 430–1
    occupational
      pensions 428
    part-time workers 429
    self-employed
      persons 429
    summary 429
  sources of law
    decisions 109
    directives 108–9
    opinions 110
    procedural law 110
    recommendations 110
    regulations 108
Security
  early proposals for EDC 7–8
  free movement of
    economically active
      persons 330–2
  free movement of goods 280
  High Representative for
    Foreign Affairs and
    Security Policy 54
  Political and Security
    Committee 68
Self-employed persons
  Equal Treatment
    Directive 429
  free movement
    personal scope 304–13
  free movement rights
    harmonization of national
      rules 322
    intervention of ECJ 322–5

  legislative
    developments 326–7
Services
  free movement of
    lawyers 327–9
  free movement rights 311–12
  widening concept of free
    movement 334–43
  see also Self-employed
    persons
Sex discrimination
  equal pay
    basis of
      comparison 408–10
    equal value work 412–14
    extension to work of equal
      value 408
    meaning of pay 404–8
    overview 403–4
    part-time workers 410–12
    remedies 414
  equal treatment
    employment terms 417–19
    equal
      opportunities 424–6
    exempt
      occupations 419–20
    legislative
      provisions 414–15
    maternity rights 420–4
    remedies 426–7
    scope 417
    underlying concept 417
  general principle of
    equality 398–9
  impact of Lisbon Treaty 432
  introduction 398
  legislative framework
    secondary
      legislation 402–3
    treaty provisions 401–2
  occupational pensions 428
  pregnant and nursing
    mothers 428
  rationale 399–401
  welfare rights
    maternity 428
    Social Security
      Directive 427–8
Sexual orientation
  concept of equal
    treatment 415–17
  general principle of
    equality 416
  secondary legislation 430–1
Single European Act
  completion of internal
    market 29
  evaluation 30
  expansion of EEA 17–18

importance 28–9
institutional and policy
changes 29–30
need for further institutional
change 30–1
'Soft law'
open method of coordination
(OMC) 134–5
source of law 122–3
Sources of law
Charter of Fundamental
Rights 101–4
conventions 105–7
Court of Justice 110–11
decisions 109
directives 108–9
fundamental rights 111–13
human rights 111–13
international
agreements 105–7
legally binding acts 109
natural justice
confidentiality 117–18
judicial review 117
legal certainty 118
legal privilege 117–18
legitimate expectations 119
non-retroactivity 118–19
other new principles 122
proportionality 119–20
unjustified
enrichment 120–1
non-discrimination 116
opinions 110
other legislative acts 109
procedural
requirements 100–1
protocols 100–1
recommendations 110
regulations 108
'soft law' 122–3
treaties 99–100, 105–7
Sovereignty
transfer of sovereign powers
to EU 71–2
UK difficulties 147
see also Competences;
Supremacy
Spain
reception of EU law 166
widening of Union 16
Special Legislative
Procedure 130–1
Standing
annulment of
community acts
interest groups and party
actions 230–1
non-privileged
applicants 226–7

restrictive
approach 234–5
failure to act (Art 265
TFEU) 237–8
illegality 249–50
State liability
development by ECJ 185–7
extensions of principle
national courts 188
private parties 187
general principle 184–5
Students
education of children 320–1
free movement rights 309–11
Subsidiarity
challenges for
non-compliance 88–9
division of competences 78
general principle 86–8
Substantive law
free movement of
economically active
persons
derogations 329–30
family members 317–20
introduction 299–301
legislative provisions 302–4
material scope of
rights 314–22
scope of basic
rights 304–13
self-employed
persons 322–9
free movement of goods
derogations 278–9
establishment of internal
market 264–70
indistinctly applicable
measures 284–91
integration
methods 259–64
introduction 255–6
legislative
provisions 256–7
overall summary 295–7
particular selling
arrangements 291–5
progress towards treaty
goals 257–9
prohibition of discrimin-
atory taxation 270–3
quantitative
restrictions 273–8
summary on tariff
barriers 273
free movement of persons
generally
conclusions 352–3
European
citizenship 337–8

general free-movement
Directives 336
services 334–6
third-country
nationals 350–2
welfare and family
rights 340–6
wholly internal
rule 346–50
non-discrimination
conclusions 433
equal pay 403–14
equal treatment 417
expansion of equality
law 430–1
general principle of
equality 398–9
introduction 398
legislative
framework 402–3
Lisbon Treaty 432
pregnant and nursing
mothers 428
rationale 399–401
secondary legislation 429
see also EU law;
Procedural law
Supranationalism 14
Supremacy of EU law
ECJ approach 138–40
international law
and 143–4
introduction 138
Member States 140–3
reception by Member States
Belgium 155
Czech Republic 162–3
Denmark 163–4
emerging trend 166–7
France 160–2
Germany 155–9
Hungary 164
Ireland 164–5
Italy 159–60
Poland 165
Spain 166
United Kingdom 146–54
UN Resolutions and 144–5
Suspensory orders 218

Tariff and tax barriers
charges having equivalent
effect (CHEE) 265–8
overview 264
prohibition of customs
duties 264–5
prohibition of discriminatory
taxation 270–3
summary on tariff
barriers 273

Taxation
  prohibition of discriminatory
    taxation
    direct and indirect
      taxation 270–1
    'similar' or 'other
      products' 271–2
    treaty provisions 270
  see also Tariff and tax
    barriers
Third-country nationals
  general treatment under
    Community law 350–2
  wholly internal rule 346–50
Time limits
  annulment of community
    acts 227
  non-contractual liability 240
  preliminary rulings 196
Trainees 309–11
Treaties
  Amsterdam
    Intergovernmental
    Conference and Treaty
    1996 33–4
  basis of legal system 93–4
  constitutional basis of
    EU 74–5
  Constitutional Treaty 37
  direct effects 172–3
  European citizenship 337–8
  free movement of
    economically active
    persons 302–3
  free movement of
    goods 256–7
  grounds for annulment 233
  legal basis for
    legislation 123–6
  Lisbon Treaty 2007 38–9
  Maastricht Treaty on
    European Union (TEU)
    1992 31–3
  Nice Intergovernmental
    Conference and Treaty
    2001 35–7

non-discrimination
  399, 401–2
sources of law 99–100, 105–7

UN Resolutions
  supremacy of EU law 144–5
Undertakings
  abuse of dominance (Art 102
    TFEU) 375
  anti-competitive agreements
    (Art 101 TFEU) 361–2
United Kingdom
  reception of EU law
    constitutional issues 146
    difficulties of
      acceptance 146
    dualist approach 146–7
    ECA 1972 147–9
    European Union Act
      2011 153–4
    judicial
      recognition 149–53
    parliamentary
      supremacy 147
  relationship with EC
    early period to 1970 9–10
    membership and
      acceptance 10–12
Unjustified enrichment 120–1

Validity 198–9
Vicarious liability 243
Voting
  Council of the Union
    forms 49–50
    qualified majority
      voting 50–2
    role 48–9
    simple majorities 49
    unanimity 49
  Parliament 55–6
  rationale for law-making
    changes 131–2

Welfare rights
  equal treatment

Social Security
  Directive 427–8
key feature of Amsterdam
  Treaty 34
widening concept of free
  movement 340–3
Western European Union 7
Wholly internal rule 346–50
Work seekers
  free movement rights 308–9
Workers
  equal pay
    basis of
      comparison 408–10
    equal value work 412–14
    extension to work of equal
      value 408
    meaning of pay 404–8
    overview 403–4
    part-time workers 410–12
    remedies 414
  equal treatment
    employment terms 417–19
    equal
      opportunities 424–6
    exempt
      occupations 419–20
    legislative
      provisions 414–15
    maternity rights 420–4
    remedies 426–7
    scope 417
    underlying concept 417
  free movement
    derogations 329–30
  free movement rights
    introduction 299–301
    legislative
      provisions 302–4
    material scope of
      rights 314–22
    scope of basic
      rights 304–13
  vicarious liability 243
**World Trade Organization
  (WTO)** 24

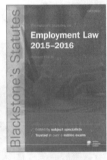

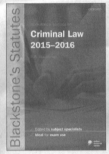